Themes in Economics

Theory, Empirics, and Policy

The main objective of the series is to publish volumes dealing with topics in economic theory and empirics with important policy implications. The series aims to publish monographs, both theoretical and empirical, on topics of contemporary interest. While topics that are important from a policy perspective are preferable, volumes in this series are one of the following types: (i) Research dealing with important economic theory topics; (ii) Rigourous empirical work on issues of contemporary importance; and (iii) Edited volumes of selected papers, either of individual authors, or those presented in Economic Theory and Policy conferences which will be conducted annually.

Some of the topics that explored in this series are: poverty, income inequality, eminent domain (land acquisition in particular), some theoretical aspects of the functioning of the market mechanism, economic and social implications of affirmative action.

More information about this series at http://www.springer.com/series/15590

Ranjan Ray

Household Behaviour, Prices, and Welfare

A Collection of Essays Including Selected Empirical Studies

Springer

Ranjan Ray
Department of Economics
Monash University
Clayton, VIC, Australia

Themes in Economics
ISBN 978-981-13-1929-7 ISBN 978-981-13-1930-3 (eBook)
https://doi.org/10.1007/978-981-13-1930-3

Library of Congress Control Number: 2018950935

This Springer imprint is published by the registered company Springer Nature Singapore Pte Ltd.
The registered company address is: 152 Beach Road, #21-01/04 Gateway East, Singapore 189721, Singapore

Foreword

How the well-being of households is affected when inflation occurs or relative prices shift, how widespread poverty is in your country, how this compares with other nations, the extent of inequality in society, and how deep the relative deprivation is of the poor compared to the rich—these are the topics that interest all of us, specialists and laity alike. But most people have no idea of the amount of effort, from data collection, through statistical analysis, to theoretical conceptualization, that goes into producing these numbers that appear in newspaper headlines and magazine essays and in tickers running beneath the main-frame of the evening television news.

This book, which is a collection of papers, written by Ranjan Ray over the years, on the above topics, mainly in the context of the Indian economy, with occasional forays to other nations, such as China, Vietnam, Canada and Australia, is an erudite and authoritative work. The value of the book lies in the wonderful, encapsulated account it gives of all the specialized work that goes on behind the production of these headline numbers concerning inequality, poverty and household welfare, in India and other economies, that all of us take an interest in but only a few fully understand. The book also goes into related areas such as commodity taxation and tax reform, which, with India's recent adoption of the Goods and Services Tax, has become a topic of popular interest.

Reading these essays not only helps one understand the full significance of some of these concepts and indicators but also makes one aware of their strengths and weaknesses. As such, **Household Behaviour, Prices and Welfare** should be of interest to students and teachers of economics, to economic journalists and media persons who report and talk about these numbers, and also, alas, to the social media trolls, wanting to give a spin that serves the interests of his or her political master.

My own interest in these topics was, initially, that of the curious bystander. This changed once I went to the world of policymaking, first in the Indian government in New Delhi in 2009 and then at the World Bank in Washington in 2012. I was actively engaged in several of the topics that this book deals with, and as a consequence, I was already familiar with some of the papers included in this volume.

At the World Bank, which is the world's premier institute for global poverty statistics, I had quickly come to appreciate the importance of in-depth analysis of the indicators of poverty, inequality and household well-being, which we use to guide us through policymaking. It is wonderful to see a robust and engaging analysis of many of these topics within the covers of one book. Ranjan Ray makes us aware of both the advantages and the pitfalls of many of these indicators and indices.

Consider the standard purchasing power parity (PPP) index, which is at the heart of intercountry welfare comparisons and would be the source of joy, anguish and complaints every time the World Bank puts out fresh PPP numbers, which prompted new intercountry comparisons. And, indeed, there is scope for questioning these indices. For instance, for large countries, such as China and India, where prices vary across geographic regions and between rural and urban areas, there is an open question concerning how representative the PPP indices are. Ideally, what one wants are different PPP indices for different groups and, if that were not available, to at least be aware of their shortcomings so that we can keep them in mind in crafting policy interventions. Ray's book does a thorough job of pointing to these conceptual problems and also providing suggestions for future research to correct them. It is in this sense that the book addresses the interests of both the policy maker and the students interested in academic work.

There was another, more personal reason that drew me to reading this book. In the early 1970s, when I was a student at the London School of Economics, among the inmates of the hostel at Fitzroy Square, where I stayed, was a small group of aspiring chartered accountants. Among those to-be accountants, setting out every morning, in their neckties and formal suits, to spend the days auditing accounts, there was one who openly envied us, the graduate students of the London School, who kept erratic hours, working late into the nights, and often chatting and debating economics hours on end. This was Ranjan Ray, who having been a student of economics in India, took a lot of interest in what we studied, and in our debates and discussions. After some months of watching us wistfully, he took a big decision. He announced he was changing his career plan and applying for admission to LSE. Soon he was my fellow student there. Having played a minor role in his career change, I wanted to read and see if that was a good decision on his part. It was.

Ithaca, New York

Kaushik Basu
Professor of Economics and Carl Marks
Professor at Cornell University

Series Editors' Preface

We have great pleasure in presenting the first volume in the new Springer series, **Themes in Economics: Theory, Empirics, and Policy**. As stated in the description on the Springer website, the main objective of the series is to publish volumes dealing with topics in economic theory and empirics with important policy implications and of contemporary relevance. Professor Ranjan Ray's collection of papers eminently meets the objectives, and we are happy that our former colleague, S. Subramanian, on the Editorial Board was successful in convincing Professor Ray to undertake this venture.

This volume is particularly appropriate as the first volume since it provides an excellent illustration of the link between theory, empirics and policy in economic research that is the key objective of this series. The essays reported in this book describe empirical studies on a variety of data sets from countries with different cultural and developmental contexts. This collection of essays covers a diverse set of topics related to household behaviour and welfare. Among others, these topics include: the distributional implications of price movements; effects of changes in relative prices on inequality and poverty; and effects of selected public delivery schemes in India on the health of its children. The volume is divided into three parts. In Part A (Chaps. 2–7), the central role played by prices in welfare comparisons is examined. In Part B (Chaps. 8–9), instead of the single-country scenario, bilateral and multilateral country contexts are considered is examined. In Part C (Chaps. 10–12), the focus is on non-money indicators such as calorie intake, hunger, child health and multidimensional poverty. Chapter 1 provides a useful overview of the material covered.

This book should prove to be a useful resource for a variety of stakeholders ranging from students and teachers of advanced undergraduate courses in economics to doctoral students, researchers and policy analysts. It contains up-to-date surveys of several of the topics covered in the volume.

Ranjan Ray is currently Professor of economics at Monash University. He has had a distinguished career of teaching and research. Apart from Monash University, the institutions where he has taught include University of Manchester, Delhi School of Economics and University of Tasmania.

Gurugram, India Satish K. Jain
Oslo, Norway Karl Ove Moene
Gurugram, India Anjan Mukherji

Acknowledgements

I thank my friend Prof. Sreenivasan (Subbu) Subramanian who as one of the then editors of the newly launched Springer Series, *Themes in Economics*, invited me to write a volume for this series. I was initially reluctant to take on the challenge of writing a book but was persuaded to take it on not only by the persistence of Subbu but also by the strong encouragement I received from the other editors of the Series, Profs. Satish Jain and Anjan Mukherjee. I owe them all my thanks and gratitude. It gave me the opportunity to link research papers from a wide range of areas in a manner that is consistent with the objectives of the Springer Series, *Themes in Economics*. I must also thank my teachers in Presidency College, Calcutta; the Delhi School of Economics; and the London School of Economics for the training I received at these institutions.

I have been incredibly lucky in having several sincere, hardworking and skilled co-authors who worked with me on the various research projects, only some of which have been reported in this volume. I thank them all for allowing me to work with them and learn from their involvement in our joint work. They are too numerous for me to name and thank them individually.

However, there is one co-author I must name—Geoffrey Lancaster. When I moved to the University of Tasmania in Hobart from the Delhi School of Economics in July 1995 and was having trouble adjusting to the Tasmanian winter from the scorching summer heat of Delhi, one of the first persons I met at work was this young happy-go-lucky lad who grew up in Tasmania and hadn't ventured much outside the island state of Australia. He was in the final year of his undergraduate degree and was looking for a supervisor to guide him on his dissertation to complete his degree. That was the trigger for a friendship and start of several joint research projects much of which has been on India. Geoff was incredibly skilled in his ability to handle data, even one with the complexity of India's National Sample Surveys, and write programs which proved invaluable for our work. He has never been to India but was very keen to learn about the country. Sadly, he passed away at a very young age. I dedicate this book to Geoff's memory.

I thank Parvin Singh for helping me with editing the manuscript to put it in a form that can be sent to the publishers and the Springer staff, especially Sagarika Ghosh, Sandeep Kaur, Jayarani Premkumar and Nupoor Singh for their editorial assistance. I also thank the various publishers, including CUP, OUP, Springer, Taylor & Francis, Wiley, for giving me permission to reproduce material from published papers in this book.

The measurement of prices, PPPs, demand estimation and welfare measures, living standards and inequality. These and more are in this excellent book by Ranjan Ray. An attractive blend of theory and measurement, the book will be a source of inspiration for all those wanting to learn about recent developments in the measurement of prices and welfare within and between countries.

—Kenneth W. Clements, *FASSA, Professor of Economics, The University of Western Australia*

This book contains a selection from the outstanding lifetime scholarly contributions of Professor Ranjan Ray which focus on the measurement of household behaviour and welfare. A distinguishing feature of the book is the ideal and balanced mixture of theory, empirics and policy. It highlights the importance of monetary and non-monetary measures in assessing welfare and poverty at the national level as well as at the global level. Through these essays, Professor Ray demonstrates his mastery over micro-economic theory and his command over econometric tools necessary to deal with diverse measurement issues such as the estimation of equivalence scales; index number methods for temporal and spatial price comparisons and compilation of purchasing power parities; optimal taxation and tax reforms; and the measurement of multidimensional poverty and deprivation. The book contains a treasure of cutting-edge techniques and empirical tools for researchers interested in measuring the distributional impact of price movements on household welfare, inequality and poverty. This book will serve as an invaluable resource for development economists, economic statisticians, researchers, policy makers and aspiring graduate students.

—D.S. Prasada Rao, *FASSA, Emeritus Professor, School of Economics, The University of Queensland*

Contents

About the Author

Ranjan Ray is Professor of Economics at Monash University, Australia. Prior to this, he was Lecturer in Econometrics (1979–1989) at the University of Manchester, UK; Professor of Public Economics (1989–1995) at the Delhi School of Economics; and Professor and Head of the Department of Economics (1995–2008) at the University of Tasmania, Australia. He has also held visiting positions at the University of British Columbia, Canada; University of Rome Tor Vergata, Italy; and Cornell University, USA. He has taught and researched in a wide range of areas. His papers have a shared focus on methodological advancement, empirical investigation and welfare-based policy application.

Chapter 1
Introduction

This monograph seeks to bring together a collection of my recent papers with co-authors covering a diverse set of topics with a shared focus on household welfare and with special reference to India. In doing so, the volume also describes other studies from other countries that share the focus on household behaviour and welfare. India has a long and rich tradition of welfare analysis based on a preference consistent framework applied to rich data sets from household budget surveys. While the earlier studies were based on grouped data sets in the Consumer Expenditure Surveys (CES) collected under the auspices of the National Sample Survey Organisation (NSSO), recent studies use the unit records from the CES that are made available to the researchers by the NSSO. Two common features of these papers are: (a) they combine methodological contributions with empirical analysis of micro-data at household-level designed to provide policy insights, and (b) they share an interest in distributive issues, namely inequality and poverty.

An attempt is made in this monograph to link the essays to provide a coherent picture on the use of household budget survey data to arrive at policy-relevant results in a wide range of areas extending from prices, purchasing power parities, real income comparisons both between and within countries, tax design and tax reforms, inequality, poverty and equivalence scales. As this illustrative list shows the topics cover a range of issues that cross the conventional divide between micro and macroeconomics. Prices play a key role in several of the essays with the focus on the distributional implications of price movements, especially on the effects of changes in relative prices on inequality and poverty. The volume documents the shift in the literature on prices from being exclusively a macrotopic featuring in the study of inflation and cross-country comparisons to one that is firmly rooted in micro-theory-based analysis of household behaviour. The link between household behaviour and welfare is a unifying feature of the monograph. A good example of a volume that demonstrates this link is the edited book by Blundell et al. (1994).

The distinctive features of India include its population size, sharp rural–urban divide and its cultural diversity. For example, the State of Uttar Pradesh alone has a population size that is comparable to the combined population of Germany, UK,

R. Ray, *Household Behaviour, Prices, and Welfare*, Themes in Economics,
https://doi.org/10.1007/978-981-13-1930-3_1

France and Italy. There are few greater examples of countries where the country-wide generalisations implicit in concepts such as purchasing power parity (PPP) of the country's currency, the national health statistics and the country's anthropometric indicators are of limited use, and aggregate country-wide statistics can be quite misleading, than in the case of India. One of the messages from the evidence presented and discussed in this book relates to the disparate, even contradictory, movements in several of the welfare indicators, besides the wide variation in their magnitudes, between the different regions of India.

The chosen studies compare household behaviour and welfare at different levels of aggregation of the regions that the households reside in, namely subnational and cross-national comparisons, both temporally and at a point in time. While the first two comparisons place the studies in the realm of micro, the third extends the interest to the macroarea. While much of the work at the subnational and national levels are on Indian data and involve intra-national comparisons, the volume also covers cross-national comparisons that are both bilateral (such as between India and China, and India and Vietnam), trilateral (such as between China, India and Vietnam) and multilateral (such as between the 200 or so countries covered in the 2011 round of the International Comparison Project). The volume does not provide comprehensive surveys of the literature on the topics of the chosen essays since they are available elsewhere in papers and monographs.

However, to make the volume self-contained, the chapters contain a limited survey of the literature that the studies draw on. Instead, the volume concentrates on the interplay of analytical framework, estimation methodology and household-level unit record data sets in yielding a set of empirical results that can be interpreted in a policy friendly manner. The volume gives primacy to the recent empirical findings on household welfare in an era of globalisation that has brought about significant changes in living standards. The essays show the usefulness of a priori-specified consumer preferences and utility maximisation-based behaviour in analysing unit record data sets. While much of the volume is of interest to researchers working on developmental issues and, more broadly, on emerging markets, the cross-national comparisons involving calculations of purchasing power parities (PPP) between national currencies are of interest to macroresearchers with a focus on developed countries.

India is quite unique since while on aggregate GDP (PPP) the size of the Indian economy is the fourth largest, behind China, EU and the USA, providing a huge market that exceeds those in many of the smaller (and much richer) OECD nations, on per capita GDP (PPP) measure, India slides down sharply in its rankings and displays all the characteristics of a developing country with high levels of poverty, illiteracy, hunger and undernourishment. India, therefore, straddles the divide between developing and developed countries in a manner that few other countries do. The focus on India, therefore, makes this monograph of wide interest to researchers and policy analysts. The Indian evidence also helps appreciation of the intra-country differences in large countries that give importance to the spatial dimensions in topics such as PPP, cost of living index, nutritional intake and anthropometric outcomes. Such an appreciation is often lacking in global comparisons between countries.

The volume can be broadly divided into three parts. Part A examines the central role played by prices in welfare comparisons. It consists of five chapters (Chaps. 2–7). Chapter 2 outlines the cost minimisation based and preference-consistent specification of demand systems modified and extended to incorporate family size and composition effects, analogous to price effects, on the household's expenditure allocation. Chapter 3 presents the alternative approaches to the measurement of changes in prices and distinguishes between the deterministic and non-stochastic approaches to price indices. It surveys some key contributions that provide a bridge between the two approaches and derives an equivalence between the deterministic and stochastic price indices. This chapter also shows how the measurement of spatial variation and temporal variation in prices in a heterogeneous country setting such as India can be integrated in a comprehensive framework that allows both sets of calculations.

Chapter 4 extends the discussion to the evaluation of the welfare implications of price changes. In particular, it explores the link between welfare analysis and the 'True Cost of Living Index' (TCLI) that, unlike the other price indices discussed in Chap. 3, is explicitly based on consumer preferences and requires a priori specification of consumers' utility function and estimation of the corresponding demand function. An important advantage of the TCLI approach, described in Chap. 4, is that it allows an investigation of the effect of relative price changes on inequality and poverty. Chapter 5 illustrates the usefulness of the methodologies discussed in Chaps. 3 and 4 by reporting the evidence from a selection of empirical studies that apply the alternative procedures discussed there. The empirical evidence on price changes, and their distributional consequences presented in Chap. 5 look at single-country studies.

Chapter 6 focusses on spatial price differences in India and their effect on State rankings and inequality. Since much of the author's work has been on India, much of the discussion in Chaps. 5 and 6 is on India, though we also report evidence from other countries, namely UK, Australia and Canada. While the evidence reported in Chap. 5 is from a selection of countries, including India, Chap. 6 is focused exclusively on India. India is of particular interest, given its large and heterogeneous population, with differences in preferences between States often exceeding that between the smaller economies in, for example the European Union. Chapters 5 and 6, which draw on, among others, Pendakur (2002), Mishra and Ray (2011), Majumder et al. (2012) and Chakrabarty et al. (2017), report on spatial price differences in Canada, the rural–urban differences in prices in India and that between the principal States of the Indian union and analyse their empirical implications for inequality and welfare.

The evidence in Chaps. 5 and 6 also highlights the sensitivity of the results to the deterministic and stochastic specifications and the need to arrive at a satisfactory trade-off between non-restrictiveness in specification and tractability in estimation. Chapter 7 moves the discussion to commodity taxes with prices still playing a central role. It defines 'optimal commodity taxes' and presents empirical evidence on whether taxes are uniform in the Indian context, and on its redistributive impact. This chapter then moves on to the issue of tax reforms and provides Indian evidence on directions of Pareto improving tax reforms and their sensitivity to demand specification.

In Part B, the volume moves from the single country to bilateral and multilateral country contexts. Part B consists of two chapters (Chaps. 8 and 9). Chapter 8 focusses on the calculation of purchasing power parities (PPP) between the national currencies and their use in welfare comparisons. Chapter 8 highlights the close connection between the use of price indices and the calculation of the PPPs. In recent years, the International Comparison Project (ICP) has occupied centre stage in providing the PPPs that are required in global and regional poverty calculations. Chapter 8 reports on studies that subject the ICP methodology to critical scrutiny and provides an alternative estimation framework that yields a set of PPPs that can be used to subject the ICP PPPs to robustness checks. The material in this chapter draws on, among others, Majumder et al. (2015, 2017).

Chapter 9 extends the discussion to describe the literature on the use of the PPPs in calculating global poverty rates. The latter issue has acquired considerable significance as we move from the Millennium Development Goals (MDGs) to the Sustainable Development Goals (SDGs), with both sets of goals providing primacy to poverty reduction, and in the light of the recent report of the Global Poverty Commission set up by the World Bank to examine the approach to poverty measurement. This section is based, largely but not exclusively, on ongoing work by the author, Ranjan Ray, with Amita Majumder and Sattwik Santra.

In Part C, which consists of four chapters (Chaps. 10–13), the volume moves beyond the exclusively money-metric framework of Parts A and B to focus on non-money indicators such as calorie intake, hunger, child health and multidimensional poverty.

Chapters 10 and 11 extend the discussion to bring in the recent developments in multidimensional deprivation that include both money-metric and non-money-metric indicators of quality of life. Following Bourguignon and Chakravarty (2003), Chakravarty and D'Ambrosio (2006), Alkire and Foster (2011), there has been a spate of studies on this topic that measure deprivation based on a lack of access by the household to a range of dimensions. There are two aspects to the measurement of multidimensional deprivation: the number of dimensions that the household is deprived in, and the spell of deprivation in each deprivation. The literature has not, until recently, distinguished between the two, and overlooked the importance of the latter since the studies have either been conducted on data from a single time period or on repeated cross sections from multiple time periods, neither of which allows examination of the spell of deprivation experienced by the same household over time. From a policy perspective, it is not only important to track how the overall multidimensional measure of poverty is moving over time, but to also identify the dimensions where the spells of deprivation are high.

With the recent availability of panel data sets, the volume reports the methodology and findings from some recent studies that extend the static multidimensional framework to distinguish between the breadth and depth of deprivation. In this concluding part C of the volume, while Chap. 10 reports the results from studies comparing multi-dimensional poverty in the static framework between regions in India, and between countries (namely, China, India and Vietnam), Chap. 11 takes a temporal view of multi-dimensional poverty on the lines mentioned above. Chapter 11 establishes the need to differentiate between 'dimensionality' and 'duration' in multidimensional measures of poverty and proposes a measure that incorporates this distinction.

The former chapter is based on, among others, Ray and Mishra (2012), Mishra and Ray (2013), Ray and Sinha (2015) while the latter reports the methodology followed in Nicholas and Ray (2012), Mishra et al. (2018), and extended in Nicholas et al. (2017). Since, as yet, India does not have a panel data that is long enough to identify dimensions recording spells of continuous deprivation, the methodology described in Chap. 11 will be empirically illustrated by reporting evidence based on panel data sets from China and Australia. Chapter 11 shows how the static multi-dimensional poverty measures can be extended to incorporate persistence in deprivation to provide evidence on the comparative spells of continuous deprivation between population subgroups in Australia and between the residents of the different regions in China. In another application of this methodology, this chapter describes a study on the multidimensional deprivation experienced by children in Australia and records systematic evidence of the higher deprivation experienced by indigenous children vis-a-vis non-indigenous children not only with respect to the number of dimensions they are deprived in, but also in the persistence of that deprivation. The empirical studies described in this chapter illustrate the policy usefulness of the methodology by identifying the population subgroups facing higher deprivation and the dimensions that are primarily contributing to that deprivation. The methodology has the potential for similar applications in other countries.

Chapter 12 provides evidence on the declining calorie intake in India co-existing with declining money-metric expenditure poverty rates. This has been a source of concern for policy makers in India with no convincing explanation provided for this mismatch between rising rates of undernourishment and falling rates of poverty. This concern is underlined by the dismal state of child health in India when the country has been performing well on most macroeconomic indicators including consistently recording during the past two decades some of the highest growth rates in the world. This chapter also provides evidence on the spatial aspect of child health in India by reporting differences between regions on the movement in the child health indicators. In recent years, the continuation of in-kind transfer mechanisms such as the Public Distribution System (PDS) and the Midday Meal Scheme (MDMS) has attracted considerable attention with many economists favouring their replacement by unconditional cash transfer such as the institution of an universal basic income (UBI) to be paid directly into the recipient's bank account. Chapter 12 provides some evidence on this issue including the nutrition-enhancing effect of PDS and MDMS and their role in reducing the 'prevalence of undernutrition'. The results sound a note of caution on disbanding, or even curtailing, in-kind transfer schemes in favour of cash transfers in India. As with much of the monograph, the spatial differences on the evidence on this issue between regions in India come out clearly making it difficult to make India wide generalisations.

The monograph ends with the principal features and main results summarised in Chap. 13. The monograph highlights the role of theory in providing an analytical framework for estimation and welfare analysis that leads to useful policy insights. It combines description of recent methodological developments with the reporting of applications on rich data sets with a focus, though not an exclusive one, on India.

The monograph covers a wide area ranging from conventional demand analysis and price indices to issues in multi-dimensional deprivation, social exclusion and an assessment of public welfare schemes in India. The volume should be a useful reference guide for teachers, researchers, and graduate students working on methodological issues in price measurement, calculation of purchasing power parities within and between countries, comparison of living standards between and within countries, developmental issues dealing with hunger, child health, inequality and poverty, and especially for those doing household survey data based empirical work on household welfare in the developing country context. The volume indicates the rich potential in micro-data sets for useful policy-relevant welfare analysis, and the role that utility theory-based demand specification can play in this regard.

References

Alkire S, Foster J (2011) Counting and multidimensional poverty measurement. J Public Econ 95 (7):476–487

Blundell R, Preston I, Walker I (1994) The measurement of household welfare. Cambridge University Press, Cambridge

Bourguignon F, Chakravarty S (2003) The measurement of multidimensional poverty. J Econ Inequality 1:25–49

Chakrabarty M, Majumder A, Ray R (2017) A framework for the simultaneous measurement of spatial variation and temporal movement in prices in a heterogeneous country: the dynamic household regional product dummy model. Rev Income Wealth (Forthcoming)

Chakravarty S, D'Ambrosio C (2006) The measurement of social exclusion. Rev Income Wealth 52(3):377–398

Majumder A, Ray R, Santra S (2017) Sensitivity of purchasing power parity estimates to estimation procedures and their effect on living standards comparisons. J Globalization Dev. https://doi.org/10.1515/jgd-2017-0006 (Forthcoming)

Majumder A, Ray R, Sinha K (2012) The calculation of rural urban food price differentials from unit values in household expenditure surveys: a new procedure and comparison with existing methods. Am J Agr Econ 94:1218–1235

Majumder A, Ray R, Sinha K (2015) Estimating purchasing power parities from household expenditure data using complete demand systems with application to living standards comparison: India and Vietnam. Rev Income Wealth 61(2):302–328

Mishra A, Ray R (2011) Prices, inequality and poverty. Rev Income Wealth 57:428–448

Mishra A, Ray R (2013) Multi-dimensional deprivation in India during and after the reforms: do the household expenditure and the family health surveys present consistent evidence? Soc Indic Res 2013(110):791–818

Mishra A, Ray R, Risse L (2018) A multidimensional dynamic measure of child disadvantage: a methodological tool for policy makers. Soc Indic Res. https://doi.org/10.1007/s11205-017-1742-x (Forthcoming)

Nicholas A, Ray R (2012) Duration and persistence in multidimensional deprivation: methodology and Australian application. Econ Rec 88:106–126

Nicholas A, Ray R, Sinha K (2017) Differentiating between dimensionality and duration in multidimensional measures of poverty: methodology with an application to China. Rev Income Wealth (Forthcoming)

Pendakur K (2002) Taking prices seriously in the measurement of inequality. J Public Econ 86:47–69 (2002)

Ray R, Mishra A (2012) Multi-dimensional deprivation in the awakening giants: a comparison of China and India on micro data. J Asian Econ 23(4):454–465

Ray R, Sinha K (2015) Multidimensional deprivation in China, India and Vietnam: a comparative study on micro-data. J Human Dev Capabilities 16(1):69–93

Chapter 2
Specification and Estimation of Demographic Demand Systems, Equivalence Scales with Selective Empirical Evidence

2.1 Demand Specification[1]

The standard approach to demand specification is to either assume a functional form for the utility function and maximise it subject to the individual's budget constraint or minimise the individual's cost or expenditure function subject to the utility set at a prespecified value. While the former exercise is referred to as the primal approach, the latter is referred to as the dual approach. While the former yields the individual's Marshallian demand function as a function of the prices of the commodities and aggregate expenditure, the latter yields the Hicksian demand function as a function of aggregate expenditure and the unobservable utility. While the former is readily estimable, the latter requires the utility to be substituted by prices and aggregate expenditure using the indirect utility function that is obtained by inverting the cost function assumed for the cost minimisation exercise. Historically, the primal approach was adopted starting with a prespecified utility function, but in recent years, the dual approach based on an expenditure or cost function has been used mainly because of its proximity to welfare analysis and cost of living indices. Given the nature of this volume, we have adopted the latter approach.

One needs to distinguish between demand estimation on a single cross section assuming that all households face the same prices for an item, and demand estimation on time series with prices varying over time. The former is referred to as Engel curve analysis, following Engel's (1895) pioneering analysis of Belgian family budget data. The focus of attention in Engel curve analysis on cross-sectional data is the effect of changes in family size and composition on the household's expenditure allocation, while that in demand estimation on time series data is the effect of changes in prices on expenditure allocation. Engel curve analysis yields estimates of 'equivalence scales' while conventional demand estimation yields estimates of own and cross-price elasticities. The common point in

[1]See Deaton and Muellbauer (1980a), Pollak and Wales (1992) for a more complete treatment.

R. Ray, *Household Behaviour, Prices, and Welfare*, Themes in Economics,
https://doi.org/10.1007/978-981-13-1930-3_2

both exercises is the estimation of expenditure elasticities that measure the response of demand for an item to an increase on total expenditure, but the interpretation changes between cross-sectional and time series analysis. This is due to the fact that in Engel curve analysis, the expenditure elasticity measures the change in demand between two households with varying level of total expenditure at a point in time, while that in demand estimation refers to change in demand due to change in total expenditure of the same household over time. This distinction has been weakened in recent years following the work of Barten (1964) which extended traditional utility functions to incorporate household size and compositional variables besides prices.

This has led to a literature that involves specification and estimation of demographic demand systems on pooled time series of cross sections allowing simultaneous estimation of family size, price and expenditure elasticities. Examples of this recent tradition include Ray (1980, 1982) on Indian data, and Pollak and Wales (1981) on UK data. The former is described in some detail below. In the Barten (1964) model, the household maximises a utility function,

$$u = u\left(\frac{q_1}{m_1}, \frac{q_2}{m_2}, \ldots \frac{q_n}{m_n}\right) \tag{2.1}$$

where $(q_1, \ldots q_n)$ are the quantities of the n goods consumed, and $m_i = m_i(b_1, \ldots, b_f)$ is a parameter which, independently of quantities, income and prices, measures the effect on utility of household composition. b_d $(d = 1, \ldots, f)$ is the number of household members in category d; m_i is called the 'specific adult equivalence scale' which is usually normalised w.r.t an adult male or a childless couple. The budget constraint, $\mu = \sum p_i q_i$ can be rewritten as $\mu = \sum p_i m_i \left(\frac{q_i}{m_i}\right)$ where μ is the aggregate household expenditure.

While Barten's (1964) original formulation was set out in primal terms and involved matrix manipulation, Muellbauer (1974) simplified the analysis by working with the indirect utility and cost or expenditure functions corresponding to the Barten household direct utility function. If we define $q_i^* = \frac{q_i}{m_i}$ as the quantity consumed per equivalent adult, and $p_i^* = p_i m_i$ as the 'equivalent adult normalised' price of an item facing the household, then the household utility maximisation can be viewed as maximising u $(q_1^*, \ldots, q_n^*)$ subject to $\mu = \sum p_i^* q_i^*$. This yields the Marshallian and Hicksian demand functions, respectively, in the Barten model as follows:

$$q_i = m_i \cdot D_i\left(\frac{\mu}{p_1 m_1}, \ldots, \frac{\mu}{p_n m_n}\right) \tag{2.2}$$

$$q_i = m_i \cdot H_i(p_1 m_1, \ldots, p_n m_n) \tag{2.3}$$

where $i = 1, \ldots, n$ and n is the number of commodities. A key feature of the Barten model that came out of Muellbauer's analysis is the 'quasi-price nature of the household composition effects' in the Barten formulation, since the p_is and the m_is appear symmetrically in the utility and demand functions.

While this made the Barten model widely applicable to any demand system by replacing q_i by q_i^*, and p_i by p_i^*, it also pointed to the restrictive manner in which the household composition effects are admitted in the Barten framework. It is clear from the Marshallian demand form in Eq. 2.2 that a change in household composition has two effects on demand for commodity i; a direct effect through a change in m_i and an indirect effect through the terms in the function, $D_i\left(\frac{\mu}{p_1 m_1}, \ldots, \frac{\mu}{p_n m_n}\right)$. In a subsequent study, Muellbauer (1977) tested on UK Family Expenditure data the underlying and central hypothesis of the Barten model, namely the quasi-price nature of household composition effects and found the hypothesis to be rejected by the data. The Barten model allows the data to be pooled across households with different family size and composition and the estimation of the price and expenditure elasticities to be performed on the pooled time series and cross-sectional data.

Muellbauer found the performance of the pooled model, following Barten, to be substantially inferior to that of the non-pooled model where the demand systems are estimated separately over the different family types. However, both the pooled and non-pooled models yielded plausible and similar values of the expenditure elasticities, the former yielded sharply lower price elasticities than the latter. This possibly reflects the implausible nature of the Barten-type quasi-price responses which are quite different from the real time series price responses. The cost function of the Barten model is given by $c(u, p_1 m_1, \ldots, p_n m_n)$. Gorman (1976) generalised the Barten model by adding a fixed cost element to the above cost function. In the Gorman framework, therefore, household composition has both a quasi-price effect and a fixed cost effect.

2.2 Temporal Comparisons of Prices and Income

Another contribution of Muellbauer (1974) is to show how the Barten model allowed the true cost of living index (TCLI) (due to Konus (1939)) and the real income index defined at the level of the individual to be extended to that of the household. While the TCLI compares the cost of reaching a fixed level of utility in two time periods, the real income index is the relative cost of reaching two utility levels at given prices. There are two variants of each index, depending on the choice of base or given year utility as the reference utility for the former, and the base or given year prices for the latter. If we define, $c(u, p)$ as the cost or expenditure function that shows the minimum cost of obtaining utility level, u, at price vector, p, then the TCLI expressions corresponding to base year utility, u_0, and given year utility, u_1, are given, respectively, by $\frac{c(u_0, p_1)}{c(u_0, p_0)}$ and $\frac{c(u_1, p_1)}{c(u_1, p_0)}$.

The corresponding real income indices are given, respectively, by $\frac{c(u_1,p_0)}{c(u_0,p_0)}$ and $\frac{c(u_1,p_1)}{c(u_0,p_1)}$. It is readily verified that the ratio of expenditures in the two time periods, $\frac{\mu_1}{\mu_0} = \frac{c(u_1,p_1)}{c(u_0,p_0)}$, is the product of the real income index (with given year prices as reference prices), and the true cost of living index (with the base year utility used as the reference utility). The Barten model allows a straightforward extension of these indices from the individual to the household level by replacing the prices, p_i, by equivalence scale normalised prices, p_i^*. We will return to this topic in more detail in the next chapter.

2.3 Cross-Sectional Welfare Comparisons Between Households

While the above discussion related to the temporal comparisons of prices and income, as measured by the cost of living index and real income index, let us now turn to cross-sectional welfare comparisons between households with varying family size and composition facing the same set of prices. The key measure here is the 'general equivalence scale' introduced by Engel (1895) and extended by Prais and Houthakker (1955) to allow item-specific equivalence scales. The equivalence scale, as its name suggests, converts households with differing size and composition into equivalent units in terms of some reference household. The scale, thus, seeks to quantify and represent in one summary measure the varying 'needs' of families that differ in household size and composition.

Viewed as a true cost of living index (TCLI) , the general equivalence scale compares two households with different composition and calculates their relative cost of enjoying the same level of utility—in other words, it seeks to answer questions such as: 'What expenditure level would make a family with one child as well off as it would be with no children and Rs. 2000? The importance of the scale in welfare economics in general and public policy discussion in particular stems from the fact that considerations of justice, equity and the like crucially involve an examination of people's 'needs' in relation to available resources. Such 'needs' will obviously vary from household to household depending on, among other things, its size and composition. Larger households will have greater needs than smaller households. Similarly, households with more children in the older category will make greater demands on certain items, less on others, than those households with more children in the younger category. Since it is the household rather than the individual that is the unit of consumption, decision making and beneficiary of public welfare programmes, it seems natural to make welfare comparisons between households in a manner similar to the way the TCLI compares individuals over time.

There have been, broadly, two approaches to the measurement of equivalence scale. The first uses nutritionist requirements of different age-sex groups to determine the scales. This method, however, has not found wide favour since rarely agree on what the 'correct' nutritional requirements are [see, e.g. Sukhatme (1978) and Dandekar (1982)]. Moreover, such requirements are likely to vary considerably over time and across countries. The second, more widely used approach, consists of calculating the scales from observed expenditure pattern of households. The approach originated with Engel's (1895) pioneering analysis of Belgian working class budget data, which was generalised by Prais and Houthakker (1955). The Engel procedure uses a household's budget share for Food as an indicator of welfare. Hence, a comparison of expenditure of households with different family size and composition but identical budget share for Food gives us the equivalence scale. In spite of the long tradition of estimation of equivalence scales, there remain severe problems in estimating and interpreting the estimated scales.

The Prais–Houthakker method leads to a serious identification problem, as noted by Forsyth (1960). McClements' (1977) suggestion of using Theil–Goldberger priors to overcome the problem has been criticised by Muellbauer (1979) on the grounds that the priors largely determine the estimates, as recently confirmed on Australian data by Bardsley and McRae (1982). Muellbauer's (1979) suggestion of using nutritionist Food priors has been similarly criticised by McClements (1979) for dominating the general scale, which he seeks to estimate, and is inconsistent with Muellbauer's own approach, generally, of not following the nutritionist method of determining equivalence scales. The Barten method, though overcoming the identification problem of Prais–Houthakker through use of price information, assumes a type of household behaviour that implies excessive quasi-price substitution in response to demographic changes and biases the estimated scales downwards.

2.4 Alternative Technique for Estimating Equivalence Scales—Generalised Cost Scaling and Price Scaling

Ray (1983) proposed an alternative technique for estimating equivalence scales. Although in the Barten–Gorman tradition of using a utility-consistent framework, it has the advantage of overcoming the identification problem by directly specifying and calculating the 'general' scale without having to rely on prior calculation of 'specific' scales. The proposed method is easy to apply, and the estimated parameters easy to interpret. This is particularly useful in view of our earlier discussion of the relevance of the scales in issues of public policy. Ray (1983) demonstrated the usefulness of the procedure by applying the methodology to pooled time series of UK budget data and obtaining plausible results. The robustness of the estimates is established by performing the empirical work under two quite different sets of circumstances involving different functional forms, different commodity and household aggregation and different number of observations but, yet, obtaining results that compare favourably with one another. The demographic technique proposed by Ray (1983) is described as follows.

The proposed demographic technique stems from viewing the general equivalence scale, $m_{0\mathrm{h}}$, as a 'true cost of living index', namely the ratio of costs of obtaining a reference utility level u at a given price level p of household h with z children and a reference household 'R' (adult couple with no children),

$$c_h(u,p,z) = m_{0\mathrm{h}}(z,u,p)c_{\mathrm{R}}(u,p) \tag{2.4}$$

If one specifies a suitable functional form for the cost function of the reference household, c_{R} (u, p), which satisfies the usual economic theoretic conditions of linear homogeneity in prices, symmetry and concavity, then choice of a suitable functional form for $m_{0\mathrm{h}}(z,u,p)$ gives us the corresponding form for the cost function of household h. Using price information and household budget data, one can then calculate the general scale directly by estimating the parameters entering m, using the estimable demand system of household, h, implied by Eq. 2.4. The direct specification of m_0 suggested by this approach, not only simplifies calculation of the general scale, but allows an easier investigation of the variation of the scale with prices and reference utility level.

This is, again, particularly useful since the variation of the scale with price, as much as the scale magnitude itself, is of relevance in welfare and income maintenance programmes. It is worth pointing out that while the Prais–Houthakker methodology almost guarantees the scale to rise with reference utility, the reverse is the case for the Barten scale. The general scale m_0 can be split into two multiplicative factors: a 'basic' component, $\bar{m}_0$, and a price and utility-varying component, Φ, where Φ represents the dependence of the general scale on the structure of relative prices and utility:

$$m_0(z,p,u) = \bar{m}_0\Phi\,(p,z,u) \tag{2.5}$$

where $\Phi(p,z,u)$ must be non-negative and homogenous of degree zero in prices p. A test of unit Φ constitutes a test of the invariance of the scale with price and utility. It is worth noting that in such an event, i.e. if $\Phi = 1$, the cost function of household h would be given by:

$$c_{\mathrm{h}}(u,p,z) = \bar{m}_0(z_{\mathrm{h}})c^{\mathrm{R}}(u,\,p) \tag{2.6}$$

Taking logs and using Shephard's Lemma, $w_i = \delta \log c/\delta \log p_i$, where w_i is budget share of item i, gives us the following relationship.

$$w_{i\mathrm{h}}(p,u,z) = w_{i\mathrm{R}}(p,u,z) \tag{2.7}$$

Equation 2.7 says that households, which enjoy the same level of utility, have identical expenditure composition which, as noted above, is the basis of the Engel model. The generalisation of the present procedure over the Engel model thus directly rests on the variation of the scale with prices, as is evident in the following relationship implied by Eqs. 2.4 and 2.5,

$$w_{ih}(u, p, z) = w_{iR}(u, p) + \frac{\delta \log \Phi}{\delta \log p_i} \tag{2.8}$$

2.5 Requirements for Identification of True Equivalence Scales and Their Interpretation as Cost of Children

Browning (1992) provides estimates of adult equivalence scales from a selection of studies in developed country contexts. The scale estimates vary considerably. This reflects an underlying difficulty in interpreting the utility-based equivalence scale estimate as the 'cost of child'. The difficulty was first pointed out by Pollak and Wales (1979) and elaborated in Pollak (1990). As noted by Browning (1992, p. 1444), 'any utility function *V(p, x, z)* can be renormalised to *F(V(p, x, z), z)*, where *F(V(p, x, z), z)* is strictly increasing in *V* without changing the demand system'. However, they generally give different values of the equivalence scale. In other words, observed behaviour cannot identify the true equivalence scales that are required in policy applications unless a 'correct normalisation' is made. Such normalisation takes the form of assumptions such as that made in the Engel model or the identifying restriction that the cost of a child is independent of base or reference utility.

This latter restriction was derived independently by Lewbel (1989) and Blackorby and Donaldson (1993) and has been referred to by them as, respectively, 'Independence of Base Utility' (IB) and 'Equivalence Scale Exactness' (ESE). As already noted above, the UK evidence reported in Ray (1983) has rejected this restriction. Note, also, that the price scaling procedure proposed in Ray (1983) and its nested specialisation that enforced price invariance of the scale satisfy the IB/ESE restriction of the invariance of the scale to reference utility. Pollak and Wales (1979) explain this problem by drawing a distinction between 'unconditional' and 'conditional preferences'. In the words of Pollak and Wales (1992, p. 85), 'the difficulty is that the preferences needed to compare alternative price–demographic situations are "unconditional preferences" (in this case, preferences over price–demographic situations) and these preferences cannot be obtained by analysing the consumption patterns of households with different demographic profiles'.

The latter are the 'conditional preferences' which correspond to the observed expenditure behaviour but are not the 'unconditional preferences' required to identify and estimate the cost of a child. The latter, it is argued, cannot be identified from observed household budget data. Again in the words of Pollak and Wales (1992, pp. 88–89), 'Conditional preferences are defined over market goods, with non-market goods held fixed at specified levels. Thus conditional preferences resemble conditional probabilities, which are "conditioned" on some specified event. Unconditional preferences, which are defined over the space of market goods and nonmarket goods, are analogous to unconditional or joint probabilities. Making situation comparisons requires knowing unconditional preferences; conditional preferences do not contain enough information to compare situations that differ in the level of market goods'. This difficulty prevents the 'true cost of living index' conventionally defined over time series data with temporal variation in prices from being used to define the adult equivalence scale based on welfare comparisons between households.

The above discussion shows that for demand data to be useful in yielding equivalence scales that are useful for policy applications involving welfare comparisons between households one requires restrictions on ordinal preferences implicit in methods proposed in the literature and, conditional on the normalisation adopted, one requires demand data to estimate the parameters of the indirect utility or cost function. Blundell and Lewbel (1991) argue that if a scale is agreed upon for a given year, then conventional 'exact price indices' can be used in conjunction with demand based preference estimates to identify changes in the scale from year to year.

2.6 Demographic Demand Systems

Ray (1983) showed that besides providing an alternative specification of the equivalence scale analogous to the 'true cost of living index', generalised cost scaling and its nested specialisation, price scaling, can be used to derive demographic demand systems that will allow simultaneous estimation of equivalence scales and demand elasticities from pooled cross section of budget surveys. In the empirical exercise in Ray (1983), two quite different frameworks were chosen and have been described as Framework 1 and Framework 2 below. Both use the same functional form for $\bar{m}_0$:

$$\bar{m}_0 = 1 + \rho z \tag{2.9}$$

where z indicates the number of children in the household, and the scales are normalised at unity for the childless couple, ρ is the basic equivalence scale, i.e. the 'cost' of a child at base year ($p = 1$). Two alternative frameworks were used for the exercise in Ray (1983).

2.6.1 *Framework 1*

A simple multiplicative form was chosen for the scale function:

$$\Phi(p, z) = \prod_{k=1}^{n} p_k^{\delta_k z} \tag{2.10}$$

where $\sum \delta_i = 0$. δ_i measures the effect of a change in the relative price of item i on the general scale, m_0. It should be noted that the δs would be identified only if there is reasonable relative price variation. This is clear from the fact that if prices move near identically over time such that the relative prices are constant, then Φ shall be close to unity regardless of the δ values.

The following non-separable generalisation of the LES [see Blundell and Ray (1984)] was chosen as the functional form for the reference household's cost function,

$$c^{R}(p, u) = \sum_i \sum_j \gamma_{ij} p_i^{1/2} p_j^{1/2} + u \prod_k p_k^{\beta_k} \tag{2.11}$$

where $\sum \beta_i = 1$ and $\gamma_{ij} = \gamma_{ji}$. Equation 2.11 nests LES when $\gamma_{ij} = 0, i \neq j$.

The estimable demographic demand system is then given by

$$\begin{aligned} w_i = {} & \delta_i z + \sum_j \gamma_{ij} \left(p_i^* p_j^*\right)^{1/2} \left(\bar{m} \prod_k p_k^{*\delta_k z)}\right) \\ & + \beta_i \left[1 - \sum_i \sum_j \gamma_{ij} \left(p_i^* p_j^*\right) 1/2 \left(\bar{m}_0 \prod_k p_k^{*\delta_k z}\right)\right] \end{aligned} \tag{2.12}$$

where $\bar{m}_0$ is given by Eq. 2.9, $p_i^* (= p_i/\mu)$ is the 'normalised price' and μ is aggregate household expenditure.

2.6.2 Framework 2

The specifications adopted in Framework 1 imply restrictive behaviour in two important respects: utility invariance of the scale and linear Engel curves. To relax these restrictive assumptions, Framework 2 proposed the following functional forms:

$$\Phi(p, u, z) = \exp\left(u \prod_k p_k^{\beta_k} \left\{\prod_k p_k^{\eta_k z} - 1\right\}\right) \tag{2.13}$$

where $\sum \beta_i = \sum \eta_i = 0$. The η_is allow dependence of the scale on both prices and utility. The direction of variation of Φ with u would depend on the magnitude of the η_is namely being positive (i.e. m_0 increasing with u) if $\prod_k p_k^{\eta_k z} > 1$, and negative otherwise. The second restrictive assumption of linear Engel curves in Framework 1 can be relaxed by assuming PIGLOG preferences for the reference household, R whose cost function is given by:

$$\log c^{R}(u,p) = \alpha_0 + \sum \alpha_i \log p_i + \frac{1}{2}\sum\sum \gamma_{ij} \log p_i \log p_j + u \prod_k p_k^{\beta_k} \quad (2.14)$$

where $\gamma_{ij} = \gamma_{ji}$, $\sum \alpha_i = 1$, $\sum \beta_i = \sum_i \gamma_{ij} = 0$. The estimable demographic demand system in budget share form is then given by,

$$w_i = \alpha_i + \sum_j \gamma_{ij} \log p_j + \beta_i^* \log[\mu/(\bar{m}_0 P)] \quad (2.15)$$

Given $\beta_i^* = \beta_i + \eta_i z$, and $\log P = P = \alpha_0 + \sum \alpha_i \log p_i + \frac{1}{2}\sum\sum \gamma_{ij} \log p_i \log p_j$

Both the demographic demand systems Eqs. 2.12 and 2.15 were estimated by Ray (1983) on pooled UK Family Expenditure Surveys (1968–79). The study was conducted on the following 4-item classification of household expenditure for Framework 1—Food; Clothing and Footwear; Fuel and Light; Durable Household Goods. The following 4-item classification was used in Framework 2—Fuel; Food; Alcohol, Clothing and Durables; Transport, Services and Other Goods. Child age effects were introduced by generalising the components of the scale function Eq. 2.5 to

$$\bar{m}_0 = 1 + \rho_1 z_1 + \rho_2 z_2 \quad (2.16)$$

$$\Phi(p,z) = \prod_k p_k^{\delta_{k1} z_1 + \delta_{k2} z_2} \quad (2.17)$$

z_1 = number of young children (0–5 years), z_2 = number of older children (5–18 years), and $\sum_k \delta_{k1} = \sum_k \delta_{k2} = 0$.

2.7 UK Evidence on Equivalence Scales

The results from estimating Eqs. 2.12 and 2.15 on UK data in Ray (1983) can be summarised as follows.

(a) In Framework 1, the parameters principally of interest here are the basic equivalence scale, ρ, and the δ_i's, which measure its variation with relative prices. The significance of δ_1 (Food) and δ_4 (Durable Household Goods) suggest rejection of the Engel model and point to the proposed methodology representing a significant improvement over Engel on likelihood-based chi-square criteria. Note, however, that on differentiating between young and older children, the price sensitivity of the scale weakens with only 2 of the 8 δ_{kd}s (k = 1, …, 4, d = 1, 2) record statistical significance. Under price invariance of the scale, a child costs around 12% of a childless couple. Allowing the scale to vary with prices opens up the possibility of substitution responses, and this leads to a drop in the basic scale estimate to around 7% of a childless couple.

(b) The results show that the 'cost' of a child is significantly and positively related to the relative price of Food.

(c) Framework 2 allows the additional dependence of 'child cost' on reference utility via the ηs. The statistical significance of the ηs confirms the variation of the equivalence scale with reference utility extending the result on the sensitivity of the scale to the structure of relative prices facing the household.

An alternative and simpler specification for the GCS functional form was proposed in Ray (1986) and the corresponding demographic demand system was estimated on UK Family Expenditure data pooled over 1968–79. Let us recall the relation between the cost functions of household h and the reference household R given above in Eq. 2.4, and the GCS form introduced in Eq. 2.5,

$$c_{\mathrm{h}}(u,p,z) = m_{0\mathrm{h}}(z,u,p)c_{\mathrm{R}}(u,p) \quad (2.4)$$

$$m_0(z,p,u) = \bar{m}_0(z)\Phi(p,z,u) \quad (2.5)$$

Following our earlier discussion, the cardinalisation adopted in GCS in Ray (1986) allows $\Phi(p,u,z)$ to be split up into a price-dependent component, Φ_1 (p, z) and a utility-dependent component Φ_2 (u, z). The general scale can be split up into multiplicative factors: $\bar{m}_0$ and Φ. $\bar{m}_0$ represents the price and utility-invariant component of m and can be interpreted as the equivalence scale in base year at base utility level. In empirical work, such a base utility level could be treated as zero so that $\bar{m}_0(z)$ becomes the equivalence scale of a 'subsistence' household at base year. The scale factor $\Phi(p, z, u)$ would then automatically show the nature of variation of the general scale both across households and over time.

$$\Phi(p,u,z) = \Phi_1(p, z)\Phi_2(u, z) \quad (2.18)$$

This is a simpler formulation than that in Ray (1983), given by Eq. 2.13 above. In Eq. 2.18, while the price-dependent component of the scale, Φ_1 (p, z), does not depend on reference utility, the utility-dependent component of the scale, Φ_2 (u, z), does not depend on prices. The price scale, Φ_1, measures the response of cost of children to relative price changes over time for a household whose welfare level u is kept constant—or, more appropriately perhaps, for the subsistence household ($u = 0$). In contrast, Φ_2 measures the response of cost of children to utility changes on constant price data, that is, as one moves across reference households within a single survey. In addition to several other restrictive assumptions, the most notable being the absence of lifecycle or intertemporal considerations, one needs to assume identical preferences and some a priori cardinalisation to identify the general equivalence scale and obtain plausible scale estimates.

The resultant 'scale' is called 'conditional', since it is conditional on preference and a particular cardinalisation. The justification of the particular cardinalisation that needs to be assumed must be (i) plausibility of the underlying story on behavioural grounds and (ii) plausibility of the estimated conditional scales in view of their subsequent policy use. We, ideally, also require a criterion that (iii) the conditional scales should be very close to the unconditional scales which they approximate. However, since the latter will not be identified on available budget data, verification of such a criterion will never be possible in practice. Assuming PIGLOG cost function given, by Eq. 2.14 above, for the reference household, R, and the following functional forms for the three components of the equivalence scales:

$$\bar{m}_0\,(z) = 1 + \rho\, z,\;\; \Phi_1\,(\mathbf{p}, \mathrm{z}) = \textstyle\prod_k p_k^{\delta_k z}\;, \Phi_2\;(u,z)\; = e^{\lambda u z} \tag{2.19}$$

The demographic demand system for household h is given by

$$w_i = \alpha_i + \delta_i\,\mathrm{z} + \textstyle\sum_j \gamma_{ij}\, \log\,(p_j) + \beta_i\, {}^{1}/(1 + \lambda z\, \prod p_k^{-\beta_k})\,\log\,({}^{\mu}/\bar{m}_0\,(z)P) \tag{2.20}$$

The demographically varying price index is given by

$$\log P = \alpha_0 + \sum \alpha_i \log p_i + \frac{1}{2}\sum\sum \gamma_{ij} \log p_i \log p_j + \sum \delta_k (z \log p_k) \tag{2.21}$$

It is also worth pointing out that the ‘unrestricted’ system, Eq. 2.20, will identify all the demographic and price–expenditure parameters satisfactorily only if there is reasonable independent variation in both prices and household size. An inspection of the log P expression above reveals, for example, that the scale ρ is identified from the δ’s only if the variation in z log p is appreciably different from that of log p_k. However, as the UK evidence presented in Ray (1986) showed, a time series of budget data from the Family Expenditure Surveys, 1968–79, contained the necessary information to yield well-determined estimates of the price parameters and, in conjunction with sensible and plausible restrictions, of the basic demographic parameters as well. The generality of the demographic demand system, Eq. 2.20, can be seen from the fact that it nests the Barten model as demonstrated below. To see this, let us go back to the starting point, the GCS, given in Eq. 2.5 and choose a different functional form for $\bar{m}_0$, although retaining that of Φ.

$$\bar{m}_0(z) = \mathrm{e}^{\varepsilon_1 z + \varepsilon_{11} z^2} \tag{2.22}$$

Given that $\Phi(p, u, z) = \prod_k p_k^{\delta_k z}\, e^{\lambda u z}, \sum \delta_i = 0.$.

Choosing the PIGLOG cost function for the reference household as before, GCS implies the following cost function for a household with z children.

$$\log c = \alpha_0 + \sum \alpha_i \log p_i + \frac{1}{2} \sum \sum \gamma_{ij} \log p_i \log p_j + u\ \beta_0 \prod_k p_k{}^{\beta_k} + \varepsilon_1 z + \varepsilon_{11} z^2 + \sum_i \delta_i (z \log p_i) + \lambda\, u\, z \tag{2.23}$$

Now, if m_i denotes the 'specific scales', then the Barten cost function for the same household is given by,

$$\alpha_0 + \sum \alpha_i \log p_i^* + \frac{1}{2} \sum \sum \gamma_{ij} \log p_i^* \log p_j^* + u\beta_0 \prod_k p_k^{*\beta_k} \tag{2.24}$$

where $p_i^* = p_i m_i$. If the specific scales are assumed to take the form

$m_i = e^{\theta_1 z}$, then it is readily verified that Eq. 2.23 nests Eq. 2.24, i.e. GCS nests Barten if the following relation holds between the GCS and Barten parameters.

$$\delta_i = \sum_j \theta_j \gamma_{ij} \tag{2.25}$$

$$\varepsilon_1 \sum_i \alpha_i \theta_i \tag{2.25a}$$

$$\varepsilon_{11} = \frac{1}{2} \sum_i \sum_j \gamma_{ij} \theta_i \theta_j \tag{2.25b}$$

$$\lambda = 0 \tag{2.25c}$$

In other words, using Eq. 2.23 as the maintained framework, we can test the Barten idea implicit in Eq. 2.24 via a nested test of the restrictions (Eqs. 2.25–2.25c). This means that Barten enforces two restrictions onto GCS, since the $(n + 2)$ independent demographic parameters of GCS are replaced by the n specific scale parameters of Barten.

The UK results presented in Ray (1986) based on demographic demand system, Eq. 2.20, can be summarised as follows.

(a) The 'cost' of a child was about 6% of a childless adult couple.
(b) The 'cost' is significantly and positively related to the relative price of Food which seems plausible in view of the dominant importance of Food in the child's consumption basket. This result is consistent with the UK evidence also reported in Ray (1983).
(c) If we ignore the price dependence of the scale, i.e. enforce the Engel restrictions, then the 'cost' goes up to around 21% of a childless couple.

(d) There is little evidence to suggest that the 'cost' alters significantly with a joint movement in reference utility and the relative price of Fuel and Alcohol.
(e) Use of genuine databased price, demographic information in conjunction with theory-based a priori restrictions can and does allow (within the proposed GCS framework) joint and efficient estimation of all the central parameters of basic interest.
(f) Using the nested specialisation of the Barten model Eq. 2.24 within the GCS form Eq. 2.23, the Barten model was easily rejected by the UK data on a log likelihood-based chi-square test. The Engel model, which can be viewed as a further specialisation of Barten with $m_i =$, i.e. all the specific scales are the same, yielded a further unacceptable fall in log likelihood implying a rejection of the Engel restrictions as well.

On the same UK FES data, Ray (1996a) provided evidence in favour of greater generality in the demographic demand literature in terms of modelling the household size and composition effects on demand and their interaction with prices. Two extensions of demographic cost functions were proposed.

2.7.1 The Generalised Non-additive Gorman Model

Gorman [1976, (52)] proposed the following demographic cost function that generalised Barten by adding a fixed cost term to the Barten component.

$$c(u,P,z) = \sum_i d_i(z)p_i + c_R(u, p_1m_1, \ldots, p_nm_n) \tag{2.26}$$

where z is the number of children in the household. Ray (1996a) proposed the following 'generalised non-additive Gorman' (GNAG) cost function:

$$c(u,P,z) = [D(P,z) + c_R(u, p_1m_1, \ldots, p_nm_n)^r]^{1/r} \tag{2.27}$$

where D is homogeneous of degree r in prices, P. The following simple form was chosen for D:

$$D = \sum_i \sum_j d^*_{ij} z p_i^{r/2} p_j^{r/2} z p_i^{r/2} p_j^{r/2}, \quad d^*_{ij} = d^*_{ji} \tag{2.28}$$

2.7.2 The Generalised Non-additive Price Scaling Model

Extended price scaling (EPS) relaxes 'Equivalence Scale Exactness' (ESE) and extends PS by adding a non-ESE term to the PS cost function.

$$c(u,P,z) = \sum_i d_i(z)p_i + m_0(P,z) + c_R(u,p_1,\ldots,p_n) \qquad (2.29)$$

EPS assumes simple additivity both between the non-ESE and ESE components and between the non-ESE parameters themselves. The 'generalised non-additive extended price scaling' (GNAEPS) cost function generalises EPS by relaxing both types of additivity and, hence, provides a convenient nesting framework for EPS (i.e. simple additivity) and its nested special cases, namely price scaling (PS) and Engel scaling. The GNAEPS cost function is given as follows.

$$c(u,P,z) = \left[D(P,z) + m_0^r(P,z)c_R^r(u,p_1,\ldots,p_n)\right]^{1/r}, \quad r > 0 \qquad (2.30)$$

where the aggregate non-ESE term, D, is homogeneous of degree r in prices P and the non-additivity parameter r performs a role analogous to that in the GNAG cost function given in Eq. 2.27. The UK-based evidence reported in Ray (1996a) rejects both the Barten and the additive Gorman models, as also the additive EPS model, thus pointing to the need for greater generality in modelling demographic demand behaviour especially the interaction between prices and household composition.

2.8 Australian Evidence on Equivalence Scales

Lancaster and Ray (1998) provide Australian evidence on equivalence scales. The motivation of this paper is to provide Australian evidence, based on micro-expenditure data, on the sensitivity of the equivalence scale to models, methods of calculation and commodities. This study compares the equivalence scale estimates between the single-equation-based methods of Engel (1895) and Rothbarth (1943) and those from the 'complete demand system'-based approaches, pioneered by Barten (1964) and modified/extended by Gorman (1976), Muellbauer (1977), Jorgenson and Slesnick (1987), Ray (1983, 1996a, b), Chatterjee et al. (1994), and Nelson (1988). This paper also contains evidence on the sensitivity of the Rothbarth scales to the choice of an 'adult good'. The Rothbarth model is dependent, for its empirical implementation, on the notion of an 'adult good'. The set of items which can be described as 'adult good' is a large one. The Australian empirical evidence, presented in Lancaster and Ray (1998) on the sensitivity of the Rothbarth scale estimates to the choice of 'adult good' is, therefore, of some policy significance.

Engel's (1895) model is based on the premise that the welfare of adults is inversely related to the share of the household budget spent on Food. This leads to the hypothesis that adults in two households with different numbers of children enjoy the same welfare if these households have the same Food share in their budget. The Engel equivalence scale, then, follows as the ratio of household expenditures that imply identical budget shares for Food in these demographically varying households. In contrast, the Rothbarth (1943) model is based on the premise that adult welfare is directly related to the level of household expenditure on 'Adult Goods'. Hence, in relation to a couple without children, one with a child needs to receive a compensation that allows it to restore its expenditure on 'Adult Goods' to its earlier prechild level. The Rothbarth equivalence scale, then, follows as the ratio of household expenditures that imply the same *level* of expenditure on 'Adult Goods' in these households.

The idea behind the Engel and Rothbarth models of linking adult welfare with, respectively, the household budget share of Food and the consumption of adult goods is simple and intuitively appealing, and this explains the popularity of these models even to this day. However, the underlying assumptions are not as innocent as they initially appear, and some are inconsistent with reality. While the Engel procedure leads to an upward bias, the Rothbarth procedure leads to a downward bias in the estimated scale. The birth of a child has two effects, each a positive one, on the household's budget share spent on Food, due to: (a) the lower per capita household expenditure in the enlarged household and (b) changed household preferences in favour of 'Food' because of the addition of a primarily Food consuming individual. The Engel equivalence scale model recognises (a) but not (b). Hence, in insisting that a household with a child be compensated to the point where its budget share on Food is restored to its prechild level, the Engel model is likely to overcompensate the household—in other words, the Engel scale suffers from an upward bias.

In contrast, the idea behind the Rothbarth model that household expenditure on adult goods is an indicator of adult welfare is based on the assumption of separability of parental preferences between their own consumption and that of their children. In other words, (a) birth of a child has no effect on parental preferences for adult goods and (b) the presence of children has income effects only on parental consumption. Notwithstanding these strong restrictions, the Rothbarth model provides a simple, intuitively appealing framework for calculating the expenditure shares of adults and children for selected adult items. However, as Nelson (1992) argues, a major limitation of the Rothbarth model stems from the existence of family 'public goods' that are characterised by their simultaneous joint consumption by adults and children. Moreover, like Engel, the Rothbarth model ignores the purely demographic impact of addition of a child to a household's preference between items.

Apart from the limitations discussed above, and the fact that they are not directly rooted in utility theory, the Engel and Rothbarth equivalence scale models do not explicitly consider prices, nor do they recognise the role that price movements may play in altering preferences. They also overlook the fact that a change in household composition may lead to change in the implicit prices a household pays for various items. To take an example—the birth of a child is likely to increase the price of outside entertainment for a couple, since babysitting services will now have to be paid for. This provides the background and justification for the demand system-based methods for equivalence scales estimation, namely the Barten and price scaling procedures described above.

The data used in Lancaster and Ray (1998) came from the 1984 and 1988–89 Household Expenditure Surveys (HES) published by the Australian Bureau of Statistics (ABS). The 1984 survey consists of 4492 households, with the information presented in a two-level record. The first level (the household record) describes demographic, income and expenditure information pertaining to each household. The expenditure is defined over 13 broad category definitions. The second level (the expenditure record) details expenditure on 422 separate commodities. These items provide the basis for more aggregated commodity groupings. All measurement is in terms of average weekly expenditure. In relation to that in the UK and other European countries, the Australian literature on equivalence scale estimation is quite recent and, without exception, the studies are on single cross-sectional data admitting no price variation. Podder (1971) made the first attempt to estimate the general equivalence scale for Australia by applying the Prais–Houthakker methodology to Food only.

The Social Welfare Policy Secretariat (SWPS) applied a modified version of the Engel method to the 1974–75 HES unit record data in a study of poverty measurement in Australia (SWPS I981). Van Hoa (1986), employing a duality approach based on the generalised Engel's law, estimated the general and commodity specific equivalence scales using the 1975–76 HES grouped data.

Kakwani (1977), using the extended linear expenditure system, estimates equivalence scales from a single cross-sectional survey incorporating a linear aggregate consumption function as the identifying restriction.

The Australian evidence reported in Lancaster and Ray (1998) can be summarised as follows:

(a) The Engel scales for both 1-adult and 2-adult households and based on the estimated linear demand specifications for the Engel relationship shows the sensitivity of the scale to the inclusion of 'Takeaway' in the calculations. The inclusion of 'Takeaway' decreases the scale for all household types.
(b) The Engel scales which seem reasonably robust tend to increase in magnitude with the introduction of higher order terms in aggregate expenditure in the estimated Food share equation.
(c) Considerable sensitivity of the Rothbarth scale to the item chosen as an 'Adult Good' thereby revealing a significant weakness in the practical application of the Rothbarth idea since there is hardly any agreement on what constitutes an 'Adult Good'. Tertiary Education, for example, gives rise to Rothbarth equivalence scales of much higher magnitude than those based on Takeaways' or 'Alcohol Taken Indoors'. Interestingly, 'Alcohol Taken Outdoors' yield significantly higher scales than 'Alcohol Taken at Home'. Unlike Engel, the introduction of quadratic terms in log real expenditure leads to a decline in the estimated Rothbarth scales for all items, the decrease being particularly sharp for 'Adult Education', and less so for 'Alcohol Outdoors'. The estimated Rothbarth scale for Tobacco shows that children exert large negative impact on a household's expenditure on this item. The presence of a child does discourage tobacco consumption at home.

(d) The Rothbarth scale seems a good deal more sensitive than the Engel scale to reference household expenditure. The Engel and Rothbarth scales also differ in the direction of changes in their magnitude with increase in reference household expenditure. While the Engel scales rise slightly with increase in household affluence, the Rothbarth scales decline, quite sharply in many cases, as we move from poor to more affluent households.
(e) The utility-based equivalence scale estimates generally lie between the Engel and Rothbarth scale estimates for Food. The Barten scales seem implausibly low and reinforce previous doubts about the usefulness of the Barten model as an equivalence scale model notwithstanding its continued popularity in the literature.

2.9 Analysis of Indian Expenditure Patterns

India has a long tradition of Engel curve analysis based on family budget data that takes the form of National Sample Surveys (NSS) collected and made available by the National Sample Survey Organisation (NSSO). The NSS is one of the oldest continuing surveys in the developing world. The NSSO collects a wide range of information that extends from land ownership, cultivation and utilisation, wage rates of skilled and unskilled labour, unemployment and labour supply at the village level to household expenditure on various items along with household characteristics. The first round of the NSS was conducted in 1950–51 which was also the year the Planning Commission was set up in India. The NSS was designed to provide the detailed information required by the Planning Commission on the extent, magnitude and patterns of poverty to help in formulating effective policies designed to reduce poverty and promote household welfare. The NSS has played a significant role in the economic development of the country.

For a long while, the NSS operated in close tandem with the Planning Commission and under the wings of Indian Statistical Institute (ISI). The founder of ISI, Professor P C Mahalanobis, was also closely involved with the Planning Commission, and this cemented the link between the ISI and the NSSO. The NSS was divested from the technical wing of the ISI in 1972, and the task of running the surveys and disseminating the information was taken over by the Ministry of Statistics and Programme Implementation of the Government of India. Since the first survey in 1950–51, the scope and coverage of the NSS has increased significantly and is now one of the largest ongoing sample surveys anywhere in the world, not just in the developing countries. Because of the early involvement of the Indian Statistical Institute in the questionnaire design and data collection, the NSS is widely respected for the high quality of the data. Until 1998, the household level data was only available to the public in grouped form, i.e. as cell averages, and this restricted the range of uses to which the NSS data could be put.

From 1998, the NSSO made available to the public the unit records, and this has led to a large increase in studies based on the NSS. With the large increase in sample size and geographical coverage, a decision was made (beginning with the 1973–1974 round) to split the rounds into two: quinquennial (or 'thick') rounds done at approximately five-year intervals on a large sample of households (about 120,000) and 'thin' rounds undertaken during intervening periods on smaller samples (approximately 35–40% of the thick-round samples). The NSS is representative of geographical regions below State level but is not representative at the district level. A central feature of the NSS, and among the most widely used of its surveys, has been the Household Expenditure Surveys (HES) or Consumer Expenditure Surveys (CES).

Thanks to the availability of such surveys, India has a long history of empirical analysis of expenditure patterns, especially cross-sectional analysis of household expenditure based on Engel curves at a point in time[2]. It is no coincidence that many of these early studies were conducted by researchers based at the ISI led by Professor Nikhilesh Bhattacharya. Most of this early work analysed the relationship between expenditure allocation over items, household size and aggregate household expenditure. There was limited role accorded to prices in influencing expenditure patterns. This largely reflected the lack of long time series of NSS cross-sectional data that would have allowed estimation of price elasticities along with expenditure and size elasticities. Bhattacharya (1967) and Joseph (1968) are early examples of analysis of Indian expenditure pattern using the 'complete demand systems' approach based on the Linear Expenditure System (LES). The lack of long time series of prices was overcome in these early studies by the use of the restrictive LES which imposed an a priori structure on the relationship between price and expenditure elasticities that allowed the former to be estimated without requiring long time series of price information.

However, such a priori relationships are now known to be empirically false thus raising questions over the accuracy of the price elasticity estimates. Bhattacharya (1967) while noting the difficulty of getting reliable estimates of price elasticities in these early attempts which had to work on data with limited price variation temporally, also, found that the expenditure elasticities were quite different from those obtained on pure time series data. Bhattacharya (1967) noted that part of the difference could be explained by the fact that in those early rounds, the NSS employed a moving reference period so households interviewed on different dates furnished accounts of different periods of 30 days (preceding the date of the interview). This distorted the estimated Engel relationship between itemwise spending and aggregate household expenditure by superimposing the seasonal variation over the true variation between households and exaggerated the extent of inequality. In more recent NSS rounds, therefore, the issue was addressed by having subrounds over shorter duration covering representative subsamples of the round sample.

---

[2]See Ray (1991) for an early review of the Indian literature on demand estimations and their welfare applications.

This is just one example of the challenges faced by researchers working with the earlier NSS data. The fact remains, therefore, that valiant efforts were made by the largely ISI-based researchers to analyse Indian expenditure patterns on NSS data and the two studies cited above are possibly the earliest anywhere to estimate a complete demand system, albeit a restrictive one, on sample survey data. Since household expenditure is a core indicator of household welfare, use and analysis of NSS HES/CES data has been central to policy formulations. With an improvement in the quality and coverage of the NSS data sets, the literature on the NSS-based demand estimations has grown exponentially and the NSS is now regarded as the prime source of information for policy relevant applications.

In recent years, the availability of time series of HES data from several rounds of the NSS accompanied by series on consumer price indices published by the Central Statistical Organisation (CSO) has facilitated attempts at 'complete demand estimation' on household budget surveys. There are now several price series with different population coverages. For example, the Ministry of Labour and Employment, Labour Bureau publishes the Consumer Price Index (CPI) of industrial workers in seven sectors, and the CPI for agricultural labourers and rural labourers. While the former (CPI-IW) has been used as a measure of urban prices, the latter (CPI-RW) has been used as a measure of urban prices in several welfare exercises such as updating of the rural and urban poverty lines. The Central Statistics Office (CSO) publishes the All India Consumer Price Index covering all the rural and urban population. Additionally, the unit records of household expenditures in NSS rounds that have been made available since 1998 containing both quantity and expenditure information has led to the use of unit values as proxies for Food prices in demand estimations on Indian data. We describe several such studies later on in this volume.

Murty (1980), Ray (1980, 1982, 1985,1996b), Coondoo and Majumder (1987) are some of the early examples of the Indian literature on 'complete demand estimation' that combined the cross-sectional variation in household expenditure from the NSS rounds pooled across years with information on temporal changes in prices published by the Government of India. Ray (1980)'s study was based on the 'Almost Ideal Demand System' of Deaton and Muellbauer (1980b).

$$w_i = \delta_i + \beta_i \log\left(\frac{\mu}{P}\right) + \sum_j \gamma_{ij} \log(p_j) + \theta_i \log(m) + v_i \tag{2.31}$$

P is the aggregate price index that is additive in log prices of the items and in the products of log prices and is given in Eq. 2.15 above, m is the general equivalence scale, size, v_i is the stochastic error term, and the other symbols are as defined earlier. Due to the limited variation in household size and composition, Eq. 2.31 did not introduce specific equivalence scales on the lines of Prais and Houthakker (1955), though this was relaxed in subsequent studies as described below.

Though set up as a 'complete demand system', Eq. 2.31 was estimated as a set of single equations with the Stone price index used as an approximation for log P. This study was based on a pooling of NSS rounds 4–23 covering the period April

1952—June 1969. A nine commodity breakdown was initially used: Food grains; milk and milk products; edible oils; meat, fish and eggs; other Food items; sugar; clothing; Fuel and Light; other non-Food items. The estimation was subsequently repeated on a more aggregated four-commodity classification where the first six items were lumped together as 'Food'. The main results included the presence of significant price effects on budget share in the nine commodity classification for many items individually and the rejection of zero price effects (as a whole, i.e. inclusive of own and cross-price effects) on budget share of Food and Clothing (rural) and Fuel and Light (urban). The estimates were generally sensible keeping in mind the poor quality of the database from the earlier NSS rounds.

Ray (1982) extended Ray (1980) by relaxing three of the restrictive features of the latter: (a) allowing the specific scales, m_i, to vary between items, (b) dispensing with the Stone price approximation for the log price index at the cost of introducing nonlinearity in the estimation and (c) estimating the system as a 'complete demand system' enforcing and testing for the symmetry restriction on the γ_{ij} s. The Barten (1964) model described earlier was used to demographically extend the 'Almost Ideal Demand' function form. The Barten-based demographic AIDS that was estimated is given as follows.

$$w_i = \alpha_i + \sum_j \gamma_{ij} \log(p_i^*) + \beta_i \log[\mu/P] \tag{2.32}$$

Note that $\log P = \alpha_0 + \sum_i \alpha_i \log\left(p_i^*\right) + \frac{1}{2}\sum_i \sum_j \gamma_{ij} \log\left(p_i^*\right) \log\left(p_j^*\right)$, and

$p_i^* = p_i m_i \cdot m_i$ is the item-specific equivalence scale. Adding Up: $\sum_i \alpha_i = 1, \sum_i \beta_i = \sum_i \gamma_{ij} = 0$, Symmetry: $\gamma_{ij} = \gamma_{ji}$.

Ray (1982) was based on the same data set as Ray (1980) and adopted the following 4-item breakdown of household expenditure: Food, Clothing, Fuel and Light, Other Non-Food items. The principal results included the following:

(a) The Barten-based demographic AIDS is a significant improvement on the non-demographic AIDS for both the rural and urban sectors on conventional likelihood criterion.
(b) The estimates of expenditure, price and family size elasticities obtained on time series data are different from corresponding estimates on pooled cross-sectional data. This is consistent with the observation of Bhattacharya (1967) from his early work on NSS data that we noted earlier.
(c) A differential nature of rural–urban expenditure pattern has emerged which is similar to that witnessed in studies on other developing economies. Rural–urban differences in preferences and spending pattern are an essential feature of large and diverse countries such as India. We return to this aspect later in this volume when we present evidence on rural–urban differences in prices in the context of estimating spatial (also called subnational) purchasing power parity within India.

(d) Ray (1982) was one of the earliest attempts at estimating a demographically extended non-restrictive demand system on pooled time series of cross-sectional data from a developing country. The elasticity estimates were found to be generally plausible in an exercise where the lack of ready and reliable retail price figures made the exercise more difficult.

While Ray (1980, 1982), Coondoo and Majumder (1987)'s studies of Indian expenditure patterns on NSS data were based on PIGLOG preferences, Ray (1985) proposed generalisations of the LES that focussed on relaxing its assumption of linear Engel curves and constant budget shares to accommodate nonlinear responses. Moreover, while the above-mentioned studies used a static framework, Ray (1985) proposed and estimated dynamic extensions that allowed the preference parameters to change over time. The dynamic extension followed Pollak (1970)'s approach of introducing habit formation and allowing a subset of the parameters to depend on lagged consumption. The following two dynamic demand models were introduced in Ray (1985).

2.9.1 Delta Scaled Dynamic QES

$$\begin{aligned} w_{it} &= z_{it}^{\delta} b_{it} + \beta_i [1 - \sum_k z_{kt}^{\delta} b_{kt}] \\ &\quad + \left[z_{it}^{\delta} c_i - \beta_i \sum\nolimits_k z_{kt}^{\delta} c_k \right] \prod_k z_{kt}^{-2\delta\beta_k} \left[1 - \sum_k z_{kt}^{\delta} b_{kt} \right]^2 \end{aligned} \tag{2.33}$$

where $z_{it} = \frac{p_{it}}{\mu_t}$, $b_{it} = b_i^* + \theta_i x_{it-1}$, $0 < \delta \le 1$, $\sum_i \beta_i = 1$.

The θ_i are the dynamic parameters which allow the b_{it} s to depend on lagged consumption, x_{it-1}, and subscripts i and t denote item and time, respectively. Equation 2.33 generalises the static QES model proposed by Howe et al. (1979) and specialises to the latter if $\delta = 1$, $\theta_i = 0$ for all i.

2.9.2 Delta Scaled Dynamic LTL

$$w_{it} = z_{it}^{\delta} b_{it} + \left(\alpha_i + \sum\nolimits_j \beta_{ij} \log p_{jt} \right) \left(1 - \sum\nolimits_k z_{kt}^{\delta} b_{kt} \right) \tag{2.34}$$

Given that $z_{it} = \frac{p_{it}}{\mu_t}$, $b_{it} = b_i^* + \theta_i x_{it-1}$, $\sum_i \alpha_i = 1$, $\sum_j \beta_{ij} = \sum_i \beta_{ji} = 0$, $\beta_{ij} = \beta_{ji}$, $0 < \delta \le 1$. Equation 2.34 extends the Linear Translog (LTL) proposed by Lau and Mitchell (1971) that extends the LES by allowing the marginal budget share to vary with prices while retaining the linearity of Engel curves. Equation 2.34 specialises to the static LTL if $\delta = 1$, and the dynamic parameters, θ_i s, are all zero. Ray (1985) estimated demand systems, Eqs. 2.33–2.34, on a 3-item breakdown, Food, Clothing and Fuel & Light, on pooled NSS data sets from NSS 7–28 rounds covering the period, 1953–54 (NSS 7th round) to 1973–74 (NSS 28th round). Notwithstanding the limited price variation over these earlier rounds of the NSS, the evidence provided support to both the delta generalisations and in favour of dynamic preferences. $\delta = 1$ was rejected in both specifications, and the dynamic parameters, the θ_is, were all highly significant.

2.10 Concluding Remarks

This chapter outlines some of the key developments in the specification of demand systems and reports the experience of estimating them from a selection of studies on data sets from different countries. This chapter describes some of the key developments in the demographic demand literature and equivalence scales that can be traced to the early work of Engel on Belgian working class data. Given the focus of this volume, this chapter reports the Indian demand literature in some greater detail than that on other countries. The emphasis in this chapter has been on describing the behavioural outcomes and of changes in family size, composition, prices and aggregate expenditure. This sets the scene for the discussion of the welfare applications of the demand estimates that we turn to in the following chapter.

References

Bardsley P, McRae I (1982) A test of McClements' method for the estimation of equivalence scales. J Public Econ 17:119–122

Barten AP (1964) Family composition, prices and expenditure patterns. In: Hart PE, Mills G, Whittaker JK (eds) Econometric analysis for national economic planning. Butterworth, London

Bhattacharya N (1967) An application of the linear expenditure system. Econ Polit Wkly, December, 2093–2098

Blackorby C, Donaldson D (1993) Household equivalence scales and welfare comparisons: a comment. J Public Econ 50:143–146

Blundell R, Lewbel A (1991) The information content of equivalence scales. J Econometrics 50:49–68

Blundell RW, Ray R (1984) Testing for linear Engel curves and additively separable preferences using a new flexible demand system. Econ J 94:800–811

Browning M (1992) Modelling the effects of children on household equivalence scales. J Econ Lit 30:1434–1475

Chatterjee S, Michelini C, Ray R (1994) Expenditure patterns and aggregate consumer behaviour: some experiments with Australian and New Zealand data. Econ Rec 70:278–291

Coondoo D, Majumder A (1987) A system of demand equations based on price independent generalized linearity. Int Econ Rev 28:213–228

Dandekar VM (1982) On measurement of undernutrition. Econ Polit Wkly, February, 203–212

Deaton AS, Muellbauer J (1980a) Economics and consumer behaviour. Cambridge University Press, Cambridge

Deaton AS, Muellbauer J (1980b) An almost ideal demand system. Am Econ Rev 70:312–326

Engel E (1895) Die Libenskosten Belgischer arbieter - familien fruher and jetzt. Int Stat Inst Bull 9:1–74
Forsyth FG (1960) The relationship between family size and family expenditure. J Roy Stat Soc: Ser A 123:367–397
Gorman WM (1976) Tricks with utility function. In: Artis MJ, Nobay AR (eds) Essays in economic analysis. Cambridge University Press, Cambridge
Howe H, Pollak RA, Wales TJ (1979) Theory and time series estimation of the quadratic expenditure system. Econometrica 47:1231–1247
Jorgenson DW, Slesnick DT (1987) Aggregate consumer behaviour and household equivalence scales. J Bus Econ Stat 5:219–232
Joseph P (1968) Application of the linear expenditure system to N.S.S. data: some further results. Econ Polit Wkly, April, 609–615
Kakwani N (1977) On the estimation of consumer unit scales. Rev Econ Stat 59:507–510
Konus AA (1939) The problem of the true index of the cost of living (1924 trans.). Econometrica 7:10–29
Lancaster G, Ray R (1998) Comparison of household equivalence scales: the Australian evidence on unit record data. Econ Rec 74:1–14
Lau LJ, Mitchell BM (1971) A linear logarithmic expenditure system: an application to US data. Econometrica 39:87–88
Lewbel A (1989) Household equivalence scales and welfare comparisons. J Public Econ 39:377–391
McClements L (1977) Equivalence scales for children. J Public Econ 8:191–210
McClements L (1979) Muellbauer on equivalence scales. J Public Econ 12:233–242
Muellbauer J (1974) Prices and inequality: the recent U.K. experience. Econ J 84:32–55
Mucllbauer J (1977) Testing the Barten model of household composition effects and the cost of children. Econ J 87:460–487
Muellbauer J (1979) McClements on equivalence scales for children. J Public Econ 12:221–231
Murty K (1980) Consumer behaviour in India: an application of the Rotterdam demand system. Eur Econ Rev 14:221–235
Nelson J (1988) Household economies of scale in consumption: theory and evidence. Econometrica 56:1301–1314
Nelson J (1992) Methods of estimating equivalence scales: an empirical investigation. Rev Income Wealth 58:295–310
Podder N (1971) The estimation of an equivalent income scale. Aust Econ Pap 10:175–187
Pollak RA (1970) Habit formation and dynamic demand functions. J Polit Econ 78:745–763
Pollak RA (1990) Distinguished fellow: Houthakker's contributions to economics. J Econ Perspect 4:141–156
Pollak RA, Wales TJ (1979) Welfare comparisons and equivalence scales. Am Econ Rev 69:216–221
Pollak RA, Wales TJ (1981) Demographic variables in demand analysis. Econometrica 49:1533–1551
Pollak RA, Wales TJ (1992) Demand system specification and estimation. Oxford University Press, Oxford
Prais SJ, Houthakker HS (1955) The analysis of family budgets. Cambridge University Press, Cambridge
Ray R (1980) Analysis of a time series of household expenditure surveys for India. Rev Econ Stat 62:595–602
Ray R (1982) The testing and estimation of complete demand systems on household budget surveys: an application of AIDS. Eur Econ Rev 17:349–369
Ray R (1983) Measuring the costs of children: an alternative approach. J Public Econ 22:89–102
Ray R (1985) A dynamic analysis of expenditure patterns in rural India. J Dev Econ 19:283–297
Ray R (1986) Demographic variables and equivalence scales in a flexible demand system: the case of AIDS. Appl Econ 18:265–278

Ray R (1991) Complete demand systems and recent welfare applications in India: a review. J Quant Econ 7:1–22

Ray R (1996a) Demographic variables in demand systems: the case for generality. Empirical Economics 21:307–315

Ray R (1996b) Nesting flexible demand functional forms: econometric evidence for India and the UK. Sankhya: Indian J Stat: Ser B 58:254–273

Rothbarth E (1943) Note on a method of determining equivalence income for families of different composition. In: Madge C (ed) War-time pattern of saving and spending, Occasional paper no. 4, appendix IV. Macmillan, London

Sukhatme PV (1978) Assessment of adequacy of diets at different income levels. Econ Polit Wkly, Special Number, p 1373

Van Hoa T (1986) Measuring equivalence scales: a new system-wide method. Econ Lett 20:95–99

Chapter 3
Alternative Approaches to Measurement of Price Movements

3.1 Introduction

Given the central role that prices play in both micro- and macroeconomic analyses,[1] it is not surprising that there is a large literature on its measurement. The topic of price measurement has a long history, almost as long as applied economic analysis itself, dating back to the nineteenth century with the work of Laspeyres and Paasche in introducing price indices that measure temporal movement in prices. Building on that early work, Fisher (1922) introduced the 'ideal price index' that is defined as the square root of the Laspeyres and Paasche price indices. The topic of price indices, and more generally the measurement of prices, is now associated with a large and still expanding literature. Several excellent and easily accessible surveys of this literature exist, and we do not wish to add to these. Examples include Allen (1975), Diewert (1981), Selvanathan and Rao (1994), Balk (1995), Clements et al. (2006).

Instead, the motivation of this chapter is to survey the literature where prices play a crucial role and show how the concepts introduced in the measurement of prices have been applied in a variety of temporal and spatial comparisons at the household, country and subnational levels.[2] While the topic of price measurement traditionally figured in macroeconomic analyses involving the use of price indices in calculating inflation and the GDP deflator, and in international comparisons of GDP and the size of economies, this survey demonstrates that prices are increas-

---

Much of the material in this chapter is contained in the survey article, Ray (2017).

---

[1]In Australia, for example, the importance of correctly measuring prices was manifest in a major review of the CPI that was undertaken in 2009 with the recommendations made public in December 2010.

[2]Since the literature on price measurement applications in economics is a vast one, this survey is not an exhaustive one but, given the space limitations, had to be selective with the focus on empirical studies that combine analytical rigour with strong policy relevance.

R. Ray, *Household Behaviour, Prices, and Welfare*, Themes in Economics,
https://doi.org/10.1007/978-981-13-1930-3_3

ingly occupying centre stage in micro-economic investigations involving welfare comparisons across households. Moreover, as discussed in the following chapter, price indices have influenced related topics such as the measurement of utility-based household equivalence scales on the lines of the exact price indices, described below, exploiting the quasi-price nature of household composition effects following the influential paper by Barten (1964) and its extension by Muellbauer (1974a).

The measurement of prices can be broadly divided into two approaches: (a) a non-stochastic approach largely based on index numbers and (b) a stochastic approach based on estimation of a set of equations that yields standard errors of estimated price parameters. Approach (a) has a longer history than approach (b) though, in recent years, there has been a steady increase in the application of the stochastic approach. Approach (a) can be further subdivided into two streams: (a1) the 'exact approach', also known as 'true cost of living indices' (TCLI), that was introduced by Konus[3] (1924, English translation in Econometrica, 1939), and (a2) the index number approach of which the Laspeyres, Paasche, Fisher and Tornqvist indices are the most well-known examples. TCLI is defined as the ratio of costs of obtaining the same standard of living, measured by indirect utility, in the two price situations, namely evaluated at the initial and given year prices.

The two situations are assumed to differ only with respect to prices. In contrast, the index number approach is based on the ratio of the costs of buying the same basket of goods in the two price situations. Unlike the index number methods, TCLI is rooted in utility theory and requires a prior specification of the utility function and estimation of the preference parameters for its application. This confers both advantage and disadvantage on (a1) vis-a-vis (a2). The principal advantage of (a1) is that it allows easier policy application by examining the effect of price changes on consumer welfare via her specified utility function and the estimated preference parameters. As Muellbauer (1974a) showed, and empirically illustrated in Muellbauer (1974b) and Ray (1985), the TCLI approach allows an examination of the distributive consequences of inflation that is not readily possible under the index number approach.

The methodology is described in more detail in the following chapter. The principal disadvantage of TCLI is that any utility specification is ad hoc and, if the results are unduly sensitive to the utility specification, then theory does not provide much guidance to the policy analyst on which set of results to use. Moreover, (a1) requires much more information that (a2) in the form of price and expenditure variation to estimate the preference parameters that is generally not available and, as Oulton (2012) notes, has not therefore been applied much in the literature. In contrast, the index number approach, or the 'approximate cost of living indices',

[3]The seminal contribution by Konus (1924) would have remained unknown to the English-speaking audience but for Schultz (1939) who took the initiative in getting an English translation published in Econometrica in 1939.

lacks the rigour of utility theory but requires much less information than the TCLI s and does not depend on ad hoc specifications of utility functions and parameter estimates. Both (a1) and (a2) share the disadvantage of depending on the choice of initial or given year as the basis for the price comparison between the two years.

There is of course some connection between (a1) and (a2) since, as Konus (1924) showed, the Laspeyres price index provides an upper limit on the TCLI based on the standard of living in the 'initial price' situation, while the Paasche price index provides a lower limit on the TCLI based on the standard of living in the 'given price' situation. However, as Schultz (1939) pointed out, since the 'initial' and 'given' year standards of living do not imply the same level of utility, the TCLIs based on initial and given year standards of living need not be equal and, hence, either TCLI can lie outside the limits provided by the Laspeyres and Paasche price indices.

The stochastic approach to price measurement has a shorter history and originated with the work of Summers (1973) in introducing the Country-Product Dummy (CPD) model to overcome the problem of missing price information in the context of calculations of the purchasing power parity (PPP) required in international comparisons. The CPD method has the advantage over fixed-weight price indices of treating the PPP as estimable parameters and hence providing standard errors that allow statistical inference.[4] The CPD was seen as a parallel system of PPP measurement to traditional price indices with nothing in common with the latter. As Rao (2005) noted, the CPD method was viewed as a 'black box due to its regression formulation' (p. 571). The CPD method therefore lacked the axiomatic properties of traditional index number formulae as laid out, for example, in Balk (1995).

However, Diewert (2005) and Rao (2005) changed this perception by establishing equivalences between the CPD method and the traditional index number methods. Diewert (2005) considers the two-country or two-period case and shows that the Geary–Khamis and Tornqvist price indices are special cases of a modified CPD framework. Rao (2005) considers a multilateral country, multicommodity framework and shows that the weighted CPD model is formally equivalent to the Rao model proposed by him in Rao (1972). In an earlier elegant contribution, Clements and Izan (1981) had shown that the Divisia price index umbers 'can be interpreted and estimated as regression coefficients under a plausible error specification' (p. 745).

[4]Strictly speaking, the TCLI approach can also be viewed as a stochastic approach since the TCLI is a function of the demand parameter estimates, and we can work out the standard errors of the estimated TCLI. However, since the estimated TCLI will be a nonlinear function of the demand parameter estimates, it is much more difficult to work out its standard error than in case of the estimated price coefficients in the CPD model.

3.2 Alternative Methods for Measuring Price Changes

3.2.1 The True Cost of Living Index (TCLI)

The TCLI is the ratio of the minimum expenditures to obtain the same standard of living, given by the indirect utility indicator, u, in two price situations. If we denote $\mathbf{p}^1$ and $\mathbf{p}^2$ as the price vector in initial and given years, respectively, and $c\ (u, \mathbf{p})$ as the cost or expenditure function, then the TCLI in year 2 with year 1 as base is given by:

$$P(\mathbf{p}^1, \mathbf{p}^2, \bar{u}) = \frac{c(\bar{u}, \mathbf{p}^2)}{c(\bar{u}, \mathbf{p}^1)} \tag{3.1}$$

$\bar{u}$ is the reference utility level. In general, namely unless preferences are homothetic, the TCLI as defined in Eq. 3.1 will depend on the reference utility level. Since the utility is unobserved, Eq. 3.1 can be converted to an observable form by substituting u by its (assumed) indirect utility expression in terms of observable prices, $\mathbf{p}$, and household expenditure, $\mathbf{x}$. If $\bar{u}$ is chosen to be that corresponding to the standard of living in the initial price situation, then the TCLI will correspond to the Laspeyres price index; if, however, $\bar{u}$ is chosen to be that in the given year, then the TCLI will correspond to the Paasche price index.

In empirical applications, the TCLI expression given by Eq. 3.1 has been extended in several directions. Following Barten (1964), and Muellbauer (1974a), the indirect utility form can be extended to include the vector of household composition, $\mathbf{z}$. The demographic parameters can be estimated from the corresponding demographic demand systems along with the price parameters. In that case, the TCLI can be extended from the individual to the household level as follows:

$$P(\mathbf{p}^1, \mathbf{p}^2, \mathbf{z}, \bar{u}) = \frac{c(\bar{u}, \mathbf{p}^2, \mathbf{z})}{c(\bar{u}, \mathbf{p}^1, \mathbf{z})} \tag{3.2}$$

Equation 3.2 defines the TCLI for a household with household composition vector $\mathbf{z}$ that is unchanged in the two price situations. Equation 3.2 allows the TCLI to be calculated separately for households with different demographic profiles. As Ray (1985) has shown on UK Family Expenditure data, the TCLI varies significantly between households with different demographic profiles so that if one pools all households with different sizes and compositions and applies Eq. 3.1 to the pooled data, the TCLI is likely to yield misleading estimates of inflation between two time periods. Note, however, that this demographic extension comes at a cost, since the TCLI will now depend not only on the assumed form for the indirect utility function, u, but also on how demographic variables are admitted into the assumed indirect utility function.

The formulation of TCLI so far has been in the context of temporal price changes between two time periods. We can adapt the TCLI to estimate spatial differences in prices, with $\mathbf{p}^1$ and $\mathbf{p}^2$ denoting the vector of prices in two regions. The initial and given years will be reinterpreted, respectively, as the numeraire or base region, and the given region. If region 1 is the numeraire region, then the TCLI will yield the spatial price index of the given region, 2, with respect to region 1. Alternatively, if 1 refers to the country as a whole, then the spatial equivalent of the temporal TCLI yields the spatial price index of each constituent region with the country as the numeraire. One can extend the TCLI concept, interpreted spatially, further treating each country as the unit, and country 1 as the base or numeraire country. In that case, Eq. (3.2) will yield the TCLI-based PPP s of the various countries with country 1's currency adopted as the numeraire currency.

3.2.2 *Fixed-Weight Price Indices and Their Application in PPP Calculations*

3.2.2.1 Fixed-Weight Price Indices in the Binary Context

Traditionally, fixed-weight indices have been proposed in the context of binary comparison of price and quantity vectors in two time periods. While the former, i.e. price index, is a scalar measure of the price changes of a vector of items between two time periods with the quantities treated as fixed, the latter, i.e. quantity index, is a scalar measure of the corresponding quantity changes between two time periods, with prices treated as fixed. In the present exposition, we will focus exclusively on price indices, though the discussion can be easily extended to quantity indices, by swapping prices with quantities. The earliest examples of such price indices are the Laspeyres and Paasche price indices.

The fixed-weight price index is the ratio of the costs of buying a fixed bundle of items in the two time periods, namely the given year and the base year. Let $\mathbf{p}_1$ and $\mathbf{p}_2$ denote the price vectors in time periods 1 and 2, and let $\mathbf{q}_1$ and $\mathbf{q}_2$ denote the corresponding quantity vectors. Year 1 is the base year, and year 2 is the given year. Then, the fixed-weight price index of year 2 with respect to year 1 is given by

$$I_{12} = \frac{\sum_{i=1}^{n} p_{i2} q_{iR}}{\sum_{i=1}^{n} p_{i1} q_{iR}} \tag{3.3}$$

i denotes item, and $\mathbf{q}_{\mathbf{iR}}$ the quantity in the reference year R. If R is the base year, then Eq. 3.1 gives us the Laspeyres price index. If R is the given year, then Eq. 3.1 gives us the Paasche price index. Laspeyres price index can be given by:

$$I_{12}^{L} = \frac{\sum_{i=1}^{n} p_{i2} q_{i1}}{\sum_{i=1}^{n} p_{i1} q_{i1}} \tag{3.4}$$

Paasche price index:

$$I_{12}^{P} = \frac{\sum_{i=1}^{n} p_{i2}q_{i2}}{\sum_{i=1}^{n} p_{i1}q_{i2}} \tag{3.5}$$

If the reference quantity $\mathbf{q_{iR}}$ of item i is the harmonic mean of the quantities of i purchased in the two years, then Eq. 3.1 gives the bilateral version Geary–Khamis (GK) proposed by Geary (1958) and Khamis (1972) in the multilateral country context.

The Laspeyres and Paasche price indices are usually considered to provide the upper and lower bounds of the 'true cost of living index' (TCLI) given by Eq. 3.1 above. Note, however, that this is not true in general, but only if the utility function is homothetic so that the TCLI is independent of the reference utility u.

As shown in Selvanathan and Rao (1994, pp. 31–34), the following inequality relationship holds in the presence of homothetic preferences;

$$I_{12}^{L} = \frac{\sum_{i=1}^{n} p_{i2}q_{i1}}{\sum_{i=1}^{n} p_{i1}q_{i1}} < P(\mathbf{p}_1, \mathbf{p}_2, u) < I_{12}^{P} = \frac{\sum_{i=1}^{n} p_{i2}q_{i2}}{\sum_{i=1}^{n} p_{i1}q_{i2}} \tag{3.6}$$

$P(\mathbf{p}_1, \mathbf{p}_2, u)$ is the TCLI between the base and given years.

Geary–Khamis price index:

$$I_{12}^{\text{GK}} = \frac{\sum_{i=1}^{n} p_{i2}q_{iR}}{\sum_{i=1}^{n} p_{i1}q_{iR}} \tag{3.7}$$

$$q_{iR} = \frac{2q_{i1}q_{i2}}{q_{i1} + q_{i2}} \tag{3.8}$$

Fisher price index is given by the square root of the product of the Laspeyres and Price Indices.

$$I_{12}^{F} = \sqrt{I_{12}^{L}}\sqrt{I_{12}^{P}} \tag{3.9}$$

Tornqvist price index is given by the weighted geometric mean of the price relative in the two years, with the weight (w) being the mean of the base (w_1) and given year (w_2) budget shares.

$$I_{12}^{T} = \prod_{i=1}^{n} \left(\frac{p_{i2}}{p_{i1}}\right)^{w_i} \tag{3.10}$$

The weights, w_i, are given by $w_i = \frac{w_{i1} + w_{i2}}{2}$.

3.2.2.2 Fixed-Weight Price Indices in the Multilateral Country Context

While the fixed-weight price indices have been used traditionally in the temporal context to measure price changes in a country between two time periods, they have been used recently in the spatial context to estimate subnational PPPs or cross-country PPP with the whole country treated as the reference region in case of the former, and a base country (typically, the USA) as the reference country in case of the latter. In this paper, we follow the latter strand in the literature. The two price indices used in the PPP calculations are[5]: Tornqvist and Fisher. Denoting c as the reference country, d as the comparison country, and n as the good, the Tornqvist index is given as a weighted geometric average of the price relatives of each good, with the weights being the average of the budget shares in c and d. The latter are denoted by s_n^c (reference country) and s_n^d (comparison country).

$$\ln P_T^{cd} = \frac{1}{2}\sum_{n=1}^{N}\left(s_n^c + s_n^d\right)\ln\frac{p_n^d}{p_n^c}. \tag{3.11}$$

The Fisher index is defined as the geometric mean of the Paasche and Laspeyres price indices. It is given as follows.

$$\ln P_F^{cd} = 0.5 \times \ln\left[\sum_{n=1}^{N} s_n^c \frac{p_n^d}{p_n^c}\right] - 0.5 \times \ln\left[\sum_{n=1}^{N} s_n^d \frac{p_n^c}{p_n^d}\right]. \tag{3.12}$$

The GEKS PPP price index for country c in country l's currency units is given by

$$\text{Tornqvist}\; P_T^c = \left(\prod_{j=1}^{M} P_T^{lj} P_T^{jc}\right)^{\frac{1}{M}}, \tag{3.13}$$

$$\text{Fisher}: P_F^c = \left(\prod_{j=1}^{M} P_F^{lj} P_F^{jc}\right)^{\frac{1}{M}} \tag{3.14}$$

M is the total number of countries, and N is the total number of commodities. In the PPP calculations reported below, India is chosen as the numeraire country, l.

[5]To save space, we have omitted a detailed description of these price indices. Details are available in Diewert (2005), who argues that these price indices can be given a regression model interpretation by demonstrating that they are special cases of the Country-Product Dummy model used in international price comparisons.

3.2.3 Stochastic Approaches to Price Measurement: The Country-Product Dummy (CPD) Model

The CPD method was originally proposed by Summers (1973) in the context of missing price information on cross-country data and has been used in the ICP rounds. The procedures are described in detail in many subsequent papers (e.g. Rao 2005; Diewert 2005). The stochastic approach in the form of the CPD model has been developed further in the context of PPP estimation, and expressions for computing standard errors of the CPD estimates under alternative stochastic specifications have been derived in Hajargasht and Rao (2010) and in Rao and Hajargasht (2016). Let p_{nc} represent the price of item n in country c (n = 1, 2,..., N; c = 1, 2, …, M). The basic statistical model underlying the CPD method can be stated as:

$$p_{nc} = a_c b_n u_{nc}, \tag{3.15}$$

where a_c and b_n are unknown parameters to be estimated from price data, and u_{cn} are independently and identically distributed random variables, assumed to follow *Lognormal* $(0, \sigma^2)$.

The above equation can be expressed as a regression equation in logarithmic form for each price observation corresponding to commodity n in country c as

$$\ln p_{nc} = \alpha_c + \gamma_n + v_{nc}, \tag{3.16}$$

or

$$y_{nc} = \ln p_{nc} = \alpha_1 D_1 + \alpha_2 D_2 + \cdots + \alpha_M D_M + \eta_1 D_1^* + \eta_2 D_2^* + \cdots + \eta_N D_N^* + v_{nc}, \tag{3.16a}$$

where D_c (c = 1, 2, …, M) and D_n^* (n = 1, 2, ..., N) are, respectively, country and commodity dummy variables and v_{nc}'s are random disturbance terms which are independently and identically (normally) distributed with zero mean and variance σ^2. Under complete price information comparisons of price levels between two countries c and d represented by PPP_{cd} can be derived as:

$$\text{PPP}_{cd} = \frac{a_d}{a_c} = \prod_{n=1}^{N} \left[\frac{p_{nd}}{p_{nc}}\right]^{1/N} \tag{3.17}$$

It is identical to the EKS (Elteto–Koves–Szulc) index used in the OECD and Eurostat comparisons for prices at the basic heading level.

3.2.4 The Household Regional Product Dummy (HRPD) Model

3.2.4.1 Specification and Estimation

The HRPD model is an extension of the CPD model for use at the household level and to calculate subnational PPP s or spatial prices within a country (with the country used as the numeraire). It was proposed in Coondoo et al. (2004) and used to calculate spatial prices in India. The model was used in Majumder and Ray (2017) to provide evidence of heterogeneity in prices at the State level in India. This study showed that the HRPD model is formally equivalent to certain well-known fixed-weight price indices under some parametric configurations analogous to the result of Diewert (2005) and Rao (2005) on the CPD model.

3.2.4.2 Description of the HRPD Model

The basic premise of the approach is the concept of quality equation due to Prais and Houthakker (1955) in which the price/unit value for a commodity paid by a household is taken to measure the quality of the commodity group consumed, and hence, the price/unit value is postulated to be an increasing function of the level of living of the household. A direct extension of the CPD model to incorporate this would be

$$p_{jrht} = \alpha_j + \beta_r + \delta_t + \theta\, y_{rht} + \varepsilon_{jrht}. \tag{3.18}$$

Here, p_{jrht} denotes the natural logarithm of the nominal price/unit value for the jth commodity (j = 1, 2, …, N) paid by the hth sample household of region r (r = 0, 1, 2, …, R) at time t (t = 1, 2, …, T), y_{rht} denotes the natural logarithm of the nominal per capita income/per capita expenditure (PCE) of the hth sample household in region r at time t, and α_j, β_r and δ_t capture the commodity effect, region effect and time effect, respectively. However, in so far as a broad measure of a household's level of living, ceteris paribus, is the effective per capita income/PCE, PCE and household demographics should be the basic explanatory variables of the price equation to be estimated on the basis of household-level data. We, therefore, extend this model by introducing household demographics.

Further, we make all the parameters time-varying and incorporate the regional effect through a formulation of both the price/unit value of individual commodities and PCE in real terms. We write our model as

$$p_{jrht} = \alpha^*_{jt} + \phi_{jrt} + \sum_{i=1}^{4} \delta^*_{jit} n_{irht} + \left(\lambda^*_{jt} + \eta^*_{jrt}\right) y_{rht} + \varepsilon_{jrht}. \tag{3.19}$$

α^*_{jt} captures the pure commodity-time effect, which is the intercept in the numeraire region for item j at time t, ϕ_{jrt} captures the interaction between time and region, and hence, $\alpha^*_{jt} + \phi_{jrt}$ is the region-specific intercept at time t. Thus, $\exp(\phi_{jrt})$ is the price relative of commodity j for region r ($\neq 0$) with the numeraire region taken as the base. δ^*_{jit}'s are the slopes with respect to demographic variables (same for all regions), λ^*_{jt} is the overall income slope (slope in the numeraire region) at time t, η^*_{jrt} captures the differential slope component of each region, and hence, $\lambda^*_{jt} + \eta^*_{jrt}$ is the region-specific income slope at time t.

Note that this model (i.e. Eq. 3.19) reduces to the basic CPD model for time t when $\phi_{jrt} = \phi_{jt}$ for all j, t; $\eta^*_{jrt} = 0$ for all j, r and t, and $\lambda^*_{jt} = 0$ for all j, t. Here, n_{irht} denotes the number of household members of the ith age-sex category present in the hth sample household in region r at time t, where i = 1, 2, 3, 4 denote adult male, adult female, male child and female child categories, respectively, and ε_{jrht} denotes the random equation disturbance term. Also, note that the term involving the demographic variables does not affect the basic structure of the CPD model.

An alternative way of interpreting the model is as follows. The same equation can be written in the form of Coondoo et al. (2004) formulation, as

$$p_{jrht} - \pi_{rt} = \alpha_{jt} + \sum_{i=1}^{4} \delta_{ijt} n_{irht} + (\lambda_{jt} + \eta_{jrt})(y_{rht} - \pi_{rt}) + \varepsilon_{jrht} \tag{3.20}$$

where

$$\alpha^*_{jt} + \phi_{jrt} = \alpha_{jt} + (1 - \lambda_{jt} - \eta_{jrt})\pi_{rt} \tag{3.21}$$

$$\delta^*_{jit} = \delta_{ijt}, \quad \lambda^*_{jt} = \lambda_{jt}, \quad \eta^*_{jrt} = \eta_{jrt}. \tag{3.22}$$

$\alpha_{jt}, \delta_{ijt}, \lambda_{jt}, \eta_{jrt}$ and π_{rt} are the parameters of the model. In principle π_{rt}'s may be interpreted as *the natural logarithm of the value of a reference basket of commodities purchased at the prices of region r in time t.* The left-hand side of Eq. 4.20 thus measures the logarithm of the price/unit value paid in real terms, and $(y_{rht} - \pi_{rt})$ on the right-hand side of Eq. 4.20 measures the logarithm of real PCE. The parameters $(\pi_{rt} - \pi_{0t})$, r = 1, 2, …, R; t = 1, 2, …, T, thus denote a set of logarithmic price index numbers for individual regions measuring the regional price level relative to that of the reference *numeraire* region (r = 0) at time t, and the spatial price index is given by the formula $\exp(\pi_{rt} - \pi_{0t})$.

Normalising $\eta_{j0t} = 0$ for the numeriare region, λ_{jt} can be interpreted as the elasticity of unit value of commodity j with respect to income in the numeraire region at time t, which may in turn be called the *quality elasticity* of commodity j in the numeraire region at time t and hence expected to be positive. Thus, η_{jrt} is the contribution of region r to the quality elasticity of commodity j over and above that of the numeriare region at time t. In other words, $(\lambda_{jt} + \eta_{jrt})$ is the *quality elasticity* of commodity j in region r at time t. Therefore, $(\lambda_{jt} + \eta_{jrt})$ is also expected to be positive.

3.2.4.3 Estimation

Let us now proceed to describe how the HRPD framework can be used to estimate spatial price indices. Following Coondoo et al. (2004), Majumder and Ray (2017) propose a two-stage estimation procedure. We write Eq. 3.13 (the first-stage equation) as:

$$\begin{aligned} p_{jrht} &= \sum_{t=1}^{T} \alpha_{jt}^{*} D_t + \sum_{t=1}^{T} \sum_{i=1}^{4} \delta_{jit}^{*} D_t n_{irht} + \sum_{t=1}^{T} \sum_{r=1}^{R} \phi_{jrt} I_r D_t \\ &\quad + \sum_{t=1}^{T} \lambda_{jt}^{*} D_t y_{rht} + \sum_{t=1}^{T} \sum_{r=1}^{R} \eta_{jrt}^{*} y_{rht} I_r D_t + \varepsilon_{jrht} \end{aligned} \tag{3.23}$$

D_t is the time dummy that takes a value 1 at time t, and 0 otherwise, and I_r is the region dummy that takes the value 1 for region r and 0 otherwise.

So, for the numeriare region, Eq. 3.15 becomes:

$$\begin{aligned} p_{j0ht} &= \sum_{t=1}^{T} \alpha_{jt}^{*} D_t + \sum_{t=1}^{T} \sum_{i=1}^{4} \delta_{jit}^{*} D_t n_{i0ht} \\ &\quad + \sum_{t=1}^{T} \lambda_{jt}^{*} D_t y_{0ht} + \varepsilon_{j0ht} \end{aligned} \tag{3.24}$$

Comparing Eqs. 3.18–3.21, which are identical equations, and using Eqs. 3.21–3.22 and the fact that for the numeraire region.

$$\alpha_{jt}^{*} = \alpha_{jt} + (1 - \lambda_{jt}) \pi_{0t}, \tag{3.24a}$$

we have

$$\phi_{jrt} = (1 - \lambda_{jt} - \eta_{jrt}) \pi_{rt} - (1 - \lambda_{jt}) \pi_{0t}. \tag{3.25}$$

Equation 3.25 constitutes the second-stage equation. It can now be estimated using the following dummy variable regression equation involving the first-stage parameter estimates for Eq. 3.23 (Recall from Eq. 3.24 that $\lambda_{jt}^{*} = \lambda_{jt}, \eta_{jrt}^{*} = \eta_{jrt}$.):

$$\hat{\phi}_{jrt} = \sum_{t=1}^{T} \sum_{r=1}^{R} \pi_{rt} \left(1 - \hat{\lambda}_{jt} - \hat{\eta}_{jrt}\right) I_r D_t - \sum_{t=1}^{T} \pi_{0t} \left(1 - \hat{\lambda}_{jt}\right) D_t + u_{jrt}. \tag{3.26}$$

Note that since $\phi_{j0t} = (1 - \lambda_{jt}) \pi_{0t} - (1 - \lambda_{jt}) \pi_{0t} = 0$, $\phi_{j0t} = 0$. This regression Eq. 3.26 will estimate π_{rt}, r = 0,1,2,....,R, t = 1,2,...,T.

Observe that π_{0t}'s are overidentified as R different estimates of these parameters may be obtained for each t by estimating Eq. 3.26 separately for r = 1, 2, ..., R. To resolve this overdeterminacy of π_{0t}'s, we propose a pooled estimation, which ensures that unique estimates of π_{0t} are obtained. Also, since we have R equations and $(R + 2)$ unknowns, viz. π_{rt}, $r = 0, 1, 2, \ldots, R$ and α_{jt} for every j, each π_{rt} is a linear function of (every) α_{jt} (which is unidentifiable and hence non-estimable, given the model). In other words, the estimated π_{rt}s will have the α_{jt}s confounded in them, thus affecting the magnitude of these estimates. The π_{rt}s estimated for a given data set will contain an additive component which is some kind of an average of the non-estimable α_{jt}'s, say $\bar{\alpha}_t$. However, for a particular time period, the spatial indices with respect to the numeraire region 0 will be given by $\exp(\pi_{rt} - \pi_{0t})$, where $\bar{\alpha}_t$ will get cancelled because it is confounded in both.

3.2.4.4 Estimation Steps

In the first stage, Eq. 3.23 is estimated for each commodity using the weighted least squares (WLS) method incorporating sample weights. In the second stage, Eq. 3.25 is estimated on the pooled data for commodity, region and time by using the weighted least squares method taking population shares of the States in India (taken from Census data closest to the respective periods) as weights. This is same as estimating the π's for each time period separately.

Finally, the spatial indices are computed by the formula $\exp(\pi_{rt} - \pi_{0t})$.[6] The HRPD model was extended in Chakrabarty et al. (2017) by making it dynamic for application in the temporal context by pooling surveys from multiple time periods. Their proposed model, namely the Dynamic Household Regional Product Dummy (DHRPD), described below in Sect. 2.4, was used in Chakrabarty et al. (2017) to examine the changing nature of spatial prices in India. The empirical results are presented later.

3.2.5 *An Engel-Based Procedure for Estimating Spatial Prices in a Large Heterogeneous Country Setting*

Coondoo et al. (2011) have proposed a procedure for estimating spatial prices that is based on Engel curve analysis and incorporates the idea of TCLI. Its main attraction rests on the fact that the procedure requires no price information, only variation in budget shares and total expenditure at the household level. The drawback is that in the absence of price information the procedure is unable to accommodate sophisticated price effects. The procedure was proposed in the sub-national context of estimating spatial price indices in India [see Majumder et al.

[6]Note that in the second-stage estimation, the dependent variable $\hat{\phi}_{jrt}$ will have standard errors (se) from step 1. One possibility could be to incorporate (1/se) as weighting factors in the second step.

(2015a) for a recent empirical application] and has been extended and applied to the cross-country context of estimating PPP s in Majumder et al. (2015a, b, c). The procedure is briefly described below.

Note that in the following description of the procedure, we have kept the subnational context in mind, but by redefining a region as a country, the subnational PPPs will become countrywide PPPs.

The procedure for estimating spatial prices for R regions, taking region 0 as base,[7] involves three stages. In the first stage, a set of item-specific Engel curves relating budget shares to the logarithm of income are estimated for each region r =0, 1, 2, …, R as follows.

$$w_{ij}^r = a_i^r + b_i^r \ln x_j^r + c_{ir}\left(\ln x_j^r\right)^2 + \varepsilon_{ij}^r, \tag{3.27}$$

i denotes item, j denotes household, ε_{ij}^r is a random disturbance term, and a_i^r, b_i^r, c_i^r are parameters that contain the price information on item i in region r.

In the second stage $a(p^r)$, r = 0, 1, 2, …, R is estimated from the following equation:

$$\hat{b}_i^r - \hat{b}_i^0 = \ln a(p^0)\left(2\hat{c}_i^0\right) - \ln a(p^r)\left(2\hat{c}_i^r\right) + e_i^r; \quad r = 1, 2, \ldots, R. \tag{3.28}$$

Here, e_i^r is a composite error term, which is a linear combination of the individual errors of estimation of the parameters a_i^r, b_i^r, c_i^r, and p^0 denotes the price vector of the base region.

In the third stage, $b(p^r)$ and $\lambda(p^r)$ r =1,2,…,R are estimated, using the normalisation $b(p^0) = \lambda(p^0) = 1$ for the base region, from the following regression equation[8]:

$$\frac{1}{\ln\left(\frac{x_j^r}{a(p^r)}\right)} = \frac{1}{b(p^r)}\left(\frac{1}{\ln\frac{x_j^0}{a(p^0)}} + 1\right) - \frac{\lambda(p^r)}{b(p^r)} + \text{error} \tag{3.29}$$

The money metric utility u_j^0 of a household of the base region that has nominal per capita income $x_j^0\left(= C\left(u_j^0, p^0\right)\right)$ is given by:

$$\frac{1}{\ln u_j^0} = \frac{1}{\ln\frac{x_j^0}{a(p^0)}} + 1. \tag{3.30}$$

[7]In the calculations reported later, we take all India as the base region, 0.

[8]The regression set-up arises because $\widehat{a(p^r)}$ and $\widehat{a(p^0)}$ are estimated values.

Using these, the TCLIs are estimated for a given reference level of utility of the base region. It may be emphasised that $a(p^r), b(p^r)$ and $\lambda(p^r)$ are estimated as composite variables, and no explicit algebraic forms for these functions are assumed. However, as already noted, being based on single-equation Engel curves, the issue of price-induced substitution effect among commodities is ignored. To incorporate such substitution among the items in the calculation of spatial prices, we need to estimate complete demand systems that require specification of functional forms for $a(p^r), b(p^r)$ and $\lambda(p^r)$ which in turn require prices for estimation. The above methodology can be extended to allow the calculation of spatial prices—see Majumder et al. (2015a) for details.

3.3 Equivalence of the HRPD and Other Systems for Measuring Price Indices

This section demonstrates the usefulness of the HRPD model by showing that it provides a general framework that can specialise to forms that are equivalent to three recently used alternative systems for measuring price indices. While in the interest of space and to avoid loss of focus of this paper which is both methodological and empirical, we have restricted the demonstration of generality of HRPD only with reference to three alternative systems, there is scope for extending the discussion to other price indices in future investigations.

3.3.1 Relating to Rao (2005) System

The second-stage equation of the HRPD model Eq. 3.25 can be written as

$$\phi_{jrt} = \left(1 - \lambda_{jt} - \eta_{jrt}\right)\pi_{rt} + \left(\lambda_{jt} - 1\right)\pi_{0t}. \tag{3.31}$$

Writing Eq. 3.23 as a regression with a partitioned regressors' matrix gives

$$Y = X_1\Pi + X_2\Pi_0 + \varepsilon, \tag{3.23a}$$

where X_1 is $NRT \times RT$, X_2 is $NRT \times T$, Π is $RT \times 1$, and Π_0 is $T \times 1$, from which expressions for the least squares estimates of Π and Π_0 are obtained as $\widehat{\Pi}_{RT\times 1} = \left(X_1'X_1\right)^{-1}X_1'\left(Y - X_2\widehat{\Pi}_0\right)$. These are the regional π's for each time period and $\widehat{\Pi}_{0_{T\times 1}} = \left(X_2'X_2\right)^{-1}X_2'\left(Y - X_1\widehat{\Pi}\right)$. These are the all-India π's for each time period.

The resulting estimates of the parameters of Eq. 3.25 are given by

$$\widehat{\pi}_{rt} = \frac{\sum_j \left(1 - \lambda_{jt} - \eta_{jrt}\right)\left(\phi_{jrt} - \left(\lambda_{jt} - 1\right)\widehat{\pi}_{0t}\right)}{\sum_j \left(1 - \lambda_{jt} - \eta_{jrt}\right)^2}, \quad r \neq 0 \tag{3.32}$$

$$\widehat{\pi}_{0t} = \frac{\sum_j \sum_r \left(\lambda_{jt} - 1\right)\left(\phi_{jrt} - \left(1 - \lambda_{jt} - \eta_{jrt}\right)\widehat{\pi}_{rt}\right)}{R \sum_j \left(\lambda_{jt} - 1\right)^2}, \quad r = 0. \tag{3.33}$$

Let $\widehat{P}_{rt} = \mathrm{e}^{\widehat{\pi}_{rt}}$ and $\widehat{P}_{0t} = \mathrm{e}^{\widehat{\pi}_{0t}}$. Then

$$\widehat{P}_{rt} = \prod_{j=1}^{N} \left(\frac{\mathrm{e}^{\phi_{jrt}}}{\widehat{P}_{0t}^{\left(\lambda_{jt}-1\right)}} \right)^{\frac{\left(1-\lambda_{jt}-\eta_{jrt}\right)}{\sum_j \left(1-\lambda_{jt}-\eta_{jrt}\right)^2}}, \quad r \neq 0 \tag{3.34}$$

$$\widehat{P}_{0t} = \prod_{j=1}^{N} \prod_{r=1}^{R} \left(\frac{\mathrm{e}^{\phi_{jrt}\left(\lambda_{jt}-1\right)}}{\widehat{P}_{rt}^{\left(\lambda_{jt}-1\right)\left(1-\lambda_{jt}-\eta_{jrt}\right)}} \right)^{\frac{1}{R \sum_j \left(\lambda_{jt}-1\right)^2}}. \tag{3.35}$$

Let $\eta_{jrt} = 2\left(1 - \lambda_{jt}\right)$, where it is required that $1 < \lambda_{jt} < 2$. These bounds are required because

(i) $\left(\lambda_{jt} - 1\right)$ needs to be >0, so that in Eq. 3.31 the coefficient of π_{0t} is positive as per the Rao (2005) system requirement,[9] and
(ii) $\lambda_{jt} < 2$ needs to be satisfied for the income slope coefficient in Eq. 3.29 to be >0, as $\left(\lambda_{jt} + \eta_{jrt}\right) = 2 - \lambda_{jt}$, when $\eta_{jrt} = 2\left(1 - \lambda_{jt}\right)$.

Then, the system becomes

$$\widehat{P}_{rt} = \prod_{j=1}^{N} \left(\frac{\left(\mathrm{e}^{\phi_{jrt}}\right)^{\frac{1}{\left(\lambda_{jt}-1\right)}}}{\widehat{P}_{0t}} \right)^{\frac{\left(\lambda_{jt}-1\right)^2}{\sum_j \left(\lambda_{jt}-1\right)^2}}, \quad r \neq 0 \tag{3.36}$$

$$\widehat{P}_{0t} = \prod_{j=1}^{N} \prod_{r=1}^{R} \left(\frac{\left(\mathrm{e}^{\phi_{jrt}}\right)^{\frac{1}{\left(\lambda_{jt}-1\right)}}}{\widehat{P}_{rt}} \right)^{\frac{\left(\lambda_{jt}-1\right)^2}{R \sum_j \left(\lambda_{jt}-1\right)^2}} \tag{3.37}$$

The system can now be written as

[9]As pointed out by Professor Ken Clements, this condition rules out inclusion of items that have unit quality elasticities (with respect to income) in the numeriare region, as $\lambda_{jt} = 1$ implies zero weight for such items.

$$\widehat{P}_{rt} = \prod_{j=1}^{N} \left(\frac{p^*_{jrt}}{\widehat{P}_{0t}} \right)^{w_{jt}}, \quad r \neq 0 \tag{3.38}$$

$$\widehat{P}_{0t} = \prod_{j=1}^{N} \prod_{r=1}^{R} \left(\frac{p^*_{jrt}}{\widehat{P}_{rt}} \right)^{\frac{w_{jt}}{R}} \tag{3.38a}$$

$$p^*_{jrt} = \left(e^{\phi_{jrt}}\right)^{\frac{1}{(\lambda_{jt}-1)}}, \quad w_{jt} = \frac{(\lambda_{jt}-1)^2}{\sum_j (\lambda_{jt}-1)^2}. \tag{3.38b}$$

Noting that $\sum_r w_{jt} = R$, Eqs. 3.38–3.38b can be interpreted as the Rao (2005) system for the temporal–spatial (analogous to country product) model. Observe that the weights w_{jt}'s are independent of r (region). See implication (ii) below.

3.3.1.1 Interpretation of the Conditions

(i) $\begin{array}{l} \eta_{jrt} = 2(1-\lambda_{jt}) \\ \Rightarrow (\lambda_{jt} + \eta_{jrt}) = 2 - \lambda_{jt} \end{array}$, which is positive under the second condition.

This implies that when the logarithm of the normalised unit values [normalised with respect to the regional composite price, $\exp(\pi_{rt})$] is regressed on the logarithm of the normalised income, the slope and intercept are independent of the regional effect (see Eq. 3.20). This also implies that the quality elasticities of the commodities are invariant across regions for all t.

(ii) ϕ_{jrt} is the additional effect of region r on the logarithm of the unit value of commodity j at period t in the absence of any household-level effect, i.e. income and demographic composition. See Eq. 3.23. When $\eta_{jrt} = 2(1-\lambda_{jt})$, this gives us:

$$\phi_{jrt} = (\lambda_{jt}-1)\pi_{rt} + (\lambda_{jt}-1)\pi_{0t} \tag{3.39}$$

This can be written as

$$\sqrt{\frac{(\lambda_{jt}-1)^2}{\sum_j (\lambda_{jt}-1)^2}} \left(\phi_{jrt} \frac{1}{(\lambda_{jt}-1)} \right) = \sqrt{\frac{(\lambda_{jt}-1)^2}{\sum_j (\lambda_{jt}-1)^2}} \pi_{rt} + \sqrt{\frac{(\lambda_{jt}-1)^2}{\sum_j (\lambda_{jt}-1)^2}} \pi_{0t}$$

Or,

$$\sqrt{w_{jt}} \left(\phi_{jrt} \frac{1}{(\lambda_{jt}-1)} \right) = \sqrt{w_{jt}}\pi_{rt} + \sqrt{w_{jt}}\pi_{0t}$$

The regression equation, for each time period, can then be written as

$$\sqrt{w_{jt}}\log(p^*_{jrt}) = \sum_{r=1}^{R} \sqrt{w_{jt}}\pi_{rt}I_r + \sqrt{w_{jt}}\pi_{0t} + u_{jrt} \tag{3.40}$$

This is of the form of Rao (2005)'s Eq. 3.3. Note that the LHS of Eq. 3.40 is $\sqrt{w_{jt}}\log(p^*_{jrt})$, where $p^*_{jrt} = (e^{\phi_{jrt}})^{\frac{1}{(\lambda_{jt}-1)}}$ is the weighted price component of commodity j in region r at time t in the regional index, and the weight w_{jt} is independent of r. Also observe that one can use OLS (as opposed to Rao's WLS), because the weights are already contained in the above equations. Both the restrictions are testable, but need to be satisfied simultaneously. One can first check for $1<\lambda_{jt}<2$ by looking at the 95% confidence interval of $\hat{\lambda}_{jt}$ and verifying that this confidence interval is contained in the interval (1, 2). If this is satisfied, the restriction $\eta_{jrt} = 2(1-\lambda_{jt})$ can be directly incorporated in Eq. 3.25 and tested using F-test.

To reformulate the weights in terms of budget shares, if we set $\lambda_{jt} = \sqrt{w^*_{jt}} + 1$, where w^*_{jt} is the median budget share of commodity j in the numeriare region at time t with respect to the total expenditure of the commodities considered. Then, $w_{jt} = w^*_{jt}$, which are Rao weights. Observe that here the second condition, that is, $1<\lambda_{jt}<2$, is automatically satisfied, because $<0<\sqrt{w^*_{jt}}<1$.

3.3.1.2 Testing

Imposing this restriction on λ_{jt} in our estimating equations, we get a set of regional price indices for each period. These can be compared with the original unrestricted ones. Also, the individual restrictions $\lambda_{jt} = \sqrt{w^*_{jt}} + 1$ can be tested using the estimates of λ_{jt} and their standard errors.

3.3.2 *Relating to Diewert (2005) System*

Starting from the second-stage Eq. 3.25, we have for $r \neq 0$, we obtain

$$\phi_{jrt} = (1-\lambda_{jt}-\eta_{jrt})\pi_{rt} + (\lambda_{jt}-1)\pi_{0t} \tag{3.41}$$

Now, let $\eta_{jrt} = 0$, that is the quality elasticities of all regions are equal to that of the numeriare region. The above equation then becomes

$$\phi_{jrt} = (1-\lambda_{jt})\pi_{rt} + (\lambda_{jt}-1)\pi_{0t} \tag{3.41a}$$

Now, define $p^{**}_{jrt} = (e^{\phi_{jrt}})^{\frac{1}{(1-\lambda_{jt})}}$. Note that here the weights are different from those in Eq. 3.38a. We then have

$$\phi_{jrt} = (1 - \lambda_{jt}) \log\left(p^{**}_{jrt}\right) = (1 - \lambda_{jt})\pi_{rt} + (\lambda_{jt} - 1)\pi_{0t}. \tag{3.41b}$$

The regression equation corresponding to Eq. 3.31 can be written as

$$\log(p^{**}_{jrt}) = \pi_{rt} - \pi_{0t} + u_{jrt}. \tag{3.42}$$

Recall that the spatial price indices are given by $\exp(\pi_{rt} - \pi_{0t})$. If we now use a weighted least squares method to estimate $(\pi_{rt} - \pi_{0t})$ from the above regression Eq. 3.42, we have

$$\widehat{\pi_{rt} - \pi_{0t}} = \sum_{j=1}^{N} \frac{w_{jt} \log(p^{**}_{jrt})}{\sum_{j=1}^{N} w_{jt}}, \tag{3.43}$$

where w_{jt} is some arbitrary weight. Observe from Eq. 3.41b that $\phi_{j0t} = 0$, so that $\log(p^{**}_{j0t}) = 0$. Hence, we can write:

$$\widehat{\pi_{rt} - \pi_{0t}} = \sum_{j=1}^{N} \frac{w_{jt} \log(p^{**}_{jrt}/p^{**}_{j0t})}{\sum_{j=1}^{N} w_{jt}} \tag{3.44}$$

By choosing w_{jt} suitably, we can establish equivalence of Eq. 3.38 with Diewert (2005) indices. If, for example, we choose the weight w_{jt} to be the harmonic mean of w^{*}_{jt} (the median budget share of commodity j in the numeriare region at time t with respect to the total expenditure of the commodities considered) and w^{*}_{j0}, Eq. 3.36 becomes the harmonic share weighted average of the logarithm of price ratios, which is of the form of Eq. 3.11 in Diewert (2005). Here again,w_{jt} is independent of r, but the regional effect is present through p^{**}_{jrt}.

3.3.3 *Relating to Hill and Syed (2014) System*

Consider Eq. 3.39 under the Rao set-up $(r \neq 0)$ [that is, $\eta_{jrt} = 2(1 - \lambda_{jt})$ and $1 < \lambda_{jt} < 2$]. Then, $\phi_{jrt} = (\lambda_{jt} - 1)\pi_{rt} + (\lambda_{jt} - 1)\pi_{0t}$.

The regression equation can be written as

$$\log(p^{*}_{jrt}) = \pi_{rt} + \pi_{0t} + u_{jrt}, \tag{3.45}$$

where p^{*}_{jrt} is as defined in Eq. 3.38a.

Now, consider the static model, i.e. fix t. We then have

$$\log(p^{*}_{jr}) = \pi_r + \pi_0 + u_{jr} \tag{3.45a}$$

This can be written as

$$\log\left(p_{jr}^{*}\right) = \sum_{r=1}^{R} \pi_r I_r + \pi_0 + u_{jr}. \tag{3.46}$$

This is of the form of Eq. 3.11 of Hill and Syed (2014), without an intercept term. Their *rural–urban* price index corresponds to our *regional* (*State-all India*) indices.

3.4 The Dynamic HRPD Model—Specification and Estimation: Simultaneous Measurement of Spatial and Temporal Variation in Prices[10]

3.4.1 Introduction

It is useful to distinguish between the literatures on the spatial and temporal variation in prices. While the former typically refers to the measurement of differences in prices faced by various behavioural units, which may be individuals or provinces or countries, at a point in time, the latter tracks the price changes faced by the same unit over a period of time. While the most prominent example of the measurement of spatial prices is that between countries and takes the form of the periodic exercises of the International Comparison Project (ICP) to estimate the purchasing power parities (PPP) between currencies, it is the temporal element in price movement in single country contexts that has attracted the bulk of the attention of the economists. The study by Rao et al. (2010) combines the spatial element in price measurement implicit in cross-country price comparisons at a point in time with the temporal element in the measurement of inflation over time by proposing an econometric methodology that extrapolates PPPs between and beyond ICP rounds based on information in benchmark years provided by the ICP.

The joint modelling of spatial and temporal prices has not been considered in the price index literature to date. The literatures on spatial and temporal prices have generally moved in parallel, with the spatial studies looking at differences in prices faced by a cross section of units at a single time period, while the temporal studies concentrate on price changes faced by a single unit over time. In case of the measurement of price movements over a long time period for a large, heterogeneous country such as India, the spatial and temporal aspects will interact to record large spatial differences in inflation over time. There was an early recognition of this interaction in the studies on India by Bhattacharyya et al. (1980, 1988) and Coondoo and Saha (1990).

The fact that the literatures on the measurement of the spatial and temporal variation in prices have moved in parallel has meant that there has been an absence

[10]See Chakrabarty et al. (2017) for a More Complete Treatment.

of a single unified framework that allows for both sets of calculations. This in turn explains the absence of dynamic specifications in the measurement of spatial price variation[11] within a country, and the absence of allowance of mutual dependence between the regional prices in the measurement of temporal price changes in a country. Chakrabarty et al. (2017) attempts to overcome both these limitations by providing a unified framework that simultaneously allows for changes in spatial variation in prices over time and also for dependence between the price movements in adjacent locations that may be due to similarities in preferences between their residents. They propose the 'Dynamic Household Regional Product Dummy (DHRPD) Model' that extends the HRPD model described above in Sect. 3.2.4.2 by allowing dependence in price movements between regions and over time. An important departure of the proposed framework from the CPD framework of Summers (1973), and its household adaptation in Coondoo et al. (2004), is that it allows the estimated spatial prices to vary over time.

The study by Chakrabarty et al. (2015) highlights the importance of jointly modelling the spatial and temporal elements of price movements, especially their interaction, in welfare applications by using them to document the differences between States and regions in India in the movements in both nominal and real expenditure inequality over time. The DHRPD model proposed in Chakrabarty et al. (2017) should be viewed as a continuation of this research agenda in the CPD framework by using a time-varying model, estimated on a pooled time series of Household Expenditure Surveys, to analyse the spatial price variation in India, both at a point in time and over time. The CPD model and its household version that is considered in Coondoo et al. (2004) are members of the class of stochastic index numbers.[12] As noted by Clements et al. (2006), an important advantage of the CPD framework that is shared by the DHRPD model is that it allows the calculation of standard errors of the price indices that is not the case with the fixed-weight price indices.

Let us start from the HRPD model given alternatively by Eqs. 3.19 and 3.20 above:

$$p_{jrht} = \alpha^*_{jt} + \phi_{jrt} + \sum_{i=1}^{4} \delta^*_{jit} n_{irht} + (\lambda^*_{jt} + \eta^*_{jrt}) y_{rht} + \varepsilon_{jrht}. \qquad (3.19)$$

$$p_{jrht} - \pi_{rt} = \alpha_{jt} + \sum_{i=1}^{4} \delta_{ijt} n_{irht} + (\lambda_{jt} + \eta_{jrt})(y_{rht} - \pi_{rt}) + \varepsilon_{jrht} \qquad (3.20)$$

[11]Exceptions include the cross-country study on ICP data by Rambaldi et al. (2010) and by Pelagatti (2010) on data from Milan. Both these studies consider the interaction between the temporal and spatial elements in price measurement via stochastic specification of the error structures in the estimating equations, similar to what is done in the present study.

[12]See Clements et al. (2006) for an excellent review of stochastic index numbers.

Let us recall the two-stage estimation procedure outlined earlier to estimate the HRPD model. This involved estimation of the second-stage equation given by Eq. 3.25 above using the dummy variable regression equation given below by Eq. 3.47 involving the first-stage parameter estimates from Eq. 3.23:

$$\hat{\phi}_{jrt} = \sum_{t=1}^{T}\sum_{r=1}^{R} \pi_{rt}\left(1 - \hat{\lambda}_{jt} - \hat{\eta}_{jrt}\right) D_r D_t - \sum_{t=1}^{T} \pi_{0t}\left(1 - \hat{\lambda}_{jt}\right) D_t + u_{jrt} \tag{3.47}$$

D_r is the region dummy that takes a value of 1 for region r (= 1,2,...,R) and 0 otherwise. Here, u_{jrt} is a composite error term arising out of a linear combination of the errors in the estimated parameters from the first-stage regression, thus yielding the regression set-up in Eq. 3.47. Also note that since $\phi_{j0t} = \left(1 - \lambda_{jt}\right)\pi_{0t} - \left(1 - \lambda_{jt}\right)\pi_{0t} = 0,\ \phi_{j0t} = 0$. This regression Eq. 3.47 will estimate π_{rt}, r = 0, 1, 2, …, R, t = 1, 2, …, T.

Observe that π_{0t}'s are overidentified as R different estimates of these parameters may be obtained for each t by estimating Eq. 3.47 separately for r = 1, 2, …, R. To resolve this overdeterminacy of π_{0t}'s, we propose a pooled estimation, which ensures that unique estimates of π_{0t} are obtained. Also, since we have R equations and (R + 2) unknowns, viz.π_{rt}, r =0, 1, 2, …, R and α_{jt} for every j, each π_{rt} is a linear function of (every) α_{jt}(which is unidentifiable and hence non-estimable, given the model). In other words, the estimated π_{rt}s will have the α_{jt}s confounded in them, thus affecting the magnitude of these estimates. The π_{rt}s estimated for a given data set will contain an additive component which is some kind of an average of the non-estimable α_{jt}'s, say $\bar{\alpha}_t$. Note, however, that for a particular time period the spatial indices with respect to the numeraire region 0 will be given by $\exp(\pi_{rt} - \pi_{0t})$, where $\bar{\alpha}_t$ will get cancelled because it is confounded in both.

But, for temporal indices some adjustment needs to be made. The temporal index at time t_2 with respect to time t_1 for region r will be given by

$$\exp(\pi_{rt_2} - \pi_{rt_1} + \bar{\alpha}_{t_2} - \bar{\alpha}_{t_1}) \tag{3.48}$$

To compute the temporal indices, therefore, we have adopted the following procedure. After estimating the parameters, $\alpha^*_{jt}, \lambda_{jt}, \pi_{0t}$, we take the average over j on both sides of Eq. 3.24a. $\bar{\alpha}_t$ is then estimated as

$$\widehat{\bar{\alpha}}_t = \widehat{\bar{\alpha}}^*_t - \left(1 - \widehat{\bar{\lambda}}_t\right)\widehat{\pi}_{0t} \tag{3.49}$$

If we allow the disturbances u_{jrt} to be correlated across different time periods, i.e. $E\left(u_{jrt}u_{jrt'}\right) \neq 0$, for all t, t', then Eq. 3.47 becomes the dynamic HRPD model. In the following empirical application, we allow the errors to follow an AR(1) process, i.e. $E\left(u_{jrt}u_{jrt-s}\right) = \rho^s$, $\rho \neq 0$, for $s \geq 0$. The dynamic HRPD model, therefore, nests the HPRD model if the AR (1) parameter, ρ, equals zero. The dynamic HPRD model can be extended further if we allow the disturbances, u_{jrt}, to be correlated between neighbouring regions, i.e. $E(u_{jrt}u_{jvt}) \neq 0$, for all t, where r and v are neighbours. In principle, both extensions can be allowed simultaneously, but, to simplify calculations, we have considered them one at a time in this study.

3.4.2 Estimation Steps

In the first stage, Eq. 3.23 is estimated, for each commodity, on household-level observations for each region and time using the least squares method incorporating household-level sampling weights. This is same as estimating the parameters for each time period separately. These regressions yield estimates of $\alpha^*_{jt}, \delta^*_{jit}, \phi_{jrt}, \lambda^*_{jt}$ and η^*_{jrt}. In the second stage, Eq. 3.47 is estimated on commodity-wise observation over region and time using the estimates from stage 1 and using the fact that $\lambda^*_{jt} = \lambda_{jt}$ and $\eta^*_{jrt} = \eta_{jrt}$ from Eq. 3.22. The following three estimation methods can be used in the second-stage estimation.

(i) Ordinary least squares method after adjusting the variables by population shares of the States (weights) in the respective periods.[13] This is same as estimating the π's for each time period separately. This is the HRPD model, or simply the model with time-varying spatial price index.
(ii) The above method in a panel framework along with an AR(1) error structure in the time dimension. This is the DHRPD model.
(iii) A maximum likelihood (ML) method for the population share adjusted item–space–time model (system of item equations) with error components that are both spatially and time-wise correlated. Here, a 'neighbour' is an adjacent region with common boundary, with a concurrence value of 1. For non-neighbours, the weights are assigned the value 0. The matrix is then normalised to a row-stochastic weight matrix. If there is a region that shares a border with two others, both have a concurrence value of 1, but the weights are 0.5. This is the DHRPD model with spatial dependence.

Finally, the spatial indices are computed by the formula $\exp(\pi_{rt} - \pi_{0t})$ and temporal indices by using Eqs. 3.48 and 3.49.

3.4.3 Testing for Time-Invariant Spatial Price Indices

We want to test $(\pi_{rt} - \pi_{0t}) = \delta_r$, say, for all t. Imposing this restriction in Eq. 3.25, we have for r =1,2,…,R

[13]The weight for all India (Region 0) is 1.

$$\phi_{jrt} = (1 - \lambda_{jt} - \eta_{jrt})(\pi_{0t} + \delta_r) - (1 - \lambda_{jt})\pi_{0t} \tag{3.50}$$

This yields the restricted model:

$$\phi_{jrt} = (1 - \lambda_{jt} - \eta_{jrt})\delta_r - \eta_{jrt}\pi_{0t} \tag{3.50a}$$

The estimating equation is:

$$\hat{\phi}_{jrt} = \sum_{r=1}^{R} \delta_r \left(1 - \hat{\lambda}_{jt} - \hat{\eta}_{jrt}\right) D_r - \sum_{t=1}^{T} \pi_{0t}\hat{\eta}_{jrt} D_t + u_{jrt} \tag{3.51}$$

3.4.4 AR(1) Structure in the Time Dimension: Introducing Price Dynamics in the Temporal Specification

To illustrate that introduction of AR(1) structure in the time dimension in Eq. 3.47 increases efficiency of the estimates under certain conditions, we consider models with and without the AR(1) error structure in a panel data set-up. We assume that after correcting for the weights (population shares), the error terms are homoscedastic. In the absence of autocorrelation, with R regions, the variance–covariance matrix of u_{jrt} is, therefore, given as:

$$\sum_{0} = \sigma_0^2 I_T \otimes I_{NR}, \tag{3.52}$$

where I_T denotes identity matrix of order $T \times T$, and I_{NR} denotes identity matrix of order $NR \times NR$. With AR(1) error structure, the error can now be written as $u_{jrt} = u^*_{jrt} + v_{jt}$, where u^*_{jrt} is homoscedastic (by our assumption) with variance σ_1^2 and $v_{jt} = \rho v_{jt-1} + \varsigma_{jt}$. Here, ρ is the autocorrelation parameter, $\varsigma_{jt} \sim N\left(0, \sigma_\varsigma^2\right)$, so that $\mathrm{Var}\left(v_{jt}\right) = \sigma^2 = \frac{\sigma_\varsigma^2}{(1-\rho^2)}$.

So, the variance–covariance matrix is of the form[14]

$$\sum_{\mathrm{AR}(1)} = \sigma_1^2 I_T \otimes I_{NR} + \sigma^2\, \Theta \otimes I_{NR}, \tag{3.53}$$

[14]It may, however, be pointed out that an identification problem may arise for $T = 4$, but only for higher-order AR process, as unobserved heterogeneity in the panel would not be distinguishable from genuine higher-order dynamics (Arellano 2003, Chap. 5).

where

$$\Theta = \begin{pmatrix} 1 & \rho & \cdots & \cdots & \rho^{T-2} & \rho^{T-1} \\ \rho & 1 & \cdots & \cdots & \rho^{T-3} & \rho^{T-2} \\ \rho^2 & \vdots & \ddots & \vdots & & \vdots \\ \vdots & \vdots & \vdots & \ddots & & \\ \rho^{T-2} & \vdots & \vdots & \vdots & 1 & \rho \\ \rho^{T-1} & \rho^{T-2} & \cdots & \cdots & \rho & 1 \end{pmatrix}_{T \times T} \tag{3.54}$$

Proposition 1 If $\sigma_0^2 > \sigma_1^2 + \sigma^2$ and $\rho \geq 0.25$,, then $(\Sigma_0 - \Sigma_{\mathrm{AR}(1)})$ is positive definite.

Now, to understand the effect on the spatial and temporal indices, consider the following. The second-stage equation can be written as

$$\phi_{jrt} = (1 - \lambda_{jt} - \eta_{jrt})\pi_{rt} + (\lambda_{jt} - 1)\pi_{0t}, \quad r \neq 0, \tag{3.55}$$

Equation 3.55 can be written in the form of partitioned matrix as $Y = X_1\Pi + X_2\Pi_0 + \varepsilon$, where X_1 is $NRT \times RT$, X_2 is $NRT \times T$, Π is $RT \times 1$ and Π_0 is $T \times 1$, and the stochastic error term, ε, is added to the specification in Eq. 3.55.

Using formula for partitioned matrices, $\hat{\Pi}_{RT\times 1} = (X_1'X_1)^{-1}X_1'(Y - X_2\hat{\Pi}_0)$ [These are the regional π's for each time period] and $\hat{\Pi}_{0T\times 1} = (X_2'X_2)^{-1}X_2'(Y - X_1\hat{\Pi})$ [These are the all India π's for each time period].

These expressions turn out to be,

$$\hat{\pi}_{rt} = \frac{\sum_j (1 - \lambda_{jt} - \eta_{jrt})(\phi_{jrt} - (\lambda_{jt} - 1)\hat{\pi}_{0t})}{\sum_j (1 - \lambda_{jt} - \eta_{jrt})^2}, \quad r \neq 0 \tag{3.56}$$

$$\hat{\pi}_{0t} = \frac{\sum_j \sum_r (\lambda_{jt} - 1)(\phi_{jrt} - (1 - \lambda_{jt} - \eta_{jrt})\hat{\pi}_{rt})}{R\sum_j (\lambda_{jt} - 1)^2}, \quad r = 0. \tag{3.57}$$

Under some simplifying assumptions, we have

$$\mathrm{Var}(\hat{\pi}_{rt} - \hat{\pi}_{0t}) = \frac{\sum_j (1 - \lambda_{jt} - \eta_{jrt})^2 \eta_{jrt}^2 \mathrm{Var}(\hat{\pi}_{0t})}{\left(\sum_j (1 - \lambda_{jt} - \eta_{jrt})^2\right)^2}. \tag{3.58}$$

Therefore, introduction of AR(1) error structure in Eq. 3.24a will have its effect on the variances of the spatial price indices only through the efficiency gain in the estimated parameter π_{0t}.

On the other hand, for the temporal indices, we have

$$\mathrm{Var}(\hat{\pi}_{rt_2} - \hat{\pi}_{rt_1}) = \frac{\sum_j (1-\lambda_{jt_2}-\eta_{jrt_2})^2(\lambda_{jt_2}-1)^2\mathrm{Var}(\hat{\pi}_{0t_2})}{\left(\sum_j (1-\lambda_{jt_2}-\eta_{jrt_2})^2\right)^2} + \frac{\sum_j (1-\lambda_{jt_1}-\eta_{jrt_1})^2(\lambda_{jt_1}-1)^2\mathrm{Var}(\hat{\pi}_{0t_1})}{\left(\sum_j (1-\lambda_{jt_1}-\eta_{jrt_1})^2\right)^2} - 2\mathrm{Cov}(\hat{\pi}_{rt_2}, \hat{\pi}_{rt_1}) \tag{3.59}$$

Under 'no-autocorrelation', the covariance term vanishes. Hence, for the temporal indices introduction of AR(1) error structure will have its effect not only through the efficiency gain in the estimated parameter π_{0t}'s, but also through the covariance term. Hence, the efficiency gain under AR(1) structure is expected to be high for the temporal indices. For the urban-rural indices, we have

$$\mathrm{Var}\left(\hat{\pi}_{rt}^U - \hat{\pi}_{rt}^R\right) = \frac{\sum_j \left(1-\lambda_{jt}^U-\eta_{jrt}^U\right)^2\left(\lambda_{jt}^U-1\right)^2\mathrm{Var}\left(\hat{\pi}_{rt}^U\right)}{\left(\sum_j \left(1-\lambda_{jt}^U-\eta_{jrt}^U\right)^2\right)^2} + \frac{\sum_j \left(1-\lambda_{jt}^R-\eta_{jrt}^R\right)^2\left(\lambda_{jt}^R-1\right)^2\mathrm{Var}\left(\hat{\pi}_{rt}^R\right)}{\left(\sum_j \left(1-\lambda_{jt}^R-\eta_{jrt}^R\right)^2\right)^2}. \tag{3.60}$$

Since both the variances on the RHS will reduce under the AR(1) structure, the urban–rural indices are expected to be more efficient compared to the situation under 'no-autocorrelation'.

3.4.5 *Spatial Autoregressive (SAR) Error Structure: Introducing Regional Price Dependence in the Cross-Sectional Specification*

To determine the effect of introducing spatial weight matrices, we ignore the AR(1) structure in time dimension, for simplicity. As in the earlier case we assume that after correcting for the weights (population shares), the error terms are homoscedastic. The spatial weight matrix (link matrix) W is given as follows

$$w_{ij} = \begin{cases} 0 & \text{if } i = j \\ 1 & \text{if } i \text{ and } j \text{ are spatially connected} \end{cases}. \tag{3.61}$$

The matrix W is normalised to a row-stochastic matrix. Under SAR scheme in our set-up, we have

$$u_{jrt} = \lambda((I_N \otimes W) \otimes I_T)u_{jrt} + v_{jrt}, \tag{3.62}$$

where λ is the spatial correlation, I_N and I_T are identity matrices of order $N \times N$ and $T \times T$, respectively, and v_{jrt} is the error term with a variance–covariance matrix of the form $\sigma_2^2 I_T \otimes I_{NR}$.

From Eq. 3.62, we have,

$$(I_{NRT} - \lambda((I_N \otimes W) \otimes I_T))u_{jrt} = v_{jrt} \tag{3.63}$$

which can be written as,

$$u = I_T \otimes (I_N \otimes (I_R - \lambda W))^{-1} v. \tag{3.63a}$$

Now, given that W is row-stochastic, the inverse term can be rewritten as

$$u = I_T \otimes \left[I_N \otimes \left(\sum_{i=0}^{\infty} \lambda^i W^i \right) \right] v \tag{3.64}$$

The variance–covariance matrix of u is given by

$$\Omega = \sigma_2^2 \left\{ I_T \otimes \left[I_N \otimes \left(\sum_{i=0}^{\infty} \lambda^i W^i \right) \right] \right\} \left\{ I_T \otimes \left[I_N \otimes \left(\sum_{i=0}^{\infty} \lambda^i W^i \right) \right] \right\}' \tag{3.65}$$

This can be written as $\Omega = \sigma_2^2 (ZZ') \otimes I_T \otimes I_N$, where $Z = \sum_{i=0}^{\infty} \lambda^i W^i$. Now, $\sum_0 - \Omega = (\sigma_0^2 I_R - \sigma_2^2 (ZZ')) \otimes I_T \otimes I_N = \sigma_2^2 \left(\frac{\sigma_0^2}{\sigma_2^2} I_T - ZZ' \right) \otimes I_T \otimes I_N$.

The maximum likelihood approach has the usual asymptotic properties. But nothing can be said about positive definiteness of $(\Sigma_0 - \Omega)$. Establishing efficiency gain introducing an AR(1) structure along with spatial autocorrelation with an additional dimension with respect to items may be analytically intractable. In finite samples, no exact results are available. OLS may perform acceptably and even be superior in terms of bias and mean squared error (Anselin 1988, p. 111). It may, however, be noted that Elhorst (2008) shows by Monte Carlo simulation that there is an efficiency gain of maximum likelihood over OLS with serial and/or spatial errors correlation.

3.5 Concluding Remarks

This chapter presents the principal alternative approaches to the measurement of prices and distinguishes between the deterministic and non-stochastic approaches to price indices. It surveys some key contributions that provide a bridge between the two approaches and derives an equivalence between the deterministic and stochastic price indices. This chapter also shows how the measurement of spatial variation and temporal variation in prices in a heterogeneous country setting such as India can be integrated in a comprehensive framework that allows both sets of calculations. In many large, emerging economies, such as Brazil, China, India and Indonesia, price differences within the country can be as large, if not larger, than price differences between smaller economies. Since prices play a crucial role in comparisons of living standards within and between countries, the subject of spatial prices in large countries with heterogeneous population is of considerable importance. This calls for improved estimates of intra-country spatial prices and their changes over time.

This chapter has described a framework, namely the 'Dynamic Household Regional Product Dummy (DHRPD) Model' that allows such an investigation, and a formal statistical test of time invariance of the estimated spatial prices. The unified framework for calculating the spatial and temporal variation in prices that is provided by the DHRPD model has potential for applications in the cross-country context as well. For example, reflecting concerns over the validity of a single economy-wide PPP for all regions and population subgroups within the country, especially for large heterogeneous countries, the International Comparison Project (ICP) has flagged its intention to move beyond the calculation of national PPPs to subnational PPPs in its next round. Chapter 5 presents evidence reported in Majumder et al. (2015b) in favour of subnational PPPs and PPPs that vary between expenditure classes. The DHRPD framework is likely to be useful in this regard, as will be seen from its successful use in the Indian context that we report in Chap. 4.

References

Allen RGD (1975) Index numbers in theory and practice. Macmillan Press, New York

Anselin L (1988) Spatial econometrics: methods and models. Kluwer Academic Publishers, Boston, London

Arellano M (2003) Panel data econometrics. Oxford University Press, New York

Balk B (1995) Axiomatic price index theory; a survey. Int Stat Rev 63:69–93

Barten AP (1964) Family composition, prices and expenditure patterns. In: Hart PE, Mills G, Whittaker JK (eds) Econometric analysis for national economic planning. Butterworth, London

Bhattacharya N, Chatterjee GS, Pal P (1988) Variations in level of living across regions and socialgroups in India, 1963–64 and 1973–74. In: Srinivasan TN, Bardhan PK (eds) Rural poverty in South Asia. Oxford University Press

Bhattacharyya SS, Joshi PD, Roychowdhury AB (1980) Regional price indices based on NSS 25th round consumer expenditure data. Sarvekshana, J NSS Organ 34:107–121

Chakrabarty M, Majumder A, Ray R (2015) Preferences, spatial prices and inequality. J Dev Stud 5111:1488–1501

Chakrabarty M, Majumder A, Ray R (2017) A framework for the simultaneous measurement of spatial variation and temporal movement in prices in a heterogeneous country: the dynamic household regional product dummy model. Forthcoming in Review of Income and Wealth

Clements K, Izan HY (1981) A note on estimating Divisia index numbers. Int Econ Rev 22:745–747

Clements K, Izan HY, Selvanathan EA (2006) Stochastic index numbers: a review. Int Stat Rev 74:235–270
Coondoo D, Majumder A, Chattopadhyay S (2011) Estimating spatial consumer price indices through Engel curve analysis. Rev Income Wealth 57:138–155
Coondoo D, Majumder A, Ray R (2004) A method of calculating regional consumer price differentials with illustrative evidence from India. Rev Income Wealth 501:51–68
Coondoo D, Saha S (1990) Between-state differentials in rural consumer prices in India: an analysis of intertemporal variations. Sankhya, Ser B 523:347–360
Diewert WE (1981) The economic theory of index numbers: a survey. In: Deaton AS (ed) Essays in the theory of consumer behaviour. Cambridge University Press, Cambridge
Diewert WE (2005) Weighted country product dummy variable regressions and index number formulae. Rev Income Wealth 51:561–570
Elhorst JP (2008) Serial and spatial error correlation. Econ Lett 100:422–424
Fisher I (1922) The making of index numbers. Houghton Mifflin, Boston
Geary RG (1958) A note on the comparison of exchange rates and PPPs between countries. J Roy Stat Soc Ser A 121:97–99
Hajargasht G, Rao DSP (2010) Stochastic approach to index numbers for multilateral price comparisons and their standard errors. Rev Income Wealth 56:S32–S58
Hill RJ, Syed I (2014) Improving international comparisons of prices at basic heading level: an application to the Asia-Pacific region. Rev Income Wealth. https://doi.org/10.1111/roiw.12116
Khamis SH (1972) A new system of index numbers for national and international purposes. J Roy Stat Soc Ser A Part I 135:96–121
Konus AA (1939) "The problem of the true index of the cost of living" (1924 trans.). Econometrica 7:10–29
Majumder A, Ray R (2017) Estimates of spatial prices in India and their sensitivity to alternative estimation methods and choice of commodities. Forthcoming in Social Indicators Research
Majumder A, Ray R, Santra S (2015a) Preferences, purchasing power parity, and inequality: analytical framework, propositions, and empirical evidence. Policy Research Working Paper 7395, World Bank
Majumder A, Ray R, Sinha K (2015b) Spatial comparisons of prices and expenditure in a heterogeneous country: methodology with application to India. Macroecon Dyn 19(5):931–989
Majumder A, Ray R, Sinha K (2015c) Estimating purchasing power parities from household expenditure data using complete demand systems with application to living standards comparison: India and Vietnam. Rev Income and Wealth 61(2):302–328
Muellbauer J (1974a) Household composition, Engel curves and welfare comparisons between households. Eur Econ Rev 5:103–122
Muellbauer J (1974b) Prices and inequality: the United Kingdom experience. Econ J 84:32–55
Oulton N (2012) How to measure living standards and productivity. Rev Income Wealth 58:424–456
Pelagatti M (2010) Price indexes across space and time and the stochastic properties of prices. In: Biggeri L, Ferrari G (eds) Price indexes in time and space: methods and practice. Springer, Berlin, pp 97–114
Prais SJ, Houthakker HS (1955) The analysis of family budgets, 2nd edn. Cambridge: Cambridge University Press
Rambaldi A, Rao DSP, Ganegodage KR (2010) Modelling spatially correlated error structures in the time-space extrapolation of purchasing power parities. In: Biggeri L, Ferrari G (eds) Price indexes in time and space: methods and practice. Springer, Berlin, pp 63–96
Rao DSP (1972) Contributions to methodology of construction of consistent index numbers. Ph.D. Thesis, Indian Statistical Institute, Calcutta
Rao DSP (2005) On the equivalence of weighted country-product-dummy CPD Method and the Rao-system for multilateral comparisons. Rev Income Wealth 51(4):571–580
Rao DSP, Hajargasht G (2016) Stochastic approach to computation of purchasing power parities in the international comparison program (ICP). J Econometrics 191:414–425

Rao DSP, Rambaldi A, Doran H (2010) Extrapolation of purchasing power parities using multiple benchmarks and auxiliary information: a new approach. Rev Income Wealth 56:S59–S98

Ray R (1985) Prices, children and inequality: further evidence for the United Kingdom, 1965–82. Econ J 95:1069–1077

Ray R (2017) The role of prices in welfare comparisons: methodological developments and a selected survey of the empirical literature. Econ Rec 93:314–332

Schultz H (1939) A Misunderstanding in index-number theory: the true Konüs condition on cost-of-living index numbers and its limitations. Econometrica 7:1–9

Selvanathan E, Rao DSP (1994) Index numbers: a stochastic approach. Macmillan, London

Summers R (1973) International price comparisons based upon incomplete data. Rev Income Wealth 191:1–16

Chapter 4
Role of Prices in Welfare Comparisons

4.1 Introduction

While the previous chapter surveyed the principal developments in the measurement of price movements, the present chapter focusses on the role that prices play in welfare comparisons between households. It provides the methodology used in selected empirical studies, reported in the following chapters, that examine the welfare implications of price changes. Such price movements are both temporal and spatial—while temporal price movements are taken into account in the context of examining changes in household welfare over time, spatial price differences are used in comparing the welfare of households residing in different countries or in different geographic locations in a large heterogeneous country at a point in time.

The pivotal position that price indices occupies in economic analysis today is not just due to the need to measure inflation over time and price differences across geographical space, but also due to the wide range of welfare-focussed policy applications that are based on price changes but extend much beyond price measurement. These include specification and estimation of equivalence scales and demographic demand systems, estimating purchasing power parities between and within countries, national income comparisons, identifying and counting the number of poor and calculation of world poverty rates, analysis of the distributional consequences of price changes both between and within countries, and the formulation of tax design and tax reforms. These are only some of the areas that have seen application of price-based concepts straddling both sides of the conventional divide between micro and macroeconomics.

Much of the interest in price measurement has historically stemmed from the central role that inflation plays in studies on aggregate data involving temporal comparisons of real national income and expenditure at the country level[1] and in cross-country comparisons of real growth rates, living standards and purchasing

[1]See Hicks (1958) and Samuelson (1950).

R. Ray, *Household Behaviour, Prices, and Welfare*, Themes in Economics,
https://doi.org/10.1007/978-981-13-1930-3_4

power of the various countries' currencies.[2] Since inflation reduces the value of a country's currency, a distinction is drawn between nominal and price-deflated real values with the latter being the focus for use in the temporal and spatial comparisons at the aggregate country level. Prices have therefore played a key role in macroeconomic analyses. However, the emphasis in traditional macrostudies on inflation was more on the aggregate price movements temporally rather than on the structure of relative prices and the distributional implications of changes in that structure over time.

Two of the key papers that established the importance of the structure of relative prices between the items of consumption in evaluating welfare changes are that of Muellbauer (1974a) and Sen (1976). Both these papers established the distributive effects of relative price movements as the link between price changes and welfare comparisons. The basis for this link is the variation in household preferences both over time and spatially across different geographical regions that leads to differentiated effect of price changes on the welfare of households both over time and at a point in time. For example, an increase in the relative price of Food vis-a-vis durable items will adversely affect the poorer households much more than the more affluent households. Given the larger share of Food in the total expenditure of the poorer households, they are much less able to move away from Food to non-Food items than the more affluent households. This drives a wedge between nominal and real expenditure inequalities since while the former uses an aggregate price index as the expenditure deflator, the latter uses a household-specific price index as the deflator that incorporates the structure of relative prices.

As the empirical evidence reported later shows, this wedge can be considerable. While Muellbauer (1974a)'s analysis was focussed on welfare comparisons between households within a country, Sen (1976)'s framework was focussed on real income comparisons between countries. Sen's methodology for the ranking of countries on real income comparisons is based on the hypothetical situation of the countries facing each other's prices, besides their own. In the illustrative application of his methodology, however, Sen used the National Sample Survey data to compare and rank States in India based on an inequality incorporated measure of household welfare. The implementation of Sen's methodology to the cross-country context is somewhat more complicated since the prices of the different items are available in different currencies and require currency conversion rates to express them in a common currency. Later in this volume, we describe in detail one such study that uses Sen's methodology in the cross-country context to rank countries on the basis of their real national expenditure.

While Muellbauer (1974a) pioneered the integration of inequality, prices and household composition in welfare analysis at the household level, Sen (1976) was one the earliest studies to draw a distinction between the size and distribution of national income and emphasised the role of both in income comparisons between countries. The contribution of Sen's paper is, in his words, to project 'distribution

[2]See, e.g. World Bank (2013).

as an integral part of real income evaluation' and provide a methodology for incorporating inequality in cross-country real income comparisons. In Sen's proposed methodology, as in Muellbauer's, the structure of relative prices plays a key role in making the income comparisons sensitive to distributive judgements. Given the pioneering nature of Muellbauer (1974a) and Sen (1976)'s papers, we describe them in some detail in this chapter as a background to the empirical studies using their framework reported later in this volume.

In the 4 decades that have elapsed since Muellbauer's and Sen's contributions, and largely stimulated by those papers, the literature on the measurement and use of prices in policy applications have extended from the traditional macrocontext studying movements in prices and quantities at the aggregate country level[3] to micro contexts at the individual and household levels incorporating distributional considerations. Analysis of the welfare implications of price changes at the household level has placed the topic of prices firmly in the micro area, and it is no longer an exclusive preserve of macroanalysis of inflation at the aggregate country level. This development was aided by the move from employing fixed-weight price indices such as Laspeyres and Paasche indices that are not utility or welfare based and understate or overstate substitution to price changes to the use of preference consistent 'true cost of living indices' (TCLI) that account properly for substitution between items. The TCLIs have made the analysis of price changes more policy friendly than before. They have made the link between preferences, prices, welfare, especially distributive issues, clearer.

A significant feature of this development is the recognition that prices can vary across households in the same time period due to changes in taste, household composition, economic circumstances and other household characteristics. Since households vary in their response to price changes depending on their preferences and economic circumstances, much of the recent price applications has been utility based giving prominence to the a priori specification of cost or expenditure functions and the estimation of the corresponding demand systems to provide estimates of the utility functional parameters required in the welfare analysis of price changes. The important role that prices are playing in distributional comparisons today is also aided by the increasing availability of household expenditure data, at the level of unit records, leading to spatial comparisons in household welfare both between and within countries on a scale not seen earlier. The empirical literature on price-based welfare applications on Indian data has occupied centre stage in this development given the long history of the National Sample Surveys (NSS) in India in providing the required household level information.

This chapter seeks to explain some of the concepts that have helped to link consumer preferences with prices and welfare and provides the framework for drawing together some of the recent studies on India, described below in Chap. 5,

[3]See Basu (2011) for an insightful analysis of inflation in the traditional aggregate country context emphasising the role of theory in reaching policy conclusions, and drawing a distinction between overall inflation and change in relative prices.

that take a micro theoretic approach to the welfare analysis of price changes. The analysis of price changes in the chosen studies includes both temporal changes at the all-India level, and spatial variation at the intra-country level adopting different methodologies and addressing a different set of price based welfare issues. The common feature in these studies is the use of a preference consistent and expenditure function-based framework that builds on the link between preferences, behaviour, welfare and equity. Another important development in this context, that we described in Chap. 2, has been the use of the preference-based 'true cost of living index' in exploiting the quasi price nature of household size and composition effects to specify equivalence scales and in extending traditional demand systems to incorporate demographic variables along with prices and aggregate expenditure in estimating their effects on household expenditure allocation between items.

The rest of this chapter is organised as follows. The following Sect. 4.2 describes the concepts and frameworks proposed in Muellbauer (1974a) in incorporating prices in inequality analysis. Section 4.3 describes the application of Sen (1976)'s methodology to spatial rankings of regions based on real expenditures taking into account spatial variation in prices and inequality. To make Sen's framework operational, one needs spatial price indices. While the previous chapter has described how the conventional price indices can be adapted to the spatial context, Sect. 4.4 describes a preference consistent methodology proposed in Majumder et al. (2012) for calculating rural—urban differences in prices. Section 4.5 describes the Muellbauer methodology for assessing the distributive effects of price movements, namely the impact of changing relative prices between items on inequality. This section also shows how that methodology can be extended to examine the effect of relative price changes on poverty. The chapter concludes with a few summary remarks in Sect. 4.6 and provides the background analytical framework for the empirical studies reported in detail in Chap. 5.

4.2 Description of the Concepts Used for Incorporating Prices in Inequality

A key concept used in inequality and poverty calculations is the 'general equivalence scale'. The 'cost of a child', or the general equivalence scale as it is more commonly known, is a concept of considerable importance in issues relating to public policy and welfare. It serves to convert households with different size and composition into comparable units by deflating their aggregate expenditures similar to the use of the price index as an expenditure deflator in temporal comparisons of household expenditure. Since the 'general equivalence scale' has already been described and discussed in Chap. 2, we provide only a very brief reference to the concept here to make this chapter self-contained. While the discussion of the equivalence scale in Chap. 2 focussed on its behavioural role in demographically extending demand systems traditionally specified as function of prices and expenditure to include family size and composition, the present discussion highlights its role along with prices in welfare comparisons between households within and between countries.

Since there is large variation in the age structure of population between developed and developing countries, the equivalence scale plays an important role not only in welfare comparisons within countries as in Muellbauer's framework, but also between countries as in Sen's exercise. Viewed as a 'True Cost of Living Index' (TCLI) , the general equivalence scale compares two households with different family size and composition and calculates their relative cost of enjoying the same level of utility—in other words, it seeks to answer questions of the form: 'What expenditure level would make a family with one child as well off as one with no children and having an expenditure level of $2000?'. The scale, thus, seeks to quantify and represent in one summary measure the changing 'needs' of a family as it expands and changes its composition with the passage of time.

The importance of the scale in welfare economics in general and public policy discussion in particular stems from the fact that considerations of equity, justice and the like crucially involve an examination of household needs in relation to available resources. Such 'needs' will obviously vary from household to household depending on, among other things, its size and composition. Larger households will have greater needs than smaller households. Similarly, households with more children in the older category will make greater demands on certain items, less on others, than those with more children in the younger category. Since it is the household rather than the individual that is the decision-making unit and beneficiary of public welfare programs, it seems natural to make welfare comparisons across households in a manner similar to the way the TCLI compares individuals over time.

The equivalence scale has figured prominently in the theoretical and empirical literature on poverty, income distribution and income maintenance programs. In the USA and the UK, for example, the scale provides the basis for many empirical studies[4] aimed at identifying and counting the poor. There has been, broadly, two approaches to the measurement of equivalence scale. The first uses nutritionist requirements of different age-sex groups to determine the scales. This method has, however, not found wide favour since 'needs' are usually regarded as a social rather than a physiological concept. Also, experts rarely agree on what the 'correct' nutritional requirements are, and moreover, such requirements are likely to vary considerably over time and across countries.

The second, more widely used approach, consists of calculating the scales from observed expenditure pattern of households and is the approach followed in this chapter. The approach, which originated with Engel's (1895) pioneering analysis of Belgian working class data and was based on Food share of total expenditure as an indicator of household welfare, was generalised by Prais and Houthakker (1955) to

[4]See Ray (1983, p. 90) for a listing of some of these studies.

allow item-specific equivalence scales. In the Engel procedure, a comparison of expenditures of households with different family size and composition but identical budget share for Food as that of the reference household gives us the Engel equivalence scale. An alternative approach, due to Rothbarth (1943), is based on the concept of 'adult goods' which are items not consumed by children. The Rothbarth scale answers questions such as: How much additional total expenditure does a household with one child need to spend to maintain the same level of expenditure on 'adult goods' as a household with no children? The Rothbarth scale is dependent on the assumption of separability of the household preferences between 'adult goods' and collectively consumed items.

The idea behind the Engel and Rothbarth models of linking household welfare with, respectively, the household budget share of Food and the consumption of adult goods is simple and intuitively appealing, and this explains the popularity of these models even to this day. However, the underlying assumptions are not as innocent as they initially appear, and some are inconsistent with reality. Muellbauer (1974a) takes as the starting point the social welfare function (SWF) which aggregates the welfare levels of the individuals. While Atkinson (1970) specifies the SWF as a function of the individual utilities which are functions of the individuals' own income levels, Sen (1997) specifies the SWF directly as a function of the individual incomes. The alternative formulations of the SWF can be expressed as follows:

$$W = G(U_1(y_1), U_n(y_n)) \tag{4.1}$$

where G is increasing, strictly quasi-concave and symmetric in the individual utility functions, $U_i\ (y_i)$ which are assumed concave and increasing in income, y_i.

$$W = F(y_1, \ldots, y_n) \tag{4.2}$$

where F is strictly quasi-concave and symmetric. Both Eqs. 4.1 and 4.2 are conditional on prices being kept constant.

In specifying W directly as a function of individual income levels, y_i, Eq. 4.2 allows interdependence between the individuals' utilities that Eq. 4.1 does not. However, in Eq. 4.1 given strict quasi-concavity of $G(.)$, equality of incomes is the optimal way of distributing a fixed total income that is not the case in Eq. 4.2. Atkinson (1970) who employs Eq. 4.1 is therefore able to define his inequality measure as a measure of the distance of the 'optimal income' from the mean income:

$$\mathrm{I} = 1 - \frac{y_e}{\bar{y}} \tag{4.3}$$

where $\bar{y}\ (= \frac{\sum y_i}{n})$ is the mean income, and y_e is the 'equally distributed equivalent income' that yields the same level of social welfare as the existing distribution of incomes. y_e is obtained from

$$F(y_1,\ldots,y_n) = F(y_e,\ldots,y_e) \tag{4.4}$$

where $F(.)$ is derived from the individualistic and non-interdependent utility functions in Eq. 4.1 rather than directly specified as function of the individual income levels as in Eq. 4.2. To make Eq. 4.4 operational, Atkinson assumed an additive form for F:

$$F = \sum g_i(y_i) \tag{4.5}$$

The assumptions of symmetry and homotheticity impose a specific form for $g_i(.)$:

$$\text{Symmetry} : g_i(y_i) = g(y_i), \quad i = 1,\ldots,n \tag{4.6}$$

$$\text{Homotheticity} : \frac{g'(y_i)}{g'(y_j)} \text{ depends only on } \frac{y_i}{y_j} \tag{4.7}$$

Muellbauer (1974a) follows Atkinson (1970) in employing SWF, W, specified as function of individual utilities as in Eq. 4.1.

Since $U_i = U_i(y_i)$ in Eq. 4.1 is assumed monotonically increasing in y_i, it can be inverted to

$$y_i = f_i(U_i) \tag{4.8}$$

Though both Muellbauer and Atkinson define the SWF as function of individual utilities as in Eq. 4.1, Muellbauer defines the inequality measure in the utility space as the proportionate distance from optimal distribution of incomes, namely the one which maximises W subject to $U = \sum U_i(y_i)$. This gives the 'equally distributed equivalent utility', U_e, as that level of utility that if obtained by all the individuals yields the same level of social welfare as the one that actually prevails.

$$G(U_1,\ldots,U_n) = G(U_e,\ldots,U_e) \tag{4.9}$$

Muellbauer's definition of inequality is then given by

$$I = 1 - \frac{U_e}{\bar{U}} \tag{4.10}$$

where $\bar{U}$ $(= \frac{\sum U_i}{n})$ is mean utility.

The 'equivalent utility' (U_e)-based Muellbauer's inequality measure in Eq. 4.10 has two principal advantages over the 'equivalent income' (y_e)-based Atkinson inequality measure in Eq. 4.3: (a) Muellbauer's formulation does not require the symmetry of the utility functions (U_i) that Atkinson's treatment requires in the income space as given by Eq. 4.6, and (b) given the equivalence of direct and indirect utility functions at the optimum, it allows W to be defined on utilities with prices changing and prices can be introduced explicitly in the inequality measures. Note that (a) is an important advantage, since the waiving of the symmetry requirement in the utility space recognises the fact that the households can be of different composition so that two households facing identical prices with identical income levels will not necessarily enjoy equal utilities.

Using the duality of direct and indirect utility functions, the SWF can be expressed as a function of indirect utilities:

$$W = G\left(V_1\left(\frac{y_1}{p}\right), \ldots, V_n\left(\frac{y_n}{p}\right)\right) \tag{4.11}$$

where the individuals have different tastes represented by the indirect utilities, V_i defined over income and a common price vector, p. Equation 4.11 opens the door to bringing in household composition via the equivalence scale, m_i, defined in Chap. 2. To do so, let us recall the Barten (1964) household utility function:

$$u = \mathrm{U}\left(\frac{q_1}{m_1}, \ldots, \frac{q_n}{m_n}\right) \tag{4.12}$$

Recalling the quasi-price nature of household composition effects in the Barten model, Eq. 4.12 corresponds to the indirect utility form:

$$\mathrm{U} = V\left(\frac{y}{p_1 m_1}, \ldots, \frac{y}{p_n m_n}\right) \equiv V\left(\frac{y}{pm}\right) \tag{4.13}$$

Assuming a functional dependence of the specific equivalence scales on household composition: $m_i = m_i(b_1, \ldots, b_f)$, where b_j, $j = 1, \ldots, f$ is the number of individuals of type j in the family, and a functional form for V in Eq. 4.13, we can estimate the parameters in the m_i functions along with the other utility function parameters in Eq. 4.13 from demand estimation on observed data on expenditures, prices and household composition. The estimation of the m_i requires some normalisation of the m_i. A convenient one that is commonly enforced is that the $m_i(b_1, \ldots, b_f)$ have the same parameters across all households. The expenditure function corresponding to the Barten household indirect utility function, given by Eq. 4.13, is as follows:

$$y = C(pm, u) \tag{4.14}$$

Then, the real income of household i of household type J with money income, $y_{i,J}$ at prices p_i relative to a reference household at prices p_0 is $C\,(p_0 m, u_{i,J})$ where $u_{i,J} = V\left(\frac{y_{i,J}}{p_i m}\right)$ and the m s are normalised at unity for the reference household. Choosing a reference household and a reference (i.e. base) year, the Atkinson type inequality indices defined over real income indices will allow the dependence of inequality on prices and household composition. Muellbauer (1974b) illustrates his proposed methodology by using the LES utility form. He defines two key index number concepts. (a) A 'true (constant utility) cost of living index' which compares prices, p_1 (given year), and p_0 (base year) is given by $\frac{C(p_1,u)}{C(p_0,u)}$ and (b) A 'real expenditure index', which compares the expenditure necessary to enjoy two utility levels, u_0 and u_1, at a given price vector, p. and is given by $\frac{C(p,u_1)}{C(p,u_0)}$.

Assuming a Barten-type household function, the 'real expenditure index' can be redefined to include household composition: $\frac{C(p_0^*,u_1)}{C(p_0^*,u_0)}$ and $\frac{C(p_1^*,u_1)}{C(p_1^*,u_0)}$, depending on which price vector is taken as reference, and as defined above, $p^* = pm$. To ensure that the vector of specific equivalence scales, m, is independent of prices, Muellbauer makes the further assumption: $\frac{m_{i0}}{m_{i1}}$ does not vary with item i; i.e., the economies of scale in households affects all goods proportionately. Assuming the LES functional form, the expenditure function (in nominal terms) for adult equivalent unit, s, in year t, is given by a $(p_t) + u_s$ b(p_t). If we take the given year utility as the reference utility, then the real expenditure for adult equivalent unit, s, in year 0 is given by $\mathrm{C}(p_0, u_{st}) = \mathrm{a}(p_0) + u_{st} b(p_0)$, where the LES indirect utility form, u_{st}, is given by $u_{st} = (y_{st} - a_t) b_t^{-1}$.

Muellbauer then makes the further assumption, $\frac{m_{iH}}{m_{iJ}} = \frac{m_{0H}}{m_{0J}}$ for i = 1,…,r. Assuming Atkinson's SWF which is additive and homothetic in individual income or expenditure:

$$W = \sum_{h=1}^{H} \left(a + \frac{b}{1+\delta} y_h^{1+\delta} \right) f(y_h) \tag{4.14a}$$

where $f(y_h)$ is the relative frequency of the hth expenditure group, the Atkinson inequality measure is given by

$$I = 1 - \left[\sum_{h=1}^{H} \left(\frac{y_h}{\bar{y}} \right)^{1+\delta} f(y_h) \right]^{1/1+\delta} \tag{4.14b}$$

where the expenditures (y_h) are expressed in per equivalent adult terms. Note that by varying δ the degree of 'inequality aversion' is varied. $I = 0$ represents perfect equality. A comparison of I (defined over real expenditures) and I (defined over nominal expenditures) gives us the egalitarian (or otherwise) nature of the price changes between base year (0) and given year (1). Muellbauer (1974b)'s exercise on UK data assumed the restrictive LES functional form. As reported in the following chapter, Ray (1985) examined the robustness of Muellbauer's empirical results by dispensing with the linearity and separability assumptions of the LES.

4.3 Spatial Price-Deflated Real Expenditure Comparisons Between Regions or Countries

The methodology proposed by Sen (1976) for real income comparisons between countries and illustrated in that paper by applying it to studying regional differences in rural standard of living in India,[5] was used in Majumder et al. (2015) to compare real expenditure among the constituent States of the Indian union. Sen (1976) was one of the earliest attempts at incorporating distributional considerations in real income comparisons between nations. He does that by proposing as a welfare measure inequality corrected mean nominal expenditure: $w_n^r = \mu_n^r(1 - G_n^r)$, where μ_n^r is mean of the nominal expenditures (x_h^r) in State r, and G_n^r is the Gini inequality measure of nominal expenditures in that State. The spatial price of State r can be used to convert the welfare measure from nominal to real terms by defining $w_R^r = \mu_R^r(1 - G_R^r)$ where μ_R^r is the mean of the real expenditures (x_h^r/S^r), G_R^r the corresponding spatially corrected real expenditure inequality, and S^r is the spatial price of State r with respect to the all-India figure which is normalised at 1.

An alternative way of incorporating spatial differences in prices in the expenditure comparisons has been proposed by Sen (1976). The welfare measure in nominal terms, w_n^r, for region r is calculated not only at that region's prices (p^r), but also at other region's prices, (p^s), i.e. $w_n^{s,r} = \mu_n^r(p^s)(1 - G_n^r(p^s))$. Sen's methodology consists of constructing the matrix W from these spatially corrected welfare values, with the diagonal elements W_{ii} being the values of the measure, w_n^r, in the various States evaluated at that State's prices, i.e. $w_n^r(p^r)$, and the off-diagonal elements denoting the corresponding values evaluated at other States' prices; i.e., the (s,r)th element denotes $w_n^r(p^s)$. Majumder, Ray and Sinha (2015) adopt Sen's recommendation to rank States from the values of the W matrix as follows: 'if the value of the diagonal element for any state 1 is larger than the value in the same row for another state 2, then we conclude that in terms of consumption state 1 has a higher rural standard of welfare' (Sen 1976, p. 35).

This gives us a 'partial ordering of a complete welfare indicator rather than a complete ordering of a partial welfare indictor' (p. 32). These pairwise comparisons may not yield unambiguous rankings; for example, State i may have a higher welfare than State j with both States' expenditures evaluated at State i's price, while State j may have a higher welfare than State i with both expenditures evaluated at State j's price. The Hasse diagrams are quite convenient in pictorially presenting the rankings, and the evidence on Indian States is reported in detail in Chap. 5. A point of interest is whether there are rural–urban differences in the spatially corrected State rankings that are shown in the Hasse diagrams.

Unfortunately, it is not always readily apparent from the Hasse diagrams if there are rural–urban differences. Majumder et al. (2015) provide evidence on rural–urban differences by constructing a distance matrix, D, whose (i,j)th element, D_{ij} is

[5]See Appendix of Sen (1976).

given by the absolute value of the distance between the spatially corrected welfare measures of States i and j, i.e., $D_{ij}^{R} = w_R^i - w_R^j$ for the rural sector and $D_{ij}^{U} = w_U^i - w_U^j$ for the urban sector. Each D matrix is, therefore, a symmetric matrix whose diagonal elements are all 0. The Mantel test (Mantel 1967), which has been widely used by evolutionists on genetic data allows linear or monotonic comparisons between the elements of two distance matrices (see Legendre and Fortin 2010) and was used here to test for rural–urban differences in the expenditure-based State rankings depicted in the Hasse diagrams.[6] The test results are reported in Chap. 5.

4.4 The Calculation of Price Differentials Between Regions in a Country with Special Reference to Rural–Urban Price Differences

Purchasing power parity (PPP) exchange rates are essential for a variety of cross-country comparisons, such as welfare comparisons involving expenditures and other values denominated in different currencies. The international statistical agencies have spent much resources on calculating PPPs between nations, (ADB 2008), but there has not been much attention on calculating PPP within nations. Yet, the considerations of preference heterogeneity and differing relative prices between nations that drive the cross-country PPP calculations, also, underline the importance of spatial prices in the context of large federal countries such as Brazil and India. The requirement of spatial prices is important in the construction of poverty lines. While PPPs of various currencies are needed in the construction of poverty lines that allow meaningful cross-country poverty comparisons, intra-country PPPs are required for construction of regional poverty lines that allow meaningful calculation of poverty estimates for the country as a whole. For example, poverty calculations in a given country based on \$1 a day poverty line, where \$1, in PPP terms, is assumed to have the same purchasing power in all regions in that country is demonstrably false. Hence, there is a need to construct intra-country PPPs that vary by regions.

While the PPP discussed above provides an overall picture of purchasing power of a region, the contribution of the items comprising the overall index is not apparent from the overall value. Yet, in terms of policy implication it may be important to identify the items that are major contributors to differential purchasing power of a country's currency unit across its regions. One may, therefore, be interested in individual item-specific PPPs and their variations. This variation could be for a particular item over space–time (e.g. rural–urban comparison), and/or

[6] See, however, Legendre and Fortin (2010) for words of caution on the use of the Mantel test, especially their observation that 'the Mantel test does not correctly estimate the proportion of the original data variation explained by spatial structures' (p. 831).

across items given space/time (e.g. Food PPP may not be the same as non-Food PPP). The variation of PPPs across items, if present, will result in a variation of the overall PPP between households because of variation in household expenditure patterns.

The motivation of Majumder et al. (2012) was to propose a procedure that allows the calculation of intra-country PPP (spatial prices) that vary across items and, hence, between household groups. The potential usefulness of the procedure is apparent in the context of large and heterogeneous countries such as the USA, Brazil and India. The Indian application of this procedure reported later illustrates the usefulness in providing evidence, both item by item and over all items, on price differences between rural and urban areas in the context of a large heterogeneous country such as India. The methodology is described below. The proposed procedure is based on an idea that is similar to the idea of quasi–price demographic effects in the Barten (1964) model that is used to estimate the general equivalence scale as a function of the item-specific equivalence scales. The proposed procedure is rooted in utility maximising demand models and generalises the conventional framework to allow commodity specific PPPs between rural and urban areas.

The extended framework is more policy friendly by enabling the calculation of item-specific rural–urban differential in prices and allows a simple test of the idea of commodity-invariant PPP underlying the conventional calculations. In modifying the prices facing a household in the Barten (1964) model, the commodity-specific equivalence scales perform a role that is similar to that played by the item-specific PPP rates in the framework that is proposed here. While household size and composition effects work through the equivalence scales in the Barten model, spatial prices work through the PPP parameters. The proposed procedure exploits this analogy to allow a simple test of the item invariance of the PPPs underlying the conventional framework just as the Barten (1964) model allowed a test of the assumption of item invariance of the specific equivalence scales underlying the Engel model.

Building on this analogy, and in a key methodological contribution, Majumder et al. (2012) shows how the introduction of preference heterogeneity through the incorporation of Barten-type quasi-price household size and composition effects on expenditure patterns helps to overcome the problem of identification of the item-specific PPP parameters similar to the manner in which the introduction of such demographic effects in the Barten framework helps to achieve identification of the item-specific equivalence scales. The proposed methodology is benchmarked against the conventional procedures by comparing the calculated rural–urban price differentials with those obtained from using the Laspeyres price index (Clements and Izan 1981; Selvanathan 1991) and the Country-Product Dummy (CPD) method (Summers 1973; Rao 2005). A significant factor behind the lack of interest in calculating PPP within nations has been the absence of data on prices on near identical items across regions within countries on a scale comparable to that between countries.

There are not been many examples of intra-country attempts to collect price information on a wide range of items between regions on a scale similar to that between countries undertaken in the International Comparison Project (ICP) of the United Nations. Yet, intra-national PPPs are as important as cross-country PPPs in view of their requirement in welfare comparisons between households living in different provinces or between rural and urban areas in a large country. Consequently, estimation of 'complete' demand systems on time series of budget surveys has, until recently, proceeded on the assumption that all households, in the same time period, face identical prices, irrespective of their region of residence or their household size and composition (see, e.g., Pollak and Wales 1992). Yet, such an assumption is false and ignores regional price differences and preference heterogeneity amongst consumers that can bias the demand estimates.

While there is a significant literature on the measurement of regional cost of living that is based mostly on US data (e.g. Koo et al. 2000) the lack of regional price data has constrained a similar literature in the context of developing countries. There is a significant early literature on regional price differentials in India (e.g. Bhattacharya et al. (1980, 1988). There is not much of a similar literature in other developing countries. The situation is now changing with the increasing availability of unit values of various items from the expenditure and quantity information on purchases of various items in the household expenditure surveys. The unit value of an item is calculated as the ratio of the value of household expenditure on that item and the corresponding quantity of purchase. Examples of some recent studies that use the unit values to construct spatial prices include Aten and Menzies (2002), Coondoo et al. (2004), Dubey and Palmer-Jones (2005), O'Donnell and Rao (2007), and Hoang (2009).

Using an alternative methodology, Hoderlein and Mihaleva (2008) also tackle the problem of insufficient price variation by constructing household specific price indices and provide evidence on UK Family Expenditure data in favour of their procedure by showing that it yields superior estimates in the form of greater precision compared to those from using aggregate price data. Coondoo, Majumder and Chattopadhyay (2011) propose an innovative methodology that allows the calculation of spatial multilateral price index numbers from consumer expenditure data using conventional Engel curve analysis without requiring any price data. Unit values cannot be used as prices due to (a) measurement errors, (b) quality effects and (c) household compositional effects on expenditure patterns. The presence of quality effects that prevent the use of raw unit values as prices has been discussed by Prais and Houthakker (1955), who refrained from using them in the estimation of price elasticities on budget data. For example, the unit value of an item, say cereals, that is consumed in the urban areas, may be higher than its rural counterpart simply because cereals consumed in urban areas is of superior quality.

A large part of rural consumption is out of home-produced items which are lower priced than urban consumption items that are mostly bought in the market. Comparison of raw unit values will, therefore, exaggerate the rural–urban differential in prices. Similarly, a larger-sized household enjoys discounted prices that a smaller household does not. Cox and Wohlgenant (1986) proposed a methodology that adjusts unit values obtained from budget surveys to correct for quality effects before they are used as prices in cross-sectional demand estimation. That methodology has been extended and used in a recent study on Vietnamese data by Hoang (2009). Gibson and Rozelle (2005) and McKelvey (2011) argue, however, that even the adjusted unit values lead to substantial biases when used as prices.

The procedure described below extends the Hoang (2009) procedure for adjusting the unit values to correct for quality- and demographic-induced taste differences for use as prices in the calculating the rural–urban price differential from budget data. Using the unit values of six Food items, calculated herein, the Quadratic Almost Ideal Demand System (QUAIDS) proposed by Banks et al. (1997) has been estimated on Indian consumer expenditure data and the overall and item-specific PPPs have been calculated at two-time points. The illustrative evidence shows considerable potential for applying the methodology in the case of other countries and for larger number of commodities.

4.4.1 Procedure for Estimating the Rural–Urban Price Differential

Let us assume that the consumer's expenditure function is given by the QUAIDS form proposed by Banks et al. (1997):

$$C(u,p) = a(p).\exp\left(\frac{b(p)}{(1/\ln u) - \lambda(p)}\right) \tag{4.15}$$

$a(p)$, $b(p)$ and $\lambda(p)$ are functions of the price vector, p, and u is the utility indicator. Let k_i denote the parameter relating to item-specific PPP between rural and urban areas. In other words, 1 unit of currency in the rural areas has the same purchasing power of item i as $1/k_i$ units of that currency in the urban areas. The $k_i's$ are item-specific PPP parameters in the demand equation that are estimable similar to the demand parameters and the PPP for item i is given by $1/k_i$.

On assuming the QUAIDS functional forms chosen for $a(p)$, $b(p)$ and $\lambda(p)$, the demand system in budget share terms is given by

$$w_i = \alpha_i + \sum_{j=1}^{n} \gamma_{ij} \log p_j + \beta_i \log(x/P) + \lambda_i[\log(x/P)]^2 \tag{4.16}$$

$$\log P = \alpha_0 + \sum_i \alpha_i \log p_i + \frac{1}{2}\sum_{i=1}^{n}\sum_{j=1}^{n} \gamma_{ij} \log p_i \log p_j \tag{4.16a}$$

Equation 4.16 holds for rural and urban areas separately. The above equation can be extended to hold for both areas as follows, using the item-specific PPPs, namely the $k_i's$, to express the urban prices in terms of the rural prices:

$$w_i = \alpha_i + \sum_{j=1}^{n} \gamma_{ij} \log p_j + D_s \sum_{j=1}^{n} \gamma_{ij} \log k_j + \beta_i \log(x/P) + \lambda_i [\log(x/P)]^2 \quad (4.17)$$

with the restrictions $\sum_{j=1}^{n} \gamma_{ij} = \sum_{i=1}^{n} \gamma_{ij} = 0$ and $\gamma_{ij} = \gamma_{ji}$, where D_s denotes the sectoral dummy (rural = 0, urban = 1). The justification for this formulation is that if we normalise the rural–urban PPP at rural prices, then, the urban price for each item, *i*, will need to be multiplied by k_i for parity with the rural prices. Equation 4.17 is, therefore, a comprehensive system with the parameters $(\alpha_i, \beta_i, \lambda_i, \gamma_{ij}, k_i)$ treated as estimable parameters. The overall rural–urban PPP can then be obtained as *1/K*, where

$$K = \frac{C^U}{C^R} \quad (4.18)$$

$C^R = C(u, p^R)$ and $C^U = C(u, p^U)$ are, respectively, the expenditure functions of the rural and urban consumer, the urban price being the PPP adjusted rural price. Extending the analogy with the equivalence scale concept, *K* is analogous to the 'cost of a child'. Equation 4.18 gives the overall PPP as the ratio of expenditures in the rural and urban areas that yield the same utility and will yield the overall PPP as a linear function of the item-specific PPPs.[7] Apart from its simplicity of estimation and interpretation, Eq. 4.18 allows the overall PPP, *K*, to depend on reference utility, *u*. In the PPP estimates reported below, we have chosen the reference utility level corresponding to the median household in the rural areas. The PPP for item *i* is given by $1/k_i$.

Unfortunately, Eq. 4.17 is unidentified since the item-specific parities (k_i's) are not all estimable. If we denote c to be the $n \times 1$ vector with a typical element, $c_i = \sum_{j=1}^{n} \gamma_{ij} \log k_j$, Γ to be the $n \times n$ matrix (γ_{ij}), and *k* to be the vector of the item-specific PPPs (k_i), then $c = \Gamma\, k$. Since by the adding up condition, Γ is less than full rank and singular, not all the k_i's can be estimated from the demand system, Eq. 4.8. We need to normalise one of the k_i's at an a priori set value. The argument is identical to that used in Muellbauer (1980) to show that the item-specific equivalence scales in the Prais and Houthakker (1955) model are unidentified and require normalisation of one of the scales. Given the arbitrary nature of any such normalisation, the Barten (1964) method of introducing quasi-price demographic effects is used to extend Eqs. 4.17–4.19 as follows.

$$w_i = \alpha_i = \alpha_i + \sum_{j=1}^{n} \gamma_{ij} \log p_j^* + \beta_i \log(x/P^*) + \lambda_i [\log(x/P^*)]^2 \quad (4.19)$$

---

[7]This is similar to the general equivalence scale in the Barten model of equivalence scales, where the general scale (m_0) is a function of the item-specific equivalence scales.

where

$$\log P^* = \alpha_0 + \sum_i \alpha_i \log p_i^* + \frac{1}{2}\sum_{i=1}^{n}\sum_{j=1}^{n} \gamma_{ij} \log p_i^* \log p_j^*, \tag{4.19a}$$

and $p_i^* = p_i k_i^{D_s}(n^A + \theta_i n^C)$, n^A and n^C being the number of adults and children in the household, respectively.

The quasi-price nature of the demographic effects on budget shares follows from the fact that n^A and n^C impact on budget share of i through the composite price–demographic term p_i^*. The PPP incorporated demographic demand system Eq. 4.19 has 2 principal advantages over Eq. 4.17, namely (a) all the item-specific PPPs (k_i) are identified and estimable in Eq. 4.17 and do not any require arbitrary normalisation,[8] and (b) Eq. 4.19 relaxes the assumption of identical preferences in Eq. 4.17 via the introduction of demographically varying preferences between households of different size and composition. Since rural and urban households differ with respect to their size and composition, (b) introduces preference heterogeneity between the two sectors as well.

The unit values (v_i) are adjusted for quality and demographic factors mentioned above as follows. Following Cox and Wohlgenant (1986) and Hoang (2009), and keeping in mind the Indian application, the unit values can be related with a set of variables through the following regression equation:

$$\begin{aligned} v_i^{hsjd} - \left(v_i^{sjd}\right)_{\text{median}} &= \alpha_i D_s + \beta_i D_j + \gamma_i \sum_j \sum_d D_j D_d + \varphi_i x^{hsjd} \\ &\quad + \omega_i f_i^{hsjd} + \sum_m b_i Z_{im}^{hsjd} + \varepsilon_i^{hsjd} \end{aligned} \tag{4.20}$$

where v_i^{hsjd} is the unit value paid by household h for item i in State j, district d and sector s, $\left(v_i^{sjd}\right)_{\text{median}}$ is the median unit value for the district in which household resides, x is household Food expenditure per capita, f is proportion of times meals consumed outside by members of that household, Z_{im} is household characteristics (these include age of the household head, gender of household head, household size, number of adult males and number of adult females in household) and D_s, D_j and D_d are dummies for sector, State and district, respectively.

While Hoang estimates Eq. 4.20 (using means in place of median being used here) and then adds the predicted residual $(\hat{\varepsilon}_i)$ to the district mean to get the quality-adjusted price for each good, the present paper adopts a slightly different methodology and uses deviation of household-level unit values from median unit

[8]The introduction of quasi-price demographic effects in the Barten (1964) model allows the use of household size and composition as identifying information for estimating all the item-specific PPPs analogous to the identification of the item-specific equivalence scales—see Muellbauer (1977).

values to represent quality effect. The quality-adjusted unit values are calculated by, first, estimating Eq. 4.20 which, for each commodity i, regresses the deviation of household's unit price from the median price in the district d, of State j, in each sector s (rural or urban), $\left(v_i^{sd}\right)_{\text{median}}$, on household characteristics. The districtwise quality-adjusted price for each item p_i is generated by adding the district median unit value for this item to the estimated residual from equation Eq. 4.6.

$$\left(p_i^{sd}\right)_{\text{median}} = \left(v_i^{sd}\right)_{\text{median}} + \left(\hat{\varepsilon}_i^{sd}\right)_{\text{median}} \tag{4.21}$$

The districtwise median of the prices calculated in Eq. 4.21 is used to represent the districtwise quality-adjusted price for each Food item i. In other words, each household is assumed to face the vector of quality-adjusted median value, using Eqs. 4.20 and 4.21, of the item in the district where the household resides. The two-step estimation procedure, therefore, consists of, first, generating the quality and demographically adjusted unit values, via estimating Eqs. 4.20 and 4.21, and then treating them as prices in the demand estimations of the Barten-extended QUAIDS model Eq. 4.19 and, subsequently, using Eq. 4.18 to calculate the overall PPP between the rural and urban areas, $1/K$. The QUAIDS equations have been estimated in linearised form, using the Stone approximation, with symmetry enforced, using SURE that allows nonzero contemporaneous covariance amongst the residuals of the various equations.

The above methodology is benchmarked against the Laspeyres index (computed using Selvanathan's (1991) procedure), obtained from the following regression equation:

$$\frac{p_i^U q_i^R}{\sqrt{p_i^R q_i^R}} = \gamma \sqrt{p_i^R q_i^R} + \varepsilon_i, \tag{4.22}$$

where U and R denote rural and urban sectors, respectively, p_i and q_i are the price and quantity of the ith commodity and ε_i is the disturbance term. The ordinary least squares estimator $\hat{\gamma}$ yields the Laspeyres index along with its standard error.

The other conventional index, with which the results have been compared, is the index computed using the Country-Product Dummy (CPD) method from the following regression equation.

$$\sqrt{w_i^s} \log p_i^s = \pi \sqrt{w_i^s} D_s + \sqrt{w_i^s} \sum_j \eta_j D_j^* + \varepsilon_i, \tag{4.23}$$

where w_i^s is the budget share of the ith item in the sth sector, D_s is the sectoral dummy and $D_j^*, j = 1, 2, \ldots, n$ are the product (item) dummies. If $\hat{\pi}$ is the ordinary least squares estimator of π, then exp $(\hat{\pi})$ yields the CPD index.

4.5 Methodology for Assessing the Distributional Consequences of Price Changes

Since expenditure pattern varies across households, primarily due to differences in their economic circumstances and in their household size and composition, differential movement in prices of items over time will have a differential impact on welfare across households. For example, inflation that is accompanied by an increase in the relative price of Food vis-a-vis non-Food items will affect the poorer household groups more adversely than the affluent ones. Similarly, if the prices of items that are consumed primarily by children increase more than those consumed primarily by adults, then households with large numbers of children will be hit harder than, say, childless households. Again, if the price increases are concentrated on items that exhibit substantial economies of scale, then inflation will hit the smaller households harder than the larger households simply because the former are unable to benefit from bulk purchase to the same extent as the latter. All that this means is that the aggregate figure of inflation published routinely by authorities may hide substantial differences in the effective inflation rates across households. The two areas where this has immediate implications are the measurement of inequality and poverty over time.

Relative price changes also have implications for the equivalence scales which are required in welfare comparisons between households, though the link is not so clear cut and direct in this case. The equivalence scales are aggregate expenditure deflators that measure the compensation, in the form of expenditure scaling, to households with children to enable them to enjoy the same level of welfare as childless households. The concept of equivalence scale, which measures compensation in relation to demographic change, is therefore similar to the concept of a true cost of living index which measures compensation in response to price changes. Since the latter depends on the reference utility level and the structure of relative prices, so will the former, unless assumed away as is done, rather unrealistically, with the use of price and expenditure-invariant equivalence scales. This link between the two concepts was established by Barten (1964)'s pioneering contribution which showed that the household composition effects that the scales measure are analogous to the price induced substitution effects estimated in conventional demand analysis.

Since such 'quasi price' demographic effects do vary with household affluence and with relative prices, the equivalence scales will be expenditure and price dependent. If equivalence scales vary with relative prices, then the expenditure deflators that adjust for differences in household size and composition will change over time with inflation and realignment of relative prices with consequent implications for the inequality and poverty calculations. This possibility is ruled out with the use of price-invariant equivalence scales or the use of household size as the expenditure deflator. The issue of price sensitivity of equivalence scales, discussed earlier, is hence not unrelated to the issue of the redistributive effect of relative price changes.

Mishra and Ray (2011) employs a parametric test of the price sensitivity of the equivalence scale based on the hypothesis that a subset of the demographic parameters estimated from the demographic demand system is individually and jointly insignificant. The approach taken there is different from that adopted in Pendakur (2002). While Pendakur (2002) specifies the demographic demand system so as to allow the equivalence scales to vary with prices, Mishra and Ray (2011) follows Ray (1983) in taking the reverse route of first specifying the equivalence scales directly as function of prices, and then working out the corresponding demographic demand system which then contains the price-invariant equivalence scales as a nested specification. The methodology of Mishra and Ray (2011) is outlined below in this section.

With regard to the direct effect of relative price changes on inequality, the point was recognised by Muellbauer (1974a) over three decades back when he distinguished between real and nominal expenditure inequality and showed the divergence between the two during the 6 years, 1964–1970, of Labour rule in the UK. Muellbauer's contribution, that included a methodology for investigating the distributional consequences of price movements, was extended to allow more realistic and flexible demand responses to price changes and applied to UK data in Ray (1985) and, more recently, to Australian data in Nicholas et al. (2010). There have not been many similar attempts on other data sets to investigate the distributional effects of relative price changes, and none on the data set of a developing country. Pendakur (2002) provided indirect evidence of the importance of price movements in inequality calculations by showing that price dependent equivalence scales affect measured family expenditure inequality in Canada, but he did not investigate directly the redistributive effect of relative price changes.

The issue of the differential impact of price changes across households is also relevant in poverty comparisons. Given their varying consumption pattern, the poor households face a price vector that is different from that faced by the non-poor. One can extend this point to argue that the effective price index varies from one poor household to another thus questioning the use of household invariant price index in making temporal adjustment to the poverty line in comparing poverty rates over time. Due to differences in the households' spending power and in their size and composition, the price index used in deflating the nominal expenditures in comparing poverty over time will vary not only between households below and above the poverty lines but also between households at varying levels of poverty. This aspect is rarely acted upon by government agencies in devising and revising poverty lines in response to price movements.

Mishra and Ray (2011) provide a unified methodology for incorporating the differential effect of price movements in the welfare comparisons involved in inequality and poverty calculations and apply it to Indian data. This paper provides evidence, reported in the following chapter, on inequality and poverty movements in India over the period, 1993/94–2004/5, and looks at the role played by the price changes in these movements. Another feature of that study is the formal statistical testing using boot strap methods of the inequality and poverty rate estimates and of their changes over time. The starting point of Mishra and Ray (2011) is the price scaling demographic technique, described earlier, of introducing demographic variables in expenditure functions:

$$c^h(u,p,z) = m_{0h}(z,p,u)\, c^R(u,p) \tag{4.24}$$

The following functional form is chosen for the utility-invariant general equivalence scale $m_{0h}(z,p)$:

$$m_{oh}(z,p) = \prod_k p_k^{\delta_k z_h} \prod_k p_k^{\varphi_k na_h}(na_h + \rho z_h), \sum_k \delta_k = 0. \tag{4.24a}$$

na_h denotes the number of adults in household h, z_h denotes the corresponding number of children, ρ is the equivalence scale. φ_k *and* δ_k denote the price sensitivity of the equivalence scale interacting with the number of adults, number of children, respectively. ρ can be interpreted as the 'cost' of a child in the base year (when p = 1) relative to an adult whose scale is normalised at 1. A test of the hypothesis that the parameters φ_k *and* δ_k are jointly insignificant constitutes a test of the price invariance of the equivalence scale.

The application of price scaling on the QAI expenditure function proposed by Banks et al. (1997) gives us the demographic QAI demand system which in budget share terms, $w_{i,h}$, is as follows.

$$\begin{aligned} w_{ih} = \alpha_i + \delta_i z_h + \sum_j \gamma_{ij} \ln p_j + \beta_i \Bigg[& lnx_h - \alpha_0 - \sum_k \alpha_k \ln p_k - \frac{1}{2}\sum_i \sum_j \gamma_{ij} \ln p_i \ln p_j \\ & - \ln(na_h + \rho z_h) - \sum_k \varphi_k na_h \ln p_k - \sum_k \delta_k z_h \ln p_k \Bigg] \\ & + \lambda_i \prod_k p_k^{-\beta_k} \Bigg[\ln x_h - \alpha_0 - \sum_k \alpha_k \ln p_k - \frac{1}{2}\sum_i \sum_j \gamma_{ij} \ln p_i \ln p_j \\ & - \ln(na_h + \rho z_h) - \sum_k \varphi_k na_h \ln p_k - \sum_k \delta_k z_h \ln p_k \Bigg]^2 \end{aligned} \tag{4.25}$$

x_h denotes the nominal expenditure of household h. In the estimations, α_o is set a priori at zero. The λ_i s. measure the quadratic expenditure effects, and if they are all 0, then Eq. 4.25 specialises to the conventional Almost Ideal Demand System.

4.5.1 Nominal and Real Expenditure Inequality and Poverty

Following Muellbauer (1974b, p. 42), we define real expenditure of household h in year t, namely $\breve{x}_{ht}$ as the minimum expenditure needed to obtain current year utility, u_t at base year price, p_0. In other words,

$$\breve{x}_{ht} = c(p_0, u_t, z_h) \tag{4.26}$$

The expression for real expenditure in case of the demographically extended QAI is given as follows:

$$\breve{x}_{ht} = \bar{m}_{oh}(z_h) \prod_k p_{kt}^{\delta_k z_h} \prod_k p_{kt}^{\phi \delta_k n a_h} a_0 \exp\left[\frac{b_0}{\left(c_t + \frac{b_t}{\ln x_t - \ln a_t - \ln \bar{m}_o - \sum_k \varphi_k n a_h \ln p_{kt} - \sum_k \delta_k z_h \ln p_{kt}} - c_0 \right)} \right] \tag{4.27}$$

$\bar{m}_{0h}(= na_h + \rho z_h)$ is the base year equivalence scale, and a_t, b_t, c_t are functions of prices, p_t. It is readily verified from Eq. 4.27 that in the base year the real and nominal expenditures are equal (i.e. $\breve{x}_{h0} = x_{h0}$), and consequently, the nominal and real expenditure inequalities will coincide. The magnitude and sign of the difference between the inequalities in real and nominal expenditures per adult equivalent, i.e. between the inequalities in $(\breve{x}_{ht}/m_{0h})$ and (x_{ht}/m_{0h}), will depend on the movement in relative prices. In the case of no change in relative prices between current year t and base year, 0, the two inequalities will coincide.

Besides the Gini inequality index, Mishra and Ray (2011) have used the Generalised Entropy inequality index, GE(α).[9] The parameter, α, can be interpreted as a measure of equality aversion. As α decreases, the index becomes more sensitive to transfers at the lower end of the distribution, and less weight is attached to transfers at the top; when $\alpha = 2$, the index attaches the same weight to transfers at all expenditure levels. The GE (α) family of inequality indices includes as special cases GE (1) and GE (2) which have been proposed by Theil (1967). The GE measure of inequality has the attractive feature that it can be decomposed into between group and within group inequality. Shorrocks (1980) has derived the entire class of measures that are decomposable under relatively weak restrictions on the form of the index. The real and nominal inequality indices which are defined over real and nominal expenditure per adult equivalent are given by I_t^R and I_t^N, respectively. $\left(I_t^R - I_t^N\right) > 0$ implies that the relative price movement has been regressive or inequality increasing, while the reverse is indicated if $\left(I_t^R - I_t^N\right) < 0$.

Analogous to the definitions of nominal and real expenditure inequalities, we can define the nominal and real poverty rates as those that omit and include, respectively, the distributional impact of price movements. The nominal poverty rates, P_t^N, are those that assume that all households face the same price vector and consequently are based on the official poverty line and its periodic revision in line with inflation as published for the various rounds by the Govt. of India and used in

[9]See Sen (1997) for the expression of the GE(α) inequality index and an analysis of its decomposability properties.

the official poverty rate calculations. In contrast, the concept of real poverty rate, P_t^R, that is proposed here bases the poverty rate calculations not on the revision of the poverty line but on the revision of the total expenditure per equivalent adult so as to compensate for the inflation and the change in relative prices, taking into account the household preferences and substitution between items by the households in response to changes in the relative prices. In other words, while the nominal poverty rates, P_t^N are the poverty rates calculated using the nominal expenditures per adult equivalent and the official poverty lines, the real poverty rates are based on the real expenditures per adult equivalent and the poverty line in the initial year.

4.6 Concluding Remarks

While the previous chapter presented the key concepts and methodologies for the measurement of price changes, both spatial variation and temporal changes, this chapter was focussed on the applications of the price indices in welfare analysis. The applications range from cross-sectional welfare comparisons between households to analysing the distributional implications of temporal movements in prices. This chapter and the earlier one lays out the concepts and frameworks used in the empirical studies, mostly focussed (but not exclusively) on India, that we report in the following chapter. As the discussion so far shows, the literature on prices has shifted from being exclusively a macrotopic featuring in the study of inflation, national income accounting and cross-country income comparisons to one that is firmly rooted in micro involving economic analysis of household behaviour, welfare and the distributional implications of changes in relative prices. This development was aided by increasing availability of data often in the form of unit records at household level that has allowed the implementation of the concepts and methodologies discussed above.

The discussion so far has also highlighted the role that theory and functional specification can play in conducting policy-driven welfare analysis. The focus on India in the rest of this volume largely reflects the interest and work of the author. It also reflects the fact that India has traditionally been the leader in providing data sets of the sort required in these studies. Some of the earliest and pioneering studies that have used prices in analysis of household welfare have been conducted on Indian data sets and mostly by researchers based at the Indian Statistical Institute. Also, being a large and heterogeneous country, India offers a spatial dimension that few countries do, an aspect that confers much interest in the empirical results on Indian prices and their welfare effects presented in the following chapter. The discussion so far has also highlighted the role that theory and functional specification can play in conducting policy-driven welfare analysis.

References

Asian Development Bank (2008) Research study on poverty-specific purchasing power parities for selected countries in Asia and the Pacific. Philippines, Manila

Aten B, Menezes T (2002) Poverty price levels: an application to Brazilian metropolitan areas. In: World Bank ICP Conference, Washington, D.C., March 11–15, 2002

Atkinson AB (1970) On the measurement of inequality. J Econ Theor 2:244–263

Banks J, Blundell R, Lewbel A (1997) Quadratic engel curves and consumer demand. Rev Econ Stat 79:527–539

Barten AP (1964) Family composition, prices and expenditure patterns. In: Hart PE, Mills G, Whitaker JK (eds) Econometric analysis for national economic planning. Butterworths, London, pp 277–292

Basu K (2011) Understanding inflation and controlling it. Econ Polit Wkly 46

Bhattacharya N, Chatterjee GS, Pal P (1988) Variations in level of living across regions and social groups in India, 1963–64 and 1973–74. In: Srinivasan TN, Bardhan PK (eds), Rural poverty in South Asia. Oxford University Press

Bhattacharyya SS, Joshi PD, Roychowdhury AB (1980) Regional price indices based on NSS 25th round consumer expenditure data. Sarvekshana, J NSS Organ 3(4):107–121

Clements KW, Izan HY (1981) A note on estimating divisia index number. Int Econ Rev 22:745–747

Coondoo D, Majumder A, Chattopadhyay S (2011) Estimating spatial consumer price indices through engel curve analysis. Rev Income Wealth 57(1):138–155

Coondoo D, Majumder A, Ray R (2004) A method of calculating regional consumer price differentials with illustrative evidence from India. Rev Income Wealth 50(1):51–68

Cox TL, Wohlgenant MK (1986) Prices and quality effects in cross-sectional demand analysis. Am J Agric Econ 68(4):908–919

Dubey A, Palmer-Jones R (2005) Prices, price indexes and poverty counts in India during 1980s and 1990s: calculation of unit value consumer price indexes, Artha Vijnana XLVII(3–4):223–258

Engel E (1895) Die Libenskosten Belgischer Arbieter-Familier Fruher und Jetzt. Bulletin de L'ltrstirur lntrrniitiiinil dr Stutistique 9:1–124

Gibson J, Rozelle S (2005) Prices and unit values in poverty measurement and tax reform analysis. World Bank Econ Rev 19(1):69–97

Hicks JR (1958) Measurement of real income. Oxford Econ Pap 10:125–162

Hoang LV (2009) Estimation of food demand from household survey data in Vietnam. DEPOCEN Working paper series, no. 2009/12, available in http://www.depocenwp.org

Hoderlein S, Mihaleva S (2008) Increasing the price variation in a repeated cross section. J Econ 147(2):316–325

Koo J, Phillips KR, Sigalla FD (2000) Measuring regional cost of living. J Bus Econ Stat 18 (1):127–136

Legendre P, Fortin MJ (2010) Comparison of the mantel test and alternative approaches for detecting complex multivariate relationships in the spatial analysis of genetic data. Mole Ecol Resour 10:831–844

Majumder A, Ray R, Sinha K (2012) Calculating Rural-Urban food price differentials from unit values in household expenditure surveys: a comparison with existing methods and a new procedure. Am J Agric Econ 94(5):1218–1235

Majumder A, Ray R, Sinha K (2015) Spatial comparisons of prices and expenditure in a heterogeneous country: methodology with application to India. Macroecon Dyn 19(5):931–989

Mantel N (1967) The detection of disease clustering and a generalized regression approach. Cancer Res 27:209–220

McKelvey C (2011) Price, unit value and quantity demanded. J Dev Econ 95(1):157–169

Mishra A, Ray R (2011) Prices, inequality and poverty: methodology and Indian evidence. Rev Income Wealth 57:427–448

Muellbauer J (1974a) Inequality measures, prices and household composition. Rev Econ Stud 41:493–504
Muellbauer J (1974b) Prices and inequality: the United Kingdom experience. Econ J 84:32–55
Muellbauer J (1977) Testing the barten model of household composition effects and the cost of children. Econ J 87:460–487
Muellbauer J (1980) The estimation of the Prais-Houthakker model of equivalence scales. Econometrica 48(1):153–176
Nicholas A, Ray R, Valenzuela R (2010) Evaluating the distributional implications of price movements: methodology, application and Australian evidence. Econ Rec 86:352–366
O'Donnell CJ, Rao DSP (2007) Predicting expenditure shares for computing PPP exchange rates, mimeographed. University of Queensland, Brisbane
Pendakur K (2002) Taking prices seriously in the measurement of inequality. J Public Econ 86:47–69
Pollak RA, Wales TJ (1992) Demand system specification and estimation. Oxford University Press
Prais SJ, Houthakker HS (1955) The analysis of family budgets. Cambridge University Press, Cambridge (2nd edition, 1971)
Rao DSP (2005) On the equivalence of weighted country-product-dummy CPD method and the Rao-System for multilateral comparisons. Rev Income Wealth 51:571–580
Ray R (1983) Measuring the costs of children: an alternative approach. J Public Econ 22:89–102
Ray R (1985) Prices, children and inequality: further evidence for the United Kingdom, 1965–82. Econ J 95:1069–1077
Rothbarth E (1943) Note on a method of determining equivalent income for families of different composition. Appendix IV in Charles Madge, War-Time pattern of saving and expenditure. Cambridge University Press, Cambridge
Samuelson PA (1950) Evaluation of real national income. Oxford Economic Papers 2:1–29
Selvanathan E (1991) Standard errors for Laspeyres and Paasche index numbers. Econ Lett 35:35–38
Sen A (1976) Real national income. Rev Econ Stud 43(1):19–39
Sen A (1997) On economic inequality. Clarendon Press, Oxford
Shorrocks A (1980) The class of additively decomposable inequality measures. Econometrica 48 (3):613–625
Summers R (1973) International price comparisons based upon incomplete data. Rev Income Wealth 19(1):1–16
Theil H (1967) Economics and information theory. North-Holland
World Bank (2013) Measuring the real size of the World economy: the framework, methodology, and results of the International Comparison Program—ICP. World Bank, Washington DC

Chapter 5
Selected Empirical Studies on Prices and Their Welfare Applications

5.1 Introduction

The previous chapters have provided the concepts, analytical framework and alternative methodologies for measuring price changes and examining their implications for household welfare. In this chapter, we describe a selection of empirical studies, mostly on India, that implement these concepts and methodologies in measuring price changes and in providing evidence on their distributive impact on household welfare. The selected studies highlight the following aspects of price changes: (a) the effect of inflation on inequality and poverty, (b) spatial differences in prices and their changes in a large heterogeneous country such as India and Canada, (c) the link between preference specification and price measurement and (d) empirical evidence on the sensitivity of welfare conclusions to the assumed demand functional form. Much of this literature not only followed the development of the concepts and methodologies for measuring and analysing price changes, but was made possible by the increasing availability of detailed information on household spending pattern and household characteristics. A significant feature of the latter development has been the availability of the data in the form of unit records that linked the information on spending on items at a disaggregated level with community and demographic characteristics for each individual household and allowed researchers to avoid the aggregation biases in welfare judgements that have affected the earlier studies.

The selected studies are all in the context of single countries though they have implications for bilateral, trilateral and multilateral country comparisons. For example, the evidence on spatial differences in price changes in India points to the need to move beyond the framework of national Purchasing Power Parities (PPP) used by the International Comparison Project (ICP) which assigns one value to the purchasing power of a country's currency, irrespective of its size and heterogeneity. We do not pursue the cross-country implications of such differences in this chapter but discuss them at length later in the volume. For example, as discussed later, the

R. Ray, *Household Behaviour, Prices, and Welfare*, Themes in Economics,
https://doi.org/10.1007/978-981-13-1930-3_5

evidence on the large differences in the purchasing power of a country's currency within the country has focussed attention on subnational PPPs in the next round of the ICP which is increasingly occupying centre stage in global income and poverty comparisons through providing the PPPs required in such comparisons. While the present chapter limits the discussion on the link between preferences, prices and welfare evaluation to the single country context, Chap. 7 follows up the discussion in the global context by providing evidence on the estimated PPPs and the magnitudes of global poverty to the methodologies for estimating the PPPs used..

5.2 Prices and Inequality: Methodological Issues and Evidence from UK, Canada and Australia

5.2.1 UK Evidence

One of the earliest studies that examined the effect of relative price changes on inequality is that of Muellbauer (1974b) on UK data. Using the parameter estimates from the linear expenditure system (LES) estimated on UK national accounts data, in conjunction with the expenditure distribution from UK Family Expenditure Surveys, Muellbauer (1974b, Table 3) calculates cost of living indices for different 1964 weekly expenditure levels for each year during 1964–72. The results show that the inflation faced by the households in the different expenditure percentiles over this period as a whole decline as we move across the expenditure distribution declining from 51.4% for households at the bottom to 44.7% for those at the top of the distribution. This translates to a divergence between changes in money (i.e. in nominal terms) and real expenditure inequality. While on both measures, UK expenditure inequality fell between 1964 and 1970, the fall in money inequality overstates the decline (in relation to real inequality) by 13–15%. This established the regressive nature of relative price changes. Much of it was due to the fact that durables which matter more to the affluent than the poorer households had below average price increases, and the reverse occurred for Food.

The use of the Atkinson (1970) inequality index defined over money and real expenditures also allowed Muellbauer (1974b, Table 5) to provide evidence on the ceteris paribus effect of increase in prices of individual items on inequality, and this shows that the items which have the largest effects though in reverse directions are the prices of Food and durables. While a 25% increase in the price of Food increases expenditure inequality by 48%, a similar increase in the price of durables reduces inequality by 40%. The result on the regressive nature of overall inflation in the UK over the period, 1964–72, is thus explained by the fact that over this period the prices of necessities such as Food and Fuel and Light increased by much more than that of Durable Household Goods. In making the link between inflation and inequality, Muellbauer (1974b) showed that (a) it is important to go beyond aggregate inflation and look at changes in relative prices of the individual items, and (b) the index of retail prices can vary between household types making it misleading to look simply at the general index of retail prices. While neither (a) nor (b) may matter during periods of low inflation, they can become quite significant in periods of large price increases.

Somewhat surprisingly, Muellbauer (1974b) does not acknowledge the earlier and pioneering work of Nikhilesh Bhattacharya and his associates at the Indian Statistical Institute a decade earlier in establishing the effect of price changes on inequality in India based on household survey data (the National Sample Surveys). An example of this early work is Iyengar and Bhattacharya (1965)[1] which considered the period, 1955–1960, and showed that (a) the average cost of living index (CLI) increased with household expenditures in the State of West Bengal during 1954 and 1955, but this trend began to weaken in the later years and actually reversed itself from 1957 onwards, (b) the CLI was more sensitive at the lower levels of household expenditure, and (c) the effect of price adjustment on the Lorenz ratio and the specific concentration coefficients was quite significant establishing the need to adjust for inflation in comparing inequalities over time. Iyengar and Bhattacharya (1965) not only provided the first evidence on the importance of adjusting inequality for price changes but as they indicate towards the end of their paper it set up the rationale 'to construct consumer price indices by levels of living, with rural–urban breakdown, for all the Indian States, and with some breakdown by items of expenditure. This project has been taken up in the Indian Statistical Institute on the basis of National Sample Survey data' (p. 56).

This early work by applied statisticians at the ISI used the Lorenz curves and concentration ratios in measuring inequality. To put Muellbauer's work in true historical perspective, his contribution was to methodologically extend that earlier work by Indian researchers by using the social welfare function-based Atkinson inequality measure. However, the basis and motivation of both types of enquiries stem from the differential spending pattern of households that translates into differentials in cost of living index across the expenditure distribution which in turn ensures that inflation is non-neutral in its effect on inequality. Muellbauer (1974b)'s principal conclusion that over the period, 1964–72, relative price changes had a large redistributive impact in the UK was challenged by Irvine and McCarthy (1980). They argued that Muellbauer's analysis based on LES parameter estimates had a major flaw in that the subsistence expenditures for 1964 using his parameter estimates exceeded the expenditures of the three lowest income groups. Clearly, concavity which is a prerequisite for welfare analysis is violated for these income groups. In other words, in Muellbauer's exercise, the LES does not obey the fundamental conditions of consumer theory for these three income groups.

Muellbauer (1974b)'s assertion that 'as long as $q_i, \geq 0$ for all i, the expenditure function satisfies all the fundamental conditions of consumer theory (concave in p, increasing in p and U), and hence the corresponding cost of living indices are also

[1]See the recently published revised edition of the widely used collection of essays in 'Poverty and Income Distribution in India' edited earlier by Srinivasan and Bardhan and now re-edited by Banerjee et al. (2017) for an account of the early contributions by Indian researchers on inequality and poverty.

valid' (p. 39, fn. 1) is incorrect. Irvine and McCarthy (1980) show, using the same methodology as Muellbauer's, that if one removed the three lowest income groups, allowed the LES parameters to change with time, and used the updated UK data from the more recent 'Blue Books', the large regressive effect of relative price changes in the UK over the period, 1964–72, disappears. Moreover, as they note, the use of LES in distributional comparisons is inappropriate since the LES-based TCLI monotonically changes with reference expenditure. The critique of Muellbauer's study by Irvine and McCarthy (1980) showed that while his methodology had considerable policy appeal by opening up the examination of the distributive effects of relative price changes and allowing the identification of items which had a particularly large effect on real expenditure inequality, it also true that 'there are substantial difficulties in developing techniques which are empirically robust without being theoretically simplistic' (Irvine and McCarthy 1980, p. 911).

Moreover, as argued in Ray (1985), Muellbauer's methodology raises the issue of sensitivity of the results to the demand functional form used in estimating the parameters that are required in analysing the distributive effect of relative price changes. Irvine and McCarthy (1980) touched on this issue by using a dynamic LES rather than the static LES used by Muellbauer, but he did not use a different demand functional form. The sensitivity of distributive judgements to preference specification can be a significant practical issue since there is no a priori reason to choose one demand functional form over another, especially if they are non-nested to one another. Ray (1985) argues that the use of the LES or any demand system which has linear Engel curves is inappropriate in distributional comparisons and then proceeds to examine on UK data the sensitivity of the normative conclusions on inequality magnitudes and their trend to the demand functional form one chooses to employ. Ray uses the price scaling technique, proposed in Ray (1983) and described earlier in this volume, to obtain demographically extended versions of the 'Nonlinear preferences system' (NLPS) proposed in Blundell and Ray (1984) and the 'Almost Ideal Demand System' (AIDS) proposed in Deaton and Muellbauer (1980). Both these demand models allow nonlinear Engel curves and non-separable preferences.

Apart from examining the sensitivity of the empirical evidence to the chosen demand forms, Ray (1985) also calculates the inequality estimates separately for childless couples and couple with one child to see if these two household types experienced differences in the magnitudes and trends in inequality in the UK over the longer time period, 1965–1982, than the one considered by Muellbauer. The principal conclusions of Ray (1985) are as follows:

(a) The inequality of childless couples differs quite significantly from that of those with one child, not only in absolute magnitude but, more importantly, in the direction of change as well. Let us give two examples: (i) between 1965 and 1970, i.e. the period considered by Muellbauer, childless couples experienced a sharp rise in inequality, while those with a child saw a decline; (ii) the reverse occurs between 1978 and 1980.

(b) Expenditure inequality among childless couples generally seems to be greater than for couples with one child. This possibly reflects the fact that couples with children are likely to be closer to each other in their circumstances and stages in their life cycle and, hence, in their earnings and spending compared to households without children. The latter, for example, could well include newly married couples on the one hand, and pensioners with no dependent children on the other.
(c) In view of such sharp demographic differences in inequality magnitudes and trends, it is inappropriate to pool all household types into a single expenditure distribution.
(d) The NLPS and AIDS inequality estimates agree generally on the directions of change in inequality, though in many cases they disagree quite substantially on the magnitude of change.

The sensitivity of movements in 'real' expenditure inequality to the adopted demand functional form reflects the dependence of the true cost of living index (TCLI) on the assumed form of the indirect utility or expenditure function. Note that the TCLI is needed to convert the distribution of money expenditures into that of real expenditure. In Ray (1985), the asymmetric manner in which nonlinear Engel curves enter either system, namely data determined in one (NLPS) and maintained in the other (AIDS), seems to have a significant impact on the calculated price responses and, hence, on the TCLI which depends on them. The Atkinson index was originally designed for a single cross section of individual money incomes with no price variation. His assumed welfare function was additive and homothetic. To extend his idea to intertemporal comparison with price variation, Muellbauer (1974a, b) redefines the welfare function such that prices explicitly enter the consumer's utility function, namely, her indirect utility function. The issue of which cardinalisation to choose thus follows inevitably from the linking of demand theory specification and estimation with the evaluation of the inequality effects of price movements.

5.2.2 Canadian Evidence

Pendakur (2002) using an alternative approach provides Canadian evidence that reiterates the importance of prices in the measurement of inequality. Pendakur (2002) focusses on the equivalence scale that is used as the expenditure deflator to adjust for differences across households in their demographic composition and on the price indices used as price deflator to adjust for different price regimes by converting nominal into real expenditures. Pendakur allows flexible deflators by allowing expenditure-dependent price deflators and price-dependent equivalence scales. The price-dependent equivalence scale used in this study is on the lines of the Price Scaled (PS) equivalence scales proposed and used on UK data by Ray (1983) as described earlier. Pendakur does not, however, allow expenditure dependence of the price-dependent equivalence scale unlike in the GCS procedure proposed and applied to the UK data in Ray (1986). The UK evidence, however, provided only weak support for expenditure dependence of the scale. Moreover, the assumption of expenditure independence of the scale is consistent with the requirement of IB/ESE needed for the welfare interpretation of the equivalence scale as the 'cost of a child'.

Pendakur (2002) reports Canadian evidence 'that using more flexible expenditure-dependent price deflators and price-dependent equivalence scales affects the level of, and trend in, measured family expenditure inequality in Canada over 1969–1997. For example, standard methods show a significant decrease in inequality between 1969 and 1978, but more flexible methods show a significant increase in inequality over this period' (p. 48). While Ray (1985)'s study provided evidence on the sensitivity of UK inequality estimates to the differences in the demand specification keeping the equivalence scale functional specification unchanged, Pendakur (2002) reported the sensitivity of the Canadian inequality estimates to a more flexible representation of the equivalence scale, conditional on the 'Quadratic Almost Ideal Demand' (QAI) model proposed in Banks et al. (1997). In different ways and on different data sets, both Ray (1985) and Pendakur (2002) confirm the above-mentioned quote from Irvine and McCarthy (1980) on the 'substantial difficulties in developing techniques which are empirically robust without being theoretically simplistic'.

Pendakur (2002)'s empirical results also point to the spatially differentiated nature of price changes in the context of a large heterogeneous country such as Canada and the importance of incorporating regional variation in prices in inequality calculations. In his words, 'measured inequality responds to whether or not variation in prices across regions is accounted for… we can see that taking regional price differences into account changes the estimated level of inequality, and pushes down the Gini coefficient in each year by as much as 0.5 percentage points. This is because regions with higher average expenditure also have higher prices, so that some inter-regional expenditure inequality is undone by inter-regional price variation. The difference between measures seems to be larger in the 1990s than in the 1980s. This is due to the greater variation in price deflators across regions in the 1990s versus the 1980s…. Taking regional price differences into account also changes the trend in measured inequality' (pp. 63–64). The estimates of price deflators presented by Pendakur (2002) show significant variation in their magnitude between the Canadian provinces and that this variation increased during the chosen period, 1969–1997. The issue of spatial variation in prices, inequality and poverty is taken up in greater detail as we report the evidence for India from a selection of studies by the author in the following section.

5.2.3 Australian Evidence

Nicholas et al. (2010) examine the distributive implications of inflation in Australia during the period, 1988/89–2003/2004. It uses the demographically extended 'Quadratic Almost Ideal Demand' (QAI) model, described earlier, estimated on a pooled cross section of the unit record files from the Household Expenditure Survey (HES) conducted by the ABS for the years 1988/9, 1993/4, 1998/9 and 2003/4. The household was chosen as the unit of analysis. The period chosen was of considerable economic significance in Australia since it started with the economic reforms under Prime Minister Bob Hawke in the late 1980s, then saw the recession of the early 1990s under Prime Minister Paul Keating, and extended to the early years of the new millennium. Nicholas et al. (2010, Table 4) present the nominal and real expenditure shares of each of 5 quintile groups, arranged in an ascending order by the corresponding per adult equivalent expenditure distribution. The shares are calculated from the nominal and real expenditures for each household in the sample of 20,463 households over the four HES data sets. The following features emerge from this table.

(a) The bottom 20% of households have expenditure shares of less than 10%, while the top 20% of households have expenditure shares of at least 38%. Between 1988 and 2003 (15 year period), there was an overall decline in the expenditure shares of the bottom two quintiles and an increase in the corresponding share of the top quintile. The trend for the lowest quintile appears to be an inverted U, as their shares first increased before declining towards the end of the study period.
(b) The decline in the expenditure share of the bottom quintile group has been particularly sharp between 1998 and 2003. The beneficiary of this regressive transfer of spending has mainly been the top quintile group.
(c) The nominal expenditure shares generally exceed the corresponding real expenditure shares for the bottom two quintile groups, while the reverse is the case for the top quintile group. Moreover, the real expenditure shares appear to be more variable over the 15 year period than those in nominal terms. In particular, the expenditure shares dropped more sharply in real terms for the two lowest quintiles, particularly between 1998 and 2003; at the same time, real expenditure shares for the top quintile registered the larger increase compared to the nominal shares. These suggest that, especially in the late 1990s and early 2000s, the relative price changes have caused regressive transfers of real spending power from the poor to the rich households.

Nicholas, Ray and Valenzuela (2010, Table 6) present the Australian nominal and real expenditure inequalities in the full sample, based on the PS-QAIDS parameter estimates and using the methodology for calculating nominal and real inequalities outlined earlier in Chap. 4. The inequality estimates were calculated using the Gini and Atkinson inequality measures, with the latter evaluated at two levels of 'inequality aversion', ϵ. Table 6 confirms that, after an initial decline in the late 1980s, there has been an increase in expenditure inequality that accelerated sharply during the period 1998–2003. Note that, while the 1990s started out in recession, most of the years in this decade was characterised by relative growth and prosperity. This can in part explain the decline in nominal inequality during this period. However, the inequality measures based on real expenditures tell a different story—they indicate a gradual worsening of inequality during this period. Moreover, the larger magnitude of real expenditure inequality over nominal expenditure inequality is a direct confirmation of the inequality increasing nature of the price movement during the 1990s and beyond. These findings are robust to the choice of the measure used in the inequality calculations.

These features of Australian inflation during the 1990s and the early years of the new millennium are seen more clearly in Figs. 5.1, 5.2 and 5.3 in Nicholas et al. (2010) which present the Lorenz curves of per equivalent adult expenditures, in nominal and real terms, in the three years beyond the base year. The Lorenz curve of real expenditure lies outside that of nominal expenditure, and the gap between the two curves has been increasing over time. The inequality increasing bias of price inflation in Australia during 2003/4 is seen most clearly in Fig. 5.1 for 2003/4 where a wide gap opens up between the two non-intersecting Lorenz curves. The overall conclusion of this study was, therefore, that inflation in Australia during the

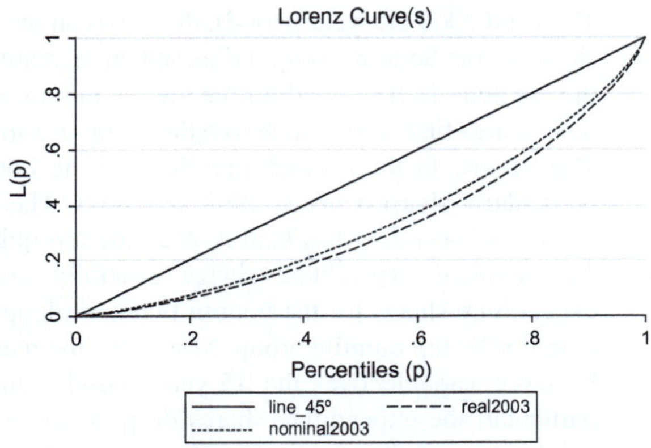

Fig. 5.1 Lorenz curves of nominal and real expenditures in 2003/4. Reproduced from Nicholas et al. (2010)

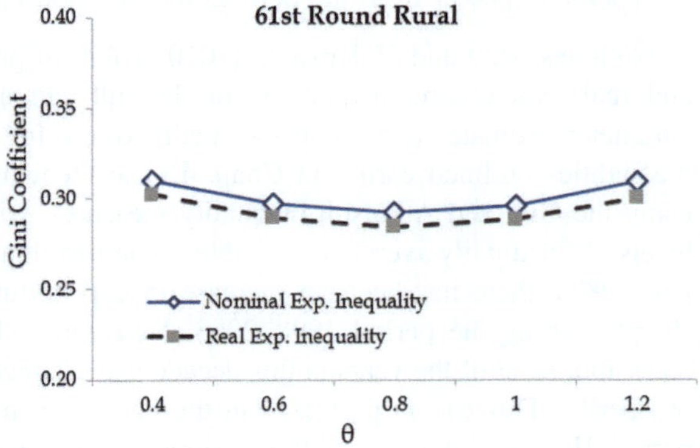

Fig. 5.2 Gini coefficient for 61st round at varying values of θ in rural. Reproduced from Mishra and Ray (2011)

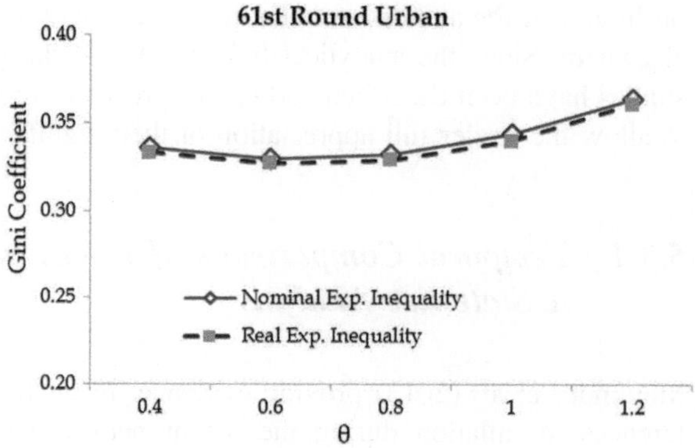

Fig. 5.3 Gini coefficient for 61st round at varying values of θ in urban sample. Reproduced from Mishra and Ray (2011)

1990s had an inequality increasing bias and that this bias increased in the late 1990s and the first part of the new millennium.

5.3 Indian Evidence on Spatial and Temporal Variation in Prices, and the Impact of Price Movements on Inequality and Poverty

India has a long history of studies on prices and on the distributive effect of inflation on inequality and poverty. We have already mentioned the early work on prices at the Indian Statistical Institute which was closely aligned to the Planning Commission and the National Sample Survey Organisation (NSSO). For some time, they even shared the same premises and researchers moved freely between these three organisations. This ensured that the work on expenditure patterns and prices had a policy focus centred on welfare. Thanks to the NSSO, India has a long history of collecting and disseminating data, on household expenditure and a variety of household characteristics, at regular intervals, referred to as NSS rounds. The Central Statistical Organisation (CSO) and the Ministry of Labour and Employment, Labour Bureau have been publishing information on price series disaggregated by items, by rural and urban areas, and covering different groups of population.

In recent years, the availability of unit record data on expenditures and quantities of Food consumption has provided an additional source of price information on Food items, namely, unit values that are increasingly used in studies on inflation. India is a large and heterogeneous country where the heterogeneity takes on various forms—for example, the rural–urban divide, differences in the Food habits between the different States, caste differences and that between the spending pattern of the affluent, middle and the poorer households. India therefore provides a particularly interesting case for the study of prices and analysing their role in affecting household welfare. In this section, we report in detail several of the recent studies on India that the author has been involved in with researchers based at the ISI and elsewhere. Since the analytical framework and the methodology adopted in these studies have been described earlier, we proceed to report the results in some detail to allow the reader full appreciation of their significance for policy formulation.

5.3.1 Temporal Comparisons of Prices in India: A Statewise Analysis

Majumder et al. (2013) provide evidence, using the TCLI, on the Statewise differences in inflation during the recent period, 1999/2000–2009/10. This paper compares alternative preference consistent methods for calculating price indices. It does so in the context of India paying special attention to the heterogeneity in preferences and price movements among the constituent States. The use of demand systems based methods allows the incorporation of price-induced substitution effects between items. This study allows such substitution effects to vary across States. The paper examines the rankings of the Indian States in terms of real expenditure and its growth under alternative temporal price scenario during the period from 1999–2000 to 2009–2010. The paper compares the growth rates both between the nominal and temporal price deflated figures and also between the price deflated growth rates under alternative forms of temporal and preference consistent price indices. The results have methodological and empirical implications that extend much beyond India.

This study uses the detailed information on household expenditures on Food and non-Food items, household size, composition and other household characteristics contained in the unit records from the 55th (July, 1999–June, 2000), 61st (July, 2004–June, 2005) and 66th (July, 2009–June, 2010) rounds of India's National Sample Surveys (NSS). All these rounds are 'thick' rounds, and based on large samples. The temporal price calculations were done at two levels of commodity aggregation:

(a) All items, employing the procedure due to Coondoo et al. (2011) described earlier in the volume that does not require price information, but requires only the household expenditures on the various items.
(b) The six principal Food items on which the NSS contained information on both expenditures and quantities allowing the calculation of unit values. This allowed the demand estimation on the major Food items treating the quality-adjusted unit values as prices. These Food items are: cereals and cereal substitutes; pulses and products; milk and milk products, edible oil, meat, fish and eggs; vegetables. The QAI-based TCLI was used to calculate the spatial price indices in each State.

The estimates of the temporal price indices obtained from using the two alternative procedures have been presented in Tables 5.1 and 5.2. An estimate of temporal price for a State that is significantly greater than one implies that the State

Table 5.1 Testing for temporal variation in price index for each of 15 major States with respect to itself in the previous NSS round, $SP_{(State,\ base)}(State,\ t)$, rural and urban, method from Coondoo et al. (2011), all items (Majumder et al. 2013)

States	Rural		Urban	
	$SP_{55}(61)$	$SP_{61}(66)$	$SP_{55}(61)$	$SP_{61}(66)$
(1)	(2)	(3)	(4)	(5)
Andhra Pradesh	1.310 (1.55)	1.559 (0.88)	1.359 (2.79)*	1.679 (0.59)
Assam	1.377 (1.22)	1.355 (0.69)	1.407 (2.20)*	1.253 (0.92)
Bihar	1.180 (1.34)	1.381 (2.25)*	1.221 (0.84)	1.405 (1.85)
Gujarat	1.155 (1.25)	1.565 (1.88)	1.344 (1.58)	1.344 (0.46)
Haryana	1.200 (0.92)	1.454 (2.24)*	1.244 (0.98)	1.454 (1.74)
Karnataka	1.084 (0.72)	1.493 (2.62)*	1.187 (1.01)	1.689 (0.76)
Kerala	1.334 (3.11)*	1.424 (1.82)	1.384 (1.02)	1.471 (1.16)
Madhya Pradesh	1.152 (1.03)	1.564 (1.39)	1.224 (1.12)	1.550 (2.06)*
Maharashtra	1.193 (1.23)	1.663 (3.42)*	1.257 (1.11)	1.527 (1.29)
Orissa	1.148 (1.19)	1.626 (1.99)*	1.227 (1.83)	1.530 (1.37)
Punjab	1.195 (3.84)*	1.485 (1.79)	1.382 (3.47)*	1.314 (0.41)
Rajasthan	1.098 (0.94)	1.580 (1.99)*	1.148 (0.69)	1.489 (1.49)
Tamil Nadu	1.204 (1.19)	1.533 (2.35)*	1.290 (2.56)*	1.355 (1.58)
Uttar Pradesh	1.174 (2.02)*	1.462 (2.23)*	1.267 (2.00)*	1.401 (0.53)
West Bengal	1.266 (3.47)*	1.427 (2.03)*	1.298 (2.52)*	1.247 (0.13)

Figures in parentheses are the *t*-statistic given by $\frac{SP_{(State,t-1)}(State,t)-1}{se(SP_{(State,t-1)}(State,t))}$, for testing PPP = 1

*Significant at 5% level

is more expensive in the current period in relation to itself in the base period, and vice versa, if the estimate is less than one. While a comparison between the tables provides evidence of the sensitivity of the estimated temporal prices to the method used and to the commodity aggregation adopted, each table allows a further comparison between the rural and urban spatial price estimates and how they have

Table 5.2 Testing for temporal variation in price index for each of 15 major States with respect to itself in the previous NSS round, $SP_{(State,\ base)}(State,\ t)$, rural and urban, method: QAIDS index, 6 items (Majumder et al. 2013)

States	Rural		Urban	
	$SP_{55}(61)$	$SP_{61}(66)$	$SP_{55}(61)$	$SP_{61}(66)$
(1)	(2)	(3)	(4)	(5)
Andhra Pradesh	1.220 (11.000)*	1.477 (25.037)*	0.980 (−1.053)	1.965 (41.196)*
Assam	1.193 (2.881)*	1.317 (8.251)*	1.317 (3.139)*	1.565 (8.803)*
Bihar	0.849 (−6.864)*	1.938 (26.573)*	1.033 (1.000)*	1.544 (12.982)*
Gujarat	1.057 (3.000)*	1.497 (15.762)*	1.042 (1.556)	1.557 (19.479)*
Haryana	1.479 (7.983)*	1.236 (10.011)*	1.107 (2.892)*	1.853 (26.896)*
Karnataka	1.151 (4.719)*	1.261 (8.254)*	0.818 (−11.375)*	1.921 (30.930)*
Kerala	1.167 (4.639)*	1.517 (23.849)*	1.216 (2.160)*	1.426 (15.672)*
Madhya Pradesh	1.042 (3.000)*	1.890 (28.535)*	1.019 (0.826)	1.831 (28.487)*
Maharashtra	1.060 (3.529)*	1.513 (18.327)*	1.006 (0.429)	1.586 (24.767)*
Orissa	0.982 (−0.667)	1.912 (29.899)*	1.003 (0.062)	1.689 (15.418)*
Punjab	0.900 (−4.762)*	1.840 (35.721)*	1.136 (3.579)*	1.334 (22.210)*
Rajasthan	0.550 (−23.684)	2.233 (34.725)*	0.835 (−2.619)*	1.884 (27.238)*
Tamil Nadu	1.024 (1.043)	1.288 (11.577)*	1.077 (4.053)	1.341 (15.945)*
Uttar Pradesh	1.150 (7.143)*	1.347 (17.861)*	1.059 (2.950)*	1.640 (37.505)*
West Bengal	1.342 (7.435)*	1.877 (17.786)*	1.262 (3.275)*	1.566 (8.210)*

Figures in parentheses are the t-statistic given by $\frac{SP_{(State,t-1)}(State,t)-1}{se(SP_{(State,t-1)}(State,t))}$, for testing PPP = 1

*Significant at 5% level

changed over the period between NSS rounds 55th (1993/94) and 66th (2009/10). The tables also report below each temporal price estimate the value of the t-statistic against the null hypothesis of no temporal price difference, i.e. price situation remained the same in the State over the two periods.

The following observations are in order:

(a) There is evidence of differential temporal movement of prices across States and sensitivity to the method of computation of the indices.
(b) In terms of magnitude, the price rise is generally higher during the period from 61st to 66th round than that from 55th to 61st round for both the rural and the urban sectors and both the indices.
(c) The QAIDS-based Food price indices are smaller in magnitude than the corresponding All-item indices (Coondoo et al. 2011) for all States except for Haryana, Karnataka and West Bengal in the rural sector and for all States in the urban sector for the period 55th–61st round. During 61st–66th round, while the urban picture is completely reversed (exceptions are Kerala, Punjab and Tamil Nadu), in the rural sector seven States have higher values for the QAIDS-based Food price indices.
(d) During the period 55th–61st round, for the rural sector, while the all-item index (Coondoo et al. 2011) shows an increase for all States, and a significant increase for Kerala, Punjab, Uttar Pradesh and West Bengal at 5% level, the QAIDS-based index records a significant decline in Food prices for Bihar, Orissa, Punjab and Rajasthan and a significant increase for all other States. In the urban sector, the QAIDS-based Food index records a significant decline for Andhra Pradesh, Karnataka and Rajasthan and a significant increase for all other States. The all-item-based index, on the other hand, shows an increase for all States and significant increase for Andhra Pradesh, Assam, Punjab, Tamil Nadu, Uttar Pradesh and West Bengal. For the latter period, both indices agree in showing an increase in price level for all States and sectors.

Two points are worth noting in the discussion of the temporal price estimates presented in Tables 5.1 and 5.2. First, the differences in the price indices between the comparable figures in Tables 5.1 and 5.2 can be explained as follows. While the former, which uses the Engel-based procedure proposed by Coondoo et al. (2011), is essentially single equation without any price effects and ignores the price-induced substitution between items, the latter is in the 'complete demand systems' tradition and does incorporate substitution effects via the joint estimation of the expenditure and price coefficients using the price information. Thus, while the former procedure is of considerable practical use, it comes with some costs as well. However, Table 5.1 relates to overall inflation since it covers all the principal items of spending, unlike the estimates of Food inflation presented in Table 5.2. Second, the picture on inflation that is presented in Table 5.2 is only a partial picture because (a) it relates only to Food items, and (b) the Food items are considered at an aggregate level. This was necessitated by the fact that the unit values that we calculated are available in the NSS reports for the Food items at an aggregate level, but this is clearly a matter for further research.

5.3.2 *Rural–Urban Food Price Differentials in India from Unit Values in Household Expenditure Surveys*

In the previous chapter, Sect. 4.4, we described the methodology proposed in Majumder et al. (2012) for estimating rural–urban price differentials in India. We now report the results from this study in some detail.

This study uses the detailed information on household expenditure on six Food items, household size, composition and other household characteristics contained in the unit records from the 55th (July 1999–June 2000) and 61st (July 2004–June 2005) rounds of India's National Sample Surveys. Both these rounds are 'thick' rounds, being based on large samples. The following 6 Food items have been considered: Cereals, gram and cereal substitutes; pulses; milk and milk products; edible oil; meat, egg and fish and vegetables. This is the most important set of Food items consumed in India. In the 55th round, these items constitute 77% of total Food expenditure for the rural sector and 73% for the urban sector. The corresponding figures are 76 and 74%, respectively, for the 61st round. The exercise was performed over 15 major States of the Indian union.

Table 5.3 presents the estimates of urban all-India PPPs (with respect to rural India) for NSS rounds 55 and 61, computed using the different methods, viz. the method proposed in Majumder et al. (2012), the Selvanathan (1991) method and the CPD method (Rao 2005). The table also presents values of the spatial price indices obtained using the recently proposed method by Coondoo et al. (2011). All the methods yield PPPs significantly different from 1 in both rounds, indicating substantial rural–urban differential in purchasing power. The PPPs using the proposed method compare fairly well with the other conventional estimates. All the procedures agree that the PPP rates are significantly different from unity. In other words, the rural Rupee has a higher purchasing power than the urban Rupee in both the NSS rounds. The single equation Engel curve-based PPP estimates turn out to be slightly higher than those using the QUAIDS system. There is general agreement that the rural–urban price differences narrowed between the 55th and 61st rounds,

Table 5.3 Estimates of all-India urban PPPs, NSS 55th and 61st rounds (Majumder et al. 2012)

Utility-based PPPs[a] $K = \frac{C^{\text{Urban}}}{C^{\text{Rural}}}$	Model (3): PPP augmented QUAIDS[b]	1.176 (5.50)[c]	1.156 (2.03)
	Coondoo et al. (2011): single equation Engel curve approach	1.293 (2.55)	1.307 (1.98)
Laspeyre's index (Selvanathan 1991)		1.168 (12.92)	1.153 (17.00)
CPD index (Rao 2005)		1.161 (5.55)	1.153 (5.67)

[a]Reference utility has been evaluated at the median per capita Food expenditure
[b]PPPs have been calculated at all-India prices and urban price $\left(p_i^U\right)$ has been taken as $p_i^U = k_i p_i^R$
[c]Figures in parentheses are the asymptotic t-statistics for testing PPP = 1. All are significant at 5% level

with the PPP moving marginally towards unity—the outlier is the single equation Engel curve-based PPP estimate.

The absence of any price information in the Engel curve-based PPP procedure of Coondoo et al. (2011) explains the much higher standard errors of the PPP estimates obtained using their procedure, along with their PPP magnitudes that are out of line with the other procedures. Table 5.3 underlines the usefulness of the use of the quality and demographically corrected unit values as prices in the other procedures—the adjusted unit values reduce the rural–urban price differential in Food prices, though maintaining the statistical significance of that difference. Unlike the other procedures which figure in Table 5.3, the Barten (1964)-based procedure proposed in Majumder et al. (2012) can go beyond the overall PPP reported there by disaggregating it among the constituent items. Table 5.4 highlights this advantage by presenting the estimates of k_i's along with the corresponding t-statistics (reported in parentheses) for NSS rounds 55 and 61. Clearly, all the k_i's are highly significant. However, in our context it is more relevant and interesting to test if these are significantly close to 1, that is, whether the item-specific rural–urban PPPs are equal or not.

Table 5.4 also presents the t-statistics for testing the latter hypothesis. It turns out that purchasing power is lower in the urban sector (with respect to rural sector) for cereals, milk and milk products and meat, egg and fish in both the rounds, but significantly so only for the 55th round. The purchasing power for vegetables is higher in the urban sector in both rounds, but significantly so for the 61st round. The PPPs for pulses and edible oils are not significantly different from 1 in either of

Table 5.4 Estimates of item-specific all-India PPP parameters, NSS 55th and 61st rounds (Majumder et al. 2012)

Commodities	NSS 55th round			NSS 61st round		
	k_i	Testing: $k_i = 1$ t-statistic $= \frac{k_i - 1}{se(k_i)}$	PPP_i	k_i	Testing: $k_i = 1$ t-statistic $= \frac{k_i - 1}{se(k_i)}$	PPP_i
Ceareals, gram and cereal substitutes	0.732 (8.05)[a]	−2.941***	1.366	0.701 (3.89)	−1.658*	1.427
Pulses	1.180 (7.75)	1.180	0.847	0.958 (4.18)	−0.181	1.044
Milk and milk products	0.778 (7.76)	−2.218**	1.285	0.941 (4.14)	−0.258	1.063
Edible oils	1.233 (8.04)	1.518	0.811	0.727 (3.66)	−1.376	1.376
Meat, egg and fish	0.724 (10.45)	−3.995***	1.381	0.857 (4.32)	−0.724	1.167
Vegetables	1.199 (4.63)	0.768	0.834	1.985 (10.34)	5.129***	0.504

[a]Figures in parentheses are the asymptotic t values. *Significant at 10% level, **significant at 5% level, ***significant at 1% level

the rounds between the two sectors. Thus, the major contributors to the reduction in the rural–urban price differential in Food prices between the two NSS rounds are cereals, milk and milk products and meat, egg and fish and they outweigh the widening price differential of vegetables. Table 5.5 provides further evidence of the difference between the item wise PPPs in India's rural and urban areas in the two rounds of the NSS. It reports the *t*-statistics of the pairwise differences between the item-specific PPPs. The numbers below the diagonal refer to the differences in NSS round 55, and those above the diagonal refer to those in NSS round 61.

Table 5.5 underlines the need to go beyond a single PPP over all items and look at the disaggregated picture between items. A closer look at Table 5.4 in conjunction with Tables 5.3 and 5.4 reveals many interesting features. Some of the major features are given below. For example, in the 55th round, cereals, milk and milk products and meat, egg and fish have PPP values above the overall PPP value of 1.176, but among these three items only the difference between PPP values of cereals and milk and milk products is significant (at 5% level), while the other pairwise comparisons give non-significant *t* values. On the other hand, in the 61st round, Cereals, Edible oils and meat, egg and fish have PPP values above the overall PPP value of 1.156, but none of the PPP pairs is significantly different from one another (at 5% level). While the PPP for pulses is highly significantly different from those of all other items in both rounds, such is the case for vegetables only in the 61st round. Thus, the statistical significances in several cases of the pairwise differences between the PPPs of various items, and in both rounds, are consistent with the formal rejection of the joint hypothesis of equality of the item wise PPPs in the likelihood ratio tests reported above.

Table 5.5 *t*-statistics for pairwise comparison of k_i's, NSS 61st round and 55th round (Majumder et al. 2012)

61st round → 55th round ↓	k_1 (cereals, gram and cereal subs.)	k_2 (pulses)	k_3 (milk and milk products)	k_4 (edible oils)	k_5 (meat, egg and fish)	k_6 (vegetables)
k_1 (cereals, gram and cereal subs.)		−1.74*	−2.01**	−0.36	−1.91*	−7.71***
k_2 (pulses)	−2.35**		9.30***	5.66***	9.77***	5.84***
k_3 (milk and milk products)	−2.06**	5.78***		−0.93	−21.58***	5.69***
k_4 (edible oils)	−2.53**	23.78***	2.39**		−1.30	−6.97***
k_5 (meat, egg and fish)	0.19	7.38***	0.59	3.04***		−8.58***
k_6 (vegetables)	−1.48	7.25***	3.76***	0.23	−1.67*	

*Significant at 10% level, **significant at 5% level, ***significant at 1% level

Note The cell (k_i, k_j) gives the *t* value for comparison between k_i and k_j, given by $\frac{k_i - k_j}{\text{std.err.}(k_i - k_j)}$

The results of Majumder et al. (2012) indicate considerable potential for the application of the procedure to other countries. As more and more countries now make available unit record information on household consumption, in quantity and expenditure terms, the methodology adopted is capable of much wider use. A fruitful extension of this study is to combine the calculation of both intra-country and intercountry PPP rates in a comprehensive exercise, with the latter based on the former. One limitation of this study is the use of unit values from the expenditure records in the household budget surveys as prices. Adjusted or not, unit values of the various items are unsatisfactory proxies for prices. While the corrections minimise the distortions in the unit values, they do not eliminate them completely. However, reliance on them is unavoidable as there is hardly any information on regional market prices. One of the messages of this study is the need to embark on a project to make available regional prices using methods such as 'price opinion' suggested by Gibson and Rozelle (2005). Clearly, a project comparable to the ICP project is needed for the availability of price information in various regions in a country using definitions that are consistent between the participating countries. Such a project is needed for the calculation of intra-country PPP rates that are as important as inter-country PPP rates. Without the former, the latter is of very limited use.

5.3.3 *Indian Evidence on the Impact of Prices on Inequality and Poverty*[2]

Mishra and Ray (2011) propose a methodology for evaluating the distributional implications of price movement for inequality and poverty measurement. The methodology is based on a distinction between inequalities in nominal expenditures, where the expenditures are either measured in nominal terms or a common price deflator is applied for all households, and inequalities in real expenditures which take into account the varying household preferences in converting the nominal to real expenditures. The empirical application to the Indian budget data sets from NSS rounds 50, 55 and 61 shows the usefulness of the proposed procedures. The relative price changes in India have tended to be inequality and poverty reducing as confirmed by formal statistical tests. The result is robust to expenditure-dependent equivalence scales. The progressivity of the relative price changes weakened in the second half of our time period as Fuel and Light overtook the composite group called 'Miscellaneous' in recording the largest price increase. This study is now reported in greater detail below.

Since expenditure pattern varies across households, primarily due to differences in their economic circumstances and in their household size and composition, differential movement in prices of items over time will have a differential impact on welfare across households. For example, inflation that is accompanied by an

[2]The material in this subsection is based on Mishra and Ray (2011).

increase in the relative price of Food vis-a-vis non-Food items will affect the poorer household groups more adversely than the affluent ones. Similarly, if the prices of items that are consumed primarily by children increase more than those consumed primarily by adults, then households with large numbers of children will be hit harder than, say, childless households. Again, if the price increases are concentrated on items that exhibit substantial economies of scale, then inflation will hit the smaller households harder than the larger households simply because the former are unable to benefit from bulk purchase to the same extent as the latter. All that this means is that the aggregate figure of inflation published routinely by authorities may hide substantial differences in the effective inflation rates across households. The two areas where this has immediate implications are the measurement of inequality and poverty over time.

Relative price changes also have implications for the equivalence scales which are required in welfare comparisons between households, though the link is not so clear-cut and direct in this case. The equivalence scales are aggregate expenditure deflators that measure the compensation, in the form of expenditure scaling, to households with children to enable them to enjoy the same level of welfare as childless households. The concept of equivalence scale, which measures compensation in relation to demographic change, is therefore similar to the concept of a true cost of living index which measures compensation in response to price changes. Since the latter depends on the reference utility level and the structure of relative prices, so will the former, unless assumed away as is done, rather unrealistically, with the use of price and expenditure invariant equivalence scales. This link between the two concepts was established by Barten (1964)'s pioneering contribution which showed that the household composition effects that the scales measure are analogous to the price-induced substitution effects estimated in conventional demand analysis. Since such 'quasi-price' demographic effects do vary with household affluence and with relative prices, the equivalence scales will be expenditure and price dependent.

If equivalence scales vary with relative prices, then the expenditure deflators that adjust for differences in household size and composition will change over time with inflation and realignment of relative prices with consequent implications for the inequality and poverty calculations. This possibility is ruled out with the use of price invariant equivalence scales or the use of household size as the expenditure deflator. The issue of price sensitivity of equivalence scales is hence not unrelated to the issue of the redistributive effect of relative price changes that motivated this study. Mishra and Ray (2011) employ a parametric test of the price sensitivity of the equivalence scale based on the hypothesis that a subset of the demographic parameters estimated from the demographic demand system is individually and jointly insignificant. The approach taken here is different from that adopted in Pendakur (2002). While Pendakur (2002) specifies the demographic demand system so as to allow the equivalence scales to vary with prices, the present study follows Ray (1983) in taking the reverse route of first specifying the equivalence scales directly as function of prices, and then working out the corresponding demographic demand system which then contains the price invariant equivalence scales as a nested specification.

With regard to the direct effect of relative price changes on inequality, the point was recognised by Muellbauer (1974b) over three decades back when he distinguished between real and nominal expenditure inequality and showed the divergence between the two during the 6 years, 1964–1970, of Labour rule in the UK. Muellbauer's contribution, that included a methodology for investigating the distributional consequences of price movements, was extended to allow more realistic and flexible demand responses to price changes and applied to UK data in Ray (1985) and, more recently, to Australian data in Nicholas et al. (2010). There have not been many similar attempts on other data sets to investigate the distributional effects of relative price changes, and none on the data set of a developing country. Pendakur (2002) provided indirect evidence of the importance of price movements in inequality calculations by showing that price-dependent equivalence scales affect measured family expenditure inequality in Canada, but he did not investigate directly the redistributive effect of relative price changes. Such an attempt for India is made in the present study.

The issue of the differential impact of price changes across households is also relevant in poverty comparisons. The criticism of the World Bank methodology for calculating poverty rates made by, among others, Reddy and Pogge (2010) is based on the idea that, given their varying consumption pattern, the poor households face a price vector that is different from that faced by the non-poor. One can extend this point to argue that the effective price index varies from one poor household to another thus questioning the use of household invariant price index in making temporal adjustment to the poverty line in comparing poverty rates over time. The issue gets more complex in international poverty comparisons since the exchange rates used in converting an internationally specified poverty line denominated in, say, the US dollar into the national currencies must be converted using exchange rates that are more relevant for the poor.

The idea here is the same due to differences in the households' spending power and in their size and composition, the price index used in deflating the nominal expenditures in comparing poverty overtime will vary not only between households below and above the poverty lines but also between households at varying levels of poverty. This aspect is rarely acted upon by government agencies in devising and revising poverty lines in response to price movements.

A logical implication of the above discussion is that, based on the same vector of item prices, each household will face a different overall effective price index depending on its expenditure allocation over the various consumption categories. Since this effective price index will vary across households, this will cause a divergence between nominal and real expenditure inequalities, and between official and 'real' poverty rates. We define nominal expenditure inequality as that which calculates inequality in per capita or per adult equivalent money expenditures, and real inequality as the measure of inequality where we deflate the money expenditures by the household-specific price indices. In case of poverty comparisons, the corresponding distinction is between poverty rates based on poverty lines used in official poverty calculations and poverty rates based on this idea of household-specific inflation adjustments to their nominal expenditures.

Much of the recent debate over poverty lines in India[3] has been between the advocates of the 'direct method', where the poverty line is specified in terms of the minimal calorie needs and advocates of the more conventional 'indirect method' based on expenditures and an expenditure-based poverty line that was originally derived from a calorie norm but then periodically revised using official price indices. The present exercise abstracts from that debate and compares the official 'indirect' method with another 'indirect method' that questions the use of the official price index in updating the poverty lines in the same manner for all households and that too using a weighting scheme to aggregate the item wise prices into an overall price index using a non-representative consumption basket for the poor. The principal motivation of Mishra and Ray (2011) paper is to provide a unified methodology for incorporating the differential effect of price movements in the welfare comparisons involved in inequality and poverty calculations and apply it to Indian data. The period considered, 1993/94–2004/5, is particularly significant for it covers the period of what is commonly referred to as first and generation economic reforms in India. This paper provides evidence on inequality and poverty movements in India over this period and looks at the role played by the price changes in these movements.

Another feature of this study is the formal statistical testing using bootstrap methods of the inequality and poverty rate estimates and of their changes over time. Since the concepts and functional specification used in Mishra and Ray (2011) have been described in Chap. 4, let us proceed to the data description, and the empirical findings of this study. This study uses the detailed information on expenditure on various items, on household size, composition and the socio-economic class of the household contained in the unit records from the 50th (July 1993–June 1994), 55th (July 1999–June 2000) and 61st (July 2004–June 2005) rounds of India's National Sample Surveys (NSS). All these rounds are 'thick' rounds being based on large samples and are comparable. These three surveys cover a reasonably long time interval (1993–2004) to make the comparisons of poverty and inequality meaningful and significant since it covers the period of economic reforms in India. The price information was obtained from published price series put out by the Government of India and the RBI.

The State-specific poverty lines are made available by the Planning Commission. Frequency weights, in the form of 'multipliers', are provided in the data sets. Households which differ in size will have different weights. The multipliers provided us with the household weights based on the number of individual members in the household. These were used in the inequality and poverty calculations reported below. Table 5.6 provides information on the sample size in the NSS data sets and the estimation samples that we have used. The estimation sample is somewhat smaller than the actual NSS sample because we excluded some of the smaller States and concentrated on the 21 major States in India. Given the sample size in various NSS rounds, as shown in Table 5.6, we have enough observations to provide

[3]See, for example, Ray and Lancaster (2005), Ray (2007), and Sen (2005).

Table 5.6 Sample size (Mishra and Ray 2011)

NSS rounds	NSS sample		Estimation sample	
	Rural	Urban	Rural	Urban
50th round	69,206	46,148	53,484	43,072
55th round	71,386	48,924	64,792	43,043
61st round	79,298	45,346	66,088	37,523

reliable estimates of inequality and poverty. This is confirmed by the well-determined estimates of inequality and poverty rates and the tight confidence intervals reported later.

The demand systems were estimated on the following fouritem breakdown of household expenditure: Food (i = 1), Fuel and Light (i = 2), Clothing, Bedding and Footwear (i = 3), and Miscellaneous (i = 4). While the Consumer Price Index for Agricultural Labourers (CPIAL) for these major commodity groupings was used as rural prices, the Consumer Price Index for Industrial Workers (CPIIW) was used as the urban prices. The 'Miscellaneous' category includes the following: education, medical care, entertainment, toilet articles. The 'Miscellaneous' category does not include consumer durables or housing. The choice of the items for inclusion in 'Miscellaneous' category and the four-item disaggregation of consumer expenditure is, principally, due to the fact that the definition of 'Miscellaneous' and the four items used here match up exactly with the published price series on these items. As Table 5.7 shows, these four expenditure categories together constitute the major share of expenditure for a median household, more so for a household below the poverty line.

Table 5.8 reports the price series of the four groups of items used in the demand estimation. The all-India price indices were obtained as the population share-weighted average of the State price indices. The CPI for agricultural workers and that for industrial workers were taken as the rural and urban price series, respectively. Fuel and Light and the composite item, called Miscellaneous, recorded the larger price increases over this period. While the Miscellaneous group had the largest price increase between rounds 50 and 55, Fuel and Light overtook this composite group in its price increase between rounds 55 and 61. There was a significant realignment of prices leading to changes in relative prices in both rural and urban areas.

Table 5.7 Expenditure share (Mishra and Ray 2011)

NSS rounds	Percentage share of Food, Fuel and Light, Clothing, Bedding and Footwear and miscellaneous categories in total expenditure					
	Median household		Households below poverty line		Household above poverty line	
50th (%)	84.3	78.8	89.0	86.4	82.2	76.1
55th (%)	78.1	73.5	80.9	79.2	77.9	72.7
61st (%)	92.7	88.2	93.6	91.3	92.5	87.2
Average (%)	85.0	80.2	87.8	85.6	84.2	78.7

Table 5.8 Prices indices for rural and urban samples with 50th round as base period (Mishra and Ray 2011)

Commodity group	Rural			Urban		
	50th	55th	61st	50th	55th	61st
Food group	1.000	1.414	1.508	1.000	1.655	1.869
Fuel and Light group	1.000	1.485	1.912	1.000	1.689	2.609
Clothing, Bedding and Footwear	1.000	1.366	1.628	1.000	1.536	1.732
Miscellaneous group	1.000	1.551	1.832	1.000	1.684	2.111

5.4 Prices and Expenditure Inequality in India

Tables 5.9 and 5.10 present the expenditure shares in rural and urban areas, respectively, of households in the five quintiles of the expenditure distribution, arranged in an ascending order of household expenditure per adult equivalent. The tables report the shares of the quintiles in terms of both nominal expenditure per adult equivalent and real expenditure per adult equivalent. There has been expenditure redistribution in both rural and urban areas from the bottom three quintiles to the top quintile throughout the reforms period and beyond (1993/94–2004/2005). The expenditure distribution in both nominal and real terms is more unequal in the urban areas compared to the rural as reflected in the lower share of the bottom three quintiles in the urban sector. A comparison of the nominal and real expenditure shares suggests that the price movements have been progressive over this period since the real expenditure shares of the lower quintiles exceed the corresponding nominal expenditure shares in NSS rounds 55 and 61,[4] and this is true in both rural and urban areas.

This is not surprising if we recall that, during this period, the price of the composite group of luxury items called Miscellaneous increased more than those of the items of necessities, notably, Food. The progressive nature of the price movements in India during the 1990s and the early part of the new millennium is seen more directly from Tables 5.11 and 5.12 which present the nominal and real expenditure inequalities in the two sectors. These tables report the inequality estimates calculated using the Gini inequality measure and the decomposable generalised entropy (GE) inequality index at varying levels of distribution sensitivity. The qualitative picture on inequality is generally robust to the inequality measure employed. Inequality has been increasing in both rural and urban areas. These tables also report the standard errors that were calculated using bootstrap methods following the procedures outlined in Mills and Zandvakili (1997), Biewen (2002) and Athanasopoulos and Vahid (2003).

The estimates are well determined and all the inequality estimates are highly significant. The confidence intervals have been shifting to the right between rounds

[4]Since the prices are normalised at unity in the base round 50, the nominal and real expenditure shares are the same in that round. This remark also holds for inequality and poverty rates.

Table 5.9 Quintile shares of total expenditure in rural areas (Mishra and Ray 2011)

Quintile	Nominal expenditure share			Real expenditure share		
	50th	55th	61st	50th	55th	61st
1	10.237	9.746	9.188	10.237	9.813	9.374
2	14.344	13.858	13.145	14.344	13.945	13.377
3	17.837	17.495	16.785	17.837	17.582	16.955
4	22.443	22.415	21.820	22.443	22.479	21.925
5	35.139	36.485	39.062	35.139	36.182	38.368

Table 5.10 Quintile shares of total expenditure in urban areas (Mishra and Ray 2011)

Quintile	Nominal expenditure share			Real expenditure share		
	50th	55th	61st	50th	55th	61st
1	9.039	8.477	7.792	9.039	8.580	7.854
2	13.399	12.940	11.593	13.399	13.065	11.679
3	17.250	16.945	15.874	17.250	17.064	15.968
4	22.621	22.657	22.446	22.621	22.735	22.558
5	37.691	38.981	42.295	37.691	38.556	41.941

Table 5.11 Nominal and real expenditure inequalities in rural areas (Mishra and Ray 2011)

Rounds	Nominal				Real			
	Gini	Generalised entropy			Gini	Generalized entropy		
		GE (0)	GE (1)	GE (2)		GE (0)	GE (1)	GE (2)
50th	0.2482	0.1009	0.1097	0.1805	0.2482	0.1009	0.1097	0.1805
SE[a]	0.0014	0.0015	0.0045	0.0489	0.0014	0.0015	0.0045	0.0489
95% UB	0.2510	0.1039	0.1186	0.2764	0.2510	0.1039	0.1186	0.2764
95% LB	0.2455	0.0979	0.1008	0.0846	0.2455	0.0979	0.1008	0.0846
55th	0.2660	0.1159	0.1254	0.1844	0.2634	0.1136	0.1220	0.1727
SE[a]	0.0012	0.0012	0.0030	0.0219	0.0011	0.0011	0.0026	0.0173
95% UB	0.2683	0.1184	0.1312	0.2272	0.2655	0.1158	0.1271	0.2066
95% LB	0.2638	0.1135	0.1196	0.1416	0.2612	0.1114	0.1170	0.1389
61st	0.2962	0.1439	0.1665	0.2724	0.2876	0.1354	0.1534	0.2324
SE[a]	0.0013	0.0015	0.0031	0.0161	0.0012	0.0013	0.0025	0.0109
95% UB	0.2988	0.1469	0.1726	0.3041	0.2900	0.1379	0.1582	0.2537
95% LB	0.2936	0.1410	0.1603	0.2408	0.2852	0.1329	0.1486	0.2110

[a]*SE* Bootstrap standard error of the estimate; *UB* upper bound; *LB* lower bound

consistent with the increase in the inequality magnitudes over time. The increase in inequality has been particularly large in both areas in the second half, namely, between 1999/2000 and 2004/2005. The nominal expenditure inequalities exceed their real counterpart in both the comparison rounds 55 and 61. This suggests that the movement in relative prices in India during this period has been progressive

Table 5.12 Nominal and real expenditure inequalities in urban areas (Mishra and Ray 2011)

Rounds	Nominal				Real			
	Gini	Generalized entropy			Gini	Generalised entropy		
		GE (0)	GE (1)	GE (2)		GE (0)	GE (1)	GE (2)
50th	0.2848	0.1336	0.1395	0.1892	0.2848	0.1336	0.1395	0.1892
SE[a]	0.0014	0.0015	0.0032	0.0206	0.0014	0.0015	0.0032	0.0206
95% UB	0.2876	0.1366	0.1458	0.2295	0.2876	0.1366	0.1458	0.2295
95% LB	0.2821	0.1307	0.1332	0.1489	0.2821	0.1307	0.1332	0.1489
55th	0.3045	0.1584	0.1866	0.7078	0.2998	0.1534	0.1762	0.5666
SE[a]	0.0034	0.0046	0.0166	0.2516	0.0030	0.0040	0.0139	0.1851
95% UB	0.3112	0.1675	0.2191	1.2009	0.3057	0.1613	0.2034	0.9294
95% LB	0.2978	0.1493	0.1542	0.2147	0.2939	0.1455	0.1490	0.2039
61st	0.3439	0.1924	0.2135	0.3365	0.3404	0.1884	0.2075	0.3173
SE[a]	0.0018	0.0022	0.0045	0.0270	0.0017	0.0020	0.0041	0.0227
95% UB	0.3474	0.1967	0.2223	0.3894	0.3437	0.1923	0.2155	0.3618
95% LB	0.3405	0.1882	0.2047	0.2836	0.3371	0.1844	0.1995	0.2727

[a]*SE* Bootstrap standard error of the estimate; *UB* upper bound; *LB* lower bound

with an inequality-reducing bias, unlike the Australian experience reported in Nicholas et al. (2010). Tables 5.11 and 5.12 also confirm that the urban expenditure distribution is more unequal than the rural in both nominal and real terms.

The above discussion has assumed the absence of economies of household size. In order to examine the role played by the economies of household size, Mishra and Ray (2011) allow size economies by generalising the equivalence scale specification mentioned in Chap. 4 via the introduction of the parameter, θ, as follows:

$$m_{oh}(z,p) = \prod_k p_k^{\delta_k z_h} \prod_k p_k^{\phi_k na_h} (na_h + \rho z_h)^\theta \tag{5.1}$$

$\theta = 1$ assumes the absence of economies of household size. As θ declines from 1, the household experiences economies of scale that increase as θ declines further towards 0, while as θ increases beyond 1, the household experiences diseconomies of scale. The precise nature of the relationship between inequality and θ has been a matter of some controversy [see Coulter et al. (1992), Banks and Johnson (1994)]. Figures 5.2 and 5.3 provide evidence from India's rural and urban areas, respectively, on this issue by plotting the graphs of nominal and real expenditure inequalities against a range of θ values varying from $\theta = 0$ to $\theta = 1.2$[5] based on the 61st round of the National Sample Survey. The gap between the two graphs is a

[5]$\theta = 0$ implies that household expenditures are uncorrected for differences in household size and composition, $0 < \theta < 1$ implies consumption economies of scale that favour larger sized households, while $\theta > 1$ implies diseconomies that favour smaller-sized households.

measure of the bias in the nominal inequalities in relation to the real expenditure inequalities.

These figures confirm that in both areas of the Indian economy, the price movement across items has been progressive resulting in a reduction of real expenditure inequality from nominal inequality during the 61st round. The figures show that this result is robust to a wide range of θ values. A comparison of Figs. 5.2 and 5.3 shows that the bias has been much less in the urban areas than in the rural. The graphs also establish a mild U-shaped relationship between inequality and economies of household size.

5.4.1 Prices and Expenditure Poverty in India

Table 5.13 presents the head-count poverty rates during the three NSS rounds considered in this study.[6] The introduction of adult–child relativities via the estimated equivalence scales leads to a sharp reduction in the nominal poverty rates from the per capita-based figures in both areas. The bootstrapped standard errors show that the poverty rates are well determined and highly significant. While the rural poverty rates register a steady decline throughout the period covered, the nominal per capita urban poverty rates record a sharp rise between 1999/2000 and 2004/2005. The overall picture conveyed by Table 5.13 is one of declining poverty in rural areas and stagnant or rising poverty in the urban areas.

A comparison of the nominal and real poverty rates based on the expenditures on the four included items shows that the nominal poverty rates that use the official poverty lines had an upward bias in relation to the real poverty rates.[7] This is also evident from the leftward shift in the 95% confidence interval as we move from the nominal to the real poverty rate estimates. This parallels the earlier result that the price movements had a progressive, inequality-reducing effect through the realignment of relative prices. The narrowing of the difference between the nominal and real poverty rates in both areas between the 55th and the 61st rounds suggests, however, that the progressive nature of the relative price changes weakened in the second half of our chosen period. This is also evident in a similar narrowing of the difference between the nominal and real expenditure inequalities between these two NSS rounds evident from Tables 5.11 and 5.12.

[6]The poverty line for the expenditure calculations based on the four included items were obtained by multiplying the official poverty lines by the median Engel ratios of the four included items to total expenditure.

[7]This is explained by the higher price increases in the 'Miscellaneous' category compared to the other items along with the fact that the budget share of this composite item has also increased significantly over this period. The nominal expenditure poverty rates that are based on the official poverty lines do not take into account these changes in the expenditure pattern and the relative prices unlike the real expenditure poverty rates that do.

Table 5.13 Head-count poverty rates (Mishra and Ray 2011)

Rounds	Rural			Urban		
	Over-expenditure on four included commodity groups[a]		Overall items	Over-expenditure on four included commodity groups[a]		Overall items
	Nominal[b] poverty rate (per equiv.)	Real poverty rate (per equiv.)	Nominal poverty Rate (percapita)	Nominal[b] poverty rate (per equiv.)	Real poverty rate (per equiv.)	Nominal poverty rate (percapita)
50th	0.0942	0.0942	0.2394	0.1130	0.1130	0.2162
SE[c]	0.0011	0.0011	0.0016	0.0013	0.0013	0.0020
95% UB	0.0964	0.0964	0.2424	0.1156	0.1156	0.2202
95% LB	0.0920	0.0920	0.2363	0.1103	0.1103	0.2122
55th	0.1123	0.0684	0.1922	0.1236	0.0792	0.1609
SE[c]	0.0011	0.0010	0.0014	0.0017	0.0014	0.0016
95% UB	0.1144	0.0703	0.1950	0.1269	0.0820	0.1641
95% LB	0.1102	0.0664	0.1894	0.1203	0.0765	0.1577
61st	0.0485	0.0308	0.1758	0.1102	0.0977	0.2689
SE[c]	0.0009	0.0006	0.0013	0.0015	0.0013	0.0017
95% UB	0.0503	0.0319	0.1783	0.1131	0.1002	0.2722
95% LB	0.0468	0.0297	0.1732	0.1074	0.0952	0.2655

[a]These included groups of item are Food; Fuel and Light; Clothing, Bedding and Footwear; Miscellaneous

[b]The nominal poverty lines used in these calculations were obtained by scaling down the official poverty lines by multiplying them by the median budget share of the four commodity groups in total expenditure (0.944 for rural and 0.919 for urban) in the 61st round

[c]*SE* Bootstrap standard error of the estimate; *UB* upper bound; *LB* lower bound

This is explained by the item wise inflation figures presented in Table 5.8. As noted earlier, while the Miscellaneous group of luxury items recorded the largest price increase among the four groups between the 50th and 55th rounds, it was overtaken by Fuel and Light, an item of necessity, during the period between the 55th and 61st rounds, thus reducing the redistributive impact of the relative price changes during the latter time period. The progressive nature of the relative price changes in India over the period covered in this study is formally established by the confidence intervals of the estimates of the difference between the nominal and real magnitudes of inequality and poverty that are presented in Table 5.14. Bootstrap methods using 10,000 replications were used to calculate the confidence intervals. The positive magnitudes of the differences and with the fact that there is no case where 0 falls within the confidence intervals confirm one of the key empirical results of this study.

Table 5.14 Differences between nominal and real expenditure inequality and between nominal and real poverty rate, per adult equivalent (Mishra and Ray 2011)

	Rural sample		Urban sample	
	Expenditure inequality[a]	Poverty rate[b] (per adult equiv.)	Expenditure inequality[a]	Poverty rate[b] (per adult equiv.)
NSS 55th round	0.00204	0.01962	0.00312	0.02524
95% CI	[0.00206, 0.00203]	[0.01926, 0.01928]	[0.00315, 0.00310]	[0.02559, 0.02489]
NSS 61st round	0.00659	0.04994	0.00247	0.02288
95% CI	[0.00663, 0.00655]	[0.05066, 0.04921]	[0.00249, 0.00246]	[0.02357, 0.02218]

[a]Expenditure inequalities are measured by Gini coefficients
[b]Head-count measure used to calculate poverty rate

Figures 5.4a and 5.5b present evidence on the impact of economies of scale of household size on the poverty calculations[8] in the rural areas and urban areas, respectively, by plotting the graphs of the nominal and real poverty rates against a range of θ values in case of NSS round 61. Once again, there is a similarity with the inequality results. The real poverty rates are lower than the nominal poverty rates and the gap between the two increases as the size economies decrease. In case of the assumed value of θ being 0.6 or less, the two poverty rates are virtually identical, and this is true of both rural and urban areas. In other words, the official poverty line-based poverty rates provide a reasonably accurate picture of real expenditure poverty only if there exist significant economies of household size in consumption. The graphs agree that there is a positive relationship between the calculated poverty rates and the assumed value of the size economies parameter, θ, used in the poverty calculations. In other words, the larger the size economies the lower the estimated poverty rate. This is explained by the fact that in the NSS data sets the larger sized households, that can take advantage of economies of household size, dominate the samples.[9]

[8]See Meenakshi and Ray (2002) for previous evidence from India, Lanjouw and Ravallion (1995) for evidence from Pakistan and Lancaster, Ray and Valenzuela (1999) for cross-country evidence from a range of developing and developed countries on the sensitivity of the poverty estimates to household size economies in consumption.

[9]Typically, two-thirds or more of the households have two or more adults and 1 or more children.

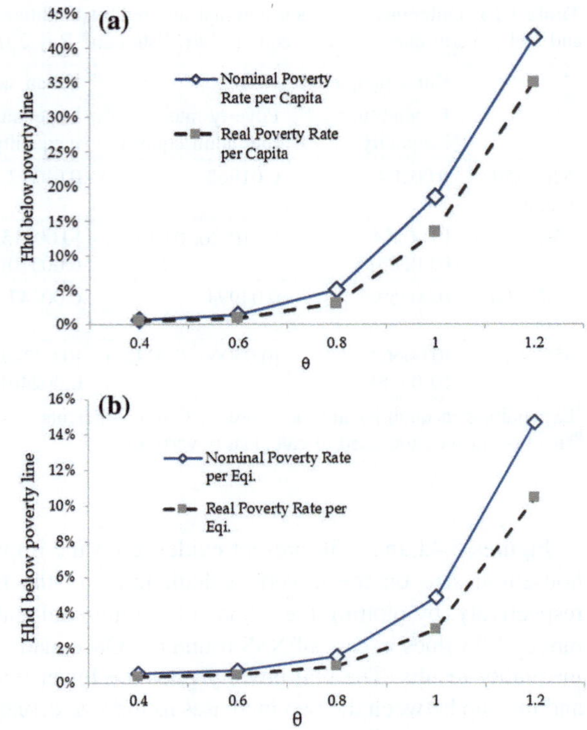

Fig. 5.4 **a** Head-count rural poverty rates at varying values of θ in 61st round. **b** Head-count rural poverty rates at varying values of θ in 61st round. Reproduced from Mishra and Ray (2011)

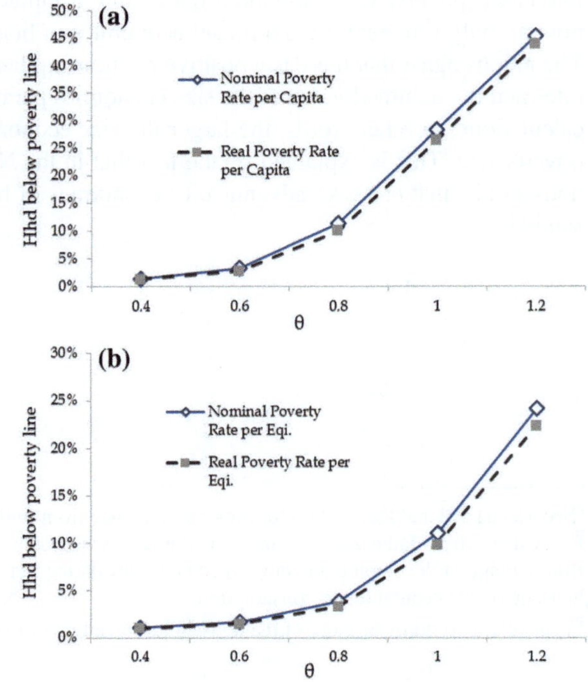

Fig. 5.5 **a** Head-count urban poverty rates at varying values of θ in 61st round. **b** Head-count urban poverty rates at varying values of θ in 61st round. Reproduced from Mishra and Ray (2011)

5.5 Concluding Remarks

This chapter reports some of the principal studies that examine the welfare implications of price changes. The evidence covered several countries with the results for India reported and discussed in greater detail than the others. Special attention was paid to reporting the effect of price changes on inequality and, in the Indian context, on poverty. The applications serve to illustrate the usefulness of unit values of the Food items, adjusted for differences in quality and family characteristics, as proxies for prices of the various items in the calculation of the price indices. The results confirm that price changes are non-neutral in their effect on distribution, though the size and the qualitative nature of the impact vary between countries and over different time periods. The Indian evidence also establishes the impact of economies of scale in household consumption on inequality and poverty. This chapter has also described a new procedure for calculating rural–urban differences in prices and illustrated it by applying to the NSS data from India to estimate the rural–urban price differential for each item and of that overall for all items. The results on the spatial differences in the temporal movement in prices point to the need for empirical evidence from a more complete treatment of spatial prices in a heterogeneous country setting and the use of such prices in the welfare ranking of its constituent regions or States. The following chapter provides such a treatment.

References

Athanasopoulos G, Vahid F (2003) Statistical inference and changes in income inequality in Australia. Econ Rec 79:412–424

Atkinson AB (1970) On the measurement of inequality. J Econ Theory 2:244–263

Banerjee A, Bardhan P, Somanathan R, Srinivasan TN (eds) (2017) Poverty and income distribution in India. Juggernaut Books, Kolkata

Banks J, Johnson P (1994) Equivalence scales relativities revisited. Econ J 104:883–890

Banks J, Blundell R, Lewbel A (1997) Quadratic Engel curves and consumer demand. Rev Econ Stat 79:527–539

Barten AP (1964) Family composition, prices and expenditure patterns. In: Hart PE, Mills G, Whittaker JK (eds) Econometric analysis for national economic planning. Butterworth, London

Biewen M (2002) Bootstrap inference for inequality, mobility and poverty measurement. J Econometrics 108:317–342

Blundell RW, Ray R (1984) Testing for linear Engel curves and additively separable preferences using a new flexible demand system. Econ J 94:800–811

Coondoo D, Majumder A, Chattopadhyay S (2011) Estimating spatial consumer price indices through engel curve analysis. Rev Income Wealth 57:138–155

Coulter FAE, Cowell FA, Jenkins SP (1992) Equivalence scale relativities and the extent of inequality and poverty. Econ J 102:1067–1082

Deaton AS, Muellbauer J (1980) An almost ideal demand system. Am Econ Rev 70:312–326

Gibson J, Rozelle S (2005) Prices and unit values in poverty measurement and tax reform analysis. World Bank Econ Rev 19(1):69–97

Irvine I, McCarthy C (1980) Further evidence on inflation and redistribution in the United Kingdom. Econ J 90:907–911

Iyengar N S, Bhattacharya N (1965) The effect of differentials in consumer price index on measures of income inequality. Sankhya Series B 27:47–56

Lancaster G, Ray R, Valenzuela MR (1999) A cross-country study of household poverty and inequality on unit record household budget data. Econ Dev Cult Change 48:177–208

Lanjouw P, Ravallion M (1995) Poverty and household size. Econ J 105:1415–1433

Majumder A, Ray R, Sinha K (2012) The calculation of rural urban food price differentials from unit values in household expenditure surveys: a new procedure and comparison with existing methods. Am J Agric Econ 94:1218–1235

Majumder A, Ray R, Sinha K (2013) Temporal comparisons of prices, expenditure and growth in India: a state-wise analysis. Indian Growth Dev Rev 6:195–211

Meenakshi JV, Ray R (2002) Impact of household size and family composition on poverty in rural India. J Policy Model 24:539–559

Mills J, Zandvakili S (1997) Statistical inference via bootstrapping for measures of inequality. J Appl Econometrics 12:133–150

Mishra A, Ray R (2011) Prices, inequality and poverty. Rev Income Wealth 57:428–448

Muellbauer J (1974a) Household composition, Engel curves and welfare comparisons between households. Eur Econ Rev 5:103–122

Muellbauer J (1974b) Prices and inequality: the United Kingdom experience. Econ J 84:32–55

Nicholas A, Ray R, Valenzuela MR (2010) Evaluating the distributional implications of price movements: methodology, application and australian evidence. Econ Rec 86:352–366

Pendakur K (2002) Taking prices seriously in the measurement of inequality. J Public Econ 86:47–69

Rao DSP (2005) On the equivalence of weighted country product dummy (CPD) method and the rao-system for multilateral price comparison. Rev Income Wealth 51(4):571–580

Ray R (1983) Measuring the costs of children: an alternative approach. J Public Econ 22:89–102

Ray R (1985) Prices, children and inequality: further evidence for the U.K., 1965–82. Econ J 95:1069–1077

Ray R (1986) Demographic variables and equivalence scales in a flexible demand system: the case of AIDS. Appl Econ 18:265–278

Ray R (2007) Changes in food consumption and the implications for food security and undernourishment: India in the 1990s. Dev Change 38:321–344

Ray R, Lancaster G (2005) On setting the poverty line based on estimated nutrient prices: condition of socially disadvantaged groups during the reform period. Econ Polit Wkly 40 (1):46–56

Reddy S, Pogge T (2010) How *Not* to Count the Poor. In: Anand S, Segal P, Stiglitz J (eds) Debates on the measurement of global poverty. Oxford University Press, Oxford

Selvanthan E (1991) Standard errors for Laspeyres and Paasche index numbers. Econ Lett 35:35–38

Sen P (2005) Of calories and things: reflections on nutritional norms, poverty lines and consumption behaviour in India. Econ Polit Wkly 30:4611–4618

Chapter 6
Spatial Differences in Prices in India, State Rankings and Inequality

6.1 Introduction

The results on India presented in the previous chapter touched on the issue of spatial differences in prices by providing evidence of regional differences in the temporal movement in prices and of rural–urban differentials in prices at a point in time. The focus of the discussion in the previous chapter was on inflation and its distributive effects rather than on the spatial differences in prices. The present chapter provides a more complete treatment by focussing exclusively on the calculation of spatial price indices and using them in the welfare ranking of the Indian States. Building on the concepts and methodologies described earlier, this chapter reports in some detail the findings from Majumder et al. (2015a, b), Chakrabarty et al. (2015, 2017) and Majumder and Ray (2017). Majumder et al. (2015a, b) contain an empirical application of Sen (1976)'s proposal for welfare ranking of regions using a distribution-sensitive welfare function that incorporates the regional price differences.

Chakrabarty et al. (2015) compare the effects of spatial and temporal changes in prices on inequality and conclude that 'the effects of temporal price inflation and spatial prices on inequality are qualitatively different'. Majumder and Ray (2017) provide evidence on the sensitivity of the estimated spatial prices to estimation methods. This study 'includes a systematic comparison between the spatial price indices from alternative models, namely the CPD and utility-based models, and the result that the utility-based methods point to a much greater extent of spatial price heterogeneity than is suggested by the CPD-type models'. Chakrabarty et al. (2017) examine the role of the stochastic specification in the estimation of the price indices. Using the framework of the 'Dynamic Household Regional Product Dummy Model' (DHRPD) described earlier, this paper concludes that 'the introduction of an AR(1) error process improves the efficiency of the estimates of parameters, urban–rural and temporal price indices under certain conditions'. We now proceed to describe the results from these studies on NSS data in detail.

R. Ray, *Household Behaviour, Prices, and Welfare*, Themes in Economics,
https://doi.org/10.1007/978-981-13-1930-3_6

6.2 Spatial Comparisons of Prices and Expenditure in a Heterogeneous Country: Methodology with Application to India[1]

There is now a large literature on the comparison of real incomes of countries across time and space. Much of it is based on the Penn World Tables (PWT), from the International Comparison Program (ICP) of the United Nations, which regularly publishes estimates of real GDP for a large panel of countries. While such comparisons are routinely done from the World Development Indicators published by the World Bank, there have been some recent attempts to make these international comparisons consistent across space and over time. Recent examples of international comparisons of real income or real expenditure include Hill (2004), Neary (2004) and Feenstra et al. (2009). Oulton (2012) sets out a preference-based algorithm for comparing living standards across countries. Most of these international income comparisons treat the whole country as a single entity and ignore the spatial dimension within the country.[2] They ignore the fact that in large countries, such as Brazil and India, there is much greater variation in prices and consumer preferences between States or provinces than between several of the smaller countries that figure in the ICP real income or inequality comparisons. As reported in Majumder et al. (2015a, b, Table 9), the order of magnitude of the coefficient of variation of the PPPs between the States in India is larger than that between several of the smaller countries in the European Union.

The variation in the PPP of a currency inside a large country can be attributed to three related but conceptually different factors: (a) intra-national spatial heterogeneity in preferences, (b) differences in prices and (c) spatial differences in household size and composition. In the context of countries such as India and Brazil, the combined impact of these three factors may lead to large spatial heterogeneity in the PPP of the country's currency. The assumption of a single PPP restricts the usefulness of the methodology adopted in such country contexts. For example, the international statistical agencies have spent much resources on calculating PPPs between nations, (Asian Development Bank 2008; Rao et al. 2010), but there has not been much attention paid to calculating PPPs within nations. Nor are these cross-country comparisons usually made on preference consistent expenditure systems that take into account substitution between items over time or the spatial differences in the magnitude of such substitution effects driven by corresponding spatial differences in prices and preferences. Yet, the considerations of preference heterogeneity and differing relative prices between nations that drive the cross-country PPP calculations, also, underline the importance of spatial prices in the context of large federal countries such as Brazil and India. In the words of

[1]The material in this section is based on Majumder et al. (2015a, b).

[2]There is also a long tradition of international inequality comparisons that treat the whole country as a single entity—examples include Hill (2000), and Almas (2012).

Oulton (2012), 'though much work has been done on estimating systems of consumer demand or producers' cost functions, the results of these studies are not typically employed by other economists in empirical work… when macro economists study inflation empirically they do not usually employ their micro-colleagues' estimates of expenditure functions'.

The recent study by Feenstra et al. (2009), while continuing the tradition of treating all countries, large and small, as homogenous, marks a departure and proposes a framework for expenditure comparisons between countries based on estimated preference parameters.[3] Majumder et al. (2015a, b), which is in this recent tradition, is motivated by an attempt to take consumer preferences and price-induced substitution into account in calculating spatial price indices, unlike much of the earlier literature as exemplified by the quote from Oulton noted above. In doing so, this paper pays major attention to the regional heterogeneity in prices and household size and composition as the principal reasons for the spatial heterogeneity in a country's PPP, namely those identified as (b) and (c) above. This paper also takes into account regional variation in preferences, namely (a) above, by calculating the intra-national PPPs using spatially different preference parameters obtained by estimating the demand systems separately for each of the constituent States. However, the paper's contribution on this is limited by the fact that it uses the same demand functional form in case of all the constituent States.

The recent evidence of Aten and Menezes (2002), Coondoo et al. (2004, 2011), Majumder et al. (2012, 2015a, b) and Deaton and Dupriez (2011) suggests that the assumption of spatial homogeneity is unlikely to be valid in the case of large heterogeneous countries with diverse preferences such as Brazil, India and Indonesia. The lack of spatial prices in large countries prevents real income comparisons between provinces since the calculation of provincial real income is dependent on the availability of regional price deflators. The heterogeneity in regional preferences over items and in the regional price movements in large countries implies that there is much greater variation between individual provinces and States in such countries than exists between several of the smaller countries in, for example, the European Union or, more generally, the list of countries that figure in the ICP project. Majumder et al. (2015a, b) recognises this and concentrates on the spatial dimension within a country rather than between countries. In a different context, namely, of monetary aggregation, Barnett (2007) has proposed a Divisia-based methodology for aggregating monetary service flows aggregated over the smaller nations of the European Union. Many of these smaller countries in Barnett (2007)'s framework are analogous to the constituent States of the Indian union considered in Majumder et al. (2015a, b).

Majumder et al. (2015a, b) uses the methodology proposed in Majumder et al. (2012) that provides for a preference consistent framework to estimate spatial

[3]See O'Donnell and Rao (2007) for an expenditure function-based approach to the estimation of price indices and comparison with those based on conventional PPP methodology of Divisia price indices.

differences in prices. This paper extends Majumder et al. (2012) in moving from urban–rural heterogeneity in that study to regional heterogeneity between the principal States of the Indian union. The study uses the estimated spatial prices in expenditure comparisons between regions in the context of a large heterogeneous country, namely India. This study is in the recent expenditure function-based tradition of Feenstra et al. (2009). It extends that study in three significant respects: (a) it introduces spatial differences in preferences and price movements within a country and moves from the multicountry context of that study to the multi region context of a single federal country, (b) it shows that the utility-based 'true cost of living index' used recently in intertemporal price comparisons can also be used in constructing spatial price indices within the country for a single time period, and (c) the expenditure function adopted is the Rank 3 functional form introduced by Banks et al. (1997) rather than its restricted Rank 2 specialisation that yields the Almost Ideal Demand System.[4] The paper compares alternative methodologies for estimating spatial prices.

The comparison is not only between the traditional approach based on Divisia price indices[5] and that based on the estimated preference parameters from complete demand systems but, within the latter approach, between that using the innovative procedure of Coondoo et al. (2011) that uses Engel curve analysis without requiring any price information and that which uses prices constructed from unit values in the household expenditure surveys. The latter is preferable in the context of long time series where it is important to take into account price-induced substitution between items and the regional heterogeneity in such substitution. The principal contribution of this paper is, therefore, empirical in comparing between the results of different methodologies in calculating spatial prices within a large federal country. Other distinguishing features of Majumder et al. (2015a, b) include the fact that it proposes formal tests of the hypothesis of no spatial differences in prices. Moreover, the paper uses the distribution-sensitive welfare measure, proposed by Sen (1976), to rank States in India and examines whether the welfare rankings have changed over the chosen period. This was a period of considerable economic significance for India because it coincided with 'second-generation reforms' that helped to make India one of the fastest growing countries in the world. Yet, not all States in India have shared equally in the progress and this puts the focus on the regional expenditure, price and welfare differences within the country as is done in this study. As Datt and Ravallion (1998) have shown that there has been considerable unevenness in economic progress among the constituent States in the Indian Union.

[4]While the use of the Rank 2 AIDS framework by Feenstra et al. (2009) was necessitated by the fact that their analytical results are conditional on such a functional form, there is now extensive empirical evidence that rejects Rank 2 demand models in favour of more general expenditure patterns.

[5]See Hulten (1973) and Hill (2000). Feenstra and Reinsdorf (2000) have shown equivalence between the Divisia approach and the 'exact approach' of the 'true cost of living indices' in case of the 'Almost Ideal Demand System'. It is not readily apparent if such equivalence extends to Rank 3 preferences such as the one considered here.

While Datt and Ravallion (1998)'s study was based on poverty rates and covered the prereforms period, the Majumder et al. (2015a, b) ranks States based on the welfare of the entire population (not just the poor) and covers the more recent period of economic reforms in India.

It may be noted that the expenditure-based welfare comparison between different regions in a large country is analogous to that between countries in international comparisons, but the former does not usually suffer from the problems posed by inconsistent data definitions in various countries faced in the latter. Moreover, the prevalence of similar institutional and cultural features in various regions in a country, along with a shared historical experience, unlike between countries, makes the intra-country welfare comparisons more meaningful than the cross-country comparisons, as noted by Datt and Ravallion (1998). Since the concepts, the prices indices and the methodologies including the Sen (1976) procedure for ranking regions based on an inequality incorporated welfare measure have been described in the earlier chapters, let us proceed to describe the data and report the results from Majumder et al. (2015a, b). This study uses the detailed information on household expenditures on Food and non-Food items, household size, composition and other household characteristics contained in the unit records from the 50th (July, 1993–June, 1994), 55th (July, 1999–June, 2000), 61st (July, 2004–June, 2005) and 66th (July, 2009–June, 2010) rounds of India's National Sample Surveys (NSS). All these rounds are 'thick' rounds and based on large samples. The period covered by these four 'thick rounds' of the NSS, 1993/94–2009/2010 is of much interest, both in India and abroad, since it saw India transformed from a slow growing economy facing a serious balance of payments crisis in 1991/2 to one of the fastest growing economies of the world. Moreover, the NSS 66th round covered the period immediately following the global financial crisis. The spatial price calculations were done for 11 principal Food items on which the NSS contained information on both expenditures and quantities allowing the calculation of unit values, and the exercise was performed for each of 15 major States in India.

The methods for calculating the indices were based on: (a) the Coondoo et al. (2011) procedure, (b) the QAIDS demand system-based procedure, (c) the Tornqvist formula and (d) the Laspeyres index. As mentioned earlier, procedure (a) avoids the requirement of price information; the latter three procedures use the quality adjusted unit values as prices. A comparison of the calculated spatial price indices between (a) and (b) shows the effect of disregarding price-based substitution in (a), but not in (b); a comparison between (b) and (c) shows the effect of using Rank 3 *vis-a-vis* Rank 2 demand systems; and comparison between (b)/(c) and (d) establishes the robustness of the evidence to the adoption of the approach of 'exact price' indices versus that of Divisia price indices. The coefficient estimates of the quality adjustment regressions of the unit values of the 11 Food items are not presented here but the interested reader is referred to Appendix Table A4 in Majumder et al. (2015a, b). Several of the coefficient estimates are highly significant. The sectoral dummy (Urban = 1, Rural = 0) is significant for 8 items (non-significant for fruits, sugar and spices) with positive values for all except milk and milk products and Pan/Tobacco, thereby generally implying higher urban price.

With the exception of milk and milk products, the more affluent households consume superior quality Food items, as evident from the positive and significant coefficient estimate of the per capita expenditure variable for most items. Household size generally goes the other way, with larger households consuming inferior quality Food items. The coefficient estimates of the district price effects, D^M_{id2} and D^M_{id3}, are mostly significant providing some support to McKelvey (2011)'s suggestion that in districts with higher prices the quality chosen will be lower. All the PPPs were calculated with these controls included in the unit value regressions. Note, however, that these additional controls have very little policy significance since the two sets of quality adjusted unit values in the 66th round are found to be nearly identical. The quality and demographically adjusted unit values of the 11 Food items in each of the 15 major States and for the whole country for the four NSS rounds, 50th, 55th, 61st and 66th, are presented in Tables 6.1, 6.2, 6.3 and 6.4, respectively, in Majumder et al. (2015a, b). Three features are worth noting: (a) there was an increase in the unit values of most of the items, with much of the increase taking place between rounds 61 and 66, i.e. the most recent period, 2004/5–2009/10. In contrast, the period between NSS rounds 55 and 61, i.e. 1999/2000–2004/5 saw relatively mild increases for most items, with even a decline in case of cereal and cereal substitutes; (b) this contains prima facie evidence of the large variation in spatial prices that motivated this study; (c) consistent with the evidence discussed in the previous chapter, the structure of spatial prices varies sharply between rural and urban areas, and over the rounds.

The estimates of the spatial price indices obtained from using the four alternative procedures for calculating spatial price indices have been presented in Tables 6.1, 6.2, 6.3 and 6.4. An estimate of spatial price for a State that is significantly greater than one implies that the State is more expensive in relation to the country as a whole, and vice versa if the estimate is less than one. While a comparison between the tables provides evidence of the sensitivity of the estimated spatial prices to the method used, each table allows a further comparison between the rural and urban spatial price estimates and how they have changed over the period between NSS rounds 50th (1993/94) and 66th (2009/10). The tables also report below each spatial price estimate the value of the t-statistic against the null hypothesis of no regional price difference, i.e. all the spatial prices are unity.[6] The following features are worth noting:

(a) The estimates are mostly, but not always, plausible. A few exceptions occur in case of the QAIDS-based estimates[7] presented in Table 6.2. The estimates are generally well determined.

[6]While the standard errors for the Laspeyres and Tornqvist indices are obtained from regression Eqs. (2.9) and (2.10), respectively, those for the Coondoo et al. (2011) and QAIDS-based price indices have been estimated using the Delta method.

[7]The few implausible estimates that are reported in case of QAIDS are restricted to the NSS 50th round and may reflect the quality of the data in the earlier rounds.

Table 6.1 Testing for Statewise variation in prices with respect to all India, S^{State} in various NSS rounds for 15 major States, rural and urban, method from Coondoo et al. (2011), 11 Food items (Majumder et al. 2015a)

States	Rural price indices				Urban price indices			
	50th round	55th round	61st round	66th round	50th round	55th round	61st round	66th round
(1)	(2)	(3)	(4)	(5)	(6)	(7)	(8)	(9)
Andhra Pradesh	1.011 (0.20)	1.008 (0.14)	1.094 (1.27)	1.161 (0.31)	0.898 (−2.80)*	0.876 (−1.81)	0.935 (−1.11)	1.088 (0.11)
Assam	1.097 (0.72)	1.078 (1.23)	1.242 (1.73)	1.077 (0.14)	1.115 (0.89)	1.081 (0.53)	1.202 (1.82)	1.061 (0.09)
Bihar	0.871 (−3.45)*	0.930 (−1.36)	0.897 (−2.56)*	0.823 (−1.21)	0.876 (−2.77)*	0.769 (−2.32)*	0.765 (−4.92)*	0.758 (−0.63)
Gujarat	1.181 (0.74)	1.213 (2.65)*	1.127 (0.92)	1.142 (0.40)	1.056 (0.61)	1.074 (0.70)	1.164 (2.20)*	1.103 (0.19)
Haryana	1.310 (2.50)*	1.374 (3.46)*	1.389 (3.93)*	1.432 (0.57)	1.051 (0.47)	1.022 (0.10)	1.053 (0.35)	1.073 (0.13)
Karnataka	0.925 (−1.39)	1.095 (1.27)	0.962 (−1.14)	0.960 (−0.10)	0.912 (−1.05)	1.009 (0.12)	0.985 (−0.12)	1.041 (0.06)
Kerala	1.351 (3.39)*	1.533 (2.34)*	1.481 (2.50)*	1.416 (0.53)	1.089 (1.56)	1.079 (0.68)	1.097 (0.51)	1.115 (0.30)
Madhya Pradesh	0.898 (−2.06)*	0.836 (−3.61)*	0.759 (−7.40)*	0.814 (−0.69)	0.886 (−5.37)*	0.797 (−5.84)*	0.768 (−3.48)*	0.782 (−0.64)
Maharashtra	0.874 (−0.90)	1.019 (0.55)	0.950 (−0.87)	1.050 (0.14)	1.097 (1.70)	1.008 (0.09)	1.029 (0.45)	1.128 (0.22)
Orissa	0.855 (−5.69)*	0.846 (−4.71)*	0.761 (−2.85)*	0.802 (−0.77)	0.929 (−0.71)	0.825 (−2.80)*	0.848 (−3.82)*	0.839 (−0.68)
Punjab	1.395 (5.49)*	1.351 (3.94)*	1.379 (3.72)*	1.412 (0.71)	1.127 (1.28)	1.023 (0.21)	1.106 (1.81)	1.101 (0.20)
Rajasthan	1.156 (2.45)*	1.179 (2.62)*	1.103 (0.78)	1.142 (0.51)	1.007 (0.15)	0.966 (−0.55)	0.903 (−1.00)	0.971 (−0.09)
Tamil Nadu	1.059 (1.03)	1.096 (0.66)	1.058 (0.74)	1.019 (0.03)	0.928 (−0.86)	1.030 (0.15)	1.053 (0.43)	1.004 (0.01)
Uttar Pradesh	0.895 (−2.51)*	0.942 (−1.19)	0.910 (−1.86)	0.899 (−0.38)	0.861 (−1.87)	0.790 (−5.97)*	0.841 (−1.92)	0.866 (−0.76)
West Bengal	1.029 (0.25)	1.101 (4.26)*	1.072 (2.61)*	1.004 (0.01)	1.097 (2.26)*	1.034 (0.73)	1.120 (0.99)	1.013 (0.05)
All India	1.000	1.000	1.000	1.000	1.000	1.000	1.000	1.000

Figures in parentheses are the t-statistics given by $\frac{S^{\text{State}}-1}{se(S^{\text{State}})}$

*Significant at 5% level

Table 6.2 Testing for Statewise variation in prices with respect to all India, S^{State} in various NSS rounds for 15 major States, rural and urban, method is QAIDS index, 11 items (Majumder et al. 2015a)

States	Rural price indices				Urban price indices			
	50th round	55th round	61st round	66th round	50th round	55th round	61st round	66th round
(1)	(2)	(3)	(4)	(5)	(6)	(7)	(8)	(9)
Andhra Pradesh	0.797 (−13.04)*	0.841 (−10.91)*	1.048 (2.13)**	1.083 (5.47)*	0.815 (−3.03)*	0.911 (−3.34)*	0.923 (−3.17)*	1.190 (7.67)*
Assam	0.812 (−4.77)*	1.150 (5.60)*	1.619 (5.76)*	0.972 (−1.03)	0.786 (−2.74)*	0.545 (−17.56)*	1.097 (1.05)	1.029 (0.58)
Bihar	1.268 (14.2)*	1.046 (7.10)*	1.122 (4.99)*	0.955 (−1.95)***	1.476 (8.69)*	1.232 (13.98)*	1.068 (1.49)	1.040 (0.83)
Gujarat	0.567 (−10.74)*	0.831 (−5.05)*	1.498 (3.16)*	0.840 (−10.91)*	0.588 (−9.13)*	0.839 (−5.91)*	1.461 (2.45)**	0.950 (−1.58)
Haryana	1.345 (9.13)*	0.891 (−4.29)*	1.360 (2.02)**	0.907 (−3.59)*	0.876 (−1.22)	1.185 (5.03)*	0.851 (−2.01)**	0.902 (−1.56)
Karnataka	0.549 (−34.07)*	0.893 (−6.92)*	0.868 (−3.81)*	0.748 (−16.14)*	0.857 (−4.43)*	0.864 (−8.12)*	0.902 (−3.34)*	1.390 (5.41)*
Kerala	0.862 (−2.28)**	1.024 (0.51)	1.222 (2.18)**	1.697 (11.54)*	0.449 (−11.86)*	0.887 (−2.17)*	0.921 (−1.47)	1.368 (4.91)*
Madhya Pradesh	0.887 (−6.61)*	0.851 (−12.51)*	0.939 (−1.92)***	0.729 (−20.64)*	1.478 (7.89)*	0.958 (−3.03)*	0.844 (−4.32)*	0.753 (−14.49)*
Maharashtra	0.840 (−8.54)*	0.901 (−8.20)*	1.165 (3.81)*	1.174 (5.39)*	0.586 (−31.89)*	0.936 (−6.42)*	1.162 (5.30)*	1.236 (5.82)*
Orissa	1.018 (0.62)	1.010 (0.77)	1.098 (2.02)**	1.031 (1.45)	1.035 (0.44)	0.982 (−0.43)	1.066 (0.76)	0.907 (−2.90)*
Punjab	1.050 (2.35)**	0.858 (−6.74)*	1.240 (5.77)*	1.093 (6.10)*	0.976 (−0.40)	1.162 (3.98)*	1.120 (1.99)**	0.881 (−7.79)*
Rajasthan	0.993	0.642	0.741	0.796	1.209	0.868	1.114	0.757

(continued)

Table 6.2 (continued)

States	Rural price indices				Urban price indices			
	50th round	55th round	61st round	66th round	50th round	55th round	61st round	66th round
(1)	(2)	(3)	(4)	(5)	(6)	(7)	(8)	(9)
	(−0.40)	(−36.40)*	(−3.37)*	(−10.95)*	(3.08)*	(−6.87)*	(0.98)	(−9.40)*
Tamil Nadu	0.977 (−0.94)	0.963 (−1.89)***	0.808 (−3.43)*	0.880 (−6.51)*	0.640 (−9.85)*	0.908 (−4.38)*	0.919 (−2.36)**	1.074 (1.64)***
Uttar Pradesh	0.962 (−3.78)*	0.901 (−13.17)*	0.990 (−0.36)	0.826 (−16.09)*	1.303 (8.68)*	1.060 (4.65)*	1.020 (0.56)	0.769 (−16.98)*
West Bengal	1.490 (10.17)*	1.219 (7.29)*	1.156 (3.95)*	1.471 (11.53)*	0.677 (−5.06)*	0.769 (−8.04)*	1.226 (5.02)*	1.546 (6.46)*
All India	1.000	1.000	1.000	1.000	1.000	1.000	1.000	1.000

Figures in parentheses are the t-statistic given by $\frac{S^{\text{State}}-1}{se(S^{\text{State}})}$

$^{*}p < 0.01$, $^{**}p < 0.05$, $^{***}p < 0.10$ are level of significance for testing PPP = 1

Table 6.3 Testing for Statewise variation in prices with respect to all India, S^{State} in various NSS rounds for 15 major States, rural and urban, method from Tornqvist GEKS Divisia index, 11 Food items (Majumder et al. 2015a)

States	Rural price indices				Urban price indices			
	50th round	55th round	61st round	66th round	50th round	55th round	61st round	66th round
(1)	(2)	(3)	(4)	(5)	(6)	(7)	(8)	(9)
Andhra Pradesh	0.965 (−1.72)***	0.979 (−4.24)*	1.032 (4.72)*	1.176 (13.74)*	1.025 (2.78)*	0.968 (−2.78)*	1.028 (3.27)*	1.295 (16.66)*
Assam	1.164 (13.32)*	1.064 (10.28)*	1.021 (2.87)*	1.077 (14.52)*	1.320 (10.46)*	1.048 (19.66)*	1.045 (5.44)*	1.081 (10.48)*
Bihar	0.974 (−2.11)*	1.056 (4.95)*	0.950 (−10.45)*	0.937 (−8.43)*	0.968 (−5.53)*	1.082 (5.31)*	0.951 (−7.84)*	0.915 (−11.59)*
Gujarat	1.025 (2.35)**	0.890 (−5.37)*	0.912 (−3.83)*	0.885 (−4.14)*	0.993 (−0.89)	0.910 (−5.53)*	0.905 (−3.14)*	0.975 (−5.62)*
Haryana	0.983 (−1.51)	0.907 (−8.61)*	0.956 (−3.79)*	0.944 (−4.69)*	0.958 (−4.26)*	0.959 (−4.26)*	0.886 (−5.99)*	0.905 (−7.38)*
Karnataka	0.920 (−3.18)*	0.935 (−5.67)*	0.979 (−3.58)*	0.923 (−23.93)*	1.023 (3.01)*	0.960 (−3.65)*	1.004 (0.77)	0.987 (−1.41)
Kerala	0.976 (−1.10)	1.013 (1.46)	1.162 (8.83)*	1.317 (13.07)*	0.935 (−6.21)*	1.008 (0.69)	1.036 (2.59)*	1.145 (9.65)*
Madhya Pradesh	0.992 (−0.59)	0.955 (−8.13)*	(0.927 (−15.66)*	0.895 (−7.96)*	0.957 (−5.02)*	0.976 (−3.32)*	0.905 (−12.27)*	1.048 (19.01)*
Maharashtra	0.982 (−1.26)	1.070 (3.86)*	0.977 (−2.84)*	0.994 (−1.44)	1.066 (9.80)*	1.162 (13.01)*	1.028 (8.51)*	0.938 (−21.12)*
Orissa	1.009 (0.57)	0.989 (−2.16)**	0.953 (−10.50)*	1.070 (5.97)*	0.979 (−1.67)***	0.977 (−2.62)*	0.986 (−2.25)**	1.085 (7.57)*
Punjab	1.106	1.109	1.192	1.120	0.975	1.052	1.029	0.868

(continued)

Table 6.3 (continued)

States	Rural price indices				Urban price indices			
	50th round	55th round	61st round	66th round	50th round	55th round	61st round	66th round
(1)	(2)	(3)	(4)	(5)	(6)	(7)	(8)	(9)
	(4.85)*	(6.37)*	(6.25)*	(3.88)*	(−4.04)*	(4.24)*	(3.36)*	(−4.61)*
Rajasthan	0.915 (−9.53)*	0.891 (−7.54)*	0.942 (−4.36)*	0.853 (−5.48)*	0.953 (−4.04)*	0.934 (−4.96)*	0.924 (−6.09)*	0.904 (−8.36)*
Tamil Nadu	1.047 (7.97)*	1.060 (9.30)*	1.022 (2.54)*	1.080 (7.38)*	1.004 (0.65)	1.026 (4.19)*	1.026 (3.65)*	1.029 (4.30)*
Uttar Pradesh	0.922 (−7.52)*	0.933 (−11.27)*	0.980 (−3.44)*	0.905 (−12.57)*	0.915 (−7.40)*	0.956 (−8.68)*	0.929 (−9.56)*	0.898 (−19.18)*
West Bengal	1.095 (3.11)*	0.938 (−3.49)*	0.955 (−3.98)*	0.924 (−5.39)*	1.184 (8.64)*	0.975 (−4.59)*	0.979 (−4.16)*	1.001 (0.28)
All India	1.000	1.000	1.000	1.000	1.000	1.000	1.000	1.000

Figures in parentheses are the t-statistics for testing significance of ln(PPP), as the estimating equation is Eq. 2.10
$^*p < 0.01$, $^{**}p < 0.05$, $^{***}p < 0.10$ are levels of significance for testing ln(PPP) = 0

Table 6.4 Testing for Statewise variation in prices with respect to all India, S^{State} in various NSS rounds for 15 major States, rural and urban, method is Laspeyres index, 11 Food items (Majumder et al. 2015a)

States	Rural price indices				Urban price indices			
	50th round	55th Round	61st round	66th round	50th round	55th round	61st round	66th round
(1)	(2)	(3)	(4)	(5)	(6)	(7)	(8)	(9)
Andhra Pradesh	1.046 (8.141)*	1.034 (4.635)*	1.078 (1.584)	1.067 (1.91)***	0.980 (−2.269)*	1.020 (0.851)	1.013 (0.308)	1.111 (2.323)*
Assam	1.249 (20.13)*	1.237 (9.599)*	1.100 (4.786)*	1.090 (3.681)*	1.102 (12.98)*	1.155 (5.885)*	1.073 (1.74)***	1.083 (4.092)*
Bihar	1.029 (1.358)	1.041 (1.298)	0.924 (−6.214)*	0.977 (−0.936)	0.972 (−0.789)	0.976 (−0.564)	0.917 (−4.305)*	0.997 (−0.180)
Gujarat	1.081 (11.79)*	1.101 (2.116)*	1.155 (2.494)*	0.960 (−0.867)	1.077 (3.569)*	1.091 (2.843)*	1.119 (2.187)*	1.008 (0.186)
Haryana	0.865 (−20.22)*	0.932 (−3.649)*	0.906 (−2.174)*	0.941 (−2.195)**	0.920 (−6.576)*	0.973 (−1.509)	0.883 (−3.579)*	0.951 (−1.77)***
Karnataka	0.974 (−0.635)	1.065 (2.865)*	1.025 (0.474)	0.959 (−0.701)	0.987 (−0.630)	1.052 (1.833)***	1.090 (1.565)	1.016 (0.246)
Kerala	1.253 (10.29)*	1.289 (22.43)*	1.229 (5.291)*	1.172 (13.71)*	1.056 (13.32)*	1.123 (12.439)*	1.077 (2.758)*	1.015 (0.657)
Madhya Pradesh	0.954 (−1.757)***	0.928 (−1.877)***	0.905 (−3.273)*	0.903 (−3.008)*	0.939 (−3.978)*	0.905 (−2.372)*	0.854 (−5.241)*	0.910 (−2.40)**
Maharashtra	0.995 (−0.129)	1.036 (0.682)	0.989 (−0.557)	1.095 (2.960)*	1.152 (2.703)*	1.116 (2.272)**	1.103 (2.442)**	1.171 (−11.02)*
Orissa	0.982 (−2.560)*	1.013 (0.343)	0.966 (−1.306)	0.916 (−3.743)*	0.922 (−5.622)*	0.950 (−1.599)	0.944 (−2.026)**	0.969 (−1.162)
Punjab	0.911 (−15.03)**	0.891 (−3.605)*	1.137 (3.473)*	1.015 (−16.49)*	0.945 (−5.338)*	0.904 (−4.669)*	1.076 (2.941)*	1.007 (0.112)
Rajasthan	0.884	0.916	0.918	0.962	0.895	0.908	0.894	0.944

(continued)

Table 6.4 (continued)

States	Rural price indices				Urban price indices			
	50th round	55th Round	61st round	66th round	50th round	55th round	61st round	66th round
(1)	(2)	(3)	(4)	(5)	(6)	(7)	(8)	(9)
	(−11.87)*	(−3.027)*	(−2.16)**	(−1.115)	(−7.264)*	(−13.54)*	(−5.367)*	(−0.944)
Tamil Nadu	1.172 (2.919)*	1.075 (1.518)	1.006 (0.185)	1.015 (0.522)	1.046 (3.775)*	1.061 (3.132)*	1.029 (0.763)	0.998 (−0.075)
Uttar Pradesh	0.854 (−12.92)*	0.879 (−3.443)*	0.946 (−1.85)***	0.969 (−0.892)	0.872 (−10.28)*	0.882 (−5.218)*	0.902 (−2.958)*	0.932 (−2.54)**
West Bengal	1.123 (5.571)*	1.136 (5.456)*	1.054 (2.139)**	0.981 (−0.719)	1.035 (2.749)*	1.071 (3.685)*	1.067 (1.547)	1.033 (0.849)
All India	1.000	1.000	1.000	1.000	1.000	1.000	1.000	1.000

Figures in parentheses are the t-statistics given by $\frac{S^{\text{State}}-1}{se(S^{\text{State}})}$

*$p < 0.01$, **$p < 0.05$, ***$p < 0.10$ are levels of significance for testing PPP = 1

(b) These tables contain widespread evidence of spatially different prices in India in each round and in each sector. Clearly, the treatment of India as a single entity in international comparisons of PPP and real expenditure is based on a false premise of spatial homogeneity.

(c) Notwithstanding wide differences in methodology, the qualitative picture on the spatial differences between the States seems remarkably robust between Tables 6.1, 6.2, 6.3 and 6.4, though the quantitative magnitudes do vary. The Rank 3 demand system-based estimated spatial price indices generally show greater variation between States and in the magnitude of their deviation from 1 than the other two procedures. The coefficients of variation (CV) of the different price indices across States are presented in Table 6.5, which corroborates this observation. Clearly, the QAIDS-based estimates show the largest variation. The fact is that, the QAIDS is a Rank 3 system and allows substitution between items in response to price changes. In contrast, among the others, although Tornqvist index allows substitution between items, it is based on a Rank 2 system (see Diewert 1967) and the rest do not allow substitution between items. This points to the usefulness of the Rank 3 demand system-based approach to calculating the 'exact' price indices.

(d) In particular, as observed in Table 6.5, the Laspeyres and Tornqvist spatial price indices pick up only the weakest evidence of spatially different prices. This reflects the fact that these Divisia price indices admit limited (and biased) price-induced substitution effects and overlook their heterogeneity between the various States enforcing a spatial homogeneity that is clearly unrealistic in the federal context of India. Since much of the literature on cross-country comparisons of PPP and real expenditure are based on Divisia price indices, these results have much wider significance that extend beyond the immediate context of India. Note, however, that even in case of these two spatial price indices, the hypothesis of spatial homogeneity is strongly rejected in case of several States (Tables 6.1, 6.2, 6.3 and 6.4).

To test for uniformity of spatial variation across price indices computed using different methods, nonparametric Levene's test was performed pairwise between indices for the different rounds.[8] Table 6.6 presents the results. The eminent features that emerge from the table are: (a) when the two Rank 3 system-based methods (Coondoo et al. and QAIDS based) are compared, except for NSS 50th round, the hypothesis of equality of variation in spatial prices is not rejected; (b) the hypothesis is rejected in all cases when the QAIDS-based index and the Tornqvist index are compared and (c) for the 66th round in the rural sector, the Laspeyres index shows significant difference in variation when compared with all other

[8]As the overall test for equality of variations would not detect the non-homogeneous index, if any, pairwise tests were performed. It may be noted that while the original Levene's test (Levene 1960) of equality of variances based on means is founded on the assumption of symmetric distributions, the nonparametric Levene test, which utilises the *method of ranks* (Nordstokke and Zumbo 2010), avoids the assumption of normality implicit in the analysis of variance.

Table 6.5 Coefficient of variation, CV, % of the different price indices, 11 items across States: NSS 50th–66th rounds, rural and urban (Majumder et al. 2015a)

Indices	CV (rural India)				CV (urban India)			
	50th round	55th round	61st round	66th round	50th round	55th round	61st round	66th round
(1)	(2)	(3)	(4)	(5)	(6)	(7)	(8)	(9)
Coondoo et al. (2011) index	17.3	17.9	20.3	19.7	10.0	11.9	14.3	12.6
QAIDS-based index	26.9	15.1	21.7	26.5	35.5	18.5	15.7	23.4
Tornqvist GEKS index	7.2	7.3	8.1	12.9	10.4	6.5	5.7	11.4
Laspeyres index	12.6	11.6	9.8	7.5	8.2	8.9	9.3	6.9

The coefficient of variation (%) of the PPPs among the following OECD small countries (with are less than 1.5 million kilometres square) during 2009–10 turned out to be 8.8
Countries are Finland, France, Germany, Greece, Ireland, Italy, Luxembourg, Netherlands and Euro Area. Data source: OECD. Stat *Extracts*

indices and in the urban sector this difference is observed with two indices, viz. the QAIDS-based index and the Tornqvist index. While (a) and (b) point to the usefulness of the Rank 3 demand system-based approach to calculating the 'exact' price indices, (c), along with the fact that Laspeyres index shows the minimum CV in the 66th round (Table 6.6), indicates the usefulness of demand system-based approach. Thus, Laspeyres methodology leads to a downward biased estimate of the level of spatial heterogeneity in prices, at least in the 66th round.

The above discussion raises the question: Does the incorporation of spatial prices have any impact on the expenditure comparisons in relation to the nominal expenditures that assume no spatial price differences? Tables 6.7, 6.8, 6.9 and 6.10 provide evidence on this issue by reporting, for each State, the spatial price-deflated real income, the real income being the State income in relation to the all-India income, for NSS rounds 50, 55, 61 and 66, respectively [these comparisons are along the line suggested by Feenstra et al. (2009)]. The quality of the unit value information in NSS round 50 is again reflected in some of the implausible estimates of real expenditure indices reported by the QAIDS-based figures in Table 6.4. These tables show considerable sensitivity of the expenditure indices to (a) the deflation of nominal indices by the spatial price deflator and (b) the spatial price estimation procedure adopted. In case of the latest NSS round available to us, namely NSS round 66, for example, the poorer States of Bihar and Uttar Pradesh do much better on the spatially price-deflated expenditure comparisons than in the nominal real expenditure comparisons that assumes spatial price homogeneity. These tables also show considerable movement in the State rankings over the period spanned by the four large NSS rounds considered in this study.

Further evidence on the sensitivity of the State rankings to the incorporation of regional price differentials via the use of spatial price deflators in the real

Table 6.6 Testing for spatial homogeneity: pairwise nonparametric Levene's test NSS 50th–66th rounds, rural and urban (Majumder et al. 2015a)

Levene's test between	*F*-statistic							
	Rural				Urban			
	50th round	55th round	61st round	66th round	50th round	55th round	61st round	66th round
(1)	(2)	(3)	(4)	(5)	(6)	(7)	(8)	(9)
Coondoo et al. index and Laspeyres index	1.012 (0.323)	1.268 (0.270)	3.192*** (0.085)	5.162** (0.031)	2.953*** (0.097)	0.061 (0.806)	2.053 (0.163)	2.465 (0.128)
Coondoo et al. index and Tornqvist index	11.103* (0.002)	3.876*** (0.059)	9.021* (0.006)	1.070 (0.310)	10.859* (0.003)	1.731 (0.199)	17.617* (0.000)	0.646 (0.428)
Coondoo et al. index and QAIDS index	0.919 (0.346)	0.063 (0.804)	0.101 (0.753)	0.410 (0.527)	13.266* (0.001)	0.001 (1.000)	0.010 (0.920)	2.678 (0.113)
Laspeyres index and Tornqvist index	4.402** (0.045)	1.366 (0.252)	2.356 (0.136)	7.548** (0.010)	1.684 (0.205)	4.821** (0.037)	11.452* (0.002)	3.656*** (0.066)
Laspeyres Index and QAIDS index	2.723 (0.110)	0.709 (0.407)	3.931*** (0.057)	12.007* (0.002)	15.291* (0.001)	2.195 (0.150)	1.712 (0.201)	21.254*** (0.000)
Tornqvist index and QAIDS index	8.607* (0.007)	3.118*** (0.088)	4.876** (0.036)	4.633** (0.040)	16.760* (0.000)	8.235* (0.008)	15.157* (0.001)	5.311** (0.029)

Figures in parentheses are p values

$*p < 0.01$, $**p < 0.05$, $***p < 0.10$ are levels of significance for testing equality of variance

Table 6.7 Statewise real expenditure comparisons[a] for 15 major States of India, rural and urban NSS 50th round, 1993–94, 11 items (Majumder et al. 2015a)

States	Rural real income					Urban real income				
	Nominal	Spatial price deflated				Nominal	Spatial price deflated			
		Coondoo et al. (2011) index	QAIDS	Tornqvist index	Laspeyres index		Coondoo et al. (2011) index	QAIDS	Tornqvist index	Laspeyres index
(1)	(2)	(3)	(4)	(5)	(6)	(7)	(8)	(9)	(10)	(11)
Andhra Pradesh	1.026	1.014	1.288	1.063	0.981	0.892	0.993	1.094	0.870	0.910
Assam	0.917	0.836	1.130	0.788	0.734	1.001	0.897	1.274	0.758	0.908
Bihar	0.776	0.891	0.612	0.796	0.754	0.771	0.880	0.522	0.797	0.793
Gujarat	1.078	0.913	1.900	1.052	0.997	0.992	0.940	1.687	0.999	0.921
Haryana	1.368	1.044	1.017	1.392	1.582	1.035	0.984	1.182	1.080	1.125
Karnataka	0.957	1.034	1.744	1.04	0.983	0.924	1.013	1.078	0.903	0.936
Kerala	1.387	1.027	1.609	1.421	1.107	1.078	0.990	2.399	1.153	1.021
Madhya Pradesh	0.896	0.998	1.011	0.903	0.939	0.891	1.005	0.603	0.931	0.949
Maharashtra	0.969	1.109	1.154	0.987	0.974	1.157	1.054	1.973	1.086	1.004
Orissa	0.781	0.913	0.767	0.774	0.795	0.879	0.946	0.849	0.898	0.953
Punjab	1.539	1.104	1.466	1.391	1.689	1.115	0.989	1.142	1.143	1.180
Rajasthan	1.146	0.991	1.154	1.253	1.296	0.927	0.921	0.767	0.973	1.036
Tamil Nadu	1.043	0.985	1.067	0.997	0.89	0.957	1.031	1.496	0.953	0.915
Uttar Pradesh	0.973	1.087	1.012	1.056	1.139	0.849	0.986	0.652	0.928	0.974
West Bengal	0.991	0.963	0.665	0.905	0.882	1.035	0.944	1.528	0.874	1.000
All India	1.000	1.000	1.000	1.000	1.000	1.000	1.000	1.000	1.000	1.000

[a] Real income (nominal) $= \frac{\text{State per capita expenditure}}{\text{All - India per capita expenditure}}$, Real income (Spatial price deflated) $= \frac{\text{Real income(nominal)}}{S^{\text{State}}}$

Table 6.8 Statewise real expenditure comparisons[a] for 15 major States of India: rural and urban NSS 55th round, 1999–00, 11 items (Majumder et al. 2015a)

States	Rural real income					Urban real income				
	Nominal	Spatial price deflated				Nominal	Spatial price deflated			
		Coondoo et al. (2011) index	QAIDS	Tornqvist index	Laspeyres index		Coondoo et al. (2011) index	QAIDS	Tornqvist index	Laspeyres index
(1)	(2)	(3)	(4)	(5)	(6)	(7)	(8)	(9)	(10)	(11)
Andhra Pradesh	0.933	0.925	1.109	0.953	0.902	0.905	1.034	0.994	0.935	0.887
Assam	0.877	0.813	0.762	0.824	0.709	0.952	0.881	1.746	0.909	0.824
Bihar	0.792	0.852	0.757	0.750	0.761	0.704	0.915	0.571	0.651	0.721
Gujarat	1.134	0.935	1.365	1.274	1.030	1.043	0.971	1.243	1.147	0.956
Haryana	1.469	1.069	1.649	1.620	1.577	1.067	1.044	0.901	1.112	1.096
Karnataka	1.028	0.939	1.151	1.100	0.965	1.066	1.056	1.234	1.111	1.013
Kerala	1.575	1.028	1.538	1.555	1.222	1.091	1.012	1.230	1.083	0.971
Madhya Pradesh	0.826	0.988	0.971	0.865	0.890	0.811	1.017	0.847	0.831	0.896
Maharashtra	1.022	1.003	1.134	0.955	0.986	1.139	1.130	1.217	0.980	1.020
Orissa	0.768	0.908	0.760	0.777	0.758	0.723	0.876	0.736	0.740	0.762
Punjab	1.528	1.131	1.780	1.378	1.715	1.051	1.027	0.905	1.000	1.163
Rajasthan	1.129	0.958	1.757	1.268	1.233	0.931	0.964	1.073	0.997	1.025
Tamil Nadu	1.057	0.964	1.098	0.997	0.984	1.137	1.104	1.252	1.108	1.071
Uttar Pradesh	0.960	1.019	1.065	1.029	1.092	0.807	1.022	0.761	0.844	0.916
West Bengal	0.935	0.849	0.767	0.996	0.823	1.014	0.981	1.318	1.040	0.946
All India	1.000	1.000	1.000	1.000	1.000	1.000	1.000	1.000	1.000	1.000

[a] $\text{Real income (nominal)} = \frac{\text{State per capita expenditure}}{\text{All - India per capita expenditure}}$, $\text{Real income (Spatial price deflated)} = \frac{\text{Real income(nominal)}}{S^{\text{State}}}$

Table 6.9 Statewise real expenditure comparisons[a] for 15 major States of India, rural and urban 61st round, 2004–2005, 11 items (Majumder et al. 2015a)

States	Rural real income					Urban real income				
	Nominal	Spatial price deflated				Nominal	Spatial price deflated			
		Coondoo et al. (2011) index	QAIDS	Tornqvist index	Laspeyres index		Coondoo et al. (2011) index	QAIDS	Tornqvist index	Laspeyres index
(1)	(2)	(3)	(4)	(5)	(6)	(7)	(8)	(9)	(10)	(11)
Andhra Pradesh	1.043	0.954	0.995	1.010	0.967	0.988	1.057	1.070	0.961	0.975
Assam	0.996	0.802	0.615	0.975	0.905	1.023	0.851	0.932	0.979	0.953
Bihar	0.768	0.856	0.684	0.809	0.832	0.660	0.863	0.618	0.694	0.720
Gujarat	1.113	0.988	0.743	1.220	0.964	1.092	0.938	0.747	1.207	0.976
Haryana	1.563	1.125	1.150	1.635	1.725	1.071	1.018	1.259	1.209	1.213
Karnataka	0.937	0.974	1.079	0.958	0.915	1.030	1.045	1.142	1.025	0.945
Kerala	1.780	1.202	1.456	1.532	1.448	1.226	1.118	1.332	1.184	1.138
Madhya Pradesh	0.796	1.049	0.848	0.859	0.880	0.809	1.054	0.958	0.894	0.947
Maharashtra	1.030	1.085	0.884	1.055	1.042	1.112	1.081	0.957	1.082	1.008
Orissa	0.729	0.959	0.664	0.765	0.754	0.715	0.843	0.671	0.725	0.757
Punjab	1.563	1.133	1.260	1.311	1.375	1.182	1.069	1.055	1.148	1.099
Rajasthan	1.033	0.937	1.395	1.096	1.125	0.855	0.947	0.767	0.925	0.957
Tamil Nadu	1.039	0.982	1.285	1.016	1.033	1.056	1.002	1.149	1.029	1.026
Uttar Pradesh	0.931	1.023	0.940	0.950	0.984	0.796	0.947	0.781	0.857	0.883
West Bengal	0.994	0.928	0.860	1.041	0.943	1.049	0.937	0.856	1.072	0.983
All India	1.000	1.000	1.000	1.000	1.000	1.000	1.000	1.000	1.000	1.000

[a]Real income (nominal) $= \frac{\text{State per capita expenditure}}{\text{All - India per capita expenditure}}$, Real income (Spatial price deflated) $= \frac{\text{Real income(nominal)}}{S^{\text{State}}}$

Table 6.10 Statewise real expenditure comparisons[a] for 15 major States of India: rural and urban 66th round, 2009–2010, 11 items (Majumder et al. 2015a)

States	Rural real income					Urban real income				
	Nominal	Spatial price deflated				Nominal	Spatial price deflated			
		Coondoo et al. (2011) index	QAIDS	Tornqvist index	Laspeyres index		Coondoo et al. (2011) index	QAIDS	Tornqvist index	Laspeyres index
(1)	(2)	(3)	(4)	(5)	(6)	(7)	(8)	(9)	(10)	(11)
Andhra Pradesh	1.144	0.985	1.056	0.973	1.072	1.086	0.998	0.913	0.838	0.977
Assam	0.910	0.845	0.936	0.845	0.835	0.864	0.814	0.840	0.799	0.798
Bihar	0.723	0.878	0.757	0.771	0.740	0.591	0.780	0.568	0.646	0.593
Gujarat	1.118	0.979	1.331	1.263	1.164	1.031	0.935	1.085	1.057	1.023
Haryana	1.493	1.042	1.646	1.582	1.587	1.082	1.008	1.199	1.195	1.138
Karnataka	0.932	0.971	1.245	1.009	0.972	1.110	1.066	0.799	1.124	1.092
Kerala	1.850	1.306	1.090	1.404	1.578	1.221	1.095	0.893	1.066	1.203
Madhya Pradesh	0.843	1.035	1.156	0.942	0.933	0.824	1.053	1.094	0.787	0.906
Maharashtra	1.100	1.047	0.937	1.106	1.004	1.213	1.075	0.982	1.293	1.036
Orissa	0.751	0.937	0.729	0.702	0.820	0.791	0.943	0.872	0.729	0.817
Punjab	1.643	1.163	1.504	1.467	1.619	1.116	1.013	1.266	1.285	1.109
Rajasthan	1.086	0.951	1.365	1.274	1.129	0.850	0.875	1.123	0.940	0.900
Tamil Nadu	1.067	1.047	1.213	0.988	1.051	0.967	0.963	0.901	0.940	0.969
Uttar Pradesh	0.873	0.971	1.057	0.964	0.901	0.815	0.942	1.060	0.907	0.874
West Bengal	0.900	0.896	0.612	0.974	0.918	0.970	0.958	0.627	0.969	0.939
All India	1.000	1.000	1.000	1.000	1.000	1.000	1.000	1.000	1.000	1.000

[a]Real income (nominal) $= \frac{\text{State per capita expenditure}}{\text{All - India per capita expenditure}}$, Real income (Spatial price deflated) $= \frac{\text{Real income(nominal)}}{S^{\text{State}}}$

expenditure comparisons, and to the spatial price used in the comparison, is provided in Table 6.11 which reports the Spearman rank correlations between the State rankings in NSS 66th round under alternative spatial price deflators used to capture movements in spatial prices. These also include the case where no deflator is used, namely what has been referred to as 'nominal' in the table. For reasons of space, we have reported only the correlation estimates in the latest round, NSS 66th round, but the picture is not very different in the earlier rounds. The off diagonal elements in the first row and the first column show the sensitivity of the State rankings to the incorporation of spatial prices in comparison with nominal ranking. The use of the spatial price deflators, via application of the Laspeyres index, seems to have the least impact on the nominal State rankings in both rural and urban areas with the correlation magnitudes upwards of 0.9. The State rankings are sensitive to the use of the other spatial price deflators. However, the variation in ranking is much more pronounced in the urban sector than in the rural sector. The overall message from Table 6.11 is that it is not only important to incorporate regional differences in prices and preferences in the expenditure comparisons, but we also need to do so through the use of preference consistent true cost of living indices based on Rank 3 demand systems.

Let us recall that the main difference between the procedures is in the treatment of price-induced substitution effects between the Food items. While the Coondoo et al. (2011) procedure ignores price-induced substitution and concentrates exclusively on the expenditure effects via the Engel curves, those using Divisia indices based on Laspeyres and Tornqvist price indices are limited by the fact that they are

Table 6.11 Rank correlation coefficient (Spearman's Rho) among Statewise, nominal and spatial price-deflated real incomes, NSS 66th round, 2009–10, rural and urban, 11 items (Majumder et al. 2015a)

Rural	Urban				
	Nominal	Deflated by Coondoo et al. index	Deflated by QAIDS index	Deflated by Tornqvist index	Deflated by Laspeyres index
Nominal		0.750**	0.204	0.847**	0.904**
		(0.001)	(0.467)	(0.000)	(0.000)
Deflated by Coondoo et al. index	0.725**		0.207	0.617*	0.793**
	(0.002)		(0.459)	(0.014)	(0.000)
Deflated by QAIDS index	0.607*	0.542*		0.393	0.389
	(0.016)	(0.037)		(0.147)	(0.152)
Deflated by Tornqvist index	0.868**	0.665**	0.771**		0.860**
	(0.000)	(0.007)	(0.001)		(0.000)
Deflated by Laspeyres index	0.932**	0.758**	0.800**	0.929**	
	(0.000)	(0.001)	(0.000)	(0.000)	

Figures in parentheses are p values
*Correlation is significant at the 0.05 level (2-tailed)
**Correlation is significant at the 0.01 level (2-tailed)

evaluated at a fixed 'reference bundle'. The QAIDS-based procedure is the most general since it admits Rank 3 demand systems and allows realistic substitution possibilities though none above Rank 3 preferences. Hence, on long time series data, the QAIDS-based procedure will be preferable, but on datasets covering limited time period but where the cross-sectional variation is much larger, and price information is scarce, the Coondoo et al. (2011) is possibly a better procedure to employ.

The State rankings and changes in the rankings are brought out clearly by the Hasse diagrams for the different rounds presented in Fig. 6.1a (rural) and Fig. 6.1b (urban). The diagrams are based on the *W* matrix (constructed from Laspeyres index) and the rule suggested by Sen (1976) on how to rank the States using the values of the distribution-sensitive mean expenditure of a State evaluated at all the States' prices, including its own prices. The Hasse diagram provides a clear representation of 210 pairwise comparisons of the States' welfare levels, 'with a downward path indicating superiority in the standard of welfare' (Sen 1976) under the assumption that all States have the same welfare function. A comparison of Fig. 3 of Sen (1976) with Fig. 6.1a of our paper brings out several similarities and some sharp differences. Kerala was ranked near the bottom in Sen's rankings based on NSS rounds 16 (1960–61) and 17 (1961–62), but it has moved up sharply to be at or near the top in Fig. 6.1a in this paper. Punjab has slipped slightly from its pre-eminent position in Sen's study, with its top ranking taken by Haryana which was carved out of the erstwhile State of Punjab. Figure 6.1a, b in our paper reveals several cases of changes in State rankings over the period spanned by the four NSS surveys. They also reveal several rural urban differences in the Hasse pictures. For example, in 61st round, rural Punjab is ranked quite highly among the rural States, but slips down several steps in the corresponding urban rankings. Overall, however, there are no major changes in the rankings over the period, 1993/94–2009/10, though the structure of the Hasse pictures has changed during this period.

Though the Hasse diagrams provide vivid representations of the State rankings, they do not constitute a formal test of pairwise differences between the alternative price situations. Such a test of differences is provided by the Mantel test, described earlier, which is based on the symmetric distance matrix consisting of pairwise distances between the States' spatially corrected welfare values using Sen (1976)'s welfare function. Table 6.12 provides the results of the Mantel (1967) test of the hypothesis of no correlation between the rural and urban distance matrices. This table provides the Mantel test statistic in all four rounds. The values of the test statistic lead to a decisive rejection of the hypothesis. The message is intuitively clear —Food being an item of necessity, there is greater closeness between the welfare distances between States in the rural and urban areas based on Food items only than the one that would be based on Food and non-Food items. This is because prices and preferences vary much more in case of non-Food items than Food items. In other words, the rural–urban differences in the welfare-based State rankings in India, with some States moving ahead of the others during this period of economic reforms and beyond, possibly shows up mainly in the expenditure on non-Food items.

(a)

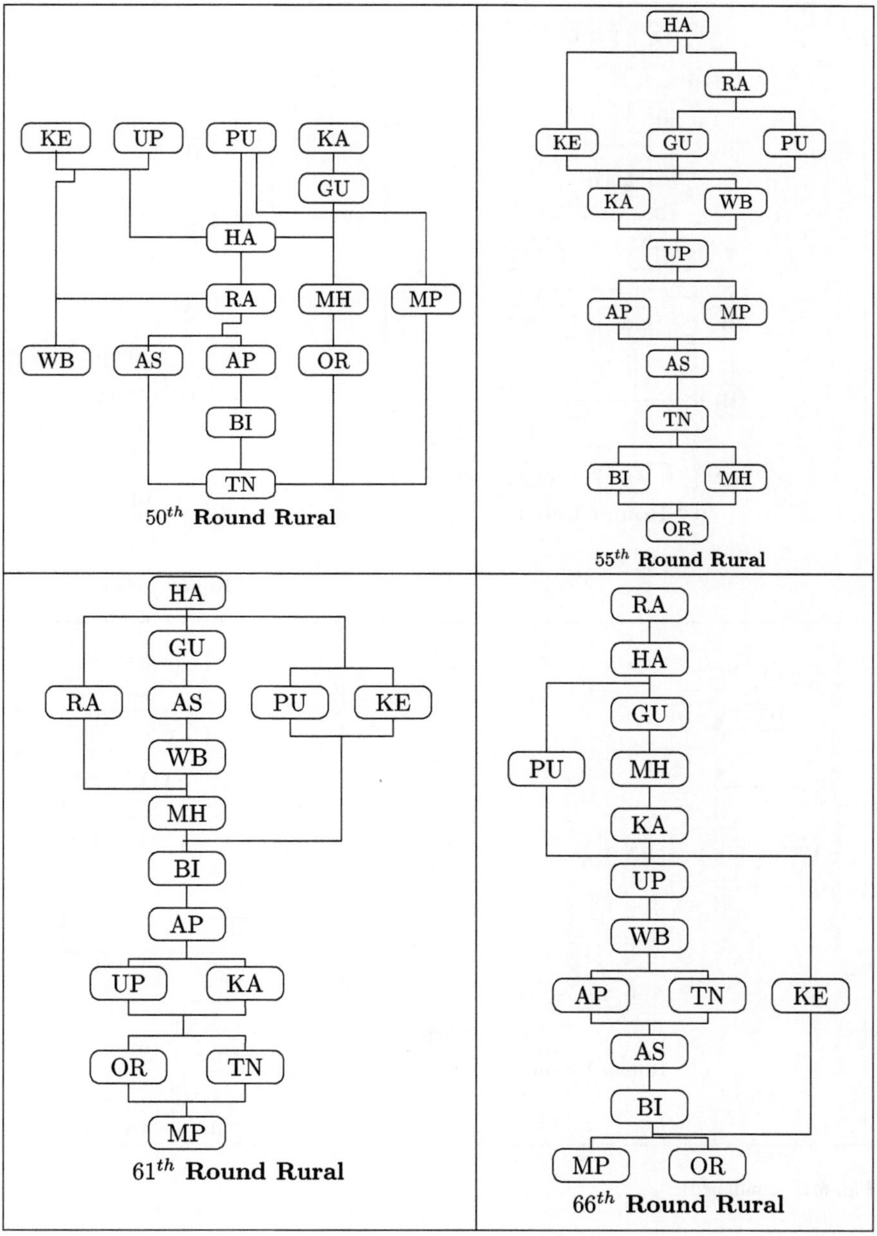

Fig. 6.1 **a** Hasse diagrams for various NSS rounds (State names have been abbreviated in these diagrams), rural India. **b** Hasse diagrams for various NSS rounds (State names have been abbreviated in these diagrams), urban India. Reproduced from Majumder et al. (2015a)

(b)

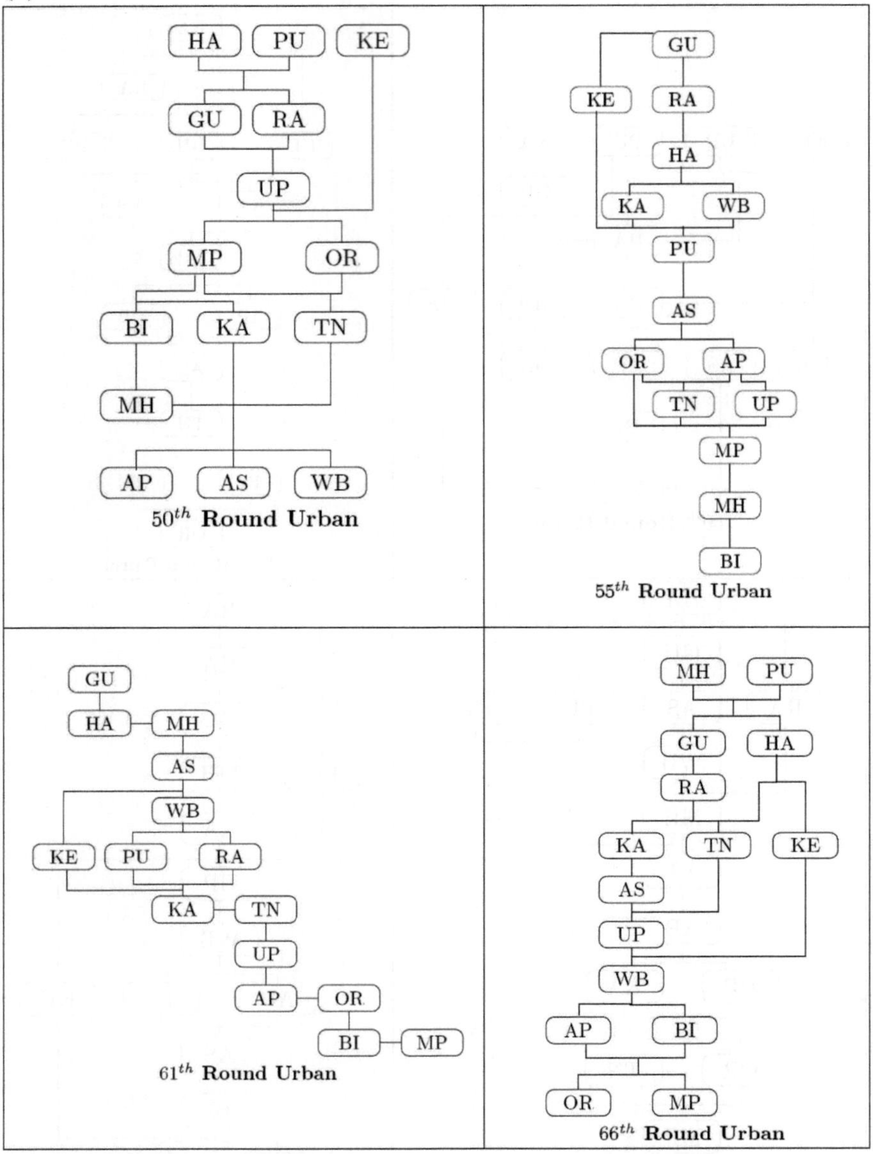

Fig. 6.1 (continued)

Table 6.12 Mantel test of no association between distances in States' welfare levels in rural and urban areas (Majumder et al. 2015a)

Spatial analysis			
	Rural versus urban	Mantel stat(r)[a]	Significance
11 Food items	NSS 50th round	0.8956*	< 0.001
	NSS 55th round	0.8482*	< 0.001
	NSS 61st round	0.8864*	< 0.001
	NSS 66th round	0.9235*	< 0.001

[a]Mantel statistic based on Pearson's product moment correlation. Estimates based on 1000 permutations
*Statistically significant at 1% level of significance

6.3 Preferences, Spatial Prices and Inequality[9]

6.3.1 Introduction

Chakrabarty et al. (2015) examine the effect of prices on inequality in the heterogeneous country context of rural India during the period of economic reforms and beyond (1999/2000–2009/2010). It proposes a framework for calculating 'exact' price indices, based on the recent 'Exact Affine Stone Index' (EASI) demand system proposed by Lewbel and Pendakur (2009), and shows its usefulness by calculating spatial prices and regionally varying temporal prices that allow for both differences in preferences between States and over time. The study finds that the nature of inflation has been regressive during the first half (1999/2000–2004/2005) and progressive during the second half (2004/5–2009/2010) and the effects of temporal price inflation and spatial prices on inequality are qualitatively different. The study of the behaviour of inequality as a country develops and experiences high growth rates is important, given that rising inequality may lead to increasing marginalisation even while the poverty rates may have declined.

The 'true cost of living index' (TCLI), or the 'exact price index', is the ratio of the expenditures for attaining the same utility level, u^*, in two price situations, $\boldsymbol{p}_1$ and $\boldsymbol{p}_0$. Denoting the former as the price vector in situation '1', and the latter as the base price vector (situation '0'), the TCLI for EASI is, in logarithmic form, given by

$$\ln P(\boldsymbol{p}_1, \boldsymbol{p}_0, u*) = \sum_{j=1}^{J} w_0^j \left(\ln p_1^j - \ln p_0^j\right) + \frac{1}{2}\sum_{j=1}^{J}\sum_{k=1}^{J} \alpha^{jk}\left(\ln p_1^j - \ln p_0^j\right)\left(\ln p_1^k - \ln p_0^k\right) \tag{6.1}$$

[9]The material in this section is based on Chakrabarty et al. (2015).

The expression on the right-hand side of Eq. 6.1 allows the calculation of both spatial and temporal prices. In case of the former, we use the median household in the distribution of households over the whole of India in a particular survey as the reference household and calculate the Statewise price indices with respect to that of the whole country normalised at one. In case of the temporal TCLI, Chakrabarty et al. (2015) use the median household in the base year as the reference household. Even in the temporal case, we keep the spatial element in mind in calculating the temporal TCLI, State by State and for all India. In the temporal case, they also calculate the TCLI s in each time period by quartiles, by taking the median household in the four quartiles in the base year as the reference household. This allows us to examine the inflation over the period; 1999/2000–2009/2010; by quartiles. In using the quartile-specific TCLI as the price deflator to convert a household's expenditure from nominal to real expenditures, we open up a divergence between nominal and real expenditure inequalities. The sign of the difference between nominal and real expenditure inequalities tells us the distributive impact of the inflation over the period considered, with a positive sign indicating that the nature of price increase has been progressive, and regressive, otherwise.

Chakrabarty et al. (2015) use the detailed rural information on household purchases of Food and non-Food items in both quantity and value terms, along with that on household size, composition and household type, contained in the unit records from the 55th (July, 1999–June, 2000), 61st (July, 2004–June, 2005), and 66th (July, 2009–June, 2010) rounds, which are the three recent rounds of India's National Sample Surveys. The study focusses on rural sector only because in India, the majority of households (about 70%) live in rural areas. Table 6.13 presents the temporal 'exact' price indices for each State and for all India in NSS Rounds 66 and 61 with respect to NSS round 55 as the base year. Table 6.13 shows that in both cases, the second half (2004/5–2009/10) witnessed a much larger increase in prices than the first half (1999/2000–2004/5) of the decade. The similarity between the qualitative pictures painted by the NSS, 10 items based 'exact' indices and the official cost of living estimates, evident from Table 6.13, confirms that the prices of the excluded items have not moved that differently from those of the included items to have large distributional implications that could question the robustness of the principal welfare conclusions of this study. Table 6.13 also underlines the spatial dimension in the price increases by recording considerable variation between the principal States in their temporal price inflation. As inflation accelerated sharply from the first half to the second half of the decade, so did the spatial dispersion in the temporal price indices between the States. By the end of the decade, a wide gulf had opened up with, for example, Punjab recording almost a doubling of prices over the period in contrast to Kerala which recorded a much lower rate of inflation. The lack of a robust picture on inflation, that holds for all the States in India, and some of the differences are quite noticeable, points to the need to investigate the spatial dimension in the context of a large federal country with heterogeneous preferences and affluence such as India to a much greater extent than has been done before.

Table 6.13 State-specific and all-India temporal price indices, rural sector base, NSS 55th round (Chakrabarty et al. 2015)

State	'Exact' indices			Official estimates[a]			
	NSS rounds			2004–2005		2009–2010	
	55th	61st	66th	CPIAL	CPIRL	CPIAL	CPIRL
Andhra Pradesh	1.000	1.092	2.010	1.126	1.123	1.741	1.730
Assam	1.000	1.049	1.616	1.078	1.084	1.615	1.632
Bihar	1.000	1.056	1.727	1.149	1.148	1.773	1.761
Gujarat	1.000	1.071	1.703	1.115	1.114	1.713	1.708
Haryana	1.000	1.125	1.862	1.147	1.150	1.879	1.857
Karnataka	1.000	1.036	1.631	1.126	1.118	1.772	1.757
Kerala	1.000	1.058	1.545	1.093	1.086	1.545	1.549
Madhya Pradesh	1.000	1.034	1.718	1.065	1.073	1.694	1.700
Maharashtra	1.000	1.072	1.844	1.155	1.155	1.855	1.838
Orissa	1.000	1.011	1.666	1.053	1.053	1.628	1.632
Punjab	1.000	1.098	1.975	1.123	1.122	1.854	1.828
Rajasthan	1.000	1.021	1.665	1.113	1.106	1.842	1.817
Tamil Nadu	1.000	1.070	1.888	1.161	1.164	1.719	1.702
Uttar Pradesh	1.000	1.097	1.755	1.140	1.142	1.777	1.756
West Bengal	1.000	1.062	1.671	1.140	1.147	1.726	1.727
Coefficient of variation (%)	–	2.84	7.48	2.97	2.96	5.51	4.91
All India (rural)	1.000	1.076	1.790	1.125	1.124	1.743	1.729

[a]These were calculated from the published figures of CPIAL and CPIRL for the years corresponding to the three NSS rounds with 1986–87 as base. The figures in this table were obtained by dividing the 2004–2005 and 2009–2010 figures by the 1999–2000 figures for each State and all India

Table 6.14 presents the Gini measure of the nominal and real expenditure inequalities (household level) both by State and for each time period. In this table, the nominal inequality refers to the case where all the households within a State face the same price, while real inequality refers to the case where we allow the prices to differ between households by quartiles. Note that the two sets of inequalities are equal in the base year, 1999/2000. The following features are worth noting. First, there is considerable variation in the magnitude of the inequalities between States. This is true of both nominal and real expenditure inequalities. Second, while in most States, the inequalities were static or even recorded a decline during 1999/2000–2004/5, there was a sharp increase in inequality, in both nominal and real terms, in most States during the second half, 2004/5–2009/10. The increase in inequality was particularly large in case of Kerala and Punjab making them two of the most unequal States in India at the end of our sample period. While the sharp increase in case of Kerala is possibly due to the increased inflow of remittances from the gulf that favoured some households over others, the inequality increase in Punjab reflects the gain for the large farmers that benefitted from growth enhancing

Table 6.14 State-specific spatial price indices with respect to all India, 66th round, rural sector (Chakrabarty et al. 2015)

State	(Set 1) evaluated using EASI parameters estimated at all-India level		(Set 2) evaluated using EASI parameters estimated at State level	
	Cox and Wohlgenant, Hoang unit value	Deaton unit value	Cox and Wohlgenant, Hoang unit value	Deaton unit value
Andhra Pradesh	1.389	1.354	1.215	1.163
Assam	1.179	1.197	1.098	1.109
Bihar	0.881	0.915	0.926	0.957
Chhattisgarh	1.032	1.029	1.021	1.004
Gujarat	0.979	0.989	1.001	1.021
Haryana	0.847	0.857	0.911	0.957
Jharkhand	0.934	0.983	0.960	0.983
Karnataka	0.991	1.014	0.993	0.976
Kerala	1.384	1.272	1.198	1.136
Madhya Pradesh	0.789	0.828	0.874	0.910
Maharashtra	1.025	1.041	1.022	1.037
Orissa	0.884	0.877	0.932	0.909
Punjab	0.859	0.867	0.925	0.954
Rajasthan	0.776	0.783	0.866	0.881
Tamil Nadu	1.351	1.297	1.190	1.127
Uttar Pradesh	0.731	0.767	0.834	0.872
Uttaranchal	0.918	0.926	0.955	0.957
West Bengal	1.037	1.055	1.024	0.999
All India (rural)	1.000	1.000	1.000	1.000
Coefficient of variation	0.2129	0.1839	0.1201	0.0921

reforms and the large subsidy to diesel and fertilisers. The increase in inequality in nearly all the States during the period, 2004/5–2009/10, is reflected in the sharp increase in inequality recorded by the all-India figures in both nominal and real terms. Third, neither the magnitude nor the direction of change in inequality over the two subperiods is identical for all the States nor is it robust between nominal and real expenditure inequality. For example, in Gujarat, while nominal inequality increased sharply during the period between NSS rounds 61 and 66, real expenditure inequality declined. In Haryana, while there was a sharp increase in nominal inequality over this subperiod, real expenditure inequality remained unchanged.

Note, however, that the qualitative result on the sharp increase in nominal expenditure inequality between rounds 61 and 66 is generally robust between States. Table 6.15 contains evidence on the distributive impact of inflation. If the

Table 6.15 State-specific and all-India Gini coefficients, nominal and temporal price-deflated, rural sector (Chakrabarty et al. 2015)

State	Gini coefficient (nominal)[a]	Gini coefficient: temporal price deflated (with respect to 55th round)			
		Within a State all households face the same price (nominal)		Within a State all households within a quartile face the same price (real)	
	55th round	61st round	66th round	61st round	66th round
Andhra Pradesh	0.226	0.204	0.265	0.202	0.250
Assam	0.189	0.141	0.232	0.128	0.219
Bihar	0.192	0.175	0.227	0.167	0.226
Gujarat	0.221	0.204	0.256	0.240	0.221
Haryana	0.243	0.232	0.287	0.260	0.260
Karnataka	0.228	0.195	0.252	0.192	0.221
Kerala	0.283	0.249	0.351	0.256	0.341
Madhya Pradesh	0.222	0.211	0.305	0.225	0.318
Maharashtra	0.240	0.207	0.246	0.214	0.235
Orissa	0.205	0.193	0.267	0.190	0.253
Punjab	0.221	0.205	0.313	0.179	0.258
Rajasthan	0.222	0.205	0.272	0.233	0.275
Tamil Nadu	0.264	0.204	0.290	0.213	0.273
Uttar Pradesh	0.232	0.211	0.253	0.226	0.253
West Bengal	0.202	0.187	0.232	0.174	0.233
All India (rural)	0.222	0.215	0.290	0.235	0.288

[a]The 'nominal' and 'temporal price-deflated' Gini coefficients are the same for the 55th round

real expenditure inequality exceeds nominal expenditure inequality, then it indicates that the relative price changes have been regressive and progressive otherwise. A comparison of the two sets of inequalities suggests that, along with the magnitude, the nature of inflation has changed between the two subperiods. The price inflation was regressive in several States during the first subperiod (1999/2000–2004/5), and this is reflected in the real expenditure inequality (0.235) exceeding the nominal inequality (0.215) in round 61 at the All India level. However, during the second subperiod, (2004/5–2009/10), with items such as Fuel, Clothing and Footwear recording much greater price increases than most of the Food items, the inflation has tended to moderate the increase in inequality via the change in relative prices. This is reflected in the fact that, in most States, the nominal expenditure inequality exceeds the real expenditure inequality in round 66, often by large margins. Note, however, that the progressive nature of the relative price changes during the subperiod, 2004/5–2009/10, only helped to slow down the inequality increase, not reverse it. At the all-India level, while the nominal inequality increased quite sharply from 0.215 in round 61 to 0.290 in round 66, the real expenditure inequality also recorded a large increase, from 0.235 to 0.288, though less in proportionate terms than the increase in nominal expenditure inequality. It is important to recognise that the second half of our sample period, which saw a sharp rise in inflation, was also associated with a sharp increase in inequality. This brings into focus the relationship between inflation and inequality, an issue we turn to in the following section.

6.3.2 The Effect of Inflation on Inequality

The above discussion suggests that high inflation is associated with a sharp increase in inequality. Inflation can worsen inequality in principally two ways: first, those at the lower end of the distribution, namely those on fixed income and the unemployed will see a slower increase in their purchasing power, if at all, in relation to those at the upper end whose earnings, mainly business income and indexed salaries, will increase with inflation; second, the less affluent households have limited substitution possibilities in relation to the more affluent households. This raises the question: what is the estimate of the elasticity of inequality with respect to prices and to the State of development? Surprisingly, there is hardly any evidence in the literature on this issue, though there is considerable evidence on the elasticity of poverty with respect to growth and prices [see, e.g. Ravallion and Datt (2002)]. To answer this question, Chakrabarty et al. (2015) created a State-level panel from the three rounds of the National Sample Surveys that have been used in this study (NSS Rounds 55, 61 and 66), and ran panel regressions with the State-level nominal and real expenditure inequality as the dependent variables.

Besides the measures of temporal and spatial prices, we tried several other State-level variables as determinants, most of which proved insignificant. All the variables were estimated in log form, so that the coefficients are readily interpreted as elasticities. Several variants of the models were estimated by using various combinations of the State-level variables. The final model that emerged is,

$$\begin{aligned} \ln G_{it} = \alpha + \beta^{\text{NFP}} \ln \text{NFP}_{it} + \beta^{\text{GOV}} \ln \text{GOV}_{it} + \beta^{TI} \ln \text{TI}_{it} \\ + \beta^{\text{SI}} \ln \text{SI}_{it} + \eta_i + \varepsilon_{it}, \end{aligned} \tag{6.2}$$

where G denotes Gini coefficient (nominal/real), NFP is the real non-farm output per capita, GOV is the (real) State development expenditure per capita, TI is the temporal index, SI is the spatial index, i stands for States, t stands for time points, and η_i is the State-specific (fixed/random) effect. The F-tests rejected pooled regression and, based on Hausman test statistic, the most efficient models (panel fixed model/ panel random model) were arrived at. The results are presented in Tables 6.16 and 6.17, with the left column in each table showing the estimated

Table 6.16 Panel regressions for Statewise overall Gini coefficients, nominal and temporal price-deflated, rural sector preferences assumed identical for all States (Chakrabarty et al. 2015)

Explanatory variables (measured in logarithms)	Dependent variable: log (Gini coefficient)	
	Within a State, all households face the same price (nominal)	Within a State, all households within a quartile face the same price
	(Fixed effects model)[a]	(Random effects model)[a]
Real non-farm output per person (NFP)	−0.111 (0.386)	0.213 (0.033)**
Real per capita State development expenditure (GOVT)	−0.110 (0.073)***	−0.206 (0.001)*
Temporal index (TI) (from Table 6.5)	0.690 (0.000)*	0.451 (0.000)*
Spatial index (SI) (from Table 6.4: set 1)	−0.293 (0.015)**	−0.204 (0.099)***
Constant	0.279 (0.747)	-2.170 (0.001)*
Likelihood ratio (LR) test: (χ_4^2)	94.66 (0.000)*	28.28 (0.000)*
Hausman test statistic: (χ_4^2)	9.74 (0.045)**	2.84 (0.585)

Figures in parentheses are the p values ($^*p < 0.01$, $^{**}p < 0.05$, $^{***}p < 0.10$ are level of significance)

[a]Among several other variants, including pooled regression, that were tried out, these turned out to be the most efficient models for the respective cases

coefficients in the panel regression of nominal inequality, the right column showing that for real expenditure inequality. Table 6.16 reports the results based on the first set of spatial prices, reported under Set 1 in Table 6.4 (columns 2–4), i.e. spatial indices evaluated using EASI parameters estimated on pooled all-India data. Table 6.17 is based on the second set of spatial prices, which are evaluated using parameters of State-specific EASI demand system.

The model adequacies are evident from the LR tests. In Table 6.16, the Hausman test statistic is consistent with the fact that in case of nominal inequality, the State dummies include several State-specific unobserved characteristics which may be correlated with the other State-specific variables, in particular the spatial indices, as the dependent variable is unadjusted for any State-specific variation. On the other hand, in case of real expenditure inequality, the State-to-State variations due to price changes have been incorporated in forming the LHS variable. Hence, the remaining impact of the State is purely random and uncorrelated with the included State-specific other variables in the regression. In contrast, in Table 6.17, both turn out to be random effects models and the difference in the nominal inequality model is due to introduction of State-specific preference consistent spatial price indices. The implication is clear. While the spatial indices in Table 6.16 contain State-specific variation only in prices, those in Table 6.17 contain variation in both prices and

Table 6.17 Panel regressions for Statewise overall Gini coefficients, nominal and temporal price-deflated, rural sector, preferences allowed to vary between States (Chakrabarty et al. 2015)

Explanatory variables (measured in logarithms)	Dependent variable: log (Gini coefficient)	
	Within a State, all households face the same price (nominal)	Within a State, all households within a quartile face the same price
	(Random effects model)[b]	(Random effects model)[b]
Real non-farm output per person (NFP)	0.191 (0.024)**	0.190 (0.054)***
Real per capita State development expenditure (GOVT)	−0.221 (0.000)*	−0.193 (0.001)*
Temporal index (TI) (from Table 6.5)	0.609 (0.000)*	0.446 (0.000)*
Spatial index (SI) (from Table 6.4: set 2)	−0.067 (0.579)	−0.166 (0.324)
Constant	−1.857 (0.001)*	−2.033 (0.002)*
Likelihood ratio (LR) test: (χ_4^2)	54.11 (0.000)*	26.57 (0.000)*
Hausman test statistic: (χ_4^2)	3.07 (0.546)	7.48 (0.112)

Figures in parentheses are the p values (*$p < 0.01$, **$p < 0.05$, ***$p < 0.10$ are level of significance

[b]Among several other variants, including pooled regression, that were tried out, these turned out to be the most efficient models for the respective cases

preferences. The remaining impact of the States in the latter case thus becomes purely random and hence the model becomes a random effects model.

To focus our attention, the tables report the estimated coefficients of the principal variables of interest in this study, namely the temporal and spatial price indices and two measures, of development, real non-farm output per person (NFP) and real per capita State development expenditure (GOVT). These tables allow interesting comparisons between the principal determinants of nominal and real expenditure inequality, and neither the magnitude nor the sign are always the same for the estimated coefficients in the panel regressions of the two inequality measures. In Table 6.15, non-farm output has no effect on nominal inequality, but has a significantly positive effect on real expenditure inequality. A plausible explanation is as follows. Since the rural sector is dominated by agriculture, an increase in non-farm output shifts the income (in real terms, as here the inequality is based on quartilewise price-deflated expenditures as opposed to the case with nominal inequality) towards that section of people, engaged in non-agricultural activities, who are generally rich and this increases inequality. Real per capita development expenditure reduces both nominal and real inequality, with the effect much greater in both size and significance for real than for nominal inequality. The elasticity estimates of −0.11 (nominal) and −0.21 (real) suggest that, ceteris paribus, with a doubling of rural development expenditure, there will be a 11% reduction in nominal inequality, and a 21% reduction in real expenditure inequality. The benefits of rural development spending are mainly felt by the less affluent households and the elasticity estimates point to a significant role that rural development schemes can play in moderating inequality increases in a period of high growth.

Of particular interest are the price elasticities of inequality, and here we distinguish between temporal and spatial prices. The temporal price elasticity is positive and highly significant in both cases, with an estimate of 0.690 for nominal inequality, and 0.451 for real inequality. A ceteris paribus doubling of temporal prices will increase nominal inequality by 69% and will increase real inequality by 45%. The lower elasticity of the latter is consistent with the results discussed in the previous section that suggested that during the period of high inflation in India that marked the second half, 2004/5–2009/10, the progressive nature of the relative price changes tended to moderate the inequality increase that is taken into account in the measure of real expenditure inequality, but not nominal expenditure inequality. Both the elasticity estimates do agree, however, that inflation has a large adverse impact on expenditure distribution. In contrast to temporal inflation, spatial prices have a negative impact on inequality which suggests that the more expensive States are associated with lower inequality. The magnitude and size of significance is larger in case of nominal inequality than for real inequality. Note, however, that spatial prices have a weaker effect than temporal prices on both measures of inequality. Table 6.17 shows a slightly different picture. Here non-farm output has significantly positive effect on both nominal real expenditure inequalities. Real per capita development expenditure reduces both nominal and real inequality, with the effect greater in both size and significance for nominal than for real inequality, with elasticity estimates of −0.22 (nominal) and −0.19 (real). While the temporal price elasticity is positive and highly significant in both cases, as in the previous case, with an estimate of 0.609 for nominal inequality, and 0.446 for real inequality, the spatial indices turn out to be negative and non-significant. One common feature of the two tables is that most of the State-specific variation in inequality is captured through the State-specific temporal price indices.

6.4 Sensitivity of Spatial Prices to Estimation Method and Choice of Commodities

Further evidence on spatial prices in India is provided in Majumder and Ray (2017). The material in this section draws heavily on that paper. This paper provides Indian evidence on subnational PPPs that point to considerable spatial price heterogeneity within the country, based on Indian National Sample Survey (NSS) data. The prices of various commodities have been generated from the household-specific unit values obtained from the information on expenditures and quantities from the NSS unit records. This paper shows that the CPD model, proposed in the cross-country context, can be adapted to the household context to estimate spatial prices in the intra-country context. As discussed earlier in this volume, the proposed CPD-based model is shown to be formally equivalent to certain well-known fixed-weight price indices under certain parametric configurations. The empirical contribution includes a systematic comparison between the spatial price indices from alternative models, namely the CPD- and utility-based models, and the result that the utility-based methods point to a much greater extent of spatial price heterogeneity than is suggested by the CPD-type models.

The results also record the sensitivity of the spatial price indices to the choice of commodities in the utility-based approach. The pairwise comparison of estimates suggests that commodity selection may be more important than model selection in its impact on the spatial price estimates, though the latter is important as well. The study provides estimates of rural–urban differentials in spatial price indices that suggest some interesting differences between the constituent States. The results make a strong case for further research on the topic of subnational PPPs in the context of large heterogeneous countries. Two significant characteristics in the literature on the measurement of prices provide a background to Majumder and Ray (2017). First, the measurement of spatial variation in prices within a country has generally proceeded separately from that of the temporal movements in prices in the country as a whole. Second, all countries (large and small) are treated as single entities with little recognition in exercises such as the ICP that the spatial price differences within a large heterogeneous country may be larger than that between smaller countries. In case of a long time period, the spatial and temporal aspects will interact to record large regional differences in inflation over time. Nowhere is this truer than in case of India where the differences between the constituent States of the Indian union are often larger than that between, say, the countries in the European Union. There was an early recognition of the interaction between the spatial and temporal aspects of price movements in India in the studies by Bhattacharya et al. (1980, 1988) and Coondoo and Saha (1990).

While the literature on price inflation has generally concentrated on temporal inflation, there is now mounting evidence on spatial variation of prices within a country. Examples include Aten and Menezes (2002) on Brazil, De Carli (2010) on Italy, Dikhanov et al. (2011) on Philippines, Majumder et al. (2012, 2015a) on India, Majumder et al. (2015b) on Vietnam and Mishra and Ray (2014) on Australia. Biggeri et al. (2008, 2010) contain proposals and procedures for estimating spatial prices, also known as subnational PPPs. Majumder and Ray (2017) add to this literature by presenting evidence for India and on the sensitivity of the estimated spatial prices to models and included commodities. This study also reports tests of homogeneity of spatial price indices between the rural and urban areas in each of the major States in India. While there is now a significant empirical literature on rural–urban differentials in prices, this paper marks a departure by providing evidence on the robustness of the estimated rural–urban differentials in the spatial price indices.

Since the principal models used in Majumder and Ray (2017) have been described earlier, we proceed to report and discuss the principal empirical results of this study. This study uses the detailed information on household purchases of Food and non-Food items in both quantity and value terms, along with that on household size, composition and household type, contained in the unit records from the 55th (July, 1999–June, 2000), 61st (July, 2004–June, 2005) and 66th (July, 2009–June, 2010) rounds of the National Sample Survey (NSS) . Since NSS goes way back in time, one can do this exercise over many years. This study focusses on the three large rounds, 55th (1999–2000), 61st (2004–2005) and 66th (2009–2010) to keep the calculations manageable and to ensure consistency in the definitions of variables between surveys. Note that only the commodities, for which unit values can be calculated, have been included in this study. The commodity groupings considered here are at a higher level of aggregation than that corresponding to Basic Headings in the computation of PPPs in the International Comparison Program. This commodity list excludes commodities such as housing, transportation and a number of durables, but the included commodities constitute approximately 63–65% of the per capita total expenditure for the two lower quartile groups and 50–60% for the two upper quartile groups for all rounds considered in Majumder and Ray (2017).

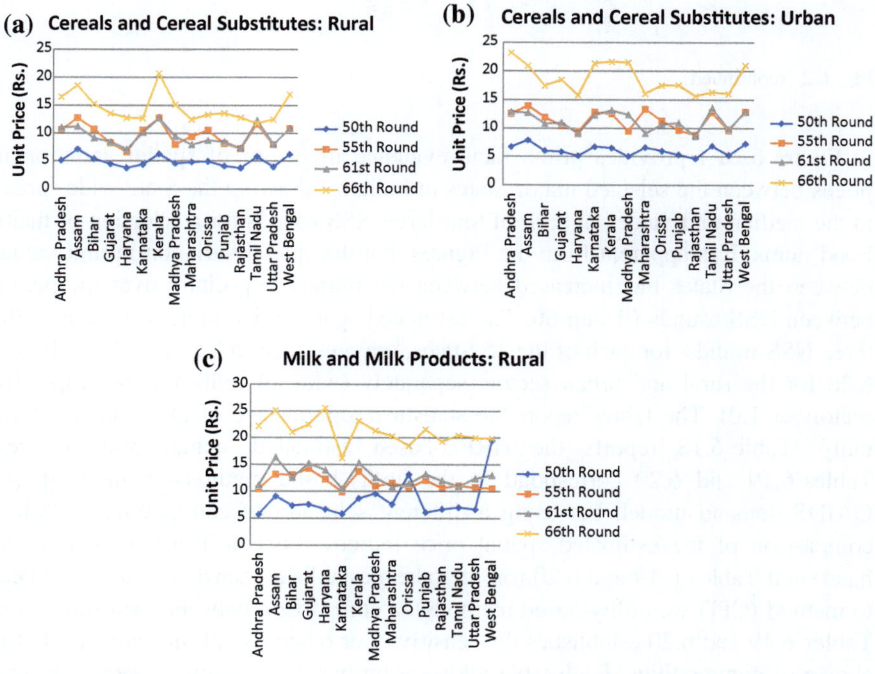

Fig. 6.2 **a** Levels of Statewise unit values of cereals and cereals substitutes, rural over the NSS rounds. **b** Levels of Statewise unit values of cereals and cereals substitutes, urban over the NSS rounds. **c** Levels of Statewise unit values of milk and milk products, rural over the NSS rounds. **d** Levels of Statewise unit values of milk and milk products, urban over the NSS rounds. **e** Levels of Statewise unit values of vegetables, rural over the NSS rounds. **f** Levels of Statewise unit values of vegetables, urban over the NSS rounds. Reproduced from Majumder et al. (2015a)

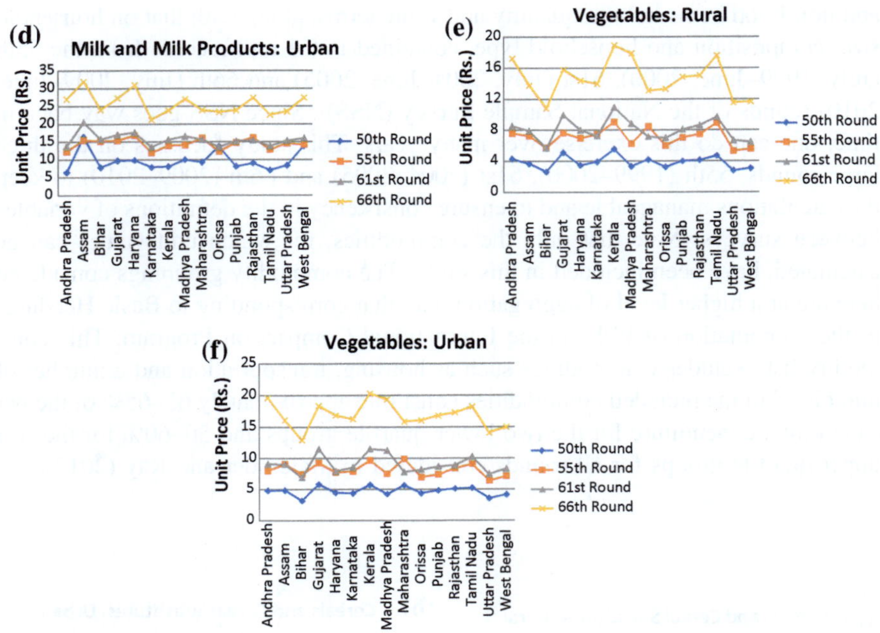

Fig. 6.2 (continued)

Figure 6.2a–f provides prima facie evidence in favour of spatial variation in prices between the selected major States in India by showing the State-wide spread in the median unit values in each of four large NSS rounds for a selection of major Food items. It is apparent from the Figures that the spatial variation in unit values between the States has increased between the rounds, especially over the period between NSS rounds 61 and 66. The estimated spatial price indices in each of the three NSS rounds, for each of the 15 States, are presented in Tables 6.18, 6.19 and 6.20 for the rural and urban sectors separately (with all India for the respective sectors at 1.0). The tables report the statistical significance of the estimates from unity. Table 6.18 reports the HRPD-based estimated spatial price indices, Tables 6.19 and 6.20 correspond to the utility-based methods, both using the QAIDS demand model, but using a different selection of commodities. While a comparison of the estimated spatial price indices between Tables 6.18 (on one hand) and Tables 6.19 and 6.20 (on the other) establishes sensitivity of the indices to method (CPD vs. utility-based methods), a comparison between the estimates in Tables 6.19 and 6.20 establishes the sensitivity or otherwise of the estimates to the choice of commodities. Each table allows a further comparison between the rural and urban spatial price indices. There is now a fair amount of empirical evidence, though by no means unanimous, on the rural–urban differential in prices, as summarised, for example, in Hill and Syed (2015), but there is hardly any evidence on rural–urban differential in spatial price indices. In interpreting the estimates in

Table 6.18 Estimates of spatial price indices, the HRPD model, 55th–66th rounds, 13 commodities (Majumder and Ray 2017)

State	Rural			Urban		
	55th round	61st round	66th round	55th round	61st round	66th round
	1999–2000	2004–2005	2009–2010	1999–2000	2004–2005	2009–2010
AP	1.026 (0.385)	1.047 (0.756)	1.077 (0.926)	0.998 (−0.043)	1.008 (0.169)	1.071 (1.086)
AS	1.156** (2.324)	1.153* (1.926)	1.126 (1.387)	1.120** (2.426)	1.109* (1.932)	1.036 (0.511)
BI	1.005 (0.162)	0.979 (−0.464)	0.993 (−0.185)	1.023 (0.859)	0.941 (−1.269)	0.931** (−2.111)
GU	1.099 (1.533)	1.085 (1.125)	1.048 (0.705)	1.091* (1.757)	1.085 (1.398)	1.053 (1.102)
HA	1.057 (0.689)	0.988 (−0.170)	1.031 (0.509)	1.049 (0.711)	1.005 (0.084)	1.009 (0.184)
KA	1.034 (0.876)	0.991 (−0.177)	0.955 (−0.740)	1.031 (0.680)	1.009 (0.176)	0.994 (−0.119)
KE	1.104 (1.109)	1.067 (0.821)	1.026 (0.325)	1.038 (0.469)	0.980 (−0.295)	0.917 (−1.343)
MA	1.056 (1.157)	1.009 (0.210)	1.034 (0.663)	1.066 (1.600)	1.084** (2.258)	1.120** (2.650)
MP	0.949* (−1.942)	0.923** (−3.164)	0.984 (−0.502)	0.975 (−0.945)	0.969 (−1.016)	0.988 (−0.312)
OR	0.994 (−0.126)	0.972 (−0.451)	0.940 (−0.837)	1.012 (0.173)	0.940 (−1.103)	0.930 (−0.969)
PU	1.062 (1.053)	1.009 (0.278)	1.045 (1.112)	1.003 (0.075)	0.994 (−0.144)	0.976 (−0.582)
RA	1.016 (0.244)	1.002 (0.023)	1.013 (0.173)	1.008 (0.161)	0.978 (−0.353)	1.007 (0.113)
TN	1.057 (0.574)	1.048 (0.395)	0.983 (−0.130)	1.057 (0.736)	1.079 (0.913)	1.018 (0.157)
UP	0.994 (−0.185)	0.956 (−1.211)	0.983 (−0.355)	1.012 (0.395))	0.971 (−0.769)	1.001 (0.028)
WB	1.076 (1.516)	1.062 (1.027)	1.005 (0.108)	1.083** (2.492)	1.072* (1.861)	1.011 (0.315)
All India	1	1	1	1	1	1

Figures in parentheses are *t*-statistics for testing index = 1
*Significant at 10% level; **significant at 5% level

Tables 6.1, 6.2 and 6.3, note, incidentally, that higher rural spatial price index for a State vis-a-vis its urban spatial price index does not mean higher rural prices.

Tables 6.18, 6.19 and 6.20 agree on an overall picture of spatial heterogeneity in prices between the 15 Indian States with several States recording rejection of the hypothesis that its spatial price index is unity. However, the CPD-based approach, that underlines the HRPD model, is much closer to spatial homogeneity than the utility-based approaches. This is consistent with the results presented in Majumder et al. (2015a) which found that the utility-based spatial price estimates record higher

Table 6.19 Estimates of spatial price indices, QAIDS method, 55th–66th rounds, 11 Food items (Majumder et al. 2015a)

State	Rural			Urban		
	55th round	61st round	66th round	55th round	61st round	66th round
	1999–2000	2004–2005	2009–2010	1999–2000	2004–2005	2009–2010
AP	0.841** (−10.91)	1.048** (2.13)	1.083** (5.47)	0.911** (−3.34)	0.923** (−3.17)	1.190** (7.67)
AS	1.150** (5.60)	1.619** (5.76)	0.972 (−1.03)	0.545** (−17.56)	1.097 (1.05)	1.029 (0.58)
BI	1.046** (7.10)	1.122** (4.99)	0.955* (−1.95)	1.232** (13.98)	1.068 (1.49)	1.040 (0.83)
GU	0.831** (−5.05)	1.498** (3.16)	0.840** (−10.91)	0.839** (−5.91)	1.461** (2.45)	0.950 (−1.58)
HA	0.891** (−4.29)	1.360** (2.02)	0.907** (−3.59)	1.185** (5.03)	0.851** (−2.01)	0.902 (−1.56)
KA	0.893** (−6.92)	0.868** (−3.81)	0.748** (−16.14)	0.864** (−8.12)	0.902** (−3.34)	1.390** (5.41)
KE	1.024 (0.51)	1.222** (2.18)	1.697** (11.54)	0.887** (−2.17)	0.921 (−1.47)	1.368** (4.91)
MA	0.901** (−8.20)	1.165** (3.81)	1.174** (5.39)	0.936** (−6.42)	1.162** (5.30)	1.236** (5.82)
MP	0.851** (−12.51)	0.939* (−1.92)	0.729** (−20.64)	0.958** (−3.03)	0.844** (−4.32)	0.753** (−14.49)
OR	1.010 (0.77)	1.098** (2.02)	1.010 (0.77)	0.982 (−0.43)	1.066 (0.76)	0.907** (−2.90)
PU	0.858** (−6.74)	1.240** (5.77)	0.858** (−6.74)	1.162** (3.98)	1.120** (1.99)	0.881** (−7.79)
RA	0.642** (−36.40)	0.741** (−3.37)	0.642** (−36.40)	0.868** (−6.87)	1.114 (0.98)	0.757** (−9.40)
TN	0.963* (−1.89)	0.808** (−3.43)	0.963* (−1.89)	0.908** (−4.38)	0.919** (−2.36)	1.074* (1.64)
UP	0.901** (−13.17)	0.990 (−0.36)	0.901** (−13.17)	1.060** (4.65)	1.020 (0.56)	0.769** (−16.98)
WB	1.219** (7.29)	1.156** (3.95)	1.219** (7.29)	0.769** (−8.04)	1.226** (5.02)	1.546** (6.46)
All India	1	1	1	1	1	1

Figures in parentheses are *t*-statistics for testing index = 1
*Significant at 10% level; **significant at 5% level

statistical significances from unity than those based on the fixed-weight Divisia price indices. That result carries over to the CPD versus utility-based comparisons, given the result shown earlier that the HRPD model is equivalent to certain fixed-weight price indices under certain price parameter configurations. Fixed-weight price indices, unlike the utility-based methods, allow limited substitution possibility between commodities. In the context of a large and heterogeneous country such as India, where the price-induced substitution between commodities

Table 6.20 Estimates of spatial price indices, QAIDS method, 55th–66th rounds, 6 Food items (Majumder et al. 2015b)

State	Rural			Urban		
	55th round	61st round	66th round	55th round	61st round	66th round
	1999–2000	2004–2005	2009–2010	1999–2000	2004–2005	2009–2010
AP	0.960** (−4.09)	0.994 (1.078)	0.994 (−0.52)	0.936** (−4.84)	0.812** (12.97)	1.079** (5.95)
AS	1.183** (7.98)	1.060 (1.25)	0.880** (−4.91)	0.884** (−3.17)	0.867** (2.59)	0.976 (0.55)
BI	0.879** (−18.81)	0.578** (−30.69)	0.751** (−17.03)	0.862** (−11.67)	0.719** (14.99)	0.797** (8.94)
GU	1.092** (2.16)	0.961** (−2.52)	0.940** (−4.15)	0.950** (−2.54)	0.887** (5.35)	0.926** (4.44)
HA	0.902** (−2.02)	1.060 (1.46)	0.860** (−10.30)	0.858** (3.17)	0.801** (8.93)	0.917** (5.01)
KA	1.001 (0.06)	0.997 (−0.11)	0.843** (−12.11)	0.917** (−5.83)	0.693** (21.91)	0.882** (8.06)
KE	1.243** (8.66)	1.246** (7.02)	1.303** (15.88)	1.003 (0.07)	1.091 (1.11)	1.115** (5.47)
MA	1.027** (1.97)	0.641** (−50.94)	0.774** (−17.58)	1.057** (4.68)	0.657** (25.73)	0.790 (16.11)
MP	0.745** (−22.46)	0.914** (−6.64)	0.985 (−0.98)	0.748** (−20.48)	0.924** (6.14)	1.049** (3.21)
OR	0.760** (−14.68)	0.546** (−36.73)	0.762** (−19.56)	0.814** (−5.11)	0.599** (15.48)	0.760** (11.58)
PU	0.971 (−0.45)	0.713** (−17.02)	0.874** (−11.80)	0.928 (−1.28)	0.941** (2.20)	0.815** (20.92)
RA	1.057 (0.86)	0.499** (−30.25)	0.712** (−26.10)	0.830** (−3.68)	0.596** (9.61)	0.763** (19.50)
TN	1.273** (8.79)	1.131** (5.29)	0.988 (−0.68)	1.020 (1.32)	1.009 (0.50)	0.930** (5.13)
UP	0.845** (−16.34)	0.777** (18.93)	0.712** (−37.93)	0.760** (−27.52)	0.677** (29.04)	0.765** (31.51)
WB	1.003 (0.013)	0.938** (−2.27)	1.322** (8.88)	0.983 (0.52)	0.920 (1.50)	1.136** (2.58)
All India	1	1	1	1	1	1

Figures in parentheses are *t*-statistics for testing index = 1
**Significant at 5% level

can vary a lot between the regions and over time, the CPD-type approach can present a picture of spatial price homogeneity that is misleading. A comparison between Tables 6.2 and 6.3 points to an overall picture of robustness in the qualitative results, though there are some noticeable differences for some States. Table 6.21 reports the sensitivity of the estimated spatial price indices to the model/method of estimation along with the choice of commodities. This table presents, for each State and separately for the rural and urban sectors, the formal tests of statistical significance of the difference between the estimated spatial price indices from two models with alternative choice of commodities.

The following general observations can be made from Table 6.21. First, there is widespread evidence of sensitivity of the spatial price estimates to the model/data used in the form of several statistical significances of the pairwise differences. Second, the estimates are generally more sensitive to the choice of commodities than to the model used. This is apparent from the fact that the last two columns in Table 6.21, which report the difference between the estimates from QAIDS (11 commodities) and QAIDS (6 commodities) in the rural and urban sectors, record the largest number of statistical significant estimates of the pairwise differences. In fact, in this case, nearly all the pairwise differences are statistically significant at 5% level of significance. Third, where the difference is significant at the 5% level, there is some uniformity between the rural and urban sectors in the sign of the estimated differences between the spatial price indices—see, for example, Kerala and West Bengal. Karnataka provides a significant exception. Table 6.22 provides evidence on rural–urban homogeneity in the spatial price index for each State and in each of the three rounds considered in this study.

Note that the numbers in Table 6.22 are estimates of rural–urban differentials in spatial price indices, not the more commonly calculated rural–urban differences in prices. It is possible for the rural spatial price index (S^{rural}) in a State to exceed its urban spatial price index $\left(S^{\text{urban}}\right)$, yet the urban prices could well be higher than rural prices in that State. Since S^{rural} and S^{urban} are not directly comparable owing to different numeraires, we use the ratio, $\left(1 - S^{\text{rural}}\right)/\left(1 - S^{\text{urban}}\right)$, to measure the distance of a State's rural spatial price index (from the respective all-India numeraire of 1.0) relative to that in its urban areas. A test of significance of this ratio to be equal to 1 in a State constitutes a test of rural–urban homogeneity in spatial prices in that State. It is interesting to note that while the CPD-based HRPD model presents a picture of rural–urban spatial price homogeneity in all the States with no statistical significances recorded anywhere this is not the case with the utility-based estimates. This reinforces the observation made earlier from Tables 6.18, 6.19 and 6.20 that the CPD-type models underplay the role of price-induced substitution between commodities that can vary considerably between regions and this leads to a distorted and misleading picture of spatial price homogeneity that is out of step with the heterogeneity portrayed by utility- and demand estimation-based methods that allow price-induced substitution. The use of the latter provides evidence of considerable spatial price heterogeneity in India both between States and between the rural and urban areas.

The main contribution of Majumder and Ray (2017) is to provide Indian evidence on subnational PPPs that point to considerable spatial price heterogeneity in India. This paper also shows that the CPD model, proposed in the cross-country context, can be adapted to the household context to estimate spatial prices within a country. The methodological contribution of this paper has been to show that the proposed CPD-based model, namely the HRPD model is formally equivalent to certain well-known fixed-weight price indices under certain parametric

Table 6.21 Comparison of models with respect to pairwise difference, D_1[a] between spatial prices within sectors, 66th round, 2009–2010, rural and urban (Majumder and Ray 2017)

State	Models					
	CPD–QAIDS 11		CPD–QAIDS 6		QAIDS 11–QAIDS 6	
	Rural	Urban	Rural	Urban	Rural	Urban
AP	−0.006 (−0.10)	−0.119* (−1.94)	0.083 (1.32)	−0.008 (−0.14)	0.089** (4.67)	0.111** (3.94)
AS	0.154* (1.68)	0.007 (0.05)	0.246** (2.71)	0.060 (0.43)	0.092** (2.53)	0.053 (0.80)
BI	0.038 (0.82)	−0.109 (−1.48)	0.242** (5.66)	0.134** (2.21)	0.204** (7.42)	0.243** (4.58)
GU	0.208* (1.94)	0.102 (1.56)	0.108 (1.01)	0.127** (2.12)	−0.100** (−4.85)	0.024 (0.69)
HA	0.124 (1.16)	0.107 (0.95)	0.171* (1.64)	0.092 (0.98)	0.047 (1.60)	−0.015 (−0.22)
KA	0.207** (3.01)	−0.396** (−4.25)	0.112* (1.65)	0.112* (1.85)	−0.095** (−4.67)	0.508** (6.91)
KE	−0.671** (−5.85)	−0.451** (−4.67)	−0.277** (−2.79)	−0.198** (−3.08)	0.394** (6.22)	0.253** (3.25)
MA	−0.139** (−2.16)	−0.115* (−1.90)	0.260** (4.54)	0.330** (7.02)	0.400** (11.53)	0.446** (10.48)
MP	0.255** (4.99)	0.235** (4.23)	−0.001 (−0.01)	−0.061 (−1.10)	−0.256** (−12.69)	−0.296** (−12.93)
OR	−0.091 (−1.33)	0.024 (0.23)	0.178** (2.69)	0.170* (1.74)	0.269** (10.96)	0.147** (3.84)
PU	−0.047 (−0.46)	0.095 (1.13)	0.171* (1.66)	0.161* (1.95)	0.219** (11.78)	0.066** (3.77)
RA	0.218** (3.72)	0.250** (3.37)	0.301** (5.33)	0.244** (3.46)	0.084** (3.87)	−0.006 (−0.21)
TN	0.103 (1.46)	−0.056 (−0.83)	−0.005 (−0.07)	0.088* (1.70)	−0.108** (−4.24)	0.144** (3.07)
UP	0.157** (4.71)	0.232** (5.46)	0.271** (8.36)	0.236** (5.77)	0.114** (8.65)	0.004 (0.27)
WB	−0.466** (−7.05)	−0.535** (−5.40)	−0.317** (−5.01)	−0.125* (−1.69)	0.149** (2.72)	0.410** (4.12)

[a]The difference is measured as D_1 = Spatial index(Model 1)-Spatial index (Model 2); figures in parentheses are the t-statistics for testing $D\_1 = 0$. The standard errors have been calculated using Delta method

*Significant at 10% level; **significant at 5% level

configurations. The empirical contribution also includes a comparison between the spatial price indices from alternative models and the result that the utility-based methods point to a much greater extent of spatial price heterogeneity than is the case with the CPD-type approaches. The results also point to the importance of the choice of commodities in the utility-based models used to calculate the Statewise spatial price indices. The bilateral model comparisons are backed up by formal tests

Table 6.22 Testing rural–urban differences, D_2^a in spatial price indices, S using different methods: 55th–66th rounds (Majumder and Ray 2017)

State	Value of *D*_2								
	Evaluated using CPD approach (13 commodities)			Evaluated using QAIDS (11 Food items)			Evaluated using QAIDS (6 Food commodities)		
	55th round	61st round	66th round	55th round	61st round	66th round	55th round	61st round	66th round
	1999–2000	2004–2005	2009–2010	1999–2000	2004–2005	2009–2010	1999–2000	2004–2005	2009–2010
AP	−11.544 (−0.05)	6.094 (0.12)	1.083 (0.07)	1.774 (1.39)	−0.627** (−4.60)	0.439** (−5.70)	0.625* (−1.87)	0.032** (−32.59)	−0.076** (−7.34)
AS	1.296 (0.17)	1.413 (0.21)	3.544 (0.19)	−0.331** (−21.48)	6.359 (0.87)	−0.959 (−1.03)	−1.578** (−4.81)	−0.451** (−3.62)	5.000 (0.44)
BI	0.214 (−0.42)	0.353 (−0.86)	0.108 (−1.53)	0.200** (−25.31)	1.809 (0.64)	−1.138 (−1.43)	0.877 (−1.39)	1.502** (4.50)	1.227 (1.46)
GU	1.095 (0.08)	1.009 (0.01)	0.905 (−0.04)	1.052 (0.19)	1.079 (0.14)	3.225 (1.08)	−1.840** (−2.54)	0.345** (−4.33)	0.811 (−0.71)
HA	1.162 (0.05)	−2.482 (−0.06)	3.402 (0.07)	−0.590** (−8.80)	−2.411** (−2.01)	0.954 (−0.07)	0.690 (−0.76)	−0.302** (−6.22)	1.687* (1.83)
KA	1.105 (0.03)	−0.994 (−0.19)	7.599 (0.09)	0.784 (−1.45)	1.343 (0.64)	−0.645** (−13.08)	−0.012** (−5.04)	0.010** (−11.15)	1.331* (1.67)
KE	2.724 (0.27)	−3.369 (−0.320)	−0.314 (−1.10)	−0.211** (−2.87)	−2.804* (−1.66)	1.895** (2.13)	81.000 (0.07)	2.703 (0.69)	2.635** (3.21)
MA	0.844 (−0.15)	0.106 (−1.37)	0.287 (−1.50)	1.541* (1.77)	1.018 (0.06)	0.737 (−1.41)	0.474** (−2.02)	1.047 (1.02)	1.076 (0.84)
MP	2.077 (0.22)	2.468 (0.34)	1.360 (0.05)	3.532** (2.11)	0.392** (−2.72)	1.096 (1.04)	1.012 (0.18)	1.132 (0.52)	−0.306** (−4.00)
OR	−0.515 (−0.20)	0.460 (−0.41)	0.863 (−0.09)	−0.550 (−1.05)	1.480 (0.23)	−0.331** (−5.21)	1.290 (1.09)	1.132* (1.67)	0.992 (−0.08)
PU	19.187 (0.04)	−1.675 (−0.09)	−1.905 (−0.37)	−0.874** (−7.35)	2.002 (0.94)	−0.781** (−10.95)	0.403 (−0.63)	4.864* (1.73)	0.681** (−4.81)

(continued)

Table 6.22 (continued)

State	Value of D_2								
	Evaluated using CPD approach (13 commodities)			Evaluated using QAIDS (11 Food items)			Evaluated using QAIDS (6 Food commodities)		
	55th round	61st round	66th round	55th round	61st round	66th round	55th round	61st round	66th round
	1999–2000	2004–2005	2009–2010	1999–2000	2004–2005	2009–2010	1999–2000	2004–2005	2009–2010
RA	2.085 (0.06)	−0.077 (−0.42)	2.052 (0.05)	2.700** (4.25)	−2.266 (−1.35)	0.840 (−1.35)	−0.335** (−3.34)	1.240* (1.77)	1.215** (2.77)
TN	0.991 (−0.01)	0.606 (−0.41)	−0.953 (−0.42)	0.404** (−2.56)	2.357 (1.12)	−1.632** (−2.57)	13.650 (1.21)	14.556 (0.46)	0.171** (−3.26)
UP	−0.532 (−0.48)	1.487 (0.22)	−14.591 (−0.03)	−1.649** (−7.04)	−0.491 (−0.91)	0.753** (−3.84)	0.646** (−7.70)	0.690** (−7.11)	1.226** (4.46)
WB	0.912 (−0.10)	0.864 (−0.14)	0.436 (−0.11)	−0.950** (−11.08)	0.691 (−1.39)	0.862 (−0.91)	−0.176 (−0.09)	0.775 (−0.36)	2.368 (1.43)

[a]The difference is measured by $D\_2 = \left(1 - S^{\text{Rural}}\right)/\left(1 - S^{\text{Urban}}\right)$, that is, the ratio of distances from the respective all-India figures
Figures in parentheses are the *t*-statistics for testing $D\_2 = 1$. The standard errors have been calculated using Delta method
*Significant at 10% level; **significant at 5% level

of statistical significances of the pairwise differences between the corresponding spatial price index estimates. Also, perhaps for the first time, this study reports the estimates of rural–urban differentials in spatial price indices, rather than prices that suggest some interesting differences between States. The overall picture is one of considerable spatial price heterogeneity in India that provides the case for further research on the topic of subnational PPPs in the context of large heterogeneous countries.

It is useful to remind the reader that the spatial price estimates reported in Majumder and Ray (2017) are based on information obtained from the household surveys rather than the CPI data. These alternative data sources differ in, among other respects, the commodities chosen, the level of commodity aggregation, the unit of behaviour and the geographical coverage. A similar difference exists between the price information used in the ICP to calculate PPP and that used by the national statistical agencies to calculate cost of living indices. This makes the spatial prices of this study not readily comparable with those from the ICP price information for the individual countries nor with the rural–urban disaggregated cost of living indices based on CPI. A satisfactory comparison of spatial price indices based on alternative sources of price information is best left for a future study.

6.5 The Simultaneous Measurement of Spatial Variation and Temporal Movement in Prices in India

While the literature on spatial variation and temporal movement in prices have grown in parallel, Chakrabarty et al. (2017) mark a departure by providing a unified treatment and proposing a comprehensive framework that allows both approaches. The proposed model, described earlier in Chap. 3, Sect. 3.4, is based on twin extensions of the household version of the 'Country-Product Dummy model' by allowing for a dynamic stochastic specification and interdependence of spatial prices of geographically adjacent regions. Tests of temporal stability and regional independence of the estimated spatial prices are proposed and applied in this paper. This study shows that the introduction of an AR(1) error process improves the efficiency of the estimates of parameters, urban–rural and temporal price indices under certain conditions. The Indian application points to a rich potential for using the proposed framework in cross-country comparisons such as the ICP exercises. The results of this study described below also reiterate the importance of the stochastic specification in the estimation of spatial prices noted in Majumder and Ray (2017). Chakrabarty et al. (2017) extend that framework by considering simultaneously both spatial and temporal variation in prices. This study uses the detailed information on household purchases of Food and non-Food items in both quantity and value terms, along with that on household size, composition and household type, contained in the unit records from the 55th (July, 1999–June, 2000), 61st (July, 2004–June, 2005), 66th (July, 2009–June, 2010) and 68th (July

Table 6.23 Wooldridge test, $F(1,194)$ for autocorrelation in panel data (Chakrabarty et al. 2017)

	Estimate of (common) ρ	*F*-statistics
Rural	0.6449	38.862**
Urban	0.6505	25.810**
Combined	0.6777	15.705**

**Significant at 5% level

2011–June 2012) rounds of India's National Sample Surveys. The overall time period considered in this study, July 1999–June 2012 is long enough for a meaningful test of the time invariance of the spatial price indices and the introduction of a dynamic stochastic specification to be of interest.

Table 6.23 presents the estimates of the AR(1) coefficient ρ (common for all periods). The Wooldridge (2002) test for autocorrelation in panel data, with Statewise items constituting a panel over the four rounds, confirms the presence of first-order autocorrelation. While π'_{rt} s of the DHRPD model may be interpreted as the natural logarithm of the value of a reference basket of items/commodities purchased at the prices of region r at time t, the estimates of the exponential of their differences with that of the numeraire region (π_{0t}) may be interpreted more readily as estimated spatial price indices, as explained earlier in Chap. 3. The estimates of the spatial prices in the four NSS rounds are presented in Tables 6.24, 6.25 and 6.26 (combined). The figures in parentheses are the t-statistics corresponding to the hypothesis that the spatial price in the State is one, i.e. no different from the numeraire region, making that State has 'average prices'. There are some, but not many, rejections of the null hypothesis. There is not much change in the estimated spatial prices over the time period spanned by NSS rounds 55, 61, 66 and 68. The changes are mainly quantitative, not qualitative ones. There is hardly any case where the spatial price of a State moves from significantly below one to significantly above one, or vice versa. A comparison between Tables 6.24 and 6.25 shows that there are several cases of rural urban differences in a State's spatial prices. Each table also allows a comparison between the estimated spatial prices in the HRPD and dynamic models. The introduction of AR(1) errors does not show any general pattern in its effect on the estimated spatial price indices. However, it does not move any State from being a cheaper State (spatial price index significantly <1) to being a more expensive State (spatial price index significantly >1), or vice versa. The rural spread in spatial prices exceeded that in the urban areas in rounds 55 and 61, as evident in the fall in the coefficient of variation (CV) in each of these rounds as we move from the rural (Table 6.24) to the urban (Table 6.25) sector. It is interesting to note, however, that the direction of change in CV between the two sectors is sharply reversed in the later rounds 66 and 68.

Table 6.27 provides direct evidence of differences between the price indices in the 15 States by presenting the estimates of the pairwise differences between States in the estimated spatial price indices in NSS round 68 under AR(1) error structure. While the upper triangular estimates correspond to the rural areas, the lower triangular estimates refer to the urban areas. Though not everywhere, there are several

Table 6.24 Estimates of spatial price indices, 55th–68th rounds, rural (Chakrabarty et al. 2017)

State	HRPD model				DHRPD model with AR(1) error terms			
	55th round	61st round	66th round	68th round	55th round	61st round	66th round	68th round
AP	1.026 (0.385)	1.047 (0.756)	1.077 (0.926)	1.087 (1.015)	1.022 (0.477)	1.052 (1.112)	1.080 (1.566)	1.093* (1.828)
AS	1.156** (2.324)	1.153** (1.926)	1.126 (1.387)	1.057 (0.857)	1.148* (1.773)	1.163** (2.065)	1.138* (1.915)	1.063 (0.886)
BI	1.005 (0.162)	0.979 (−0.464)	0.993 (−0.185)	0.943** (−2.010)	0.963 (−1.152)	0.931** (−2.246)	0.941* (−1.928)	0.909** (−3.166)
GU	1.099 (1.533)	1.085 (1.125)	1.048 (0.705)	1.067 (0.890)	1.085 (1.301)	1.073 (1.157)	1.012 (0.144)	1.056 (0.640)
HA	1.057 (0.689)	0.988 (−0.170)	1.031 (0.509)	1.007 (0.139)	1.059 (0.677)	1.003 (0.038)	1.048 (0.556)	1.024 (0.269)
KA	1.034 (0.876)	0.991 (−0.177)	0.955 (−0.740)	0.977 (−0.400)	1.047 (0.740)	0.999 (−0.018)	0.966 (−0.600)	1.001 (0.015)
KE	1.104 (1.109)	1.067 (0.821)	1.026 (0.325)	1.037 (0.419)	1.093 (1.276)	1.080 (1.163)	1.035 (0.432)	1.052 (0.622)
MA	1.056 (1.157)	1.009 (0.210)	1.034 (0.663)	1.063 (1.464)	1.053 (1.087)	1.007 (0.159)	1.032 (0.695)	1.065 (1.346)
MP	0.949* (−1.942)	0.923** (−3.164)	0.984 (−0.502)	0.962 (−1.208)	0.941 (−1.433)	0.918** (−2.120)	0.985 (−0.367)	0.960 (−1.017)
OR	0.994 (−0.126)	0.972 (−0.451)	0.940 (−0.837)	0.932 (−1.019)	0.987 (−0.219)	0.978 (−0.387)	0.945 (−1.003)	0.935 (−1.206)
PU	1.062 (1.053)	1.009 (0.278)	1.045 (1.112)	1.054 (0.912)	1.056 (0.658)	1.029 (0.353)	1.053 (0.623)	1.064 (0.744)
RA	1.016 (0.244)	1.002 (0.023)	1.013 (0.173)	0.950 (−0.615)	1.010 (0.207)	1.009 (0.184)	1.018 (0.388)	0.959 (−0.915)
TN	1.057	1.048	0.983	1.029	1.063	1.059	1.000	1.032

(continued)

Table 6.24 (continued)

State	HRPD model				DHRPD model with AR(1) error terms			
	55th round	61st round	66th round	68th round	55th round	61st round	66th round	68th round
	(0.574)	(0.395)	(−0.130)	(0.187)	(1.067)	(1.009)	(−0.004)	(0.533)
UP	0.994 (−0.185)	0.956 (−1.211)	0.983 (−0.355)	0.920** (−2.145)	0.991 (−0.336)	0.967 (−1.238)	0.988 (−0.458)	0.927** (−2.924)
WB	1.076 (1.516)	1.062 (1.027)	1.005 (0.108)	1.016 (0.329)	1.070 (1.480)	1.068 (1.495)	1.006 (0.144)	1.018 (0.411)
All India	1	1	1	1	1	1	1	1
CV	0.050	0.057	0.047	0.055	0.052	0.062	0.051	0.058
Estimate of (common) ρ					0.6449			

Figures in parentheses are *t*-statistics for testing index = 1
*Significant at 10% level; **significant at 5% level

Table 6.25 Estimates of spatial price indices, 55th–68th rounds, urban (Chakrabarty et al. 2017)

State	HRPD model				DHRPD model with AR(1) error terms			
	55th round	61st round	66th round	68th round	55th round	61st round	66th round	68th round
AP	0.998 (−0.043)	1.008 (0.169)	1.071 (1.086)	1.033 (0.543)	0.980 (−0.503)	1.000 (0.005)	1.076* (1.724)	1.040 (0.960)
AS	1.120** (2.426)	1.109* (1.932)	1.036 (0.511)	1.053 (0.787)	1.110 (0.995)	1.103 (0.973)	1.038 (0.367)	1.055 (0.509)
BI	1.023 (0.859)	0.941 (−1.269)	0.931** (−2.111)	0.915* (−1.728)	1.018 (0.345)	0.940 (−1.301)	0.939 (−1.368)	0.921* (−1.757)
GU	1.091* (1.757)	1.085 (1.398)	1.053 (1.102)	1.059 (1.366)	1.093* (1.829)	1.072 (1.536)	1.036 (0.810)	1.051 (1.118)
HA	1.049 (0.711)	1.005 (0.084)	1.009 (0.184)	0.990 (−0.197)	1.051 (0.629)	1.008 (0.103)	1.010 (0.139)	1.001 (0.010)
KA	1.031 (0.680)	1.009 (0.176)	0.994 (−0.119)	1.028 (0.471)	1.024 (0.516)	0.988 (−0.277)	0.978 (−0.483)	1.013 (0.267)
KE	1.038 (0.469)	0.980 (−0.295)	0.917 (−1.343)	0.898 (−1.303)	0.999 (−0.017)	0.983 (−0.272)	0.926 (−1.521)	0.926 (−1.540)
MA	1.066 (1.600)	1.084** (2.258)	1.120** (2.650)	1.113** (2.417)	1.066* (1.932)	1.067** (1.987)	1.105** (2.975)	1.103** (3.018)
MP	0.975 (−0.945)	0.969 (−1.016)	0.988 (−0.312)	0.966 (−0.825)	0.973 (−0.641)	0.967 (−0.809)	0.990 (−0.236)	0.960 (−0.958)
OR	1.012 (0.173)	0.940 (−1.103)	0.930 (−0.969)	0.854** (−2.578)	1.002 (0.031)	0.933 (−0.945)	0.935 (−0.861)	0.875* (−1.815)
PU	1.003 (0.075)	0.994 (−0.144)	0.976 (−0.582)	0.973 (−0.527)	1.002 (0.034)	0.999 (−0.011)	0.980 (−0.309)	0.990 (−0.159)
RA	1.008 (0.161)	0.978 (−0.353)	1.007 (0.113)	0.959 (−0.885)	1.011 (0.199)	0.975 (−0.499)	0.999 (−0.013)	0.965 (−0.693)
TN	1.057	1.079	1.018	1.042	1.056	1.067*	1.020	1.041

(continued)

Table 6.25 (continued)

State	HRPD model				DHRPD model with AR(1) error terms			
	55th round	61st round	66th round	68th round	55th round	61st round	66th round	68th round
	(0.736)	(0.913)	(0.157)	(0.331)	(1.452)	(1.721)	(0.511)	(1.044)
UP	1.012 (0.395))	0.971 (−0.769)	1.001 (0.028)	0.996 (−0.101)	1.003 (0.101)	0.967 (−1.103)	0.993 (−0.236)	0.978 (−0.705)
WB	1.083** (2.492)	1.072* (1.861)	1.011 (0.315)	1.030 (0.713)	1.076* (1.728)	1.067 (1.578)	1.014 (0.346)	1.029 (0.703)
All India	1	1	1	1	1	1	1	1
CV	0.038	0.055	0.054	0.069	0.040	0.053	0.050	0.061
Estimate of (common) ρ					0.6505			

Figures in parentheses are *t*-statistics for testing index = 1
*Significant at 10% level; **significant at 5% level

Table 6.26 Estimates of spatial price indices, 55th–68th rounds, combined sample (Chakrabarty et al. 2017)

State	HRPD model				DHRPD model with AR(1) error terms			
	55th round	61st round	66th round	68th round	55th round	61st round	66th round	68th round
AP	1.005 (0.087)	1.026 (0.511)	1.071 (0.937)	1.062 (0.795)	1.001 (0.018)	1.025 (0.577)	1.067 (1.357)	1.063 (1.319)
AS	1.119** (2.065)	1.129** (1.949)	1.088 (1.024)	1.050 (0.751)	1.119 (1.356)	1.130 (1.580)	1.094 (1.233)	1.051 (0.665)
BI	0.977 (−0.873)	0.929* (−1.764)	0.979 (−0.353)	0.901** (−3.283)	0.953 (−1.314)	0.904** (−2.886)	0.956 (−1.284)	0.887** (−3.612)
GU	1.086 (1.642)	1.065 (0.931)	1.045 (0.818)	1.074 (1.313)	1.071 (1.193)	1.045 (0.797)	1.018 (0.328)	1.060 (1.047)
HA	1.021 (0.282)	0.991 (−0.144)	0.987 (−0.262)	0.981 (−0.452)	1.026 (0.305)	0.998 (−0.019)	0.993 (−0.090)	0.986 (−0.173)
KA	1.027 (0.670)	1.007 (0.148)	0.996 (−0.070)	0.999 (−0.023)	1.025 (0.434)	0.995 (−0.093)	0.982 (−0.343)	1.006 (0.112)
KE	1.050 (0.576)	0.986 (−0.193)	0.955 (−0.665)	0.950 (−0.606)	1.026 (0.380)	0.993 (−0.112)	0.961 (−0.601)	0.968 (−0.487)
MA	1.045 (0.929)	1.038 (0.852)	1.059 (1.200)	1.088** (2.158)	1.046 (1.048)	1.034 (0.796)	1.042 (0.944)	1.082* (1.799)
MP	0.945** (−2.217)	0.934** (−2.425)	0.974 (−0.601)	0.946 (−1.592)	0.938 (−1.466)	0.924* (−1.874)	0.969 (−0.756)	0.940 (−1.486)
OR	0.966 (−0.795)	0.933 (−1.113)	0.919 (−1.110)	0.905 (−1.426)	0.960 (−0.658)	0.928 (−1.280)	0.914 (−1.485)	0.899* (−1.796)
PU	1.010 (0.192)	0.974 (−0.719)	0.989 (−0.291)	1.003 (0.053)	1.013 (0.164)	0.983 (−0.230)	0.991 (−0.119)	1.006 (0.082)
RA	0.994 (−0.091)	0.981 (−0.262)	0.969 (−0.456)	0.941 (−0.881)	0.997 (−0.064)	0.976 (−0.502)	0.974 (−0.534)	0.946 (−1.153)
TN	1.046	1.061	0.982	1.028	1.052	1.060	0.989	1.026

(continued)

Table 6.26 (continued)

State	HRPD model				DHRPD model with AR(1) error terms			
	55th round	61st round	66th round	68th round	55th round	61st round	66th round	68th round
	(0.518)	(0.611)	(−0.140)	(0.185)	(0.987)	(1.159)	(−0.215)	(0.508)
UP	0.974 (−0.739)	0.931 (−1.982)	0.953 (−1.080)	0.916** (−2.152)	0.972 (−0.979)	0.933** (−2.496)	0.950* (−1.841)	0.914** (−3.188)
WB	1.064 (1.571)	1.051 (1.107)	0.995 (−0.113)	1.021 (0.478)	1.057 (1.190)	1.048 (1.069)	0.992 (−0.188)	1.017 (0.368)
All India	1	1	1	1	1	1	1	1
CV	0.048	0.061	0.047	0.063	0.047	0.059	0.048	0.063
Estimate of (common) ρ					0.6777			

Figures in parentheses are *t*-statistics for testing index = 1
*Significant at 10% level; **significant at 5% level

Table 6.27 Pairwise difference between spatial prices within sectors, DHRPD model with AR(1) error terms, 68th round, rural and urban (Chakrabarty et al. 2017)

Urban	Rural														
	AP	AS	BI	GU	HA	KA	KE	MA	MP	OR	PU	RA	TN	UP	WB
AP		0.030 (0.343)	0.185** (3.151)	0.037 (0.368)	0.070 (0.683)	0.093 (1.226)	0.042 (0.429)	0.029 (0.409)	0.133** (2.070)	0.158** (2.133)	0.029 (0.295)	0.134** (1.978)	0.061 (0.779)	0.166** (2.924)	0.075 (1.104)
AS	0.014 (0.125)		0.155** (2.009)	0.007 (0.064)	0.040 (0.349)	0.062 (0.690)	0.012 (0.107)	−0.001 (−0.016)	0.103 (1.266)	0.128 (1.434)	−0.001 (−0.005)	0.104 (1.236)	0.031 (0.336)	0.136* (1.798)	0.045 (0.532)
BI	−0.119* (−1.940)	−0.134 (−1.148)		−0.147 (−1.600)	−0.115 (−1.241)	−0.092 (−1.474)	−0.143 (−1.630)	−0.156** (−2.785)	−0.052 (−1.062)	−0.026 (−0.430)	−0.155* (−1.714)	−0.051 (−0.952)	−0.123* (−1.855)	−0.019 −(0.493)	−0.110** (−2.062)
GU	0.010 (0.167)	−0.004 (−0.035)	0.130** (2.032)		0.032 (0.260)	0.055 (0.532)	0.004 (0.037)	−0.009 (−0.087)	0.096 (0.999)	0.121 (1.178)	−0.008 (−0.064)	0.097 (0.986)	0.024 (0.227)	0.129 (1.414)	0.038 (0.383)
HA	−0.040 (−0.480)	−0.054 (−0.419)	0.080 (0.948)	−0.050 (−0.592)		0.023 (0.219)	−0.028 (−0.230)	−0.041 (−0.408)	0.064 (0.658)	0.089 (0.859)	−0.040 (−0.326)	0.065 (0.653)	−0.008 (−0.078)	0.096 (1.052)	0.005 (0.054)
KA	−0.028 (−0.434)	−0.042 (−0.357)	0.092 (1.402)	−0.038 (−0.576)	0.012 (0.141)		−0.051 (−0.508)	−0.064 (−0.869)	0.041 (0.598)	0.066 (0.851)	−0.063 (−0.616)	0.042 (0.585)	−0.031 (−0.381)	0.073 (1.207)	−0.018 (−0.246)
KE	−0.115* (−1.792)	−0.129 (−1.095)	0.005 (0.073)	−0.125* (−1.889)	−0.075 (−0.873)	−0.087 (−1.284)		−0.013 (−0.137)	0.091 (0.997)	0.117 (1.180)	−0.012 (−0.103)	0.092 (0.981)	0.020 (0.191)	0.124 (1.436)	0.033 (0.352)
MA	0.063 (1.165)	0.049 (0.431)	0.183** (3.225)	0.053 (0.930)	0.103 (1.301)	0.091 (1.545)	0.178** (3.003)		0.104 (1.686)	0.130* (1.796)	0.001 (0.008)	0.106 (1.608)	0.033 (0.426)	0.137** (2.539)	0.046 (0.705)
MP	−0.080 (−1.356)	−0.095 (−0.821)	0.039 (0.638)	−0.091 (−1.472)	−0.041 (−0.493)	−0.053 (−0.833)	0.034 (0.539)	−0.143** (−2.655)		0.025 (0.380)	−0.104 (−1.098)	0.001 (0.017)	−0.072 (−1.002)	0.033 (0.708)	−0.058 (−0.978)
OR	−0.165** (−2.049)	−0.179 (−1.405)	−0.045 (−0.553)	−0.175** (−2.131)	−0.125 (−1.267)	−0.137 (−1.644)	−0.050 (−0.598)	−0.228** (−2.972)	−0.085 (−1.053)		−0.129 (−1.272)	−0.024 (−0.347)	−0.097 (−1.204)	0.008 (0.127)	−0.084 (−1.191)
PU	−0.050 (−0.659)	−0.065 (−0.519)	0.069 (0.880)	−0.061 (−0.775)	−0.011 (−0.114)	−0.023 (−0.287)	0.064 (0.800)	−0.114 (−1.563)	0.030 (0.390)	0.114 (1.218)		0.105 (1.082)	0.032 (0.304)	0.137 (1.527)	0.045 (0.469)
RA	−0.075 (−1.147)	−0.089 (−0.754)	0.044 (0.658)	−0.085 (−1.264)	−0.035 (−0.407)	−0.047 (−0.687)	0.040 (0.569)	−0.138** (−2.275)	0.005 (0.080)	0.090 (1.056)	−0.025 (−0.302)		−0.073 (−0.974)	0.032 (0.623)	−0.059 (−0.937)
TN	0.000 (0.005)	−0.014 (−0.123)	0.120** (2.012)	−0.010 (−0.168)	0.040 (0.492)	0.028 (0.453)	0.115* (1.855)	−0.063 (−1.212)	0.081 (1.413)	0.165** (2.094)	0.051 (0.678)	0.075 (1.188)		0.105 (1.612)	0.014 (0.182)

(continued)

Table 6.27 (continued)

Urban	Rural														
	AP	AS	BI	GU	HA	KA	KE	MA	MP	OR	PU	RA	TN	UP	WB
UP	−0.063 (−1.191)	−0.077 (−0.688)	0.057 (1.027)	−0.073 (−1.320)	−0.023 (−0.297)	−0.035 (−0.614)	0.052 (0.897)	−0.126** (−2.689)	0.018 (0.333)	0.102 (1.349)	−0.012 (−0.171)	0.012 (0.207)	−0.063 (−1.254)		−0.091* (−1.778)
WB	−0.011 (−0.183)	−0.025 (−0.219)	0.109* (1.765)	−0.021 (−0.343)	0.029 (0.348)	0.017 (0.263)	0.104 (1.624)	−0.074 (−1.366)	0.069 (1.174)	0.154* (1.915)	0.040 (0.518)	0.064 (0.982)	−0.011 (−0.195)	0.052 (0.986)	

For both the upper and lower triangular parts the differences are (row State-column State). Figures in parentheses are *t*-statistics of the difference
*Significant at 10% level; **significant at 5% level

statistically significant pairwise differences between the spatial prices providing evidence of regional price heterogeneity in both the sectors of the Indian economy. To test whether the pairwise differences are same between the two sectors, both qualitatively and quantitatively, we transformed the matrix in Table 6.27 by changing the signs of the elements in the lower triangular part [because for both the upper and lower triangular parts the differences are (row State-column State)] and then tested for symmetry of the transformed matrix. The test rejected the hypothesis of symmetry[1]. Hence, the pattern of pairwise differences between the estimated spatial price indices is different in the two sectors. This is another significant result since it shows that not only are there rural–urban spatial price differences, but that the pairwise differences between the spatial price indices themselves vary between the two sectors of the Indian economy. To our knowledge, no previous study has provided evidence of such an extent of spatial price heterogeneity in the context of a large developing country.

The stochastic specifications of the DHRPD equations used to estimate the spatial and temporal price indices that have been presented so far have assumed independence between the errors across different States and regions. There could be several reasons for doubting the validity of this assumption. For example, cultural and historical affinity between proximate States, such as, Gujarat and Maharashtra, Bengal and Bihar, Karnataka and Andhra Pradesh, could lead to correlation between the regional observations of the omitted variables that will destroy the assumed independence between the errors across the regions. Chakrabarty et al. (2017) relax this assumption and compute the indices incorporating spatial dependence between States. To preserve parsimony in the number of estimated parameters, this study imposes a structure that allows a limited interdependence without adding too many parameters. One such structure, which seems reasonable a priori, allows interdependence between neighbouring or adjacent States, not otherwise. The 'neighbouring States' have been defined in this study as contiguous States in India that share a common border. Table 6.28 provides the tests of significance of regional dependence using Moran's I (Moran 1950) and Geary's C (Geary 1954) test statistics for global spatial autocorrelation for continuous data. The former is based on cross-products of the deviations from the mean. Moran's I is

Table 6.28 Tests of spatial autocorrelation (Chakrabarty et al. 2017)

Test		Rural	Urban	Combined
Moran's coefficient I	Observed value	0.442	0.327	0.500
	Expected value	−0.001	−0.001	−0.001
	z score (test based on normality)	16.673 (0.000)*	12.340 (0.000)	18.831 (0.000)
Geary's coefficient C	Observed value	0.436	0.601	0.420
	Expected value	1.000	1.000	1.000
	z score (test based on normality)	−17.033 (0.000)	−12.048 (0.000)	−17.518 (0.000)

*Figures in parentheses are the p values. All are highly significant

similar but not equivalent to a correlation coefficient. It varies from −1 to +1. In the absence of autocorrelation and regardless of the specified weight matrix, the expectation of Moran's I statistic is $-1/(n - 1)$, which tends to zero as the sample size n increases. A Moran's I coefficient larger than $-1/(n - 1)$ indicates positive spatial autocorrelation, and a Moran's I less than $-1/(n - 1)$ indicates negative spatial autocorrelation. Geary's C statistic is based on the deviations in responses of each observation with one another.

Geary's C ranges from 0 (maximal positive autocorrelation) to a positive value for high negative autocorrelation. Its expectation is 1 in the absence of autocorrelation and regardless of the specified weight matrix (Sokal and Oden 1978). If the value of Geary's C is less than 1, it indicates positive spatial autocorrelation. Table 6.28 clearly demonstrates the presence of significant positive spatial autocorrelation with both Moran's I and Geary's C agreeing on the sign of the spatial autocorrelation. Table 6.29 presents the spatial indices for the rural, urban and combined samples in the presence of correlation between the stochastic errors in the neighbouring States. A comparison between the second half of Table 6.26 and the last four columns of Table 6.29 provides evidence on the impact of allowing regional dependence between the errors on the spatial price estimates. Both sets of estimates relate to the combined rural urban samples in each State and are conditional on the AR(1) error specification. The comparison shows several cases where the spatial price estimates need to be revised on admitting regional dependence. There are some cases, such as Bihar and Uttar Pradesh in round 68, where a strong statistical significance in the absence of regional dependence weakens to insignificance in the presence of regional dependence. Though the qualitative picture seems fairly robust between Tables 6.26 and 6.29, there are several cases of non-negligible changes to the magnitude of the spatial price estimates.

6.6 Conclusion

The focus of this chapter has been on the estimation of spatial prices in India and on the spatial differences in the temporal changes in prices. This chapter also reports the evidence on the implications of admitting spatial differences in prices on inequality. A key feature of this chapter has been the estimation of spatial prices in a framework that jointly allows both spatial and temporal variation in prices. Moreover, while admitting the presence of first-order autoregressive effects in the specification of the error term on the time series part, the estimation allowed in the cross-sectional part the presence of regional dependence in prices via correlated movement in prices of the neighbouring States in India. The results highlight the importance of both the stochastic and deterministic specifications in the estimation of the spatial prices. The significance of the results is underlined by the fact that the period considered includes the period of economic reforms in India.

Interest in the results should extend beyond India. In many large, emerging economies, such as Brazil, China, India and Indonesia, price differences within the

Table 6.29 Estimates of spatial price indices, DHRPD model with AR(1) errors and dependence on neighbouring States, 55th–68th rounds (Chakrabarty et al. 2017)

State	Rural				Urban				Combined			
	55th round	61st round	66th round	68th round	55th round	61st round	66th round	68th round	55th round	61st round	66th round	68th round
AP	0.971 (−0.189)	1.023 (0.121)	1.056 (0.290)	1.073 (0.432)	0.976 (−0.281)	0.998 (−0.019)	1.076 (0.686)	1.045 (0.485)	0.902 (−0.646)	0.935 (−0.445)	0.972 (−0.199)	0.987 (−0.096)
AS	1.219 (1.149)	1.252 (1.114)	1.231 (1.057)	1.155 (0.876)	1.065 (0.609)	1.057 (0.473)	0.990 (−0.083)	1.014 (0.139)	1.126 (0.636)	1.165 (0.862)	1.129 (0.758)	1.082 (0.531)
BI	0.992 (−0.053)	0.996 (−0.025)	1.011 (0.059)	0.962 (−0.259)	1.026 (0.267)	0.946 (−0.553)	0.945 (−0.559)	0.923 (−0.911)	0.994 (−0.037)	0.965 (−0.232)	1.027 (0.188)	0.935 (−0.514)
GU	1.027 (0.164)	1.032 (0.167)	0.993 (−0.037)	1.033 (0.204)	1.143 (1.333)	1.128 (1.110)	1.095 (0.841)	1.097 (0.981)	1.092 (0.503)	1.093 (0.552)	1.073 (0.476)	1.106 (0.711)
HA	0.987 (−0.084)	0.929 (−0.401)	0.985 (−0.084)	0.980 (−0.125)	1.135 (1.191)	1.105 (0.855)	1.113 (0.904)	1.079 (0.765)	1.154 (0.776)	1.172 (0.898)	1.173 (0.979)	1.143 (0.879)
KA	0.967 (−0.200)	0.949 (−0.279)	0.930 (−0.393)	0.951 (−0.317)	0.999 (−0.011)	0.959 (−0.393)	0.959 (−0.386)	1.021 (0.210)	0.864 (−0.892)	0.842 (−1.142)	0.830 (−1.332)	0.869 (−1.043)
KE	1.046 (0.267)	1.046 (0.228)	0.995 (−0.027)	1.021 (0.125)	1.000 (−0.001)	0.969 (−0.291)	0.924 (−0.739)	0.919 (−0.922)	0.896 (−0.661)	0.861 (−0.969)	0.827 (−1.334)	0.839 (−1.318)
MA	0.983 (−0.106)	0.955 (−0.256)	0.999 (−0.003)	1.033 (0.201)	1.085 (0.828)	1.086 (0.760)	1.129 (1.112)	1.130 (1.285)	0.961 (−0.238)	0.945 (−0.366)	0.978 (−0.152)	1.044 (0.305)
MP	0.885 (−0.841)	0.880 (−0.760)	0.954 (−0.273)	0.943 (−0.392)	0.998 (−0.018)	0.991 (−0.089)	1.020 (0.197)	0.983 (−0.197)	0.929 (−0.455)	0.935 (−0.456)	0.998 (−0.015)	0.974 (−0.201)
OR	0.982 (−0.123)	1.000 (−0.001)	0.958 (−0.252)	0.951 (−0.343)	0.989 (−0.126)	0.924 (−0.813)	0.923 (−0.805)	0.868* (−1.697)	0.944 (−0.358)	0.940 (−0.421)	0.921 (−0.608)	0.905 (−0.781)
PU	0.988 (−0.077)	0.971 (−0.157)	0.999 (−0.007)	1.032 (0.190)	1.086 (0.786)	1.106 (0.847)	1.086 (0.703)	1.071 (0.692)	1.145 (0.735)	1.158 (0.838)	1.191 (1.065)	1.176 (1.065)
RA	0.937	0.954	0.956	0.919	1.081	1.057	1.079	1.019	1.081	1.128	1.103	1.055

(continued)

Table 6.29 (continued)

State	Rural				Urban				Combined			
	55th round	61st round	66th round	68th round	55th round	61st round	66th round	68th round	55th round	61st round	66th round	68th round
	(−0.433)	(−0.258)	(−0.250)	(−0.565)	(0.766)	(0.502)	(0.668)	(0.203)	(0.440)	(0.727)	(0.644)	(0.378)
TN	1.002 (0.012)	1.002 (0.010)	0.946 (−0.296)	1.003 (0.019)	1.004 (0.044)	1.011 (0.096)	0.998 (−0.014)	1.068 (0.649)	0.875 (−0.802)	0.858 (−0.992)	0.803 (−1.550)	0.898 (−0.771)
UP	0.939 (−0.418)	0.927 (−0.431)	0.949 (−0.301)	0.900 (−0.717)	1.053 (0.547)	1.027 (0.256)	1.056 (0.497)	1.033 (0.340)	1.050 (0.283)	1.034 (0.212)	1.061 (0.401)	1.016 (0.113)
WB	1.117 (0.689)	1.139 (0.689)	1.075 (0.397)	1.077 (0.469)	1.046 (0.447)	1.025 (0.217)	0.967 (−0.305)	0.985 (−0.152)	1.060 (0.328)	1.063 (0.374)	1.020 (0.132)	1.043 (0.294)
All India	1	1	1	1	1	1	1	1	1	1	1	1
CV	0.079	0.092	0.075	0.068	0.050	0.061	0.069	0.071	0.102	0.116	0.121	0.101

country can be as large, if not larger, than price differences between smaller economies. Since prices play a crucial role in comparisons of living standards within and between countries, the subject of spatial prices in large countries with heterogeneous population is of considerable importance. This calls for improved estimates of intra-country spatial prices and their changes over time. This has implications for the International Comparison Project (ICP) which focusses on price comparisons between countries rather than within countries. The treatment of spatial differences in prices runs in parallel with that on price differences between expenditure classes that we focussed on earlier when discussing the effect of price changes on inequality. The discussion on spatial differences in prices could be considered as an extension of the earlier discussion on that between expenditure classes. Later on in this volume, we provide evidence on the effect of admitting such price differences between expenditure classes on the PPP s between currencies.

References

Almas I (2012) International income inequality: measuring PPP bias by estimating engel curves for food. Am Econ Rev 102:1093–1117

Asian Development Bank (2008) Research study on poverty-specific purchasing power parities for selected countries in Asia and the Pacific. Asian Development Bank, Manila

Aten B, Menezes T (2002) Poverty price levels: an application to Brazilian metropolitan areas. Paper presented at World Bank ICP conference, Washington, DC, March 11–15

Banks J, Blundell R, Lewbel A (1997) Quadratic Engel curves and consumer demand. Rev Econ Stat 79:527–539

Barnett WA (2007) Multilateral aggregation-theoretic monetary aggregation over heterogeneous countries. J Econometrics 136:457–482

Bhattacharya N, Chatterjee GS, Pal P (1988) Variations in level of living across regions and social groups in India, 1963–64 and 1973–74. In: Srinivasan TN, Bardhan PK (eds) Rural poverty in South Asia. Oxford University Press

Bhattacharyya SS, Joshi PD, Roychowdhury AB (1980) Regional price indices based on NSS 25th round consumer expenditure data. Sarvekshana, J NSS Organ 3(4):107–121

Biggeri L, De Carli R, Laureti T (2008) The interpretation of the PPPs: a method for measuring the factors that affect the comparisons and the integration with the CPI work at regional level. Paper presented at the joint UNECE/ILO meeting on consumer price indices, May 8–9, Geneva

Biggeri, L. et al. (2010), "Sub National PPPs based on integration with CPIs", Research Project, Draft Proposal, Paper presented at the 2nd ICP Technical Advisory Group Meeting, Washington DC, February 17–19

Chakrabarty M, Majumder A, Ray R (2015) Preferences, spatial prices and inequality. J Dev Stud 51:1488–1501

Chakrabarty M, Majumder A, Ray R (2017) A framework for the simultaneous measurement of spatial variation and temporal movement in prices in a heterogeneous country: the dynamic household regional product dummy model. Forthcoming in Review of Income and Wealth, https://doi.org/10.1111/roiw.12266

Coondoo D, Majumder A, Chattopadhyay S (2011) Estimating spatial consumer price indices through Engel curve analysis. Rev Income Wealth 57:138–155

Coondoo D, Majumder A, Ray R (2004) A method of calculating regional consumer price differentials with illustrative evidence from India. Rev Income Wealth 50:51–68

Coondoo D, Saha S (1990) Between-state differentials in rural consumer prices in India: an analysis of intertemporal variations. Sankhya, Series B 52(3):347–360

Datt G, Ravallion M (1998) Why have some Indian states done better than others at reducing rural poverty? Economica 65:17–38

Deaton A, Dupriez O (2011) Spatial price differences within large countries. Working Paper 1321, Woodrow Wilson School of Public and International Affairs, Princeton University

De Carli R (2010) Intra-National Price Level Differentials: The Italian Experience. In: Biggeri L, Ferrari G (eds) Price indexes in time and space: methods and practice. Springer, Berlin, pp 115–130

Diewert W (1967) Exact and superlative index numbers. J Econometrics 4(2):115–145

Dikhanov Y, Palanyandy C, Capilit E (2011) Subnational purchasing power parities toward integration of international comparison program and the consumer price index: the case of Philippines. ADB Economics Working Paper Series, no. 290, Asian Development Bank

Feenstra RC, Ma H, Rao DSP (2009) Consistent comparisons of real incomes across time and space. Macroecon Dyn 13(S2):169–193. https://doi.org/10.1017/S1365100509090221

Feenstra RC, Reinsdorf MB (2000) An exact price index for the almost ideal demand system. Econ Lett 66:159–162

Geary RC (1954) The contiguity ratio and statistical mapping. Incorporated Stat 5(3):115–145

Hill RJ (2000) Measuring substitution bias in international comparisons based on additive purchasing power parity methods. Eur Econ Rev 44:145–162

Hill RJ (2004) Constructing price indexes across space and time: the case of the European Union. Am Econ Rev 94:1379–1410

Hill RJ, Syed IA (2015) Improving international comparisons of prices at basic heading level: an application to the Asia-Pacific region. Review of Income and Wealth 61:515–539

Hulten CR (1973) Divisia index numbers. Econometrica 41(6):1017–1025

Levene H (1960) Robust tests for equality of variances. In: Olkin Ingram, Ghurve Sudhish, Hoeffding Wassily, Madow William, Mann Henry (eds) Contributions to probability and statistics: essays in honor of Harold Hotelling. Stanford University Press, Stanford, CA, pp 278–292

Lewbel A, Pendakur K (2009) Tricks and hicks the EASI demand system. Am Econ Rev 99:827–863

Majumder A, Ray R (2017) Estimates of spatial prices in India and their sensitivity to alternative estimation methods and choice of commodities. Soc Ind Res 131:145–167

Majumder A, Ray R, Sinha K (2012) The calculation of rural–urban food price differentials from unit values in household expenditure surveys: a new procedure and comparison with existing methods. Am J Agric Econ 94:1218–1235

Majumder A, Ray R, Sinha K (2015a) Spatial comparisons of prices and expenditure in a heterogeneous country: methodology with application to India. Macroecon Dyn 19:931–989

Majumder A, Ray R, Sinha K (2015b) Estimating purchasing power parities from household expenditure data using complete demand systems with application to living standards comparison: India and Vietnam. Rev Income Wealth 61(2):302–328

Mantel N (1967) The detection of disease clustering and a generalized regression approach. J Am Assoc Cancer Res 27(2):209–220

McKelvey C (2011) Price, unit value and quantity demanded. J Dev Econ 95:157–169

Mishra A, Ray R (2014) Spatial variation in prices and expenditure inequalities in Australia. Econ Rec 90(289):137–159

Moran PAP (1950) Notes on continuous stochastic phenomena. Biometrika 37(17–23):1950

Neary JP (2004) Rationalizing the Penn World Table: true multilateral indices for international comparisons of real income. Am Econ Rev 94(5):1411–1428

Nordstokke DW, Zumbo BD (2010) A new nonparametric test for equal variances. Psicologica 31:401–430

O'Donnell CJ, Rao DSP (2007) Predicting expenditure shares for computing PPP exchange rates. Unpublished, University of Queensland, Brisbane, Australia

Oulton N (2012) How to measure living standards and productivity. Rev Income Wealth 58:424–456
Rao DSP, Rambaldi A, Doran H (2010) Extrapolation of purchasing power parities using multiple benchmarks and auxiliary information: a new approach. Rev Income Wealth 56:S59–S98
Ravallion M, Datt G (2002) Why has economic growth been more pro-poor in some states of India than others? J Dev Econ 68:381–400
Sen A (1976) Real national income. Rev Econ Stud 43(1):19–39
Sokal RR, Oden NL (1978) Spatial autocorrelation in biology. 1. Methodology. Biol J Linn Soc 10:199–228
Wooldridge JM (2002) Econometric analysis of cross section and panel data. MIT Press, Cambridge, MA

Chapter 7
Optimal Commodity Taxes and Tax Reforms

7.1 Introduction

Direct taxes are an important instrument at the hands of the government to reduce inequality. Conventional wisdom suggests that since indirect taxes are generally regressive, the share of direct taxes should increase and that of indirect taxes should decrease if the government wishes to use fiscal policy to tackle inequality. However, in India, the reverse has been the case with direct taxes accounting for 61% of total taxes in 2009–10, which dropped to 56% in 2013–14. Since Prime Minister Narendra Modi has assumed office, it has dropped further, with direct taxes accounting for 51% of total taxes in 2015–16. In contrast, indirect taxes have been outpacing direct taxes with the share of indirect taxes in total tax revenue increasing steadily over the years. Consequently, indirect taxation has gained in importance as an instrument for revenue raising and in securing redistribution. With the recent introduction of Goods and Services Tax (GST) in India that replaces State sales taxes, the subject of commodity taxation has gained in importance in the context of fiscal policy in India. Though unlike GST rates elsewhere, the GST rates in India allow a limited degree of non-uniformity in taxes between commodities, nevertheless the move reflects a drive towards uniformity. This encourages a return to the classical question in public finance: Should commodity taxes be uniform or differentiated? Given an existing set of commodity tax rates, what should the direction of welfare-improving tax changes be?

The objective of this chapter is on providing empirical evidence on these issues, which are focussed largely but not exclusively on India. While much of the literature on optimal commodity taxes has been analytical concentrating on the conditions for commodity taxes to be uniform at the optimum, the empirical evidence on optimal commodity taxes has been less extensive. One thing that comes through in the analytical literature on optimal commodity taxes is the sensitivity of the structure of such taxes to assumptions on consumer preferences. This chapter reports in some detail the analytical and empirical evidence on the link between

R. Ray, *Household Behaviour, Prices, and Welfare*, Themes in Economics,
https://doi.org/10.1007/978-981-13-1930-3_7

preference specification and optimal commodity taxation, especially on the question posed earlier; Should the commodity taxes be uniform or differentiated? This question has recently assumed added significance in the Indian context in the light of the move to the GST. While the empirical evidence is mostly from India, we also report evidence on optimal commodity taxes from Australia where there was a move to GST in 2000. This chapter also reviews the evidence on the redistributive role of optimal commodity taxes.

Following Ahmad and Stern (1984), the literature has drawn a distinction between tax design and tax reforms. While the former corresponds to optimal taxation, the latter is more practical in that it seeks to explore directions of commodity tax changes that are welfare improving but are revenue neutral with respect to the current vector of tax rates. Ray (1999) has drawn a further distinction between 'marginal' and 'non-marginal' commodity tax reforms. This chapter will describe the studies dealing with these issues, reporting in some detail the empirical evidence, especially that on the sensitivity of the results to the assumed form for consumer preferences in the form of the chosen utility and demand systems. Along with the evidence on optimal commodity taxes, the results on tax reforms will underline the link between the planner's attitude to social welfare as exemplified by her 'inequality aversion', on the lines of Atkinson (1970)'s social welfare function-based inequality measure, and the directions of welfare-improving tax changes.

The plan of this chapter is as follows. Section 7.2 presents the framework for the optimal commodity taxes and reports some of the principal analytical results in the literature. Section 7.3 reports the empirical evidence on optimal commodity tax rates and on their redistribution. Section 7.4 extends the discussion to commodity tax reforms and reports evidence from India and Australia. Section 7.5 examines the implication of allowing tax evasion in the optimal commodity tax model and reports empirical evidence on the sensitivity of the optimal tax rates to tax evasion. Section 7.6 concludes the chapter.

7.2 Optimal Commodity Taxes

7.2.1 The One-Consumer Model

One of the aims of this chapter is to show that optimal commodity tax theory provides a rich analytical structure for the derivation of tax rules, admittedly under alternative sets of specialised conditions, and allows numerical calculations thus yielding hard empirical evidence on tax rates that are of considerable use to the policy analyst. No attempt is made here to survey the large literature on optimal commodity taxes and tax reforms. Several such surveys are available—for example Sandmo (1976), Atkinson and Stiglitz (1980, Chaps. 12, 14), Stern (1987), Slemrod (1990), Myles (1995, Chaps. 4, 6) and Ray (1997). It is important to distinguish between tax design and tax reforms. While the former refers to a movement from an initial state of no taxes to one where they are 'optimal', the latter investigates the direction of social welfare increasing, revenue-neutral commodity tax changes to the existing structure of taxes. Tax reform calculations require less information than tax design since, while the former require knowledge of price and expenditure elasticities only at the point of observed behaviour, the latter require knowledge of the income, price responses globally, specially, at points quite different from the current position.

The two aspects of taxation are not unrelated, however, since 'optimal taxation' can be viewed as the limiting state of a sequence of tax reforms when there is no further possibility of further social welfare increasing tax changes. As described later, Murty and Ray (1989) exploit this relation between commodity tax design and tax reform to propose a computational algorithm that allows optimal commodity taxes taking into account the dependence of prices, quantities, taxes and elasticities on one another. The assumption of goods–leisure separability is maintained throughout the discussion. As Ebrahimi and Heady (1988) point out, this is a crucial assumption for tax design and tax reform. Let q, p, t denote $(n \times 1)$ vectors of consumer prices, producer prices and consumer taxes. Let $u(x)$, $v(q, u)$ denote the individual's direct and indirect utility function, respectively, where x denotes the vector of commodity demand, and $\mu = q'x$ is aggregate expenditure. At the optimum,

$$v(q, u) = u(x) \tag{7.1}$$

Assuming no taxes on wage income so that the government's entire requirement is to be raised through commodity taxes, the revenue constraint is given by

$$R = R_0 \sum_{i=1}^{n} t_i X_i \tag{7.2}$$

where t_i is defined as the difference between consumer price (q_i) and producer price (p_i). This implies the assumption of constant producer prices, i.e. full shifting of taxes to the consumer. The latter has been shown to be consistent with the more general assumption of constant returns to scale. The optimal tax problem involves choosing the set of commodity taxes t_i $(i = 1, \ldots, n)$ that maximises $u(x)$ subject to the revenue constraint Eq. 7.2 and the individual's budget constraint, namely

$$\sum_{i=1}^{n} q_i x_i = wl \tag{7.3}$$

where w is the wage rate and l is labour supplied. The first-order conditions, after routine manipulation, give rise to the following formulation due to Samuelson (1951, reprinted in 1986).

$$\sum_{i=1}^{n} t_i s_{ki} = -v x_k \tag{7.4}$$

Given s_{ki} is the derivative of the compensated demand curve, i.e. the Slutsky substitution effect (hence, $s_{ki} = s_{ik}$), and v is not indexed on k. In other words, the optimal tax structure involves an equi-proportionate movement along the compensated demand curve for all goods. Notwithstanding the elegance of Eq. 7.4, it does not convey much useful practical advice for the design of commodity taxes. To do so, we either need to consider special cases or make further assumptions. Let us consider the case, examined initially by Corlett and hague (1953), of a three-goods model consisting of labour and two-taxed goods. Equation 7.4, then, becomes,

$$t_1 s_{11} + t_2 s_{12} = -v x_1 \tag{7.5}$$

$$t_1 s_{21} + t_2 s_{22} = -v x_2 \tag{7.6}$$

Solving Eqs. 7.5–7.6, we obtain

$$t_1 = -v \frac{x_1 s_{22} - x_2 s_{12}}{s_{11} s_{22} - s_{12}^2} \tag{7.7}$$

$$t_2 = -v \frac{x_2 s_{11} - x_1 s_{21}}{s_{11} s_{22} - s_{12}^2} \tag{7.8}$$

Using the principal requirements of utility and demand theory, it can be shown that Eqs. 7.7–7.8 imply the following,

$$\tilde{t}_1 \gtreqless \tilde{t}_2 \quad \text{according as } \sigma_{10} \lesseqgtr \sigma_{20} \tag{7.9}$$

where $\tilde{t}_1 = t_1/q_1$ is the tax rate and σ_{10} is the compensated cross-elasticity of i (1, 2) with wage, where labour is denoted by '0'. In other words, at the optimum, the good which is to be taxed at the highest rate is the one with the lowest compensated cross-elasticity of labour. Alternatively, this can be stated as follows.

Proposition 1 In a two-goods, one-consumer model, the consumer good which is more complementary with labour (i.e. substitutable for leisure) should be taxed at a lower rate than one which is a substitute for labour (i.e. complementary with leisure).

In the general case of n commodities and leisure, Atkinson and Stiglitz (1972) derive the following two propositions under alternative set of assumptions. The first of these is originally due to Ramsey (1927).

Proposition 2 If there is constant marginal disutility of labour, and the marginal utility of good I is free of consumption of good j, then the optimal commodity tax rate is inversely proportional to the price elasticity of demand.

Proposition 3 In the one-consumer model, if labour supply is completely inelastic, then the optimal commodity tax rate is uniform or, alternatively, labour should bear all the tax.

Both these propositions can be extended as follows.

Proposition 4 [Atkinson and Stiglitz (1972)] When the utility function is directly additive, the optimal commodity tax rate is inversely proportional to the income elasticity of demand.

Proposition 5 [Sandmo (1976)] If there exists utility separability between consumption and labour, and the consumer's preference is homothetic, then the optimal commodity tax rate is uniform.

7.2.2 *The Many-Consumers Model*

The discussion above has concentrated on efficiency, ignoring equity considerations, since it is based on a one-consumer economy. The extension to the many-person case, due to Diamond and Mirrlees (1971), allows equity considerations, in addition to efficiency, and brings out the conflict between the two in the design of commodity taxes. Following Diamond and Mirrlees (1971), and exploiting the equality between direct and indirect utility at the optimum, we define social welfare V over individuals' indirect utilities, so that it is specified as a function of prices. For much of the following discussion, we assume identical preferences, and that the difference between individuals is in wage income only. Let $v^h(q, \mu^h)$, x^h denote, respectively, individual h's ($h = 1, \ldots, H$) indirect utility function and her vector of commodity demand. Then,

$$V(q, \mu) = W[v^1(q, \mu^1), v^2(q, \mu^2), \ldots, v^H(q, \mu^H)] \tag{7.10}$$

If $X(q)$ denotes the aggregate demand vector, then

$$X(q, \mu^1, \mu^2, \ldots, \mu^H) = \sum_{h=1}^{H} x^h(q, \mu^h) \tag{7.11}$$

The revenue constraint is now given by

$$R = R_0 = \sum_{i=1}^{n} t_i X_i \tag{7.12}$$

where R_0 is set exogenously by the authorities.

The optimal tax problem involves maximising W, given by Eq. 7.10, with respect to taxes, subject to the revenue constraint in Eq. 7.12. Assuming, as before, full shifting of taxes so that differentiation with respect to taxes and prices are formally equivalent, optimal commodity taxes imply the following relationship [see Atkinson and Stiglitz (1980, Chap. 12) for derivation].

$$\frac{\sum_{i=1}^{n}\sum_{h=1}^{H} t_i S_{ki}^h}{\sum_{h=1}^{H} x_i^h} = -\left[1 - \sum_{h=1}^{H} \frac{b_h}{H}\frac{x_k^h}{\overline{x_k}}\right] \tag{7.13}$$

where S_{ki}^h is individual h's Slutsky (compensated) quantity response of item k to unit change in price of i, $\overline{x_k}$ is the mean demand for k, and b^h is given by,

$$b^h = \frac{\beta_h}{\lambda} + \sum_{i=1}^{n} t_i \frac{\delta x_i^h}{\delta \mu^h} \tag{7.14}$$

$\beta_h = \delta W / \delta v^h$. α^h is individual h's gross social marginal utility of income, α^h is h's private marginal utility of income, and λ can be interpreted as the social 'cost' in welfare terms of raising an extra unit of revenue. Following Diamond (1975), b^h is net social marginal utility of income measured in terms of government revenue. It is *net* in the sense that it measures both the gain in social welfare due to an increase in income to h, and the increase in payments of h due to this increase in income.

Equation 7.13 is the many-person generalisation of Eq. 7.4, with an essential feature of the latter lost in the generalisation, namely, that the RHS of Eq. 7.13 is *not* invariant to the choice of commodity k. The tax rule, given by Eq. 7.13, shows that the reduction in aggregate compensated demand for the kth commodity due to the introduction of the optimal tax system should be inverse related to the correlation between b^h and x_k^h. Hence, goods consumed by those with high b^hs, typically necessities, should attract lower taxes. Equation 7.13, therefore, incorporates equity considerations, via the b^hs, in addition to efficiency. It is worth noting that b^h, which is endogenous to the optimal tax system, is dependent via β^h, partly on the a priori social welfare function, W, and partly on the structure of the consumer's income effects, $(\frac{\delta x_i^h}{\delta \mu^h})$. Like its one-consumer counterpart, Eq. 7.13 is not a particularly useful guide for tax design since it does not yield explicit expressions for optimal commodity taxes. A large part of the literature of optimal commodity taxes in a many-person economy has been concerned with the derivation of alternative sets of sufficient conditions for optimally uniform commodity taxes. Though these conditions are quite restrictive, economists tend to focus on the uniform commodity tax case as a benchmark similar to the focus on the perfectly competitive model, for example. The following propositions summarise the principal results on optimal commodity taxes in a many-person economy. We state these results in order of increasing generality about assumptions on the nature of Engel curve relationship across individuals.

Proposition 7 [Atkinson (1977)] If (a) consumers have identical preferences and they are given by the Linear Expenditure System, (b) consumers differ in wage income only, and (c) an optimal income tax is in force, then uniform commodity taxation is optimal.

Proposition 8 [Deaton (1979)] If (a) consumers have identical preferences and demand functions have linear Engel curves, (b) consumers differ in their wage income only, (c) leisure is weakly separable from goods, and (d) optimal linear income tax is in force, then uniform commodity taxation is optimal.

Proposition 9 [Deaton and Stern (1986)] If (a) households have non-identical preferences but these preferences exhibit linear and parallel Engel curves differing only in intercepts dependent on household composition, (b) an optimal 'demogrant' scheme linear in observable household characteristics exists, (c) leisure is weakly separable from goods, and (d) optimal linear income tax is in force, then uniform commodity taxation is optimal.

Proposition 10 [Atkinson and Stiglitz (1976)] If (a) consumers have identical preferences, (b) consumers differ in their wage income only, (c) leisure is weakly separable from goods, and (d) optimal nonlinear income tax is in force, then uniform commodity taxation is optimal.

Ray (1986b) examines the implication of relaxing the assumption of linear Engel curves, while retaining a linear income tax, within the framework of the Restricted Nonlinear Preferences (RNLPS) demand system introduced by Blundell and Ray (1984). The RNLPS is given by,

$$x_i^h = \frac{1}{q_i}\,\delta_i^h(\mu^h) + \frac{\beta_i}{q_i}\,\mu^h, \quad \sum \beta_i = 1 \tag{7.15}$$

where

$$\delta_i^h = q_i^\alpha \gamma_i \mu^{h^{1-\alpha}} - \beta_i \sum_k q_k^\alpha \gamma_k \mu^{h^{1-\alpha}} \tag{7.15a}$$

$(\beta_i, \gamma, \alpha)$ are the demand system parameters, and α, if different from unity, allows nonlinear Engel curves.

Let us define

$$\overline{\delta_i} = \frac{1}{H}\sum_h \delta_i^h \tag{7.16a}$$

$$\delta_i^* = \sum_h \frac{b^h}{H\bar{b}}\,\delta_i^h \tag{7.16b}$$

Ray (1986b) proves the following result.

Proposition 11 If (a) consumers have non-identical preferences, (b) preferences exhibit nonlinear and non-parallel Engel curves of the RNLPS form, (c) leisure is weakly separable from goods, and (d) an optimal linear income tax is in force, then a sufficient condition for optimally uniform commodity taxes as follows:

$$\overline{\delta_{\imath}} - \delta_i^* = \imath\left(1 - \frac{1}{\alpha}\right)\frac{1}{H}\sum_{h=1}^{H}\left(\tilde{\Phi}^h \mu^h \frac{\delta w_i^h}{\delta \mu^h}\right) \tag{7.17}$$

Given $\imath$ is the uniform commodity tax rate, w_i^h is the budget share of item I in household h, and $\tilde{\Phi}^h = S_{i0}^h / \left(\delta x_i^h / \delta \mu^h\right)$ is the proportionality factor implied by weak separability between goods and leisure, with S_{i0}^h denoting individual h's Slutsky (compensated) quantity response of item i to unit change in the wage rate.

Equation 7.17 yields, as special cases, certain well-known sufficiency conditions for uniform commodity taxes.

Case 1 If Engel curves are linear, i.e. $\alpha = 1$, Eq. 7.17 will be automatically satisfied, since $\overline{\delta_{\imath}} = \delta_i^*$ in this case, and both sides of Eq. 7.17 will equal zero. Note that this includes the case of LES preferences considered by Atkinson (1977) [see Proposition 7].

Case 2 If the γ_is are all zero, i.e. the goods' utility function is of the Cobb Douglas form, then again Eq. 7.17 will be satisfied since both sides will be zero, and commodity taxes will be uniform. This is a well-known result in the literature.

Case 3 If the b^hs are all equal, then $\imath = 0$ is the solution. In such a case, commodity taxes will not only be uniform but will be zero leaving the government to raise revenue by direct taxes. Note that this result is true even in the presence of nonlinear Engel curves [see Atkinson and Stiglitz (1980, Chap. 14)].

7.3 Empirical Evidence on Optimal Commodity Taxes

7.3.1 Introduction

Although, as already noted, it is widely recognised that calculations on optimal tax rates depend quite crucially on assumptions about consumer preferences, the empirical evidence on how the tax rates vary with utility and demand specification seem virtually non-existent. Most existing studies on optimal tax rates and tax reforms (see, e.g. Atkinson and Stiglitz 1972; Harris and Mackinnon 1979; Ahmad and Stern 1984) have done so using additively separable utility functions, for example those corresponding to the Direct Addilog System, the Linear Expenditure System or its homothetic specialisation, the Cobb–Douglas system. Although in the absence of a poll tax and in the many-person case the first two systems do not ***necessarily*** imply uniform taxes, they distort consumer behaviour considerably and this restricts the usefulness of the tax rates generated by them. Ray (1986a) provides empirical evidence on optimal commodity tax rates on Indian budget data departing from the assumption of linearity and separability that characterised the earlier literature. Given the importance of commodity taxes in India and, more generally, in developing countries, the methodology, data set and the empirical results of this study are described in some detail here.

Ray (1986a) attempts to answer the following questions:

(i) How sensitive are the estimated 'optimal' commodity tax rates to demand specification?
(ii) How sensitive are the 'optimal' tax rates to variation in the government's 'inequality aversion'?
(iii) What redistributive impacts are implied by the alternative sets of 'optimal' tax rates calculated in (i) and how do they compare across demand specification and inequality aversion?

The methodology adopted in this study involves solving the Ramsey first-order conditions at a given time period as a set of simultaneous equations, with the 'optimal' commodity tax rates being the unknown, estimable parameters. The exercise is carried out for alternative demand systems, and the corresponding sets of commodity tax rates compared. The empirical results, reported later, show considerable sensitivity of tax rates to demand specification. Before proceeding, it is necessary to make the following points:

(1) The term 'optimality', as used in Ray (1986a), needs to be very carefully interpreted since it is strictly conditional upon the particular configuration of prices and expenditure levels ***observed*** at a particular time. It will be unwise for the reader to interpret the present tax estimates, literally and unconditionally, as optimal taxes which, strictly speaking, they are not. For taxes to be strictly interpreted as optimal, the calculations must allow for the dependence of expenditure and price levels on taxes via a simulation algorithm which ***simultaneously*** arrives at the optimal value of all these variables. This, however, was not done in Ray (1986a), mainly for computational reasons.

Instead, this study used as given actual prices and expenditure levels. As Ahmad and Stern (1984, p. 269) have recently pointed out: 'one is taking current prices, given demands and given demand responses and asking what would the tax component in the price have to be in order to be described as optimum' (in a model where the Ramsey assumptions apply, particularly 100 per cent shifting).

(2) The evidence in Ray (1986a) is on 'optimal tax rates', and not tax reforms. It is important to distinguish between the two, since sensitivity of the calculated 'optimal' tax rates to demand specification does not ***necessarily imply*** similar sensitivity of directions for tax reform. The latter is an interesting exercise in itself, and one such study [Murty and Ray (1989)] is described in the following Section.
(3) While Ray (1986a) permits nonlinear Engel curves and non-separable preferences via the Restricted Nonlinear Preferences System (RNLPS) demand system employed, this study continued the tradition in this area of assuming weak separability between goods and leisure. The absence of wage and earnings data makes it imperative that demand is analysed conditional on total commodity expenditure and prices with no mention of labour supply behaviour. Such a treatment can only be rationalised by assuming weak separability

between goods and leisure. In common with other studies, an income tax is ruled out by assumption, indirect taxes are passed on fully to the consumer, and all households face identical prices at a given point in time.

7.3.2 Methodology

Let us recall the social welfare maximising exercise yielding the optimal tax rates. This involves the government maximising a social welfare function, expressed in the Bergson–Samuelson form as a function $W(V^1, V^2, \ldots, V^H)$ of the indirect utilities of the H individuals, given their demand function $x_h(q, \mu_h)$. More formally, the government chooses t_i $(i = 1, \ldots, n)$ to

$$\max_{t \varepsilon \mathrm{T}} W\left[V^1(q, \mu_1), V^2(q, \mu_2), \ldots, V^H(q, \mu_H)\right]$$

subject to $\sum_{i=1}^{n} t_i \left(\sum_{h=1}^{H} x_i^h\right) \leqq R_0$

The corresponding Lagrangian is

$$\mathrm{L} = \mathrm{W}(\mathrm{V}^1, \mathrm{V}^2, \ldots \mathrm{V}^{\mathrm{H}}) + \lambda \left[\sum_{i=1}^{n} t_i \left(\sum_{h=1}^{H} x_i^h\right) - R_0\right] \tag{7.18}$$

Let us denote $\tilde{t}_i = t_i/q_i$ to be the indirect tax paid per unit of consumer price, q_i. The first-order equations can be written as

$$-\sum_{h=1}^{H} \beta^h x_i^h + \lambda\left[\mathrm{H}\,\overline{X}_i + \sum_{k=1}^{n} \tilde{t}_k\, q_k \frac{\delta X_k}{\delta q_i}\right] = 0, \quad i = 1, \ldots, \mathrm{n} \tag{7.19}$$

$$R_0 = \sum_{i=1}^{n} \tilde{t}_i\, q_i X_i \tag{7.20}$$

where $\beta^h = (\delta W/\delta V^h)$. η^h is the 'social marginal utility of income' of h, $X_i = \sum_{h=1}^{H} x_i^h$, $\overline{X}_i = X_i/H$.

Equations 7.19–7.20 is the basic estimating system in the study [Ray (1986a)] with $\tilde{t}_i$ and λ treated as estimable parameters. λ can be interpreted as the social 'cost' in welfare terms of raising an extra unit of revenue. For a particular survey period, namely NSS 28th round in Ray (1986a) and assuming that the revenue requirement R_0 is fixed exogenously by the authorities, Eqs. 7.19–7.20 containing $(n + 1)$ equations can be solved for the $(n + 1)$ unknowns $\{\tilde{t}_i, \lambda\}$. To estimate the above system of equations, one requires, besides data on individual (x_i^h) and aggregate demand (X_i), information on β^h and the price responses, $\frac{\delta X_k}{\delta q_i}$. The price responses are obtained from the demand parameter estimates. To measure β^h, Ray (1986a) chooses the following utility function due to Atkinson (1970).

$$U^h(\mu) = \frac{k\mu^{h^{1-\varepsilon}}}{1-\varepsilon}, \varepsilon \neq 1 \quad (7.21a)$$

$$U^h(\mu) = k \log \mu^h, \varepsilon = 1. \quad (7.21b)$$

where $\varepsilon \geq 0$ is interpreted as the planner's 'inequality aversion', with higher ε representing greater aversion. Normalising $\beta^1 = 1$ for the poorest household in the sample, we obtain the following expression for the social marginal utility of income.

$$\beta^h = \left[\frac{\mu^1}{\mu^h}\right]^{\varepsilon} \quad (7.22)$$

Equation 7.22 implies that the 'social marginal utility of income' for the poorest household is unity and declines monotonically with an increase in household affluence at a rate determined by ε. The sensitivity of the commodity tax rates is examined with respect to the price-expenditure elasticities from the widely used Linear Expenditure System (LES) and its one-parameter (α) generalisation, namely the Restricted Nonlinear Preferences System (RNLPS) mentioned earlier. Let us now turn to the question of redistribution implied by the 'optimal' tax rates. The redistributive effect of indirect taxation in the context of a developing economy like India is likely to be as important an issue as efficiency. In deriving measures of redistribution for the two demand systems, Ray (1986a) follows the approach of Sah (1983) and assumes that the public budget is balanced and that the real income gain to the 'worst off' is taken as the measure of redistribution. Let 1 be the worst-off household. Denoting T_h to be the indirect taxes paid by household h, the public budget constraint is $\sum_h T_h = 0$ which incorporates the assumption that indirect taxation is viewed purely as a redistributive mechanism between the various households. If T_1 measures 'redistribution' to the worst-off household 1 with aggregate expenditure, μ_1, then for the LES, Ray (1986a) derives, in proportionate terms, an expression for redistribution as follows.

$$-\frac{T_1}{\mu_1} = \sum_{i=1}^{n} \tilde{t}_i a_i \left(\frac{\mu}{\mu_1} - 1\right) \quad (7.23)$$

Given a_i is the 'subsistence quantity' in the LES and $\mu(= \frac{\sum \mu^h}{H})$ is the mean expenditure. The corresponding expression for the RNLPS is given by

$$-\frac{T_1}{\mu_1} = \sum_{i=1}^{n} \tilde{t}_i\, a_i \left(\frac{\mu^*}{\mu} - 1\right) \quad (7.24)$$

where $\mu^* = \sum \mu_h / \sum \mu_h^{1-\alpha}$, and α is the parameter that generalises the RNLPS over LES. Note that if $\alpha = 1$, Eq. 7.24 becomes identical to the LES measure Eq. 7.23.

7.3.3 Data and Results

Ray (1986a) was based on the time series of household budget surveys in urban India, published annually as National Sample Survey Reports. The required price elasticities were obtained from the demand systems estimated on 60 observations from pooled NSS data covering 7th–28th rounds (excluding the 26th and 27th rounds whose reports were not available). The tax rates were then calculated using the cross-sectional expenditure information for NSS, 28th round and so the conditional 'optimal tax estimates' are to be taken to be valid for the survey period of NSS 28th round, namely 1973–74 only. The exercise was based on a nine-commodity breakdown of aggregate expenditure, including a disaggregation of the category 'Food' into six principal constituents. Table 7.1 presents the 'optimal' tax rates for the two demand systems calculated at sample mean for NSS, 28th round and at various levels of 'inequality aversion' (ε). The tax rates for the two demand systems are much closer to one another at low levels of ε than at high levels—fairly substantial differences exist at high levels of 'inequality aversion'. In many cases, comparable estimates differ not only in their absolute magnitude but, more crucially, in their sign as well. In relation to RNLPS, for example, the LES overestimates quite substantially the 'optimal' subsidy on cereals for 'Rawlsian-minded' tax authorities ($\varepsilon = 5.0$). Still more significant is the result that a 'Rawlsian-minded' authority ($\varepsilon = 3.0, 5.0$) believing in the LES would proceed to impose fairly significant-sized taxes on Sugar and Tea and Fuel and Light, while its counterpart, believing in the LES generalisation, RNLPS, would actually be providing a subsidy to these items. It is, incidentally, worth noting that some of the tax estimates in Table 7.1, especially for the relatively smaller items of expenditure, are quite implausible, possibly, reflecting the quality of the recorded price-expenditure data for these items.

The most important point of similarity between the two sets of tax rates is that both demand systems suggest a rough move towards uniform taxes, at least for the major items, at low levels of inequality aversion ($\varepsilon = 0.1$). It should be noted, however, that neither the LES nor the RNLPS strictly implies proportional taxes for the sense of 'optimality' used here. The two demand systems also agree that, as 'inequality aversion' (ε) increases, a positive tax on cereals is replaced by a subsidy which increases in magnitude—the exact reverse is the case for the principal 'luxury' item, other non-Food. The principal result of interest in this study is the relative robustness of 'optimal' tax rates to demand systems at low levels of 'inequality aversion' but their extreme sensitivity at high levels. This seems to suggest an interconnection between the inequality aversion parameter, ε, and the nonlinearity parameter, α. Since the estimated α (= 0.236) is a long way from unity,

Table 7.1 Estimates of t_i and λ in the many-person case[a] (Ray 1986a)

Item	Parameter	Demand system	Alternative degree of inequality aversion (ε)				
			$\varepsilon = 0.1$	$\varepsilon = 0.5$	$\varepsilon = 1.5$	$\varepsilon = 3.0$	$\varepsilon = 5.0$
1. Cereals	$\tilde{t}_1$	LES	0.139	−0.365	1.569	−2.181	−2.222
	$\tilde{t}_1$	RNLPS	0.143	−0.136	0.999	−1.593	−1.643
2. Milk and milk products	$\tilde{t}_2$	LES	0.033	0.187	0.594	0.829	0.847
	$\tilde{t}_2$	RNLPS	0.039	0.144	0.528	0.844	0.875
3. Edible oils	$\tilde{t}_3$	LES	0.748	0.921	1.379	1.665	1.720
	$\tilde{t}_3$	RNLPS	0.683	0.727	0.914	1.107	1.167
4. Meat, fish and eggs	$\tilde{t}_4$	LES	0.773	1.066	1.771	2.162	2.246
	$\tilde{t}_4$	RNLPS	0.845	1.015	1.547	1.962	2.087
5. Sugar and tea	$\tilde{t}_5$	LES	0.023	0.077	0.246	0.358	0.370
	$\tilde{t}_5$	RNLPS	0.053	0.007	−0.087	−0.114	−0.110
6. Other Food	$\tilde{t}_6$	LES	0.135	0.253	0.515	0.624	0.608
	$\tilde{t}_6$	RNLPS	0.155	0.196	0.298	0.332	0.302
7. Clothing	$\tilde{t}_7$	LES	−0.029	0.141	0.538	0.727	0.730
	$\tilde{t}_7$	RNLPS	−0.050	0.103	0.558	0.849	0.854
8. Fuel and Light	$\tilde{t}_8$	LES	0.068	0.108	0.215	0.268	0.261
	$\tilde{t}_8$	RNLPS	0.105	0.024	−0.216	−0.383	−0.409
9. Other non-Food	$\tilde{t}_9$	LES	−0.078	0.065	0.396	0.560	0.576
	$\tilde{t}_9$	RNLPS	−0.101	0.011	0.342	0.564	0.592
	λ	LES	1.590	0.779	0.236	0.109	0.070
	λ	RNLPS	1.667	0.761	0.191	0.079	0.050

[a]Note that these calculations are only for NSS (urban) 28th round

the calculated price elasticities are highly sensitive to the relaxation of the linearity/separability assumptions. At low levels of ε, such sensitivity does not matter from the view point of tax calculations since, for an inequality-neutral tax authority, the main motive for a differentiated tax system, namely securing redistribution, being largely absent, the 'efficient' tax system would resemble uniformity, irrespective of what the calculated price elasticities turn out to be. However, at high levels of ε the sensitivity of price responses to demand systems will be translated to a similar sensitivity of tax estimates, since the calculated price responses will become all that more important. To take a simple but extremely illustrative example, Fuel and Light is a 'luxury' on LES estimates but not on RNLPS-based calculations. A 'highly inequality averse' tax authority therefore favours a large tax for this item in one case (LES) but a large subsidy in the other. This is highlighted by the complete reversal in the relationship between the 'optimal' tax rate for this item and ε, as between the two demand systems. A similar reversal occurs for Sugar and Tea as well. Overall, the empirical evidence from both the demand systems suggests non-uniform commodity taxes at the 'optimum' with 'optimality' used in the restrictive sense of being conditional on observed behaviour.

Table 7.2 shows the redistributive impact of the 'optimal' tax rates for LES and RNLPS demand systems calculated using Eqs. 7.23–7.24, respectively.

The calculations were performed for a hypothetical household whose aggregate expenditure equals half that of the sample average. The real income gain, implied by the LES tax rates, seems to become significant only at very high levels of 'inequality aversion' (ε). However, allowing for nonlinear Engel curves makes the 'efficiency'-based tax rates look a good deal *less* progressive—indeed, for this particular household it implies a redistribution away from itself. The estimated redistribution suggest that for the chosen survey, i.e. NSS (urban) 28th round, the RNLPS tax rates imply a real income gain only for *very poor* households, namely those with less than 4% of the sample average. In other words, a lot fewer households gain under the RNLPS tax rates than under LES; however, for those that do gain under the former, the size of the gain is a good deal larger than under LES. Ray (1986b) extends Ray (1986a) by estimating the redistribution brought about by the actual commodity tax rates in rural and urban areas using the measure of redistribution $\left(\frac{T_1}{\mu_1}\right)$ given by Eq. 7.24.

Based on the nine-commodity breakdown of consumer expenditure in Ray (1986a) and the LES, RNLPS demand parameter estimates obtained in that study, the actual indirect tax rates for this nine-commodity classification calculated by Ahmad and Stern (1984), Ray (1986b, Table 2) reports the effect of relaxing linear Engel curves in consumer behaviour on the redistribution. This table is reproduced as Table 7.3 here. The calculations were performed at two expenditure (μ) levels: Rs. 30 and Rs. 50 which correspond to individuals within the bottom 30% of the expenditure distribution. The limited redistribution possibilities of indirect taxation, pointed out by Sah (1983) and also seen in the evidence based on optimal tax rates presented in Ray (1986a) and reported in Table 7.2, are confirmed in Ray (1986b). In fact, the picture looks a good deal worse. *Both* the hypothetical households, far

Table 7.2 Redistributive impact of 'optimal' indirect taxes[a] $(-T_1/\mu_1)$ (Ray 1986a)

Alternative degree of inequality aversion (ε)					
$\varepsilon = 0.1$		$\varepsilon = 1.5$		$\varepsilon = 5.0$	
LES	RNLPS	LES	RNLPS	LES	RNLPS
0.070	0.070	0.343	−1.13	0.447	−1.80

[a] $\mu_1 = \frac{1}{2}\mu$, μ = 'average expenditure' $\sum \mu_h/H$

Table 7.3 Redistribution for India based on actual indirect tax rates $\left(-\frac{T_L}{\mu_L}\right)$ (Ray 1986b)

Expenditure Level	Rural		Urban	
	Linear Engel Curve	Nonlinear Engel Curve	Linear Engel Curve	Nonlinear Engel Curve
Rs. 20	0.105	−0.031	0.220	−0.038
Rs. 50	0.004	−0.039	0.037	−0.041

from gaining, are actual net losers in the nonlinear case. Since India is a typical developing country which relies on indirect taxes as its main source of revenue, the result suggests that the possibilities of securing significant redistribution through relying on indirect taxation alone are very limited indeed.

7.3.4 An Algorithm for Calculating Optimal Commodity Taxes

A computational difficulty in calculating optimal commodity tax rates, using the first-order conditions, Eqs. 7.19–7.20, stems from the need to generate the demand, the price levels, and the price elasticities at the optimum and use them rather than the observed values as done in Ray (1986a). Murty and Ray (1989) propose and implement an improved procedure for calculating optimal commodity taxes that takes into account the simultaneous interdependence of taxes, expenditure and price levels/responses, thus making the calculated taxes truly optimal. If λ_i ($I = 1, \ldots, n$) denotes the marginal social cost of raising an extra unit of revenue, then

$$\lambda_i = -\frac{\frac{\delta V}{\delta t_i}}{\frac{\delta R}{\delta t_i}} \tag{7.25}$$

where V, R are given by Eq. 7.10 and Eq. 7.12, respectively. If $\lambda_i \neq \lambda_j$, then social welfare can be increased by reducing taxes on commodities with higher than average λ_is, and raising taxes on others until the λ_is are all equal, when commodity taxes are optimal. The optimal tax algorithm is based on this principle and is given as follows.

Change taxes according to

$$\Delta t_i^{(r)} = [\bar{\lambda}^{(r-1)} - \lambda_i^{(r-1)}] \tag{7.26}$$

where the superscript r denotes the round of the iterative procedure, $\bar{\lambda}$ is the expenditure weighted mean of the λ_is, and k ($0 < k < 1$) is the step length fixed exogenously for a particular set of tax calculations. At each round in the iterative procedure, the demand levels, elasticities, social welfare weights, etc., are recalculated at the new vector of commodity taxes. Murty and Ray (1989) show that the procedure ensures revenue neutrality between initial and optimal commodity taxes.

The initial rural estimates of the marginal social cost of raising revenue, λ_i^0(with corresponding rankings in parentheses) at two widely dispersed levels of inequality aversion ($\varepsilon = 2.0, 25.0$) for the alternative demand systems RNLPS, LES are presented in Table 4. The table also contains the corresponding urban estimates for LES and the λ-rankings as reported by Ahmad and Stern (1984) from their computations on pooled rural and urban data using the LES. The following results emerge from Table 7.4:

Table 7.4 Initial estimates ($\lambda_i^0 s$) and ranking of $\lambda_i s$ (Murty and Ray 1989)

Commodities	Effective taxes	RNLPS		LES				λ rankings as reported by Ahmad and Stern (1984, Table 1(a))	
		Rural	Rural	Rural		Urban		Rural and urban data pooled	
		ε = 2.0	ε = 25.0	ε = 2.0	ε = 25.0	ε = 2.0	ε = 25.0	ε = 2.0	ε = 5.0
1. Cereals	−0.052	0.039(2)	0.029(2)	0.068(2)	0.028(2)	0.056(2)	0.015(3)	(2)	(2)
2. Milk and milk products	0.009	0.005(7)	0.003(7)	0.013(7)	0.003(7)	0.012(8)	0.002(9)	(9)	(9)
3. Edible oils	0.083	0.018(3)	0.013(3)	0.039(3)	0.012(3)	0.028(5)	0.006(6)	(4)	(5)
4. Meat, fish and eggs	0.014	0.016(4)	0.011(4)	0.033(5)	0.011(4)	0.026(6)	0.009(4)	(5)	(4)
5. Sugar and tea	0.069	0.014(5)	0.009(5)	0.029(6)	0.009(5)	0.032(4)	0.007(5)	(5)	(6)
6. Other Foods	0.114	0.011(6)	0.004(6)	0.035(4)	0.004(6)	0.039(3)	0.016(2)	(3)	(3)
7. Clothing	0.242	0.004(9)	0.002(9)	0.012(8)	0.002(9)	0.009(9)	0.003(8)	(7)	(8)
8. Fuel	0.247	0.045(1)	0.033(1)	0.081(1)	0.034(1)	0.057(1)	0.021(1)	(1)	(1)
9. Other non-Food	0.133	0.005(7)	0.003(7)	0.011(9)	0.003(7)	0.015(7)	0.005(7)	(8)	(7)

Note Figure in parentheses denotes rankings of the λ_is

(1) The rural sample yields identical rankings of $\bar{\lambda}_i^0$ for both levels of inequality aversion with RNLPS but not with LES. The $\bar{\lambda}_i^0$ rankings for the two demand systems are identical in the Rawlsian case of very high inequality aversion ($\varepsilon = 25.0$).
(2) The urban sample, in contrast, reveals sensitivity of the $\bar{\lambda}$-rankings to ε.
(3) The LES ranking of the $\bar{\lambda}_i$s is quite sensitive to the rural/urban data employed. The above results underline the importance of allowing for rural/urban differences in India's expenditure pattern. The assumption of identical preferences between rural and urban areas underlines use of pooled rural/urban data in applied welfare analysis. If untrue, such pooling is likely to yield misleading estimates of optimal commodity taxes and indicate false directions of tax reform, as confirmed by Table 7.4.

The optimal commodity taxes obtained using the iterative procedure are presented in Table 7.5. Murty and Ray (1989) report that their experience with the proposed procedure has been very encouraging—they seldom faced convergence problems (except at low values of ε) with the $\bar{\lambda}_i^{(r)}$ converging towards one another from iteration 2 onwards, and particularly rapidly from iteration 25. In all of the cases reported in Table 7.5, convergence was attained within 200 iterations. Convergence was faster with the RNLPS parameter estimates than with their linear counterparts. Three features of Murty and Ray (1989)'s exercise deserve mention.

(a) The estimates reported in Table 7.5 were found to be truly optimal by checking that they are invariant to choice of step length k, and to alternative sets of revenue-neutral commodity taxes as starting values.
(b) The iterative procedure was found to be monotonically increasing in social welfare. The 'proportionate social gain' measure, S, due to King (1983), and β_h-weighted sums of equivalent and compensating gains of tax change all increased monotonically as the process iterated towards the optimum.

Table 7.5 Estimates of optimal commodity taxes, t_i (Murty and Ray 1989)

Commodities	Rural			Urban	
	RNLPS		LES	LES	
	$\varepsilon = 2.0$	$\varepsilon = 25.0$	$\varepsilon = 25.0$	$\varepsilon = 2.0$	$\varepsilon = 25.0$
1. Cereals	−0.571	−0.647	−0.651	−0.678	−0.733
2. Milk and milk products	−0.190	−0.050	−0.104	0.051	0.197
3. Edible oils	0.048	−0.009	0.483	1.210	0.347
4. Meat, fish and eggs	−0.151	−0.136	−0.116	0.103	0.166
5. Sugar and tea	−0.312	−0.255	−0.242	−0.233	−0.252
6. Other Foods	−0.009	−0.085	0.887	0.397	0.379
7. Clothing	0.151	0.330	0.156	0.358	0.537
8. Fuel	−0.103	−0.238	0.160	0.422	0.054
9. Other non-Food	1.087	1.292	0.711	0.318	0.506
$\lambda_i = \lambda_j = \bar{\lambda}$	0.398	0.164	0.153	0.615	0.175

Note t_i represents tax revenue for a Rupee's producer price worth of final consumer demand

(c) The demand regularity conditions, namely non-negativity of Hicksian demand and negative semi-definiteness of the Slutsky substitution matrix, were satisfied at all points in the iterative process and at the optimum.

Table 7.5 shows that, for either demand system, the optimal commodity taxes are far from uniform. The table also confirms the sensitivity of optimal commodity tax estimates to demand functional form as obtained in Ray (1986a). The tax estimates reveal significant rural/urban differences. The LES figures, for example, show that comparable estimates not only differ markedly in absolute magnitude, but for some items they do not even agree on the sign. A significant feature of these calculations is that Murty and Ray (1989) have allowed the social marginal utility of income, β_h, to depend on prices and hence vary with each iteration. The β_h estimates at the initial, i.e. observed vector of prices, and at the optimum are presented in Table 7.6. For a Rawlsian planner (e = 25.0) with maximin preferences, the welfare weights—not surprisingly—remain the same. However, for $\varepsilon = 2.0$, the weights do change significantly over the iterations.

7.4 Commodity Tax Reforms

7.4.1 Marginal Commodity Tax Reforms

The algorithm for calculating optimal commodity taxes described above yield in the initial round a ranking of the λ_i^0s which provide the direction of marginal tax changes that are Pareto improving but are revenue neutral with respect to the existing vector of tax rates. In an influential paper, Ahmad and Stern (1984) proposed the theory and methodology of marginal commodity tax reforms and illustrated the proposed methods with an empirical discussion of the possibilities of tax reform in India. A 'welfare-improving tax reform' is defined as a vector of tax changes which increases social welfare but does not decrease tax revenue. Ahmad and Stern (1984) demonstrate how, given a social welfare function and data on taxes and expenditure, directions of welfare improve reform can be found. Let us recall the definition of λ_i as the marginal cost in terms of social welfare of raising an extra unit of revenue from increasing the tax on that good. We can, therefore, find welfare-improving tax reform if, for example, λ_i exceeds λ_j. In that case, we increase aggregate social welfare at constant revenue by increasing taxes on the jth good by an amount sufficient to raise one unit of revenue, and decreasing taxes on the ith good by an amount sufficient to lose one unit of revenue. Clearly, the possibility of welfare-improving tax reforms exists as long as the λ_is are not equal. When they are, commodity taxes are optimal.

Table 7.6 Estimates of social welfare weights (β_h) of the households (Murty and Ray 1989)

Expenditure class (Rs.)	Rural				Expenditure class (Rs.)	Urban			
	RNLPS: $\varepsilon = 2.0$		RNLPS: $\varepsilon = 25.0$			LES: $\varepsilon = 2.0$		LES: $\varepsilon = 25.0$	
	Initial	At optimum	Initial	At optimum		Initial	At optimum	Initial	At optimum
10–15	1.000	1.000	1.000	1.000	10–15	1.000	1.000	1.000	1.000
15–20	0.142	0.332	0.000	0.000	15–20	0.399	0.473	0.000	0.000
20–30	0.034	0.114	0.000	0.000	20–30	0.163	0.216	0.000	0.000
30–35	0.017	0.065	0.000	0.000	30–35	0.097	0.135	0.000	0.000
35–40	0.012	0.047	0.000	0.000	35–40	0.071	0.101	0.000	0.000
40–50	0.007	0.032	0.000	0.000	40–50	0.048	0.069	0.000	0.000
50–60	0.005	0.021	0.000	0.000	50–60	0.031	0.047	0.000	0.000
60–70	0.003	0.015	0.000	0.000	60–70	0.022	0.033	0.000	0.000
70–80	0.002	0.011	0.000	0.000	70–80	0.016	0.025	0.000	0.000
80–100	0.002	0.008	0.000	0.000	80–100	0.011	0.017	0.000	0.000
100–150	0.001	0.005	0.000	0.000	100–150	0.006	0.009	0.000	0.000
150–200	0.000	0.003	0.000	0.000	150–200	0.003	0.005	0.000	0.000
200 & above	0.000	0.000	0.000	0.000	200–300	0.001	0.002	0.000	0.000
					300 and above	0.000	0.001	0.000	0.000

Using Roy's identity and the definition of the revenue constraint, λ_i can be expressed in terms of observables as follows:

$$\lambda_i = \frac{\sum_h \beta^h e_i^h}{E_i - \sum_{k=1}^n R_k E_{ki}} \tag{7.27}$$

As already defined, β^h is the social marginal utility of income to h, $e_i = q_i x_i^h$ is money expenditure on i by h, $E_i = \sum_h e_i^h$ is aggregate money expenditure on i, $R_k = t_k X_k$ is tax revenue from good k, and E_{ki} is the aggregate uncompensated price elasticity of k with respect to price of i. The following comments are in order. First, to calculate the λ_is, we require four items of information: the money demands, e_i^h, the welfare weights, β^h, the taxes, t_k and the aggregate price elasticities, E_{ki}. Second, we require information on demand levels and elasticities only at observed point of behaviour. Third, we do not need to calculate elasticities for each individual, only aggregate elasticities are required. The marginal tax reform calculations thus impose far fewer data requirements than optimal commodity taxes. Finally, the theory of marginal commodity tax reforms is limited in scope in three respects: (i) while it can indicate the *direction* of reforms, it says nothing about the *size* of the reform, (ii) while, in general, there will be many welfare-improving directions of reform, the theory is unable to tell us which to choose, and (iii) the analysis is marginal in the sense that it is restricted to small movements from the status quo.

7.4.2 Non-marginal Commodity Tax Reforms and Price Dependent Welfare Weights

Ray (1999) extends the marginal tax reform framework of Ahmad and Stern (1984) by (i) allowing the social welfare weights, β_h, to vary with prices, q, and (ii) proposing a framework for evaluating non-marginal tax changes that are welfare improving but do not decrease tax revenue. To allow price dependence, the social welfare weights are written as

$$\beta^h = \frac{\delta V[v^1(q,\mu^1), v^2(q,\mu^2), \ldots, v^H(q,\mu^H)]}{\delta v^h(q,\mu^h)} \cdot \frac{\delta v^h(q,\mu^h)}{\delta \mu^h} \tag{7.28}$$

β^h is therefore, implicitly, a function of consumer price, q and taxes, t. In the tax calculations on Australian data, Ray (1999) departs from conventional practice described in Sect. 7.4.1 in allowing price dependent welfare weights as expressed in Eq. 7.28. The non-marginal tax reforms are based on the following second-order approximations to the incremental impact of unit change in tax (hence, consumer price, q) on social welfare, government revenue.

$$\frac{\Delta V}{\Delta q_i} \approx \frac{\delta V}{\delta q_i} + \frac{\Delta q_i}{2}\frac{\delta^2 V}{\delta q_i^2} \tag{7.29}$$

$$\frac{\Delta R}{\Delta q_i} \approx \frac{\delta R}{\delta q_i} + \frac{\Delta q_i}{2}\frac{\delta^2 R}{\delta q_i^2} \tag{7.30}$$

Using Roy's identity and ignoring the term $(\frac{\Delta q_i}{2}\sum_k t_k \frac{\delta^2 X_k}{\delta q_i^2})$ as small and negligible, Eqs. 7.29–7.30 yield after manipulations the following expressions,

$$\frac{\Delta V}{\Delta q_i} \approx -\sum\nolimits_h \beta^h x_i^h \left[1 + \frac{\Delta q_i}{2q_i}\left(\frac{\delta \log \beta^h}{\delta \log q_i} + \frac{\delta \log x_i^h}{\delta \log q_i}\right)\right] \tag{7.31}$$

$$\frac{\Delta R}{\Delta q_i} \approx \left(1 + \frac{\Delta q_i}{q_i} e_{ii}\right) X_i + \sum\nolimits_k \frac{\widetilde{t_k}}{q_i} E_k e_{ki} \tag{7.32}$$

where the partial derivatives are evaluated at prereform prices. Substituting Eqs. 7.31–7.32 in $\lambda = -\frac{\Delta V}{\Delta t_i} / \frac{\Delta R}{\Delta t_i}$, we obtain the following second-order approximation-based expression λ_i^n for the true λ_i'

$$\lambda_i^n = \frac{\sum_h \beta^h e_i^h \left[1 + \frac{\delta_i}{2}\left(\frac{\delta \log \beta^h}{\delta \log q_i} + e_{ii}^h\right)\right]}{(1 + \delta_i\, e_{ii})\, \widehat{E_i} + \sum_k \widetilde{t_k}\, \widehat{E_k} e_{ki}} \tag{7.33}$$

Given, $\delta_i = \frac{\Delta q_i}{q_i}$ is the proportionate change in consumer price due to the tax change, and the hats denote predicted values at post-reform prices.

For convenience, the corresponding expression λ_i^m in case of marginal tax changes is given by

$$\lambda_i^m = \frac{\sum_h \beta^h e_i^h}{E_i + \sum_k \widetilde{t_k}\, E_k e_{ki}} \tag{7.34}$$

λ_i^n extends λ_i^m in the following manner:

(i) the increased accuracy of the second-order approximations in measuring quantity response to price change as reflected in the additional presence of the individual household's own price elasticity, e_{ii}^h, in the numerator of λ_i^n, and the aggregate own price elasticity, e_{ii} in the denominator;

(ii) the dependence of β_h on prices as measured by their elasticities, $\delta \log \beta^h / \delta \log q_i$; and

(iii) the size of the contemplated tax change of i, as measured by δ_i.

$\bar{\lambda}_i^m$ will be close to $\bar{\lambda}_i^n$ only for infinitesimally small tax changes $\delta_i \approx 0$, unless the social welfare weights are price invariant, and the own price elasticities are zero for all households. Therefore, unlike $\bar{\lambda}_i^m$, calculation of $\bar{\lambda}_i^n$ requires knowledge of (a) size of the tax change, (b) individual price elasticities for all households and (c) predicted household demand at post-reform prices. Ray (1999) uses the non-marginal tax reform framework to provide Australian empirical evidence based on non-retired two adult households from 1984, 1988–89 and 1993–94 Household Expenditure Surveys (HES) published by the Australian Bureau of Statistics (ABS). The Australian evidence shows considerably more sensitivity to demand specification in the non-marginal framework than in the marginal framework. The tax reforms are more sensitive to the presence of price effects on budget share than to higher-order income effects through the square of the log expenditure variable in Rank 3 demand. Household composition changes have little effect on commodity tax reform. The significance of the marginal/non-marginal distinction for tax reforms increases sharply with the size of the contemplated tax change and with inequality aversion. A Rawlsian planner is much less likely to use the marginal tax reform framework than an utilitarian one. The failure of marginal tax reforms to recognise the realignment of relative prices brought about by the tax change, and neglect of their impact on behaviour and welfare leads to misleading directions of desirable tax changes. As the Australian evidence shows, this results in an understatement of the importance of demand specification in the tax calculations.

7.5 Optimal Commodity Taxes in the Presence of Tax Evasion

7.5.1 Introduction

The literature on tax evasion and its implications for optimal tax theory has concentrated on income rather than commodity taxes (see Cowell (1990) for a survey). The problem of commodity tax evasion has received relatively little attention. In developing countries—for example, India—where indirect taxes play a much larger role than direct taxes, commodity tax evasion is of commodity tax evasion is of considerable policy importance. Ray (1998) introduces commodity tax evasion in the traditional optimal tax framework with heterogeneous individuals and investigates if and how the principal analytical and empirical evidence on optimal commodity taxes is modified as a result of the extension. The model is briefly described below. It builds on the many-person optimal commodity tax model described earlier. The notations are the same as used earlier, with new notations used for the extension to tax evasion. Let α_i denote the proportion of sales reported in industry i, and let $\alpha_i^*(= 1-\alpha_i)$ denote the proportion of sales evaded. We assume $0 < \alpha_i < 1$ to avoid the possibility of corner solution. Let $g_i(\alpha_i^*)$, which is increasing and convex in α_i^*, be the firm's resource cost of evasion per unit of output produced. The tax authorities audit a fraction of firms Φ_i $(0 < \Phi_i < 1)$. Firms caught cheating pay a fine $(\imath - 1)$ proportional to the fine evaded. If t_i is the specific tax on item i, as before, then the 'expected tax',t_i^e, is given by

$$t_i^e = (1 - \Phi_i)\alpha_i t_i + \Phi_i(t_i + (\imath - 1)(1 - \alpha_i)t_i) = (\alpha_i + \alpha_i^* \Phi_i \imath)t_i \tag{7.35}$$

The firm in industry i maximises 'expected profits' that, per unit of output, are given by

$$\prod_i^e = q_i - c_i - g_i(\alpha_i^*) - t_i^e \tag{7.36}$$

where q_i is, as before, the consumer price, and c_i is the unit cost of production. The first- and second-order conditions for optimal α_i^* that maximise expected profits are given by

$$g_i'(\alpha_i^*) = (1 - \Phi_i \imath)t_i \tag{7.37a}$$

$$g_i''(\alpha_i^*) > 0, \tag{7.37b}$$

where g_i', g_i'' denote the first and second derivatives of g_i with respect to α_i^*. Note that $\Phi_i \imath < 1$ is required for an interior solution. Let the government's audit cost be denoted by $d(\Phi)$ which is an increasing function of the audit probabilities Φ. Assuming full shifting of taxes, the following relationships hold:

$$q_i = c_i + g_i + t_i^e \tag{7.38}$$

$$R = R_0 = \sum_{i=1}^{n} t_i^e X_i - d(\Phi) \tag{7.39}$$

Given R and R_0 are, respectively, the net revenue and a priori specified revenue constraint. The optimal tax problem involves maximising 7.38 with respect to t_i subject to Eqs. 7.38–7.39. The first-order conditions are as follows

$$\sum_{h=1}^{H} \beta^h q_i x_i^h \frac{\delta q_i}{\delta t_i} = \lambda \left[q_i X_i \frac{\delta t_i^e}{\delta t_i} + \sum_{j=1}^{n} t_j^e X_j e_{ji} \frac{\delta q_i}{\delta t_i} \right] \tag{7.40}$$

where β^h is the welfare weight of household h, e_{ji} is the aggregate price elasticity of j with respect to i, and λ is the Lagrange multiplier of the revenue constraint. It is readily verified that Eq. 7.40 generalises Eq. 7.19 to the presence of commodity tax evasion. Assuming that, given prices, the social welfare function is additive of the form used by Atkinson (1970), β^h is given by $(\mu^1/\mu^H)^{\varepsilon}$, where $\mathcal{E} \geq 0$ denotes inequality aversion. Now, from Eq. 7.35 and Eq. 7.38, we have, respectively,

$$\frac{\delta t_i^e}{\delta t_i} = \widetilde{\alpha_\imath} + (1 - \Phi_i \imath) t_i \frac{\delta \alpha_i}{\delta t_i} \tag{7.41}$$

$$\frac{\delta q_i}{\delta t_i} = \widetilde{\alpha_\imath} + (1 - \Phi_i \imath)\, t_i \frac{\delta \alpha_i}{\delta t_i} - g_i' \frac{\delta \alpha_i}{\delta t_i} \tag{7.42}$$

where $\widetilde{\alpha_\imath} = \alpha_i + \alpha_i^* \Phi_i \imath$. Equation 7.37a implies

$$\frac{\delta \alpha_i}{\delta t_i} = -\frac{(1 - \Phi_i \imath)}{g_i''} \tag{7.43}$$

Substituting Eq. 7.43 into Eqs. 7.41–7.42 and the resulting expressions into Eq. 7.40 and rearranging terms, we obtain,

$$\sum_{h=1}^{H} \beta^h q_i x_i^h = \lambda [E_i A_i + \sum_k \widetilde{\alpha_k} e_{ki} \widetilde{t_k} E_k] \tag{7.44}$$

where

$$A_i = \frac{\delta t_i^e / \delta t_i}{\delta p_i / \delta t_i} = 1 - \frac{(1 - \Phi_i \imath) g_i'}{\widetilde{\alpha_\imath} g_i''} \leq 1 \tag{7.44a}$$

$E_i = q_i X_i$ is aggregate expenditure on i, $\widetilde{t_k} = \frac{t_k}{q_k}$ is the tax rate, and e_{ki} is the uncompensated price elasticity of k with respect to i. Equation 7.44 is a generalisation of the traditional first-order conditions for optimal commodity taxes and specialise to the latter if there is no tax evasion, i.e. $A_i = 1$, $\alpha_i = 1$, $\alpha_i^* = 0$. Equation 7.40 holds if taxes are optimal. If they are not, then λ will be indexed on i, i.e. λ_i will vary with i. In that case,

$$\lambda_i = \frac{\sum_{h=1}^{H} \beta^h q_i x_i^h}{E_i A_i + \sum_k \widetilde{\alpha_k} e_{ki} \widetilde{t_k} E_k} \tag{7.45}$$

Following Ahmad and Stern (1984), λ_i can be interpreted as the marginal social cost of raising revenue and generalises the expression used by them to the case of tax evasion. If there is no inequality aversion ($\mathcal{E} = 0$) and if the tax rates are uniform, ($\widetilde{t_\imath} = \widetilde{t}$), then Eq. 7.45 implies,

$$\lambda_i = \frac{1}{A_i + \frac{\widetilde{t}}{E_i} \sum_k \widetilde{\alpha_k} e_{ki} E_k} \tag{7.46}$$

Because the right-hand side varies with i, $\lambda_i \neq \lambda_j$, hence uniform commodity tax rates will not be optimal even in case of no inequality aversion. This marks an important departure from the conventional case of no tax evasion ($A_i = 1$, $\widetilde{\alpha}_k = 1$ for all k) and can be formally stated as the following proposition.

Proposition A
In the presence of commodity tax evasion, uniform tax rates will not generally be optimal even for a utilitarian tax authority. If the uncompensated cross-price elasticities are very small, i.e. $e_{ki} \sim 0$ for $i \neq k$, so that $e_{ii} = -1$, then Eq. 7.45 implies

$$\lambda_i = \frac{\sum_{h=1}^{H} \beta^h q_i x_i^h}{E_i(A_i - \widetilde{\alpha}_i \widetilde{t}_i)} \quad (7.47)$$

Recalling that the tax rate $\widetilde{t}_i$ will be optimal if λ_i is invariant to i, Eq. 7.47 leads us to the following proposition.

Proposition B
If the uncompensated cross-price elasticities are very small, then the optimal commodity tax rate will be given by

$$\widetilde{t}_i = \frac{1}{\widetilde{\alpha}_i}\left[A_i - \rho \frac{\sum_{h=1}^{H} \beta^h q_i x_i^h}{E_i}\right] \quad \text{(where7.48)}$$

ρ is determined by the revenue constraint.

The above discussion raises the question: What is the magnitude of revision to the optimal tax rates required to accommodate the presence of commodity tax evasion? Ray (1998) argues that no explicit, unconditional statements can be made about the magnitude of revision. Consider the case where there are a large number of items such that the uncompensated cross-price elasticities are small and negligible, i.e. $e_{ki} \sim 0$ for $k \neq i$. Let $\widetilde{t}_i^{(1)}$, $\widetilde{t}_i^{(2)}$ denote the optimal tax rate in the presence and absence of tax evasion, respectively, and let λ, $\bar{\lambda}$ denote the shadow cost of funds in the two cases. Then, Ray (1998) derives the following relation:

$$\widetilde{t}_i^{(1)} = \frac{1}{\widetilde{\alpha}_i}\left[\frac{\bar{\lambda}}{\lambda}\widetilde{t}_i^{(2)} + \frac{1}{e_{ii}}\left(\frac{\bar{\lambda}}{\lambda} - A_i\right)\right] \quad (7.49)$$

Equation 7.49 is a convenient formula for adjusting the traditional optimal tax estimates, $\widetilde{t}_i^{(2)}$, to incorporate tax evasion. Clearly, if there is no tax evasion, then $\widetilde{\alpha}_i = 1$, $\bar{\lambda} = \lambda$, and $A_i = 1$, so that $\widetilde{t}_i^{(1)} = \widetilde{t}_i^{(2)}$, and no revision is required. This is the baseline case. Equation 7.49 shows that, among others, the magnitude of the own price elasticity of an item has a crucial impact on the magnitude of revision to its optimal tax estimate required by the presence of tax evasion.

7.5.2 Empirical Evidence

Ray (1998) provides empirical evidence from India on the sensitivity of the optimal commodity taxes to assumptions on commodity tax evasion. The chosen data was a nine-item disaggregation of consumer expenditure across 13 expenditure classes from the 32nd round of the National Sample Survey. Equations 7.44–7.44a were solved corresponding to alternative a priori values of the tax evasion parameter (α_i^*), audit probability (Φ_i) and inequality aversion (ε) using LES parameter estimates. The rate of tax evasion and the audit probabilities were assumed invariant across industries ($\alpha_i = \alpha$, $\Phi_i = \Phi$). The following functional form for g_i (α_i^*) was chosen to satisfy the a priori features mentioned earlier.

$$g_i(\alpha_i^*) = \left(1 - \alpha_i^{*2}\right)^{-\frac{1}{2}} - 1 \tag{7.50}$$

Table 7.7 shows considerable sensitivity of the optimal tax estimates to under-reporting to sales—the higher the tax evasion, the larger the absolute magnitudes of tax and subsidy. The tax evasion parameter, α_i^*, has an effect on the optimal tax estimates similar to that of the inequality aversion parameter, ε, in traditional optimal tax calculations that have been described earlier. Table 7.6 suggests that the introduction of tax evasion in the many-person optimal commodity tax model with heterogeneous individuals makes the optimal taxes more redistributive and non-uniform. Table 7.8 reports estimates of optimal commodity taxes (t_i) and of tax evasion (α_i^*) with the latter now endogenised, assuming the functional form for tax evasion given by Eq. 7.50, and using the conditions for optimal α_i, given by Eqs. 7.37a–7.37b. The estimates are conditional on an assumed audit probability (Φ) of 0.3. The iterative procedure, used to calculate the optimal α_i, took account of all interdependencies in the optimal tax equations. The estimates for milk and milk products; meat, fish and eggs; other Food; clothing; and other non-Food all confirm that a larger penalty for evasion leads to an increase in the optimal sales reporting. Table 7.8 also provides evidence of considerable non-uniformity across items in the optimal rate of tax evasion.

Table 7.7 Sensitivity of optimal commodity taxes to tax evasion (Ray 1999)

Item	$\alpha^* = 0.8$		$\alpha^* = 0.4$		$\alpha^* = 0.2$		$\alpha^* = 0.0$	
	t	t^e	t	t^e	t	t^e	t	t^e
1. Cereals	−1.096	−0.746	−0.383	−0.322	−0.296	−0.273	−0.258	−0.258
2. Milk and milk products	0.573	0.390	0.237	0.199	0.204	0.187	0.189	0.189
3. Edible oils	−0.119	−0.081	0.060	0.050	0.070	0.064	0.073	0.073
4. Meat, fish and eggs	0.166	0.113	0.138	0.116	0.128	0.118	0.123	0.123
5. Sugar and tea	−0.130	−0.089	0.054	0.045	0.065	0.059	0.068	0.068
6. Other Foods	0.052	0.035	0.118	0.099	0.116	0.107	0.115	0.115
7. Clothing	1.064	0.724	0.378	0.318	0.323	0.298	0.303	0.303
8. Fuel	−0.452	−0.307	−0.049	−0.041	−0.013	−0.012	0.002	0.002
9. Other non-Food	0.802	0.545	0.306	0.257	0.262	0.241	0.245	0.245

Note $\tau = 1.50, \beta = 0.40, \varepsilon = 2.0$

Table 7.8 Simultaneous estimation of optimal commodity taxes and optimal tax evasion (Ray 1999)

Item	$\tau = 1.5$				$\tau = 5.0$	
	$\varepsilon = 2.0$		$\varepsilon = 25.0$		$\varepsilon = 2.0$	
	α_k	t	α_k	t	α_k	t
1. Cereals	1.0	−0.452	1.0	−0.695	1.0	−0.271
2. Milk and milk products	0.092	0.232	0.122	0.311	0.219	0.236
3. Edible oils	0.022	0.055	1.0	−0.064	1.0	−0.021
4. Meat, fish and eggs	0.053	0.134	0.036	0.089	0.100	0.101
5. Sugar and tea	0.020	0.051	1.0	−0.072	1.0	−0.028
6. Other Foods	0.042	0.106	0.013	0.032	0.095	0.096
7. Clothing	0.188	0.496	0.344	1.039	0.378	0.476
8. Fuel	1.0	−0.158	1.0	−0.470	1.0	−0.137
9. Other non-Food	0.153	0.396	0.250	0.689	0.338	0.406

Note $\beta = 0.4$. Tax evasion, $\alpha_k^* = 1 - \alpha_k$

7.6 Conclusion

This chapter discusses the topic of commodity taxes that is an important issue in the policy formulation in developing countries. In India that was the focus of much of the discussion, the share of indirect taxes in total revenue has been increasing. Moreover, with the recently introduced GST replacing a plethora of sales taxes and designed to simplify the tax system, indirect taxation has increased in its importance in India in the policy settings of the government. This chapter reviews some of the rules guiding the setting of commodity tax rates and illustrates the analytical discussion by selectively reporting the empirical evidence from some of the studies on optimal taxes and tax reforms. The discussion highlights the close connection between assumptions on consumer preferences and the optimal commodity tax rates that are meant to inform the policy analyst. The sensitivity of the optimal commodity tax rates to departures from an assumed linearity of Engel curves and separable preferences underlines the importance of using a realistic preference framework in arriving at accurate policy prescriptions. The empirical evidence establishes the case for non-uniform commodity tax rates and shows that indirect taxation can play only a limited role in securing redistribution. The discussion in this chapter also includes commodity tax evasion that, unlike income tax evasion, has not figured much in the literature. The result that commodity tax rules are sensitive to the recognition of tax evasion and its incorporation in the analytical modelling is a result of considerable policy significance.

References

Ahmad E, Stern NH (1984) The theory of reform and Indian indirect taxes. J Public Econ 25:259–298

Atkinson AB (1970) On the measurement of inequality. J Econ Theor 2:244–263

Atkinson AB (1977) Optimal taxation and the direct versus indirect tax controversy. Can J Econ 10:590–606

Atkinson AB, Stiglitz J (1972) The structure of indirect taxation and economic efficiency. J Public Econ 1:97–119

Atkinson AB, Stiglitz J (1976) The design of tax structure: direct versus indirect taxation. J Public Econ 9:55–75

Atkinson AB, Stiglitz J (1980) Lectures in public economics. McGraw Hill, New York

Blundell RW, Ray R (1984) Testing for linear Engel curves and additively separable preferences using a new flexible demand system. Econ J 94:800–811

Corlett WJ, Hague DC (1953) Complementarity and the excess burden of taxation. Rev Econ Stud 21:21–30

Cowell F (1990) Tax sheltering and the cost of evasion. Oxford Econ Pap 42(1):231–243

Deaton AS (1979) Optimally uniform commodity taxes. Econ Lett 2:357–361

Deaton AS, Stern NH (1986) Optimally uniform commodity taxes, taste differences and lump sum grants. *Econ Lett* 20: 263–266

Diamond PA (1975) A many person Ramsey tax rule. J Public Econ 4:335–342

Diamond PA, Mirrlees J (1971) Optimal taxation and public production: tax rules. Am Econ Rev 61:261–278

Ebrahimi E, Heady C (1988) Tax design and household composition. *Econ J* (Conference Supplement) 98: 83–96

Harris RG, Mackinnon JG (1979) Computing optimal tax equilibria. J Public Econ 11:197–212

King MA (1983) Welfare analysis of tax reforms using household data. J Public Econ 21:183–214

Murty MN, Ray R (1989) A Computational procedure for calculating optimal commodity taxes with illustrative evidence from Indian budget data. Scand J Econ 91:655–670

Myles G (1995) Public Economics. Cambridge University Press, Cambridge

Ramsey FP (1927) A contribution to the theory of taxation. Econ J 37:47–61

Ray R (1986a) Sensitivity of 'Optimal' commodity tax rates to alternative demand functional forms: an econometric case study of India. J Public Econ 31:253–268

Ray R (1986b) Redistribution through commodity taxes: the non-linear Engel curve case. Public Finan/Finan Publ 41:277–284

Ray R (1997) Issues in the design and reform of commodity taxes: analytical results and empirical evidence. J Econ Surv 11:353–388

Ray R (1998) The design of commodity taxes in the presence of tax evasion with illustrative evidence from India. Public Finan/Finan Publ 26:503–518

Ray R (1999) Marginal and non-marginal commodity tax reforms with rank two and rank three demographic demand systems. Oxford Econ Pap 51:689–712

Sah RK (1983) How much redistribution is possible through commodity taxes? J Public Econ 20:89–101

Samuelson P (1986) Theory of optimal taxation. *J Public Econ* 30: 137–143. This was circulated earlier as unpublished memorandum for the US Treasury (1951)

Sandmo A (1976) Optimal Taxation: an introduction to the litereature. J Public Econ 6:37–54

Slemrod J (1990) Optimal taxation and optimal tax systems. J Econ Perspect 4:157–178

Stern NH (1987) Uniformity verus selectivity in tax structure: lessons from theory and policy. Discussion paper no. 9, *Development economics research programme*, July

Chapter 8
Purchasing Power Parities and Their Role in International Comparisons

8.1 Introduction

In this chapter, we move from the single country context of the previous chapters to the international context. The focus of this chapter is on purchasing power parities (PPP) and their robustness to procedures. PPPs can be viewed as cost of living index calculated spatially across countries with different currencies. It is analogous to measurement of price changes over time, with the numeraire currency in the PPP context being the counterpart of the base year in the time series context. While the alternative procedures for PPP estimation have been described in the discussion on price indices in Chap. 3, this chapter extends that discussion by describing studies that estimate and apply PPPs in welfare comparisons between countries. Conversion rates of one currency into another are required for a variety of reasons such as international comparison of living standards, ranking of countries by their per capita GDP and in cross-country inequality and poverty comparisons. Market exchange rates are inappropriate for such comparisons because they are based on tradeable items only. The PPPs provide the adjustments required to market exchange rates such that the price of an item in two countries is identical if expressed in a common currency.

The PPP rates are based on a much wider selection of items than market exchange rates including both tradeable and non-tradeable items. Asian countries such as China and India rank much higher on per capita GDP if PPP rates are used instead of market exchange rates. The United Nations International Comparison Project (ICP) carries out detailed price comparisons across countries to arrive at the PPP values required for a variety of cross-country comparisons such as the ones mentioned above. Given the crucial role that PPPs play in international comparisons, there has been considerable controversy on the PPP values that should be used as deflators. While Clements, Wu and Zhang (2006) provide a method of comparison of consumption patterns between countries that is free of currency units, the requirement of PPP is, in general, unavoidable in most cross-country

R. Ray, *Household Behaviour, Prices, and Welfare*, Themes in Economics,
https://doi.org/10.1007/978-981-13-1930-3_8

comparisons. Recent examples of international comparisons of real income or real expenditure include Hill (2004), Neary (2004) and Feenstra et al. (2009). Oulton (2012a) sets out a preference-based algorithm for comparing living standards across countries. PPP rates are also required in intra-national comparisons since a country's currency unit does not have the same purchasing power in all regions in that country. The issue of intra-national PPP takes the form of spatial prices. The role that PPPs perform in converting an internationally denominated poverty line, for example, 1 US $ a day, into that of different countries expressed in their own currencies is analogous to the role that spatial prices play inside a country in converting the national poverty line into regional poverty lines taking into account regional prices and preferences.

While considerable resources have been spent by the statistical agencies on calculating PPP rates between countries, as is evident from the scale of the ICP project, the issue of intra-national PPPs has received much less attention. In large heterogeneous countries such as Brazil and India, the requirement of intra-national PPP rates, i.e. spatial prices, is as important as that of the international PPP rates in the cross-country context. This is evident from the recent attempts of Aten and Menezes (2002) on Brazil and Coondoo et al. (2004, 2011), Majumder et al. (2012) on India to calculate spatial prices. The evidence in these studies shows that cross-country PPP rates at the aggregate level that do not take into account the regional diversity in countries such as Brazil and India are likely to be seriously misleading. Setting aside the issue of regional diversity, the idea of a distribution-invariant PPP that is supposed to hold for all the expenditure classes, rich and poor alike, is another important issue of interest. This is an assumption that has been criticised in the poverty context by Reddy and Pogge (2007). If untrue, as the present results suggest, this is yet another indictment of the all-purpose, single-value, countrywide PPPs that come out of high-profile projects such as the ICP.

In view of its importance, the methodologies adopted to calculate the PPP have received considerable critical scrutiny. For example, Hill (2000) and Almas (2012) analyse and quantify the PPP bias in the widely used Penn World Table incomes of various countries. One of the most prominent methods adopted in the PPP calculations has been the Country-Product Dummy Method (CPD), due to Summers (1973), that is based on the idea of hedonic price regressions, and was originally proposed to deal with the problem of missing observations in international price comparisons. The CPD method has been analysed and extended by Diewert (2005) and Rao (2005). Coondoo et al. (2004) extend the CPD methodology by using it in conjunction with the idea of a 'quality or price equation', due to Prais and Houthakker (1955), to calculate spatial prices in the Indian context. The methodology proposed by Coondoo et al. (2004) has been used in modified form in the cross-country context by Deaton et al. (2004) to calculate PPP rates between India and Indonesia. The latter study is not based on any preference-consistent 'complete' demand system. In contrast, Oulton (2012a) takes an expenditure function-based approach, but does not consider the spatial dimension within each country in the cross-country expenditure comparisons.

A key limitation of the CPD approach is that it does not take into account the preferences of the consumer as revealed by her estimated demand pattern. Notwithstanding the fact that the PPP is analogous to the concept of a true cost of living index (TCLI), and the increasing availability of household survey data that provides the necessary information for a preference-consistent, demand system-based approach to PPP calculations, such an approach is conspicuous by its absence. Recent studies that come closest to this spirit are O'Donnell and Rao (2007) who estimate demand systems to calculate PPP between Ethiopia and Uganda, Majumder et al. (2015) who used a preference-based approach to calculate the PPPs between India and Vietnam, and Majumder et al. (2016) who extended that study to consider the trilateral case of India, Indonesia and Vietnam. The latter two studies are described in detail in this chapter. The rest of this chapter is organised as follows. The International Comparison Program (ICP) that is the main producer of the PPPs used globally is described, and its limitations are discussed in Sect. 8.2. Section 8.3 describes the methodology and results of the study of Majumder et al. (2015) on PPP between India and Vietnam and its welfare application, while Sect. 8.4 extends the discussion to describe the study of Majumder et al. (2016) on estimating PPP between India, Indonesia and Vietnam. Both these studies compare the PPPs obtained using the alternative preference-based methodology with those from the ICP. These studies also illustrate the application of the PPPs to welfare comparison between countries. Section 8.5 widens the discussion by reporting the methodology and results from a recent study by Majumder et al. (2017) on the sensitivity of the PPPs to estimation procedures and their effect on living standards comparisons. Section 8.6 concludes the chapter.

8.2 Purchasing Power Parities and the International Comparison Program

8.2.1 Purchasing Power Parities Meaning and Their Usage

The International Comparison Program (ICP) that is centrally directed from the global office of the World Bank is, by any measure, truly impressive in the scale of the exercise and highly ambitious in what it claims to achieve. As the volume (World Bank 2013) that describes the objectives, methodology and the data sets of the ICP, 2005, exercise States in its title, it seeks to measure the 'real size' of the world economy, even though it is not clear what 'real' really means. It does so by calculating 'purchasing power parity' (PPP) rates between the various countries' currencies and using the PPPs rather than the market exchange rates in converting the national accounts of various countries and their components, denominated in local currencies, into a common currency, typically, the US dollar. PPPs are also required for a variety of welfare comparisons between countries such as poverty and expenditure comparisons and, more generally, in standard of living comparisons that require all currencies to be converted to a common currency. As is well known, market exchange rates are inappropriate for currency conversions since they do not measure the 'true' purchasing power of a currency. For example, on market exchange rates, the price of a haircut in India seems incredibly cheap to an American visiting India or, conversely, a taxi ride in Australia will be almost as expensive as plane travel between two cities in India. PPP provides the adjustments required to market exchange rates such that the price of an item in two countries is identical if expressed in a common currency. A working definition of the PPP is provided in World Bank (2013, p. 19), namely that 'it represents the number of currency units required to purchase the amount of goods and services equivalent to what can be bought with one unit of currency unit of the base or reference or numeraire country'.

There are several reasons for the divergence between the market exchange rates and the PPP rates (however measured). The short-term factors include the capital movements between countries, interest rate movements, speculation in foreign exchange markets. The longer-term factors include the fact that the exchange rates are almost exclusively dependent on the relative prices of tradeable items, while standard of living comparisons between countries should include both tradeable and non-tradeable items, especially in the context of developing countries. Consequently, the PPP rates are based on a much wider selection of items than market exchange rates including both tradeable and non-tradeable items. It is not surprising, therefore, that the PPP rates deviate from exchange rates much more for developing countries than the developed ones. Asian countries such as China and India rank much higher on per capita GDP if PPP rates are used instead of exchange rates, though not high enough to provide any comfort. Some would argue that the PPP rates make these two economies look misleadingly better, since these two countries are now ranked the 'second and third largest economies' on the 2011 PPP rates applied to the GDP, ignoring the fact that the rankings come down sharply once they are converted to per capita figures. Rather absurdly, India leapfrogs from tenth to third place between the ICP 2005 and the ICP 2011 PPPs, and this is paraded as a great achievement by the international community, ignoring the fact that India has many more mouths to feed in 2011 than it did in 2005.

The use of PPPs has provided some comfort to authorities in developing countries who have used them to argue that the 'real size' of their economies is much higher than shown by the exchange rate converted figures. This is against a background of an upward revision in the PPP rates in the 2005 ICPs from the 1993 PPP figures for both China and India making both these two countries seem a lot poorer than what we thought previously. The recently released latest ICP figures for India from its 2011 exercise [see World Bank (2014)] show that the ratio of PPP to market exchange rates, also referred to as the 'price level index' (PLI), has hardly changed for India between 2005 and 2011, notwithstanding the high growth rate recorded by India over the latter half of this period. Intuition suggests that for countries experiencing large increase in affluence by her middle classes, as India did, the price of non-tradeable items will increase disproportionately, and this will increase the PLI towards unity. That has not happened for India, and that itself raises doubts on the validity of the latest PPPs. It is, therefore, difficult to make much sense of these PPP-based pronouncements.

One does not need to take PPP calculations seriously if national policy makers are not obsessed with international comparisons, but unfortunately they are. In poverty comparisons, for example, there is as much interest in how the poverty rates compare between countries (which require PPP rates) as in how a country's poverty rates have behaved over time (which do not require PPP rates if we fix the national poverty line in the local currency and adjust it for inflation). In the 'globalised' world that we live in, nation states cannot be oblivious to outside perceptions on their economies, and this is why PPPs acquire an importance, however exaggerated that importance may be. For example, the famous, but rather dubiously calculated, international poverty line (IPL) specification at US $1.25 a day at 2005 PPPs is only valid if the 2005 PPPs are, even setting aside the other issues that arise from methodological differences between this IPL and the US $1 a day IPL used previously. Yet, notwithstanding the serious problems that have been noted with both IPL specifications [see, e.g. Reddy and Pogge (2007)], they are extensively used in cross-national poverty comparisons. In fact, the Indian Planning Commission has outdone the World Bank by using poverty lines denominated in Indian Rupees that are even more miserly than the PPP-converted IPL used by the World Bank!

8.2.2 The International Comparison Program: Background, Methodology and Limitations

The ICP was started in 1967 on a modest scale by researchers based at the University of Pennsylvania working under the umbrella of the United Nations Statistical Commission. During the period, 1967–70, the PPP calculations by the ICP were based on 10 countries—initially 6, increasing to 10 in 1970. Since then, the scale of the exercise has increased steadily with the coverage extending to more countries and more items and with improvements in the methodology. As the exercise became more complex and expensive, the gap between ICP rounds increased. The 2005 ICP was the most comprehensive to date involving 146 countries and was conducted and funded, for the first time, by the Global Office of the World Bank. The latest round is ICP, 2011, which involved nearly 200 countries and whose results have been released only recently (World Bank 2014). The 2005 ICP had three defining characteristics that distinguished it from earlier rounds: (a) this was the first time both China and India participated fully making the ICP, 2005, exercise truly global and giving it a credibility that was lacking previously; (b) the use of a sophisticated global linking mechanism that involved 'moving from the use of a Ring list priced by a few countries for linking to the development of a set of global core products that will be picked by all countries' (World Bank 2013, p. XXXI), (c) notwithstanding the important role played by the regional offices, this was the most centralised ICP operation with the involvement of the World Bank, and the focus on intercountry PPPs with the US dollar as the numeraire, rather than on intra-regional and subnational PPPs that the regional offices[1] are better placed to provide.

On (c), all the regions had to feed the price information keeping in mind a set of 155 'basic headings' that was centrally determined and expected to hold globally. There have been examples of regional PPP calculations such as the one on poverty-specific PPPs in the Asia-Pacific region (ADB 2008) and on PPPs generally in Asia and the Pacific (ADB 2007). The latter exercises were conducted regionally by the Asian Development Bank rather than the World Bank. The methodology for calculating PPP started with collecting prices at the level of individual item. As stated in Ch. 1 of the World Bank Handbook (World Bank 2013), 'the ICP starts with the price data at the item level. These price data are combined to yield PPPs at the basic heading level where a basic heading level is identified as the lowest level aggregate for which the information on expenditure is available on from the national accounts. The ICP has 155 basic headings. Some examples of basic headings are: rice, lamb, mutton, …' (p. 24). To put it simply,[2] the methodology for calculating the intercountry PPP starts with simple price relatives at the 'item' level that are aggregated to the level of 155 'basic headings' using simple averages that in turn are further aggregated into 126 'classes'. The next step is to combine these 126 classes to form 61 broad commodity groups that are further aggregated into 26 categories that form the final platform on which the PPP results are based and published. The Fisher and Tornqvist indices are used to calculate the elements of the matrix of the bilateral PPPs between the participating countries, and these elements are averaged over all the countries to provide the estimates of multilateral PPPs.

The latter is done so as to satisfy the important property of transitivity: it stipulates that the PPP computed between two countries, *j* and *k*, should be the same whether it is computed directly or indirectly through a third country. In other words, the PPP between India and Vietnam can be obtained from the PPP of each country vis-a-vis the USA as the product of the PPP of India and USA multiplied by the PPP between USA and Vietnam. Unfortunately, the principle of transitivity which seems an innocent principle has restrictive implications, such as the dependence of the bilateral PPPs on the third country through which these are derived and referred to as the 'star country'. More generally, PPPs between India and other Asian countries will depend on the PPPs of the currencies of all the participating countries, rich and poor alike, many of whom have substantially different consumer preferences from India and the country it is being compared to. This is a big price to pay for the multilateral comparisons. Later in this piece, we will provide some empirical evidence on the distortion to the bilateral PPPs in the trilateral PPPs that

[1]It is surprising that notwithstanding the involvement of China and India in the ICP, 2005, neither country's statistical office was represented in the ICP Technical Advisory Group. The role of these two countries' statistical offices seems to have been limited to the micro-level operations of feeding price data to a centrally dictated chain rather than being actively involved at the global/macrolevel of providing advice and influencing the programme itself.

[2]The process is much more complex—the reader is referred to World Bank (2013) for details.

the mere addition of a third country can make, and too a country from Asia with reasonably similar tastes and preferences to the comparing countries. Further, the use of fixed Divisia price indices rather than the 'exact price indices' based on the utility-based concept of 'true cost of living index' either ignores or exaggerates the substitution response to price changes, and this distorts the PPP estimates.

Moreover, it is very difficult to calculate the standard errors of the price indices that have been used, and so the reader is unable to assess the reliability and precision of the PPP estimates. This can be addressed through the use of the 'Country-Product Dummy' (CPD) method due to Summers (1973) which treats the PPP as an estimable parameter, but the method has yet to be used widely in the PPP calculations. The ICP PPPs as calculated and published have three other limitations that are particularly significant in the context of large and heterogeneous countries such as China and India. First, the treatment of large countries as single entities with the same value of the PPP assumed to hold in every region of the country. This overlooks the large regional variation in prices and expenditure patterns inside these countries. In China, for example, it is well known that the coastal provinces experienced much sharper growth than the inland provinces, making the publication of a single countrywide PPP and the use of that PPP to calculate 'real GDP', of very limited value, if any. A similar criticism can be made regarding the PPP calculations for India.

We have presented in an earlier chapter evidence on spatial heterogeneity in prices and real expenditures in India in the form of intra-national PPPs to underline this limitation. Second, notwithstanding huge increase in the scale of operations and the complexity in the procedures adopted, one basic deficiency in the ICP remains, namely the collection of prices without regard to the fact, supported by mounting evidence, that the poor face substantially higher prices and, often, they do not have access to many of the 'items' that are constituents of the 'basic headings'. It is therefore not clear whose PPP is being calculated, certainly not that of the poor. Since one of the main uses of the ICP PPPs has been the calculation of the IPL, this is a significant (mis)use of the published ICP numbers!! We provide below evidence on the distribution sensitivity of the PPPs. Third, even setting aside the issue of intra-national PPPs, discussed above, the calculation of a single PPP in bilateral comparisons is also very misleading. For example, as we report below, in the India vs Vietnam PPP calculations, the overall PPP can hide significant differences between the rural-to-rural and urban-to-urban PPPs of the Indian Rupee vis-a-vis the Vietnamese Dong.

8.3 Estimating Purchasing Power Parities Between India and Vietnam

8.3.1 *Motivation and Description*

This section describes in detail the methodology and results of the study on bilateral PPP between India and Vietnam and its robustness by Majumder et al. (2015). The principal motivation of Majumder et al. (2015) is to propose a preference-consistent and unified framework for the estimation of PPPs within and between countries. The paper proposes a three-step methodology. In step 1, the study estimates prices from household-level unit values after adjusting for quality, demographic and regional effects. In step 2, the quality-adjusted unit values are used to estimate preference parameters from a 'complete' demand system. In step 3, the estimated demand parameters are used to calculate spatial prices within a country, and PPP between countries, using the 'exact' approach of a 'true cost of living index' (TCLI). The usefulness of this three-step methodology is illustrated by applying it to estimate PPPs both within and between India and Vietnam using a recent demand system. The paper contains a systematic comparison of the expenditure function-based PPPs in the spirit of the 'exact price indices' with those from using the CPD procedure and the Divisia price indices.

The usefulness of the proposed methodology is illustrated by using the spatial prices and the cross-country PPPs to compare of levels of living between India and Vietnam based on Food expenditures. The exercise follows the methodology proposed in Oulton (2012a) for calculating prices as true cost of living indices. The comparison of living standards between India and Vietnam extends the cross-country expenditure comparisons in Feenstra et al. (2009), Oulton (2012b) by using PPPs that vary across expenditure percentiles and a welfare measure that, following Sen (1976), is sensitive to inequality changes. The paper reports the sensitivity of the welfare comparisons to the PPPs used, namely between the welfare rankings obtained using the 'demand system'-based methodology on Food expenditures proposed here with those using PPPs that are currently available. The results underline the policy significance of our results by pointing to a picture of high sensitivity of the welfare comparisons to the PPPs used during a period that overlaps partly with the recent global financial crisis.

In view of the absence of studies that estimate intercountry PPPs using a preference-consistent framework, this study fills a significant gap in the literature. In the spirit of combining the spatial dimension in each country with the cross-country aspect, the study by Majumder et al. (2015) calculates the PPP rates between the two countries both in aggregate and separately for the rural and the urban areas and provides evidence on their movement over time. A significant contribution of this study is that it tests for invariance of intercountry PPP across expenditure classes and hence departs from the practice of assuming that the PPPs between countries is the same for all households irrespective of their affluence, an assumption that has been criticised in the poverty context by Reddy and Pogge (2007), as mentioned earlier. To the best of our knowledge, this assumption has not been tested before. Another key distinguishing feature of this study is that it concentrates on Food-based PPPs and departs from the practice in the ICP and other studies of considering all items, both Food and non-Food, in the PPP calculations. Consistent with the point made by Reddy and Pogge (2007), PPPs based on Food items alone are more relevant in welfare comparisons such as poverty calculations that require price indices that are more relevant for the poor.

While the PPPs from the ICP are an improvement from the market exchange rates by considering a wider basket of goods, namely tradeable and non-tradeable items, they go overboard by including a host of items which hardly figure in the consumption basket of the ultra-poor. This is a serious limitation of the ICP PPPs, given that one of the main uses of PPPs is to convert poverty lines denominated in US dollar into that in local currencies. As we report later in the levels of living comparisons, the results from using the ICP PPPs are quite different from those using the distribution-sensitive and preference-consistent PPPs obtained in this study. Moreover, the present results provide significant evidence of rural–urban heterogeneity in the PPPs and in the welfare comparisons between India and Vietnam. Perhaps for the first time, Majumder et al. (2015) estimate the PPP exchange rates between two countries (India and Vietnam) taking account of their regional heterogeneity in preferences and prices. The heterogeneity in preferences between (and within) India and Vietnam is explicitly taken into account by estimating the Rank 3 Quadratic Almost Ideal System (QAIDS), due to Banks, Blundell and Lewbel (1997), separately for (i) India and Vietnam, (ii) in each country, separately for its rural and urban areas and (iii) within each sector, separately for each of the constituent States and regions in India and Vietnam, respectively.

QAIDS is estimated in its true, nonlinear form rather than its linear approximate version that has been used in several recent applications [see, e.g. O'Donnell and Rao (2007)]. Other distinguishing features of Majumder et al. (2015) include the modification of the procedure due to Cox and Wohlgenant (1986) and Hoang (2009) to generate the quality-adjusted prices of Food items based on unit values from the household surveys that are subsequently used in the demand estimation, and the incorporation of demographic effects in the estimated quality equations.[3] The methodological contribution of this study has wider application than the immediate PPP context of this study since the quality-adjusted Food prices, obtained from the hedonic price regressions using the unit values from the household surveys, will help in constructing Food poverty lines in both countries that can validate, or otherwise, the poverty lines currently in use.

8.3.2 Framework and Methodology

The methodology views the PPP as a true cost of living index as follows.

$$\text{PPP}(A,B) = \frac{C^A(u^r, p^A)}{C^B(u^r, p^B)}. \tag{8.1}$$

[3]See McKelvey (2011) for recent Indonesian evidence on the ability of unit values and market prices to act as satisfactory proxies of one another.

where u^r denotes reference utility, C^A and C^B denote the expenditure function of the comparison country/region, A, and the base country/region, B, respectively, and p^A and p^B denote the corresponding vector of prices in the two countries/regions. Equation 8.1 gives us spatial prices when A and B refer to regions inside a country, and PPP when A and B refer to different countries. The TCLI-based approach of estimating PPPs adopted in this study has the following principal advantage over that adopted in the World Bank's ICP exercise. In using a reference utility, rather than a reference commodity bundle, to calculate the PPPs, the present approach sidesteps comparability issues on definition of items or commodities that arise in international comparisons based on reference commodity bundles. The same commodity may have different meanings in different countries. In some cases, an item in one country may not even exist in another. This posed non-trivial problems in the ICP. As noted in Oulton (2012a, p. 449), for example, this resulted in several of the 106 items included under 'Basic Headings' in the 2005 ICP to record zero expenditure in some countries and had to be excluded from the common reference basket.

In contrast, the mapping from the commodity space to utility space in the cross-country comparisons, implicit in the use of the TCLI approach, implies that one can consider all the principal items of consumption in one country without having to worry about whether they are consumed or have identical meaning in another. This is not to claim however that comparability issues do not arise in the present context as well, but to note that in working with broad aggregates or composite items, such as cereals and cereal substitutes, that have roughly similar meaning in the two countries, the present study minimises the distortions and problems caused by working with a finer classification of items and avoids the problem of inconsistent item definitions and zero expenditures noted above. Consequently, the present approach does not require information on prices for a finer classification of items, nor does the present study calculate PPPs for each item, unlike in the earlier study on spatial prices within India (Majumder et al. 2012). The disadvantage of the present approach, however, is that it requires demand estimates of 'complete demand systems' and that sets a severe constraint on the number of items that can be considered, since the complexities of demand estimation multiply with the number of items included in the demand estimation. Another disadvantage that follows from this is that the assumption of additive separability between the constituent items within a group is unlikely to hold, and is a price we need to pay to keep the demand estimation manageable.

Incidentally, we should note that the use of two Asian countries in the present study that have similar, though not identical, Food consumption patterns helps to minimise the comparability issues that arise in international comparisons. The issue of consistency in the definition of items is much less severe within a country and does not affect the calculation of spatial prices as in Majumder et al. (2012). Hence, while the TCLI approach has been widely used in the intra-country context, this is one of the first studies to extend that to the cross-country context. The contribution of this study is to show, that if one works with broad item groupings that have roughly similar meaning in the countries being compared, the rich information contained in the unit values available in the Household Expenditure Surveys, can be used to calculate PPPs both within and between countries using a consistent methodology. Though both spatial prices and cross-country PPPs are estimated as 'true cost of living indices' (TCLI) in this study, it is important to draw a conceptual distinction between the spatial prices/PPPs, which involve cross-sectional price comparisons, and the TCLI, which measures temporal price movements. The former, unlike the TCLIs, not only capture the price differences but also other differences such as changes in demographic characteristics and in tastes. The spatial prices/PPPs should not, therefore, be viewed strictly as TCLIs. Hence, while the TCLIs can be estimated on time series data pooled over different time periods, we cannot estimate the spatial prices/PPPs by pooling data over different regions or over different countries.

Moreover, one cannot pool the Indian and Vietnamese expenditure data sets since that will require economically relevant exchange rates between the two currencies which are not available. The calculation of such exchange rates is, indeed, one of the principal motivations of this study. Unless preferences are homothetic, a possibility that is rejected by the evidence presented in Oulton (2012b), the spatial prices/PPP are dependent on reference utility, u^r, and, hence, on reference expenditure. This provides the background to the evidence presented later on the sensitivity of the PPPs between the two countries to reference expenditure. The general cost function underlying quadratic logarithmic (QL) systems, [e.g. the Quadratic Almost Ideal Demand System (QAIDS) of Banks et al. (1997) and the Generalised Almost Ideal Demand System (GAIDS) of Lancaster and Ray (1998)], is of the form,

$$C(u,p) = a(p) \cdot \exp\left(\frac{b(p)}{(1/\ln u) - \lambda(p)}\right), \tag{8.2}$$

Given p is the price vector, $a(p)$ is a homogeneous function of degree one in prices, $b(p)$ and $\lambda(p)$ are homogeneous functions of degree zero in prices, and u denotes the level of utility. The budget share functions corresponding to the cost function given in Eq. 8.2 are of the form,

$$w_i = a_i(p) + b_i(p) \ln\left(\frac{x}{a(p)}\right) + \frac{\lambda_i(p)}{b(p)}\left(\ln\frac{x}{a(p)}\right)^2, \tag{8.3}$$

where x denotes nominal per capita expenditure and i denotes item of expenditure. Using Eq. 8.1, the corresponding true cost of living index (TCLI) in logarithmic form comparing price situation p^A with price situation p^B is given by,

$$\ln P(p^A, p^B, u^r) = \left[\ln a(p^A) - \ln a(p^B)\right] + \left[\frac{b(p^A)}{\frac{1}{\ln u^r} - \lambda(p^A)} - \frac{b(p^B)}{\frac{1}{\ln u^r} - \lambda(p^B)}\right] \tag{8.4}$$

Given u^r is the reference utility level. The first term of the RHS of Eq. 8.4 is the logarithm of the basic index (measuring the cost of living index at some minimum benchmark utility level) and the second term is the logarithm of the marginal index. Note that for $p^A = \theta p^B, \theta > 0, a(p^A) = \theta a(p^B)$, so that the basic index takes a value θ and hence, may be interpreted as that component of TCLI that captures the effect of uniform or average inflation on the cost of living. On the other hand, for $p^A = \theta p^B$ the marginal index takes a value of unity. Hence, the marginal index may be interpreted as the other component of TCLI that captures the effect of changes in the relative price structure. The specific functional forms of $a(p^r), b(p^r)$ and $\lambda(p^r)$ for QAIDS in Eq. 8.2 are as follows, $\ln a(p^r) = \alpha_0 + \sum_{i=1}^n \alpha_i \ln p_i^r + \frac{1}{2}\sum_{i=1}^n \sum_{j=1}^n \gamma_{ij} \ln p_i^r \ln p_j^r$ where $b(p^r) = \prod_{i=1}^n p_i^{r\,\beta_i}$, $\lambda(p^r) = \sum_{i=1}^n \lambda_i \ln p_i^r$, and p_i^r is the price of item i in region r. The resulting budget share equations are given by,

$$w_i^r = \alpha_i + \sum_{j=1}^n \gamma_{ij} \log p_j^r + \beta_i \log(x/a(p^r)) + \lambda_i[\log(x/a(p^r))]^2 \tag{8.5}$$

Given a reference utility level, the regional PPPs can be calculated from Eq. 8.4 using the estimated parameters and information on prices. Based on the level (country/region/sector) of data used, estimation of demand system in Eq. 8.5 yields the estimates of $a(p^r)$, $b(p^r)$ and $\lambda(p^r)$, where superscript r denotes country/region/sector, as the case may be. Substitution in Eq. 8.4 and taking exponential yields the PPP between countries/regions/sectors, conditional on prespecified reference utility, u^r, in each situation. A comparison among regions yields spatial prices and that between countries measures the purchasing power parity between countries. In the empirical work, we have used the utility level corresponding to median expenditure in the base country, India, as the reference utility level, u^r, to calculate the PPPs and have compared them with those at other percentile points of the expenditure distribution—see Oulton (2012b) for a full description of the 2005 ICP.

8.3.3 The Procedure to Generate Quality-Adjusted Unit Values as Prices (Food Items)

The PPPs based on complete demand systems require price information for estimation of the price parameters. Such information is missing in most data sets. We use as proxies for prices[4] the unit values for Food items obtained by dividing expenditure values by quantities. However, the raw unit values need to be adjusted for quality and demographic effects. To do so, we adopt the following procedure. The unit values, v_i, are adjusted for quality and demographic factors following Cox

[4]See Atella et al. (2004) for an alternative methodology for constructing spatial prices in cross sections using the variability of budget shares that do not require quantity information.

and Wohlgenant (1986) and Hoang (2009), through the following regression equation,

$$\begin{aligned} v_i^{hsjd} - \left(v_i^{sjd}\right)_{\text{median}} &= \alpha_i D_s + \beta_i D_j + \gamma_i \sum_j \sum_d D_j D_d + \varphi_i x^{hsjd} \\ &\quad + \omega_i f_i^{hsjd} + \sum_m b_i Z_{im}^{hsjd} + \varepsilon_i^{hsjd}, \end{aligned} \tag{8.6}$$

where, v_i^{hsjd} is the unit value paid by household h for item i in State/province j, district d and sector s, $\left(v_i^{sjd}\right)_{\text{median}}$ is the median unit value for the district in which the household resides, x is the household Food expenditure per capita, f is the proportion of times meals consumed outside by that household and D_s, D_j and D_d are dummies for sector, State/province and district, respectively. While Huang estimates Eq. 8.6 using *mean* (in place of *median* being used here) unit prices and then adds the predicted residual $(\widehat{\varepsilon}_i)$ to the district *mean* to get the quality-adjusted price for each good, the present paper uses deviation of household-level unit prices from *median* unit prices to represent quality effect. The quality-adjusted unit prices are calculated by, first, estimating Eq. 8.6 which, for each commodity i, regresses the deviation of household's unit price from the median price in the district d, of State/province j in each sector s (rural or urban), $\left(v_i^{sjd}\right)_{\text{median}}$, on household characteristics.

Next, the districtwise quality-adjusted price for each item is generated by adding the district median unit value for this item to the estimated residual from Eq. 8.6.

$$\left(p_i^{sjd}\right)_{\text{median}} = \left(v_i^{sjd}\right)_{\text{median}} + (\widehat{\varepsilon_i^{sjd}})_{\text{median}} \tag{8.7}$$

The districtwise median of the prices calculated in Eq. 8.7 is used to represent the districtwise quality-adjusted price for each Food item i in State/province j. In other words, each household is assumed to face the vector of quality-adjusted median value, using Eqs. 8.6 and 8.7, of the item in the district where the household resides. The use of district level information on unit values allows us to consider price variation among districts and, hence, the present empirical exercise goes beyond previous studies that rarely went beyond State level variation in prices and preferences.

8.3.4 *Comparing Levels of Living Between India and Vietnam*

The methodology proposed by Sen (1976) for real income comparisons between countries is used to compare the levels of living between India and Vietnam as measured by their spending on Food items. Following Sen (1976), we consider, as a welfare measure, the inequality corrected mean per capita Food spending in the 2 countries: $W_I = \mu_I(1 - G_I), W_V = \mu_V(1 - G_V)$, where μ, G denote the mean per capita Food expenditure (over the principal Food items) and Gini Food expenditure inequality, respectively. The superscripts *I*, *V* refer to India and Vietnam, respectively. The ratio, W_V/W_I, is a measure of the relative level of living in Vietnam vis-a-vis India. To calculate this ratio, we converted the Indian Food expenditures (in Rupees) to Vietnamese Dong using the PPPs obtained in this study. Recognising the dependence of the calculated PPP on the reference expenditure and spatial differences in preferences and prices, we provide below the welfare ratios calculated separately for rural and urban areas using the corresponding PPPs. Besides the rural–urban differences in the levels of living comparison, Majumder et al. (2015) also provides evidence on the sensitivity of the welfare comparisons to the PPPs used, namely between those that allow them to vary across expenditure percentiles, and those which do not. Note that, while the Gini expenditure inequalities are unit free and consequently will be the same after conversion of the Food expenditures from one currency into another, this will not be the case if the PPPs are allowed to vary with reference expenditure as is the case here. The temporal comparison of the welfare ratio allows us to incorporate the movements in PPPs over time. As reported later, the PPP produced by the ICP understates the depreciation of the Dong vis-a-vis the Rupee over the period, 2004-5 to 2008 and consequently overstates sharply the welfare level of the Vietnamese relative to the Indian consumer during the recent global financial crisis.

8.3.5 Description of the Indian and Vietnamese Data Sets

The Indian data came from the 55th (July, 1999–June, 2000), 61st (July, 2004–June, 2005) and 66th (July, 2009–June, 2010) rounds of India's National Sample Surveys (NSS) on consumer expenditure. All these rounds are 'thick' rounds, being based on large samples. The exercise was performed over 15 major States of the Indian union, with each State subdivided into rural and urban sectors. The data from the unit records (household level) were used in the estimation. The Vietnamese data came from the Vietnamese Living Standard Survey (VLSS) in 1997/98, and the Vietnamese Household Living Standard Surveys (VHLSS) of 2004 and 2008. The 1997/98 Vietnam Living Standards Survey was the second VLSS survey conducted by the General Statistics Office (GSO) of Vietnam, with technical support from the World Bank and financial support from the UNDP (United Nations Development Program) and SIDA (Swedish International Development Cooperation Agency). The VHLSS 2004 and 2008 are parts of the Vietnam household living standard survey conducted every two years between 2002 and 2010. The VHLSS questionnaires are the same as those of the VLSS surveys except that some modules are simplified and some modules are not included.

The household expenditure module used in the present analysis remains same across the VLSS and VHLSS surveys. For the purpose of this study, the eight major regions of Vietnam are grouped into three regions for rural and urban areas separately. North Vietnam consists of Red River Delta, Northeast and Northwest; Central Vietnam consists of North Central coast, South Central Coast and Central highlands; and South Vietnam consists of South East and Mekong Delta. The empirical exercise was conducted on the following six Food items in each country[5]: cereals and cereal substitutes; pulses; milk and milk products; edible oil; meat, fish and eggs and vegetables. These are well defined Food items whose meaning does not change much between India and Vietnam. Also, the data sets contained household-level quantity and expenditure information that goes down to district level in both the countries. Further details on the data, the QAIDS demand estimates and the quality adjustment regression estimates have been presented in Sect. 8.3 of Majumder et al. (2015).

8.3.6 Results

8.3.6.1 Spatial Food Prices in India and Vietnam

Table 8.1 presents the Food PPPs (along with their standard errors) based on the QAIDS parameter estimates for each of the 15 major States in India (rural and urban), with All India (for the respective sectors) as base, for the three NSS rounds —55th, 61st and 66th. The QAIDS was estimated for each State separately and for each of the three rounds, along with that for all India which pooled the data over these 15 major States. Several features are worth noting: first, the regional or spatial Food PPPs are generally well determined; second, in several cases, though not always, the State PPPs are considerably different from the all-India PPP normalised value of 1; prominent examples are the poorer States of Bihar, Orissa and Uttar Pradesh where 1 Rupee buys much more than what it buys elsewhere; third, there is rural–urban agreement on the PPPs in all the three rounds with a reasonable degree of stability in the PPP values over this period; fourth, the idea that a Rupee buys the same everywhere in India, underlying the conventional between-country PPP calculations in ICP, is inconsistent with the picture portrayed in Table 8.1 which rejects, in case of several States, the hypothesis that the spatial price is one.

Table 8.2 presents the corresponding QAIDS Food PPPs for the three regions of Vietnam (rural and urban), with all Vietnam (for the respective sectors) as base, for 1998, 2004 and 2008 along with their standard errors. The PPPs are less well determined than in India, which largely reflects the much smaller sample size in VLSS/VHLSS compared to the NSS. The affluent southern region is the most

[5]These are the dominant Food items that constituted nearly three fourth of total Food spending in each country.

Table 8.1 Spatial[a] Food prices in India, QAIDS-based (Majumder et al. 2015)

States	Rural[b]			Urban		
	NSS 55th round	NSS 61st round	NSS 66th round	NSS 55th round	NSS 61st round	NSS 66th round
Andhra Pradesh	0.960* (−4.09)	0.994 (1.078)	0.994 (−0.52)	0.936* (−4.84)	0.812* (12.97)	1.079* (5.95)
Assam	1.183* (7.98)	1.060 (1.25)	0.880* (−4.91)	0.884* (−3.17)	0.867* (2.59)	0.976 (0.55)
Bihar	0.879* (−18.81)	0.578* (−30.69)	0.751* (−17.03)	0.862* (−11.67)	0.719* (14.99)	0.797* (8.94)
Gujarat	1.092* (2.16)	0.961* (−2.52)	0.940* (−4.15)	0.950* (−2.54)	0.887* (5.35)	0.926* (4.44)
Haryana	0.902* (−2.02)	1.060 (1.46)	0.860* (−10.30)	0.858* (3.17)	0.801* (8.93)	0.917* (5.01)
Karnataka	1.001 (0.06)	0.997 (−0.11)	0.843* (−12.11)	0.917* (−5.83)	0.693* (21.91)	0.882* (8.06)
Kerala	1.243* (8.66)	1.246* (7.02)	1.303* (15.88)	1.003 (0.07)	1.091 (1.11)	1.115* (5.47)
Madhya Pradesh	0.745* (−22.46)	0.914* (−6.64)	0.985 (−0.98)	0.748* (−20.48)	0.924* (6.14)	1.049* (3.21)
Maharashtra	1.027** (1.97)	0.641* (−50.94)	0.774* (−17.58)	1.057* (4.68)	0.657* (25.73)	0.790 (16.11)
Orissa	0.760* (−14.68)	0.546* (−36.73)	0.762* (−19.56)	0.814* (−5.11)	0.599* (15.48)	0.760* (11.58)
Punjab	0.971 (−0.45)	0.713* (−17.02)	0.874* (−11.80)	0.928 (−1.28)	0.941* (2.20)	0.815* (20.92)
Rajasthan	1.057 (0.86)	0.499* (−30.25)	0.712* (−26.10)	0.830* (−3.68)	0.596* (9.61)	0.763* (19.50)
Tamil Nadu	1.273* (8.79)	1.131* (5.29)	0.988 (−0.68)	1.020 (1.32)	1.009 (0.50)	0.930* (5.13)
Uttar Pradesh	0.845* (−16.34)	0.777* (18.93)	0.712* (−37.93)	0.760* (−27.52)	0.677* (29.04)	0.765* (31.51)
West Bengal	1.003 (0.013)	0.938* (−2.27)	1.322* (8.88)	0.983 (0.52)	0.920 (1.50)	1.136* (2.58)
All India	1.000	1.000	1.000	1.000	1.000	1.000

[a]The State's median household is the comparison household, and the all-India median household is the reference household

[b]Figures in parentheses are the t-statistic given by $\frac{S^{\text{State}}-1}{se(S^{\text{State}})}$

*$p < 0.01$, **$p < 0.05$, ***$p < 0.10$ are level of significance for testing PPP = 1

expensive region with the Dong buying less there than in the rest of the country. A comparison with the spatial prices in India in Table 8.1 shows that the spread in Food prices between the most expensive (Southern) region and the least expensive (Central) region is much smaller than in India. However, as in India, the qualitative picture is robust between the rural and urban sectors and is stable over the period covered by the three Vietnamese surveys.

Table 8.2 Spatial[a] Food prices in Vietnam, QAIDS-based (Majumder et al. 2015)

	1998[b]		2004		2008	
Region	Rural	Urban	Rural	Urban	Rural	Urban
North Vietnam	0.886*** (−9.39)	1.076 (1.31)	0.872*** (−21.79)	1.083*** (5.66)	1.095* (9.24)	0.986 (−0.66)
Central Vietnam	1.011 (0.81)	0.922* (−1.84)	0.979*** (−2.69)	0.976 (−1.26)	0.960* (−3.53)	0.850* (−5.82)
Southern Vietnam	1.112*** (7.51)	1.135*** (3.46)	1.128*** (14.19)	1.023* (1.92)	0.911* (−4.99)	0.995* (−0.15)
All Vietnam	1.000	1.000	1.000	1.000	1.000	1.000

[a]The region's median household is the comparison household, and the all Vietnam median household is the reference household

[b]Figures in parentheses are the t-statistic given by $\frac{S^{\text{State}}-1}{se(S^{\text{State}})}$

*$p < 0.01$, **$p < 0.05$, ***$p < 0.10$ are level of significance for testing PPP = 1

8.3.6.2 Purchasing Power Parity Between India and Vietnam

Table 8.3 compares the QAIDS Food-based PPP rates between the Indian Rupee and the Vietnamese Dong with that from using the CPD method (Rao 2005), and the conventional Divisia (DIV), Paasche (PA), Laspeyres (LA) and Fisher (FI) price indices. The QAIDS-based Food PPP rates are obtained by inserting the QAIDS parameter estimates in the two countries in the cost functions in Eq. 8.1 and then evaluating both of them at a (common) reference utility level. The latter is expressed in terms of observable variables by inverting the QAIDS expenditure function to obtain an observable expression for indirect utility, u. The reference utility level, u^r, chosen for the PPP calculations in Table 8.3 is that for the household with median per capita Food expenditure in India. Hence, while the denominator in Eq. 8.1 is simply the median per capita household expenditure on Food in India, the numerator is obtained by using the Vietnamese coefficient estimates along with the reference utility level of the median Indian household which is calculated by inverting the estimated QAIDS expenditure function, Eq. 8.2, for India. The CPD index is obtained from the following regression equation.

$$\sqrt{w_i^r}\log p_i^r = \pi\sqrt{w_i^r}D_r + \sqrt{w_i^r}\sum_j \eta_j D_j^* + \varepsilon_i, \tag{8.8}$$

where w_i^r is the budget share of the *i*th item in the *r*th country, $D_r, r = I$ (India) and V (Vietnam), is the country dummy and $D_j^*, j = 1, 2, \ldots, n$ are the product (item) dummies. If $\hat{\pi}$ is the ordinary least square squares estimator of π, then $\exp(\hat{\pi})$ yields the CPD index. The DIV, PA, LA and FI indices are given, respectively, by the following formulae,

Table 8.3 Food PPP of Vietnam with respect to India (India = 1) using alternative procedures[a] (Majumder et al. 2015)

Year	Sector	QAIDS-based estimates	CPD index (Rao 2005)	Divisia index	Paasche index	Laspeyres index	Fisher index
1999–2000	Rural	387.67 (152.53)	333.36 (20.33)	361.153	274.779	608.632	408.949
	Urban	418.86 (338.80)	360.94 (19.13)	405.367	335.625	629.104	459.503
	All	414.43 (124.09)	346.74 (15.26)	382.56	278.633	640.348	422.4
2004–2005	Rural	385.65 (167.37)	322.58 (26.77)	343.723	192.32	558.731	327.803
	Urban	344.23 (122.35)	407.05 (27.68)	318.353	191.794	521.634	316.3
	All	344.23 (122.35)	388.89 (22.55)	318.353	191.794	521.634	316.3
2008	Rural	838.35 (232.90)	1025.47 (53.32)	587.390	539.688	680.643	606.081
	Urban	889.92 (395.24)	1079.17 (57.20)	614.310	559.601	746.356	646.268
	All	811.37 (193.42)	1054.62 (42.18)	587.457	544.917	680.812	609.086

[a]Figures in parentheses are the asymptotic standard errors

$$\mathrm{DIV} = \exp\left[0.5\sum_{i=1}^{k}\left(w_i^V + w_i^I\right)\log\left(\frac{p_i^V}{p_i^I}\right)\right]; \mathrm{PA} = \frac{\sum_i p_i^V q_i^V}{\sum_i p_i^I q_i^V};$$

$$\mathrm{LA} = \frac{\sum_i p_i^V q_i^I \sum_i}{\sum_i p_i^I q_i^I}; \text{and } \mathrm{FI} = \sqrt{\mathrm{LA.PA}}.$$

The following results are worth noting from Table 8.3.

(a) The QAIDS-based PPP estimates vary between rural and urban areas and reconfirm the picture of rural–urban heterogeneity in each country that was evident from the spatial prices reported earlier.
(b) There has been reasonable stability in the PPPs both between methods and over time in the first two periods. The picture changed dramatically in the third period, 2004/5–2008/9 with the Dong slipping sharply against the Rupee. This is explained by the large increases in the prices of cereals and cereal substitutes, and meat, fish and eggs in Vietnam, reported earlier, which dwarfed that in India over this period, along with the fact that the latter item features much more prominently in the Vietnamese diet than in the Indian diet. Large parts of India are vegetarians and do not consume this item at all.
(c) There is reasonable agreement in the first two periods between the PPP rates from QAIDS and that from the CPD, Divisia and Fisher Indices. However, the Paasche and Laspeyres PPPs vary considerably from one another and the rest,

as one expects from the use of these fixed-basket-based price indices. The Fisher index that averages out the large and reverse biases in Paasche and Laspeyres is much closer to the Divisia, CPD and QAIDS PPP rates, though differences still remain across the alternative procedures.

(d) The picture of rough stability in the PPPs across procedures changes drastically in 2008–9 with the PPP rates varying widely. The Fisher and Divisia PPP rates are in line with one another, but the CPD PPP rates move to values that are much higher than the rest. The QAIDS-based PPP rates are also much higher than the Fisher's and Divisia PPP rates but are intermediate, almost half way, between them and the CPD rates. The explanation, once again, lies in the large inflation in Food prices in Vietnam during this period dwarfing that in India.

(e) To see how the Food PPP rates presented in Table 8.3 compared with PPP rates reported elsewhere, Majumder et al. (2015) calculated the Re/Dong PPP rates for these years from the PPP rates of these currencies reported in http://www.economywatch.com/economic-statistics/economic-indicators/Implied_PPP_Conversion_Rate/. The Re/Dong PPP rates are 304.02, 321.27 and 383.34. The corresponding Re/Dong PPP rates from figures reported in the website https://uqicd.economics.uq.edu.au/[6] are 261.42 in 1998 and 292.83 in 2005. No PPP rates are available from the latter for the years beyond 2005. These are PPP rates based on all items, Food and non-Food, while the PPP rates of Table 8.3 are based on Food items only. The 2005 QAIDS-based PPP rates are much closer to the former than the latter which seems to be biased downwards in relation to both the other sets of PPPs. However, the QAIDS-based PPPs, as also the other Food PPPs, move far ahead of the PPPs from the former website during the last period, 2008–9. Once again, the explanation lies in the sharp rise in Vietnamese Food prices that puts the Food PPPs out of line with the PPPs based on all items. As reported below, this has dramatic implications for the estimates of the relative welfare level of the Vietnamese and the Indian household vis-a-vis one another.

Table 8.4 presents the QAIDS-based Food PPPs between India and Vietnam calculated at five different reference utility levels, namely at 30% ("ultra-poor"), at 50% ("poor"), at 200% ("rich") and at 300% ("ultra-rich") of median household expenditure of the NSS 61st round data, besides at the median expenditure itself, for rural, urban and rural–urban combined sectors. Table 8.4 also presents the pairwise differences in the PPP values along with the associated t-statistics. Both the sectors agree that the PPP increases with household affluence. In the rural sector and at the all country level, all the t-statistics are highly significant. In the urban sector, the PPPs differ significantly in the middle section of the population. Thus, Table 8.4 provides evidence of the sensitivity of the PPP estimates to the reference household, an issue that received hardly any attention in the literature. The evidence also confirms large variation across the PPPs corresponding to the reference households, especially in the rural areas, less in the urban. At the all country level, for example,

[6]See Rao et al. (2010) for the methodology for the PPP rates reported in the website.

Table 8.4 Pairwise comparison of QAIDS-based Food PPPs evaluated at different reference utility levels, Vietnam and India for 2004–05 (Majumder et al. 2015)

	Expenditure points	Per capita expenditure (Rs.)	PPP[a] (India = 1)	Difference with PPP of[b]			
				30% of median	50% of median	Median	200% of median
Rural	30% of median	83.29	294.50 (132.50)				
	50% of median	124.94	328.53 (146.51)	34.03* (14.35)			
	Median	249.88	385.65 (167.37)	91.95* (34.13)	57.12* (21.39)		
	200% of median	499.76	438.48 (340.51)	143.98* (31.61)	109.95* (24.14)	52.83* (11.60)	
	300% of median	749.65	466.05 (243.08)	171.55* (34.16)	137.52* (27.38)	80.40* (16.01)	27.57* (5.49)
Urban	30% of median	97.78	333.73 (372.94)				
	50% of median	146.67	350.78 (388.61)	17.05 (1.50)			
	Median	293.33	379.13 (402.44)	45.40* (3.85)	28.35** (2.40)		
	200% of median	586.67	405.98 (850.97)	72.25* (3.64)	55.20* (2.78)	26.85 (1.35)	
	300% of median	880.00	420.78 (530.05)	87.05* (4.12)	70.00* (3.31)	41.65** (1.97)	14.80 (0.70)
All	30% of median	87.88	260.37 (98.70)				
	50% of median	131.82	290.73 (108.99)	30.36* (9.79)			
	Median	263.64	344.23 (122.35)	83.86* (24.28)	53.50* (15.49)		
	200% of median	527.28	397.94 (363.39)	137.57* (17.02)	107.21* (13.26)	53.71* (6.64)	
	300% of median	790.92	428.56 (192.14)	168.19* (19.41)	137.83* (15.90)	84.33* (9.73)	30.62* (3.53)

[a]Standard errors in parenthesis
[b]t-statistic in parenthesis
$*p < 0.01$, $**p < 0.05$, $***p < 0.10$. All estimates are based on LQAIDS estimates for six Food items

the PPP of 260.37 Dong per Rupee for an 'ultra-poor' household at 30% of median expenditure is considerably lower than the PPP figure of 344.23 Dong per Rupee for a median household. It is clear that the provision of a single PPP that is intended for use at all levels of affluence severely restricts its usefulness especially in cross-country welfare comparisons. This has the policy implication that in poverty calculations using the US $1[7] a day poverty line, one needs to use different PPPs in calculating the number of 'ultra-poor' and the 'poor' in a given country. This adds to the evidence, presented above, on the need to use regionally varying cross-country PPPs (in cross-country inequality and poverty comparisons) and regional poverty lines (in intra-national poverty comparisons).

A comparison of the Food PPP estimates of Tables 8.3 and 8.4 shows wide variation between them. The reason for the large difference between the estimates in Tables 8.3 and 8.4 is twofold: (a) while the former reports expenditure-invariant PPPs, the latter shows their variation over the expenditure percentiles; (b) while the former compares the PPPs between alternative procedures, the latter reports only the QAIDS-based PPPs. Note that the QAIDS-based PPP figure of 344.23 Dong per Rupee at the all country level in 2004–5, and evaluated at the median, is the common point of reference for both tables. The central message from a comparison of Tables 8.3 and 8.4 is that not only does the PPP vary sharply between alternative procedures, it varies sharply between the expenditure percentiles as well. The policy significance of the sensitivity of PPP to regions, expenditure percentiles and procedures is underlined by the discussion in the following section which shows the sensitivity of the levels of living comparisons in India and Vietnam to the PPP used in converting the expenditure figures to a common currency.

8.3.6.3 Comparing the Levels of Living Between India and Vietnam

Table 8.5 reports the values of the 2004–5 Sen (1976) welfare index, namely the inequality-adjusted mean expenditure on the six Food items in the two countries. The last column reports the ratio of the Sen (1976) welfare values in the two countries. The table compares the relative welfare of the Vietnamese vis-a-vis the Indian, under alternative PPP rates used in converting the Indian expenditures from Rupees to Dong. The table shows the impact of allowing the PPPs to vary across different expenditure percentiles on the relative levels of living. This table also allows rural–urban comparison. The following points are worth noting.

(a) All the PPPs agree that, in 2004–5, the Vietnamese enjoyed a higher standard of living than the Indian. This is confirmed by Table A16 in the Appendix which reports the summary budget share of Food in the two countries. Consistent with Engel's law, the higher budget share of Food in India than in Vietnam indicates a lower level of living in the former vis-a-vis the latter. Note, however, that a comparison of the Food shares at the mean or median, rather than by each expenditure percentile, may exaggerate differences in the expenditure pattern between India and Vietnam just as the use of a utility-invariant PPP exaggerates the differences in their living standards, as reported below.

[7]This is separate from the argument of Reddy and Pogge (2007) on whether the $1 a day (or $1.25 a day as has been used lately) is an appropriate figure to use as the international poverty line.

Table 8.5 Comparison of Food expenditure-based welfare between India and Vietnam, 2004–05 (Majumder et al. 2015)

Year		Sector	India			Vietnam			$\frac{W_V}{W_I}$
			Expenditure on six Food items (μ_I) (1000 Dongs)	Gini (G_I)	Sen's Welfare $W_I = \mu_I (1 - G_I)$	Expenditure on six Food items (μ_V) (1000 Dongs)	Gini (G_V)	Sen's Welfare $W_V = \mu_V (1 - G_V)$	
2004–05	Varying PPP between expenditure percentiles	Rural	119.31	0.2878	84.97	118.77	0.2778	85.77	1.01
		Urban	132.97	0.2840	95.21	170.04	0.3209	115.48	1.21
		All	116.81	0.3041	81.29	131.33	0.2884	93.46	1.15
	Median PPP	Rural	68.74	0.2517	51.44	118.77	0.2778	85.77	1.67
		Urban	95.22	0.2663	69.87	170.04	0.3209	115.48	1.65
		All	77.28	0.2628	56.97	131.33	0.2884	93.46	1.64
	ICP[a] PPP	Rural	88.38	0.2517	66.13	118.77	0.2778	85.77	1.30
		Urban	104.29	0.2663	76.52	170.04	0.3209	115.48	1.51
		All	94.17	0.2628	69.42	131.33	0.2884	93.46	1.35

[a]ICP PPP rates against USD 1 in 2005: India (14.669), Vietnam (4712.75), Dong/INR = 321.27

(b) All the PPPs agree that the welfare disparity between India and Vietnam is higher in case of the urban residents than the rural ones.
(c) The similarity ends there. The use of expenditure percentile-specific PPPs sharply reduces the welfare disparity between India and Vietnam in relation to the others.
(d) The use of the ICP PPP leads to a magnitude of welfare disparity that lies between that from the use of expenditure-specific and expenditure-invariant Food PPPs considered in this paper. The key point from Table 8.5 is that the use of a fixed, utility-invariant PPP exaggerates differences in the levels of living between India and Vietnam.

Table 8.6 shows how the relative welfare levels between the two countries have moved over the period spanned by the three NSS rounds/VLSS-VHLSS surveys. This table brings out the divergence between the magnitudes of the welfare ratios corresponding to the QAIDS-based PPP rates and those from the PPP rates obtained from the website mentioned earlier. The 2004–5 snapshot is not quite the complete picture. There is a wide divergence between the two in the earlier and later years. If we focus on the period between 2004/5 and 2008/9, we see that both the PPPs agree that, due to the much higher Food inflation in Vietnam than in India, there has been a large decline in the relative welfare of the Vietnamese over this period. There is general agreement that over the period, 2004–8, the picture of relative affluence of the Vietnamese household gave way to one of relative deprivations in relation to the Indian household. However, the use of the non-demand systems and all item-based PPPs greatly understates the extent of this decline in relation to the preference-consistent Food PPPs proposed in this study. Consequently, by the end of the period considered in this study, the former exaggerates greatly the relative welfare of the Vietnamese in relation to the latter. This is dramatised by the result that in 2008–9, while the Food PPPs show that urban Vietnam experienced a welfare level that is half that in urban India, the all item PPPs record the exact reverse with urban Vietnam ahead of urban India by around 30%. This is an indictment of the all item PPPs that underplay the role of high Food inflation in increasing deprivation both within and between countries.

8.4 Unified Framework for Estimating Intra- and Intercountry Food PPPs

The study by Majumder et al. (2015), described in the previous section, involving a bilateral comparison between India and Vietnam was extended in Majumder et al. (2016). The latter study that is described below, besides adding Indonesia to the comparison, calculates item-specific PPPs following the Barten (1964)-based methodology proposed and used in Majumder et al. (2012) to estimate spatial prices in India. This study highlights the importance of estimating and using item-specific PPPs in cross-country comparisons by formally testing and rejecting the assumption

Table 8.6 Temporal movement in the relative welfare values and sensitivity to the PPP used (Majumder et al. 2015)

Year		Sector	India			Vietnam			$\frac{W_V}{W_I}$
			Expenditure on six Food items (μ_I) (1000 Dongs)	Gini (G_I)	Sen's Welfare $W_I = \mu_I (1 - G_I)$ (1000 Dongs)	Expenditure on six Food items (μ_V) (1000 Dongs)	Gini (G_V)	Sen's Welfare $W_V = \mu_V (1 - G_V)$ (1000 Dongs)	
1999[a]	Median PPP	Rural	99.98	0.2493	75.05	56.52	0.3604	36.15	0.48
		Urban	140.54	0.2616	103.78	115.19	0.2592	85.33	0.82
		All	119.75	0.2650	88.02	73.41	0.3313	49.09	0.56
	ICP PPP	Rural	78.40	0.2493	58.86	56.52	0.3604	36.15	0.61
		Urban	102.01	0.2616	75.32	115.19	0.2592	85.33	1.13
		All	87.85	0.2650	64.57	73.41	0.3313	49.09	0.76
2004–05[b]	Median PPP	Rural	68.74	0.2517	51.44	118.77	0.2778	85.77	1.67
		Urban	95.22	0.2663	69.87	170.04	0.3209	115.48	1.65
		All	77.28	0.2628	56.97	131.33	0.2884	93.46	1.64
	ICP PPP	Rural	88.38	0.2517	66.13	118.77	0.2778	85.77	1.30
		Urban	104.29	0.2663	76.52	170.04	0.3209	115.48	1.51
		All	94.17	0.2628	69.42	131.33	0.2884	93.46	1.35
2008[c]	Median PPP	Rural	424.84	0.2475	319.71	148.39	0.3444	97.28	0.30
		Urban	555.96	0.2730	404.21	309.84	0.2636	228.16	0.56
		All	450.14	0.2657	330.53	186.60	0.3253	125.90	0.38
	ICP PPP	Rural	194.26	0.2475	146.19	148.39	0.3444	97.28	0.67
		Urban	239.49	0.2730	174.12	309.84	0.2636	228.16	1.31
		All	212.68	0.2657	156.16	186.60	0.3253	125.90	0.81

[a]ICP PPP rates against USD 1 in 1998: India (12.46), Vietnam (3789.65), INR/Dong = 304.02
[b]ICP PPP rates against USD 1 in 2005: India (14.669), Vietnam (4712.75), INR/Dong = 321.27
[c]ICP PPP rates against USD 1 in 2008: India (16.863), Vietnam (6464.29), INR/Dong = 383.34

of item-invariant PPPs and by providing empirical evidence that they do make a difference to the welfare comparisons between countries. Majumder et al. (2016) provide PPPs based on Food items only which may be more relevant for poverty comparisons. The econometric estimation of the PPPs, both item-specific and overall, allows us to report their standard errors and conduct tests of hypotheses on the PPPs that are not possible with the conventional price indices-based PPPs. This is an advantage that the Barten (1964)-based PPP procedure shares with the Country-Product Dummy (CPD) approach of estimating the PPPs.[8] Majumder et al. (2016) illustrates the advantage of this approach by directly estimating the price level indices (PLI) which is defined as the ratio of the PPP to the exchange rate. This study reports the tests of the equality of PLI between items and of each of the PLI being significantly differing from unity. Ravallion (2013) suggests that, as a country grows and approaches the developed countries in affluence, their PLIs will move towards unity in what is called a 'dynamic Penn effect'. However, very little is known about the PLIs of developing countries vis-a-vis one another, other than the magnitudes implied by their PLIs with respect to the USA. Majumder et al. (2016) provide a departure by reporting the matrix of the estimated PLIs between the three countries, India, Indonesia and Vietnam considered there.

8.4.1 Estimating Equation

The QAIDS demand equation, in expenditure share form, augmented to incorporate the item-specific PPPs (k_i) as estimable parameters, is given by

$$w_i = \alpha_i + \sum_{j=1}^{n} \gamma_{ij} \log p_j^* + \beta_i \log\left(x/P^*\right) + \left(\frac{\lambda_i}{\prod_{k=1}^{n} p_k^{*\beta_k}}\right)\left(\log\left(x/P^*\right)\right)^2 \quad (8.9)$$

where

$$\log P^* = \alpha_0 + \sum_i \alpha_i \log p_i^* + \frac{1}{2}\sum_{i=1}^{n}\sum_{j=1}^{n} \gamma_{ij} \log p_i^* \log p_j^* \quad (8.9a)$$

and $p_i^* = p_i k_i^{D_s} \sqrt{n}$, with the restrictions $\sum_{j=1}^{n} \gamma_{ij} = \sum_{i=1}^{n} \gamma_{ij} = 0$ and $\gamma_{ij} = \gamma_{ji}$, where D_s denotes the sectoral dummy (rural = 0, urban = 1) and $\sqrt{n}$ is the OECD equivalence scale, n being the household size. The item-specific PPPs, namely the $k_i' s$, express the urban prices in terms of the rural prices or, alternatively, the PPP of the comparison country in terms of the reference country.

[8] See, also, Clements et al. (2006) for an alternative and promising stochastic approach to index numbers where 'uncertainty and statistical ideas play a central role'.

8.4.2 Data Description

The data for this study comes from Household Expenditure Surveys conducted in the three countries, India, Indonesia and Vietnam. The three surveys chosen covered periods that, though not identical, had large degree of overlaps between them making the calculation of cross-country PPPs meaningful. The Indian data came from the 66th round (July 2009–June 2010) of India's National Sample Surveys (NSS) on consumption expenditure. The Indonesian data came from the Indonesian Social and Economic Survey (SUSENAS) 2011, collected by the Central Statistical Agency of the Government of Indonesia. The Vietnamese data came from the Vietnamese Household Living Standard Surveys (VHLSS) of 2010.

8.4.3 Preference-Consistent PPPs Between India, Indonesia and Vietnam

Table 8.7 presents the item-specific cross-country PPPs (along with their standard errors). While the k_is denote the item-specific PPPs of the Indonesian Rupiah and Vietnamese Dong with respect to the Indian Rupee, $1/k_i$ denotes the PPP of the Indian Rupee with respect to the other two currencies. In keeping with the spatial aspect of this study, the PPPs reported in Table 8.7 correspond to rural–rural (left half) and urban–urban (right half) comparisons of purchasing power of the respective countries' currency units. The PPP estimates are mostly well determined, and there is evidence of considerable variation of the PPPs between items in both the rural and urban sectors. The coefficient of variation (CV) between the item-specific PPPs records greater variability in the PPPs in Vietnam than in Indonesia. The variation is higher in the rural areas than in the urban in both countries. Much of the fluctuation in the PPPs is on account of the smaller Food items, such as pan/tobacco/intoxicants and beverages. Since there are issues of comparability and differences in the meaning of these items between countries, this result should be treated with some caution. Nevertheless, as Table 8.6 reports, the hypothesis of item invariance of the PPPs (i.e. $k_i = K$ for all i) is easily rejected on a likelihood ratio test for both sectors. This table also underlines the importance of the intra-country spatial price differences by establishing several cases of large differences in the PPPs between the rural and urban sectors, most noticeably, for the principal Food items, cereals and cereal substitutes, milk and milk products, and vegetables. The idea of a single PPP between countries that hold for all items and for both the rural and urban sectors is convincingly rejected by the evidence contained in Table 8.7.

Table 8.7 Estimates of item-specific intercountry PPP parameters, k_i and the corresponding PPPs, $1/k_i$, Indonesia and Vietnam with India as base[a] (Majumder et al. 2016)

Commodities (i)	Rural				Urban			
	Indonesia		Vietnam		Indonesia		Vietnam	
	k_i	$1/k_i$	k_i	$1/k_i$	k_i	$1/k_i$	k_i	$/k_i$
Cereals/ grams	0.00975	102.62	0.0025	349.83	0.0055	190.30	0.00193	518.59
	(26.67)[b]		(30.27)		(24.77)		(27.73)	
Milk and milk products	0.00651	153.56	0.0085	119.75	0.01249	80.07	0.0082	118.76
	(18.72)		(19.55)		(25.43)		(32.24)	
Edible oil	0.00789	126.1	0.0101	92.53	0.0125	78.40	0.0037	305.49
	(27.43)		(29.78)		(34.30)		(17.13)	
Meat, fish and egg	0.01276	78.35	0.0030	313.01	0.0096	105.63	0.0012	618.89
	(25.15)		(25.26)		(41.60)		(18.76)	
Vegetables	0.00651	153.62	0.0017	792.64	0.0051	169.20	0.00566	176.71
	(49.27)		(11.98)		(58.69)		(11.63)	
Fruits	0.00867	115.28	0.0037	325.37	0.0032	255.43	0.0221	44.22
	(22.28)		(30.69)		(28.89)		(12.55)	
Pan/tobacco/intoxicants	0.01066	93.79	0.0215	46.19	0.0125	79.66	0.0020	370.08
	(23.48)		(20.07)		(23.59)		(14.22)	
Beverages	0.00269	371.36	0.0012	816.86	0.0057	182.54	0.0013	614.55
	(27.78)		(12.11)		(21.21)		(18.88)	
Value of log likelihood (LL2)	18355.11		6515.7		18349.4		6467.527	

(continued)

Table 8.7 (continued)

Commodities (i)	Rural				Urban			
	Indonesia		Vietnam		Indonesia		Vietnam	
	k_i	$1/k_i$	k_i	$1/k_i$	k_i	$1/k_i$	k_i	$/k_i$
Chi-square (d.f. 7) statistics for testing equality of $\boldsymbol{k_i}$'s [c]	186.72***		108.33***		175.94***		101.92***	
Simple average of itemwise PPPs (APPP)		149.42		357.02		142.65		345.91
Weighted[d] average of itemwise PPPs		119.20		360.06		123.38		466.34
Coefficient of variation (CV) of APPP (%)		62.63		83.83		46.40		64.64

[a]That is, for India $k(i) = 1$ for all commodities, where i denotes commodities
[b]Figures in parentheses are the asymptotic t-statistics. All are significant at 1% level
[c]These are computed as 2(LL2-LL1), where LL1 is taken from the relevant rows of the last column of Table 8.3
***Significant at 1% level
[d]The weights are budget shares of respective countries and sectors

8.5 Sensitivity of PPP Estimates to Estimation Procedures

In this section, we move from the bilateral and trilateral country contexts of Sects. 8.3 and 8.4, respectively, to the global context involving all the countries covered by the ICP. We report some of the findings from Majumder et al. (2017) which conducted a systematic comparison of the PPP estimates from a wide range of procedures including the ICP PPPs. Besides the preference-based TCLI PPPs which have been described earlier, this study considered the PPPs from the Gini–Elteto–Koves–Szulc (GEKS), Geary–Khamis (GK), equally weighted Geary–Khamis (EWGK) and the CPD procedures. Before presenting the results on sensitivity of the estimated PPPs to differences in procedures, we describe briefly the alternative methodologies considered in the study.

8.5.1 Description of the Alternative PPP Estimation Procedures

8.5.1.1 The ICP Methodology

The ICP distinguishes between 'below basic headings' and 'above basic headings' in the procedures it uses to calculate the PPP. An early description of the ICP exercise when it was conducted under the auspices of the UN is contained in United Nations (1992). A more recent description of the ICP methodology is contained in World Bank (2013)—see, in particular, the contributions by Rao (Chaps. 1 and 4) and Diewert (Chaps. 5 and 6) in that volume.[9] The ICP follows a hierarchical approach for estimating the PPPs. Basic heading (BH) is the lowest level at which the PPPs are estimated. The BH PPPs are then aggregated to calculate PPPs for different uses in cross-country comparisons. In this study, we will restrict ourselves to the PPP estimation procedure above the BH levels, building on the prices constructed from below the BH levels. While the unweighted CPD method (described below) is used by the ICP below the BH level to deal with the problem of missing price information, the commonly used methods of aggregation for computing PPPs for GDP or consumption and other major aggregates above the BH level are the GEKS, Iklé, GK and the Rao or weighted CPD methods. The GK method that is favoured by the ICP in producing PPPs for GDP comparisons by aggregating the BH PPPs has the unique advantage '*that it produces additive results that have the property of matrix consistency, where the results can be compared down the basic headings and across countries for any basic heading or aggregation. There are strong arguments that gross domestic product should retain this property even after conversion to another currency since it is in accord with standard national*

[9]To save space, we have provided a brief description of the ICP exercise. The reader is referred to United Nations (1992) and World Bank (2013) for more details.

accounting practice. Such additive consistency is advantageous not only because it permits an easier analysis of the structure of the aggregates (e.g., it enables the calculation of distribution percentages), but also because it allows comparison across countries'. (United Nations 1992, p. 52).

As pointed out in the same UN document, '*In the usual G-K application, countries are accorded the weight of their own total GDP in the aggregation .... This accords with standard national accounts methodology, where prices embedded in national accounts are an average weighted by the quantities produced in each region ... Most other methods of aggregation use a weighting system that accords the same importance to each country ... EKS type systems give the same importance to, say, Luxembourg, as to France, even though France's economy is over 50 times larger than that of Luxembourg ... systems such as EKS tend to produce somewhat larger differences between per capita incomes between rich and poor countries than the G-K method'*. (United Nations 1992, p. 53). The GK method is not without its disadvantages either. It is not superlative unlike the Fisher and Tornqvist price indices; i.e., it does not approximate the preference-consistent 'true cost of living index'. A more serious objection to GK, noted by Dikhanov (1994) and Hill (2000) and reiterated below, stems from its use of the concept of the 'world price' of an item defined as the consumption weighted average of prices in all the participating counties which will therefore be heavily slanted towards the prices of the richer countries (Gershenkron effect). Hill (2000) argues '*using a single reference price vector to compare countries introduces substitution bias. As a result, additive methods (such as GK) tend to overestimate the per capita incomes of countries whose relative prices differ substantially from the reference prices used in the comparison'*. (p. 146). The GK method overvalues the expenditure on non-tradeable items in the poorer countries and that will tend to understate poverty. Since the GK method has featured prominently in successive ICP exercises, especially in generating PPPs used in GDP comparisons, empirical evidence on the size of the 'Gershenkeron effect' that we provide later is of interest. Iklė (1972), Dikhanov (1994), and Hill (2000) have, therefore, proposed alternative variants of the GK method, referred to as 'equally weighted GK' (EWGK). This is designed to reduce the size of the 'Gershenkeron effect', while retaining the 'additivity' property of GK. Hill (2000) proposed version of EWGK, which is simpler than that of the others, is used here to estimate the EWGK PPPs for comparison with the PPPs from the other procedures. This discussion shows that there is no single procedure that dominates all the others. Until the 2005 ICP, GK was the main aggregation procedure used in the ICP, though the GEKS procedure has been used in the Eurostat-OECD region since 1985.

An important principle that multilateral PPP estimation ought to satisfy, and is respected by the ICP, is the transitivity principle, which is as follows:

$$\mathrm{PPP}_{jk} = \mathrm{PPP}_{jm} \cdot \mathrm{PPP}_{mk}. \tag{8.10}$$

In words, the PPP between countries j and k, $j, k = 1, 2, \ldots, M$, can be obtained as the product of the PPP between j and m, and that between m and k. This property guarantees the level of internal consistency required in international comparisons. The ICP exercise satisfies several other principles in the multilateral PPP calculations. The principal ones are additivity, base invariance and fixity principle. Additivity (already mentioned above), in the words of Rao in World Bank (2013, Chap. 1, p. 35), '*(additivity) ensures that the additive nature of the national accounts within a country, expressed in national currency units, is also maintained when international comparisons are made'*. Base Invariance—all countries should be treated equally in deriving the matrix of PPPs that satisfy transitivity. This principle was satisfied by the 2005 ICP by choosing a 'star country' through which all the other countries are compared, then treating each country as a star country and taking the geometric average of the 146 participating countries. As Rao notes in World Bank (2013, p. 34), this procedure gives identical results to the application of the GEKS procedure. Fixity principle—this principle '*stipulates that the relative volumes in the global comparisons between any pair of countries belonging to a given region should be identical to the relative volumes of the two countries established in the regional comparisons to which they belong*' (World Bank 2013, p. 37). In other words, the real GDPs of India and Pakistan as countries in the South Asia region should be identical to the ratio of their GDP from the global comparisons. This principle, which was developed in the 2005 ICP round, was implemented through the idea of 'Ring Countries' that linked the various regions. The more recent ICP, namely the 2011 ICP round, changed the Ring approach '*to a global core list approach in which all participating countries were asked to include a common set of items in the regional list of products they surveyed*'. (World Bank 2015).

8.5.1.2 Gini–Elteto–Koves–Szulc (GEKS) Index

The GEKS method is a generic method, proposed independently by Eltetö and Köves (1964), and Szulc (1964), which generates transitive indices from a matrix of binary indices which satisfy the country reversal test but not transitivity. Let I_{jk} represent a price index (or PPP) for country k with country j as base such that $I_{jk} \cdot I_{kj} = 1$. Then, the GEKS index is given by,

$$GEKS_{jk} = \prod_{l=1}^{M} \left(I_{jl} \cdot I_{lk}\right)^{\frac{1}{M}} \tag{8.11}$$

The GEKS index can be implemented once the binary index number formula to compute I_{jk} is chosen. The Fisher binary index is the most commonly used index.[10]

[10]Note that if the Fisher index is replaced by Tornqvist formula, the GEKS index can be derived from the stochastic CPD approach of Rao described below. However, Balk (2009) recently provided an overview of various multilateral methods and endorsed the GEKS-Fisher method as a centre-stage method, particularly from the economic approach to international comparisons.

8.5.1.3 The Geary–Khamis (GK) Index

Let p_{ij} and q_{ij} denote the price and quantity of commodity i for country j, $i = 1, 2, \ldots, N$ and $j = 1, 2, \ldots, M$. Let P_i and PPP_j, respectively, denote the international price of ith commodity and the purchasing power parity of jth currency. The Geary–Khamis method defines the international prices and the purchasing power parities through the following system of $(M + N)$ equations,

$$P_i = \sum_{j=1}^{M} \left(\frac{q_{ij}}{\sum_{j=1}^{M} q_{ij}} \frac{p_{ij}}{\text{PPP}_j} \right); \text{PPP}_j = \frac{\sum_{i=1}^{N} p_{ij} q_{ij}}{\sum_{i=1}^{N} P_i q_{ij}} \tag{8.12}$$

In general, the above system of equations, a set of $(M + N)$ linear homogeneous equations in as many unknowns, has a unique positive solution for the P_i's and PPP_j's apart from an undetermined scalar multiplicative factor [see Geary (1958), Rao (1971) and Khamis (1972)]. As defined above, the GK method is multilateral since the 'international price', P_i, is defined in Eq. 8.3 as the quantity weighted average of prices in all the countries. It is possible, however, to define a bilateral GK with the 'international price' defined as the weighted average of only the countries being compared. While multilateral GK is transitive, bilateral GK is not. However, multilateral GK has the disadvantage of violating the 'characteristicity' requirement of Drechsler (1973) that stipulates that the PPP between two countries should depend on the prices and expenditures in those two countries alone.

8.5.1.4 The Equally Weighted Geary–Khamis (EWGK) Index

Given that the GK index gives greater weight to the price vectors of larger countries when determining the reference price vector resulting in the 'Gershenkeron effect' explained above, an equally weighted variant of the index has been proposed.[11] The equally weighted Geary–Khamis method defines the international prices and the purchasing power parities through the following system of $(M + N)$ equations.

$$P_i = \sum_{j=1}^{M} \left(\frac{w_{ij}}{\sum_{j=1}^{M} w_{ij}} \frac{p_{ij}}{\text{PPP}_j} \right); \text{PPP}_j = \frac{\sum_{i=1}^{N} p_{ij} q_{ij}}{\sum_{i=1}^{N} P_i q_{ij}} \tag{8.13}$$

Given w_{ij} denotes the share of good i in the expenditure of country j.

[11]See Balk (2009), Eq. (43) and Hill (2000), Eq. (10).

8.5.1.5 The CPD PPP

The Country-Product Dummy (CPD) model was originally proposed by Summers (1973) to calculate relative price levels between countries in the context of missing price information. The CPD PPPs are estimated from the following equation,

$$y_{ij} \equiv \ln p_{ij} = \alpha_1 D_1 + \alpha_2 D_2 + \cdots + \alpha_M D_M + \eta_1 D_1^* + \eta_2 D_2^* + \cdots + \eta_N D_N^* + v_{ij}, \tag{8.14}$$

where D_j (j = 1, 2, …, M) and D_i^* (i = 1, 2, …, N) are, respectively, country and commodity dummy variables, and v_{ij}'s are random disturbance terms which are independently and identically (normally) distributed with zero mean and variance σ^2.

Under complete price information comparisons of price levels between two countries j and k, represented by PPP_{jk} can be derived as,

$$\text{PPP}_{jk} = \frac{\alpha_k}{\alpha_j} = \prod_{i=1}^{N} \left[\frac{p_{ik}}{p_{ij}}\right]^{1/N} \tag{8.15}$$

However, Rao (2005), in the spirit of the standard index number approach, proposed that a more appropriate procedure would be to find estimates of the parameters that are likely to track the more important commodities more closely. This is achieved by minimising a weighted residual sum of squares, with each observation weighted according to the expenditure share of the commodity in a given country.

Thus, the generalised CPD method suggests that estimation of Eq. 8.15 be conducted after weighting each observation according to its value share. This is equivalent to the application of ordinary least squares after transforming the equation premultiplied by $\sqrt{w_{ij}}$, where w_{ij} is the budget share of item i in country j. The equation thus becomes,

$$\sqrt{w_{ij}} \ln p_{ij} = \sqrt{w_{ij}} \sum_{j=1}^{M} \alpha_j D_j + \sqrt{w_{ij}} \sum_{i=1}^{N} \eta_i D_i^* + u_{ij} \tag{8.16}$$

Rao (2005) has shown that PPPs resulting from the least squares estimation of the above weighted CPD equation are equivalent to a system of expenditure share weighted log-change system. The Rao system is given by, $PPP_j = \prod_{i=1}^{N} \left(\frac{p_{ij}}{P_i}\right)^{w_{ij}}$, setting one country as the numeraire, and

$$P_i = \prod_{j=1}^{M} \left(\frac{p_{ij}}{\text{PPP}_j}\right)^{\frac{w_{ij}}{\sum_{j=1}^{M} w_{ij}}} \tag{8.17}$$

Here, P_i, $i = 1, 2, \ldots, N$ are the international average prices (at the numeraire country's currency) of commodities. PPP_j is the PPP of country j with respect to the numeraire country. Note that $\sum_{i=1}^{N} w_{ij} = 1$, the sum of budget shares in country j. The equivalence of purchasing power parities and international prices derived from the application of the weighted CPD method with those arising out of the Rao system for multilateral comparisons implies that the weighted CPD method is a natural method of aggregation at all levels of aggregation within the context of international comparisons.

The basic CPD model, given by Eq. 8.14 above, has the advantage that, as it is based on stochastic formulation, it allows the use of a range of econometric tools and techniques that are not normally used in the computation of PPPs. In particular, the regression approach provides estimated standard errors for all the coefficients. An added advantage is that the stochastic formulation of CPD given by Eqs. 8.14 and 8.16 can be extended to allow regionally correlated price movements via admitting spatially correlated errors. The empirical literature on subnational and cross-country PPPs is generally based on the assumption that there is no interdependence between the price movements in the various regions of a country or between that in the various countries. There is some evidence to the contrary in early work reported by Aten (1996) on subnational PPPs, and by Rao (2001) on cross-country PPPs.

8.5.2 Empirical Evidence on the PPP Comparisons Between Procedures

The PPP calculations in this paper relate to the ICP round, 2011. The ICP group in the World Bank made the price and expenditure information for 2011 available. Majumder et al. (2017) constructed the prices for item groups at the basic heading (BH) level by considering the item prices (in LCU) within the BH taking into account the importance matrix provided by the World Bank. As a standard practice, Majumder et al. (2017) report the PPPs in terms of price level indices (PLIs), given by the ratio of PPP to the exchange rate with the Indian Rupee being the numeraire currency. Table 8.8 presents the alternative sets of PLIs that allow comparison of the ICP 2011 PLIs against those from the alternative procedures, namely the CPD, GEKS, GK and EWGK for 178 countries. The countries have been arranged according to seven ICP regions, viz. 'Africa', 'Asia and the Pacific', 'Commonwealth of Independent States (CIS)', 'Eurostat-OECD', 'Latin America', 'Western Asia' and 'the Caribbean'. The regionwise and overall correlation coefficients between the alternative PPPs are close to 0.9. The high correlations set the ground for comparison between the alternative PPPs as well as with ICP PPPs. The following features may be noted from Table 8.8a–d:

(i) In terms of PLI being greater or less than unity, there is agreement among almost all the PPPs, with the exception of few countries in the Africa, Asia and the Pacific and CIS regions, although there is variation in magnitudes. Consistent with the Balassa–Samuelson hypothesis, developed countries in the affluent Eurostat-OECD region much richer than India record PLIs well above one, while countries poorer than India in the Asia and the Pacific region and in Latin America record PLIs marginally above or below one.

(ii) As is evident from the table, the results are sensitive to the procedure of price aggregation at the BH level. This is corroborated by the fact that there are considerable discrepancies between figures in the ICP and other columns.

(iii) The discrepancies between the ICP figures and the others in the regions 'Africa' and 'Asia and the Pacific' are of particular concern, as in these regions the need to use accurate PPPs is at its peak, given the high poverty rates in these regions and their disproportionately large contribution to global poverty. Here, the CPD-, GEKS-, GK- and EWGK-based PLIs are lower than the ICP-based PLIs for many countries.

(iv) Given our earlier remarks on the 'Gershenkeron effect' affecting the GK procedure, the GK PPPs are of special interest in these comparisons. An interesting observation that can be made from Table 8.8 is that the GK PLIs are, for most countries, higher than the GEKS PLIs. What is particularly striking is that the differential between the two sets of PLIs is quite large for the affluent countries in the Eurostat-OECD region with the GK PLIs exceeding the GEKS PLIs by multiples of nearly 2 in some cases (e.g. Canada, UK and the USA). In contrast, the differential comes down sharply for the poorer countries in Africa and the Asia-Pacific region to almost parity, with some countries even recording lower PLI values for the GK than the GEKS. This is consistent with the 'Gershenkeron effect' which overstates the price level index in many of the affluent countries and hence makes India and other developing countries look lot less poor in relation to such countries. In other words, the upward bias in the GK PLIs vis-a-vis the others is more evident in case of countries such as the USA, UK and Canada with price structures vastly different from those in the less affluent countries. This is also evident from a comparison of the PPPs in Appendix Table A1 with a nearly twofold increase in the GK PPPs over the GEKS PPPs for affluent countries such as Australia, New Zealand, Canada, UK and the USA, but much less so for the less developed countries.

(v) The EWGK PLIs are also of interest since EWGK, while retaining the additivity property of GK, is designed to exhibit less of the upward bias than the GK procedure. Table 8.8 shows that this is indeed the case, with the EGWK PLIs in Table 8.8 being more in line with the GEKS estimates than the GK estimates. This is particularly evident in case of the affluent countries such as the USA, UK and Canada where the EGWK PLIs are quite close to the GEKS PLIs. It is significant that in case of several of these affluent countries it is the ICP PPPs that are quite out of line with the others, often exceeding them by a large margin.

Table 8.9 presents the TCLI PPPs for the countries for which the unit records from the Household Expenditure Surveys were used to calculate the PPPs. Along with the overall TCLI PPPs, the table also presents PPPs based on other methods for comparison. As indicated earlier, the unit-level data enables us to compute expenditure group-specific PPPs. The PPPs calculated for expenditure quintiles have also been reported in the table. It may be observed that in terms of order of magnitude, the TCLI-based overall PPPs compare fairly well with the others with some discrepancies, which may possibly be attributed to non-homotheticity of preferences in the QAIDS-based TCLI set-up. It is interesting to note that this table brings out an advantage of the TCLI procedure by providing evidence on the large variation in the PPP between expenditure quintiles and is consistent with the evidence presented in Majumder et al. (2015) on PPPs between India and Vietnam that vary between expenditure classes. This brings into question the current practice of using single countrywide PPPs in cross-country comparisons.

8.6 Concluding Remarks

Purchasing power parities (PPPs) play a crucial role in cross-country comparisons of a variety of country indicators such as GDP and national income, and in calculations of global poverty. The PPPs are used to convert the country-level statistics in local currency units to a numeraire currency such as the US dollar. As the number of studies involving cross-country comparisons has proliferated, the importance of the PPPs used in the comparisons has grown. Consequently, the profile of the International Comparison Project (ICP) that produces the PPPs used in the global calculations has grown as well. This chapter reviews the alternative PPP procedures that are available and reports PPP estimates from studies involving bilateral, trilateral and fully multilateral country comparisons. The studies surveyed here show that, given the publicly available information, one can use alternative methodologies to come up with PPPs that provide counterfactuals to the ICP PPPs.

The key message that stands out from the evidence reported in this chapter is that the PPPs vary by region and by expenditure classes, and this suggests that the next round of the ICP should integrate calculation of subnational and class-specific PPPs with that of the aggregate PPPs between countries taking note of regional heterogeneity in preferences (within and between countries) and between the expenditure classes. The results on sensitivity of the PPPs to procedures underline the need to subject the principal conclusions to robustness checks and, in particular, check for the accuracy of the PPPs used by benchmarking them against the PPPs from alternative procedures. In nearly all the studies on global poverty, for example, the ICP PPPs have been used uncritically. The lack of robustness of the PPPs makes it imperative to experiment with a range of PPPs in the poverty calculations. This volume now turns to this issue in the following chapter.

Table 8.8 Alternative price level indices, PLIs for 2011, numeraire in Indian rupee (Majumder et al. 2017)

Region	Country	ICP	CPD	GEKS	GK	EWGK	Region	Country	ICP	CPD	GEKS	GK	EWGK
a													
Africa	Algeria	1.319	1.268	1.236	1.183	1.227	Africa	Liberia	1.730	1.454	1.435	1.307	1.343
	Angola	2.487	1.716	1.480	1.437	1.554		Madagascar	1.067	0.789	0.804	0.751	0.821
	Benin	1.464	1.111	1.108	1.286	1.549		Malawi	1.556	1.458	1.611	1.699	2.221
	Botswana	1.982	1.731	1.789	2.038	2.074		Mali	1.428	1.358	1.404	1.402	1.443
	Burkina Faso	1.439	1.239	1.369	1.399	1.535		Mauritania	1.209	1.008	1.048	1.076	1.384
	Burundi	1.152	1.129	1.129	1.046	1.500		Mauritius	1.919	1.575	1.686	1.902	1.602
	Cameroon	1.509	1.349	1.158	1.157	1.447		Morocco	1.589	1.600	1.860	2.030	2.086
	Cape Verde	1.872	1.432	1.290	1.630	1.104		Mozambique	1.687	1.594	1.623	1.686	1.789
	Central African Republic	1.723	1.776	1.813	1.822	2.097		Namibia	2.197	1.733	0.872	0.498	0.176
	Chad	1.632	1.467	1.505	1.556	1.678		Niger	1.483	1.526	1.785	1.677	1.736
	Comoros	1.894	1.615	1.417	1.051	1.301		Nigeria	1.572	1.354	1.489	1.504	1.583
	Congo, Dem. Rep.	1.784	1.780	2.010	2.087	2.289		Rwanda	1.296	1.136	0.993	0.868	1.095
	Congo, Rep.	1.949	1.905	1.868	1.900	1.888		Senegal	1.611	1.646	1.701	1.770	2.019
	Côte d'Ivoire	1.552	1.534	1.257	1.175	1.319		Seychelles	1.881	1.848	1.948	2.261	2.140
	Djibouti	1.767	1.724	1.768	2.008	2.446		Sierra Leone	1.229	1.151	1.159	1.123	0.841
	Egypt, Arab Republic	0.897	0.792	0.851	0.922	0.843		South Africa	2.188	1.925	2.147	2.402	2.211
	Equatorial Guinea	2.147	1.466	1.438	1.196	1.026		Sudan	1.677	1.448	1.720	1.970	2.333
	Ethiopia	0.973	0.938	0.996	1.047	1.328		Swaziland	1.753	1.215	1.316	1.588	1.683
	Gabon	2.362	2.227	2.154	2.416	2.449		São Tomé and Principe	1.719	1.636	1.629	1.893	2.220
	Gambia, The	1.104	1.077	1.094	1.086	1.148		Tanzania	1.143	1.040	1.144	1.060	1.212
	Ghana	1.576	1.369	1.419	1.451	1.423		Togo	1.480	1.485	1.529	1.585	1.634

(continued)

Table 8.8 (continued)

Region	Country	ICP	CPD	GEKS	GK	EWGK	Region	Country	ICP	CPD	GEKS	GK	EWGK
	Guinea	1.166	1.287	1.405	1.576	1.962		Tunisia	1.477	1.455	1.507	1.745	1.574
	Guinea-Bissau	1.565	1.719	1.681	1.582	1.837		Uganda	1.147	1.204	1.106	1.109	1.323
	Kenya	1.243	1.030	1.026	1.068	1.145		Zambia	1.599	1.501	1.547	1.780	2.116
	Lesotho	1.676	1.424	1.485	1.588	1.691		Zimbabwe	1.637	1.523	1.655	1.791	2.110

Region	Country	ICP	CPD	GEKS	GK	EWGK	Region	Country	ICP	CPD	GEKS	GK	EWGK
b													
Asia and The Pacific	Bangladesh	1.025	0.956	0.956	1.104	1.116	Comm. and independent States	Armenia	1.363	1.541	1.483	1.804	1.913
	Bhutan	1.119	0.965	0.936	1.065	1.147		Azerbaijan	1.191	1.360	1.301	1.365	1.396
	Brunei Darussalam	2.151	1.889	1.619	1.510	1.347		Belarus	0.914	1.025	0.957	1.116	1.055
	Cambodia	1.112	1.024	1.050	1.145	1.019		Kazakhstan	1.603	1.337	1.312	1.630	1.467
	China	1.801	1.674	1.859	2.166	2.094		Kyrgyzstan	1.049	0.955	0.911	1.054	1.142
	Fiji	2.080	1.615	1.529	1.716	1.535		Moldova	1.305	1.294	1.365	1.499	1.477
	Hong Kong SAR, China	2.388	1.899	2.326	2.464	2.078		Russian Federation	1.684	1.666	1.583	1.887	1.792
	India	1.000	1.000	1.000	1.000	1.000		Tajikistan	1.073	1.105	1.062	1.045	1.035
	Indonesia	1.417	1.311	1.227	1.482	1.379		Ukraine	1.193	1.227	1.245	1.462	1.475
	Lao PDR	1.054	0.976	0.956	0.938	0.930	Eurostat-OECD	Albania	1.565	1.464	1.442	1.633	1.721
	Macao SAR, China	2.176	1.693	1.838	2.114	1.814		Australia	5.173	3.815	3.797	4.280	3.845
	Malaysia	1.610	1.366	0.865	0.644	0.609		Austria	3.937	2.984	2.970	3.447	3.276
	Maldives	2.163	1.692	1.674	2.137	1.836		Belgium	4.057	2.893	2.654	3.209	2.761
	Mongolia	1.360	1.310	1.160	1.308	1.421			1.822	1.879	1.861	2.025	2.092

(continued)

Table 8.8 (continued)

Region	Country	ICP	CPD	GEKS	GK	EWGK	Region	Country	ICP	CPD	GEKS	GK	EWGK
								Bosnia and Herzegovina					
	Myanmar	0.935	0.815	0.352	0.175	0.063		Bulgaria	1.555	1.586	1.629	1.882	1.762
	Nepal	1.071	0.672	0.625	0.581	0.438		Canada	4.281	3.323	3.210	3.603	3.347
	Pakistan	0.905	0.787	0.655	0.557	0.600		Chile	2.434	2.289	2.237	2.620	2.403
	Philippines	1.358	1.024	0.786	0.682	0.513		Croatia	2.473	2.315	2.444	2.971	2.874
	Singapore	2.960	2.214	2.822	2.633	2.003		Cyprus	3.244	2.798	3.004	3.308	3.279
	Sri Lanka	1.135	1.117	0.987	1.041	0.949		Czech Republic	2.533	2.179	2.163	2.618	2.568
	Taiwan, China	1.712	1.574	1.507	1.617	1.247		Denmark	5.251	3.917	3.857	4.681	4.311
	Thailand	1.314	0.985	1.045	1.036	0.917		Estonia	2.489	2.239	2.099	2.514	2.531
	Vietnam	1.090	0.899	0.826	0.867	0.704		Finland	4.405	3.558	3.841	4.449	4.153
Region	Country	ICP	CPD	GEKS	GK	EWGK	Region	Country	ICP	CPD	GEKS	GK	EWGK
c													
Eurostat-OECD	France	3.963	3.041	3.180	3.783	3.377	Eurostat-OECD	Slovakia	2.326	2.280	2.246	2.732	2.630
	Germany	3.616	2.804	2.765	3.283	2.874		Slovenia	3.017	2.669	2.569	3.065	2.939
	Greece	3.284	2.851	2.889	3.419	3.464		Spain	3.467	2.611	2.577	3.280	2.948
	Hungary	2.009	1.837	1.826	2.251	2.131		Sweden	4.738	3.398	3.297	4.028	3.755
	Iceland	3.889	3.505	3.735	4.269	4.248		Switzerland	6.023	3.899	3.645	4.657	3.975
	Ireland	4.357	3.048	2.948	3.755	3.371		Turkey	1.995	1.962	1.975	2.240	2.153
	Israel	3.761	2.785	2.781	3.274	2.670		United Kingdom	3.921	2.922	3.056	3.775	3.440
	Italy	3.694	3.097	3.041	3.747	3.217		United States	3.332	2.552	2.601	3.061	2.302

(continued)

Table 8.8 (continued)

Region	Country	ICP	CPD	GEKS	GK	EWGK	Region	Country	ICP	CPD	GEKS	GK	EWGK
	Japan	4.555	3.853	3.810	4.035	3.635	Latin America	Bolivia	1.345	1.196	1.206	0.909	0.994
	Korea, Rep.	2.555	2.198	1.793	1.875	1.408		Brazil	2.961	2.899	3.734	3.888	3.779
	Latvia	2.322	2.131	2.217	2.817	2.500		Colombia	2.067	1.808	2.110	2.388	2.211
	Lithuania	2.109	2.144	2.224	2.622	2.603		Costa Rica	2.252	1.937	1.748	2.288	1.858
	Luxembourg	4.890	3.027	3.043	3.658	3.115		Dominican Republic	1.688	1.525	1.528	1.527	1.503
	Macedonia, FYR	1.469	1.441	1.535	1.790	1.801		Ecuador	1.728	1.521	1.463	1.452	1.444
	Malta	2.689	2.531	2.568	3.030	2.826		El Salvador	1.667	1.606	1.489	1.399	1.333
	Mexico	2.063	1.857	1.890	2.287	2.152		Guatemala	1.565	1.208	0.992	1.228	0.734
	Montenegro	1.801	1.709	1.721	1.962	1.976		Haiti	1.643	1.119	1.440	1.485	1.547
	Netherlands	3.994	2.835	2.779	3.382	2.763		Honduras	1.744	1.522	1.510	1.359	1.301
	New Zealand	3.887	3.106	3.081	3.515	3.400		Nicaragua	1.275	1.123	0.975	0.915	0.702
	Norway	5.880	5.110	4.845	5.786	5.307		Panama	1.743	1.612	1.759	1.853	1.876
	Poland	1.954	1.676	1.756	2.151	1.949		Paraguay	1.740	1.699	1.769	1.963	1.998
	Portugal	3.086	2.589	2.617	3.204	2.789		Peru	1.768	1.573	1.646	1.698	1.635
	Romania	1.840	1.753	1.695	2.063	1.960		Uruguay	2.677	2.307	2.020	2.738	2.162
	Russian Federation	1.684	1.666	1.583	1.887	1.792		Venezuela, RB	2.114	2.475	2.189	2.136	1.872
	Serbia	1.783	1.845	1.799	2.178	2.097							

(continued)

Table 8.8 (continued)

d

Region	Country	ICP	CPD	GEKS	GK	EWGK
The Caribbean	Anguilla	2.900	2.437	2.150	2.564	1.794
	Antigua and Barbuda	2.383	2.000	1.965	1.842	1.510
	Aruba	2.751	2.438	2.762	3.315	3.153
	Bahamas, The	3.531	2.401	2.799	3.576	2.870
	Barbados	3.728	2.592	2.982	4.304	3.790
	Belize	1.841	1.663	1.254	1.331	1.096
	Bermuda	5.899	3.715	4.315	4.975	4.455
	Cayman Islands	4.168	3.728	4.183	5.195	5.172
	Curaçao	2.477	2.361	2.676	2.967	2.879
	Dominica	2.374	2.152	2.022	2.125	2.035
	Grenada	2.351	2.145	2.068	2.373	2.485
	Jamaica	2.247	2.378	2.203	2.489	2.617
	Montserrat	2.646	2.400	2.406	2.713	2.620
	St. Kitts and Nevis	2.374	2.468	2.271	2.573	2.392
	St. Lucia	2.409	2.055	2.008	2.393	2.372
	St. Vincent and the Grenadines	2.285	2.158	2.102	2.257	2.057
	Suriname	1.746	1.739	1.720	1.797	1.761
	Trinidad and Tobago	2.180	2.171	2.184	2.323	2.541
	Turks and Caicos Islands	3.974	2.443	2.580	3.023	2.370
	Virgin Islands, British	3.879	2.463	3.210	3.232	3.159

Region	Country	ICP	CPD	GEKS	GK	EWGK
West Asia	Bahrain	1.893	1.583	1.357	1.604	1.339
	Egypt, Arab Republic	0.897	0.792	0.851	0.922	0.843
	Iraq	1.396	1.419	1.434	1.850	1.997
	Jordan	1.383	1.406	1.472	1.599	1.708
	Kuwait	2.214	1.874	1.899	2.206	2.272
	Oman	1.678	1.639	1.769	1.913	1.939
	Palestinian Territory	2.077	1.702	1.726	1.717	1.682
	Qatar	2.605	1.917	2.187	3.173	3.206
	Saudi Arabia	1.623	1.492	1.574	1.811	1.874
	Sudan	1.677	1.448	1.720	1.970	2.333
	United Arab Emirates	2.518	1.867	2.187	2.886	2.886
	Yemen	1.161	1.125	1.173	1.285	1.253

Table 8.9 Alternative PPPs and TCLI-based PPPs from household-level data, base country: India, 2011 (Majumder et al. 2017)

Country	ICP PPP (Numeraire: Indian rupee)	CPD PPP	GEKS PPP	GK PPP	EWGK PPP	TCLI-based PPPs					
						Overall	Quintile 1	Quintile 2	Quintile 3	Quintile 4	Quintile 5
Iraq	35.882	36.465	36.856	47.536	51.304	41.932	45.060	45.705	40.995	37.678	29.124
Malawi	5.195	4.867	5.376	5.673	7.415	7.166	5.718	7.244	7.116	7.461	6.811
Tanzania	38.494	35.042	38.535	35.692	40.833	30.080	23.887	29.605	29.047	31.053	30.117
Vietnam	479.060	394.883	363.134	380.955	309.393	639.906	562.399	663.861	635.605	628.115	542.026

References

Asian Development Bank (ADB) (2007) Purchasing power parities and real expenditures, 2005 international comparison program in Asia and the Pacific. Economics and Research Department of Asian Development Bank, Manila, December

Asian Development Bank (ADB) (2008) Research study on poverty- specific purchasing power parities for selected countries in Asia and the Pacific. Asian Development Bank, Manila

Almas I (2012) International income inequality: measuring PPP Bias by estimating engel curves for food. Am Econ Rev 102:1093–1117

Atella V, Menon M, Perali F (2004) Estimation of unit values in cross sections without quantity information and implications for demand and welfare analysis. In: Dagum C, Ferrari G (eds) Household behaviour, equivalence scales, welfare and poverty. Physica, New York

Aten B (1996) Evidence of spatial autocorrelation in international prices. Rev Income Wealth 42:149–163

Aten B, Menezes T (2002) Poverty price levels: an application to Brazilian Metropolitan areas. In: World Bank ICP conference, Washington DC, March 11–15, 2002

Balk B (2009) Aggregation methods in international comparisons: an evaluation. In: Prasada Rao DS (ed) Purchasing power parities of currencies: recent advances in methods and applications. Edward Elgar, Cheltenham, UK, pp 59–85

Banks J, Blundell R, Lewbel A (1997) Quadratic engel curves and consumer demand. Rev Econ Stat 79:527–539

Barten AP (1964) Family composition, prices and expenditure patterns. In: Hart PE, Mills G, Whitaker JK (eds) Econometric analysis for national economic planning. Butterworths, London, pp 277–292

Clements K, Izan HY, Selvanathan E (2006a) Stochastic index numbers: a review. Int Stat Rev 74 (2):235–270

Clements K, Wu Y, Zhang J (2006b) Comparing international consumption patterns. Empirical Economics 31:1–30

Coondoo D, Majumder A, Chattopadhyay S (2011) Estimating spatial consumer price indices through engel curve analysis. Rev Income Wealth 57(1):138–155

Coondoo D, Majumder A, Ray R (2004) A method of calculating regional consumer price differentials with illustrative evidence from India. Rev Income Wealth 50(1):51–68

Cox TL, Wohlgenant MK (1986) Prices and quality effects in cross-sectional demand analysis. Am J Agr Econ 68(4):908–919

Deaton AS, Friedman J, Alatas V (2004) Purchasing power parity exchange rates from household survey data: India and Indonesia. Working Paper No. 173, Research Program in Development Studies, Woodrow Wilson School, Princeton University

Diewert WE (2005) Weighted country product dummy variable regressions and index number formulae. Rev Income Wealth 51:561–570

Dikhanov Y (1994) Sensitivity of PPP-based income estimates to choice of aggregation procedures. Paper presented at the 23rd general conference of the International Association for Research in Income and Wealth, held at St. Andrews, New Brunswick, Canada

Drechsler L (1973) Weighting of index numbers in multilateral international comparisons. Rev Income Wealth 19(1):17–34

Eltetö Ő, Köves P (1964) On an index computation problem in international comparisons. Statiztikai Szemle 42:507–518 (in Hungarian)

Feenstra RC, Ma H, Rao DSP (2009) Consistent comparisons of real incomes across time and space. Macroecon Dyn 13(Supplement):169–193

Geary RG (1958) A note on the comparison of exchange rates and PPPs between countries. J Roy Stat Soc A 121:97–99

Hill RJ (2000) Measuring substitution bias in international comparisons based on additive purchasing power parity methods. Eur Econ Rev 44:145–162

Hill RJ (2004) Constructing price indexes across space and time: the case of the European Union. Am Econ Rev 94:1379–1410
Hoang LV (2009) Estimation of food demand from household survey data in Vietnam. DEPOCEN Working paper series, no. 2009/12. Available at: http://www.depocenwp.org
Iklė DM (1972) A new approach to the index number problem. Quart J Econ 86:188–211
Khamis SH (1972) A new system of index numbers for national and international purposes. J Roy Stat Soc A, Part I 135:96–121
Lancaster G, Ray R (1998) Comparison of alternative models of household equivalence scales: the Australian evidence on unit record data. Econ Rec 74:1–14
Majumder A, Ray R, Santra S (2017) Sensitivity of purchasing power parity estimates to estimation procedures and their effect on living standards comparisons. J Globalization Dev 8:1. https://doi.org/10.1515/jgd-2017-0006
Majumder A, Ray R, Sinha K (2012) The calculation of rural urban food price differentials from unit values in household expenditure surveys: a new procedure and comparison with existing methods. Am J Agr Econ 94:1218–1235
Majumder A, Ray R, Sinha K (2015) Estimating purchasing power parities from household expenditure data using complete demand systems with application to living standards comparison: India and Vietnam. Rev Income Wealth 61(2):302–328
Majumder A, Ray R, Sinha K (2016) A unified framework for the estimation of intra and inter country food purchasing power parities: India, Indonesia and Vietnam. Indian Growth Dev Rev 9(1):2–31
McKelvey C (2011) Price, unit value and quantity demanded. J Dev Econ 95(1):157–169
Neary JP (2004) Rationalizing the Penn world table: true multilateral indices for international comparisons of real income. Am Econ Rev 94:1411–1428
O'Donnell CJ, Rao DSP (2007) Predicting expenditure shares for computing PPP exchange rates. Unpublished, University of Queensland, Brisbane, Australia
Oulton N (2012a) How to measure living standards and productivity. Rev Income Wealth 58:424–456
Oulton N (2012b) The wealth and poverty of nations: true PPPs for 141 countries. CEP Discussion Paper No. 1080, London School of Economics
Prais SJ, Houthakker HS (1955) The analysis of family budgets. Cambridge University Press, Cambridge (2nd edition, 1971)
Rao DSP (1971) Existence and uniqueness of a new class of index numbers. Sankhy a, Series B 33:341–354
Rao DSP (2001) Weighted EKS and generalised CPD methods for aggregation at basic heading level and above basic heading level. Mimeographed, Joint World Bank–OECD seminar on purchasing power parities: recent advances in methods and applications, Washington DC, available in http://www.oecd.org/std/prices-ppp/2424825.pdf
Rao DSP (2005) On the equivalence of weighted country-product-dummy CPD method and the rao-system for multilateral comparisons. Rev Income Wealth 51:571–580
Rao DSP, Rambaldi A, Doran H (2010) Extrapolation of purchasing power parities using multiple benchmarks and auxiliary information: a new approach. Rev Income Wealth 56(Special Issue): S59–S98
Ravallion M (2013) Price levels and economic growth: making sense of revisions to data on real incomes. Rev Income Wealth 59(4):593–613
Reddy S, Pogge T (2007) How not to count the poor. In: Anand S, Stiglitz J (eds) Measuring global poverty. Oxford University Press, Oxford
Sen A (1976) Real national income. Rev Econ Stud 43:19–39
Summers R (1973) International price comparisons based upon incomplete data. Rev Income Wealth 19(1):1–16
Szulc B (1964) Index numbers of multilateral regional comparisons. Przeglad Statystyczny 11:239–254 (in Polish)

United Nations (1992) Handbook of the international comparison programme, Department of Economic and Social Development Statistical Division, Studies in Methods, Series F, No. 62, United Nations, New York

World Bank (2013) Measuring the real size of the world economy: the framework, methodology, and results of the international comparison program (ICP). World Bank, Washington, DC

World Bank (2014) Purchasing power parities and real expenditures of world economies; summary of results and findings of the 2011 international comparison program. World Bank, Washington, DC

World Bank (2015) Purchasing power parities and the real size of world economies: a comprehensive report of the 2011 international comparison program. World Bank, Washington, DC

Chapter 9
Using PPPs in Calculation of Global and Regional Poverty Rates

9.1 Introduction

One of the central applications of the Purchasing Power Parity (PPP) concept is in the calculation of global and regional poverty rates. PPPs play a crucial role in global poverty enumeration since they are used both in the construction of the international poverty line (IPL) from the poverty lines of the 15 poorest countries (as is the current practice) and in the application of the IPL to estimate the poverty numbers and poverty rates in each country. Both the construction and application of the IPL require the availability of currency conversion factors that measure the 'true purchasing power' of a country's currency expressed in terms of a global currency such as the US dollar. PPPs are designed to perform that role. The International Comparison Project (ICP) which is housed in the World Bank is charged with the task of producing the PPPs that are to be used in the global poverty enumerations. With the reduction and the eventual elimination of global poverty figuring high on the agenda of policy makers everywhere, appearing explicitly as targets in the Millennium and Sustainable Development Goals, the profile of the ICP has grown as it periodically updates the PPPs in the light of new data from the individual countries.

The ICP has a large budget in providing and periodically updating the PPPs based on a large-scale exercise involving nearly 200 countries. In the previous chapter, we have provided evidence of the sensitivity of PPPs to alternative procedures using the ICP PPPs as a benchmark for robustness. In this chapter, we carry that discussion forward by reporting the results obtained by Majumder et al. (2017b) on the sensitivity of the global and regional poverty rates to the PPPs used. In view of the scale of the exercise and the resources involved, the ICP updates the PPPs at fairly long time intervals. Given the need to update the global poverty figures at closer intervals than the ICP exercise, this chapter then visits the wider issue of identifying the key determinants of the PPPs for generating their estimates between the ICP rounds. Indeed, so high is poverty reduction and its eventual

R. Ray, *Household Behaviour, Prices, and Welfare*, Themes in Economics,
https://doi.org/10.1007/978-981-13-1930-3_9

elimination in the global policy agenda that the World Bank recently constituted a committee under the Chairmanship of the eminent British economist, the late Professor Anthony Atkinson, to provide fresh thinking on the way we view and measure poverty. This chapter contains a critical review of the Report of the Global Poverty Commission which is an important document for future poverty enumeration.

The plan for the rest of this chapter is as follows. The background and the main results of the study on global and regional poverty in Majumder et al. (2017b), with the focus on the link between PPP and poverty estimates, are presented in Sect. 9.2. Section 9.3 reports the results from Majumder et al. (2015) of estimation of the PPPs between countries and over time, exploring in particular the link between PPP changes and movements in intra-country inequality. Section 9.4 contains a critical evaluation of the recent Report of the Commission on Global Poverty. Section 9.5 concludes the chapter.

9.2 PPP and Poverty Rates

9.2.1 Background and Motivation

With 2015 marking the end of the era for the Millennium Development Goals (MDG) and the start of that for Sustainable Development Goals (SDG), with reduction of global poverty featuring prominently in both sets of goals, there has recently been a surge of studies that seek to quantify the magnitude of global poverty. Examples include Cruz et al. (2015), Ferreira et al. (2016), Jolliffe and Prydz (2015), Kakwani and Son (2016). The literature on estimating global poverty[1] can be traced back to Ahluwalia et al. (1979) with the next major contribution by Ravallion et al. (1991). In the nearly 4 decades that have elapsed since the Ahluwalia et al. (1979) study, the complexity of the exercise has grown many fold with an increase in the number of countries included in the poverty enumeration. The complexity has been reflected in changes in the manner the 'international poverty line' (IPL) has been defined and implemented in successive poverty counts. While the Ahluwalia et al. (1979) study was based on the Indian poverty line used as the IPL, Ravallion et al. (1991) provided the first dollar-a-day poverty line at 1985 PPPs. This study, which was designed to answer a set of poverty-related questions on world poverty and give aggregate results for 86 countries in the mid-1990s, was conducted as a background paper for the World Development Report, 1990.

[1]See Ravallion (2016) for a recent comprehensive review of poverty measures and the related literature.

Since this was the first time the concept of an 'international poverty line' was proposed and implemented, let us explain how the $1 a day figure was arrived at Ravallion et al. (1991) proposed measuring global poverty by the standards of the poorest countries, based on a survey of national poverty lines. Drawing on 33 national poverty lines for the 1970s and 1980s (for both developed and developing economies), Ravallion, Datt and van de Walle proposed a line of $23 a month ($0.76 a day) at 1985 consumption PPP. That value was the predicted poverty line for the poorest country in the sample of 88 countries (Somalia), based on a regression model that ran a semi-log regression of the national poverty line on per capita mean consumption and per capita mean consumption square (all at 1985 PPP). This value was quite close to the poverty line of India. As Ravallion et al. (1991, pp. 348/349) note: 'Thus, India's poverty line is very close to the poverty line we would predict for the poorest country, and as such, can be considered a reasonable lower bound to the range of admissible poverty lines for the developing world.

A more generous, and more representative, absolute poverty line for low-income countries is $31, which (to the nearest dollar) is shared by six of the countries in our sample, namely Indonesia, Bangladesh, Nepal, Kenya, Tanzania, and Morocco and two other countries are close to this figure (Philippines and Pakistan). We shall use both these poverty lines, interpreting the lower line as defining "extreme absolute poverty"'. The higher line of $31 a month ($1.02 a day) was therefore considered to be more representative of the poverty lines in low-income countries. Subsequently, the higher line became more accepted in the World Bank and internationally, and it became known the '$1 a day' (at 1985 PPP). It was re-estimated to $1.08 at 1993 PPPs by Chen and Ravallion (2001). This was not a major revision since it simply involved re-evaluating the $1 a day poverty line at 1993 PPPs. Subsequently, in the first major update of the $1 a day poverty line, proposed in World Development Report, 1990, Ravallion et al. (2009) revised the $1 a day poverty line at 1985 PPP to $1.25 a day at 2005 PPP based on an updated and expanded set of countries compared to what was used in Ravallion et al. (1991).

As explained by Ravallion et al. (2009, pp. 166/167), 'The new data set on national poverty lines differs from the old (Ravallion et al. 1991) data set in four main respects. First, while the data were drawn from sources for the 1980s (with a mean year of 1984) the new data are all post-1990 (mean of 1999), such that in no case do the proximate sources overlap. Second, the new data set covers 88 developing economies (74 with complete data for the subsequent analysis), while the old data set included only 22 developing economies (plus 11 developed countries). Third, the old data set used rural poverty lines when there was a choice, whereas the new one estimates national average lines. Fourth, the old data set was unrepresentative of sub-Saharan Africa, with only five countries from that region (Burundi, Kenya, South Africa, Tanzania, and Zambia), whereas the new data set has a good spread across regions, including 25 countries in sub-Saharan Africa. The proportion of African countries in the old sample was about half what it should have been to be considered representative of poor countries. The sample bias in the Ravallion, Datt, and van de Walle data set was unavoidable at the time (1990), but it can now be corrected.' (p. 166/167).

In the latest round of the ICP, namely the 2011 ICP round led to another revision of the IPL. The IPL, now defined as the mean of the poverty lines of the 15 poorest countries, mostly from Africa, yields IPL at around $1.90 a day at 2011 PPP. While Ferreira et al. (2016, Table 6) arrive at the IPL figure of $1.88 a day, Jolliffe and Prydz (2015, Table 2) arrive at a lower value of $1.82. Using a different methodology based on the concept of 'equivalent poverty lines', Kakwani and Son (2016) obtain the IPL as a weighted average of the equivalent poverty lines of 66 countries and arrive at the IPL figure of $1.78 a day. Since many of the households in the poverty count are bunched around the IPL, any movement in the IPL specification, however small, is likely to lead to large changes in the global poverty numbers. It is well-established that global poverty measures are sensitive to estimates of relative prices across countries, as reflected in the large changes in global poverty estimates with new rounds of PPPs becoming available over past decades. Deaton (2001, 2010) has provided good summaries of these large changes and likened the new rounds of PPP data to 'earthquakes', based on the 1985 PPPs to the 1993 PPPs and the 1993 PPPs to the 2005 PPPs. Chen and Ravallion (2010) comment on the large changes due to the PPPs. With the release of the 2011 PPPs, once again the global picture of global poverty changed, albeit less significantly than previous revisions (Ferreira et al. 2016; Jolliffe and Prydz 2015). While there is no consensus between Jolliffe and Prydz (2015), Ferreira et al. (2016) and Kakwani and Son (2016) on the exact figure to be used for the IPL, these three studies, as indeed all the global poverty enumerations so far, have all been based on the ICP PPPs. This raises the question: How robust are the global poverty numbers to departures from the ICP PPPs?

Majumder et al. (2017b) addresses this question and provides empirical evidence. There is no clear answer to this question in the literature nor is there any evidence on the robustness of the ICP PPPs themselves to changes in the ICP methodology. Given that the ICP uses the Gini-Elteto-Koves-Szulc (GEKS) multilateral price index in aggregation of ICP PPP basic heading data, in an attempt to partially answer this question Majumder et al. (2017b) examines the sensitivity of measures of relative prices (and poverty) to using CPD (and various spatial versions) and GEKS methods, using price data provided by the World Bank. It also verifies how these PPPs track the published 2011 ICP PPPs, which are used as benchmark. The poverty issue has recently taken on an added importance with the Global Poverty Commission (World Bank 2016) recommending that from now till 2030 the PPPs to be used in the poverty count should be frozen at the 2011 ICP values with the inflation adjustment made every year at the country level in line with the CPIs of each country. This makes it imperative to examine the sensitivity of poverty measures to the PPPs used. Taking advantage of the fact that the CPD method allows stochastic formulation, this study provides further results on the sensitivity of the CPD PPPs and the corresponding poverty counts to allowing spatially correlated movements in prices between countries by admitting a more general error specification.

9.2.2 The Spatial CPD Model

The alternative PPP procedures used in Majumder et al. (2017b) have been explained earlier. The only model that has not been encountered earlier is the spatial CPD model that extends the basic CPD model to allow regionally correlated price movements via admitting spatially correlated errors. The empirical literature on subnational and cross-country PPPs is generally based on the assumption that there is no interdependence between the price movements in the various regions of a country or between that in the various countries. There is some evidence to the contrary in early work reported by Aten (1996) on subnational PPPs, and by Rao (2001) on cross-country PPPs. The Spatial CPD model is given by

$$y_{ij} = \alpha_1 D_1 + \alpha_2 D_2 + \cdots \alpha_M D_M + \beta_1 D_1^* + \beta_2 D_2^* + \cdots + \beta_N D_N^* + \varepsilon_{ij} \tag{9.1}$$

where D_j and D_i^* are, respectively, the country and commodity (product) dummy variables in the standard CPD model. Here, ε the vector of ε_{ij}'s is specified as follows:

$$\varepsilon = \boldsymbol{\rho S}\varepsilon + \eta \tag{9.1a}$$

Given $\boldsymbol{\rho}$ is the overall spatial correlation and η_{ij}'s are i.i.d. with mean 0 and variance σ^2, $\boldsymbol{S}$ is a spatial weight matrix of order $\boldsymbol{NC} \times \boldsymbol{NC}$. The spatial weight matrix can be of various types depending on the neighbourhood criteria, based on distance, in general. One possible neighbourhood criterion, in the cross-country context, can be defined as follows. $\boldsymbol{S}_{jk} = 1$ if j and k refer to the same region and same item and $j \neq k$, $\boldsymbol{S}_{jk} = 0$ otherwise. $\boldsymbol{\rho}$ can be estimated using maximum likelihood methods in the joint estimation of the two equations. Another possible neighbourhood criterion is to define neighbours in terms of inverse of distance between centroids of two countries. We have provided PPP estimates employing both types of spatial CPD models, referred to below in Tables 9.3a–d as CPD-S1 (Region Cluster) and CPD-S2 (Inverse Distance between Centroids), respectively.

9.2.3 Data Sources and Description

The PPP calculations in this paper relate to the ICP round, 2011. Along with the ICP PPPs from published reports (with India as the numeraire country), we report the following indices, namely, the GEKS, weighted CPD and its two spatially correlated generalisations. The ICP PPPs are used as benchmark. Three points are worth noting here: (i) as opposed to the PPP for 'Individual consumption expenditure by households' (ICEH), which is the PPP used for international poverty monitoring by the World Bank and others, we have used the ICP PPPs for 'Actual individual consumption' (AIC); (ii) although ICP uses the GEKS procedure above the BH level, we independently calculated these PPPs using the price information described below in Sect. 9.2.3.1,[2] and (iii) the base country has been moved from USA to India. The change in base has been made as India shares many of the features of a developing country including high poverty rates, but at the same time provides a market and an economy size that places it in the top tier of nations. In addition, poverty comparisons amongst developing countries can be made using these PPPs directly, without reference to USA. The poverty calculations are based on the PovcalNet program.

9.2.3.1 Price Data

The ICP group in the World Bank made the price and expenditure information for 2011 available. We constructed the prices for item groups at the basic heading (BH) level by considering the item prices in local currency units (LCU) within the BH taking into account the importance matrix provided by the World Bank. For their analysis, Majumder, Ray and Santra (2017b) considered the average (geometric mean) prices of similar items (having the same units of measurement) with the highest importance. It needs to be mentioned here that (i) the World Bank makes available prices at the basic heading (BH) level, but these are in PPPs (US $ = 1), not in LCUs and (ii) ICP does not use averages of item prices, instead price data are aggregated using CPD method to derive basic heading PPPs. It is worth noting that of the exercise objective is to look at sensitivity of PPPs to alternative procedures and that the price aggregates used in the computation of the GEKS and CPD models are the same. ICP PPPs are used only as benchmark.

9.2.4 Results

9.2.4.1 The Alternative Sets of PPPs

Tables 9.1a–d present, for all the countries participating in the 2011 ICP, the five sets of PPPs corresponding to the ICP (published), the GEKS, the weighted CPD and its two spatially correlated generalisations given by Eqs. (9.1)–(9.1a). Note that unlike the conventional format, Tables 9.1a–d presents the PPPs with the Indian Rupee as the numeraire. The following points are worth noting. First, within the CPD framework, the introduction of spatial correlation between price movements in

[2]While GEKS forms the basis for PPP computations within ICP, there are many stages involved in PPP compilation. First, PPPs are compiled at the regional level and then linked through Global Core prices maintaining fixity. Therefore, applying GEKS to all the countries is not the same as applying GEKS within ICP. Hence, one would expect differences between our computations of GEKS and ICP PPPs. Consequently, the poverty estimates for 2011 presented in the results section are expected to be different from the poverty estimates used in the World Bank's official poverty estimates. However, we only try to examine the comparability in terms of order of magnitude.

Table 9.1 Alternative purchasing power parities, PPPs for 2011, Numeraire in Indian Rupee (Majumder et al. 2017b)

Region	Country	ICP	GEKS	CPD	CPD-S1 (Region Cluster)	CPD-S2 (Inverse Distance between Centroids)	Region	Country	ICP	GEKS	CPD	CPD-S1 (Region Cluster)	CPD-S2 (Inverse Distance between Centroids)
a													
Africa	Algeria	2.062	1.932	1.981	1.99	1.98	Africa	Liberia	0.037	0.031	0.031	0.03	0.03
	Angola	4.996	2.973	3.447	3.49	3.48		Madagascar	46.309	34.873	34.217	34.66	34.40
	Benin	14.801	11.202	11.231	11.22	11.22		Malawi	5.195	5.376	4.867	4.95	4.89
	Botswana	0.290	0.262	0.254	0.25	0.25		Mali	14.437	14.193	13.735	13.92	13.78
	Burkina Faso	14.552	13.841	12.527	12.58	12.42		Mauritania	7.395	6.409	6.163	6.27	6.21
	Burundi	31.130	30.494	30.518	30.90	31.10		Mauritius	1.181	1.037	0.969	0.98	0.97
	Cameroon	15.253	11.706	13.641	13.82	13.71		Morocco	0.276	0.322	0.277	0.28	0.28
	Cape Verde	3.164	2.180	2.420	2.44	2.41		Mozambique	1.051	1.011	0.993	1.01	1.00
	Central African Republic	17.419	18.330	17.953	18.28	18.05		Namibia	0.342	0.136	0.270	0.27	0.27
	Chad	16.499	15.216	14.829	14.57	14.71		Niger	14.995	18.045	15.431	15.45	15.36
	Comoros	14.360	10.748	12.249	12.03	11.94		Nigeria	5.184	4.912	4.464	4.53	4.49
	Congo, Rep.	35.145	39.599	35.070	35.23	34.93		Rwanda	16.717	12.803	14.652	14.85	14.82
	Congo, Dem.	19.711	18.889	19.256	19.52	19.29		Senegal	16.285	17.197	16.643	16.86	16.54
	Côte d'Ivoire	15.691	12.713	15.514	15.69	15.59		Seychelles	0.499	0.517	0.490	0.49	0.49
	Djibouti	6.727	6.733	6.566	6.49	6.52		Sierra Leone	114.179	107.708	106.962	108.75	107.00
	Egypt, Arab Republic	0.115	0.109	0.101	0.10	0.10		South Africa	0.340	0.334	0.299	0.30	0.30
	Equatorial Guinea	21.712	14.536	14.824	14.63	14.68		Sudan	0.096	0.098	0.083	0.08	0.08
	Ethiopia	0.352	0.361	0.340	0.33	0.34		Swaziland	0.273	0.205	0.189	0.19	0.19

(continued)

Table 9.1 (continued)

Region	Country	ICP	GEKS	CPD	CPD-S1 (Region Cluster)	CPD-S2 (Inverse Distance between Centroids)	Region	Country	ICP	GEKS	CPD	CPD-S1 (Region Cluster)	CPD-S2 (Inverse Distance between Centroids)
	Gabon	23.877	21.778	22.521	22.78	22.46		São Tomé and Principe				606.56	600.27
	Gambia, The	0.697	0.691	0.680	0.67	0.65		Tanzania	38.494	38.535	35.042	35.21	34.90
	Ghana	0.051	0.046	0.044	0.04	0.04		Togo	14.966	15.461	15.011	15.19	15.06
	Guinea	165.403	199.346	182.576	180.93	176.37		Tunisia	0.045	0.045	0.044	0.04	0.04
	Guinea-Bissau	15.827	16.995	17.382	17.52	17.62		Uganda	61.989	59.763	65.103	65.65	65.14
	Kenya	2.365	1.952	1.959	1.99	1.98		Zambia	166.554	161.138	156.330	156.36	155.50
	Lesotho	0.261	0.231	0.222	0.22	0.23		Zimbabwe	0.035	0.035	0.033	0.03	0.03
b													
Asia And The Pacific	Bangladesh	1.628	1.519	1.519	1.54	1.54	Commonwealth And Independent States	Armenia	10.880	11.836	12.298	12.34	12.36
	Bhutan	1.119	0.936	0.965	0.95	0.94		Azerbaijan	0.020	0.022	0.023	0.02	0.02
	Brunei Darussalam	0.058	0.044	0.051	0.05	0.05		Belarus	109.735	114.905	123.162	124.24	123.87
	Cambodia	96.712	91.308	89.079	90.19	90.01		Kazakhstan	5.037	4.122	4.201	4.25	4.21
	China	0.249	0.257	0.232	0.23	0.23		Kyrgyzstan	1.037	0.901	0.944	0.94	0.94
	Fiji	0.080	0.059	0.062	0.06	0.06		Moldova	0.328	0.343	0.325	0.33	0.33
	Hong Kong SAR, China	0.398	0.388	0.317	0.32	0.32		Russian Federation	1.059	0.995	1.048	1.06	1.04
	India	1.000	1.000	1.000	1.000	1.000		Tajikistan	0.106	0.105	0.109	0.11	0.11
	Indonesia	266.380	230.556	246.329	247.45	247.01		Ukraine	0.204	0.213	0.209	0.21	0.21
	Lao PDR	181.329	164.455	167.919	169.13	168.57	Eurostat-OECD	Albania	3.400	3.132	3.180	3.21	3.20
	Macao SAR, China	0.374	0.316	0.291	0.30	0.30		Australia	0.107	0.079	0.079	0.08	0.08
	Malaysia	0.106	0.057	0.090	0.09	0.09		Austria	0.061	0.046	0.046	0.05	0.05

(continued)

Table 9.1 (continued)

Region	Country	ICP	GEKS	CPD	CPD-S1 (Region Cluster)	CPD-S2 (Inverse Distance between Centroids)	Region	Country	ICP	GEKS	CPD	CPD-S1 (Region Cluster)	CPD-S2 (Inverse Distance between Centroids)
	Maldives	0.677	0.524	0.529	0.54	0.53		Belgium	0.063	0.041	0.045	0.05	0.05
	Mongolia	36.881	31.458	35.527	36.23	35.75		Bosnia and Herzegovina	0.055	0.056	0.057	0.06	0.06
	Myanmar	16.380	6.164	14.278	14.16	14.20		Bulgaria	0.047	0.049	0.048	0.05	0.05
	Nepal	1.698	0.991	1.065	1.06	1.06		Canada	0.091	0.068	0.070	0.07	0.07
	Pakistan	1.673	1.212	1.456	1.47	1.45		Chile	25.222	23.183	23.718	23.44	23.78
	Philippines	1.261	0.729	0.950	0.96	0.95		Croatia	0.284	0.280	0.265	0.27	0.26
	Singapore	0.080	0.076	0.060	0.06	0.06		Cyprus	0.050	0.046	0.043	0.04	0.04
	Sri Lanka	2.689	2.339	2.645	2.66	2.64		Czech Republic	0.960	0.820	0.826	0.84	0.82
	Taiwan, China	1.081	0.951	0.994	0.99	0.99		Denmark	0.603	0.443	0.450	0.46	0.45
	Thailand	0.858	0.683	0.644	0.65	0.65		Estonia	0.038	0.032	0.035	0.03	0.03
	Vietnam	479.060	363.134	394.883	398.14	394.89		Finland	0.068	0.059	0.055	0.06	0.05
c													
Eurostat-OECD	France	0.061	0.049	0.047	0.05	0.05	Eurostat-OECD	Slovakia	0.036	0.035	0.035	0.03	0.03
	Germany	0.056	0.043	0.043	0.04	0.04		Slovenia	0.047	0.040	0.041	0.04	0.04
	Greece	0.051	0.045	0.044	0.04	0.04		Spain	0.053	0.040	0.040	0.04	0.04
	Hungary	8.651	7.863	7.910	7.94	7.88		Sweden	0.659	0.459	0.473	0.48	0.47
	Iceland	9.677	9.293	8.722	8.82	8.71		Switzerland	0.114	0.069	0.074	0.08	0.07
	Ireland	0.067	0.045	0.047	0.05	0.05		Turkey	0.072	0.071	0.071	0.07	0.07
	Israel	0.288	0.213	0.214	0.22	0.22		United Kingdom	0.052	0.041	0.039	0.04	0.04
	Italy	0.057	0.047	0.048	0.05	0.05		United States	0.071	0.056	0.055	0.06	0.05

(continued)

Table 9.1 (continued)

Region	Country	ICP	GEKS	CPD	CPD-S1 (Region Cluster)	CPD-S2 (Inverse Distance between Centroids)	Region	Country	ICP	GEKS	CPD	CPD-S1 (Region Cluster)	CPD-S2 (Inverse Distance between Centroids)
	Japan	7.789	6.515	6.588	6.65	6.59	Latin America	Bolivia	0.200	0.179	0.178	0.18	0.18
	Korea, Rep.	60.669	42.568	52.186	52.48	52.03		Brazil	0.106	0.134	0.104	0.11	0.10
	Latvia	0.025	0.024	0.023	0.02	0.02		Colombia	81.836	83.559	71.604	73.49	72.41
	Lithuania	0.112	0.118	0.114	0.11	0.11		Costa Rica	24.404	18.934	20.983	21.29	20.86
	Luxembourg	0.075	0.047	0.047	0.05	0.05		Dominican Republic	1.379	1.248	1.245	1.27	1.27
	Macedonia, FYR	1.392	1.455	1.366	1.37	1.37		Ecuador	0.037	0.031	0.033	0.03	0.03
	Malta	0.041	0.040	0.039	0.04	0.04		El Salvador	0.036	0.032	0.034	0.03	0.03
	Mexico	0.549	0.503	0.494	0.50	0.50		Guatemala	0.261	0.166	0.202	0.20	0.20
	Montenegro	0.028	0.027	0.026	0.03	0.03		Haiti	1.426	1.251	0.972	0.97	0.97
	Netherlands	0.062	0.043	0.044	0.04	0.04		Honduras	0.706	0.611	0.616	0.62	0.61
	New Zealand	0.105	0.084	0.084	0.09	0.08		Nicaragua	0.613	0.468	0.540	0.54	0.53
	Norway	0.706	0.582	0.614	0.61	0.60		Panama	0.037	0.038	0.035	0.03	0.03
	Poland	0.124	0.112	0.106	0.11	0.11		Paraguay	155.704	158.318	152.030	151.69	151.98
	Portugal	0.048	0.040	0.040	0.04	0.04		Peru	0.104	0.097	0.093	0.09	0.09
	Romania	0.120	0.111	0.115	0.12	0.11		Uruguay	1.108	0.836	0.955	0.96	0.95
	Russian Federation	1.059	0.995	1.048	1.06	1.04		Venezuela, RB	0.194	0.201	0.227	0.23	0.23
	Serbia	2.802	2.827	2.899	2.93	2.91							

(continued)

Table 9.1 (continued)

Region	Country	ICP	GEKS	CPD	CPD-S1 (Region Cluster)	CPD-S2 (Inverse Distance between Centroids)	Region	Country	ICP	GEKS	CPD	CPD-S1 (Region Cluster)	CPD-S2 (Inverse Distance between Centroids)
d													
The Caribbean	Anguilla	0.168	0.124	0.141	0.14	0.14	Western Asia	Bahrain	0.015	0.011	0.013	0.01	0.01
	Antigua and Barbuda	0.138	0.114	0.116	0.12	0.12		Egypt, Arab Republic	0.115	0.109	0.101	–	–
	Aruba	0.106	0.106	0.094	0.09	0.09		Iraq	35.882	36.856	36.465	36.55	36.50
	Bahamas, The	0.076	0.060	0.051	0.05	0.05		Jordan	0.021	0.022	0.021	0.02	0.02
	Barbados	0.160	0.128	0.111	0.11	0.11		Kuwait	0.013	0.011	0.011	0.01	0.01
	Belize	0.079	0.054	0.071	0.07	0.07		Oman	0.014	0.015	0.014	0.01	0.01
	Bermuda	0.126	0.092	0.080	0.08	0.08		Palestinian Territory	0.159	0.132	0.130	0.13	0.13
	Cayman Islands	0.075	0.075	0.067	0.07	0.07		Qatar	0.204	0.171	0.150	0.15	0.16
	Curaçao	0.095	0.103	0.091	0.09	0.09		Saudi Arabia	0.130	0.126	0.120	0.12	0.12
	Dominica	0.137	0.117	0.125	0.13	0.12		Sudan	0.096	0.098	0.083	–	–
	Grenada	0.136	0.120	0.124	0.12	0.12		United Arab Emirates	0.198	0.172	0.147	0.15	0.15
	Jamaica	4.136	4.055	4.377	4.41	4.36		Yemen	5.319	5.372	5.153	5.24	5.18
	Montserrat	0.153	0.139	0.139	0.14	0.14							
	St. Kitts and Nevis	0.108	0.098	0.097	0.10	0.10							
	St. Lucia	0.137	0.131	0.143	0.14	0.14							
		0.139	0.116	0.119	0.12	0.11							

(continued)

Table 9.1 (continued)

Region	Country	ICP	GEKS	CPD	CPD-S1 (Region Cluster)	CPD-S2 (Inverse Distance between Centroids)	Region	Country	ICP	GEKS	CPD	CPD-S1 (Region Cluster)	CPD-S2 (Inverse Distance between Centroids)
	St. Vincent and the Grenadines												
	Suriname	0.132	0.122	0.125	0.13	0.12							
	Trinidad and Tobago	0.122	0.120	0.122	0.12	0.12							
	Turks and Caicos Islands	0.299	0.300	0.298	0.30	0.30							
	Virgin Islands, British	0.085	0.055	0.052	0.05	0.05							

countries in the same region has little effect on the PPPs. Second, while the orders of magnitudes are comparable among the five sets of indices, the calculated GEKS and CPD PPPs differ in many cases from that of the ICP PPPs. Although generalised statements cannot be made on the sign of the difference between the ICP and the other PPPs that hold in all cases, in several countries the ICP PPPs exceed the other PPPs, often by quite a large margin. This is particularly true of several of the poorer countries in Africa and Asia with consequent implications for the poverty rates.

9.2.4.2 Comparing the Poverty Lines and the Poverty Rates Between PPPs

Table 9.2 compares the International Poverty Lines (IPLs) (specified in Indian Rupees) between the values implied by the five sets of PPPs. The reader will recall that the IPL is defined as the mean of the national poverty lines of the 15 poorest countries converted to the Indian Rupee at PPP. This table also presents evidence for these 15 countries on the discrepancy between their national poverty lines and the IPL converted back to the Local Currency Units (LCU) of these countries. In many cases, the discrepancy is considerable suggesting wide divergence between the national poverty rates and the globally relevant poverty rates for these 15 countries. The table also shows that the IPL based on ICP PPPs is lower in relation to the other PPPs. Though in absolute magnitude the difference is not considerable, this is likely to have some impact on the country-specific poverty rates and on the distribution of the poor population between the ICP regions since many of the globally poor households are very close to the IPL.

Table 9.3a–d compares the five sets of poverty rates for each country. There are several instances of large variation in the poverty rates at the individual country level between alternative sets of PPPs, especially for several African and South Asian countries. In contrast, the poverty rates are quite robust to PPPs in case of the affluent countries in the EUROSTAT-OECD region. This is also true of countries in the Caribbean region. Consistent with the comparison of PPPs within the CPD framework in Table 9.1a–d and the picture of robustness of PPPs from the last three columns of numbers, Table 9.3a–d confirms that the introduction of spatially correlated price movements has very little effect on the CPD poverty rates at the country level. Table 9.4 compares the regional poverty rates, which are obtained as the population-weighted averages of the poverty rates of the countries in the region. It may be noted from Table 9.4 that the computed GEKS and CPD poverty rates track the ICP poverty rates quite well at the regional level, although the CPD values for the CIS region is somewhat out of line from the others. While generalised statements are again not possible, these tables show that the variation between the poverty rates are more between the ICP, GEKS and CPD PPPs than between the non-spatial and spatial CPD PPPs. There are large regional variations, but the rankings of the regions remain same across all PPPs.

Table 9.2 Poverty lines of the 15 poorest countries using alternative methods, 2011 (Majumder et al. 2017b)

Region	Country	National poverty line (Local Currency Unit) NPL (LCU)	Poverty line in PPP (Numeraire: Indian Rupee)					Converted Poverty Line in Local Currency Unit using Mean Poverty Line in PPP (Numeraire: Indian Rupee) CNPL (PPP-LCU)					Ratio of NPL(LCU) to CNPL(PPP-LCU)				
			ICP	GEKS	CPD	CPD-S1	CPD-S2	ICP	GEKS	CPD	CPD-S1	CPD-S2	ICP	GEKS	CPD	CPD-S1	CPD-S2
Africa																	
	Chad	295.8	17.9	19.4	20.0	20.3	20.1	433.4	425.6	416.4	407.2	413.7	0.68	0.70	0.71	0.73	0.72
	Ethiopia	10.0	28.4	27.8	29.5	30.1	29.7	9.3	10.1	9.5	9.3	9.5	1.08	0.99	1.05	1.08	1.05
	Gambia, The	17.8	25.5	25.7	26.1	26.5	27.3	18.3	19.2	19.1	18.7	18.3	0.97	0.92	0.93	0.95	0.97
	Ghana	2.2	43.0	47.7	49.5	48.9	49.3	1.3	1.3	1.3	1.3	1.3	1.64	1.71	1.76	1.75	1.75
	Guinea-Bissau	478.8	30.3	28.2	27.6	27.3	27.2	415.7	475.4	488.1	489.7	495.6	1.15	1.01	0.98	0.98	0.97
	Malawi	97.5	18.8	18.1	20.0	19.7	19.9	136.5	150.4	136.7	138.3	137.5	0.72	0.65	0.71	0.70	0.71
	Mali	434.8	30.1	30.6	31.7	31.2	31.6	379.2	397.0	385.7	389.0	387.6	1.15	1.10	1.13	1.12	1.12
	Mozambique	18.5	17.7	18.4	18.7	18.4	18.5	27.6	28.3	27.9	28.2	28.3	0.67	0.66	0.67	0.66	0.66
	Niger	313.0	20.9	17.3	20.3	20.3	20.4	393.9	504.8	433.3	431.8	432.2	0.80	0.62	0.72	0.72	0.72
	Rwanda	351.2	21.0	27.4	24.0	23.7	23.7	439.1	358.1	411.5	415.0	416.8	0.80	0.98	0.85	0.85	0.84
	Sierra Leone	4365.9	38.2	40.5	40.8	40.2	40.8	2999.1	3012.9	3003.7	3038.9	3009.5	1.46	1.45	1.45	1.44	1.45
	Tanzania	474.5	12.3	12.3	13.5	13.5	13.6	1011.1	1077.9	984.1	984.0	981.5	0.47	0.44	0.48	0.48	0.48
	Uganda	1536.8	24.8	25.7	23.6	23.4	23.6	1628.2	1671.7	1828.2	1834.5	1832.2	0.94	0.92	0.84	0.84	0.84
South Asia	Nepal	34.96	20.59	35.27	32.81	32.87	32.33	44.60	27.73	29.92	29.72	29.81	0.78	1.26	1.17	1.18	1.17
CIS	Tajikistan	4.72	44.54	45.01	43.23	42.99	43.32	2.78	2.93	3.07	3.07	3.06	1.70	1.61	1.54	1.54	1.54
Mean			26.27	27.97	28.08	27.94	28.13										

CPD-S1 and CPD-S2 are CPD methods with spatially autocorrelated errors. S1 is based on neighbours defined as countries belonging to the same ICP region and S2 is based on neighbourhood as a function of inverse of distance between Centroids of two countries.

Table 9.3 Poverty rates, % by country and region under alternative PPPs: 2011[a], Numeraire in Indian Rupee (Majumder et al. 2017b)

Region	Country	ICP	GEKS	CPD	CPD-S1 (Region cluster)	CPD-S2 (Inverse distance between centroids)
a						
Africa	Angola	26.69	10.16	14.65	14.82	14.91
	Benin	47.71	34.16	34.58	34.20	34.60
	Botswana	15.25	14.09	13.41	12.91	13.11
	Burkina Faso	49.55	50.45	43.88	43.83	43.42
	Burundi	71.79	74.11	74.29	74.55	75.04
	Cameroon	25.22	16.01	18.82	19.08	19.03
	Central African Republic	61.68	66.54	65.80	66.38	66.18
	Chad	34.01	33.46	32.44	31.63	32.18
	Comoros	10.72	5.39	8.73	8.42	8.38
	Congo, Rep.	25.53	26.20	35.68	35.90	35.76
	Côte d'Ivoire	25.36	19.72	27.63	27.88	27.88
	Djibouti	16.19	18.03	17.51	16.93	17.19
	Ethiopia	25.53	31.78	27.57	25.99	27.18
	Gabon	6.31	5.54	6.60	6.65	6.56
	Gambia, The	39.96	42.52	41.74	40.60	39.96
	Ghana	21.01	19.06	18.23	18.41	18.37
	Guinea	27.53	44.76	38.78	37.82	36.37
	Guinea-Bissau	60.53	67.40	68.17	68.23	68.92
	Kenya	29.73	23.80	24.12	24.55	24.55
	Lesotho	57.26	55.04	53.60	53.90	54.65
	Liberia	61.98	53.58	54.71	54.71	54.31
	Madagascar	77.72	67.48	65.15	65.59	65.51
	Malawi	67.55	71.47	67.64	68.23	67.96
	Mali	41.51	44.59	42.60	43.25	42.92
	Mauritania	8.42	6.71	4.52	4.66	4.61
	Mauritius	0.40	0.27	0.21	0.21	0.21
	Morocco	2.08	4.97	2.95	2.97	2.97
	Mozambique	65.56	66.83	66.20	66.74	66.81
	Namibia	18.86	1.55	13.12	13.35	13.23
	Niger	42.19	61.12	50.16	49.87	49.90
	Nigeria	47.77	48.34	43.39	43.87	43.81
	Rwanda	56.73	44.54	52.92	53.37	53.64
	São Tomé and Princ.	25.96	26.39	25.62	24.82	24.63
	Senegal	33.62	39.31	37.98	38.28	37.89

(continued)

Table 9.3 (continued)

Region	Country	ICP	GEKS	CPD	CPD-S1 (Region cluster)	CPD-S2 (Inverse distance between centroids)
	Sierra Leone		44.84		45.49	44.80
	South Africa	14.45	15.57	12.68	12.49	12.88
	Sudan	10.93	13.77	8.87	8.94	8.93
	Swaziland	39.16	29.18	26.03	25.23	25.81
	Tanzania	39.75	44.68	38.08	38.13	37.91
	Togo	48.44	53.25	51.92	52.22	52.12
	Tunisia	1.30	1.84	1.59	1.71	1.62
	Uganda	27.94	29.15	35.58	35.82	35.76
	Zambia	61.27	62.35	61.45	61.22	61.26
	Zimbabwe	21.40		17.27	17.60	17.59
b						
East Asia and the Pacific	China	9.44	11.84	6.35	6.27	6.42
	Fiji	2.73	0.82	1.50	1.41	1.50
	Indonesia	10.71	7.34	8.36	8.34	8.53
	Malaysia	0.16	0.00	0.10	0.10	0.11
	Mongolia	0.17	0.12	0.24	0.25	0.24
	Philippines	10.14	1.22	3.91	3.92	3.92
	Thailand	0.03	0.01	0.01	0.01	0.01
	Vietnam	2.26	0.89	1.28	1.31	1.29
South Asia	Bhutan	1.62	1.01	1.15	1.02	1.02
	India	16.41	20.12	20.38	20.07	20.47
	Maldives	2.93	1.57	2.55	2.55	2.55
	Nepal	10.84	1.68	2.16	2.16	2.16
	Pakistan	4.87	0.87	3.10	3.22	3.10
	Sri Lanka	1.09	0.72	1.51	1.51	1.52
CIS	Armenia	0.92	2.00	2.44	2.44	2.53
	Azerbaijan	0.00	0.00	0.53	0.53	0.57
	Kazakhstan	0.01	0.01	0.01	0.01	0.01
	Kyrgyzstan	0.42	0.27	0.35	0.34	0.35
	Moldova	0.06	0.22	0.11	0.11	0.15
Eurostat-OECD	Albania	0.46	0.46	0.46	0.46	0.46
	Australia	0.67	0.67	0.67	0.67	0.67
	Austria	0.42	0.37	0.37	0.37	0.37
	Belgium	0.43	0.38	0.40	0.40	0.40
	Bosnia and Herzegovina	0.06	0.06	0.07	0.07	0.07
	Bulgaria	1.87	2.04	1.99	1.99	1.99
	Canada	0.34	0.34	0.34	0.34	0.34

(continued)

Table 9.3 (continued)

Region	Country	ICP	GEKS	CPD	CPD-S1 (Region cluster)	CPD-S2 (Inverse distance between centroids)
	Chile	0.94	0.94	0.96	0.93	0.96
	Croatia	0.73	0.73	0.70	0.70	0.70
	Cyprus	0.03	0.03	0.03	0.03	0.03
	Czech Republic	0.04	0.04	0.04	0.04	0.04

c

Region	Country	ICP	GEEKS	CPD	CPD-S1 (Region cluster)	CPD-S2 (Inverse distance between centroids)
Eurostat-OECD	Denmark	1.22	1.22	1.22	1.22	1.22
	Estonia	1.08	0.95	1.03	0.98	0.98
	Finland	0.08	0.08	0.08	0.08	0.08
	France	0.08	0.07	0.07	0.07	0.07
	Germany	0.19	0.18	0.18	0.18	0.18
	Greece	2.17	2.16	2.16	2.13	2.14
	Hungary	0.05	0.05	0.05	0.05	0.05
	Iceland	0.32	0.32	0.32	0.32	0.32
	Ireland	0.50	0.39	0.41	0.41	0.41
	Israel	0.39	0.39	0.39	0.39	0.39
	Italy	1.22	1.17	1.17	1.17	1.17
	Japan	0.35	0.35	0.35	0.35	0.35
	Latvia	1.18	1.18	1.10	1.10	1.10
	Lithuania	0.84	0.87	0.86	0.86	0.86
	Luxembourg	0.32	0.30	0.30	0.30	0.30
	Macedonia, FYR	0.70	1.17	0.90	0.90	1.04
	Mexico	4.70	4.50	4.43	4.45	4.45
	Montenegro	0.21	0.21	0.21	0.21	0.21
	Netherlands	0.38	0.38	0.38	0.38	0.38
	Norway	0.21	0.18	0.21	0.18	0.18
	Poland	0.28	0.27	0.27	0.27	0.27
	Portugal	0.46	0.38	0.38	0.38	0.38
	Romania	4.18	4.13	4.39	4.36	4.36
	Russian Federation	0.04	0.04	0.05	0.06	0.05
	Serbia	0.05	0.05	0.10	0.10	0.10
	Slovakia	0.30	0.34	0.34	0.34	0.34

(continued)

Table 9.3 (continued)

Region	Country	ICP	GEKS	CPD	CPD-S1 (Region cluster)	CPD-S2 (Inverse distance between centroids)
	Spain	1.53	1.45	1.45	1.45	1.45
	Sweden	0.64	0.62	0.62	0.62	0.62
	Switzerland	0.10	0.10	0.10	0.10	0.10
	Turkey	0.00	0.05	0.05	0.00	0.05
	UK	0.82	0.81	0.81	0.81	0.81
	USA	1.33	1.00	1.00	1.00	1.00
d						
Latin America	Bolivia	7.61	7.20	7.11	7.07	7.07
	Brazil	4.84	6.88	5.05	5.14	5.06
	Colombia	5.86	6.83	5.17	5.34	5.29
	Costa Rica	1.66	1.13	1.37	1.37	1.37
	Dominican Rep.	2.21	1.81	1.81	1.90	1.95
	Ecuador	5.27	4.57	4.80	4.79	4.79
	El Salvador	3.69	3.22	3.99	3.97	3.79
	Guatemala	10.01	4.79	7.28	7.12	7.24
	Haiti	52.12	50.28	40.82	40.75	40.77
	Honduras	17.43	15.49	15.74	15.63	15.70
	Nicaragua	9.44	6.36	8.34	8.23	8.23
	Panama	3.48	4.02	3.33	3.27	3.29
	Paraguay	4.55	5.64	5.10	5.10	5.10
	Peru	3.53	3.46	3.15	3.06	3.07
	Uruguay	0.25	0.12	0.20	0.20	0.20
	Venezuela, RB	8.76	9.34	10.44	10.73	10.66
The Caribbean	Belize	12.59	8.18	12.30	12.30	12.37
	Jamaica	1.18	1.43	1.84	1.84	1.84
	St. Lucia	31.00	26.04	27.11	27.09	25.85
	Suriname	21.14	21.41	21.41	21.41	21.41
	Trinidad and Tobago	2.42	2.97	2.94	2.90	2.88

[a]Table 3 gives the values for only those countries for which all the four poverty rates (ICP, GEKS, CPD, CPD-S1, and CPD-S2) could be computed. At the time the exercise was done, the poverty rates (from POVCALNET) for Western Asia were not available

This table also shows that at the aggregate world level the introduction of spatial correlation in the CPD framework does not lead to any significant revision in the world poverty rate. The global poverty rate corresponding to ICP and GEKS is slightly higher than that corresponding to the non-spatial CPD and the two variants

Table 9.4 Regional Poverty Rates, % under Alternative PPPs, 2011 (Majumder et al. 2017b)

Region*	2011 PPPs				
	ICP	GEKS	CPD	CPD-S1 (Region cluster)	CPD-S2 (Inverse distance between centroids)
Africa	35.38	35.96	33.53	33.55	33.64
Commonwealth of independent States	0.17	0.27	1.30	1.30	1.31
East Asia and the Pacific	8.70	9.46	5.89	5.84	5.97
South Asia	14.66	17.12	17.15	16.98	17.29
Eurostat-OECD	1.05	0.96	0.95	0.95	0.96
Latin America	6.76	7.54	6.41	6.48	6.43
The Caribbean	5.69	5.18	5.69	5.68	5.63
World	11.62	12.64	11.34	11.29	11.42

*Based on Table 9.3a–d. The singleton countries have been omitted

of the spatial CPD, although the changes are all within 1% point of each other. Therefore, relative to the many other data uncertainties about global poverty, the methodological choice of GEKS versus CPD in aggregating PPPs above the country level seems to have relatively small impacts on the understanding of global poverty. In fact, the global poverty estimates appear largely 'robust' to the choice of using GEKS versus CPD variants in aggregating PPPs. However, at the country level there are large variations. Figure 9.1a–d presents some selected scatter plots of the GEKS and CPD (non-spatial)-based poverty rates (y-axis) against the ICP values (x-axis). As can be clearly seen, the country-level variations between poverty rates from the different PPPs in 'Africa' and 'Asia and the Pacific' regions are quite high compared to the variations in 'Eurostat-OECD' and 'Latin America' regions.

Table 9.5 compares the regional composition of the 'extremely poor' global population, defined as those living on less than the IPL a day, under the five sets of PPPs. While for East Asia and the Pacific, the ICP PPPs show a larger value for the share of the 'extremely poor' global population, for South Asia, the ICP PPPs show a smaller value in relation to the GEKS and CPD models. For other regions, all the values are quite robust. Majumder et al. (2017b) builds on the study by Majumder et al. (2017a), which examined the sensitivity of regional rankings based on living standards to the PPPs used. The former extends the latter by moving from living standards to poverty rates, introducing spatial correlation in the CPD framework and providing evidence on the impact of regionally correlated price movements on the poverty rates. One of the positive features of both studies is the demonstration that one can come up with independently estimated PPPs that do not require the elaborate and expensive procedure set up by the ICP and can arrive at robust poverty rates at the regional and global level.

(a)

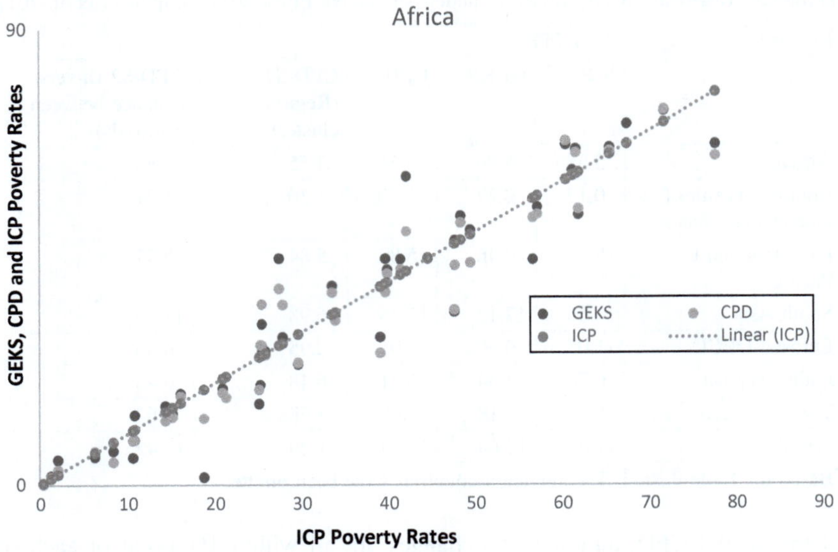

(b)

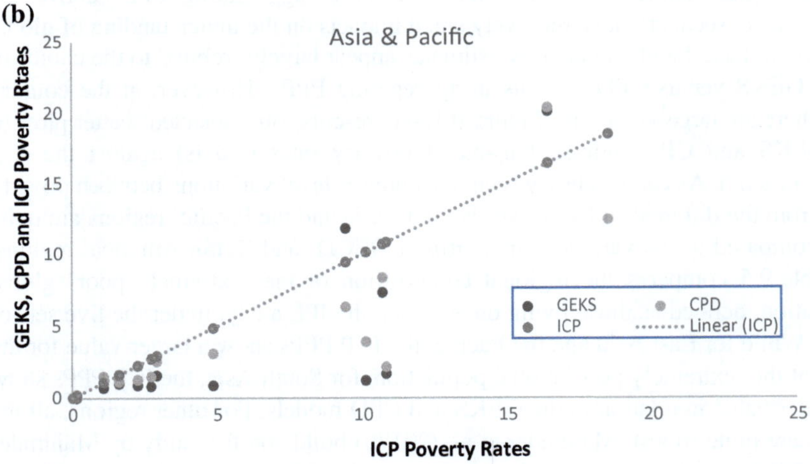

Fig. 9.1 a–d Scatter plot of poverty rates (against ICP rates) for selected regions. Reproduced from Majumder et al. (2017b)

(c)

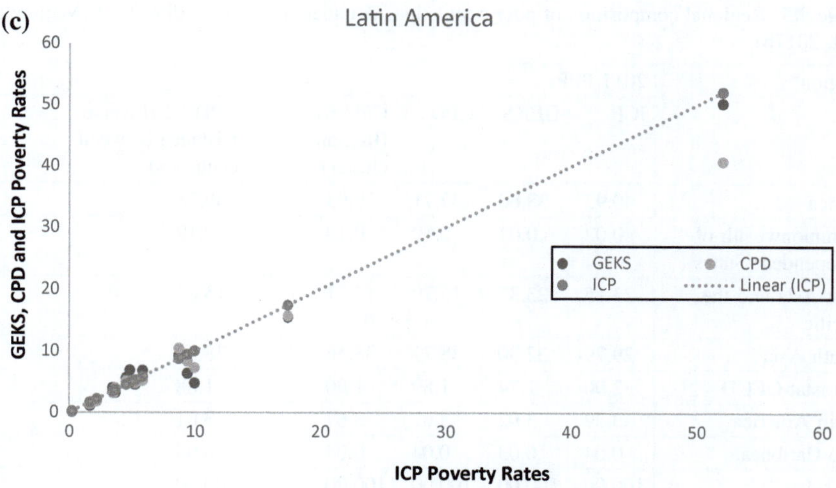

(d)

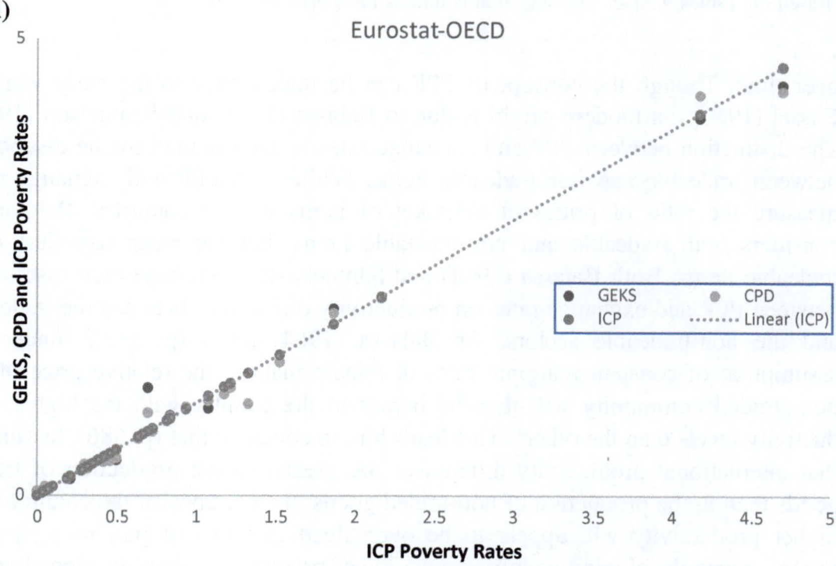

Fig. 9.1 (continued)

9.3 Determinants of PPP Changes Between Countries and Over Time

Before presenting the estimates reported in Majumder et al. (2015) on the key determinants of PPP, let us discuss briefly the origin of the PPP concept itself and some of the controversies in the recent literature on how a country's PPP changes

Table 9.5 Regional composition of poor population, % under alternative PPPs, 2011 (Majumder et al. 2017b)

Region*	2011 PPPs				
	ICP	GEKS	CPD	CPD-S1 (Region cluster)	CPD-S2 (Inverse Distance between centroids)
Africa	40.92	38.60	39.71	39.93	39.58
Commonwealth of independent States	0.02	0.03	0.19	0.19	0.19
East Asia and the Pacific	23.15	23.37	15.79	15.71	15.88
South Asia	29.79	32.30	38.77	38.56	38.83
Eurostat-OECD	2.06	1.74	1.89	1.90	1.88
Latin America	3.79	3.92	3.62	3.67	3.61
The Caribbean	0.04	0.03	0.04	0.04	0.04
World	100.00	100.00	100.00	100.00	100.00

*Based on Tables 9.3a–d. The singleton countries have been omitted

over time. Though the concept of PPP can be traced back to the early work of Cassel (1916), its modern origin is due to Balassa (1964) and Samuelson (1964). The distinction between PPP and exchange rates is underpinned by the distinction between tradeable and non-tradeable items. While both PPP and exchange rates measure the ratio of prices of a basket of items in two countries, the former considers both tradeable and non-tradeable items, but the latter considers only tradeable items. Both Balassa (1964) and Samuelson (1964) base their distinction between PPP and exchange rates on productivity differences between the tradeable and the non-tradeable sectors. As Balassa (1964) notes (p. 585), 'under the assumption of constant marginal rates of transformation, the relative price of the non- traded commodity will thus be higher in the country with the higher productivity levels than the other'. This leads him to conclude that (p. 586), 'assuming that international productivity differences are greater in the production of traded goods than in the production of non-traded goods, the currency of the country with higher productivity will appear to be overvalued in terms of purchasing power parity'. Since developing countries have lower productivity than developed countries, this argument leads to what Ravallion (2013a) terms the 'static Penn effect', where the 'price level index', defined as the ratio of the PPP to the exchange rate is higher in the developed countries. Ravallion (2013a) extends this argument to claim that with economic growth, the developing countries witness productivity gains in the traded goods sector leading to the 'dynamic Penn effect' whereby there is a positive association between changes in economic growth and that in the 'price level index'. The Balassa Samuelson analysis is reinforced by Bhagwati (1984) who argues that services, a typical non-tradeable item, are cheaper in developing countries. Though the distinction is not always emphasized in the literature, Balassa (1964) draws a distinction between the 'absolute' and 'relative' interpretations of the PPP doctrine that views the PPP as 'equilibrium exchange rates.'[3] While, according to the first interpretation, PPP tends to approximate the equilibrium rates of exchange, according to the second interpretation, 'changes in relative prices would indicate the necessary adjustments in exchange rates' (Balassa 1964, p. 584). Though the equivalence is not exact, the 'static Penn effect' corresponds to the absolute interpretation of the PPP doctrine while the relative interpretation corresponds to the 'dynamic Penn effect'. As we report below, while Majumder et al. (2015) finds no evidence in favor of the 'static Penn effect', which involves cross-sectional PPP comparisons between countries in a given year, it does find robust evidence in favor of a 'dynamic Penn effect' which relates to the same country over time. The latter has, recently, been the subject of controversy between Ravallion (2013a, b) and Inklaar (2013) with the former claiming robust evidence in favor of a 'dynamic Penn effect', and the latter denying such an effect.

The information for performing the cross-country empirical exercises conducted by Majumder et al. (2015) was constructed from a variety of data sources, mostly from information published by the World Bank on its website. The data sources and explanation of variables have been listed in Appendix A of that paper. That study investigated the effect of movements in the real per capita expenditure, exchange rate, inflation (as measured by the GDP deflator) and, crucially, the intra-country inequality on PPP changes. It ran panel regressions on cross-country data sets from the ICP years, 1993, 1996,[4] 2005 and 2011. Following the suggestion in Inklaar (2013, p. 616), the panel regressions 'unpacked' the exchange rate from the PPP and used the following specification that extends Inklaar's Eq. (9.2) to include income inequality:

$$ln\left(\frac{\text{PPP}_{it}}{\text{PPP}_{it-1}}\right) = \alpha + \beta_1 ln\left(\frac{P_{it}}{P_{it-1}}\right) + \beta_2 ln\left(\frac{Y_{it}}{Y_{it-1}}\right) + \beta_3 ln\left(\frac{E_{it}}{E_{it-1}}\right) + \beta_4 ln\left(\frac{In_{it}}{In_{it-1}}\right) + \varepsilon_{it} \tag{9.2}$$

PPP is the purchasing power parity, P is the GDP deflator that is used as a measure of inflation,[5] Y is the GDP per capita at national prices, E is the nominal exchange rate, In is Gini measure of inequality, ε denotes the error term which

[3]This view has however been challenged by Rogoff (1996) who points to the 'PPP puzzle', namely, the need to 'reconcile the extremely high short-term volatility of real exchange rates with the glacial rate… at which deviations from PPP seem to die out' (p. 664). In a rare departure from the Balassa Samuelson framework, Rogoff (1996) points to the role of transportation costs and tariffs in explaining the 'PPP puzzle'.

[4]There was a small ICP in 1996, as reported in Ravallion (2013a).

[5]The GDP deflator was defined as the ratio of GDP evaluated at current international dollar to GDP calculated at constant 2011 international dollar. This contrasts with the definition used by both Inklaar and Ravallion. This was done for, basically, three reasons: (1) since PPP constitutes the dependent variable, it seems more appropriate to measure price changes in terms of PPP; (2) the use of current and constant US Dollars may lead to misleading results because the effect of US inflation will be embedded in it as the study uses a long time span and (3) the ratios in local currency units are not comparable as the base years vary with countries.

includes omitted effects, i denotes country, t denotes time. The existence of 'Dynamic Penn effect' (DPE) is denoted by the term $\left[\beta_2 \ln\left(\frac{Y_{it}}{Y_{it-1}}\right) + \beta_3 \ln\left(\frac{E_{it}}{E_{it-1}}\right)\right]$, with the maintained hypothesis of a DPE given by the joint parametric restrictions, $\beta_2 > 0$ and significant and $\beta_3 = 1$.

The 'Static Penn effect' (SPE), that was the basis of the original Balassa Samuelson formulation, is contained in the a-temporal version of (9.2) involving PPP variation between countries at a point in time.

$$\ln(\text{PPP}_{it}) = \tilde{\alpha} + \tilde{\beta}_1 ln(P_{it}) + \tilde{\beta}_2 ln(Y_{it}) + \tilde{\beta}_3 ln(E_t) + \tilde{\beta}_4 ln(In_t) + \varepsilon_{it} \quad (9.3)$$

The existence of 'Static Penn effect' (SPE) is denoted by the maintained hypothesis consisting of the joint parametric restrictions, $\tilde{\beta}_2 > 0$ and significant, and $\tilde{\beta}_3 = 1$.

Figures 1, 2, 3 and 3a in Majumder et al. (2015), not reproduced here for space reasons, provide graphical evidence on the issue. Figure 1 provides a visual representation of one of the necessary conditions for 'Static Penn effect' by plotting PPP against Y in logarithmic scale in each of the 4 ICP years, 1993, 1996, 2005 and 2011. There is clearly a positive relationship between the two in each year. This is also true of the corresponding relationship between PPP and exchange rate in Fig. 2. Figure 3 shows that there is also prima facie evidence in favour of a positive relationship between PPP and intra-country inequality. This evidence becomes much stronger once we control for the other determinants. While Fig. 3 depicts the relationship between PPP and intra-country inequality year by year, Fig. 3a shows the corresponding relationship on the combined data set pooled over the 4 years. The increasing relationship looks much stronger in Fig. 3a which introduces the temporal movement in the inequality changes that seem to reinforce and strengthen the positive relationship between PPP and inequality.

Table 9.6 provides the estimates of Eq. (9.3) for 2005 and 2011. Here evidence of the 'Static Penn effect' is not observed in either year. Although $\tilde{\beta}_2 > 0$ and significant, the test for $\tilde{\beta}_3 = 1$ strongly rejects the hypothesis in both years. Effect of the GDP deflator is non-significant. The evidence on the effect of inequality (interacted with the countries classified into 'low' and 'middle and upper' income levels) on PPP is mixed. Effects are positive for both years for the low-income countries, but significant only in 2005. For the higher-income countries, the effects are non-significant.[6] A possible explanation for the differential effect of the low- and high-income countries could be that with increase in income while low-income countries almost certainly move towards consumption of tradeable goods, the higher-income countries, who are already consuming tradeable goods, move towards consumption of luxurious non-tradeable items (like recreation, services of maids).

[6]When the two groups are merged, the overall effect of inequality turns out to be non-significant for both years.

Table 9.6 Regression results of static inequality augmented Inklaar equations dependent variable: ln (PPP)

Explanatory variables	Estimated parameters	
	Year 2005	Year 2011
ln (GDP Deflator)	0.405 (0.740)	Omitted due to collinearity
ln (GDPPC)	0.627*** (0.000)	0.227*** (0.000)
ln (exchange rate)	0.357** (0.016)	0.769*** (0.000)
Inequality		
Low-income countries	4.200** (0.045)	0.227 (0.577)
Higher-income countries	1.709 (0.245)	−0.147 (0.619)
Constant	−6.607*** (0.000)	−2.373*** (0.000)
R^2	0.9182	0.9856
No. of observations	107	101
No. of countries	107	101
F-statistic for testing $\tilde{\beta}_3 = 1$	21.86*** (0.000)	38.59*** (0.000)

Source Majumder et al. (2015)
Note (1) Figures in parentheses are the *p* values. ** significant at 5% level; *** significant at 1% level

Turning now to the pooled ICP data sets over the 4 years, the following was the estimable form of Eq. (9.2).

$$D\ln(\mathrm{PPP}_{it}) = \mathrm{Trend} + \alpha_1 D\ln(GDP\mathrm{Deflator}_{it}) + \alpha_2 D\ln(GDP_{it}) + \alpha_3 D\ln(E_{it}) + \beta DZ_{it} + \epsilon_{it} \quad (9.4)$$

Note:

a. Trend is adjusted by the gap (no. of years) between two time periods. It is used to remove country-specific fixed effects.
b. The operator D denotes difference over time, i.e. $Dx_t \equiv x_t - x_{\text{previous}\,t}$.
c. $t \in \{1993, 1996, 2005, 2011\}$.
d. Z_{it} is a vector of interaction terms between inequality and two groups of countries (the 'low income countries' and 'higher income countries' consisting of lower middle, upper middle, high-income non-OECD and high-income OECD countries) and β is a vector of the associated coefficients.[7]

[7]The results are robust to alternative classification of countries (e.g. merging the 'lower middle income' group with the 'low income' group).

Table 9.7 Regression results of Dynamic Inklaar Eq. (9.4) without the inequality variable–dependent variable: D ln (PPP)

Explanatory Variables	Estimated parameters	
Trend	−0.000 (0.995)	
D ln (GDP deflator)	0.325 (0.278)	0.323 (0.153)
D ln (GDPPC)	0.555* (0.074)	0.555** (0.050)
D ln (exchange rate)	0.749*** (0.003)	0.749*** (0.003)
R^2	0.6846	0.6846
No. of observations	311	311
No. of countries	120	120
F-statistic for testing $\alpha_3 = 1$	1.25 (0.275)	1.26 (0.273)

Source Majumder et al. (2015)
Note (1) Figures in parentheses are the *p* values. **significant at 5% level; ***significant at 1% level (2) The operator *D* denotes difference over time

Table 9.7 presents the estimates of Eq. (9.4) without the inequality variables. Since the information on inequality is available for only a subset of the countries, Table 9.7 allowed estimation on the maximum number of observations available in the pooled sample. Note that the evidence in favor of a 'Dynamic Penn effect' is quite strong (for both with and without the 'Trend' variable) with the highly significant positive estimates of the coefficients of per capita GDP variable and exchange rate variable and non-rejection of the hypothesis of $\alpha_3 = 1$. The coefficient of the GDP deflator variable is positive, but non-significant. The trend variable has little or no effect on the estimates.

Table 9.8 presents a more complete picture by reporting the estimates of Eq. (9.4) with the inequality variable included on the right-hand side. Table 9.8 presents robust evidence of a positive relationship between PPP and intra-country inequality for countries with PPP less than the exchange rate.[8] Note from the table that the inclusion or omission of the trend variable has little effect on the strong statistical significance of the inequality coefficient estimate in case of the low-income countries. A comparison between the first two columns of estimates of Table 9.8 shows that the enforcement of the restriction that the exchange rate coefficient, $\alpha_3 = 1$, which means that we are estimating the changes in the

[8]In the 'low income group' in 98% cases, PPP is less than the exchange rate.

Table 9.8 Regression results of Dynamic Inklaar Eq. (9.4) with the inequality variable–dependent variable: D ln (PPP)

Explanatory variables	Parameter estimates with trend		Parameter estimates without trend
Trend	−0.000 (0.990)	−0.023 (0.344)	–
D ln (GDP deflator)	0.343 (0.182)	0.334* (0.096)	0.338 (0.160)
D ln (GDPPC)	0.563** (0.041)	0.921 (0.158)	0.563** (0.030)
D ln (exchange rate)	0.756*** (0.003)	1 (constrained)	0.757*** (0.003)
D Inequality			
Low-income countries	3.980*** (0.004)	5.241*** (0.007)	3.980*** (0.005)
Higher-income countries	0.041 (0.941)	−0.444 (0.396)	0.041 (0.941)
R^2	0.6898		0.6898
No. of observations	303	303	303
No. of countries	119	119	119
F-statistic for testing $\alpha_3 = 1$	1.18 (0.288)		1.43 (0.245)

Source Majumder et al. (2015)
Figures in parentheses are the *p* values. *significant at 10% level; **significant at 5% level; ***significant at 1% level

price-level index (PLI) rather than in the PPP, increases quite sharply the magnitude of the estimated inequality effect. Note, also, from the first and third columns of estimates that the existence of the DPE ($\alpha_2 > 0, \alpha_3 = 1$) is robust to the inclusion of the inequality variable, and as in Table 9.7, the Trend variable has no visible effect on the estimates.

(2) **Low-income countries** are those as specified by World Bank. **Higher-income countries** include lower-middle, upper-middle, high-income non-OECD and high-income OECD countries.

9.4 Report of the Commission on Global Poverty: A Critique

9.4.1 Background and Motivation of the Commission on Global Poverty

While 2015 marked the end of the era of the Millennium Development Goals (MDG), 2016 ushered in the era of the Sustainable Development Goals (SDG). The topic of global poverty provided a link between the two sets of goals of the UN. While the MDG s set a target of halving over the period, 1990–2015, the number of 'extremely poor people' defined as those living on less than 1.25 US $ a day at 2005 PPP, the SDGs set a target of eliminating by 2030 'extreme poverty' which uses the updated definition of the poverty line at $1.90 a day at 2011 PPP. The setting of targets obviously requires monitoring of the progress toward the goals defined by the targets. In case of the poverty targets, the enumeration and monitoring of poverty numbers globally has been the responsibility of the World Bank. While the ILO is charged with the responsibility for producing and monitoring the statistics on employment, the WHO with that on health, UNICEF with child welfare, the World Bank has the responsibility of enumerating and monitoring global poverty. The link between ILO and employment, between WHO and health, between UNICEF and child welfare is quite natural and follows from the very name of these UN agencies and the very rationale for their existence.

In contrast, the connection between the World Bank and global poverty is more a product of history than deliberate design. One of the earliest studies of global poverty was by Ahluwalia et al. (1979), and all these authors happened to be working at the World Bank. The next major piece of work on global poverty was due to Ravallion et al. Walle (1991) and, once again, all these authors were working at the World Bank. Over the next 25 years that have elapsed since the Ravallion et al. (1991) paper appeared, the World Bank has firmly established itself as the global organisation that has the ultimate responsibility for the enumeration and monitoring of global poverty. This manifested itself in the publication of the two papers on global poverty earlier this year by Ferreira et al. (2016), and Jolliffe and Prydz (2016) and it is no coincidence that all the authors of these papers are working at the World Bank. The enumeration of global poverty requires the specification of a 'global poverty line', typically specified in a global currency such as the US dollar, and the availability of the various countries' purchasing power parities (PPP) that are required to convert the global poverty line into the local currency denominated poverty lines.

PPPs are considered more reliable than exchange rates since they are based on the entire basket of items consumed by the individual, unlike the market exchange rates which are based only on tradeable items. Specifying the 'global poverty line', also referred to as the 'international poverty line' (IPL), and the PPP estimation present conceptual problems and impose data requirements that have made the task of poverty enumeration and monitoring a complex one on a scale that is far greater than most other cross-country exercises. The study by Ahluwalia et al. (1979) avoided this complexity by basing the global poverty line on the poverty line for India. Moreover, their study was based on a sample of only 36 countries and consequently the PPP requirement was much less than that today. The Ravallion et al. (1991) paper was the earliest to base the 'global poverty line' on the poverty lines of a number of countries, 33 to be precise, including both developing and developed countries. That practice continues even today with the 33 countries having been replaced by the '15 poorest countries' for whom the national poverty lines are available, and the global poverty line is defined as the mean of these 15 national poverty lines converted to the US dollar at the prevailing PPPs.

As the number of countries entering the global poverty calculations has grown from the 36 in Ahluwalia et al. (1979) to 86 in Ravallion et al. (1991) to nearly 200 economies in the recent studies mentioned above, the scale of the International Comparison Project (ICP) that produces the required PPPs has grown exponentially such that it is now housed in the World Bank further cementing the link between the World Bank and the monitoring of global poverty. Since the unit records from households survey based micro information used by the ICP to arrive at their PPP s is available only to those working in the World Bank, it is no surprise that all the published studies on global poverty have used the ICP PPPs. Whatever robustness checks that have been carried out on the specified international poverty line (IPL) used by the World Bank have worked with the ICP PPPs. It is against this background of close and continuing involvement of the World Bank in the monitoring of global poverty that the then Chief Economist and Senior Vice President of the World Bank, Kaushik Basu, convened in 2015 a high-level Commission under the Chairmanship of the eminent British economist, Sir Anthony Atkinson, along with an Advisory Board of 23 renowned economists 'to advise the World Bank on the methodology currently used for tracking poverty in terms of people's consumption, given that prices change over time and purchasing power parities across nations shift…and to give advice on other dimensions and relativities of poverty and deprivation that ought to be measured' (World Bank 2016, p. viii). It is to the credit of Basu that, for the first time in its history, the World Bank sought outside expert advice on its monitoring of global poverty, especially since what the Bank reports on global poverty numbers will be crucial in the assessment of progress on poverty reduction. The Report was completed and made available to the public very recently (World Bank 2016). The contents of the Report of the Poverty Commission are of special interest to the Indian policy makers since India contributes more than other countries to the global count of poor.

9.4.2 The Write up of the Report and Its Main Recommendations: A Critique

The report of the Commission reads very well, which is not surprising since the Chair, Professor Atkinson, is known not only for his outstanding contributions to the topic of poverty and inequality but also for the elegance and lucidity of his writings. Unfortunately, the editing and the sequential structure of the report left considerable room for improvement. As it stands, it is too lengthy and is unlikely to engage non-economists and policy makers who will not be that interested in the detailed description of the economists' contributions to the topic. Of the three chapters constituting the report, the third chapter, titled, 'Making it Happen', is the most significant contribution and should have appeared as the first chapter along with the two recommendations that it contains, one on 'major investment in statistical sources' (Recommendation 20) and the other calling for regular auditing of the IPL by an outside body (Recommendation 21). Both these recommendations deserve full support. I am afraid many a reader will have lost patience and interest by the time he/she waded through the first 100 pages. It would have been useful to have a summary of each chapter in dot point form. Let us now turn to the centrepiece of the Report, namely the 21 recommendations that it makes to the World Bank. For reasons of space, I do not write them out in full here, since the recommendations along with the World Bank's response are mentioned in the cover note to the Report put out by the Bank-see http://pubdocs.worldbank.org/en/733161476724983858/MonitoringGlobalPovertyCoverNote.pdf. I urge the reader to read these recommendations carefully. I will focus on the more important of the recommendations and subject them to scrutiny. The 21 recommendations follow the sequence of the three chapters as they appear in the report: Recommendations 1-10 deal with 'Monitoring Extreme Poverty', recommendations 11-19 with 'Complementary Indicators and Multidimensionality', and recommendations 20, 21 with the practical sounding 'Making it Happen'.

Recommendation 1 reiterates the current practice of defining 'extreme poverty' in terms of an 'international poverty line' expressed in each country in terms of the currency of that country. This should be read in conjunction with recommendation 10 that the global poverty estimates should be updated up to 2030 on the basis of the IPL specified in local currency and in line with domestic inflation as measured by the national CPI. The crucial part is the suggestion that the PPP to be used in specifying the IPL as the starting point will be the 2011 ICP PPPs, which will henceforth be frozen at their 2011 PPP values and that the PPPs form the further ICP rounds will not be incorporated until 2030. The task of updating the poverty lines in line with inflation all the way to 2030 will fall entirely on the domestic CPI s of the various countries. These two recommendations are the centrepiece of the

Poverty Commission Report and, yet, are the most problematic. It is well known that the ICP PPPs are based on a different basket of items than the CPI, and until the inconsistency is ironed out through successive rounds of the ICP, it is unwise to switch overnight from one to the other. The recommendation to freeze the use of the ICP PPPs at the estimates from the 2011 round assumes a degree of accuracy of the 2011 ICP PPPs that hasn't been established yet. Note also that a similar point was made by a panellist when the Poverty Commission's Report was launched in Washington on 13 July, 2016. This panel member (Andrew Dabalen) drew attention to significant problems with the 2011 ICP PPPs in certain regions (especially the Middle Eastern and North African region, MENA) that seriously bias the regional and global poverty rates based on those PPPs.

A more fundamental objection is that the idea of a single 'international poverty line' to be applied to all countries regardless of their economic status and regional location makes little sense, especially if one recalls that such a poverty line is obtained as the mean of the poverty lines of the 15 'poorest countries'. Nearly all these countries are in Africa with abysmal levels of poverty. It follows trivially that the poverty line thus obtained will be set at too low a level for countries such as India or Indonesia with significantly higher rates of growth. In other words, the bar for a household to cross from poor to a non-poor status will be set at too low a level for such countries. This will underestimate poverty in two of the most populous countries in the world (China, India) and, consequently, will bias downwards the magnitude of global poverty. More seriously, for countries such as India and Indonesia, it will give the policy makers in these countries a false sense of satisfaction regarding poverty eradication. In richer countries, the enforcement of the 'international poverty line' will forcibly reduce the poverty count to zero and will let the authorities there off the hook. A more sensible suggestion is to abandon the concept of a single international poverty lines and define, instead, regional poverty lines based on the national poverty lines in the various ICP regions. Alternatively, multiple 'international poverty lines' could be defined based on the national poverty lines of countries grouped by their level of affluence and development.

Consistent with its failure to question the concept of a globally specified 'international poverty line', the Poverty Commission does not scrutinise the multilateral estimation strategy underlining the calculation of the ICP PPPs. It is odd that, notwithstanding the close connection between PPP estimation and poverty enumeration, so little time and space is spent by the Commission on examining the PPP methodology used by the ICP. Does it make sense to base the PPPs of all the countries, including the poorest developing countries, on the US dollar? If one needs to work out PPPs between two countries, A and B, not involving the USA, isn't it odd that one has to divide the PPPs of A and B by one another to obtain the PPP between A and B? The Commission does recognise in passing the oddity of this practice, but does not act on it. More fundamentally, is a multilateral estimation strategy defensible in estimating PPPs between two countries which have little in common with the remaining (n-2) countries? Why, for example, in bilateral welfare comparisons between India and Vietnam, should one be forced to use the ICP PPPs which are based on the price and quantity information from all the countries participating in the ICP, many of whom are far removed geographically, developmentally and culturally, from both India and Vietnam? Yet another shortcoming of the ICP PPPs is that they are mostly based on fixed weight price indices that are not utility or preference consistent unlike the 'exact' or 'true cost of living indices. Another issue that does not appear anywhere in the Report is that of subnational PPPs that question the appropriateness of using a single economy-wide number as a country's PPP. The ICP seems to be ahead of the Commission on Global Poverty in this regard since it has signalled subnational PPPs as one of its priorities in the next phase of its research.

The report's recommendation no. 18 to 'include a multidimensional poverty indicator based on the counting approach' ought to be welcomed. This is in line with the recent literature on multidimensional poverty measurement and will align the World Bank's poverty statistics with that reported in the Human Development Reports. However, the Report of the Global Poverty Commission overlooks the recent literature on dynamic multi-dimensional poverty measures surveyed, for example, in Alkire et al. (2015, Ch. 9). As noted in Nicholas and Ray (2012), such an approach allows the analyst to incorporate both the persistence and duration of deprivation across multiple dimensions. This requires panel data that can be accommodated in the implementation of Recommendation 20, namely that 'there should be a major investment in statistical sources and analysis, with these activities being accorded a high priority in the work of the World Bank'. The report notes in passing the need to have panel data since it is important not only to count and monitor poverty but also to distinguish between transitory and persistent poverty and incorporate that in the global poverty measures. The report takes a static view of poverty in both the unidimensional and multidimensional contexts, notwithstanding a recent literature on dynamic extensions of static poverty measures in both. This limits the report's policy appeal since more important than simply tracking the aggregate poverty numbers is the need to identify and count those households that are experiencing persistent poverty and identify the dimensions that are recording the longest and uninterrupted spells of deprivation.

Since we currently don't have panel data sets across a range of countries needed to undertake such an exercise, the Report lost the opportunity to show the lead by urging the Bank to move to a dynamic framework for poverty enumeration and monitoring. It ought to have made a specific mention of the need to provide the required panel databases across countries over a realistic time frame as a recommendation. The need to subject the World Bank's poverty enumeration to regular auditing by an outside body noted in recommendation 21 is another of the Poverty Commission's recommendations that is timely and deserves to be strongly supported by all the stakeholders. Perhaps predictably, the senior management of the

World Bank has rejected this recommendation and refused to subject the Bank to outside scrutiny. Hopefully, sooner rather than later, the Bank will be forced to adopt this recommendation and make its poverty counting and monitoring a more transparent exercise.

9.5 Concluding Remarks

As the Millennium Development Goals (MDG) gave way to the Sustainable Development Goals (SDG), one set of targets that has received much attention is that relating to poverty reduction. While MDG and the SDG differ in the set of indicators, goals and targets, poverty reduction is common to both sets of goals. The idea is for the SDG to take off from where the world poverty was when the MDG era ended in 2015. This set off a spate of recent studies on poverty enumeration at the level of regions and the world as a whole. Such cross-national poverty comparisons require two crucial ingredients: an 'international poverty line' (IPL) denominated in a common currency, typically the US dollar, and a set of country-specific PPPs that allow the IPLs to be converted to the local currency units. While much of the sensitivity analyses of world and regional poverty rates has been with respect to variation in the national poverty lines and in the IPLs, what is lacking has been similar sensitivity exercise with respect to the PPPs used in the country-level poverty calculations. Almost universally, the ICP PPPs have been used since they are the only ones that are publicly available. The results of Majumder et al. (2017b) that have been reported in this chapter suggest that the link between PPP and poverty rates needs to be explored in much greater detail, both analytically and empirically, that has been the case so far.

The significant role that PPPs play in the calculations of global inequality and poverty rates points to the need to calculate and update the PPPs at closer time intervals than is done by the ICP. This leads to the question: How does the PPP of a country's currency change with economic growth? It raises the wider issue of identifying the key determinants of PPP changes over time. This chapter attempts to provide some Light on these issues by reporting the empirical evidence from Majumder et al. (2015) that suggests a link between intra country inequality and PPP along with results in favour of a 'dynamic Penn effect' as suggested by Ravallion (2013a).

References

Ahluwalia M, Carter N, Chenery H (1979) Growth and poverty in developing countries. J Dev Econ 6(3):299–341

Alkire S, Foster J, Seth S, Santos MS, Roche JM, Ballon P (2015) Multidimensional poverty measurement and analysis. Oxford University Press, Oxford, UK

Aten B (1996) Evidence of spatial autocorrelation in international prices. Rev Income Wealth 42:149–163

Balassa B (1964) The purchasing power parity doctrine: a reappraisal. J Polit Econ 72(6):584–596

Bhagwati J (1984) Why are services cheaper in poor countries. Econ J 94(374):279–286

Cassel G (1916) The present situation of the foreign exchanges. Econ J 26(103):319–323

Chen S, Ravallion M (2001) How well did the world's poorest fare in the 1990s? Rev Income Wealth 47(3):283–300

Chen S, Ravallion M (2010) The developing world is poorer than we thought, but no less successful in the fight against poverty. Quart J Econ 125(4):1577–1625

Cruz M, Foster J, Quillin B, Schellekens P (2015) Ending extreme poverty and sharing prosperity: progress and policies, (Policy Research Note). In: Development economics. World Bank Group, Washington, DC

Deaton A (2001) Counting the world's poor: problems and possible solutions. The World Bank Research Observer 16(2):125–147

Deaton A (2010) Price indexes, inequality, and the measurement of world poverty. Am Econ Rev 100(1):5–34

Ferreira F, Chen S, Dabalen A, Dikhanov Y, Hamadeh N, Jolliffe D, Narayan A, Prydz E, Revenga A, Sangraula P, Serajuddin U, Yoshida N (2016) A global count of the extreme poor in 2012: data issues, methodology and initial results. J Econ Inequality 14(2):141–172

Inklaar R (2013) Price levels and economic growth: making sense of the revisions to data on real incomes: a comment. Rev Inc Wealth 59(4):614–622

Jolliffe D, Prydz E (2015) Global poverty goals and prices: how purchasing power parity matters. In: Policy research working paper 7256, Development Research Group, World Bank

Jolliffe D, Prydz E (2016) Estimating international poverty lines from comparable national thresholds (English). Policy Research, Working Paper, No. WPS 7606; Paper is funded by the Knowledge for Change Program (KCP). World Bank Group, Washington, DC. http://documents.worldbank.org/curated/en/837051468184454513/Estimating-international-poverty-lines-from-comparable-national-thresholds

Kakwani N, Son HH (2016) Global poverty estimates based on 2011 purchasing power parity: where should the new poverty line be drawn? J Econ Inequality 14(2):173–184

Majumder A, Ray R, Santra S (2015) Preferences, purchasing power parity, and inequality: analytical framework, propositions, and empirical evidence. In: World bank policy research working paper 7395, Washington, DC

Majumder A, Ray R, Santra S (2017a) Sensitivity of purchasing power parity estimates to estimation procedures and their effect on living standards comparisons. J Globalization Dev 8 (1):1–25

Majumder A, Ray R, Santra S (2017b) Sensitivity of regional and global poverty rates to alternative purchasing power parities. In: Forthcoming in Indian Growth and Development Review

Nicholas A, Ray R (2012) Duration and persistence in multidimensional deprivation: methodology and australian application. Econ Rec 88:106–126

Rao DSP (2001) Weighted EKS and generalised CPD methods for aggregation at basic heading level and above basic heading level, mimeographed. In: Joint World Bank-OECD seminar on purchasing power parities: recent advances in methods and applications. Washington DC, available in http://www.oecd.org/std/prices-ppp/2424825.pdf

Ravallion M (2013a) Price levels and economic growth: making sense of revisions to data on real incomes. Rev Income Wealth 59(4):593–613

Ravallion M (2013b) Reply to Robert Inklaar. Rev Income Wealth 59(4):623–628
Ravallion M (2016) Toward better global poverty measures. J Econ Inequality 14(2):227–248 (Springer; Society for the Study of Economic Inequality)
Ravallion M, Datt G, van de Walle D (1991) Quantifying absolute poverty in the developing world. Rev Income Wealth 37:345–361
Ravallion M, Chen S, Sangraula P (2009) Dollar a day revisited. In: World bank economic review, vol 23, Issue 2. World Bank Group, pp 163–184
Rogoff K (1996) The purchasing power parity puzzle. J Econ Lit 34(2):647–668
Samuelson P (1964) Theoretical notes on trade problems. Rev Econ Stat 46(2):145–154
World Bank (2016) Monitoring global poverty. Report of the Commission on Global Poverty. World Bank, Washington, DC

Chapter 10
Multidimensional Deprivation: Comparison Within and Between Countries

10.1 Introduction

The discussion so far has focussed on household welfare based on money metric variables such as prices and expenditure. In this chapter and the next, the volume widens the discussion to include a household's inability to enjoy some of the basic necessities of life such as drinking water, Fuel, electricity, toilet and medical care. Notwithstanding significant improvement in levels of living, many parts of the world still experience lack of access to several of these dimensions. Poverty measures and, more broadly, an exclusive reliance on variables that can be quantified in money terms, often fail to capture the true extent of human misery both globally and in pockets inside countries. The motivation of this chapter and the next is to provide evidence from studies that compare between and within countries taking a multidimensional view of deprivation. Deprivation is a better indicator of 'illfare' than 'poverty' since many households who are above the 'poverty line' may be severely distressed due to lack of access to a range of basic necessities of life. In this chapter, we take a static view of multidimensional deprivation examining its movements over time ignoring dynamic elements that capture persistence and duration in that deprivation. Such elements are considered in the following chapter. The topic of multidimensional deprivation sits well in this volume because of its methodological interest combined with a policy application based on empirical evidence. Keeping this in mind, this chapter reports in detail the methodology and results from two studies, Mishra and Ray (2013) and Ray and Sinha (2015). A common feature of these studies is that, besides their adoption of a static multidimensional framework and a common methodology, both involve comparison of deprivation over time and between regions. While the former study is at a subnational level and compares multidimensional deprivation between the principal States in India, the later involves comparison between countries, namely China, India and Vietnam. Both studies are based on unit level household records from concurrent surveys.

R. Ray, *Household Behaviour, Prices, and Welfare*, Themes in Economics,
https://doi.org/10.1007/978-981-13-1930-3_10

Inspired by the work of Sen (1985, 1999), there is now widespread agreement that deprivation is multidimensional and cannot be adequately captured by unidimensional measures such as the expenditure poverty rate, and that nations should not be ranked simply by their per capita GDP. An early practical consequence of this new approach was the adoption of the Human Development Index (HDI) by the United Nations Development Programme in its first Human Development Report in 1990 (UNDP 1990). The HDI, that implements the idea of multidimensional deprivation, is a simple unweighted average of measures of literacy, life expectancy and per capita GDP. Two key criticisms of the HDI are (a) it is a composite index that measures average achievement in three basic dimensions of human development rather than that of the most deprived who need to be targeted in policy interventions and (b) it ignores the distribution of deprivation between attributes and between households. The former limitation led to the formulation in 1997 by the UNDP of the Human Poverty Index (HPI) that, like the HDI, is also a composite index but is focussed on those with low incomes, and its use in the 1997 Human Development Report (UNDP 1997). The HPI has subsequently been generalised by Chakravarty and Majumder (2005) to allow incorporation of a wider set of dimensions and general nonlinear functional forms that satisfy a set of poverty axioms. The second limitation has seen the introduction of alternative multidimensional measures of deprivation in several recent contributions that take the individual or household, rather than the country, as the unit of analysis. These measures are based on the number of dimensions that a household is deprived in and then aggregating the household-level information into an overall measure of multidimensional deprivation. Examples of contributions that adopt a multidimensional approach to poverty or deprivation include Bourguignon and Chakravarty (2003), Chakravarty and D'Ambrosio (2006), Jayaraj and Subramanian (2010), and Alkire and Foster (2011).

A key difference between the earlier HDI, HPI and the more recent multidimensional deprivation, poverty measures is that while the former starts with the dimensions and aggregates the dimension-specific deprivation rates (as percentage of population) into an overall measure, the latter starts with the household and then aggregates the household-specific deprivation rates (as the proportion of dimensions) into the overall measure. Since the latter need household-level data, the informational requirements of the recent multidimensional deprivation measures are much greater than the earlier aggregated measures such as HDI, which were based on national averages. The trade-off is that the recent measures are more policy friendly in allowing the identification of dimensions and population subgroups that are the prime contributors to deprivation and need to be targeted in policy interventions. Though the terms 'poverty' and 'deprivation' are used interchangeably in the recent literature on multidimensional deprivation, the former refers to households that are identified as 'poor' based on a poverty line cut-off, similar in spirit to the traditional poverty concept but based on multiple dimensions, while the latter refers to the deprivation faced by the entire population. Alkire and Foster (2011), Alkire and Santos (2010), are examples of the former, while Chakravarty and D'Ambrosio (2006) and Jayaraj and Subramanian (2010) are examples of the latter. In the following discussion, we will refer to the former as 'multidimensional poverty' (MDP) and the latter as 'multidimensional deprivation' (MDD). The rest of the chapter is organised as follows. The basic framework of multidimensional deprivation is described and contrasted with that of multidimensional poverty in the next Sect. 10.2. The next two Sects. 10.3 and 10.4 report in detail the data sets and evidence from the studies mentioned above. The chapter concludes with a few summary remarks in Sect. 10.5.

10.2 Measuring Multidimensional Deprivation (MDD) and Multidimensional Poverty (MDP), the Contrasting Approaches

Though MDD and MDP are used synonymously in recent literature, the former is a measure of the dimensions failure of all households, while the latter measures the deprivation of only a subset of households defined as the 'poor'. While measurement of MDD requires only a dimension-specific cut-off that defines deprivation in that dimension, i.e. a 'dimension failure', MDP requires an additional cut-off in terms of the minimum number of 'dimension failures' that defines a 'poor' household. The dependence of MDP measure on two a priori specified cut-offs increases its subjectivity over MDD. The poverty line cut-off exposes the MDP measure to controversy over what that poverty line should be that has characterised the conventional unidimensional poverty measures. This can be a significant issue in international comparisons since what is a reasonable cut-off in one society may not be so in another. MDD avoids this since it does not require an arbitrary definition of a 'poor' household. Both measures encompass the 'union' (i.e. deprivation failure in one or more dimensions) and 'intersection' (i.e. deprivation in all dimensions) measures as limiting cases. The principal advantage of MDP over MDD is that it is decomposable in not only population subgroups, but also in dimensions. In other words, MDP allows not only the identification of subgroups that require targeted intervention (that MDD does as well), it also allows the identification of dimensions that are the prime contributors of deprivation (that MDD does not allow except in the union case).

Following the notation used by Jayaraj and Subramanian (2010), let n_j denote the number of households that are deprived in exactly j dimensions, $j \in \{0, 1, \ldots, K\}$ where the total number of households be denoted by n. Then, three possible headcount rates of deprivation are,

$$H^I = \frac{n_K}{n} \tag{10.1}$$

$$H^U = \frac{(n_1 + n_2 + \cdots + n_K)}{n} = \sum_{j=1}^{K} H_j \tag{10.2}$$

$$H_{j^*} = \frac{(n_{j^*} + \cdots + n_K)}{n} = \sum_{j=j^*}^{K} H_j \tag{10.3}$$

where $H_j = \frac{n_j}{n}, j \in \{1, \ldots, K\}$ and H^I, H^U and H_{j^*} are headcount rates of MDD. While H^I, the 'intersection method', denotes headcount deprivation rates of households who are derived in all the K dimensions; H^U, the 'union method' denotes the corresponding headcount rates of households that are deprived in at least one dimension. While H^I understates the magnitude of deprivation, H^U overstates it. Alternatively, H^I measures the magnitude of extreme deprivation, while H^U measures the aggregate of mild, moderate and extreme deprivation. A compromise is H_{j^*}, which lies between H^I and H^U, where j^* is specified a priori. It approaches the former when j^* moves towards K and approaches the latter when j^* moves towards 1. The MDD measure, as formulated by Jayaraj and Subramanian (2010), is defined as,

$$\pi_\alpha = \sum_{j=1}^{K} \left(\frac{j}{K}\right)^{\alpha} H_j, \quad \alpha \geq 0 \tag{10.4}$$

The parameter α in the above equation performs a role analogous to that of the α in case of the Atkinson (1970) and Foster, Greer and Thorbecke (1984) measures. As α increases from 1 to higher values, π_α gives greater weight to the deprivation rates of households that are deprived in more and more dimensions and, at very high α values, it measures the magnitude of extreme deprivation. At $\alpha = 0$, π_α coincides with the union measure, H^U. As $\alpha \to \infty$, π_α approaches the intersection measure, H^I. The MDP measure can be briefly described as follows. Let z_c denote the cut-off in a dimension that defines a household's deprivation in that dimension. Let k denote the minimum number of dimensions in which a household must be deprived in order to be classified as 'poor'. Let q denote the number of multidimensionally poor households, and let $c_i (i = 1, \ldots, q)$ denote the number of dimensions that 'poor' household i is deprived in. The MDP measure, M_0, which has been used in the HDR, 2010 (UNDP 2010) is a special case of the M_α class introduced by Alkire and Foster (2011) and is given by,

$$M_0(k) = \left(\frac{q}{n}\right) \left(\sum_{i=1}^{q} \frac{c_i}{qK}\right) \tag{10.5}$$

where k is the total number of dimensions. M_0 is the product of two components, namely $H = \frac{q}{n}$, which measures the proportion of people who are multidimensionally poor, and $A = \sum \frac{c_i}{qK}$, which measures the 'intensity of poverty'. The latter reflects the proportion of the weighted deprivation indicators, K, in which, on average, the poor households are deprived. M_0 can also be written as $\sum \left(\frac{c_i}{nK}\right)$, which measures the total number of deprivations experienced by the poor households divided by the maximum number of deprivations possible (i.e. if each of the poor households was deprived in every dimension). The two measures π_α and $M_0(k)$ will coincide if $\alpha = 1$ for the former, and $k = 1$ for the latter, i.e. $\pi_1 = M_0(1)$. In this case, both indices will measure 'the ratio of the number of instances of deprivation that actually obtains to the maximum possible number of such instances' (Jayaraj and Subramanian 2010, p. 56).

10.3 Multidimensional Deprivation in India During and After the Reforms

In this section, we describe the study by Mishra and Ray (2013). The chief motivation of this study is to examine the magnitude of social exclusion or deprivation in India and its changes during and after the reforms using composite multidimensional indices that consider a wider range of deprivation dimensions that have been considered previously. The welfare comparisons are carried out at the State level with rural and urban areas distinguished in the comparisons. The study pays special attention to the backward classes. It extends the recent multidimensional study on India by Jayaraj and Subramianan (2010) considering a wider range of welfare indicators and, most notably, includes mothers' and child health in the analysis. Almost uniquely, India now offers two parallel large-scale data sets that contain household-level information in unit record form that allow calculation and comparison of the deprivation measures between the data sets. A feature of this study is that it examines the robustness of the evidence on deprivation by comparing the results from successive rounds of two large-scale surveys, namely the well-established and widely used National Sample Surveys (NSS) and the more recent National Family Health Surveys (NFHS) which, quite conveniently for us, cover (near) identical years and span virtually the same overall time period. The study was conducted both at the aggregate country level of all India and at the level of the constituent States.

If we introduce superscript h to the MDD measure given by Eq. 10.4 to denote State 'h', so that π_α^h is the deprivation measure of State 'h', then

$$\pi_\alpha^h = \sum_{j=1}^{K} (j/K)^\alpha H_j^h \tag{10.6}$$

The ratio $\delta^h = \frac{\pi_\alpha^h}{\pi_\alpha}$ measures the percentage contribution of the State h to overall deprivation of the country as a whole. If we deflate the δ^h by the population share, s^h, of State 'h', i.e. define $\eta^h = \delta^h / s^h$, then $\eta^h > 1$ suggests that State 'h' is more deprived than the region/country as whole, and less deprived if $\eta^h < 1$. Note that, in the context of this study, 'h' can also refer to members of the scheduled classes/tribes (SC/ST), so that η^h will be used as a convenient measure to assess if the SC/ST households are more deprived or less deprived than the others.

10.3.1 Data Sets

Mishra and Ray (2013) are based on two of the largest data sets available anywhere, namely the National Sample Survey (NSS) and the National Family Health Survey (NFHS) in India. The NSS data set, which has a longer history of collection and usage, combines detailed quantitative information at the household level on expenditure on various items with qualitative information on the socio-economic class of the household, the household's access to basic utilities such as clean Fuel for cooking, electricity. This study is based on the unit records from the Consumer Expenditure Surveys (CES) carried out in the 50th (July 1993–June 1994), 55th (July 1999–June 2000), 61st rounds (July 2004–June 2005) of the NSS. Apart from the fact that this covers the period of economic reforms in India, the information is available at household and at State level allowing a decomposition of the all-India deprivation between States, and between the SC/ST and the other socio-economic groups. This study considers the following five deprivation dimensions in the NSS: energy for clean Fuel, electricity for lighting, education of head of household head, Food expenditure and clothing expenditure. While the first two use qualitative information on whether the household has access or not to that utility, we defined a household to be deprived on the last three dimensions if (a) the household head has not obtained primary education, (b) if the household's spending on Food, clothing is less than half the corresponding median value spending in that State sample.

The second data set used here is the National Family Health Surveys (NFHS). The NFHS[1] is a large-scale, multiround survey conducted in a representative sample of households throughout India. So far, three rounds of NFHS, namely NFHS 1 and NFHS 3 have been completed and this study is based on all three of them. The NFHS 1, which was conducted in 1992–93, collected extensive information on population, health, and nutrition, with an emphasis on women and young children. NFHS 2 was conducted in 1998–99 in all 26 States of India with added features on the quality of health and family planning services, reproductive health, anaemia, the nutrition of women and status of women.

NFHS 3 was carried out in 2005–06 with added information on the body mass index (BMI) status of the mother of the children. Information on the following deprivation dimensions is available in all the NFHS rounds: Access to drinking water, electricity, clean Fuel for cooking, 'pucca' house, toilet facility, bicycle, radio, education of the household head, whether the household belongs to the poorest wealth quintile, and the child's long- and short-term health status (i.e. stunted or not, wasted or not). NFHS 2 contains additional information on the mother's BMI status, while NFHS 3 contains information on the child's anaemic status. Consistent with our earlier treatment in the NSS, a household is considered educationally deprived if the household head did not receive primary education. Unlike the NSS, the NFHS has the additional complication in that while the information on the non-health deprivation dimensions is at the household level, the health

[1]See the NFHS website, www.nfhsindia.org for further details.

information is available at the individual level. To translate the individual level information to the household level, we adopted the following definition of household-level health deprivation. A household was considered deprived on account of the long- and short-run health of its children if 60% or more of its children (0–3 years) are 'stunted' and 'wasted',[2] respectively. Exploiting the information in NFHS 3, this was extended to the child's anaemic status, and a household was considered deprived if 60% or more of its children in age group of 0–3 years suffered from severe anaemia. If the mother's BMI was outside the range 18.5 and 30, the household was considered deprived on account of the mother's health.

10.3.2 Results

The dimension-specific headcount rates of deprivation using Eqs. 10.1 and 10.2 (with $\alpha = 1$) in the three NSS rounds, 50, 55 and 61 are presented for rural and urban areas in Tables 10.1 and 10.2, respectively. The corresponding deprivation rates for NFHS 1 and NFHS 3 are presented in Tables 10.3 and 10.4 for rural areas and Tables 10.5 and 10.6 in urban areas, respectively. The overall picture is one of declining headcount rates over the chosen period across all States, in both rural and urban areas, for both household groups, and in case of both data sets. The rural areas record higher headcount rates than the urban in case of both data sets, with the NSS-based evidence suggesting that energy for clean Fuel and education of the household head lead the expenditure dimensions in the deprivation rates. The NFHS-based results also show wide variation between dimensions on the head-count rates with access to drinking water, clean Fuel, 'pucca house' and toilet facility among those with the highest rates of deprivation. Stunted children lead on deprivation magnitude among the health variables. Though there has been an all-round decline in the deprivation rates, the progress has been quite uneven between the dimensions, and between the States, with stunting of very young children (0–3 years) being one where the progress has been the least. While such declines in deprivation magnitudes are not surprising in the context of overall progress during the 1990s and the early part of the new millennium, the NSS 61st round and NFHS 3 evidence suggest that there is still considerable deprivation in some of the dimensions even at the end of our chosen period. Another result that holds generally is the higher rate of deprivation faced by the SC/ST households though, more in case of some dimensions, less for others. It is significant that SC/ST households record larger health deprivation than the others, with the gap being particularly large in case of stunting, less on account of wasting or the mother's BMI.

---

[2]A child (0–3 years) is considered 'stunted' or 'wasted' if that child's z score of height for age and of weight for height is less than 2, respectively. This is consistent with the definition of child malnourishment adopted in the literature [see, for example, Svedberg (1990)],

Table 10.1 Dimension-specific headcount rates for rural areas (Mishra and Ray 2013)

States								Headcount ratio in deprivation dimension							
				50th round NSS				55th round NSS				61st round NSS			
	Clean Fuel for cooking	Electricity for lighting	Education of head of household head[a]	Food expen-diture[b]	Clothing expen-diture[b,c]	Clean Fuel	Electricity for lighting	Education of head of household head[a]	Food expen-diture[b]	Clothing expen-diture[b,c]	Clean Fuel	Electricity for lighting	Education of head of household head[a]	Food expen-diture[b]	Clothing expen-diture[b,c]
Andhra Pradesh	0.93	0.44	0.74	0.03	0.20	0.88	0.31	0.75	0.02	0.13	0.79	0.15	0.62	0.04	0.14
Assam[d]	0.97	0.67	0.55	0.02	0.15	0.93	0.63	0.57	0.03	0.13	0.89	0.41	0.38	0.01	0.11
Bihar[d]	0.94	0.92	0.70	0.03	0.15	0.92	0.93	0.70	0.01	0.11	0.90	0.82	0.54	0.02	0.08
Gujarat	0.89	0.30	0.64	0.05	0.13	0.82	0.19	0.61	0.02	0.11	0.75	0.16	0.44	0.04	0.08
Jammu & Kashmir	0.89	0.19	0.64	0.02	0.09	0.69	0.03	0.50	0.01	0.13	0.82	0.02	0.54	0.01	0.06
Karnataka	0.95	0.40	0.69	0.05	0.15	0.88	0.23	0.63	0.04	0.12	0.89	0.12	0.54	0.02	0.07
Kerala	0.91	0.38	0.35	0.06	0.23	0.83	0.30	0.39	0.04	0.15	0.78	0.18	0.27	0.06	0.13
Madhya Pradesh[d]	0.99	0.51	0.75	0.05	0.14	0.96	0.34	0.69	0.03	0.10	0.94	0.29	0.53	0.03	0.11
Maharashtra	0.79	0.37	0.57	0.07	0.12	0.74	0.24	0.51	0.02	0.11	0.73	0.19	0.38	0.04	0.08
Orissa	0.95	0.79	0.75	0.03	0.16	0.96	0.75	0.71	0.03	0.14	0.88	0.60	0.57	0.04	0.11
Punjab[d]	0.88	0.12	0.62	0.04	0.18	0.72	0.08	0.54	0.02	0.12	0.73	0.05	0.45	0.03	0.08
Rajasthan	0.96	0.55	0.75	0.05	0.11	0.94	0.48	0.68	0.01	0.08	0.93	0.49	0.62	0.03	0.06
Tamil Nadu	0.93	0.41	0.61	0.05	0.16	0.84	0.24	0.58	0.05	0.13	0.78	0.13	0.45	0.04	0.09
Uttar Pradesh[d]	0.96	0.78	0.68	0.05	0.15	0.91	0.73	0.60	0.02	0.10	0.90	0.65	0.52	0.03	0.09
West Bengal	0.79	0.84	0.59	0.02	0.13	0.90	0.74	0.57	0.03	0.10	0.80	0.60	0.49	0.02	0.10
C.V.[e]	0.07	0.47	0.16	0.38	0.23	0.10	0.67	0.16	0.41	0.16	0.09	0.78	0.20	0.45	0.25
All India	0.92	0.57	0.64	0.04	0.15	0.87	0.47	0.61	0.02	0.12	0.83	0.36	0.48	0.03	0.10
SC/ST	0.95	0.71	0.77	0.07	0.21	0.94	0.61	0.74	0.04	0.16	0.91	0.47	0.59	0.05	0.14
Non-SC/ST	0.91	0.51	0.59	0.03	0.13	0.85	0.41	0.56	0.02	0.09	0.80	0.31	0.43	0.02	0.08

[a]If the education of the head of the household is below primary, he is considered to be deprived
[b]For Food, Clothing and transport export expenditure, the threshold for being deprived is half of the median expenditure per capita on the respective category for that State
[c]For Food expenditure, recall period is 30 days while for Clothing expenditure, it is 365 days
[d]Assam includes Manipur, Meghalaya and Tripura; Punjab includes Haryana, Himachal Pradesh and Delhi; Uttar Pradesh, Madhya Pradesh and Bihar include Uttaranchal, Chhattisgarh and Jharkhand since their inception (here only for 61st round)
[e]Coefficient of variation

Table 10.2 Dimension-specific headcount rates for urban areas (Mishra and Ray 2013)

States															
								Headcount ratio in deprivation dimension							
				50th round NSS				55th round NSS				61st round NSS			
	Clean Fuel for cooking	Electricity for lighting	Education of head of household head[a]	Food expen-diture[b]	Clothing expen-diture[b,c]	Clean Fuel	Electricity for lighting	Education of head of household head[a]	Food expen-diture[b]	Clothing expen-diture[b,c]	Clean Fuel	Electricity for lighting	Education of head of household head[a]	Food expen-diture[b]	Clothing expen-diture[b,c]
Andhra Pradesh	0.43	0.15	0.41	0.05	0.21	0.28	0.08	0.35	0.03	0.16	0.37	0.07	0.39	0.04	0.18
Assam[d]	0.59	0.18	0.23	0.02	0.21	0.38	0.13	0.24	0.02	0.19	0.41	0.10	0.22	0.01	0.17
Bihar[d]	0.70	0.33	0.38	0.04	0.17	0.59	0.29	0.36	0.03	0.17	0.56	0.30	0.33	0.04	0.15
Gujarat	0.22	0.10	0.33	0.05	0.17	0.17	0.06	0.29	0.02	0.12	0.22	0.06	0.25	0.03	0.12
Jammu & Kashmir	0.19	0.01	0.23	0.02	0.19	0.13	0.02	0.27	0.00	0.12	0.21	0.01	0.30	0.02	0.09
Karnataka	0.42	0.15	0.33	0.07	0.19	0.32	0.09	0.29	0.05	0.15	0.38	0.06	0.28	0.05	0.12
Kerala	0.74	0.21	0.29	0.06	0.23	0.58	0.11	0.23	0.05	0.16	0.59	0.09	0.23	0.09	0.13
Madhya Pradesh[d]	0.49	0.12	0.35	0.05	0.16	0.41	0.06	0.35	0.04	0.10	0.49	0.07	0.33	0.04	0.12
Maharashtra	0.20	0.08	0.24	0.11	0.16	0.17	0.04	0.23	0.06	0.13	0.22	0.05	0.20	0.09	0.11
Orissa	0.62	0.28	0.37	0.06	0.18	0.53	0.27	0.38	0.04	0.16	0.57	0.23	0.37	0.04	0.14
Punjab[d]	0.22	0.04	0.28	0.07	0.18	0.15	0.03	0.28	0.04	0.15	0.17	0.03	0.25	0.05	0.13
Rajasthan	0.43	0.10	0.38	0.06	0.16	0.32	0.07	0.32	0.02	0.13	0.44	0.09	0.33	0.03	0.07
Tamil Nadu	0.50	0.18	0.35	0.06	0.18	0.29	0.08	0.28	0.07	0.16	0.31	0.06	0.27	0.06	0.13
Uttar Pradesh[d]	0.50	0.23	0.41	0.05	0.16	0.43	0.18	0.40	0.04	0.13	0.44	0.20	0.36	0.05	0.13
West Bengal	0.47	0.26	0.33	0.05	0.17	0.43	0.18	0.32	0.03	0.15	0.43	0.16	0.29	0.04	0.13
C.V.[e]	0.40	0.56	0.19	0.38	0.11	0.44	0.74	0.18	0.49	0.15	0.35	0.79	0.20	0.48	0.22
All India	0.43	0.15	0.32	0.06	0.18	0.32	0.10	0.30	0.04	0.14	0.35	0.09	0.28	0.05	0.13
SC/ST	0.62	0.30	0.51	0.12	0.27	0.52	0.21	0.49	0.07	0.23	0.53	0.18	0.42	0.08	0.18
Non-SC/ST	0.40	0.13	0.29	0.05	0.16	0.18	0.08	0.26	0.03	0.13	0.32	0.08	0.24	0.04	0.12

[a] If the education of the head of the household is below primary, he is considered to be deprived
[b] For Food, clothing and transport export expenditure, the threshold for being deprived is half of the median expenditure per capita on the respective category for that State
[c] For Food expenditure, recall period is 30 days while for Clothing expenditure, it is 365 days
[d] Assam includes Manipur, Meghalaya and Tripura; Punjab includes Haryana, Himachal Pradesh and Delhi; Uttar Pradesh, Madhya Pradesh and Bihar include Uttaranchal, Chhattisgarh and Jharkhand since their inception (here only for 61st round)
[e] Coefficient of variation

Table 10.3 Dimension-specific headcount rates for rural areas NFHS 1 (Mishra and Ray 2013)

States	Headcount ratio in deprivation dimension												
	Access to source of drinking water on its premises	Access to electricity for lighting	Access to clean Fuel for cooking	Access to 'Pucca' house	Access to toilet facility	Education of the head of the household head[a]	Access to bicycle	Access to radio	Belongs to poorest wealth quintile	Share of stunted children[b]	Share of wasted children[b]	BMI of the mother[c]	Share of anaemic children[b]
Andhra Pradesh	0.88	0.46	0.95	0.81	0.92	0.62	0.71	0.65	0.17	NA	NA	NA	NA
Assam[d]	0.72	0.72	0.95	0.99	0.45	0.42	0.65	0.70	0.22	0.45	0.12	NA	NA
Bihar[d]	0.62	0.93	0.99	0.93	0.92	0.61	0.66	0.79	0.37	0.58	0.18	NA	NA
Gujarat	0.62	0.30	0.82	0.81	0.83	0.44	0.68	0.69	0.16	0.44	0.18	NA	NA
Jammu & Kashmir	0.68	0.16	0.84	0.78	0.94	0.52	0.78	0.41	0.10	0.37	0.12	NA	NA
Karnataka	0.84	0.47	0.95	0.95	0.91	0.54	0.73	0.57	0.17	0.44	0.14	NA	NA
Kerala	0.38	0.46	0.94	0.84	0.34	0.18	0.79	0.42	0.02	0.25	0.11	NA	NA
Madhya Pradesh[d]	0.87	0.47	0.98	0.97	0.95	0.58	0.58	0.77	0.32	NA	NA	NA	NA
Maharashtra	0.74	0.37	0.89	0.93	0.90	0.45	0.66	0.68	0.19	0.47	0.18	NA	NA
Orissa	0.86	0.80	0.98	0.95	0.95	0.52	0.54	0.73	0.34	0.47	0.20	NA	NA
Punjab[d]	0.57	0.12	0.89	0.70	0.86	0.52	0.53	0.54	0.03	0.37	0.11	NA	NA
Rajasthan	0.80	0.58	0.98	0.75	0.93	0.65	0.72	0.75	0.36	0.39	0.16	NA	NA
Tamil Nadu	0.82	0.45	0.94	0.86	0.92	0.42	0.65	0.65	0.11	NA	NA	NA	NA
Uttar Pradesh[d]	0.57	0.80	0.99	0.92	0.93	0.55	0.46	0.72	0.37	0.57	0.14	NA	NA

(continued)

Table 10.3 (continued)

States	Headcount ratio in deprivation dimension											
	Access to source of drinking water on its premises	Access to electricity for lighting	Access to clean Fuel for cooking	Access to 'Pucca' house	Access to toilet facility	Education of the head of the household head[a]	Access to bicycle	Access to radio	Belongs to poorest wealth quintile	Share of stunted children[b]	Share of wasted children[b]	BMI of the mother[c]	Share of anaemic children[b]
West Bengal	0.77	0.86	0.99	0.90	0.81	0.46	0.52	0.63	0.37	NA	NA	NA	NA
C.V.[e]	0.20	0.47	0.06	0.10	0.22	0.23	0.16	0.18	0.58	0.21	0.22	NA	NA
All India	0.70	0.55	0.95	0.87	0.84	0.51	0.62	0.66	0.23	0.47	0.15	NA	NA
SC/ST	NA	NA	NA	NA	NA	NA	NA	NA	NA	NA	NA	NA	NA
Non-SC/ST	NA	NA	NA	NA	NA	NA	NA	NA	NA	NA	NA	NA	NA

[a]If the education of the head of the household is below primary, he is considered to be deprived

[b]For share of stunted, wasted and anaemic children in a household, the threshold for being deprived is 60% or more of the total children in the household. It has to be noted that for calculating 'share of anaemic children', only children suffering from severe anaemia are considered to be deprived

[c]If the BMI of the mother is less than 18.5 and more than 30, she is considered to be deprived

[d]Assam includes Manipur, Meghalaya and Tripura; Punjab includes Haryana, Himachal Pradesh and Delhi; Uttar Pradesh, Madhya Pradesh and Bihar include Uttaranchal, Chhattisgarh and Jharkhand since their inception (here only for NFHS 3)

[e]Coefficient of variation

Table 10.4 Dimension-specific headcount rates for rural areas NFHS 3 (Mishra and Ray 2013)

States	Headcount ratio in deprivation dimension											
	Access to source of drinking water on its premises	Access to electricity for lighting	Access to clean Fuel for cooking	Access to 'Pucca' house	Access to toilet facility	Education of the head of the household head[a]	Access to bicycle	Access to radio	Belongs to poorest wealth quintile	Share of stunted children[b]	Share of wasted children[b]	BMI of the mother[c]	Share of anaemic children[b]
Andhra Pradesh	0.81	0.15	0.83	0.55	0.73	0.53	0.55	0.85	0.16	0.38	0.09	0.47	0.02
Assam[d]	0.95	0.43	0.84	0.88	0.19	0.33	0.49	0.62	0.15	0.33	0.13	0.28	0.01
Bihar[d]	1.00	0.81	0.97	0.88	0.84	0.60	0.47	0.71	0.35	0.44	0.18	0.46	0.01
Gujarat	0.53	0.17	0.78	0.51	0.70	0.37	0.49	0.76	0.12	0.42	0.14	0.49	0.03
Jammu & Kashmir	0.70	0.10	0.80	0.60	0.49	0.44	0.80	0.35	0.04	0.26	0.11	0.32	0.02
Karnataka	0.84	0.16	0.89	0.62	0.78	0.50	0.61	0.71	0.17	0.37	0.14	0.42	0.02
Kerala	0.93	0.11	0.79	0.17	0.05	0.12	0.63	0.48	0.02	0.17	0.13	0.18	0.00
Madhya Pradesh[d]	0.97	0.36	0.97	0.91	0.92	0.49	0.44	0.82	0.52	0.42	0.20	0.46	0.02
Maharashtra	0.63	0.29	0.81	0.69	0.80	0.34	0.55	0.75	0.22	0.38	0.11	0.46	0.02
Orissa	1.00	0.62	0.97	0.74	0.89	0.43	0.37	0.80	0.48	0.36	0.13	0.45	0.01
Punjab[d]	0.65	0.06	0.81	0.49	0.55	0.39	0.45	0.64	0.03	0.29	0.10	0.32	0.02
Rajasthan	0.86	0.46	0.97	0.65	0.92	0.55	0.60	0.80	0.35	0.36	0.14	0.37	0.05
Tamil Nadu	0.85	0.16	0.83	0.40	0.83	0.37	0.50	0.66	0.19	0.22	0.17	0.35	0.02
Uttar Pradesh[d]	0.99	0.72	0.96	0.87	0.84	0.50	0.24	0.69	0.36	0.46	0.08	0.38	0.02

(continued)

Table 10.4 (continued)

States	Headcount ratio in deprivation dimension											
	Access to source of drinking water on its premises	Access to electricity for lighting	Access to clean Fuel for cooking	Access to 'Pucca' house	Access to toilet facility	Education of the head of the household head[a]	Access to bicycle	Access to radio	Belongs to poorest wealth quintile	Share of stunted children[b]	Share of wasted children[b]	BMI of the mother[c]	Share of anaemic children[b]
West Bengal	0.99	0.65	0.97	0.81	0.55	0.45	0.35	0.70	0.36	0.34	0.13	0.48	0.01
C.V.[e]	0.18	0.72	0.09	0.32	0.39	0.28	0.27	0.19	0.69	0.23	0.25	0.23	0.58
All India	0.86	0.36	0.88	0.69	0.66	0.43	0.47	0.69	0.24	0.36	0.13	0.39	0.02
SC/ST	0.90	0.45	0.94	0.79	0.76	0.52	0.55	0.77	0.36	0.41	0.15	0.42	0.02
Non-SC/ST	0.84	0.32	0.86	0.63	0.61	0.38	0.44	0.66	0.18	0.34	0.12	0.37	0.02

[a]If the education of the head of the household is below primary, he is considered to be deprived

[b]For share of stunted, wasted and anaemic children in a household, the threshold for being deprived is 60% or more of the total children in the household. It has to be noted that for calculating 'share of anaemic children', only children suffering from severe anaemia are considered to be deprived

[c]If the BMI of the mother is less than 18.5 and more than 30, she is considered to be deprived

[d]Assam includes Manipur, Meghalaya and Tripura; Punjab includes Haryana, Himachal Pradesh and Delhi; Uttar Pradesh, Madhya Pradesh and Bihar include Uttaranchal, Chhattisgarh and Jharkhand since their inception (here only for NFHS 3)

[e]Coefficient of variation

Table 10.5 Dimension-specific headcount rates for urban areas NFHS 1 (Mishra and Ray 2013)

States	Headcount ratio in deprivation dimension												
	Access to source of drinking water on its premises	Access to electricity for lighting	Access to clean Fuel for cooking	Access to 'Pucca' house	Access to toilet facility	Education of the head of the household head[a]	Access to bicycle	Access to radio	Belongs to poorest wealth quintile	Share of stunted children[b]	Share of wasted children[b]	BMI of the mother[c]	Share of anaemic children[b]
Andhra Pradesh	0.51	0.15	0.37	0.35	0.30	0.25	0.44	0.35	0.01	NA	NA	NA	NA
Assam[d]	0.40	0.27	0.55	0.88	0.06	0.19	0.45	0.43	0.02	0.31	0.07	NA	NA
Bihar[d]	0.36	0.34	0.65	0.43	0.35	0.26	0.40	0.45	0.05	0.49	0.18	NA	NA
Gujarat	0.32	0.12	0.28	0.41	0.29	0.23	0.42	0.41	0.00	0.39	0.14	NA	NA
Jammu & Kashmir	0.18	0.00	0.16	0.21	0.23	0.22	0.60	0.21	0.00	0.27	0.09	NA	NA
Karnataka	0.45	0.15	0.41	0.62	0.26	0.24	0.49	0.31	0.02	0.35	0.14	NA	NA
Kerala	0.34	0.24	0.75	0.69	0.16	0.15	0.64	0.35	0.00	0.18	0.09	NA	NA
Madhya Pradesh[d]	0.39	0.10	0.46	0.51	0.25	0.22	0.31	0.42	0.01	NA	NA	NA	NA
Maharashtra	0.33	0.13	0.17	0.39	0.18	0.18	0.58	0.42	0.01	0.34	0.13	NA	NA
Orissa	0.59	0.31	0.68	0.68	0.50	0.25	0.31	0.45	0.03	0.30	0.14	NA	NA
Punjab[d]	0.21	0.04	0.18	0.22	0.19	0.21	0.42	0.33	0.00	0.37	0.09	NA	NA
Rajasthan	0.27	0.13	0.48	0.16	0.34	0.31	0.48	0.41	0.03	0.40	0.26	NA	NA
Tamil Nadu	0.55	0.19	0.48	0.59	0.30	0.18	0.51	0.38	0.01	NA	NA	NA	NA
Uttar Pradesh[d]	0.18	0.19	0.47	0.33	0.20	0.28	0.35	0.45	0.02	0.49	0.12	NA	NA

(continued)

Table 10.5 (continued)

States	Headcount ratio in deprivation dimension												
	Access to source of drinking water on its premises	Access to electricity for lighting	Access to clean Fuel for cooking	Access to 'Pucca' house	Access to toilet facility	Education of the head of the household head[a]	Access to bicycle	Access to radio	Belongs to poorest wealth quintile	Share of stunted children[b]	Share of wasted children[b]	BMI of the mother[c]	Share of anaemic children[b]
West Bengal	0.60	0.29	0.60	0.49	0.17	0.24	0.51	0.45	0.04	NA	NA	NA	NA
C.V.[e]	0.37	0.56	0.42	0.44	0.41	0.18	0.22	0.18	0.92	0.26	0.39	NA	NA
All India	0.34	0.15	0.39	0.43	0.23	0.22	0.45	0.38	0.01	0.37	0.12	NA	NA
SC/ST	NA	NA	NA	NA	NA	NA	NA	NA	NA	NA	NA	NA	NA
Non-SC/ST	NA	NA	NA	NA	NA	NA	NA	NA	NA	NA	NA	NA	NA

[a]If the education of the head of the household is below primary, he is considered to be deprived

[b]For share of stunted, wasted and anaemic children in a household, the threshold for being deprived is 60% or more of the total children in the household. It has to be noted that for calculating 'share of anaemic children', only children suffering from severe anaemia are considered to be deprived

[c]If the BMI of the mother is less than 18.5 and more than 30, she is considered to be deprived

[d]Assam includes Manipur, Meghalaya and Tripura; Punjab includes Haryana, Himachal Pradesh and Delhi; Uttar Pradesh, Madhya Pradesh and Bihar include Uttaranchal, Chhattisgarh and Jharkhand since their inception (here only for NFHS 3)

[e]Coefficient of variation

Table 10.6 Dimension-specific headcount rates for urban areas NFHS 3 (Mishra and Ray 2013)

States	Headcount ratio in deprivation dimension												
	Access to source of drinking water on its premises	Access to electricity for lighting	Access to clean Fuel for cooking	Access to 'Pucca' house	Access to toilet facility	Education of the head of the household head[a]	Access to bicycle	Access to radio	Belongs to poorest wealth quintile	Share of stunted children[b]	Share of wasted children[b]	BMI of the mother[c]	Share of anaemic children[b]
Andhra Pradesh	0.27	0.03	0.17	0.11	0.10	0.26	0.42	0.76	0.02	0.24	0.07	0.26	0.02
Assam[d]	0.68	0.11	0.35	0.61	0.01	0.16	0.41	0.52	0.02	0.25	0.11	0.21	0.01
Bihar[d]	0.88	0.26	0.50	0.38	0.27	0.33	0.37	0.62	0.10	0.34	0.20	0.33	0.02
Gujarat	0.17	0.03	0.20	0.07	0.12	0.15	0.27	0.62	0.01	0.36	0.12	0.29	0.02
Jammu & Kashmir	0.17	0.01	0.15	0.19	0.14	0.27	0.50	0.30	0.00	0.20	0.08	0.17	0.02
Karnataka	0.60	0.04	0.28	0.19	0.17	0.21	0.47	0.59	0.03	0.28	0.13	0.30	0.02
Kerala	0.75	0.06	0.58	0.08	0.02	0.10	0.45	0.47	0.01	0.15	0.08	0.14	0.00
Madhya Pradesh[d]	0.55	0.04	0.27	0.23	0.19	0.16	0.21	0.60	0.03	0.28	0.22	0.34	0.02
Maharashtra	0.20	0.03	0.14	0.12	0.08	0.14	0.43	0.56	0.01	0.29	0.11	0.33	0.01
Orissa	0.70	0.16	0.52	0.35	0.41	0.18	0.20	0.71	0.13	0.28	0.10	0.29	0.02
Punjab[d]	0.28	0.01	0.13	0.08	0.09	0.18	0.42	0.55	0.00	0.27	0.11	0.24	0.02
Rajasthan	0.19	0.04	0.30	0.12	0.15	0.19	0.29	0.63	0.01	0.24	0.19	0.39	0.03
Tamil Nadu	0.56	0.05	0.20	0.15	0.13	0.17	0.39	0.54	0.02	0.20	0.17	0.26	0.02
Uttar Pradesh[d]	0.57	0.11	0.36	0.20	0.13	0.27	0.23	0.58	0.03	0.37	0.06	0.29	0.02

(continued)

Table 10.6 (continued)

States	Headcount ratio in deprivation dimension												
	Access to source of drinking water on its premises	Access to electricity for lighting	Access to clean Fuel for cooking	Access to 'Pucca' house	Access to toilet facility	Education of the head of the household head[a]	Access to bicycle	Access to radio	Belongs to poorest wealth quintile	Share of stunted children[b]	Share of wasted children[b]	BMI of the mother[c]	Share of anaemic children[b]
West Bengal	0.59	0.06	0.28	0.10	0.04	0.21	0.48	0.51	0.01	0.20	0.11	0.29	0.01
C.V.[e]	0.50	0.98	0.49	0.75	0.74	0.30	0.28	0.18	1.25	0.23	0.40	0.24	0.44
All India	0.45	0.06	0.25	0.19	0.11	0.19	0.37	0.58	0.02	0.28	0.12	0.28	0.02
SC/ST	0.56	0.10	0.38	0.31	0.21	0.28	0.45	0.65	0.05	0.35	0.14	0.31	0.03
Non-SC/ST	0.42	0.05	0.22	0.16	0.09	0.17	0.36	0.56	0.02	0.25	0.12	0.27	0.01

[a]If the education of the head of the household is below primary, he is considered to be deprived

[b]For share of stunted, wasted and anaemic children in a household, the threshold for being deprived is 60% or more of the total children in the household. It has to be noted that for calculating 'share of anaemic children', only children suffering from severe anaemia are considered to be deprived

[c] If the BMI of the mother is less than 18.5 and more than 30, she is considered to be deprived

[d]Assam includes Manipur, Meghalaya and Tripura; Punjab includes Haryana, Himachal Pradesh and Delhi; Uttar Pradesh, Madhya Pradesh and Bihar include Uttaranchal, Chhattisgarh and Jharkhand since their inception (here only for NFHS 3)

[e]Coefficient of variation

The estimates of multidimensional deprivation, both Statewise and for all India calculated using the measure given by Eq. 10.6 at various values of α, are presented in Tables 10.7 and 10.8 for NSS rural, urban, respectively, and in Tables 10.9 and 10.10 for NFHS rural, urban, respectively. These tables also report, in parenthesis, the percentage contribution of a State to all-India deprivation exploiting the decomposable property of the multidimensional deprivation measure that is used here. The Statewise figures do not differ from one another all that much at low values of α, but they do vary widely as we consider higher values of α, i.e., the more deprived households. The Statewise rankings implied by the values of π are in line with expectations, for example, the poorer States of Bihar and Uttar Pradesh record much higher levels of deprivation at high α values than the richer States of Gujarat and Punjab. This is true of both data sets, and for all the three rounds considered for each survey. Consistent with the results on the dimension-specific headcount rates presented earlier, these tables provide robust evidence that there has been a general decline in deprivation in India during the reforms and the post-reforms period. Note, however, from the all-India figures that the urban areas did not experience much of a decline in deprivation during the post-reforms period. In fact, both the NSS and the NFHS provide robust evidence that there has been either no change or a small increase in urban deprivation during the second half of our sample period.

This is consistent with the earlier finding (Ray and Mishra 2012), based on unidimensional expenditure measures using the NSS, that the welfare gain in the urban areas has been much more marginal during the post-reform years, and that once the sharp increase in urban inequality is taken into consideration there has been a net decline in urban welfare during the latter period. The generally higher deprivation magnitudes reported by the NFHS over the NSS is due to a combination of the inclusion of the health indicators and the use of a wider range of non-health indicators in case of the NFHS data set. Consistent with our earlier discussion, these tables confirm that the SC/ST households suffer higher deprivation than the non-SC/ST households. Note, however, that the difference between the deprivation magnitudes of these two socio-economic groups increases with α and comes into prominence at high values of α, i.e. when one considers extreme deprivation or, alternatively stated, the most deprived households. Note also that this divide between the SC/ST and non-SC/ST households is much sharper in the urban areas than in the rural, especially if we limit the comparisons to the non-health dimensions of the NSS.

Figure 10.1 provides graphical account of the relationship between economic prosperity of a State and deprivation rate by plotting the deprivation measure, $\pi(\alpha)$, against State per capita household expenditure[3] (obtained from the NSS) at α values of 1 and 3. The graphs confirm the negative relationship for both data sets and for both α values. Three interesting features are worth noting: first, the downward sloping graphs seem to flatten out at some point which suggests that relying solely

[3]For the purpose of these graphs, we have pooled the rural and urban data and treated the rural and urban areas of the State as separate points, giving us a scatter of 30 points for each data set.

Table 10.7 Measures of multidimensional deprivation for rural areas, NSS (Mishra and Ray 2013)

States	50th round NSS					55th round NSS					61st Round NSS				
	Population share	Measures of multidimensional[b] deprivation at[d]				Population share	Measures of multidimensional[b] deprivation at[d]				Population share	Measures of multidimensional[b] deprivation at[d]			
		π_0	π_1	π_2	π_3		π_0	π_1	π_2	π_3		π_0	π_1	π_2	π_3
Andhra Pradesh	0.06	0.95	0.47	0.26	0.17	0.07	0.92	0.42	0.22	0.12	0.06	0.85	0.34	0.16	0.09
		(6.2)	(6.3)	(6.4)	(6.6)		(6.4)	(6.4)	(6.2)	(6.1)		(5.7)	(5.6)	(5.5)	(5.4)
Assam[a]	0.10	0.98	0.47	0.26	0.16	0.10	0.95	0.46	0.25	0.15	0.11	0.91	0.36	0.17	0.09
		(10.3)	(10.2)	(10.1)	(10.0)		(9.6)	(10.1)	(10.4)	(10.7)		(11.5)	(11.0)	(10.4)	(9.9)
Bihar[a]	0.11	1.00	0.55	0.32	0.20	0.12	0.99	0.54	0.31	0.19	0.10	0.98	0.47	0.25	0.15
		(11.2)	(12.6)	(13.4)	(13.8)		(12.3)	(14.4)	(15.8)	(16.6)		(10.8)	(12.6)	(13.7)	(14.2)
Gujarat	0.04	0.92	0.40	0.21	0.12	0.04	0.88	0.35	0.16	0.09	0.03	0.81	0.29	0.13	0.07
		(3.4)	(3.0)	(2.8)	(2.6)		(3.5)	(3.0)	(2.7)	(2.5)		(2.8)	(2.4)	(2.2)	(2.1)
Jammu & Kashmir	0.01	0.93	0.37	0.17	0.09	0.01	0.78	0.27	0.11	0.05	0.03	0.87	0.29	0.11	0.05
		(1.3)	(1.1)	(0.9)	(0.7)		(0.7)	(0.6)	(0.4)	(0.3)		(2.8)	(2.3)	(1.8)	(1.4)
Karnataka	0.04	0.96	0.45	0.24	0.15	0.04	0.92	0.38	0.18	0.10	0.04	0.91	0.33	0.14	0.07
		(4.2)	(4.0)	(3.9)	(3.9)		(4.0)	(3.6)	(3.3)	(3.1)		(3.8)	(3.3)	(2.8)	(2.4)
Kerala	0.04	0.93	0.39	0.20	0.12	0.04	0.86	0.34	0.17	0.09	0.04	0.82	0.29	0.13	0.07
		(3.4)	(2.9)	(2.7)	(2.7)		(3.3)	(2.8)	(2.6)	(2.6)		(3.5)	(3.0)	(2.7)	(2.6)
Madhya Pradesh[a]	0.09	0.99	0.49	0.27	0.17	0.08	0.97	0.42	0.21	0.12	0.08	0.95	0.38	0.18	0.10
		(8.8)	(8.9)	(8.9)	(8.8)		(8.7)	(8.2)	(7.7)	(7.4)		(8.9)	(8.7)	(8.5)	(8.5)
Maharashtra	0.06	0.89	0.38	0.19	0.11	0.06	0.84	0.32	0.15	0.08	0.06	0.80	0.28	0.13	0.07
		(6.1)	(5.3)	(4.9)	(4.7)		(5.3)	(4.5)	(4.0)	(3.7)		(5.7)	(4.9)	(4.5)	(4.4)
Orissa	0.05	0.99	0.54	0.32	0.21	0.05	0.98	0.52	0.31	0.20	0.05	0.95	0.44	0.24	0.15
		(5.1)	(5.6)	(6.1)	(6.4)		(5.0)	(5.8)	(6.5)	(7.1)		(5.3)	(6.0)	(6.7)	(7.3)
Punjab[a]	0.08	0.92	0.37	0.18	0.10	0.08	0.83	0.30	0.12	0.06	0.09	0.81	0.27	0.11	0.05
		(7.7)	(6.4)	(5.4)	(4.8)		(7.0)	(5.4)	(4.3)	(3.6)		(7.8)	(6.3)	(5.1)	(4.3)

(continued)

Table 10.7 (continued)

States	50th round NSS					55th round NSS					61st Round NSS				
	Population share	Measures of multidimensional[b] deprivation at[d]				Population share	Measures of multidimensional[b] deprivation at[d]				Population share	Measures of multidimensional[b] deprivation at[d]			
		π_0	π_1	π_2	π_3		π_0	π_1	π_2	π_3		π_0	π_1	π_2	π_3
Rajasthan	0.05	0.97	0.48	0.27	0.17	0.06	0.95	0.44	0.23	0.13	0.05	0.95	0.43	0.22	0.13
		(5.0)	(5.2)	(5.2)	(5.2)		(5.6)	(5.6)	(5.6)	(5.5)		(5.7)	(6.2)	(6.5)	(6.6)
Tamil Nadu	0.05	0.94	0.43	0.23	0.14	0.05	0.88	0.37	0.18	0.10	0.04	0.82	0.30	0.13	0.07
		(4.7)	(4.4)	(4.3)	(4.3)		(4.7)	(4.3)	(4.0)	(3.9)		(3.9)	(3.5)	(3.1)	(2.9)
Uttar Pradesh[a]	0.15	0.98	0.52	0.31	0.19	0.16	0.96	0.47	0.26	0.15	0.15	0.94	0.44	0.23	0.14
		(15.7)	(17.2)	(18.1)	(18.8)		(16.9)	(18.0)	(18.7)	(19.0)		(15.3)	(17.4)	(19.0)	(20.1)
West Bengal	0.07	0.96	0.47	0.26	0.16	0.07	0.96	0.47	0.26	0.16	0.07	0.92	0.40	0.21	0.12
		(6.9)	(7.0)	(6.9)	(6.8)		(6.9)	(7.4)	(7.7)	(7.9)		(6.6)	(7.1)	(7.5)	(7.8)
C.V.[c]	0.53	0.03	0.13	0.20	0.25	0.56	0.07	0.20	0.29	0.36	0.50	0.07	0.19	0.30	0.37
		(0.55)	(0.62)	(0.67)	(0.70)		(0.60)	(0.69)	(0.75)	(0.79)		(0.54)	(0.63)	(0.71)	(0.76)
SC/ST	0.30	0.99	0.54	0.33	0.21	0.29	0.98	0.50	0.28	0.17	0.30	0.95	0.43	0.23	0.14
		(30.6)	(34.4)	(37.3)	(39.6)		(30.9)	(34.2)	(36.9)	(39.2)		(32.0)	(35.3)	(38.2)	(40.9)
Non-SC/ST	0.70	0.95	0.43	0.23	0.13	0.71	0.91	0.39	0.20	0.11	0.70	0.87	0.34	0.16	0.08
		(69.4)	(65.6)	(62.7)	(60.4)		(69.1)	(65.8)	(63.1)	(60.8)		(68.0)	(64.7)	(61.8)	(59.2)
All India	1.00	0.96	0.47	0.26	0.16	1.00	0.93	0.43	0.23	0.13	1.00	0.90	0.37	0.18	0.10

[a]Assam includes Manipur, Meghalaya and Tripura; Punjab includes Haryana, Himachal Pradesh and Delhi; Uttar Pradesh, Madhya Pradesh and Bihar include Uttaranchal, Chhattisgarh and Jharkhand since their inception (here only for 61st round)

[b]The dimensions of deprivation included here are 5. The household is defined as deprived if it does not have access to clean Fuel for cooking (mainly LPG, kerosene and electricity); access to electricity for lighting; education of the household head in below primary; monthly per capita Food expenditure is less than the half of the median Food expenditure in that particular State and yearly per capita cloth expenditure is less than half of the median cloth expenditure in that particular State

[c]Coefficient of variation

[d]Figures in parenthesis represent the percentage contribution of a State to all-India deprivation exploiting the decomposable property of the multidimensional deprivation measure at various values of α

Table 10.8 Measures of multidimensional deprivation for urban areas, NSS (Mishra and Ray 2013)

States	50th round NSS					55th round NSS					61st round NSS				
	Population share	Measures of multidimensional[b] deprivation at[d]				Population share	Measures of multidimensional[b] deprivation at[d]				Population share	Measures of multidimensional[b] deprivation at[d]			
		π_0	π_1	π_2	π_3		π_0	π_1	π_2	π_3		π_0	π_1	π_2	π_3
Andhra Pradesh	0.08	0.60	0.25	0.13	0.08	0.08	0.50	0.18	0.08	0.05	0.06	0.57	0.21	0.10	0.05
		(8.3)	(8.8)	(9.2)	(9.4)		(7.7)	(7.8)	(7.9)	(7.9)		(6.8)	(7.0)	(7.0)	(6.9)
Assam[a]	0.06	0.66	0.24	0.11	0.06	0.05	0.53	0.19	0.09	0.05	0.07	0.55	0.18	0.08	0.04
		(6.7)	(6.3)	(5.9)	(5.6)		(5.5)	(5.4)	(5.4)	(5.2)		(7.4)	(6.8)	(6.1)	(5.4)
Bihar[a]	0.05	0.76	0.32	0.17	0.10	0.06	0.68	0.29	0.15	0.09	0.07	0.66	0.28	0.14	0.09
		(7.0)	(7.6)	(8.0)	(8.2)		(7.5)	(8.8)	(10.0)	(10.6)		(8.3)	(9.6)	(11.0)	(12.2)
Gujarat	0.06	0.48	0.17	0.08	0.05	0.06	0.42	0.13	0.05	0.03	0.05	0.40	0.14	0.06	0.03
		(4.6)	(4.2)	(4.0)	(3.9)		(5.1)	(4.5)	(3.9)	(3.6)		(3.7)	(3.5)	(3.3)	(3.2)
Jammu & Kashmir	0.01	0.41	0.13	0.05	0.02	0.01	0.39	0.11	0.04	0.02	0.02	0.44	0.13	0.04	0.02
		(0.9)	(0.7)	(0.5)	(0.4)		(1.0)	(0.8)	(0.6)	(0.5)		(2.0)	(1.5)	(1.2)	(0.9)
Karnataka	0.06	0.58	0.23	0.12	0.08	0.06	0.50	0.18	0.08	0.05	0.05	0.52	0.18	0.08	0.04
		(5.8)	(6.0)	(6.2)	(6.4)		(5.4)	(5.4)	(5.4)	(5.5)		(5.0)	(4.8)	(4.6)	(4.5)
Kerala	0.04	0.77	0.30	0.15	0.09	0.04	0.65	0.23	0.10	0.05	0.05	0.64	0.22	0.10	0.06
		(5.4)	(5.5)	(5.4)	(5.3)		(5.6)	(5.4)	(5.2)	(5.1)		(5.6)	(5.5)	(5.3)	(5.3)
Madhya Pradesh[a]	0.08	0.63	0.23	0.11	0.06	0.08	0.55	0.19	0.08	0.04	0.08	0.60	0.21	0.09	0.05
		(8.7)	(8.3)	(7.8)	(7.4)		(8.4)	(8.1)	(7.6)	(7.1)		(8.6)	(8.4)	(8.1)	(7.7)
Maharashtra	0.12	0.44	0.16	0.08	0.05	0.12	0.40	0.13	0.05	0.03	0.12	0.39	0.13	0.06	0.03
		(9.3)	(8.5)	(8.2)	(8.4)		(9.2)	(8.0)	(7.2)	(6.9)		(9.0)	(8.5)	(8.3)	(8.5)
Orissa	0.02	0.70	0.30	0.17	0.11	0.02	0.64	0.28	0.15	0.10	0.03	0.65	0.27	0.14	0.09
		(2.7)	(3.1)	(3.4)	(3.8)		(2.8)	(3.3)	(3.9)	(4.5)		(3.6)	(4.1)	(4.8)	(5.3)
Punjab[a]	0.09	0.47	0.16	0.07	0.04	0.10	0.42	0.13	0.05	0.02	0.11	0.39	0.12	0.05	0.03

(continued)

Table 10.8 (continued)

States	50th round NSS					55th round NSS					61st round NSS				
	Population share	Measures of multidimensional[b] deprivation at[d]				Population share	Measures of multidimensional[b] deprivation at[d]				Population share	Measures of multidimensional[b] deprivation at[d]			
		π_0	π_1	π_2	π_3		π_0	π_1	π_2	π_3		π_0	π_1	π_2	π_3
		(7.0)	(6.1)	(5.3)	(4.8)		(8.1)	(6.9)	(5.8)	(5.0)		(7.9)	(7.0)	(6.2)	(5.7)
Rajasthan	0.04	0.59	0.23	0.11	0.06	0.05	0.50	0.17	0.07	0.04	0.04	0.56	0.19	0.08	0.04
		(4.3)	(4.2)	(4.1)	(4.0)		(4.7)	(4.5)	(4.1)	(3.7)		(4.6)	(4.4)	(4.0)	(3.6)
Tamil Nadu	0.08	0.64	0.25	0.13	0.08	0.08	0.50	0.18	0.08	0.04	0.08	0.50	0.17	0.07	0.04
		(9.1)	(9.1)	(9.2)	(9.2)		(7.7)	(7.5)	(7.4)	(7.4)		(7.9)	(7.3)	(6.7)	(6.3)
Uttar Pradesh[a]	0.12	0.63	0.27	0.14	0.09	0.12	0.59	0.24	0.12	0.07	0.12	0.59	0.24	0.12	0.07
		(12.6)	(13.9)	(14.8)	(15.3)		(13.9)	(15.5)	(16.8)	(17.5)		(12.9)	(14.5)	(15.9)	(17.0)
West Bengal	0.07	0.64	0.26	0.13	0.08	0.07	0.58	0.22	0.11	0.07	0.06	0.56	0.21	0.10	0.06
		(7.5)	(7.7)	(8.0)	(8.2)		(7.6)	(8.2)	(8.8)	(9.5)		(6.8)	(7.1)	(7.5)	(7.9)
C.V.[c]	0.47	0.18	0.25	0.31	0.36	0.46	0.18	0.28	0.39	0.47	0.44	0.17	0.26	0.35	0.44
		(0.43)	(0.46)	(0.50)	(0.52)		(0.45)	(0.49)	(0.55)	(0.59)		(0.41)	(0.46)	(0.52)	(0.58)
SC/ST	0.16	0.80	0.36	0.21	0.14	0.17	0.72	0.30	0.16	0.10	0.19	0.69	0.28	0.14	0.09
		(21.3)	(25.0)	(28.6)	(31.6)		(24.0)	(27.9)	(31.8)	(35.0)		(25.8)	(29.0)	(32.3)	(35.1)
Non-SC/ST	0.84	0.55	0.20	0.10	0.06	0.83	0.47	0.16	0.07	0.04	0.81	0.48	0.16	0.07	0.04
		(78.7)	(75.0)	(71.4)	(68.4)		(76.1)	(72.1)	(68.2)	(65.0)		(74.3)	(71.0)	(67.7)	(64.9)
All India	1.00	0.59	0.23	0.12	0.07	1.00	0.52	0.19	0.09	0.05	1.00	0.52	0.19	0.09	0.05

[a]Assam includes Manipur, Meghalaya and Tripura; Punjab includes Haryana, Himachal Pradesh and Delhi; Uttar Pradesh, Madhya Pradesh and Bihar include Uttaranchal, Chhattisgarh and Jharkhand since their inception (here only for 61st round)

[b]The dimensions of deprivation included here are 5. The household is defined as deprived if it does not have access to clean Fuel for cooking (mainly LPG, kerosene and electricity); access to electricity for lighting; education of the household head in below primary; monthly per capita Food expenditure is less than the half of the median Food expenditure in that particular State and yearly per capita cloth expenditure is less than half of the median cloth expenditure in that particular State

[c]Coefficient of variation

[d]Figures in parenthesis represent the percentage contribution of a State to all-India deprivation exploiting the decomposable property of the multidimensional deprivation measure at various values of α

Table 10.9 Measures of multidimensional deprivation for rural areas NFHS (Mishra and Ray 2013)

States	NFHS 1					NFHS 2					NFHS 3				
	Population share	Measures of multidimensional[b] deprivation at[d]				Population share	Measures of multidimensional[b] deprivation at[d]				Population share	Measures of multidimensional[b] deprivation at[d]			
		π_0	π_1	π_2	π_3		π_0	π_1	π_2	π_3		π_0	π_1	π_2	π_3
Andhra Pradesh	0.05	1.00	0.74	0.58	0.48	0.04	1.00	0.70	0.53	0.42	0.04	1.00	0.66	0.47	0.35
		(4.9)	(5.2)	(5.5)	(5.7)		(4.2)	(4.4)	(4.5)	(4.6)		(4.1)	(4.2)	(4.3)	(4.3)
Assam[a]	0.08	1.00	0.67	0.49	0.37	0.10	1.00	0.65	0.46	0.35	0.13	1.00	0.60	0.39	0.28
		(8.1)	(7.9)	(7.6)	(7.4)		(9.6)	(9.3)	(9.0)	(8.6)		(13.3)	(12.4)	(11.6)	(10.9)
Bihar[a]	0.07	1.00	0.76	0.60	0.50	0.11	1.00	0.75	0.60	0.51	0.04	1.00	0.71	0.54	0.43
		(7.3)	(8.0)	(8.5)	(9.0)		(10.9)	(12.1)	(13.3)	(14.3)		(4.2)	(4.6)	(5.0)	(5.3)
Gujarat	0.04	1.00	0.63	0.45	0.34	0.04	1.00	0.63	0.44	0.33	0.04	0.99	0.58	0.38	0.27
		(4.3)	(3.9)	(3.7)	(3.6)		(3.7)	(3.5)	(3.3)	(3.2)		(3.8)	(3.4)	(3.2)	(3.0)
Jammu & Kashmir	0.04	1.00	0.61	0.42	0.31	0.04	1.00	0.58	0.37	0.25	0.04	1.00	0.56	0.34	0.23
		(3.5)	(3.1)	(2.8)	(2.6)		(4.0)	(3.5)	(3.0)	(2.7)		(4.0)	(3.5)	(3.0)	(2.7)
Karnataka	0.05	1.00	0.70	0.52	0.41	0.05	1.00	0.67	0.49	0.38	0.07	1.00	0.66	0.47	0.36
		(5.2)	(5.2)	(5.2)	(5.2)		(4.7)	(4.7)	(4.6)	(4.6)		(6.5)	(6.8)	(6.9)	(6.9)
Kerala	0.05	1.00	0.54	0.33	0.22	0.03	1.00	0.53	0.31	0.20	0.04	1.00	0.50	0.27	0.16
		(5.1)	(4.0)	(3.3)	(2.8)		(3.2)	(2.5)	(2.0)	(1.6)		(3.6)	(2.8)	(2.2)	(1.7)
Madhya Pradesh[a]	0.08	1.00	0.77	0.62	0.52	0.09	1.00	0.72	0.55	0.44	0.10	1.00	0.72	0.55	0.44
		(8.0)	(9.0)	(9.7)	(10.3)		(8.9)	(9.4)	(9.8)	(10.1)		(10.1)	(11.3)	(12.3)	(13.1)
Maharashtra	0.04	1.00	0.67	0.50	0.39	0.04	1.00	0.67	0.49	0.38	0.05	0.99	0.64	0.46	0.35
		(4.0)	(3.9)	(3.9)	(3.8)		(3.5)	(3.5)	(3.5)	(3.5)		(4.8)	(4.9)	(5.0)	(5.0)
Orissa	0.06	1.00	0.76	0.60	0.50	0.06	1.00	0.75	0.61	0.51	0.05	1.00	0.72	0.56	0.45
		(5.6)	(6.1)	(6.5)	(6.8)		(6.0)	(6.7)	(7.4)	(8.0)		(5.2)	(5.8)	(6.4)	(6.9)
Punjab[a]	0.11	0.99	0.58	0.38	0.26	0.11	0.99	0.56	0.35	0.23	0.12	1.00	0.55	0.34	0.22
		(11.4)	(9.7)	(8.4)	(7.3)		(10.8)	(9.1)	(7.7)	(6.6)		(12.0)	(10.4)	(9.0)	(7.9)

(continued)

Table 10.9 (continued)

States	NFHS 1					NFHS 2					NFHS 3				
	Population share	Measures of multidimensional[b] deprivation at[d]				Population share	Measures of multidimensional[b] deprivation at[d]				Population share	Measures of multidimensional[b] deprivation at[d]			
		π_0	π_1	π_2	π_3		π_0	π_1	π_2	π_3		π_0	π_1	π_2	π_3
Rajasthan	0.08	1.00	0.73	0.58	0.48	0.09	1.00	0.69	0.52	0.41	0.05	1.00	0.69	0.51	0.41
		(7.8)	(8.3)	(8.8)	(9.2)		(9.3)	(9.6)	(9.8)	(9.9)		(4.9)	(5.2)	(5.6)	(5.9)
Tamil Nadu	0.04	1.00	0.71	0.54	0.42	0.04	1.00	0.66	0.47	0.36	0.04	1.00	0.63	0.44	0.33
		(4.0)	(4.1)	(4.2)	(4.2)		(3.8)	(3.7)	(3.6)	(3.5)		(4.4)	(4.4)	(4.4)	(4.3)
Uttar Pradesh[a]	0.15	1.00	0.70	0.53	0.42	0.14	1.00	0.71	0.53	0.42	0.14	1.00	0.69	0.51	0.40
		(15.3)	(15.6)	(15.7)	(15.7)		(13.5)	(14.2)	(14.6)	(14.8)		(14.1)	(15.2)	(16.0)	(16.7)
West Bengal	0.06	1.00	0.75	0.60	0.50	0.04	1.00	0.71	0.55	0.44	0.05	1.00	0.67	0.49	0.38
		(5.6)	(6.1)	(6.5)	(6.9)		(3.8)	(4.0)	(4.2)	(4.4)		(5.2)	(5.4)	(5.7)	(5.8)
C.V.[c]	0.48	0.00	0.10	0.17	0.23	0.52	0.00	0.10	0.18	0.25	0.56	0.00	0.11	0.19	0.26
		(0.48)	(0.48)	(0.50)	(0.52)		(0.52)	(0.55)	(0.58)	(0.62)		(0.56)	(0.56)	(0.58)	(0.61)
SC/ST	NA	NA	NA	NA	NA	0.32	1.00	0.74	0.58	0.48	0.33	1.00	0.70	0.52	0.41
		(NA)	(NA)	(NA)	(NA)		(31.5)	(34.7)	(37.2)	(39.3)		(32.8)	(35.7)	(38.0)	(39.9)
Non-SC/ST	NA	NA	NA	NA	NA	0.69	1.00	0.64	0.45	0.34	0.67	1.00	0.61	0.41	0.30
		(NA)	(NA)	(NA)	(NA)		(68.5)	(65.1)	(62.4)	(60.3)		(67.2)	(64.2)	(61.9)	(60.0)
All India	1.00	1.00	0.69	0.52	0.41	1.00	1.00	0.67	0.49	0.38	1.00	1.00	0.64	0.45	0.34

[a]Assam includes Manipur, Meghalaya and Tripura; Punjab includes Haryana, Himachal Pradesh and Delhi; Uttar Pradesh, Madhya Pradesh and Bihar include Uttaranchal, Chhattisgarh and Jharkhand since their inception (here only for NFHS 3)

[b]The dimensions of deprivation included here are 13. The household is defined as deprived if it does not have access to drinking water on its own premises; access to electricity for lighting; access to clean Fuel for cooking (mainly LPG, kerosene, electricity and biogas); access to 'pucca' house; access to any description of toilet including pit latrine; education of the household head is below primary; access to cycle as a basic minimum transport; access to radio as a basic source of entertainment; falling in the poorest wealth quintile; share of stunted children (in 0–3 years of age) in the household is 60% or more; share of wasted children (in 0–3 years of age) in the household is 60% or more; BMI of the mother in the household is less than 18.5 or above 30; and share of anaemic (suffering from severe anaemia only) children (in 0–3 years of age) in the household is 60% or more

[c]Coefficient of variation

[d]Figures in parenthesis represent the percentage contribution of a State to all-India deprivation exploiting the decomposable property of the multidimensional deprivation measure at various values of α

Table 10.10 Measures of multidimensional deprivation for urban areas, NFHS (Mishra and Ray 2013)

States	NFHS 1					NFHS 2					NFHS 3				
	Population share	Measures of multidimensional[b] deprivation at[d]				Population share	Measures of multidimensional[b] deprivation at[d]				Population share	Measures of multidimensional[b] deprivation at[d]			
		π_0	π_1	π_2	π_3		π_0	π_1	π_2	π_3		π_0	π_1	π_2	π_3
Andhra Pradesh	0.04	1.00	0.43	0.24	0.16	0.03	0.98	0.43	0.23	0.14	0.09	0.99	0.42	0.21	0.11
		(4.2)	(4.5)	(4.9)	(5.2)		(3.4)	(3.7)	(4.1)	(4.6)		(9.2)	(9.1)	(9.0)	(8.9)
Assam[a]	0.08	0.99	0.44	0.23	0.14	0.07	1.00	0.45	0.24	0.14	0.09	0.99	0.47	0.25	0.14
		(8.1)	(9.0)	(9.2)	(9.1)		(6.6)	(7.4)	(7.9)	(8.2)		(9.1)	(10.0)	(10.6)	(11.0)
Bihar[a]	0.05	0.97	0.44	0.26	0.18	0.03	0.99	0.48	0.28	0.18	0.03	0.99	0.51	0.30	0.20
		(4.9)	(5.6)	(6.4)	(7.4)		(2.9)	(3.5)	(4.1)	(4.8)		(3.2)	(3.9)	(4.7)	(5.6)
Gujarat	0.05	0.97	0.37	0.19	0.12	0.06	0.98	0.38	0.18	0.10	0.03	0.98	0.36	0.16	0.08
		(5.1)	(4.9)	(4.9)	(4.9)		(5.6)	(5.4)	(5.3)	(5.2)		(3.1)	(2.7)	(2.4)	(2.2)
Jammu & Kashmir	0.04	0.95	0.31	0.13	0.07	0.03	0.97	0.36	0.15	0.07	0.02	0.97	0.39	0.18	0.09
		(3.7)	(3.0)	(2.5)	(2.1)		(3.4)	(3.0)	(2.7)	(2.3)		(2.1)	(2.0)	(1.8)	(1.7)
Karnataka	0.06	0.97	0.42	0.23	0.15	0.05	0.97	0.40	0.20	0.11	0.05	0.99	0.46	0.24	0.14
		(5.6)	(6.0)	(6.4)	(6.7)		(5.3)	(5.3)	(5.4)	(5.6)		(4.7)	(5.1)	(5.4)	(5.8)
Kerala	0.05	0.99	0.45	0.24	0.15	0.03	0.99	0.44	0.22	0.12	0.02	0.98	0.44	0.22	0.12
		(4.5)	(5.1)	(5.3)	(5.3)		(3.0)	(3.2)	(3.2)	(3.1)		(2.3)	(2.4)	(2.4)	(2.4)
Madhya Pradesh[a]	0.06	1.00	0.43	0.23	0.14	0.07	0.98	0.45	0.25	0.16	0.09	0.98	0.42	0.21	0.12
		(6.4)	(6.8)	(7.0)	(7.2)		(7.0)	(7.8)	(9.0)	(10.1)		(9.1)	(9.0)	(9.0)	(9.2)
Maharashtra	0.07	0.97	0.36	0.17	0.09	0.13	0.99	0.39	0.17	0.09	0.14	0.98	0.39	0.18	0.09
		(6.7)	(6.3)	(5.6)	(5.1)		(12.6)	(12.2)	(11.3)	(10.1)		(13.8)	(12.8)	(11.7)	(10.5)
Orissa	0.05	0.98	0.49	0.30	0.21	0.03	0.99	0.52	0.33	0.24	0.03	0.99	0.50	0.30	0.21
		(4.8)	(6.0)	(7.2)	(8.2)		(3.3)	(4.2)	(5.5)	(7.1)		(2.7)	(3.2)	(3.9)	(4.8)
Punjab[a]	0.24	0.95	0.31	0.13	0.07	0.19	0.97	0.33	0.13	0.06	0.13	0.98	0.39	0.18	0.09
		(23.1)	(18.8)	(15.3)	(12.7)		(18.9)	(15.7)	(12.7)	(10.2)		(13.2)	(12.3)	(11.2)	(10.1)

(continued)

Table 10.10 (continued)

States	NFHS 1					NFHS 2					NFHS 3				
	Population share	Measures of multidimensional[b] deprivation at[d]				Population share	Measures of multidimensional[b] deprivation at[d]				Population share	Measures of multidimensional[b] deprivation at[d]			
		π_0	π_1	π_2	π_3		π_0	π_1	π_2	π_3		π_0	π_1	π_2	π_3
Rajasthan	0.04	0.97	0.39	0.21	0.13	0.06	0.98	0.39	0.19	0.10	0.03	0.98	0.39	0.18	0.10
		(4.2)	(4.2)	(4.3)	(4.5)		(6.3)	(6.2)	(6.1)	(5.9)		(2.7)	(2.5)	(2.4)	(2.3)
Tamil Nadu	0.05	1.00	0.47	0.27	0.17	0.07	0.98	0.43	0.22	0.13	0.06	0.98	0.43	0.22	0.12
		(5.1)	(6.0)	(6.7)	(7.1)		(7.0)	(7.4)	(7.8)	(8.2)		(6.0)	(6.2)	(6.2)	(6.3)
Uttar Pradesh[a]	0.10	0.96	0.37	0.18	0.11	0.08	0.98	0.40	0.19	0.11	0.12	0.98	0.43	0.22	0.13
		(9.5)	(9.0)	(8.9)	(8.8)		(7.5)	(7.4)	(7.5)	(7.5)		(11.4)	(11.6)	(12.0)	(12.6)
West Bengal	0.04	1.00	0.49	0.28	0.19	0.07	0.99	0.42	0.20	0.11	0.07	0.99	0.44	0.22	0.12
		(4.0)	(4.9)	(5.6)	(6.0)		(7.3)	(7.6)	(7.6)	(7.4)		(7.2)	(7.4)	(7.3)	(7.2)
C.V.[c]	0.74	0.02	0.14	0.24	0.31	0.64	0.01	0.12	0.24	0.36	0.61	0.01	0.10	0.20	0.31
		(0.72)	(0.56)	(0.44)	(0.37)		(0.64)	(0.52)	(0.43)	(0.37)		(0.61)	(0.58)	(0.56)	(0.54)
SC/ST	NA	NA	NA	NA	NA	0.19	0.99	0.49	0.28	0.18	0.21	0.99	0.48	0.27	0.16
		(NA)	(NA)	(NA)	(NA)		(18.7)	(22.7)	(26.9)	(30.9)		(20.8)	(23.4)	(26.2)	(29.1)
Non-SC/ST	NA	NA	NA	NA	NA	0.82	0.98	0.38	0.17	0.09	0.79	0.98	0.41	0.20	0.10
		(NA)	(NA)	(NA)	(NA)		(81.3)	(77.4)	(73.3)	(69.3)		(79.2)	(76.7)	(73.9)	(71.0)
All India	1.00	0.97	0.39	0.20	0.12	1.00	0.98	0.40	0.19	0.11	1.00	0.98	0.42	0.21	0.12

[a]Assam includes Manipur, Meghalaya and Tripura; Punjab includes Haryana, Himachal Pradesh and Delhi; Uttar Pradesh, Madhya Pradesh and Bihar include Uttaranchal, Chhattisgarh and Jharkhand since their inception (here only for NFHS 3)

[b]The dimensions of deprivation included here are 13. The household is defined as deprived if it does not have access to drinking water on its own premises; access to electricity for lighting; access to clean Fuel for cooking (mainly LPG, kerosene, electricity and biogas); access to 'pucca' house; access to any description of toilet including pit latrine; education of the household head is below primary; access to cycle as a basic minimum transport; access to radio as a basic source of entertainment; falling in the poorest wealth quintile; share of stunted children (in 0–3 years of age) in the household is 60% or more; share of wasted children (in 0–3 years of age) in the household is 60% or more; BMI of the mother in the household is less than 18.5 or above 30; and share of anaemic (suffering from severe anaemia only) children (in 0–3 years of age) in the household is 60% or more

[c]Coefficient of variation

[d]Figures in parenthesis represent the percentage contribution of a State to all-India deprivation exploiting the decomposable property of the multidimensional deprivation measure at various values of α

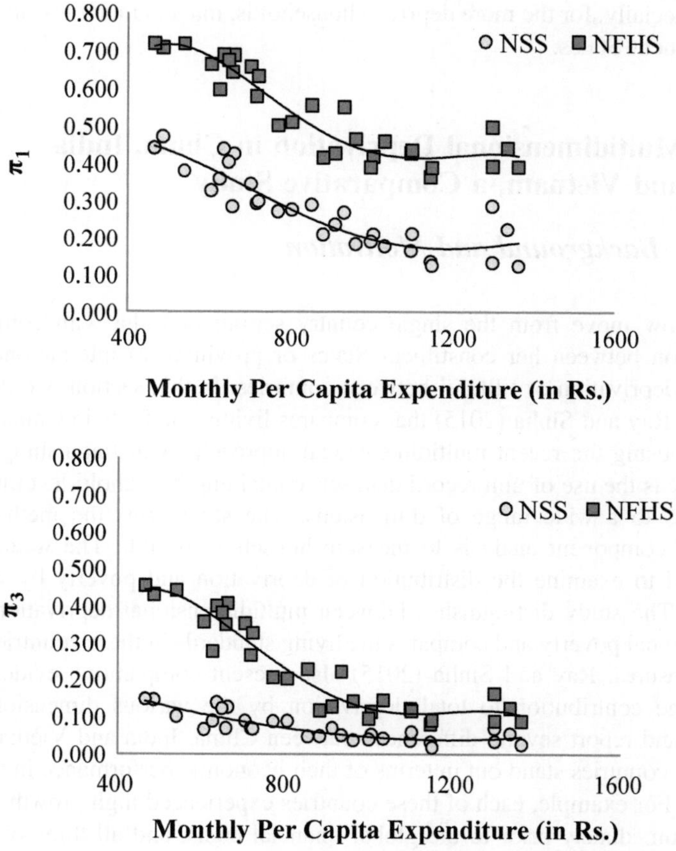

Fig. 10.1 NSS 61 and NFHS 3 graphs for rural and urban combined. Reproduced from Mishra and Ray (2013)

on overall economic prosperity will not drive deprivation to zero or to negligible values—more interventionist policy and direct anti-deprivation measures need to be implemented; second, as we increase α, i.e. if we consider the more deprived households, economic progress leads to a faster decline in the NFHS-based deprivation by nudging them from 'severely deprived' to 'moderately deprived' group of households[4]; third, in case of the poorer States, the gap between NFHS-based deprivation and NSS-based deprivation is much larger for higher values of α but the gap declines much faster for the higher α value as we move from the poorer to the more affluent States. The last feature is not surprising since health deprivation, which drives the wedge between the NSS and the NFHS deprivation

[4]Since the decline is much less rapid for the NSS, this suggests that the improvement in the deprivation occurs mainly because of the health-based deprivation dimensions.

rates, especially, for the more deprived households, matters much less in case of the more affluent States.

10.4 Multidimensional Deprivation in China, India and Vietnam, a Comparative Study

10.4.1 Background and Motivation

Let us now move from the single country setting of India with comparison of deprivation between her constituent States or provinces to international comparisons of deprivation or 'illfare' between countries. In this section, we describe the study by Ray and Sinha (2015) that compares living standards in China, India and Vietnam using the recent multidimensional approach. A distinguishing feature of this study is the use of unit record data sets containing household-level information on access to a wide range of dimensions. The study uses the methodology of principal component analysis to measure household wealth. The wealth index is then used to examine the distribution of deprivation and poverty by wealth percentiles. The study distinguishes between multidimensional deprivation and multidimensional poverty and compares the living standards in these countries based on both measures. Ray and Sinha (2015) also present comparative evidence on the percentage contribution to total deprivation by the various dimensions in each country and report several differences between China, India and Vietnam.

These countries stand out in terms of their economic performance in the last two decades. For example, each of these countries experienced high growth rates in the period immediately prior to the global financial crisis, and all three of them continued to record satisfactory growth rates even after the financial crisis. According to estimates of annual growth rates of GDP made available by the World Bank on its website (http://data.worldbank.org/indicator/NY.GDP.MKTP.KD.ZG), in 2011 China had an annual growth rate of 9.3 per cent, India had a growth rate of 6.3 per cent and Vietnam was growing at 6.0 per cent. The high growth rates translated to large reductions in aggregate poverty rates in each country. China and India, which have been referred to as 'awakening giants' by Bardhan (2010), have recorded some of the highest growth rates seen anywhere, thereby, generating a large literature comparing their economic performances. Much of this literature is based on macroindicators such as growth rates, and very little of the comparisons are based on living standards.

The inclusion of Vietnam adds to the interest of this study. Vietnam is a particularly interesting example because, following the 'Doi Moi' ('renovation') reforms in the mid-1980 s, there has been a dramatic improvement in living standards as measured by the conventional monetary indicators—see World Bank (2000) and the volume edited by Glewwe et al. (2004). Ray and Sinha (2015), which is described and its empirical results reported in this section, provide evidence on whether the improvement in Vietnamese performance revealed by the macrofigures translated to a decline in MDD during the 1990s and beyond. The inclusion of Vietnam also helps to put the performances of India and China in perspective. The robustness of the evidence on multidimensional poverty to the use of MDD or MDP measure following the distinction between the two is a significant point of departure of this study from other recent studies all of which have used one or the other.

10.4.2 Data Sets

The Chinese database came from the China Health and Nutrition Surveys (CHNS). These surveys conducted during the period 1989–2006 used a multistage, random cluster process to draw a sample of over 4000 households in nine Chinese provinces. A detailed description of the CHNS database is available in Popkin et al. (2010). The Indian database came from the National Family Health Surveys (NFHS). These are large-scale surveys conducted during 1992–2006 on a representative sample of households throughout India. Three rounds of this survey, NFHS 1 to NFHS 3, conducted in 1992–93, 1998–99 and 2005–06, respectively, are used in this study. The Vietnamese data came from Vietnamese Living Standard Surveys (VLSS) that were carried out in 1992/93 and 1997/98 and Vietnamese Household Living Standard Survey (VHLSS) of 2002 and 2004. These surveys were part of the household surveys conducted in several developing countries with technical assistance from the World Bank [for details see World Bank (2000)].

Since the main focus of this study is estimation of MDD and MDP, considerable care was taken to ensure consistency in the definition and treatment of 'dimensions of deprivation and poverty' both across countries and over time. For example, the study adopted the UN definition of deprivation of water and improved sanitation facility across all the countries.

The wealth index constructed for the analysis uses a set of household assets and characteristics that are (i) common for all survey rounds; (ii) common in all the three countries (China, India and Vietnam). For each country separate PCA for rural and urban areas were done to find eigenvector of factor scores associated with the first principal component of wealth for a common year (1998–99). In a PCA, all variables with a positive factor score are generally associated with high socio-economic status (SES) and variables with negative factor scores are associated with poor SES (Vyas and Kumaranayeke 2006). The results from PCA presented in the Appendix to Ray and Sinha (2015) suggest that having no toilet facility with a negative score is associated with poor SES, which is in line with expectations. However, it is also interesting to note that having a shared public toilet is associated with poor SES in urban India and with high SES in rural India.

10.4.3 Results

Dimension-specific headcount rates (HCR) of deprivation in the three countries in each year/round are presented in Tables 10.11, 10.12 and 10.13. There has generally been a decline in deprivation in all dimensions across the wealth quintiles in both rural and urban areas. The improvement has been more in some dimensions, less in others, but there has been all-round progress. A comparison between the 'awakening giants' shows that, while China outperforms India on progress in access to drink water, electricity and education (i.e., literacy of household head), it does not do as well on access to hospital. Vietnam has done particularly well on the latter recording an impressive increase in access to hospital over the period, 1997/8–2004. Another common feature is that rural deprivation is generally higher than urban, though the rural/urban difference is smaller in China than elsewhere.

The wealth Lorenz curves (LC) for the three countries in 1992/93 presented in Fig. 10.2. China is clearly Lorenz dominated by both India and Vietnam. This is consistent with the finding of India's NCAER, that the inequality of Indian income in 2004–5 was much higher than in China (Bardhan 2010, p. 97). It is not possible to have an unambiguous ranking of wealth inequality between India and Vietnam because of their intersecting Lorenz curves. This raises the issue of correspondence between wealth and deprivation on which we present some evidence later. As we report below, the disconnect between wealth and deprivation and, in particular, the understatement of deprivation in dimensions by that in wealth for the less well off makes it misleading to draw welfare conclusions based on wealth alone.

The dimension-specific HCR is combined into a single number, via the MDD measure, π_α, and reported for the three countries at three α values in Tables 10.14, 10.15 and 10.16. Consistent with the dimension-specific deprivation rates, there has been a general improvement in MDD in each country and across the wealth percentiles and in both rural and urban areas. These tables also exploit the subgroup decomposability of the MDD measure to report (in parenthesis) the deprivation share of rural and urban population, and of the three wealth percentiles. As expected, a disproportionately larger share of deprivation is borne by rural households in the lower wealth percentiles. The imbalance in the deprivation distribution, both between the rural and urban areas and between the wealth percentiles, increases as we increase α, i.e. if we restrict our analysis to households who are deprived in more and more dimensions. While the rural share of deprivation has declined in India, it has held steady in China and Vietnam. The rural–urban gap in deprivation in India narrowed sharply during the period, 1998/99–2005/6, to the point that in 2005/06 deprivation was (almost) equally shared between the two areas, if one recalls that the rural share of India's population is much greater than the urban share. The deprivation shares by wealth percentiles show that the bottom 50% of the households arranged in an increasing order by their 'wealth', as constructed in this study, endure a share of deprivation that is much higher than 50% at all the α values. The deprivation share for this bottom 50% (by wealth) increases to between 85 and 90% at $\alpha = 4$, i.e. for the more deprived households.

Table 10.11 Dimension-specific HCRs in China[a] (Ray and Sinha 2015)

Year	No drink water	No elec-tricity	No Fuel	No toilet	No bicy-cle	No radio	House-hold head illiterate	No hos-pital	Wait time (>15 min)	No drink water	No elec-tricity	No Fuel	No toilet	No bicy-cle	No radio	House-hold head illiterate	No hos-pital	Wait time (>15 min)	No drink water	No elec-tricity	No Fuel	No toilet	No bicy-cle	No radio	House-hold head illiterate	No hos-pital	Wait time (>15 min)
	Rural China									Urban China									Overall China								
1989	0.324	0.101	0.965	0.762	0.205	0.712	0.180	0.835	0.519	0.133	0.017	0.752	0.398	0.187	0.472	0.206	0.278	0.662	0.261	0.073	0.895	0.643	0.199	0.633	0.189	0.652	0.566
1991	0.270	0.056	0.939	0.682	0.204	0.587	0.172	0.909	0.428	0.076	0.003	0.671	0.381	0.188	0.387	0.207	0.264	0.706	0.208	0.039	0.854	0.586	0.199	0.523	0.183	0.703	0.517
1993	0.219	0.021	0.922	0.697	0.208	0.577	0.167	0.907	0.334	0.126	0.003	0.571	0.344	0.220	0.372	0.168	0.328	0.612	0.191	0.015	0.815	0.589	0.212	0.514	0.167	0.730	0.419
1997	0.113	0.009	0.781	0.666	0.278	0.595	0.149	0.928	0.275	0.085	0.003	0.394	0.320	0.302	0.368	0.131	0.342	0.526	0.104	0.007	0.652	0.551	0.286	0.519	0.143	0.733	0.358
2000	0.147	0.011	0.726	0.658	0.305	0.628	0.112	0.906	0.167	0.083	0.004	0.356	0.253	0.336	0.446	0.103	0.442	0.378	0.127	0.009	0.607	0.528	0.315	0.569	0.109	0.757	0.235
2004	0.123	0.004	0.725	0.612	0.390	0.757	0.086	0.924	0.183	0.092	0.003	0.338	0.196	0.458	0.578	0.088	0.477	0.318	0.113	0.003	0.598	0.475	0.412	0.698	0.087	0.777	0.227
2006	0.132	0.004	0.617	0.577	0.431	0.853	0.118	0.905	0.135	0.072	0.002	0.261	0.174	0.486	0.677	0.108	0.477	0.357	0.112	0.003	0.501	0.445	0.449	0.796	0.114	0.765	0.208
	Bottom 20 percentile																										
1989	0.467	0.475	0.998	0.856	0.294	0.925	0.233	0.904	0.444	0.305	0.059	1.000	0.898	0.403	0.797	0.318	0.492	0.644	0.413	0.338	0.999	0.870	0.330	0.883	0.261	0.768	0.510
1991	0.458	0.276	1.000	0.906	0.289	0.749	0.249	0.971	0.278	0.154	0.005	0.991	0.878	0.416	0.719	0.317	0.489	0.552	0.362	0.190	0.997	0.897	0.329	0.740	0.270	0.818	0.365
1993	0.328	0.097	1.000	0.918	0.313	0.847	0.242	0.973	0.256	0.316	0.010	0.995	0.845	0.388	0.650	0.272	0.617	0.354	0.324	0.070	0.999	0.896	0.336	0.787	0.251	0.865	0.286
1997	0.213	0.044	0.998	0.904	0.367	0.789	0.186	0.975	0.255	0.267	0.004	0.932	0.898	0.407	0.619	0.216	0.631	0.390	0.231	0.031	0.976	0.902	0.380	0.733	0.196	0.862	0.299
2000	0.267	0.053	0.993	0.918	0.349	0.795	0.165	0.965	0.119	0.288	0.016	0.852	0.864	0.377	0.626	0.175	0.681	0.191	0.274	0.041	0.948	0.900	0.358	0.741	0.168	0.874	0.142
2004	0.114	0.014	0.968	0.912	0.418	0.842	0.161	0.956	0.132	0.246	0.011	0.886	0.721	0.532	0.675	0.157	0.743	0.214	0.158	0.013	0.941	0.849	0.455	0.787	0.160	0.886	0.159
2006	0.171	0.017	0.900	0.922	0.486	0.917	0.193	0.934	0.091	0.240	0.007	0.698	0.684	0.594	0.826	0.205	0.764	0.191	0.193	0.014	0.834	0.844	0.522	0.888	0.197	0.878	0.124
	20th to 50th percentile																										
1989	0.433	0.015	0.999	0.907	0.247	0.802	0.187	0.818	0.492	0.147	0.011	0.986	0.555	0.207	0.569	0.224	0.405	0.580	0.340	0.014	0.994	0.792	0.234	0.726	0.199	0.684	0.521
1991	0.365	0.004	1.000	0.824	0.221	0.713	0.166	0.916	0.388	0.119	0.006	0.943	0.558	0.161	0.445	0.236	0.412	0.675	0.288	0.005	0.982	0.741	0.202	0.629	0.188	0.758	0.478
1993	0.273	0.001	1.000	0.863	0.192	0.615	0.159	0.910	0.265	0.153	0.000	0.827	0.476	0.241	0.469	0.218	0.427	0.596	0.237	0.001	0.947	0.745	0.207	0.571	0.177	0.762	0.366
1997	0.173	0.000	0.975	0.852	0.259	0.656	0.178	0.961	0.253	0.064	0.003	0.567	0.444	0.346	0.394	0.179	0.394	0.545	0.137	0.001	0.839	0.717	0.288	0.569	0.178	0.772	0.350
2000	0.151	0.001	0.938	0.880	0.306	0.706	0.143	0.949	0.136	0.057	0.003	0.499	0.270	0.401	0.488	0.141	0.470	0.375	0.120	0.002	0.796	0.683	0.337	0.636	0.143	0.794	0.213
2004	0.177	0.000	0.894	0.841	0.386	0.786	0.090	0.960	0.178	0.091	0.002	0.423	0.160	0.533	0.667	0.112	0.486	0.323	0.149	0.001	0.740	0.618	0.434	0.747	0.097	0.805	0.225
2006	0.173	0.001	0.780	0.817	0.441	0.867	0.137	0.940	0.110	0.051	0.002	0.315	0.117	0.585	0.729	0.120	0.468	0.327	0.135	0.002	0.632	0.595	0.487	0.824	0.132	0.790	0.179

(continued)

Table 10.11 (continued)

Year	No drink water	No electricity	No Fuel	No toilet	No bicycle	No radio	Household head illiterate	No hospital	Wait time (>15 min)	No drink water	No electricity	No Fuel	No toilet	No bicycle	No radio	Household head illiterate	No hospital	Wait time (>15 min)	No drink water	No electricity	No Fuel	No toilet	No bicycle	No radio	Household head illiterate	No hospital	Wait time (>15 min)
	Rural China									Urban China									Overall China								
	50th to 100th percentile																										
1989	0.200	0.002	0.931	0.637	0.144	0.572	0.155	0.817	0.565	0.055	0.003	0.513	0.103	0.087	0.283	0.149	0.117	0.719	0.153	0.002	0.794	0.461	0.125	0.477	0.153	0.587	0.616
1991	0.139	0.001	0.879	0.507	0.159	0.447	0.145	0.880	0.512	0.021	0.000	0.388	0.086	0.115	0.224	0.147	0.091	0.783	0.101	0.001	0.721	0.371	0.145	0.375	0.146	0.626	0.599
1993	0.142	0.001	0.844	0.508	0.175	0.443	0.141	0.879	0.407	0.035	0.002	0.250	0.066	0.140	0.203	0.097	0.153	0.725	0.109	0.001	0.662	0.372	0.164	0.370	0.127	0.656	0.505
1997	0.038	0.001	0.579	0.460	0.254	0.481	0.117	0.889	0.296	0.025	0.002	0.078	0.018	0.233	0.253	0.068	0.197	0.568	0.034	0.001	0.412	0.313	0.247	0.405	0.100	0.659	0.386
2000	0.098	0.000	0.495	0.423	0.286	0.515	0.072	0.858	0.205	0.017	0.000	0.074	0.002	0.280	0.348	0.052	0.330	0.453	0.072	0.000	0.360	0.288	0.284	0.461	0.066	0.688	0.284
2004	0.095	0.001	0.525	0.352	0.381	0.705	0.053	0.889	0.206	0.030	0.000	0.066	0.007	0.383	0.486	0.046	0.364	0.356	0.074	0.001	0.374	0.239	0.382	0.633	0.051	0.716	0.255
2006	0.091	0.000	0.407	0.296	0.403	0.819	0.076	0.872	0.168	0.019	0.000	0.060	0.007	0.389	0.590	0.064	0.370	0.438	0.067	0.000	0.291	0.200	0.398	0.743	0.072	0.705	0.258

[a]All the dimensions have been described in Table A1.1 in Appendix 1 of Ray and Sinha (2015)

Table 10.12 Dimension-specific HCR in India[a] (Ray and Sinha 2015)

Year	No drink water	No elec-tricity	No Fuel	No toilet	No bicy-cle	No radio	Illiterate house-hold head	No hos-pital	Wait time (>15 min)	No drink water	No elec-tricity	No Fuel	No toilet	No bicy-cle	No radio	Illiterate house-hold head	No hos-pital	Wait time (>15 min)	No drink water	No elec-tricity	No Fuel	No toilet	No bicy-cle	No radio	Illiterate house-hold head	No hos-pital	Wait time (>15 min)
	Rural India									Urban India									All India								
1992–93	0.329	0.526	0.937	0.812	0.622	0.632	0.480	0.063	N/A	0.086	0.142	0.392	0.299	0.534	0.361	0.206	0.069	N/A	0.251	0.403	0.763	0.649	0.594	0.546	0.393	0.065	N/A
1998–99	0.283	0.459	0.870	0.771	0.563	0.645	0.406	0.600	0.154	0.075	0.073	0.459	0.369	0.496	0.434	0.165	0.706	0.199	0.216	0.335	0.738	0.642	0.541	0.577	0.329	0.634	0.168
2005–06	0.238	0.327	0.220	0.687	0.500	0.653	0.392	0.182	0.182	0.098	0.050	0.700	0.222	0.504	0.566	0.185	0.289	0.220	0.175	0.202	0.437	0.476	0.502	0.614	0.298	0.230	0.199
										Bottom 20th Percentile																	
1992–93	0.782	0.938	0.990	0.996	0.782	0.975	0.649	0.052	N/A	0.298	0.623	0.840	0.776	0.744	0.729	0.456	0.079	N/A	0.628	0.838	0.942	0.926	0.770	0.897	0.588	0.061	N/A
1998–99	0.518	0.951	0.899	1.000	0.916	0.978	0.623	0.591	0.103	0.216	0.317	0.893	0.868	0.666	0.760	0.338	0.570	0.192	0.412	0.729	0.897	0.954	0.828	0.902	0.523	0.584	0.134
2005–06	0.396	0.831	0.122	0.987	0.574	0.920	0.566	0.154	0.161	0.229	0.235	0.340	0.626	0.652	0.829	0.353	0.204	0.220	0.320	0.558	0.222	0.822	0.610	0.879	0.469	0.177	0.188
										20th to 50th percentile																	
1992–93	0.269	0.778	0.989	0.957	0.717	0.796	0.587	0.063	N/A	0.073	0.050	0.512	0.403	0.573	0.434	0.237	0.076	N/A	0.206	0.545	0.836	0.780	0.671	0.680	0.475	0.067	N/A
1998–99	0.241	0.655	0.918	0.969	0.528	0.763	0.479	0.611	0.139	0.065	0.024	0.621	0.552	0.602	0.503	0.193	0.690	0.211	0.187	0.462	0.827	0.842	0.550	0.684	0.392	0.635	0.161
2005–06	0.181	0.417	0.134	0.909	0.611	0.791	0.482	0.166	0.180	0.063	0.012	0.620	0.173	0.634	0.715	0.222	0.275	0.237	0.128	0.235	0.352	0.579	0.621	0.757	0.366	0.215	0.205
										50th to 100th percentile																	
1992–93	0.183	0.209	0.884	0.653	0.501	0.397	0.348	0.067	N/A	0.008	0.003	0.141	0.047	0.427	0.170	0.088	0.062	N/A	0.128	0.143	0.648	0.460	0.478	0.325	0.265	0.065	N/A
1998–99	0.228	0.157	0.828	0.562	0.460	0.451	0.283	0.596	0.182	0.023	0.003	0.185	0.055	0.362	0.260	0.078	0.772	0.193	0.162	0.107	0.622	0.400	0.429	0.390	0.217	0.653	0.185
2005–06	0.152	0.096	0.309	0.412	0.439	0.515	0.264	0.200	0.189	0.015	0.001	0.891	0.042	0.399	0.409	0.093	0.329	0.208	0.090	0.053	0.575	0.243	0.421	0.467	0.186	0.259	0.198

[a]All the dimensions have been described in Table A1 in Appendix 1 of Ray and Sinha (2015)

Table 10.13 Dimension-specific HCR in Vietnam[a] (Ray and Sinha 2015)

Year	No drink water	No elec- tricity	No toilet	No bicycle	House- hold head illiterate	No radio	No hos- pital	No drink water	No elec- tricity	No toilet	No bicycle	House- hold head illiterate	No radio	No hos- pital	No drink water	No elec- tricity	No toilet	No bicy- cle	House- hold head illiterate	No radio	No hospital
	Rural Vietnam							Urban Vietnam							Overall Viet Nam						
1992–93	0.235	0.612	0.525	0.352	0.755	0.146	0.997	0.110	0.121	0.271	0.208	0.558	0.084	0.994	0.210	0.514	0.474	0.323	0.716	0.134	0.997
1997–98	0.196	0.293	0.413	0.275	0.570	0.375	0.879	0.068	0.017	0.161	0.225	0.513	0.484	0.816	0.159	0.214	0.340	0.260	0.554	0.406	0.861
2002	0.191	0.186	0.650	0.311	0.719	0.613	0.119	0.065	0.026	0.250	0.328	0.720	0.402	0.093	0.161	0.149	0.556	0.315	0.719	0.564	0.112
2004	0.163	0.097	0.612	0.292	0.789	0.531	0.191	0.057	0.018	0.221	0.321	0.784	0.389	0.226	0.137	0.078	0.516	0.299	0.788	0.496	0.200
											Bottom 20 percentile										
1992–93	0.443	1.000	0.964	0.767	0.897	0.219	0.998	0.333	1.000	0.833	0.667	0.833	0.222	1.000	0.441	1.000	0.962	0.764	0.895	0.219	0.998
1997–98	0.439	0.964	0.778	0.639	0.678	0.349	0.891	0.128	0.487	0.564	0.615	0.436	0.282	0.846	0.426	0.943	0.768	0.638	0.667	0.346	0.889
2002	0.469	0.740	0.989	0.603	0.740	0.852	0.100	0.183	0.123	0.612	0.613	0.756	0.557	0.078	0.401	0.594	0.899	0.606	0.744	0.782	0.095
2004	0.402	0.399	0.978	0.615	0.794	0.408	0.157	0.164	0.078	0.644	0.578	0.799	0.454	0.144	0.344	0.321	0.897	0.606	0.795	0.419	0.153
											20th to 50th percentile										
1992–93	0.296	0.940	0.626	0.407	0.807	0.151	0.995	0.321	0.964	0.571	0.071	0.607	0.071	1.000	0.297	0.940	0.625	0.398	0.802	0.149	0.995
1997–98	0.264	0.313	0.536	0.388	0.589	0.345	0.895	0.033	0.000	0.283	0.133	0.633	0.633	0.733	0.254	0.299	0.524	0.377	0.591	0.358	0.888
2002	0.228	0.127	0.852	0.421	0.746	0.683	0.104	0.067	0.006	0.312	0.351	0.748	0.434	0.094	0.190	0.098	0.724	0.404	0.747	0.624	0.101
2004	0.195	0.041	0.820	0.356	0.835	0.544	0.193	0.046	0.003	0.242	0.345	0.824	0.411	0.223	0.159	0.031	0.677	0.353	0.832	0.511	0.200
											50th to 100th percentile										
1992–93	0.090	0.236	0.259	0.163	0.718	0.091	0.999	0.196	0.022	0.217	0.087	0.348	0.022	0.978	0.092	0.231	0.258	0.161	0.709	0.090	0.998
1997–98	0.048	0.002	0.184	0.067	0.527	0.396	0.863	0.010	0.000	0.093	0.072	0.320	0.443	0.784	0.046	0.002	0.180	0.067	0.518	0.398	0.859
2002	0.065	0.007	0.418	0.140	0.723	0.466	0.140	0.017	0.000	0.069	0.203	0.697	0.316	0.099	0.053	0.006	0.336	0.155	0.716	0.431	0.130
2004	0.055	0.002	0.337	0.137	0.790	0.574	0.212	0.021	0.000	0.033	0.215	0.780	0.349	0.267	0.046	0.002	0.263	0.156	0.787	0.519	0.225

[a]All the dimensions have been described in Table A1 in Appendix 1 of Ray and Sinha (2015)

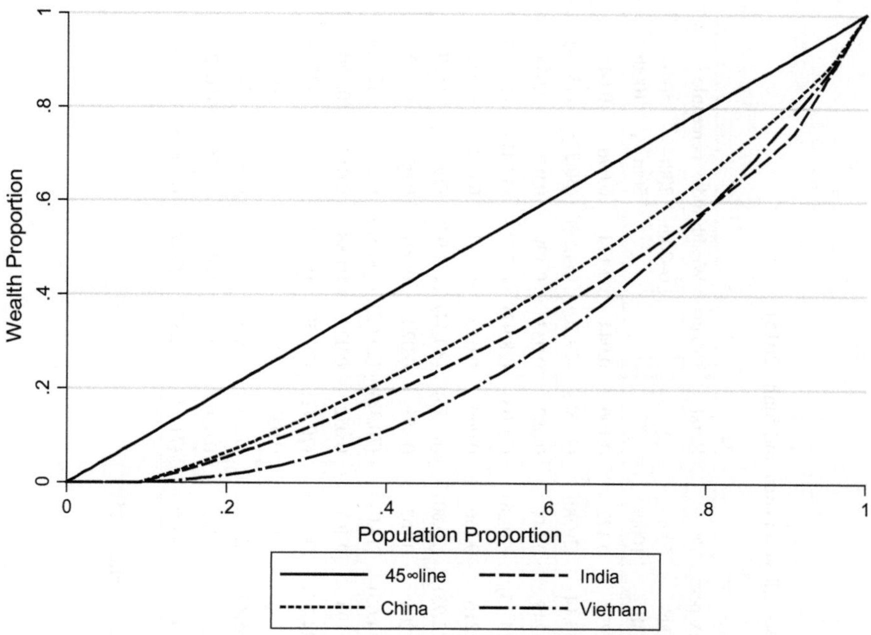

Fig. 10.2 Lorenz curve for wealth in China, India and Vietnam, 1992/1993. Reproduced from Ray and Sinha (2015)

Table 10.17 compares the dimension-specific deprivation rates between the three countries for the common year, 1992–93, and a common battery of eight dimensions. While India lags behind China on access to electricity and literacy, her deprivation rates on access to drink water, Fuel and in several other dimensions are quite comparable. Vietnam provides an interesting background to the India/China comparison, and her deprivation rates generally lie between that in the two large countries. In general, on these dimension-specific deprivation rates, Vietnam is closer to India than to China. The above discussion is largely based on the MDD measure that considers the deprivation in the whole population, not just the 'poor'. Table 10.18 looks at the 'multidimensionally poor' households by reporting (on the left-hand side) the HCR of the percentage of such households who are deprived in 1, 2, 3,…, 8 dimensions in the common year, 1992/93 in the three countries. The right-hand side reports the estimated M_0 (k) measure (MDP) at a variety of cut-offs (k) adopted for the definition of the 'poor'. The M_0 estimates are not directly comparable with the π_α estimates reported earlier since, apart from the fact that M_0 looks at only the poor, while π_α considers the entire population, there is no direct equivalence between the k (cut-off in M_0) and α (in π_α).

The MDP estimates do decline as the adopted cut-off k increases but at varying rates between the three countries. The decline is much sharper in China than in India and Vietnam. The MDP estimates of M_0 in Table 10.18 show that India and Vietnam were both multidimensionally poorer than China in 1992/93 at all the

Table 10.14 Multidimensional deprivation, contribution to deprivation in China[a], CHNS, all years (Ray and Sinha 2015)

	π_1^b					π_2^b					π_4^b				
Year	Rural	Urban	Wealth index percentile			Rural	Urban	Wealth index percentile			Rural	Urban	Wealth index percentile		
			0–20th	20th–50th	50th–100th			0–20th	20th–50th	50th–100th			0–20th	20th–50th	50th–100th
1989	0.511	0.345	0.597	0.500	0.374	0.286	0.155	0.377	0.272	0.172	0.106	0.044	0.174	0.096	0.048
	(59.70)	(40.30)	(40.56)	(34.01)	(25.43)	(64.94)	(35.06)	(45.96)	(33.14)	(20.90)	(70.80)	(29.20)	(54.59)	(30.27)	(15.14)
1991	0.472	0.320	0.552	0.474	0.343	0.246	0.133	0.323	0.245	0.144	0.082	0.033	0.129	0.079	0.035
	(59.58)	(40.42)	(40.32)	(34.65)	(25.03)	(64.84)	(35.16)	(45.38)	(34.35)	(20.26)	(71.03)	(28.97)	(53.18)	(32.47)	(14.35)
1993	0.450	0.305	0.535	0.446	0.330	0.224	0.124	0.303	0.216	0.136	0.069	0.030	0.113	0.061	0.032
	(59.62)	(40.38)	(40.82)	(34.02)	(25.16)	(64.36)	(35.64)	(46.24)	(32.95)	(20.80)	(69.56)	(30.44)	(54.97)	(29.63)	(15.40)
1997	0.422	0.274	0.512	0.428	0.284	0.202	0.107	0.279	0.205	0.107	0.058	0.024	0.097	0.058	0.022
	(60.59)	(39.41)	(41.83)	(34.95)	(23.21)	(65.50)	(34.50)	(47.28)	(34.65)	(18.07)	(70.38)	(29.62)	(54.52)	(32.95)	(12.53)
2000	0.407	0.267	0.494	0.414	0.278	0.190	0.099	0.262	0.194	0.101	0.052	0.022	0.088	0.053	0.020
	(60.40)	(39.60)	(41.66)	(34.88)	(23.46)	(65.66)	(34.34)	(47.13)	(34.75)	(18.13)	(70.41)	(29.59)	(54.72)	(33.08)	(12.20)
2001	0.423	0.283	0.490	0.424	0.303	0.200	0.107	0.255	0.203	0.115	0.057	0.023	0.081	0.059	0.024
	(59.88)	(40.12)	(40.26)	(34.86)	(24.88)	(65.29)	(34.71)	(44.51)	(35.41)	(20.08)	(71.07)	(28.93)	(49.39)	(35.87)	(14.74)
2006	0.419	0.291	0.499	0.419	0.304	0.198	0.108	0.264	0.198	0.113	0.056	0.023	0.087	0.056	0.022
	(59.05)	(40.95)	(40.84)	(34.31)	(24.85)	(64.68)	(35.32)	(45.98)	(34.43)	(19.59)	(71.15)	(28.85)	(52.65)	(34.04)	(13.31)

[a]The percentage contribution of each subgroup's π to overall π appears in parenthesis

[b]These π s are based on the nine dimensions described in Table A1 in Appendix 1 of Ray and Sinha (2015)

Table 10.15 Multidimensional deprivation, contribution to deprivation in India[a], NFHS, all years (Ray and Sinha 2015)

	π_1^b					π_2^b					π_4^b				
Year	Rural	Urban	Wealth index percentile			Rural	Urban	Wealth index percentile			Rural	Urban	Wealth index *Quintile*		
			0–20th	20th–50th	50th–100th			0–20th	20th–50th	50th–100th			0–20th	20th–50th	50th–100th
1992–93	0.489	0.232	0.628	0.473	0.279	0.273	0.091	0.414	0.257	0.111	0.105	0.024	0.198	0.090	0.025
	(67.82)	(32.18)	(45.48)	(34.29)	(20.22)	(74.96)	(25.04)	(52.93)	(32.90)	(14.18)	(81.24)	(18.76)	(63.32)	(28.82)	(7.86)
1998–99	0.528	0.331	0.662	0.527	0.352	0.313	0.143	0.462	0.304	0.154	0.135	0.040	0.249	0.119	0.042
	(61.49)	(38.51)	(42.99)	(34.19)	(22.83)	(68.69)	(31.31)	(50.19)	(33.04)	(16.77)	(77.05)	(22.95)	(60.72)	(29.13)	(10.15)
2005–06	0.376	0.315	0.472	0.384	0.277	0.168	0.119	0.243	0.167	0.094	0.046	0.024	0.079	0.041	0.016
	(54.41)	(45.59)	(41.64)	(33.94)	(24.43)	(58.63)	(41.37)	(48.22)	(33.14)	(18.64)	(65.97)	(34.03)	(58.19)	(30.32)	(11.49)

[a]The percentage contribution of each subgroup's π to overall π appears in parenthesis

[b]These π s are based on the nine dimensions described in Table A1 in Appendix 1 of Ray and Sinha (2015)

Table 10.16 Multidimensional deprivation, contribution to deprivation in Vietnam[a], VLSS, All Years (Ray and Sinha 2015)

	π_1^b					π_2^b					π_4^b				
Year	Rural	Urban	Wealth index percentile			Rural	Urban	Wealth index percentile			Rural	Urban	Wealth index percentile		
			0–20th	20th–50th	50th–100th			0–20th	20th–50th	50th–100th			0–20th	20th–50th	50th–100th
1992–93	0.518	0.335	0.754	0.601	0.363	0.311	0.146	0.583	0.380	0.150	0.147	0.048	0.372	0.174	0.034
	(60.70)	(39.30)	(43.90)	(34.99)	(21.12)	(68.07)	(31.93)	(52.38)	(34.15)	(13.47)	(75.42)	(24.58)	(64.24)	(29.94)	(5.82)
1997–98	0.425	0.328	0.666	0.472	0.299	0.224	0.131	0.475	0.249	0.106	0.091	0.031	0.281	0.087	0.018
	(56.45)	(43.55)	(46.37)	(32.84)	(20.79)	(63.08)	(36.92)	(57.25)	(30.02)	(12.73)	(74.91)	(25.09)	(72.92)	(22.50)	(4.58)
2002	0.382	0.260	0.580	0.409	0.258	0.185	0.094	0.369	0.194	0.087	0.064	0.021	0.177	0.056	0.015
	(59.46)	(40.54)	(46.52)	(32.81)	(20.68)	(66.32)	(33.68)	(56.75)	(29.82)	(13.43)	(75.56)	(24.44)	(71.31)	(22.71)	(5.99)
2004	0.369	0.287	0.491	0.390	0.282	0.164	0.105	0.266	0.174	0.098	0.045	0.021	0.096	0.045	0.017
	(56.31)	(43.69)	(42.21)	(33.52)	(24.28)	(60.95)	(39.05)	(49.39)	(32.32)	(18.29)	(68.23)	(31.77)	(60.77)	(28.61)	(10.62)

[a]The percentage contribution of each subgroup's π to overall π appears in parenthesis

[b]These π s are based on the seven of the nine dimensions described in Table A1 in Appendix 1 of Ray and Sinha (2015)

Table 10.17 Comparison of dimension-specific HCRs between China, India and Vietnam in 1992–93[a] (Ray and Sinha 2015)

Year: 1992–93	No drink water	No electricity	No Fuel	No toilet	No bicycle	No radio	Household head illiterate	No hospital
China								
All	0.190	0.015	0.794	0.589	0.204	0.502	0.164	0.709
Rural	0.220	0.021	0.913	0.698	0.207	0.576	0.169	0.883
Urban	0.122	0.002	0.518	0.335	0.196	0.331	0.152	0.305
0–20th wealth percentile	0.324	0.070	0.999	0.894	0.331	0.785	0.254	0.866
20–50th wealth percentile	0.239	0.001	0.935	0.739	0.204	0.570	0.175	0.772
50–100th wealth percentile	0.105	0.001	0.624	0.370	0.151	0.343	0.120	0.606
India								
All	0.251	0.403	0.763	0.649	0.594	0.546	0.393	0.065
Rural	0.329	0.526	0.937	0.812	0.622	0.632	0.480	0.063
Urban	0.086	0.142	0.392	0.299	0.534	0.361	0.206	0.069
0–20th wealth percentile	0.628	0.838	0.942	0.926	0.770	0.897	0.588	0.061
20–50th wealth percentile	0.206	0.545	0.836	0.780	0.671	0.680	0.475	0.067
50–100th wealth percentile	0.128	0.143	0.648	0.460	0.478	0.325	0.265	0.065
Vietnam								
All	0.210	0.514	0.887	0.474	0.323	0.716	0.134	0.997
Rural	0.235	0.612	0.965	0.525	0.352	0.755	0.146	0.997
Urban	0.110	0.121	0.573	0.271	0.208	0.558	0.084	0.994
0–20th wealth percentile	0.441	1.000	0.989	0.962	0.764	0.895	0.219	0.998
20–50th wealth percentile	0.297	0.940	0.992	0.625	0.398	0.802	0.149	0.995
50–100th wealth percentile	0.092	0.231	0.938	0.258	0.161	0.709	0.090	0.998

[a]All the dimensions have been described in Table A1 in Appendix 1 of Ray and Sinha (2015)

Table 10.18 Multidimensional poverty index in China, India and Vietnam in 1992/1993 (Ray and Sinha 2015)

Poverty Cut-off (k)	Multidimensional headcount ratio (H)						M_0					
	Rural	Urban	All	Wealth index (percentile)			Rural	Urban	All	Wealth Index (percentile)		
				0–20	20–50	50–100				0–20	20–50	50–100
China												
1	0.989	0.792	0.929	1.000	0.998	0.859	0.466	0.269	0.407	0.565	0.458	0.310
2	0.950	0.596	0.842	1.000	0.968	0.703	0.461	0.245	0.396	0.565	0.454	0.290
3	0.856	0.420	0.723	0.984	0.860	0.535	0.438	0.201	0.367	0.561	0.428	0.249
4	0.581	0.221	0.471	0.850	0.558	0.265	0.335	0.126	0.272	0.511	0.315	0.147
5	0.241	0.079	0.192	0.459	0.193	0.083	0.164	0.053	0.131	0.315	0.131	0.054
6	0.083	0.022	0.065	0.188	0.062	0.017	0.065	0.017	0.050	0.145	0.048	0.013
7	0.016	0.003	0.012	0.045	0.008	0.001	0.014	0.003	0.010	0.039	0.007	0.001
8	0.000	0.000	0.000	0.001	0.000	0.000	0.000	0.000	0.000	0.001	0.000	0.000
India												
1	0.987	0.809	0.930	1.000	0.985	0.869	0.551	0.261	0.458	0.707	0.533	0.314
2	0.947	0.543	0.818	0.999	0.923	0.683	0.546	0.228	0.444	0.707	0.525	0.291
3	0.857	0.349	0.695	0.983	0.819	0.505	0.523	0.179	0.413	0.703	0.499	0.246
4	0.710	0.210	0.551	0.930	0.712	0.303	0.469	0.127	0.359	0.683	0.459	0.171
5	0.515	0.115	0.388	0.824	0.536	0.125	0.372	0.080	0.278	0.631	0.372	0.082
6	0.290	0.049	0.213	0.608	0.264	0.024	0.231	0.039	0.170	0.498	0.203	0.018
7	0.091	0.012	0.066	0.293	0.021	0.002	0.081	0.011	0.059	0.262	0.019	0.002
8	0.003	0.001	0.002	0.012	0.000	0.000	0.003	0.001	0.003	0.012	0.000	0.000
Vietnam												
1	1.000	0.999	1.000	1.000	1.000	1.000	0.574	0.365	0.531	0.784	0.650	0.435
2	0.992	0.847	0.963	1.000	1.000	0.984	0.573	0.346	0.526	0.784	0.650	0.433
3	0.927	0.542	0.850	1.000	1.000	0.843	0.556	0.269	0.497	0.784	0.650	0.397

(continued)

Table 10.18 (continued)

Poverty Cut-off (k)	Multidimensional headcount ratio (H)						M_0					
	Rural	Urban	All	Wealth index (percentile)			Rural	Urban	All	Wealth Index (percentile)		
				0–20	20–50	50–100				0–20	20–50	50–100
4	0.745	0.285	0.653	1.000	0.974	0.488	0.487	0.173	0.423	0.784	0.640	0.264
5	0.513	0.151	0.441	0.994	0.780	0.141	0.372	0.106	0.318	0.780	0.543	0.091
6	0.287	0.067	0.243	0.826	0.340	0.021	0.234	0.054	0.197	0.675	0.268	0.016
7	0.109	0.023	0.092	0.381	0.097	0.002	0.101	0.021	0.085	0.342	0.086	0.001
8	0.016	0.006	0.014	0.067	0.008	0.000	0.017	0.006	0.015	0.067	0.008	0.000

Table 10.19 Percentage contribution of each dimension to the multidimensional poverty index: China, India and Vietnam in 1992–93[a] (Ray and Sinha 2015)

Group	No drinking water	No electricity	No Fuel	No toilet	No bicycle	No radio	Household head illiterate	No hospital	M_0
China									
All China	6.01%	0.47%	25.08%	18.59%	6.44%	15.85%	5.17%	22.39%	0.396 (100%)
Rural	5.96%	0.56%	24.78%	18.93%	5.62%	15.62%	4.58%	23.95%	0.461 (100%)
Urban	6.23%	0.10%	26.41%	17.07%	10.02%	16.87%	7.73%	15.57%	0.245 (100%)
0–20th wealth percentile	7.16%	1.55%	22.08%	19.77%	7.33%	17.36%	5.61%	19.14%	0.565 (100%)
20–50th wealth percentile	6.58%	0.03%	25.71%	20.34%	5.60%	15.69%	4.82%	21.23%	0.454 (100%)
50–100th wealth percentile	4.54%	0.03%	26.91%	15.96%	6.51%	14.79%	5.15%	26.11%	0.290 (100%)
India									
All India	7.01%	11.29%	20.81%	18.02%	15.16%	15.00%	11.00%	1.72%	0.444 (100%)
Rural	7.50%	12.00%	21.09%	18.49%	14.02%	14.43%	11.05%	1.41%	0.546 (100%)
Urban	4.50%	7.63%	19.39%	15.61%	21.00%	17.88%	10.71%	3.28%	0.228 (100%)
0–20th wealth percentile	11.09%	14.80%	16.76%	16.36%	13.61%	15.85%	10.47%	1.07%	0.707 (100%)
20–50th wealth percentile	4.85%	12.93%	19.64%	18.34%	15.40%	15.94%	11.35%	1.56%	0.525(100%)

(continued)

Table 10.19 (continued)

Group		No drinking water	No electricity	No Fuel	No toilet	No bicycle	No radio	Household head illiterate	No hospital	M_0
50–100th wealth percentile		5.38%	6.10%	26.02%	19.28%	16.43%	13.15%	11.13%	2.52%	0.291(100%)
Vietnam										
All Vietnam		4.79%	11.95%	21.00%	11.08%	7.90%	17.51%	2.98%	22.79%	0.526(100%)
Rural		4.92%	13.14%	21.05%	11.29%	7.95%	17.07%	2.97%	21.60%	0.573(100%)
Urban		3.98%	4.32%	20.68%	9.73%	7.58%	20.30%	2.99%	30.42%	0.346(100%)
0–20th wealth percentile		7.04%	15.95%	15.78%	15.34%	12.20%	14.29%	3.49%	15.92%	0.784(100%)
20–50th wealth percentile		5.71%	18.09%	19.07%	12.02%	7.66%	15.43%	2.87%	19.15%	0.650(100%)
50–100th wealth percentile		2.67%	6.68%	27.10%	7.44%	4.67%	20.48%	2.59%	28.38%	0.433(100%)
Percentage contribution for k = 2, 4, 6										
China	k = 2	6.01%	0.47%	25.08%	18.59%	6.44%	15.85%	5.17%	22.39%	0.396(100%)
	k = 4	7.31%	0.67%	21.70%	18.49%	7.47%	18.18%	6.09%	20.07%	0.272(100%)
	k = 6	11.46%	1.97%	16.16%	15.48%	13.66%	15.63%	9.86%	15.78%	0.050(100%)
India	k = 2	7.01%	11.28%	20.81%	18.02%	15.16%	15.00%	11.00%	1.71%	0.444(100%)
	k = 4	7.73%	12.73%	18.83%	17.39%	14.14%	15.46%	11.90%	1.53%	0.359(100%)
	k = 6	9.45%	14.21%	15.80%	15.50%	14.61%	15.14%	13.64%	1.64%	0.170(100%)
Vietnam	k = 2	4.79%	11.95%	21.00%	11.08%	7.90%	17.51%	2.98%	22.77%	0.526(100%)
	k = 4	5.84%	14.22%	18.81%	12.86%	9.14%	16.53%	3.48%	19.11%	0.421(100%)
	k = 6	8.46%	14.58%	15.48%	14.24%	12.53%	14.34%	4.91%	15.45%	0.197(100%)

[a] All the dimensions have been described in Table A1 in Appendix 1 of Ray and Sinha (2015)

cut-offs (k). The Indian and Vietnamese estimates of poverty are much closer to one another than to the Chinese estimates. In spite of her remarkable progress in the decade since the '*Doi Moi* reforms', as documented in Glewwe et al. (2004), Vietnam was, in 1992/93, the multidimensionally poorest country in this group of countries. This is also true of the MDD estimates of π_α reported in Tables 10.14, 10.15 and 10.16, with Vietnam recording the highest levels of MDD. The large multidimensional poverty estimates of Vietnam in the 1990s should not detract from her remarkable progress in the past decade. As noted by Glewwe et al. (2004, p. vii), 'Vietnam's economic and social achievements in the 1990s are nothing short of amazing, arguably placing it among the top two or three performers among all developing countries'. Overall, the picture portrayed by the MDD estimates is quite consistent with that portrayed by the MDP figures.

A significant advantage of the MDP measure, M_0, over the MDD measure, π_α is that the former allows dimensional decomposability unlike the latter except in the degenerate case where $\alpha = 1$. Table 10.19 reports, in the top half, the percentage contribution to overall deprivation in the three countries by each of the eight dimensions in M_0 at the cut-off of $k = 2$. Lack of access to drinking water and electricity is a greater source of poverty in rural areas than in the urban in India and Vietnam, less so in China. Consistent with the earlier discussion, lack of literacy of the household head is a larger source of poverty in India than in China. Lack of literacy matters still less in Vietnam compared to China. Lack of access to clean Fuel and lack of access to toilets accounted for 35–40% of MDP in all the three countries. In all these countries, the contribution of lack of drinking water and of electricity to poverty declines, i.e., they matter less and less, as we move up the wealth distribution. Lack of access to Fuel is a significant source of MDP even for the well-off households (i.e. those in the top 50% of the wealth distribution) in all the three countries. The bottom half of Table 10.19 reports the percentage contributions and the M_0 values at three cut-off values used to define the 'poor'. These show that the picture on the contributions of the dimensions to MDP is generally robust to the cut-off used to define the multidimensionally poor.

The evidence on the nature of correspondence between wealth and deprivation is presented in Fig. 10.3, which compares the Lorenz curve for wealth with the pseudo-Lorenz curves for MDD and MDP in each country for two combinations of MDD and MDP, i.e. deprivation in two dimensions ($\alpha = 2$ and $k = 2$) and four dimensions ($\alpha = 4$ and $k = 4$). The latter show the deprivation and poverty share of the households arranged in an increasing order of household wealth as is done in the former. As expected, the Lorenz curve for wealth bulges towards the x-axis, the pseudo-Lorenz curves for deprivation and poverty bulge towards the y-axis, away from the 45° line. Deviation from the 45° line reflects the inequity in wealth, deprivation and poverty, respectively. The fact that MDP considers only the poor explains the fact that the pseudo-Lorenz curve of the M_0 measure lies outside that of the MDD measure, π_α. It is also worth noting that the gap between the pseudo-Lorenz curves of deprivation and poverty is much smaller in China than in the other countries, which possibly suggests that the difference between 'deprivation' and 'poverty' is much less significant in China than elsewhere.

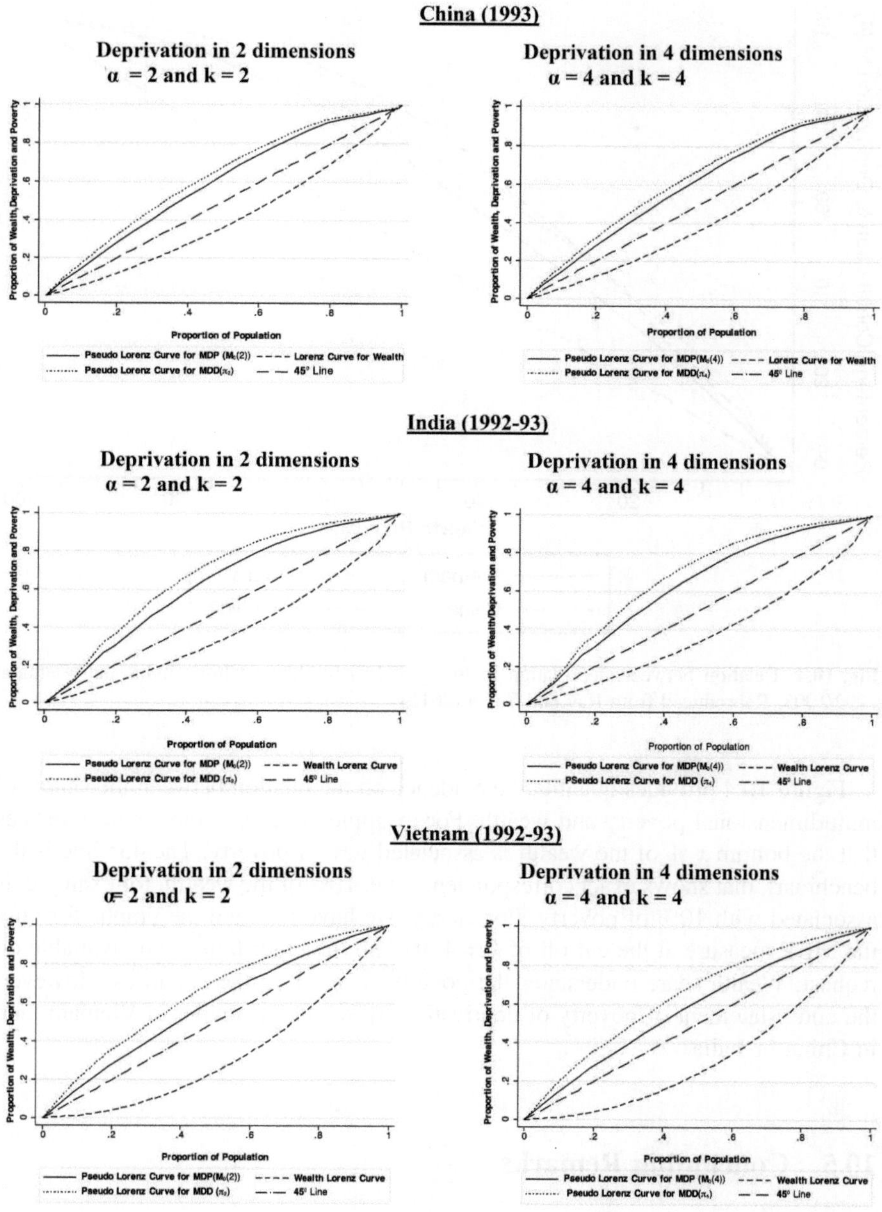

Fig. 10.3 Comparison of Lorenz curves for wealth and pseudo-Lorenz curves for deprivation, poverty. Reproduced from Ray and Sinha (2015)

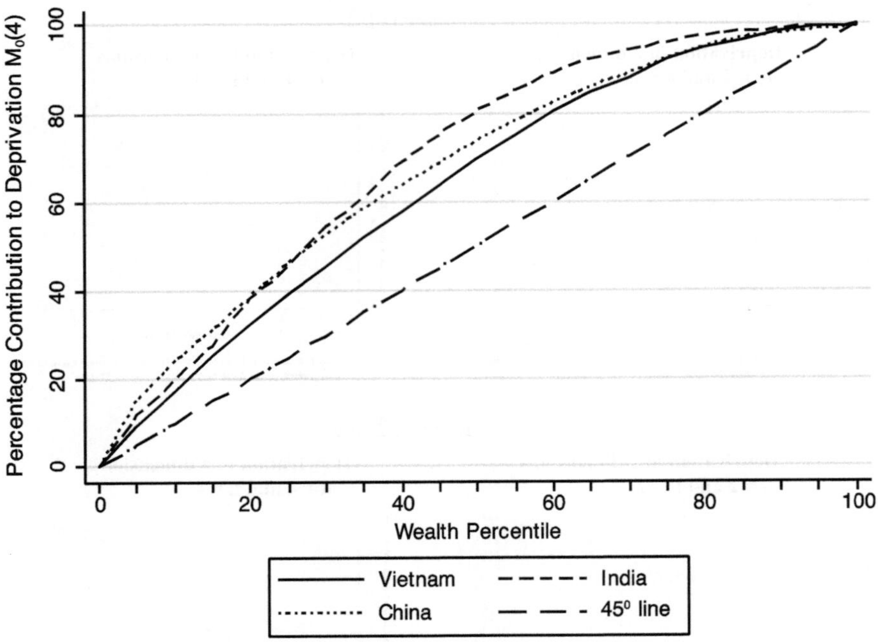

Fig. 10.4 Relation between deprivation in living and in wealth in China, India and Vietnam, 1992/1993. Reproduced from Ray and Sinha (2015)

Figure 10.4 provides quantitative evidence on the relation between the shares of multidimensional poverty and wealth. For example, a (x, y) combination indicates that the bottom x % of the wealth is associated y % of poverty. The 45° line is the benchmark that shows exact correspondence, i.e. 10% of the wealth, for example, is associated with 10% of poverty. For clarity, we have reported the graphs for only the MDP measure at the cut-off of $k = 4$, though the other figures are available on request. Wealth share understates the poverty share in all the countries. However, the understatement of poverty or deprivation by wealth is smaller in Vietnam than in China or India.

10.5 Concluding Remarks

This chapter documents the move from purely money metric measures such as income or expenditure poverty rates to multidimensional deprivation and multidimensional poverty as welfare, or perhaps more appropriately described as, 'illfare' measures. While at the aggregate country level per capita income has given way to Human Development Index (HDI) in ranking countries, at the household level an exclusive reliance on income or expenditure poverty rates has now given way to an all—encompassing multidimensional approach based on information on a household's lack of access to a range of dimensions. Countries are now routinely ranked in the Human Development Reports (HDR) according to both their HDI and their Multidimensional Poverty Index (MPI). Not only has the empirical literature reflected this change in approach, the move to the multidimensional measures has been made possible by the increasing availability of household-level data often in unit record form providing information on a variety of household characteristics and access to a range of dimensions.

Both as illustration and as case studies, this chapter describes closely two empirical exercises on multidimensional deprivation involving welfare comparisons, one at the subnational level between households across regions within a country, the other involving similar comparison between countries. Both these studies, as is the multidimensional deprivation literature as a whole, are very policy driven in not only quantifying the overall extent of deprivation, but in identifying the dimensions where the deprivation is acute, and in identifying population subgroups that fare the worst and are crying out for targeted intervention. However, the adaptation of the multidimensional literature as discussed in this chapter for policy application still has a way to go. In adopting a static framework and using data from repeated cross sections, the literature surveyed in this chapter has ignored issues such as duration and persistence of deprivation. The latter requires a dynamic extension of the measures to focus on these temporal elements and the availability of panel data for empirical investigation of such issues. We now turn to these issues in the following chapter.

References

Alkire S, Foster J (2011) Counting and multidimensional poverty measurement. J Public Econ 95 (7):476–487

Alkire S, Santos M (2010) Acute multidimensional poverty: a new index for developing countries. In: Human Development Research Paper 2010/11

Atkinson A (1970) On the measurement of inequality. J Econ Theory 2:244–263

Bardhan P (2010) Awakening giants, feet of clay: assessing the economic rise of China and India. Princeton University Press, Princeton and Oxford

Bourguignon F, Chakravarty S (2003) The measurement of multidimensional poverty. J Econ Inequality 1:25–49

Chakravarty S, D'Ambrosio C (2006) The measurement of social exclusion. Rev Income Wealth 52(3):377–398

Chakravarty S, Majumder A (2005) Measuring human poverty: a generalized index and an application using basic dimensions of life and some anthropometric indicators. J Human Dev 6 (3):275–299

Foster JE, Greer J, Thorbecke E (1984) A class of decomposable poverty measures. Econometrica 52:761–766

Glewwe P, Agrawal N, Dollar D (eds) (2004) Economic growth, poverty, and household welfare in Vietnam. World Bank, Washington

Jayaraj D, Subramanian S (2010) A Chakravarty-D'Ambrosio view of multidimensional deprivation: some estimates for India. Econ Polit Wkly XLV(6):53–65

Mishra A, Ray R (2013) Multi-dimensional deprivation in India during and after the reforms: do the household expenditure and the family health surveys present consistent evidence? Soc Indic Res 2013(110):791–818
Popkin BM, Shufa D, Zhai F, Zhang B (2010) Cohort profile: The China health and nutrition survey-monitoring and understanding socio-economic and health change in China, 1989–2011. Int J Epidemiol 39:1435–1440
Ray R, Mishra A (2012) Multi-dimensional deprivation in the awakening giants: a comparison of China and India on micro data. J Asian Econ 23(4):454–465
Ray R, Sinha K (2015) Multidimensional deprivation in China, India and Vietnam: a comparative study on micro data. J Human Dev Capabilities 16(1):69–93
Sen AK (1985) Commodities and capabilities. North-Holland, Amsterdam
Sen AK (1999) Development as freedom. Oxford University Press, Oxford
UNDP (1990) Concept and measurement of human development. Human Development Report. Oxford University Press, New York
UNDP (1997) Human development to eradicate poverty. Human Development Report. Oxford University Press, New York
UNDP (2010) The real wealth of nations: pathways to human development. Human Development Report. Oxford University Press, New York
Vyas S, Kumaranayeke L (2006) Constructing socio-economic status indices: how to use principal component analysis. Health Policy Planning 21(6):459–468
World Bank (2000) Vietnam-attacking poverty: Vietnam development report, 2000. World Bank, Hanoi

Chapter 11
Dynamic Extensions of Multidimensional Poverty Measures with Selected Empirical Applications

11.1 Introduction

A key limitation of the multidimensional deprivation literature discussed in the previous chapter has been the static nature of the measures which do not distinguish between transitory and permanent deprivation in particular dimensions. While the availability of panel data provided an impetus for the introduction of dynamic considerations in the literature on deprivation, such extensions are restricted to the unidimensional context. Examples of recent contributions include Calvo and Dercon (2007), Foster (2009), Bossert et al. (2010) and Gradin et al. (2012). There have been relatively few attempts to introduce dynamic considerations in the multidimensional deprivation context. This chapter extends the discussion of the previous chapter to describe the methodology and empirical results of three recent studies that extend the multidimensional deprivation measurement literature to incorporate dynamic considerations. The studies described in this chapter are that by Nicholas and Ray (2012) on Australian data and by Nicholas et al. (2017) on Chinese data. The choice of Australia and China in these two studies was largely dictated by the fact that these countries are among the few that provide the necessary information on panel of households covering their access or otherwise to a range of dimensions over a reasonably long period of time. While the contribution of both studies is primarily methodological, their empirical results draw attention to the differences in economic advancement between population subgroups over time. To add to the evidence in support of the usefulness of the dynamic approach to the measurement of multidimensional deprivation, this chapter reports the principal results of a study by Mishra et al. (2018) that examines child disadvantage in Australia using a holistic, dynamic measure that not only accounts for multiple sources of disadvantage but also for the persistence of disadvantage throughout a child's life. A significant feature of this study is the evidence it provides that shows the higher deprivation faced by indigenous children vis-a-vis non-indigenous children in Australia.

R. Ray, *Household Behaviour, Prices, and Welfare*, Themes in Economics,
https://doi.org/10.1007/978-981-13-1930-3_11

Nicholas and Ray (2012) proposes dynamic extensions of some recent multidimensional deprivation measures and applies them to study deprivation in Australia using panel data. In incorporating dynamic considerations, this paper draws a distinction between persistence and duration of deprivation. While 'persistence' of deprivation denotes the number of uninterrupted spells of deprivation, 'duration' denotes the total number of periods of deprivation, i.e. including both interrupted and uninterrupted spells.[1] The Australian application illustrates the usefulness of the dynamic extension. The proposed methodology allows for the identification of population subgroups and deprivation dimensions that are characterised by recurring and persistent deprivation so that they can be directly targeted in policy intervention. Nicholas et al. (2017), which is the second study that is described in this chapter, is an advancement of Nicholas and Ray (2012) by proposing a dynamic multidimensional poverty measure that is sensitive to the within-individual distribution of deprivations across dimensions and time. The proposed measure combines features from a static multidimensional measure (Alkire and Foster 2011) and a time-dependent unidimensional measure (Foster 2009).

The new measure separately identifies—and can therefore be decomposed according to—the proportion of the poverty score attributable to: (i) the concentration of deprivations within periods; (ii) the concentration of deprivations within dimensions. In doing so, it allows for a poverty ranking that is robust to assumptions about the trade-off between the two components. Previous measures have not allowed for the features proposed in Nicholas et al. (2017) due to the inability to calculate the exact contribution of each dimension to overall poverty. This study overcomes this limitation by adapting to the measure the Shapley decomposition proposed in Shorrocks (2013) (based on Shapley 1953). The measure is applied to data from China, 2000–2011. The rest of this chapter is organised as follows. Section 11.2 describes the analytical framework, the axioms, and the measure proposed in Nicholas and Ray (2012) along with the data description and the empirical results from its application on Australian panel data. Section 11.3 contains the description of the corresponding items in Nicholas et al. (2017)'s study on Chinese panel data. Section 11.4 reports the results of Mishra et al. (2018) that applies the methodology described in Sect. 11.2 to the measurement and analysis of child disadvantage in Australia. The chapter concludes with a few summary remarks in Sect. 11.5.

11.2 Duration and Persistence in Multidimensional Deprivation

Chakravarty and D'Ambrosio (2006) (henceforth CD), using an axiomatic framework, propose a class of multidimensional deprivation measures that are population subgroup decomposable. Several other recent papers have also proposed multidimensional measures based on an axiomatic framework [see, for example, Bossert

[1]See Bossert et al. (2010) for a similar distinction in the unidimensional context.

et al. (2007)]. The CD framework is adopted in Nicholas and Ray (2012) since subgroup decomposability allows different population groups within Australia to be compared and analysed. Additionally, the specific forms of the measure suggested in CD allow flexibility in terms of additional properties that may be useful for different policy questions. The proceeding subsections will present a new generalisation of the class of measures used in CD and Jayaraj and Subramanian (2010) (henceforth JS) where the duration and persistence of deprivation are explicitly taken into account.

11.2.1 Analytical Framework

11.2.1.1 The Multidimensional Deprivation Index

Assume we observe, for all *N* individuals in the population of interest, *K* different dimensions of deprivation and *T* equally spaced periods of time. We say that an individual i is deprived in dimension j at time t when $x_{ijt} < h_j$, where $i \in \{1, 2, \ldots, N\}$, $j \in \{1, 2, \ldots, K\}, t \in \{1, 2, \ldots, T\}, x_{ijt}$ is individual i's attribute level in dimension j at time t, and w_j is a cut-off point that determines whether or not an individual is considered deprived in a particular dimension. For example, in the dimension 'health', x may be the individual's body mass index, in which case w would be some threshold below which the individual would be considered underweight and therefore deprived in the health dimension. Deprivation in itself need not be classified as a dichotomous outcome, i.e. either deprived or not deprived. A general specification discussed in Atkinson (2003) and applied in Alkire and Foster (2010) allows the *depth* of deprivation in a particular dimension/period to be taken into account.

$$d_{ijt}^{\gamma} = \begin{cases} \left(1 - \frac{x_{ijt}}{h_j}\right)^{\gamma} & \text{if } x_{ijt} < h_j \\ 0 & \text{otherwise} \end{cases} \tag{11.1}$$

where $\gamma \geq 0$ is a sensitivity parameter along the lines of the poverty measure due to Foster et al. (1984). γ allows the individual weight given to a dimension to increase with the depth of deprivation in that particular dimension.

However, the types of variables used in multidimensional studies often come from survey questions that are either qualitative and/or dichotomous in nature (e.g., whether an individual has access to a certain good or service or not). In such cases, deprivation has to be represented by a restriction on (1), namely by specifying $\gamma = 0$. In other words, $d_{ijt}^{0} = 1$ when an individual is deprived in dimension j at time t and $d_{ijt}^{0} = 0$, otherwise.[2] Given this, each individual i can be said to have an

[2]As in JS and CD, this means that properties focusing on the depth of deprivation in a particular dimension as discussed in Bourguignon and Chakravarty (2003) will not be satisfied by the measures we adopt here. Instead, we emphasise the desirable properties across (as opposed to within) dimensions, as well as across time.

individual deprivation profile, which is a matrix $\boldsymbol{D_i} = \begin{pmatrix} d^0_{i11} & \cdots & d^0_{i1T} \\ . & \cdots & . \\ d^0_{iK1} & \cdots & d^0_{iKT} \end{pmatrix}$ where $d_{ijt} \in \{0, 1\} \forall j \in \{1, 2, \ldots, K\}$, $t \in \{1, 2, \ldots, T\}$ and $i \in \{1, 2, \ldots, N\}$. The *individual deprivation score* μ_i is a function $f : \boldsymbol{D_i} \rightarrow \boldsymbol{R}$ where $\boldsymbol{R}$ is the set of real numbers.[3] The *population deprivation profile* is a vector $\boldsymbol{\rho} = (\mu_1, \ldots, \mu_N)$ of individual scores in non-decreasing order. The *multidimensional deprivation index* Ω is then a function $g : \boldsymbol{\rho} \rightarrow \boldsymbol{R}$.

11.2.1.2 Desirable Properties

Property [i] Subgroup Decomposability (SD). The class of population subgroup decomposable measures requires that for any partitioning of the population, the overall index must be a population share-weighted average of the subgroup indices. Property [ii] Normalisation (NN). Normalisation requires that $\Omega \in [0, 1]$ with 1 being the maximum deprivation possible, and 0 being no deprivation. Properties [i] and [ii] allow comparability of the measure across different populations with different numbers of deprivation dimensions and/or time periods. **SD** can be satisfied by a simple sum of individual scores. For **NN** to be satisfied while preserving **SD**, the following specification is adopted.

$$\Omega = \frac{\sum_{i=1}^{N} \frac{\mu_i}{\mu_{\max}}}{N} \tag{11.2}$$

Equation 11.2 has a useful interpretation as the average individual deprivation score ratio in the population of interest. Property [iii] Dimensional Monotonicity (KM). This requires that for any time t and any individual i, Ω increases as the number of dimensions in which individual i is deprived in increases. Property [iv] Durational Monotonicity (TM). This requires that for any dimension j and any individual i, Ω increases as the number of periods in which individual i is deprived in increases.

Properties [iii] and [iv] can be satisfied by initially adopting a simple 'counting' approach to μ_i; that is, the input into the function f is simply the count of individual i's deprivations, $\sum_j^K \sum_t^T d^0_{ijt}$. Note the counting approach renders the measure unable to discriminate between different sources of deprivation since it is only the number of deprivations and not the dimension from which deprivation comes from

[3]Given that μ_i takes as its input the $(T \times K)$ matrix $\boldsymbol{D_i}$, there can in principle be a maximum of $2^{(T*K)}$ different types of individual scores, one for each possible permutation of the individual deprivation profile.

that count towards the score. If there is reason to believe that certain dimensions are more important than others, relative weights can be applied to them. Atkinson (2003) notes that weights on dimensions should ideally be proportional; however, he also recognises that weights may be different if different variables are more relevant to different subsets of the population. This issue is further pursued in the discussion of the empirical application in Sect. 11.3. An additional concern that arises from the lack of identification of particular dimensions is that even when there is reason to believe that all dimensions carry equal weight, certain specific combinations of them may lead to more severe cases of deprivation. For example, numerous individuals may consider being unemployed and being unhealthy a superior State to being unemployed and being poor. These specific interactions among dimensions, if known a priori, can be incorporated into the current measure by considering not just different combinations of the elements of $\boldsymbol{D}_i$, but also different permutations. While this is beyond the scope of the present study, an interesting avenue for future research would be the development of a framework for empirically identifying interactions among dimensions in terms of their contribution towards overall deprivation.

Using the counting approach, μ_i in Eq. 11.2 can be expressed in terms of individual i's deprivation profile over K dimensions and T time periods, so that Eq. 11.2 becomes Eq. 11.3 as follows,

$$\Omega_\alpha = \frac{\sum_{i=1}^{N}\left(\frac{\sum_j^K \sum_t^T d_{ijt}^0}{T*K}\right)^\alpha}{N} \tag{11.3}$$

$\alpha \geq 0$ allows for the sensitivity of the aggregate index to the distribution of deprivations among individuals, in this case across time and dimensions. It is analogously applied in the unidimensional poverty context by Gradin et al. (2012). When $\alpha = 0$, Eq. 11.3 gives us the headcount ratio of individuals in the population deprived in at least one dimension j for at least one time period t. When $\alpha = 1$, the weight for each individual is increasing in a linear fashion as the count of deprivations increases. As $\alpha \to \infty$, the index gives us a headcount ratio of individuals in the population deprived in all dimensions for all time periods. Following Atkinson's (2003) discussion of counting approaches to multidimensional deprivation, note that $\alpha > 1$ also implies that the cross-derivative of μ_i with respect to any two different dimensions is positive, implying that the deprivations themselves are complements in the deprivation function, while $0 < \alpha < 1$ implies they are substitutes. Equation 11.3 can be seen as a generalisation of both JS and CD. In JS, the two time periods 1992–93 and 2005–06 were considered separately; therefore, Ω_α was calculated with $T = 1$ and a different Ω_α provided for each time period. Although by observing the measure $\left(\Omega_\alpha|_{t=(1992-93)}\right) > \left(\Omega_\alpha|_{t=(2005-06)}\right)$ one can conclude that deprivation has been reduced over time, it becomes problematic to compare subgroups within the population over the period in question.

This is because in some periods one subgroup may do better than the other, but the reverse may be true for other periods, in which case it no longer becomes clear how to conclude if one group is doing better than the other over the whole period. Equation 11.3, taking into account the full length of time over which one is interested in, is able to produce a single conclusive index for subgroup comparison. CD was able, to some extent, to circumvent the issue of subgroup comparison over time. They use EU data over six years of observation (1994–99). By defining ($d_{ijt}^{0} = 1$) as deprivation in a particular dimension j for *at least 4 out of 6* years, they are able to directly compare subgroups. However, it is not clear why at least 4 out of 6 years constitutes an interesting definition. This would exclude all individuals, who, for example, have been extremely unhealthy in the health dimension for 3 years, or who have been unemployed for 3 years. Given that one has data on the dimensions for every year, why limit what the data can tell us? Additionally, from a policy perspective, it would be useful to differentiate and identify short-term versus long-term deprivation. Also, property TM is not satisfied by their aggregation in terms of each individual t, since their measure discriminates neither between being deprived in say, 4, 5 or 6 years, nor between those deprived in 1, 2 or 3 years. The duration-augmented measure proposed in Eq. 11.3 can be seen as a multidimensional analogue to Foster's (2007) 'duration-adjusted P_α measure' in the unidimensional context, which adjusts the standard headcount ratio of poverty by the average periods of poverty experienced by the individual.

11.2.1.3 Additional Properties

When $\alpha > 1$ in Eq. 11.3, two additional properties emerge. Property [v] Dimensional Transfer Principle (KT). Assume that there are two individuals a and b where for some individual deprivation function $f : \boldsymbol{D}_i \rightarrow \boldsymbol{R}, \mu_a > \mu_b$. If individual a suffers one additional dimension of deprivation but individual b's deprivation is reduced by one dimension, the aggregate measure must register an overall increase in deprivation. Property [vi] Durational Transfer Principle (TT). Assume that there are two individuals a and b where for some individual deprivation function $f : D_i \rightarrow R, \mu_a > \mu_b$. If individual a suffers one additional period of deprivation but individual b's deprivation is reduced by one period, the aggregate measure must register an overall increase in deprivation. Both properties KT and TT are analogous to the *Pigou–Dalton transfer principle* in the context of income transfers [see, for example, Shorrocks and Foster (1987)]. Both properties are desirable since they essentially give increasingly larger weights to individuals with additional deprivations. This means that policy makers that seek to reduce deprivation [as measured by the deprivation index in Eq. 11.3] would do so by first reducing the deprivation of individuals who have multiple counts of deprivation. When $\alpha > 2$ *transfer sensitivity* axioms along the lines of Shorrocks and Foster (1987) are satisfied, the measures used in JS and CD satisfy KM, and when $\alpha > 1$ in their measures, KT is satisfied as well. However, our generalised measure satisfies the additional properties of TM, as well as TT when $\alpha > 1$. When comparing subgroups of a population over a period of time, this measure has the advantage of giving increasing importance not only to those who experience a wider variation of deprivations, but also those who have experienced them for longer periods of time.

11.2.1.4 Incorporating Persistence

While Eq. 11.3 may incorporate the *duration* of deprivation (i.e., the count of periods in which an individual is deprived in a particular dimension), it does not explicitly consider *persistence*, that is, the deprivation of an individual in a particular dimension over *consecutive* periods. Bossert et al. (2010) consider, in the unidimensional poverty context, a measure in which an individual who is poor in consecutive periods is given more weight relative to another who even though is deprived for the same total number of periods, moves in and out of a State of poverty. As they say, 'the negative effects of a two-period spell are much harder to handle than two one-period spells that are interrupted by one (or more) period(s) out of poverty'. This may not always be true in the multidimensional case. One can, for example, imagine that being unemployed for three consecutive periods and then being employed for three consecutive periods is superior to alternating in and out of employment for six periods since one incurs an 'adjustment cost' when changing States. However, information on the level of persistence is useful in many situations, and given our emphasis on the dynamics of deprivation, we specify a measure that further generalises Eq. 11.3. Each d_{ijt}^{0} can be said to belong to a deprivation spell, which is a sequence of uninterrupted deprivation periods in a particular dimension. c_{ijt} is the *length* of the deprivation spell associated with a particular d_{ijt}^{0}.

$$P\Omega_{\alpha} = \frac{\sum_{i=1}^{N}\left(\frac{\sum_{j}^{K}\left(\sum_{t}^{T}\left[d_{ijt}^{0} * s\right]\right)}{T * K}\right)^{\alpha}}{N} \tag{11.4}$$

Given that $s \in [0, 1]$ is a non-negative increasing function of c_{ijt} that takes on the maximum value of 1 when the deprivation in question ($d_{ijt}^{0} = 1$) is part of a $c = T$ period spell.[4] Equation 11.4 incorporates into a multidimensional framework Gradin et al.'s (2012) unidimensional generalisation of persistence weights. This allows the multidimensional index to satisfy the following property while retaining properties [i]–[vi]. Property [vii] Durational Persistence Monotonicity (TPM). This requires that for any individual i, dimension j and period t, Ω increases as c_{ijt} increases. Choosing a functional form for s means explicitly defining an aggregate trade-off between one additional dimension of deprivation against being deprived

[4]Equation (11.4) moves beyond a simple counting approach since it uses information on permutations of deprivation across the time dimension, and not simply combinations.

for an additional consecutive period. Following Gradin et al. (2012) and extending their idea to the multidimensional context, we specify $s = \left(c_{ijt}/T\right)^{\beta}$ where $\beta \geq 0$ is a parameter that determines the sensitivity of the index to the length of individual deprivation spells.[5] In the empirical application, we set $\beta = 1$. This means that every additional period of deprivation in a particular dimension increases each associated period of deprivation by the equivalent of $1/T$ additional dimensions of deprivation. For example, consider an individual's deprivation profile for $K = 1$ and $T = 4$; $\boldsymbol{D_i} = (1, 1, 0, 0)$. Using Eq. (11.4) and $s = \left(c_{ijt}/T\right)$, $\mu_i = \left(\frac{1*2/4 + 1*2/4 + 0*2/4 + 0*2/4}{4}\right)^{\alpha}$, where deprivation in $t = (1, 2)$ is each multiplied by $2/4$ to indicate that they belong to a spell of 2 out of a maximum of 4 periods. For robustness, we also consider results from $\beta = 3$ in the empirical application.

11.2.1.5 Identifying Dimensions

The generalisation found in Eq. 11.4 also yields a useful option for policy purposes. Though it may be useful, policy-wise, to identify which subgroups of the population are the most deprived, it is also useful to identify the dimensions in which individuals tend to be deprived for the longest periods of time and for the longest spells. A measure using the full form of Eq. 11.4 will be unable to do this since it simply takes the sum of deprivations and does not discriminate between the different kinds of dimensions. Consider however a specific form of Eq. 11.4 where $K = 1$.

$$P\Omega_{\alpha}\big|_1 = \frac{\sum_{i=1}^{N}\left(\frac{\sum_t^T\left[d_{i1t}^0 * \left(\frac{c_{i1t}}{T}\right)^{\beta}\right]}{T}\right)^{\alpha}}{N} \tag{11.5}$$

Depending on the choice of α, $P\Omega_{\alpha}\big|_1$ potentially satisfies TT, TM and TPM but loses KT and KM since each dimension is considered separately; that is, it produces one $P\Omega_{\alpha}\big|_{\mathrm{j}}$ for each of the dimensions of interest. When $\alpha = 0$ in Eq. 11.5, we get the headcount ratio of those with at least 1 period of deprivation in the dimension of interest. When $\alpha = 1$, the measure assigns larger weights to groups deprived for more periods and for longer spells, but the weights increase in a linear fashion. When $\alpha > 1$, we get **TT**.

Since Eq. 11.5 satisfies the basic property of subgroup decomposability, we can calculate it for separate population subgroups for each deprivation dimension. Note that both the measures proposed in Eqs. 11.4–11.5 incorporate the duration and persistence of deprivation. $P\Omega_{\alpha}$ is recommended when the point of the analysis is to

[5]The three parameters used in this study, α, β, and γ, correspond to the same parameters in Gradin et al.'s (2011) unidimensional model, except that α only applies to deprivation across time in their specification, but α applies to both time and dimensions here.

examine overall deprivation of individuals across both the *range* of deprivation (by the number of dimensions a person is deprived in at any given time) and the *duration* and/or *persistence* of deprivation. On the other hand, $P\Omega_{\alpha}|_{j}$ is recommended when the point of the analysis is the identification of particular dimensions over which deprivation may be particularly recurring and/or persistent.

11.2.2 Data and Choice of Dimensions, Weights and Sub-groups

11.2.2.1 HILDA Data Set and Sampling

The Household Income and Labour Dynamics in Australia (HILDA) Survey is a nationally representative household-based panel study which began in 2001 and is conducted annually. The HILDA Survey is funded, by the Australian Government through Department of Families, Housing, Community Services and Indigenous Affairs (FaHCSIA) while responsibility for the design and management of the survey rests with the Melbourne Institute of Applied Economic and Social Research (University of Melbourne). The HILDA Survey is a broad social and economic longitudinal survey, with particular attention paid to family and household formation, income and work. The HILDA Survey began with a large national probability sample of Australian households occupying private dwellings. The Wave 1 panel consisted of 7682 households and 19,914 individuals. The sample that is used in this study is Release 8, which has surveys of households from 2001 to 2008. Although new entrants were included in subsequent waves, the study adopts a fully balanced panel and restricts observations to those who have completed the Person Questionnaires and Self-Completion Questionnaires in every period. Since the questionnaires were administered to those of 15 years of age or above at the initial survey, the sample consists of individuals who were between 15 and 84 years old in 2001. More than 80% of the sample is aged between 20 and 60 years.

HILDA's eight period balanced panel of individual respondents consists of 8414 individuals in each wave. However, because the study uses crucial information from the Self-Completion Questionnaire, it is only able to achieve a sample size of 4175 individuals per year. This raises the question of representativeness of the information from the subsample used in relation to the larger full respondent sample. Appendix B in Nicholas and Ray (2012) compares the means between samples and suggests that the reduced sample are more highly educated, more likely to have been employed and more likely to have a larger income. The difference in the mean household incomes between the included sample and the parent sample is of the order of 4%. Hence, the estimates reported later will tend to underestimate deprivation. The study therefore weights the results presented in the next section with sample weights provided by HILDA. The weights are designed to correct for parts of the population that are undersampled or that tend to attrite from surveys; this mostly includes those who are homeless, those living in institutions, those without permanent dwellings and those living in unregistered and isolated dwellings. These weights sum to the population level and are then rescaled to sum to the sample size. If some individuals are more likely to be sampled, they receive a lower weight and therefore their characteristics have a smaller influence on the calculated averages. As with most poverty or deprivation studies, such weights will tend to reduce but not completely remove the downward bias of the estimates.

11.2.2.2 Dimensions

Eight dimensions of deprivation are considered in this study. The choice of these deprivation dimensions is consistent with, but not identical to, the Eurostat (2000) definition of social exclusion adopted in both Chakravarty and D'Ambrosio (2006) and Bossert et al. (2007). A prime consideration in the choice of dimensions was their availability for each of the eight years considered in this study. Unfortunately, the HILDA data was unable to provide consistent and objective information on the domains of housing conditions such as the number of rooms in the house and access to utilities such as telephones and the Internet. Like most current multidimensional studies, the data limitation means the results will have to be interpreted in the Light of the available variables, and not as a comprehensive measure of deprivation. However, in contrast to the European Community Household Panel data, HILDA was able to provide more data on the domain of health, notably through the use of the 36 question SF-36 survey (Ware et al. 2000) which aggregates responses on the survey to construct subscale indices in areas such as physical functioning and mental health. The dimensions used for this study are as follows in Table 11.1.

Table 11.1 Dimensions used in this study (Nicholas and Ray 2012)

Dimension/name	Description
(i) Utilities	Inability to pay utilities bill on time in the last year
(ii) Rent	Inability to pay mortgage/rent on time in the last year
(iii) Raise 2k	Inability to raise $2000 in an emergency
(iv) Heating	Unable to afford heating in the last year
(v) Meals	Unable to afford meals in the last year
(vi) Gen health	On a general health scale of 0–100, failure to cross 20
(vii) Phy health	On a physical health scale of 0–100, failure to cross 20
(viii) Unem	Unemployed based on the ABS (2001) definition: the individual has not worked in the last week, has looked for work within the last four weeks, and was available to start work in the last week

These eight dimensions can be grouped into three broad categories: 'material resources' (dimensions i–v); 'health' (dimensions vi and vii); and 'employment' (dimension viii). While health and material resources have often been considered in multidimensional approaches (e.g. the HDI and HPI) employment captures a dimension that may be more relevant to the 'social exclusion' framework in developed countries, since it captures one's right to 'participate in the basic economic … activities of the society in which he lives' (Eurostat 2000). Unemployment is also similarly adopted in Scutella et al. (2009), Atkinson et al. (2002), and measured from an 'illfare' perspective by Paul (1992) who notes that aside from reducing income, unemployment 'deteriorates human skills and leads to mental illness'. One would expect many of the dimensions to be empirically correlated, especially within each broad category, and even (to a lesser extent) across categories (e.g. material well-being and unemployment). However, there are information gains so long as there are unique features of each dimension that are not captured by the others. For example, more Food cannot make up for a lack of access to accommodation. While it is likely that those with low incomes tend to be unable to afford both, it is also possible that there are non-income factors that affect access to accommodation, but not access to Food. Atkinson (2003) gives the example, 'if … a family is prevented by discrimination from living in a better housing, then the housing (variable) acquires an independent significance' since income alone cannot entirely explain the lack of access to the good.

There are two potential issues relating to the assignment of weights. The first relates to 'double counting' in the sense that some dimensions may essentially be capturing the same aspect of deprivation. The second is that even assuming that each dimension captures a unique aspect of deprivation, one may not want to treat all of them equally. The weight to attach to each dimension is largely dependent on the variables available, and the population of interest. Where data is available, a useful approach to weights is found in Bossert et al. (2009) where dimensions are weighted based on the views of society regarding the importance of those dimensions ('consensus weighting'). Given the lack of such data in our Australian application, we consider the simpler approach suggested in Atkinson (2003) where all dimensions are initially weighted equally. When the eight dimensions are weighted equally, the broad category of material resources (dimensions i–v) receives the largest weight of 5/8, while health (dimensions vi and vii) receives 2/8 and unemployment 1/8 (dimension viii). The heavier weight afforded to material resources is consistent with other multidimensional studies such as Scutella et al. (2009) and Bossert et al. (2009) while unemployment is afforded the least weight since it is less relevant to some individuals who are out of the labour force. To test the robustness of our results to the potential bias caused by either of the two concerns, we repeat our calculations by varying the weighting schemes across the three broad categories. This method of adopting a 'nested constellation of weights' associated with larger groupings of dimensions is also used in Foster (2007).

11.2.2.3 Subgroups

Nicholas and Ray (2012) exploit the subgroup decomposability property of the multidimensional measures in proposing measures of relative deprivation between subgroups. The two such comparisons are between: (a) residents of urban, regional and remote areas, and (b) homeowners and non-homeowners. Each of these comparisons has taken on significance in the context of recent political and economic developments in Australia. While the residents of regional and remote Australia are disadvantaged due to the tyranny of distance from modern facilities, the huge pressure on infrastructure, accommodation, transport, etc, in the cities tends to have an adverse effect of the welfare of the residents living in the metropolitan centres. It is not clear, a priori, which group is more deprived and the results presented later are both surprising and informative. The distinction between homeowners and non-homeowners is of interest for several reasons. The sharp rise in house prices in recent years suggests that house ownership is imposing increasing financial constraints on households, in which case non-ownership may become a more attractive lifestyle choice. Homeowners have a higher percentage of people who are old-aged and pensioners living on fixed incomes. In contrast, non-homeowners are a much more heterogenous group of individuals. Additionally, as the literature on labour mobility suggests, homeowners may be more likely to be unemployed due to their lower labour mobility. On the other hand, the results in Nicholas et al. (2010) showed that during a period proximate to that considered here 'the regressive nature of relative price changes affected the renters much more than non-renters', suggesting that costs of living increased for non-homeowners faster than that for homeowners. Due to these diverse factors, it is not clear whether homeowners or non-homeowners are more deprived.

11.2.3 Results from the Australian Application

Table 11.2 reports the pairwise correlation magnitudes (along with the p values) of the average duration of deprivation in the eight dimensions with one another and with the per capita adjusted household income,[6] averaged over the period, 2001–2008. By using each individual's average (whether duration, or income) over the eight time periods, we avoid the issue of simply correlating dummy variables and also deal with individual fixed effects (which may overstate correlations). The correlation magnitudes are all highly significant, though in absolute terms none of them seem particularly high. In general, a longer spell of deprivation in one dimension is positively correlated with a longer spell in another. An increase in

---

[6]This variable is constructed for each individual using the individual's household 'financial year disposable household income' in the HILDA survey which was then adjusted with the OECD equivalence scale of $\sqrt{n}$ where n is the number of members in the household to which that individual belongs.

Table 11.2 Pairwise correlation, *p* values in parentheses (Nicholas and Ray 2012)

	Heating	Meals	Raise 2k	Rent	Utilities	Genhealth	Phyhealth	Unem
Heating	1							
Meals	0.5065	1						
	(0.00)							
Raise 2k	0.3733	0.3806	1					
	(0.00)	(0.00)						
rent	0.2593	0.4099	0.339	1				
	(0.00)	(0.00)	(0.00)					
Utilities	0.3551	0.4623	0.4498	0.685	1			
	(0.00)	(0.00)	(0.00)	(0.00)				
Genhealth	0.164	0.1558	0.2048	0.0505	0.0994	1		
	(0.00)	(0.00)	(0.00)	(0.00)	(0.00)			
Phyhealth	0.0971	0.1093	0.1321	0.0388	0.0641	0.4344	1	
	(0.00)	(0.00)	(0.00)	(0.01)	(0.00)	(0.00)		
Unem	0.1762	0.1842	0.2828	0.1849	0.2239	−0.0058	−0.0207	1
	(0.00)	(0.00)	(0.00)	(0.00)	(0.00)	(0.71)	(0.18)	
Aveinc	−0.1383	−0.1371	−0.2467	−0.1444	−0.2066	−0.1063	−0.1053	−0.12
	(0.00)	(0.00)	(0.00)	(0.00)	(0.00)	(0.00)	(0.00)	(0.00)

average income does lead to a reduction in the duration of deprivation in all dimensions, though much more for some (e.g. inability to raise $2000 in an emergency) than for others. Notwithstanding their statistical significances, the evidence of weak correlation between average income and the average duration of deprivation suggests that large income changes will be required to bring about significant decrease in deprivation across all the dimensions. This in turn suggests that policy interventions directed at particular aspect of deprivation may be more effective. This Australian evidence of weak correlation between the income and the non-income deprivation measures is consistent with the South African evidence of Klasen (2000) and the Spanish evidence of Ayala et al. (2011).

The headcount ratios of deprivation, reported by dimensions in each year, are presented in Table 11.3. These deprivation rates are for the common group of 4175 individuals that constitute the panel over this period, 2001–2008. There has been a decline in deprivation in most dimensions during this period, notably in the ability to raise $2000 in an emergency and the ability to pay rent and utilities on time. Deprivation scores based on Eq. 11.3 are calculated for each of the alternative subgroups mentioned previously, where *N* is imputed according to each subgroup's size. The corresponding ratios of the deprivation scores between the comparison subgroups are presented in Table 11.5. These show the relative distance (in terms of deprivation) in the bilateral comparisons between subgroups. These are dimensions that exhibit the highest deprivation rates and that are closely linked to income. This is not surprising since for the average individual in the sample, nominal income has increased by over 50% over the eight years. On the other hand, deprivation in the health dimensions has not changed much over the years. To confirm if overall deprivation has been falling over time, we use the aggregation adopted in JS where one Ω_α is calculated for each time period; this was referred to in Sect. 11.2 as $\Omega_\alpha|_t$, which is a special case of Eq. (11.3) when $T = 1$. Table 11.4 presents the results and confirms that there has been a decline in deprivation over time consistent with the headcount ratios reported in Table 11.3. The decline in deprivation is true of all the α values.

Deprivation scores based on Eq. 11.3 are calculated for each of the alternative subgroups mentioned previously, where N is imputed according to each subgroup's size. The corresponding ratios of the deprivation scores between the comparison subgroups are presented in Table 11.5. These show the relative distance (in terms of deprivation) in the bilateral comparisons between subgroups. In terms of subgroups, those residing in the urban areas and non-homeowners are at relative disadvantage with respect to the rest of the population. Though the higher urban deprivation scores are somewhat surprising, the difference of the urban scores with the scores from regional and remote areas is marginal. In contrast, non-homeowners suffer much higher deprivation than their comparison subgroups. As α increases, the ratio of the indices of the homeowner/non-homeowner subgroups declines quite sharply.

Table 11.3 Headcount ratios of deprivation at time t in dimension j (Nicholas and Ray 2012)

	Heating	Meals	Raise 2k	Rent	Utilities	Genhealth	Phyhealth	Unem
2001	0.02	0.03	0.11	0.06	0.15	0.03	0.02	0.03
2002	0.02	0.03	0.09	0.06	0.14	0.02	0.02	0.03
2003	0.02	0.03	0.09	0.06	0.12	0.03	0.02	0.02
2004	0.02	0.02	0.08	0.05	0.11	0.03	0.02	0.02
2005	0.01	0.02	0.07	0.05	0.10	0.03	0.02	0.02
2006	0.01	0.02	0.06	0.04	0.09	0.03	0.02	0.02
2007	0.01	0.02	0.06	0.04	0.09	0.03	0.02	0.01
2008	0.01	0.02	0.06	0.04	0.08	0.03	0.03	0.01

Table 11.4 Deprivation scores aggregated across dimensions (Nicholas and Ray 2012)

	2001	2002	2003	2004	2005	2006	2007	2008
$\alpha = 0$	0.263	0.239	0.225	0.203	0.187	0.176	0.181	0.176
$\alpha = 1$	0.055	0.049	0.046	0.042	0.038	0.035	0.037	0.034
$\alpha = 3$	0.006	0.005	0.004	0.004	0.004	0.003	0.004	0.003

Table 11.5 Dimension and time-aggregated deprivation score ratios between population subgroups (Nicholas and Ray 2012)

Urban/regional			Urban/remote			Homeowner/non-owner		
$\alpha = 0$	$\alpha = 1$	$\alpha = 3$	$\alpha = 0$	$\alpha = 1$	$\alpha = 3$	$\alpha = 0$	$\alpha = 1$	$\alpha = 3$
1.16	1.04	1.15	1.17	1.07	1.19	0.52	0.26	0.14

This suggests that the relative deprivation between these subgroups increases as more weight is given to individuals who are deprived. This means that not only do the average non-homeowner (typically renters) suffer more counts of deprivation than the rest of the population, those who are deprived are more likely to be deprived in multiple dimensions and over a longer period of time.

Note that the higher level of urban deprivation in relation to that in regional and remote areas may simply be a data artefact rather than indicative of an urban/non-urban divide in favour of the latter. The chosen dimensions, necessitated by the availability of information in the HILDA data set, do not include ones such as access to high-speed Internet, telecommunications, and access to medical and education facilities where those living in regional and remote areas are likely to be much more deprived than their urban counterparts. The results should therefore only be interpreted conditional on the choice of dimensions; a wider choice of dimensions is likely to reverse the difference in overall deprivation between the urban and non-urban population that is recorded in Table 11.5. Table 11.6 presents the persistence-augmented counterparts to the estimates reported in Table 11.5 using the measure given by Eq. 11.4. The subgroup ratios are presented for $\beta = (1, 3)$, where β is the sensitivity of the index with regards to persistence. That is, a higher value of β implies greater weight to deprivations associated with longer spells. A comparison of Tables 11.5 and 11.6 shows that the incorporation of persistence does not change the results significantly. However, as we increase β from 1 to 3, marginally increasing gaps between all three subgroup comparisons suggest that those who suffer more counts of deprivation (whether across time or dimensions), also tend to suffer them persistently (i.e. for consecutive periods).

The other advantage of using the persistence-augmented index according to Eq. 11.4 is the ability to establish a dominance relation between two population subgroups without the need to assume a particular form of numerical values for the individual scores. These dominance criterion can be represented diagrammatically by curves (called 'D-curves' in JS) that show on the y-axis the proportion of population that have a category deprivation score equal to or less than the score on the x-axis. The dominance relation is satisfied when the D-curve of one subgroup lies entirely above the D-curve of another subgroup, in which case we can say that the former is more deprived than the latter. Figure 11.1 depicts the D-curves for the 'urban' and 'remote' subgroups (the 'regional' group was removed as it closely follows that of the 'remote' area). Notice that the curves for the two subgroups intersect at some point, indicating that the dominance criteria alone are unable to allow us to conclude if one group is more deprived than the other. In contrast, Fig. 11.2 confirms that, even according to

Table 11.6 Persistence-augmented deprivation score ratios between population subgroups (Nicholas and Ray 2012)

	Urban/regional			Urban/remote			Homeowner/non-owner		
	$\alpha = 0$	$\alpha = 1$	$\alpha = 3$	$\alpha = 0$	$\alpha = 1$	$\alpha = 3$	$\alpha = 0$	$\alpha = 1$	$\alpha = 3$
$\beta = 1$	1.16	1.03	1.31	1.17	1.09	1.34	0.52	0.24	0.17
$\beta = 3$	1.16	1.03	1.35	1.17	1.08	1.37	0.52	0.24	0.12

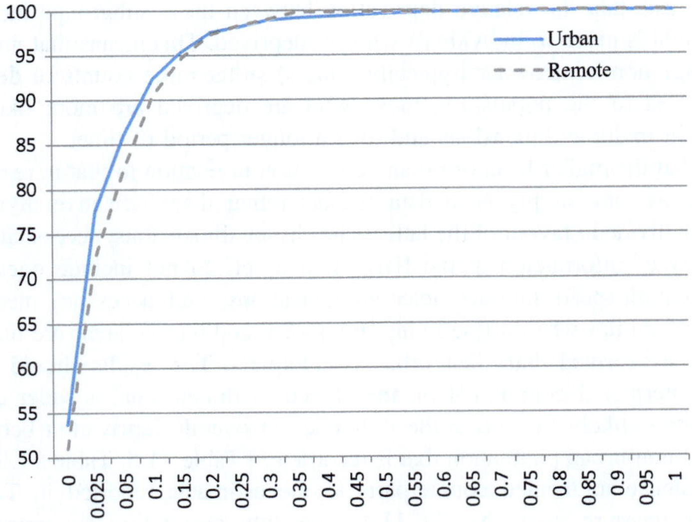

Fig. 11.1 D-curves for urban versus remote resident subgroups. Reproduced from Nicholas and Ray (2012)

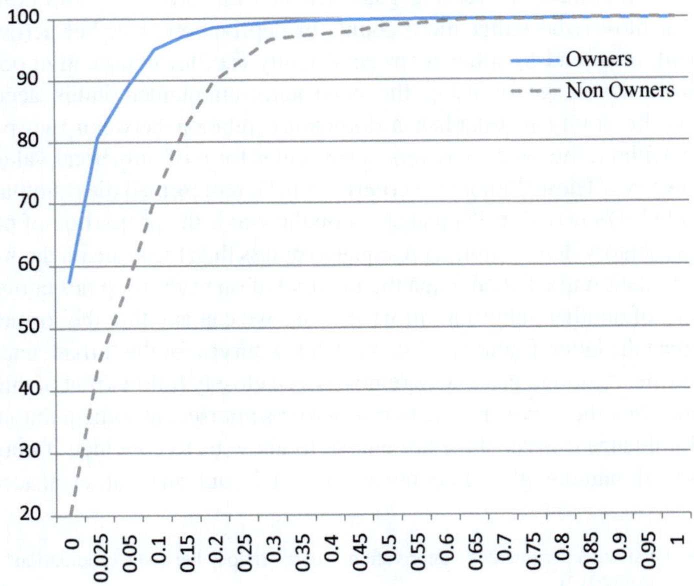

Fig. 11.2 D-curves for homeowners versus non-homeowners. Reproduced from Nicholas and Ray (2012)

Table 11.7 Income deprivation score ratios between population subgroups (Nicholas and Ray 2012)

	Urban/regional			Urban/remote			Homeowner/ non-owner		
	$\alpha = 0$	$\alpha = 1$	$\alpha = 3$	$\alpha = 0$	$\alpha = 1$	$\alpha = 3$	$\alpha = 0$	$\alpha = 1$	$\alpha = 3$
Income only	0.77	0.69	0.65	0.71	0.68	0.65	0.51	0.38	0.26
Income, health, unemployment[a]	0.94	0.77	0.64	0.40	0.22	0.69	0.64	0.40	0.22

[a]All three major dimensions are equally weighted

the dominance relation, the non-homeowners are more deprived than the homeowners since the curve for the later lies entirely above the curve for the former. For a simple comparison with a more traditional measure, Eq. 11.3 is estimated using a single dimension ($K = 1$)—income—where an individual is considered deprived in the dimension if he/she belongs to the lowest income decile at time t.[7] The subgroup ratios for income deprivation are presented in the 'income only' row in Table 11.7. The second row presents the corresponding score ratios if we aggregate the 8 dimensions of deprivation (see Table 11.4) into three equally weighted dimensions, with 1–5 aggregated into 'income', 6–7 into 'health', and unemployment left intact.

On purely income terms, the urban residents are the least deprived in comparison with the residents in regional and remote areas. That this result can be misleading is evident from the fact that it is inconsistent with the multidimensional deprivation scores presented in Table 11.5. While urban residents are more affluent than their non-urban counterparts, they turn out to be more deprived if one considers a wider range of welfare indicators. This is probably due to the heavy demand on social infrastructure and increased costs of living in urban areas. This is also evident from the fact that, with the introduction of non-income deprivation indicators in the second row of Table 11.7, the urban/regional divide weakens, and we approach the picture in Table 11.5. However, the urban/remote divide widens substantially from the first to the second row of Table 11.7. This suggests that the non-income dimensions, namely health and unemployment impact much more adversely on the households in the remote areas than those living elsewhere. On the other hand, the result on the higher deprivation of the non-homeowners versus homeowners is robust between the multidimensional estimates of Table 11.5 and its unidimensional income counterparts in Table 11.7.

While we have so far focussed on multidimensional deprivation at the individual level, it is of policy interest to identify the specific dimensions in which individuals tend to be deprived for longer periods. This is especially true after identifying subgroups of the population who should be targeted. As is evident from Tables 11.2 and 11.7, income is not strongly correlated with the various deprivation indicators, in which case policies targeted at specific dimensions are warranted. Dimension-specific

[7]When $\alpha = 0$ the deprivation ratio can be interpreted as the fraction of the population that belong to the lowest income decile for at least one out of the eight periods.

Table 11.8 Persistence-augmented deprivation scores ratios disaggregated according to dimension and subgroups (Nicholas and Ray 2012)

	Urban/regional			Urban/remote			Homeowner/non-owner		
	$\alpha = 0$	$\alpha = 1$	$\alpha = 3$	$\alpha = 0$	$\alpha = 1$	$\alpha = 3$	$\alpha = 0$	$\alpha = 1$	$\alpha = 3$
Heating	0.918	0.735	0.736	0.829	0.618	0.318	0.262	0.221	0.095
Meals	0.825	0.869	0.908	0.701	0.823	0.846	0.246	0.185	0.137
Raise 2k	0.786	0.766	0.715	0.783	0.700	0.665	0.295	0.153	0.082
Rent	0.982	1.268	2.219	0.868	1.258	1.981	0.380	0.256	0.138
Utilities	0.901	0.842	0.709	0.789	1.009	1.569	0.419	0.317	0.275
Genhealth	0.800	0.786	0.870	0.917	0.748	0.700	0.473	0.417	0.453
Phyhealth	0.916	0.776	0.580	0.842	0.719	0.534	0.496	0.563	0.611
Unem	1.007	1.027	1.067	0.994	1.040	0.407	0.406	0.248	0.082

deprivation rates incorporating the duration and persistence of deprivation are calculated using Eq. 11.5 where one $P\Omega_{\alpha}|_j$ is estimated for each dimension. The score ratios are presented in Table 11.8. The variation in the deprivation divide between dimensions is apparent at higher α values, less so at lower α values. For example, at $\alpha = 3$, while the duration and persistence in inability to pay rent/mortgage highlights the urban/non-urban deprivation divide in favour of the latter, the deprivation gap between homeowners and non-homeowners is primarily driven, in favour of the former, by the duration and persistence of unemployment and in the inability to raise 2K.

11.3 Differentiating Between Dimensionality and Duration in Multidimensional Measurement of Poverty

11.3.1 Introduction

Nicholas et al. (2017) develop a multidimensional poverty measure that is sensitive to the within-individual distribution of deprivations across dimensions and time. The new measure combines features from a static multidimensional measure (Alkire and Foster 2010) and a time-dependent unidimensional measure (Foster 2009). The proposed measure separately identifies—and can therefore be decomposed according to—the proportion of the poverty score attributable to: (i) the concentration of deprivations within periods; (ii) the concentration of deprivations within dimensions. In doing so, it allows for a poverty ranking that is robust to assumptions about the trade-off between the two components. Previous measures have not allowed for the features proposed here due to the inability to calculate the exact contribution of each dimension to overall poverty. This is overcome this by adapting to the measure the Shapley decomposition proposed in Shorrocks (2013) (based on Shapley 1953). The measure is applied to data from China, 2000–2011.

This section describes the framework and methodology adopted in Nicholas et al. (2017) and the empirical results of the application of their new measure to Chinese panel data.

The principal motivation of this paper is to contribute to the relatively scant literature on time-dependent multidimensional measures of poverty by construction a measure that is:

(**C1**) sensitive to the distribution of deprivations *across* individuals, even when deprivations are only measured in an ordinal manner.
(**C2**) sensitive to the distribution of deprivations *within* individuals, thus allocating different weights to individuals with different distributions of deprivations across time and dimensions despite each individual having the same count of deprivations. Specifically, a higher weight is allotted to individuals who experience deprivations across multiple dimensions within the same period ('dimensional convexity'), as well as to individuals who experience deprivations across multiple periods within the same dimension ('duration convexity').
(**C3**) decomposable into three components, notably, the component of poverty due the count of deprivations; the component of poverty due to allowing for dimensional convexity; and the component of poverty due to allowing for duration convexity.

An example is provided to help elucidate these contributions in the next subsection. It is important to note that, while desirable, the literature has shied away from measures satisfying the properties above due to the desirability of *dimensional decomposability*, a property where the contribution of each dimension to overall poverty can be additively decomposed. This is violated when poverty is a non-linear function of the count of dimensions of deprivation. We overcome this problem by applying the Shapley decomposition proposed in Shorrocks (2013, based on Shapley 1953) specifically adapted to suit our proposed measure. To the best of our knowledge, this method has not been applied to dimensional decomposition with the exception of Datt (2013) who has applied the technique to the static multidimensional case. In being able to differentiate between 'dimensional convexity' and 'duration convexity', the proposed measure also has the advantage of allotting different weights to both features and, consequently, is also able to provide a test of the robustness of a ranking of subgroups (such as provinces within the country) to assumptions about the trade-off between the two features.

Nicholas et al. (2017) apply the proposed time-dependent multidimensional poverty measure to longitudinal data from China (2000–2011). China is particularly useful to illustrate the application of our measure since while it is now well accepted that China has seen one of the largest poverty reductions over the past few decades, questions of how this differs across provinces and different subgroups are less established. While traditional static measures such as AF are well suited for characterising changes in poverty over time for one specific group, they are less suited for comparisons across groups, since different groups may improve or decline at different periods of time. To our knowledge, this is the first attempt at analysing poverty in China on longitudinal data using a time-dependent multidimensional poverty measure. As Lahoti et al. (2015) report, the reduction in Chinese poverty has been so dramatic that the headcount rate of world poverty alters sharply depending on the inclusion or exclusion of China from the calculations.

Consequently, considerable attention has been paid by economists to studying poverty in China—see, for example, Bardhan (2010, Chap. 7), and the chapter by Park and Wang (2014) in the recent volume on China edited by Fan et al. (2014). Thanks to the increasing availability of data, there has been in recent years a significant literature on multidimensional poverty in China. Examples include Labar and Bresson (2011), Mishra and Ray (2012), Ray and Sinha (2015) who perform a static analysis of multidimensional poverty in China using the measure due to AF while You et al. (2014) examine the intertemporal aspect of multidimensional poverty using the measure due to Dutta et al. (2003). The study by Nicholas et al. (2017) contributes to this recent literature by providing the first time-dependent analysis of multidimensional poverty in China. They provide a ranking of subgroups according to provinces, gender and rural/urban residency, as well as a ranking of dimensional contributions. In addition, these rankings are assessed for robustness to the choice of the weight allotted to dimensional versus duration convexity.

11.3.2 Examples for Contributions

While straightforward in its interpretation and implementation, the popular ‘counting’ approach to poverty measurement faces several limitations when attempting to fully utilise the wealth of information over multiple dimensions and periods contained in panel data. Consider below the deprivation profiles $\boldsymbol{D_n}$ of three individuals, A, B and C. Each entry in the profile takes a value of 1 if an individual $n \in \{A, B, C\}$ is deprived in a particular dimension $j \in \{1, 2, 3\}$ at time $t \in \{1, 2, 3\}$, and a value of 0 otherwise. The rows represent the dimensions j and the columns, the periods t.

$$\boldsymbol{D_A} = \begin{pmatrix} 1 & 0 & 0 \\ 0 & 1 & 0 \\ 0 & 0 & 1 \end{pmatrix} \quad \boldsymbol{D_B} = \begin{pmatrix} 1 & 0 & 0 \\ 1 & 0 & 0 \\ 1 & 0 & 0 \end{pmatrix} \quad \boldsymbol{D_C} = \begin{pmatrix} 1 & 1 & 1 \\ 0 & 0 & 0 \\ 0 & 0 & 0 \end{pmatrix}$$

Consider a counting measure of poverty where deprivation is measured simply as the average count of deprivations. If we treat all three dimensions and time periods as equally valued and treat all three individuals as poor, then such a measure would score all three individuals as equally deprived. Such a measure would therefore be insensitive to: (i) the distribution of deprivations *across* the profiles; and (ii) the distribution of deprivations *within* the profiles.

We examine each of the proposed contributions in the context of the example:

(i) ***C1 (sensitivity to between-individual rearrangement)***:

Existing approaches are insensitive to 'rearrangements' across the deprivation profiles. If the deprivation of individual A at $j = 2, t = 2$ is switched with the equivalent for individual B, individual A would now have two counts of deprivations, and individual B would have four. While deprivation is now more concentrated in individual B, a poverty score that simply takes the average count of deprivations would remain the same. This insensitivity to the distribution of deprivations across individuals is relaxed to a lesser extent in AF's static measure through the use of the α parameter, which at $\alpha > 1$ gives increasing sensitivity to transfers across individuals, where 'transfers' exclude rearrangements of the entries as just described. In addition, such sensitivity only arises when deprivations are cardinal. Sensitivity to rearrangement, however, can be achieved by the exponentiation of each individual's deprivation count ratio by some parameter, which would be analogous to the $\alpha > 1$ parameter of the original Foster et al. (1984) measure. The reluctance to do so in the multidimensional literature has stemmed primarily from the desirability of dimensional decomposability, that is, the ability to identify the proportion of contribution of each dimension to the total poverty score, which is in principal violated when individual deprivation scores are not a linear function of the count of deprivations (for a discussion, see Alkire and Foster 2016). We are able to overcome this through the use of the general Shapley decomposition method proposed in Shorrocks (2013), which, broadly, allows any output (in our case, the poverty index) to be allocated among the contributors (in our case, the dimensions of deprivation), even if the output is a nonlinear function of the contributions.

(ii) ***C2 (sensitivity to within-individual rearrangement)***:

While the exponentiation of each individual's deprivation count ratio would make the poverty measure sensitive to the distribution of deprivations *across* individuals, the measure would continue to rank all three individuals A, B and C as equally deprived since it is not sensitive to the distribution *within* individuals.

The lack of such differentiation is problematic in many applications. Stiglitz et al. (2009), for example, highlight that 'the consequences for quality of life of having multiple disadvantages [across different domains] far exceed the sum of their individual effects' (Stiglitz et al. 2009, p. 15). The importance of recognising the increasing cost of multiple deprivations (for any given period) is discussed in detail in Datt (2013). This is captured by the property 'dimensional convexity', which scores individual B as more deprived than individual A.

There is also an underlying belief that *recurring* deprivations within the same dimension incur an increasing cost on the individual (see Gradin et al. 2012; Hoy and Zheng 2011; Sengupta 2009). This is captured by the property 'duration convexity', which scores individual C as more deprived than individual A.

(iii) ***C3 (within-profile decomposability)***:

While in many applications individuals B and C should be ranked as more deprived than individual A, it is not clear if individual B should be ranked as more, less or equally deprived as individual C. Our proposed measure allows one to weight the component due to dimensional convexity and duration convexity differently according to the analyst's priors, while simultaneously ensuring that individuals B and C are never ranked as less deprived than individual A. In doing so, the proposed measure becomes decomposable into three components, notably the component of poverty due to: the count of deprivations; dimensional convexity; and duration convexity.

Overall, our measure allows for a deeper look into the 'black box' of the aggregate poverty score and allows us to differentiate subgroups that may have similar counts of deprivation, but a very different distribution of said deprivations. This allows us to identify subgroups of the population that contain individuals who not only have the most counts of deprivations, but who also experience them across the widest variety of dimensions in any given period, and/or who also experience them for the most periods in any given dimension. This also allows us, when doing dimensional decomposition, to allot more weight not only to dimensions which have longer average durations, but also to dimensions that occur within individuals who simultaneously suffer from the widest variety of deprivation.

11.3.3 Analytical Framework

11.3.3.1 Notation

Consider a population of N individuals, J different dimensions of deprivation and T equally spaced periods of time. x_{njt} is individual $n \in \{1, 2, \ldots, N\}$'s *achievement* in dimension $j \in \{1, 2, \ldots, J\}$ at time $t \in \{1, 2, \ldots, T\}$. Each n can be said to have an *individual achievement profile* $\boldsymbol{A_n} = \begin{pmatrix} x_{n11} & \cdots & x_{n1T} \\ . & \cdots & . \\ x_{nJ1} & \cdots & x_{nJT} \end{pmatrix}$. The *population achievement profile* is a vector $\boldsymbol{\rho} = (\boldsymbol{A}_1, \ldots, \boldsymbol{A}_N)$. Define the identification vector $\boldsymbol{v} = (c_1, \ldots, c_N)$ where c_n takes the value 1 if the individual is considered *poor*, and 0 otherwise. We return to the issue of whom to consider poor at the end of this section. A poverty index is a function $g(\boldsymbol{\rho}; \boldsymbol{v})$ that produces a single non-negative real number for any observed vector $\boldsymbol{\rho}$ and appropriately defined vector $\boldsymbol{v}$. We say that n is *deprived* in dimension j at time t when $x_{njt} < F_j$, where F_j is a deprivation cut-off that determines whether or not an individual is considered deprived in a particular dimension at a particular time and $\boldsymbol{F}$ the vector of such cut-offs. For example, in the dimension 'health', x may be the individual's body mass index, in which case F_{health} would be some threshold below which the individual would be considered underweight and therefore deprived in the health dimension.

For brevity, we assume these cut-offs do not vary across time, though the methodology allows for such an extension.

It is common for $\boldsymbol{\rho}$ to be transformed into the *population deprivation profile* $\boldsymbol{\delta} = (\boldsymbol{D}_1, \ldots, \boldsymbol{D}_N)$ where $\boldsymbol{D}_n$ is the *individual deprivation profile*, a $J \times T$ matrix where each element of $\boldsymbol{A}_n$ is transformed into deprivations defined as follows:

$$d^{\alpha}_{njt} = \begin{cases} \left(1 - \frac{x_{njt}}{F_j}\right)^{\alpha} & \text{if } x_{njt} < F_j \, \forall j, t \\ 0 & \text{otherwise} \end{cases} \tag{11.6}$$

where $\alpha \geq 0$ is a sensitivity parameter. When achievement levels are ordinal in at least one dimension, it is common to restrict $\alpha = 0$ such that $d^{\alpha}_{njt} \in \{0, 1\} \forall j, t$. The function $h : \boldsymbol{D}_n \rightarrow R_+$ produces a deprivation score s_n for each individual. Following Bourguignon and Chakravarty (2003), AF, and the majority of axiom-based multidimensional measures, Nicholas et al. (2017) restrict their framework to the class of subgroup decomposable measures of the form

$$m(\boldsymbol{\rho}; \boldsymbol{v}) = \frac{1}{N} \sum_{n=1}^{N} [h(\boldsymbol{D}_n) \times c_n] \tag{11.7}$$

Their key contribution is therefore with regards to the form of $h(\boldsymbol{D}_n)$ that yields contributions **C1**, **C2** and **C3**. Following the 'dual cut-off' method of the AF class of poverty measures, the poverty indicator function c_n takes the form

$$c_n = \begin{cases} 1 & \text{if } \sum_{t=1}^{T} \sum_{j=1}^{J} d^{0}_{njt} \geq z \\ 0 & \text{otherwise} \end{cases} \tag{11.8}$$

where $(J \times T) \geq z \geq 1$. At $z = 1$ we have the equivalent of the union method of identification, and at $z = (J \times T)$, the intersection method. Notice, however, that unlike the AF method, deprivations are counted both across dimensions and time. This opens up the possibility of identifying the poor using an additional cut-off. Clearly, the choice of who to consider poor will affect the final poverty score. Yalonetzky (2014), for example, shows that in the static multidimensional case (e.g. AF), the idea of robustness to changes in parameter choices becomes exponentially demanding and unlikely to be satisfied when there are more than two dimensions. However, since the contribution of the proposed measure is the expansion of ways in which to quantify the *depth* of poverty among the poor $[h(\boldsymbol{D}_n)]$, rather than whom to consider poor (c_n), the axioms are defined independent of identification choices. For ease of exposition, the union method of identification is adopted in both the examples and empirical application.

11.3.3.2 Dimensional and Durational Convexity, Contribution C2

Recall the three individuals from the introduction. Differentiating between them requires that the poverty measure assigns an increasingly higher weight to deprivations that share either the same period or the same dimension. This yields two properties that can be stated formally as follows. Let the $m \in \{1...M\}$ where M is the number of poor individuals in the population.

(**Axiom 1**): *Dimensional Convexity*

$$\frac{\partial^2 g}{\partial d^{\alpha}_{mjt} \partial d^{\alpha}_{mj't}} > 0 \quad \forall j' \neq j$$

The effect of an increase in any of an individual's deprivation on the aggregate poverty score is a strictly positive function of the deprivations in *other dimensions* that share the *same period* as the deprivation in question.

(**Axiom 2**): *Durational Convexity*

$$\frac{\partial^2 g}{\partial d^{\alpha}_{mjt} \partial d^{\alpha}_{mjt'}} > 0 \quad \forall t' \neq t$$

The effect of an increase in any of an individual's deprivation on the aggregate poverty score is a strictly positive function of the deprivations in *other periods* that share the *same dimension* as the deprivation in question. Notice that in the three-person example, it has been suggested that B and C are more deprived than A, but it is unclear if B is equally or more deprived than C, or vice versa. We may, for example, consider C to be more deprived than B from a simple policy perspective: C's long-lasting deprivation in a specific dimension can be targeted for future poverty reduction and should therefore be given more weight. One may instead take the opposite stance and suggest that while B's poverty was relatively more transient than C, it was 'broader' at the time it occurred and may reflect a vulnerability to shocks. We seek a measure that allows the analyst such flexibility in deciding how important *dimensional convexity* should be relative to *durational convexity*. In addition, even in situations where the choice of whom to weight more heavily is not clear, our measure provides a means of checking for robustness by considering the entire range of such trade-offs.

Any super additive form for $h(\boldsymbol{D_n})$ will satisfy both axioms. However, we also require that $h(\boldsymbol{D_n})$ differentiates between the effects of *dimensional convexity* versus *durational convexity* on the aggregate poverty score. Our poverty measure therefore consists of two delineated components, the first of which only satisfies *dimensional convexity*, and the second of which only satisfies *durational convexity*. Consider then the following measure of poverty that satisfies only *dimensional convexity*,

$$\Omega^{\text{dimension}} = \frac{1}{N}\sum_{n=1}^{N}\left(\frac{1}{T}\sum_{t=1}^{T}\left(\frac{1}{J}\sum_{j=1}^{J} d_{njt}\right)^{\beta}\right) \times c_n \tag{11.9}$$

Notice that $\Omega^{\text{dimension}}$ is a modification of the AF index—instead of using α raised over each d_{njt}, β is raised over the average count of deprivation over dimensions, thus allowing *dimensional convexity* as is done in Chakravarty and D'Ambrosio (2006), Jayaraj and Subramaniam (2010) and Datt (2013). The measure $\Omega^{\text{dimension}}$ is then simply a modified AF index calculated for each period separately, and then averaged over these periods. Because it is only averaged over periods, it fails to satisfy *durational convexity*, just as we had required. Similarly, the following measure satisfies only *durational convexity*,

$$\Omega^{\text{duration}} = \frac{1}{N}\sum_{n=1}^{N}\left(\frac{1}{J}\sum_{j=1}^{J}\left(\frac{1}{T}\sum_{t=1}^{T} d_{njt}\right)^{\beta}\right) \times c_n \tag{11.10}$$

Ω^{duration} is a modification of the individual-level Foster (2009) chronic measure, and a special case of the more general Gradin et al. (2012) measure. The measure Ω^{duration} is calculated for each dimension, and then averaged over the dimensions, thus failing to satisfy *dimensional convexity*.

The final poverty measure is then a convex combination of both measures

$$\Omega = \frac{1}{N}\sum_{n=1}^{N}\left(\delta\frac{1}{T}\sum_{t=1}^{T}\left(\frac{1}{J}\sum_{j=1}^{J} d_{njt}\right)^{\beta} + (1-\delta)\frac{1}{J}\sum_{j=1}^{J}\left(\frac{1}{T}\sum_{t=1}^{T} d_{njt}\right)^{\beta}\right) \times c_n \tag{11.11}$$

where $1 \geq \delta \geq 0$ and $\beta > 0$. Setting $\beta > 1$ and $\delta > 0$ ensures *dimensional convexity* while $\beta > 1$ and $\delta < 1$ ensures *durational convexity*. At $\beta = 1$ the measure collapses into a simple double-sum of the count of deprivations. β is analogous to the FGT α parameter: following the literature a reasonable value would be 2. As is common in these class of measures, each dimension can be assigned a different weight. Ω is a simple combination of existing measures from two independent extensions in the poverty measurement literature. While *dimensional convexity* and *durational convexity* are satisfied (independently) by those measures, they are rarely explicitly stated as a desirable property since the focus is usually on the 'transfer' or inequality-sensitivity properties of the measure. Unlike many other applications, the α parameter in Ω no longer has to be chosen but is instead set to 1 in the cardinal case, and 0 in the ordinal case, which means that there is effectively a net increase of only one parameter relative to the Alkire Foster (AF) model. This is because *dimensional convexity* and *durational convexity* are in fact sufficient conditions for certain standard 'transfer-type' properties. Because there are two additively separable components in Eq. 11.11, the parameter δ allows a clear linear weighting choice between the two. Of course, it is never clear a priori what the value of δ should be. When ranking, for example, two groups of individuals, one useful criteria is simply that both terms $\Omega^{\text{dimension}}$ and Ω^{duration} have higher scores in one group relative to the other, in which case the poverty ranking would be robust to any choice of δ. Nonetheless, in cases where such robustness does not hold, it is useful to understand how *dimensional convexity* and *durational convexity* are affecting the score.

11.3.3.3 Shapley Decomposition

Notice from Eq. 11.11 that the contribution of every dimension to overall poverty is a function of the other dimensions that occur jointly with it through the term $\Omega^{\text{dimension}}$, meaning that the measure is not directly decomposable according to dimensions. However, the Shapley decomposition procedure found in Shorrocks (2013) can be applied here to yield an exact (additive) decomposition. Effectively, since every dimension's contribution to the overall score is a function of the other dimensions that are present, the Shapley decomposition reports the dimension's contribution averaged over every possible combination of other dimensions. We describe the general procedure below. Notice from Eq. 11.11 that because the second term Ω^{duration} is simply an average over all dimensions, it is *directly* additively decomposable according to dimensions. The first term $\Omega^{\text{dimension}}$, however, is not *directly* additively decomposable when $\beta \neq 1$, and will require a Shapley decomposition to yield an additive decomposition. Define $\Omega_{j|D=0}$ as the overall poverty score when all deprivations associated with dimension j are set to 0. The dimension score $\Omega_j = \Omega - \Omega_{j|D=0}$ is therefore the marginal contribution of dimension j to Ω. Because Ω has two components, we have,

$$\Omega_j = \delta\left(\Omega^{\text{dimension}} - \Omega^{\text{dimension}}_{j|D=0}\right) + (1-\delta)\left(\Omega^{\text{duration}} - \Omega^{\text{duration}}_{j|D=0}\right) \tag{11.12}$$

For any $\beta > 0$, the second bracketed term is simply: $(1-\delta)\frac{1}{N}\sum_{n=1}^{N}\frac{1}{J}\left[\frac{\sum_t^T d_{nj't}}{T}\right]^{\beta}$ $\times c_n$. When $\beta \neq 1$, the first term is a function of the order in which dimension j' is removed. For any J number of dimensions there are a total of $K = 2^{J-1}$ orders in which j' can be removed. Let $\Omega^{\text{dimension}}[k]$ be the score $\Omega^{\text{dimension}}$ at order $k \in \{1\ldots K\}$ and let $\Omega^{\text{dimension}}_{j|D=0}[k]$ be the score $\Omega^{\text{dimension}}$ when all deprivations associated with dimension j is set to 0 at order k. Shapley's decomposition therefore yields,

$$\Omega_j = \delta\frac{1}{K}\sum_{k=1}^{K}\left(\Omega^{\text{dimension}}[k] - \Omega^{\text{dimension}}_{j|D=0}[k]\right) + (1-\delta)\frac{1}{N}\sum_{n=1}^{N}\frac{1}{J}\left[\frac{\sum_t^T d_{nj't}}{T}\right]^{\beta}\times c_n \tag{11.13}$$

A dimension's proportion contribution to overall poverty is then simply $\gamma_j = \frac{\Omega_j}{\Omega}$ where $\sum_{j=1}^{J} \gamma_j = 1$. One may find it strange that the dimensional decomposition in Eq. 11.13 uses the Shapley rule for only the first-half of the equation; this is done simply for brevity: when the Shapley rule is applied to the second-half of Eq. 11.13, it yields exactly the same score as a *direct* additive decomposition would. In this sense, the direct additive decomposition common in the literature can be seen as a special case of the Shapley decomposition method. The approach detailed above yields two terms for each dimension.

11.3.4 Data Description and Summary Features

To apply the multidimensional poverty measure proposed in this paper we require a sufficiently 'long' longitudinal data set to take advantage of the time-dependent aspect of the measure. While there are several longitudinal data sets from developing countries, the China Health and Nutrition Survey (CHNS) is the longest: we use data spanning 2000–2011. The present study follows Labar and Bresson (2011) in conducting the analysis of multidimensional poverty in China on the CHNS database. The CHNS is an ongoing international project between the Carolina Population Center at the University of North Carolina at Chapel Hill and the National Institute of Nutrition and Food Safety at the Chinese Centre for Disease Control and Prevention. This project was designed to examine the effects of health, nutrition and family planning policies and programs implemented by the national and local governments and to see how the social and economic transformation is affecting the health and nutritional status of the population. A detailed description of the CHNS database has been presented in Popkin et al. (2010). The surveys took place over a three-day period using a multi-stage, random cluster process to draw a sample of over 4000 households in nine provinces that vary substantially in geography, economic development, public resources and health indicators. Nicholas et al. (2017) converted household level information to the individual level by assuming that the household's access to a facility such as drinking water or electricity is the same for all individuals in that household.

Only individuals aged 18 years and above in the first year of the panel were included in construction of the balanced panel. Following the nature of the available information in the CHNS data set, the chosen dimensions contained a mix of some at the household level and others at the level of the individual. Deprivation at the household level is converted to individual-level deprivation by assuming that if a household is deprived in a particular dimension (e.g. Fuel or electricity), so are all members of that household. The summary statistics, year and dimension-wise, of the deprivation rates in China are presented in Table 11.9. While some dimensions such as access to Fuel, Toilet and Radio/TV recorded large improvements over the period, the opposite is true for other dimensions such as abnormal blood pressure

Table 11.9 Summary deprivation rates by dimension and time for China (Nicholas et al. 2017)

Year	Toilet	Fuel	Electricity	Drink water	Vehicle	Radio/ TV	BMI	Illness	Blood pressure	Compulsory education	Average	Household Income < 0.5 * Median[a]
2000	0.573	0.642	0.0048	0.569	0.214	0.274	0.086	0.129	0.653	0.635	0.378	0.694
2004	0.519	0.648	0.0038	0.546	0.284	0.143	0.089	0.223	0.682	0.553	0.369	0.602
2006	0.481	0.586	0.0041	0.502	0.308	0.083	0.097	0.207	0.702	0.531	0.350	0.547
2009	0.427	0.424	0.0025	0.464	0.307	0.020	0.098	0.226	0.773	0.553	0.329	0.360
2011	0.412	0.384	0.0086	0.433	0.322	0.023	0.112	0.206	0.771	0.560	0.323	0.297
Average	0.482	0.537	0.0048	0.503	0.287	0.109	0.096	0.198	0.716	0.565	0.378	0.499

[a]Income used as a benchmark and not an actual dimension

and BMI, which highlights the importance of taking into account the time-aspect of deprivation at the dimensional level since this would not be picked up by comparing static multidimensional measures over time. Interestingly, the average deprivation score across dimensions show very minor improvements over time (from 0.378 in 2000 to 0.323 in 2011) while the comparison household half-median income shows large improvements, once again highlighting the differences in information conveyed by these measures.

11.3.5 Results

We illustrate the usefulness of Ω by first comparing across subgroups of the CNHS. The comparisons are: (1) between females and males; (2) between individuals in rural and urban regions; (3) between the nine provinces chosen for the CNHS. For each of these comparisons, we first consider the poverty ranking provided by five specifications (Table 11.10), all of which are special cases or components of Ω, starting with the simplest measure $\Omega(\beta = 1)$ and adding additional elements until we reach $\Omega(\beta = 2)$. By introducing small changes to each measure we can ascertain the source of any changes in rankings. To allow all observations to input their variation into the measure, the union approach is adopted in these calculations (i.e. $z = 1$). Table 11.11 shows us the results for female/male, rural/urban and provincial subgroup comparisons. For both the female/male and rural/urban comparisons we have that all five specifications agree. This means the rankings are highly robust to changes in the measure's sensitivity to the between- and within-individual distribution of deprivations.

Notice that for the score $\Omega(\beta = 2, \delta = 0.5)$, the gap between females and males is relatively small (0.2324 vs. 0.2302) relative to the gap between rural and urban residents (0.2609 vs. 0.1364). This suggests that the size of the deprivation gap between groups are in themselves insufficient to tell us how robust differences in the

Table 11.10 Five specific measures of poverty, based on Ω (Nicholas et al. 2017)

Measure	Description
i. $\boldsymbol{\Omega}(\boldsymbol{\beta} = 1)$	Baseline: sum the count of deprivations and average them over individuals
ii. $\boldsymbol{\Omega}^{\mathbf{I}}$ $(\boldsymbol{\beta} = 2)$	Baseline measure (i), but with each individual deprivation profile squared prior to averaging over individuals, thus allowing sensitivity to across-individual distribution
iii. $\boldsymbol{\Omega}^{\mathbf{dimension}}$ $(\boldsymbol{\beta} = 2)$	Measure (ii) with the addition of Ω^{II}
iv. $\boldsymbol{\Omega}^{\mathbf{duration}}$ $(\boldsymbol{\beta} = 2)$	Measure (ii) with the addition of Ω^{III}
v. $\boldsymbol{\Omega}(\boldsymbol{\beta} = 2, \boldsymbol{\delta} = 0.5)$	Measure (ii) with the addition of an equally weighted combination of Ω^{II} and Ω^{III}

Table 11.11 Poverty scores for female/male; rural/urban and subgroup comparisons (Nicholas et al. 2017)

Measure	Female	Male	Rural	Urban	Henan	Guizhou	Heilong-jiang	Shandong	Liaoning	Hubei	Hunan	Guangxi	Jiangsu
$\boldsymbol{\Omega}(\boldsymbol{\beta} = 2, \boldsymbol{\delta} = 0.5)$	0.2324	0.2302	0.2609	0.1364	0.3019	0.2725	0.2554	0.2461	0.2228	0.2111	0.2107	0.1905	0.1846
$\boldsymbol{\Omega}^{\mathbf{dimension}}$ $(\boldsymbol{\beta} = 2)$	0.1668	0.1633	0.1912	0.0819	0.2222	0.2092	0.1801	0.1735	0.1550	0.1505	0.1498	0.1336	0.1239
$\boldsymbol{\Omega}^{\mathbf{duration}}$ $(\boldsymbol{\beta} = 2)$	0.2979	0.2970	0.3306	0.1910	0.3815	0.3358	0.3306	0.3188	0.2906	0.2718	0.2716	0.2474	0.2453
$\boldsymbol{\Omega}^{\mathbf{I}}$ $(\boldsymbol{\beta} = 2)$	0.1583	0.1550	0.1823	0.0749	0.2146	0.1991	0.1738	0.1643	0.1476	0.1411	0.1415	0.1241	0.1158
$\boldsymbol{\Omega}^{\mathbf{II}}$ $(\boldsymbol{\beta} = 2)$	0.0085	0.0083	0.0089	0.0070	0.0076	0.0101	0.0063	0.0092	0.0074	0.0094	0.0082	0.0094	0.0080
$\boldsymbol{\Omega}^{\mathbf{III}}$ $(\boldsymbol{\beta} = 2)$	0.1396	0.1420	0.1483	0.1161	0.1669	0.1367	0.1568	0.1545	0.1430	0.1306	0.1301	0.1232	0.1294
Ranking by specification													
(i) $\boldsymbol{\Omega}(\boldsymbol{\beta} = 1)$	1	2	1	2	1	2	3	4	5	7	6	8	9
(ii) $\boldsymbol{\Omega}^{\mathbf{I}}$ $(\boldsymbol{\beta} = 2)$	1	2	1	2	1	2	3	4	5	7	6	8	9
(iii) $\boldsymbol{\Omega}^{\mathbf{dimension}}$ $(\boldsymbol{\beta} = 2)b$	1	2	1	2	1	2	3	4	5	6	7	8	9
(iv) $\boldsymbol{\Omega}^{\mathbf{duration}}$ $(\boldsymbol{\beta} = 2)$	1	2	1	2	1	2	3	4	5	6	7	8	9
(v) $\boldsymbol{\Omega}(\boldsymbol{\beta} = 2, \boldsymbol{\delta} = 0.5)$	1	2	1	2	1	2	3	4	5	6	7	8	9

A higher rank indicates more deprived. $a = 0; z = 1$ in all specifications

groups will be to changes in weights allotted to the breadth (Ω^{II}) and length (Ω^{III}) sensitive components. Looking at the three components, Ω^{I}, Ω^{II} and Ω^{III}, we can see that Females are more deprived in Ω^{I} and Ω^{II} relative to males, whereas rural residents are more deprived than their urban counterparts in all three components, with the Ω^{I} component nearly triple that of the urban residents. The rankings at the provincial level are once again largely robust: in fact, the ranking are all robust to the choice of δ. However, the Hubei—Hunan comparison yields some interesting information: while Hubei has a smaller average count of deprivations (apparent from it ranking lower at $\Omega, \beta = 1$, it has both a larger concentration of deprivations in dimensions (Ω^{II}) and in specific periods of time (Ω^{III}). As we move from specification (i)–(ii), rankings do not change, suggesting that introducing FGT-type between-individual distribution sensitivity makes little difference for Hubei—Hunan. However, the rankings change when we take into account within-individual distributions of deprivations [specifications (iii)–(v)].

One thing to notice in all these subgroup comparisons is that size of the Ω^{III} component is relatively larger than Ω^{II}, meaning that deprivations are more likely to be repeated across time, rather than spread out across dimensions. While the choice of δ is never obvious since the notion of whether additional periods in the same dimension should be weighted more heavily than additional dimensions in the same period is highly subjective, we have shown that rankings robust to δ with respect to groups of provinces can be established using $\Omega^{dimension}$ and $\Omega^{duration}$. The scores associated with each of the three components are useful for comparisons across subgroups. For example, Henan is the province that has both the highest average count of deprivations, $(\Omega, \beta = 1)$ and the largest concentration of these deprivations across time in specific dimensions (Ω^{III}). However, in terms of Ω^{II}, only Heilongjiang and Liaoning are ranked lower than Henan. Instead, Guizhou, with the second highest average count of deprivations, $(\Omega, \beta = 1)$ has the largest concentration of deprivations across dimensions in specific periods (Ω^{II}) but has a Ω^{III} component that is surpassed by Liaoning, Shandong, Heilongjiang and Henan. In the next section, we explore in greater detail the heterogeneity in deprivation across Henan and Guizhou through the use of dimensional decomposition.

11.4 Multidimensional Nature of Child Disadvantage[8]

The goal of improving child welfare and alleviating child impoverishment is a crucially important objective shared by all countries around the world. However, any efforts to address this objective can only be effective if the factors which contribute to child disadvantage can be clearly discerned. The fact that the well-being of children depends on their needs being adequately met across a

[8]This section is largely based on Mishra et al. (2018).

multitude of dimensions—including health, safety, material provisions, educational development, emotional security and social inclusion—makes it a challenging task for policymakers to identify the areas in which children are experiencing the most severe instances of disadvantage and, hence, where to direct their policy attention. In addition to accounting for the fact that child well-being spans across a multitude of dimensions, policymakers also ideally need to identify the demographic groups of children that encounter relatively worse levels of disadvantage than others, so as to ensure that resources are being channelled towards those who are most vulnerable.

The need for policy and welfare analyses to adopt a robust holistic approach towards measuring and comparing child disadvantage is the main motivation of the study by Mishra et al. (2018) that is described in this section. The focus on childhood disadvantage makes a valuable contribution to efforts to tackle the broader issue of social and economic disadvantage among the total population, since impoverishment during childhood can set an individual on a downward trajectory towards poorer life outcomes in adulthood. The issue of child disadvantage is one that affects the whole of society, as the children of today will form the social and human capital of tomorrow, determining a nation's economic growth and overall well-being in the future.

While much of the empirical literature on multidimensional poverty and deprivation has examined well-being at a household level or among the adult population: relatively few were designed to focus exclusively on the welfare of children, let alone vulnerable subgroups of children population. Indeed, although the measurement of poverty has a long history, a high-level focus on child poverty is relatively recent: it was only in 2006 that the UN General Assembly first adopted a universal definition of child poverty (UNICEF 2007). Of the vast body of literature that examines the well-being of children in a developed country context, very few have methodologically applied the axiomatic approach of Alkire and Foster (2011). The only exception, to our knowledge, is Minujin and Nandy (2012) whose collection of country-level case studies focused on the conceptualisation and measurement of child well-being and included several studies that adopted multidimensional measures. Minujin and Nandy (2012) observed that 'a common finding in all [studies] is that child poverty (with its negative impact on child well-being) is very prevalent. Not only is it widespread, in some instances it is on the increase' (p. 569).

Mishra et al. (2018) is the first empirical application of a dynamic multidimensional measure of disadvantage specifically designed for, and applied to, the child population in a developed nation. Following the approach outlined earlier in this chapter, their analysis draws a distinction between the 'persistence' and 'duration' of disadvantage. Persistence refers to the number of consecutive spells of disadvantage that a child experiences over a given period, while duration refers to the cumulative total of all spells of disadvantage experienced in that period which may or may not be consecutively timed. Identifying instances of ongoing or persistent disadvantage has become a significant concern for policymakers, heightening the relevance of this methodological tool. Mishra et al. (2018) demonstrate the applicability of this methodological approach using a representative sample of the Australian child population.

The demographic breadth of the data sets used in this study allowed the application in a comparative manner across sub-groups of children within the Australian child population. Given the high importance placed on improving the living standard of the Indigenous population in Australia, who are more likely to experience higher rates of impoverishment and disadvantage than the non-Indigenous population, the study focuses on examining the experiences of Indigenous children relative to the total the Australian child population.[9] Despite living in a developed and affluent country, many Indigenous Australians experience levels of impoverishment that not only fall well below the living standards experienced by most Australians, but are on par with the levels of impoverishment faced by some of the poorest populations in developing countries. This methodological approach can aid policymakers' understanding of the dimensions of well-being where the gap between Indigenous children and non-Indigenous children generates the most profound impacts and, hence, aid in formulating targeted policy actions. The focus on comparing Indigenous and non-Indigenous well-being is particularly relevant in the context of the Australian Government's concerted efforts to 'close the gap' across a set of key statistical indicators of quality of life outcomes.

To quantify and analyse the well-being of Australian children, Mishra et al. (2018) uses data available from the Longitudinal Study of Australian Children (LSAC). The LSAC is a geographically representative nation-wide survey of all Australian children which started in 2004 and is conducted every two years. The analysis uses the 'K-cohort' of children who were born between March 1999 and February 2000. They use wave 1 through to wave 5 of the LSAC which enables us to track children from the age of 4–5 years to 12–13 years. The study only includes children who were present in the all the five waves. After cleaning the data for missing observations and invalid responses, a total of 3557 children are available for each wave, comprising our balanced panel.

Given that, in Australia, there is significant concern over impoverished living standards and poorer lifetime outcomes that afflict the Indigenous population, the study demonstrates the way in which the indicators need be tailored to befit the circumstances of the population of interest. To analyse the extent and nature of disadvantage among the Australian Indigenous child population, the study uses data from the Longitudinal Study of Indigenous Children (LSIC). LSIC is a geographically representative survey of Indigenous Australian children, which began in 2008 and is collected annually. The study uses the 'K-cohort' of children who were born between December 2003 and November 2004, and waves 1–6 of the data, which follow children from 3½–5 years of age up to age 8½–10 years. After constructing a balanced panel comprised only of children who participated in all six

[9]In Australia, the 'Indigenous' population refers to the Aboriginal and Torres Strait Islander people who are the original inhabitants of the land.

waves of LSIC, and account for missing or invalid observations, there remains a total of 321 Indigenous children

The surveys share a common objective which, generally expressed, is to identify ways to improve the well-being of Australian children. More specifically, LSAC, which is a geographically representative sample of the total Australian child population, aims to 'identify policy opportunities for improving support for children and their families and for early intervention and prevention strategies'.[10] LSIC acknowledges the particular circumstances facing Indigenous children, specifically articulating its objective to 'improve understanding of issues faced by Aboriginal and Torres Strait Islander children, their families and communities [and] improve the policy response to these issues'.[11] As such, LSIC has formulated survey questions that are specifically designed to inform policies aiming to improve the well-being of Indigenous children. While the majority of the survey items used in this analysis are common to both the LSIC and LSAC data sets, there are some differences that reflect LSIC's cultural specificity and the more difficult circumstances that Indigenous children are more likely to experience compared to non-Indigenous children. These points of difference between some of the indicators enable us to develop culturally sensitive measurements. An additional point of difference between the two data sets is that there are some marginal differences in the way that the children's age groups are categorised, which are acknowledged in the presentation of the results in Mishra et al. (2018).

A description of the indicators used for each dimension for the LSAC and LSIC data sets are presented in Tables 11.12 and 11.13 respectively. The variables have been designed so that the individual's State of disadvantage takes a value of $d = 1$ (instead of $d = 0$) if they satisfy the criteria for disadvantage. In some circumstances, it is the *absence* of a factor which enhances well-being that generates the state of disadvantage. In other circumstances, it is the *presence* of a factor which diminishes well-being that generates the state of disadvantage. Whether the state of disadvantage is defined positively (by virtue of the presence of a factor) or negatively (by virtue of the absence of a factor) does not matter for the purposes of the calculations. For both the data sets, the child is the sampling unit and responses are collected from the questionnaires completed by the main caregiver (who is usually a parent) and the child's teacher.

The main differences in the indicators used for the total sample of Australian children in LSAC and for the Indigenous children sample in LSIC relate to material well-being, educational well-being and community connectedness. These differences are sensitive to some of the most notable disparities in quality of life that are observed between these two demographic groups, including the fact that Indigenous population have statistically much lower rates of school attendance, higher rates of

[10]As stated on the LSAC website www.growingupinaustralia.gov.au.

[11]As stated on the LSIC website www.dss.gov.au/about-the-department/national-centre-for-longitudinal-studies/overview-of-footprints-in-time-the-longitudinal-study-of-indigenous-children-lsic.

Table 11.12 Description of indicators used for all Australian children in LSAC

Dimension	Indicator(s)	Description of indicator
Health	Weight	Measurement of child's Body Mass Index (BMI)
	Use of medical care	Whether the child needs or uses more medical care, mental health or educational services than is usual for most children of the same age
Family relationships	Home activities with family	Whether the parent involved the child in everyday home activities (such as cooking or caring for pets) during the past week
	Outdoor activities with family	Whether the parent involved the child in outdoor activities (such as playing games or sport) during the past week
Community connectedness	Community activities	Whether the child attended any community-related activities (such as going to a playground, swimming pool, cinema, sporting event, museum, concert, community/school event, library, religious service) with the parent or other family member, during the past month
Material well-being	Extra-cost activities	Whether the child regularly participated in any extra-cost activities (such as sports coaching, team sports, music/ art/drama lessons, community groups, language classes) during the past 6-12 months
	Access to computer	Whether the child has access to a computer or internet at home
Educational well-being	Talk about school	Frequency with which the parent talks to the child about school
	School performance	Child's performance at school compared to other children of the same age
Emotional well-being	Bullied	Whether the child has been bullied at school during the past year
Exposure to risky behavior	Drug and Alcohol problems	Whether anyone in the child's household had an Alcohol or drug problem during the past year

Note Indicators are based on the questionnaire items used in the Longitudinal Study of Australian Children (LSAC)
Source Mishra et al. (2018)

housing overcrowding and more excessive Alcohol consumption in the community. Given the impoverishment already faced by the Indigenous population, and the fact that geographic isolation can tend to exacerbate levels of disadvantage by limiting access to infrastructure and resources, the study uses the subgroup decomposability property of the multidimensional poverty measure to examine differences between Indigenous children who live in urban areas and those who live in remote areas. This element of distinction within this analysis can aid in designing targeted policy interventions.

Tables 11.14 and 11.15 present the child disadvantage headcount rates for all Australian children and only indigenous children as calculated from the LSAC and LSIC data sets, respectively. A comparison of Tables 11.14 and 11.15 shows that across nearly all indicators, Indigenous children experience higher rates of

Table 11.13 Description of indicators used for Indigenous children in LSIC

Dimension	Indicator(s)	Description of indicator
Health	Body weight	Measurement of child's Body Mass Index (BMI)
Family relationships	Home activities with family	Whether the parent or another family member did any of the following activities with the child in the past week: read a book, tell a story, play indoors, housework/cooking, help with chores
	Outdoor activities with family	Whether the parent or another family member did any of the following activities with the child in the past week: play outdoors, go to the playground; participate in organised sports/dance activities (If the above indicator is not available) Whether the parent knows where your child is, when they are away from home
Community connectedness	Safety of community	Parent's perception of the safety of the community
	Suitability of community for children	Parent's perception of how suitable the community is for young children
Material well-being	Housing size per person	Number of bedrooms in home, deflated/adjusted for number of people in household
	Housing quality	Whether the home needs repairs or an important fixture is not working
Educational well-being	School attendance	Whether the child attends playgroup/daycare/childcare/preschool/kinder/school?
	Educational development/resources	Whether the teacher helps the child's educational development (gives advice to parent about how they help child at home; gives information community services that can help child; understands needs of Indigenous families; informs parents about how to be involved in school)
Emotional well-being	Bullied	Whether the child has been bullied at school during the past year
Exposure to risky behavior	Drug and Alcohol problems	Whether anyone in the household had an Alcohol or drug problem during the past year

Note Indicators are based on the questionnaire items used in the Longitudinal Study of Indigenous Children (LSIC)
Source Mishra et al. (2018)

disadvantage than the full sample of Australian children. Of the most acute differences, rates of disadvantage in body weight are around twice as high among the Indigenous child population, and rates of exposure to Alcohol and drug problems are around seven times higher. The only dimension in which Indigenous children experience relatively lower rates of disadvantage than the full sample of Australian children is family well-being, potentially signifying that Indigenous families tend to be more connected to the children by way of spending time with them.

Table 11.14 Child disadvantage headcount rates, disaggregated by indicator and age for all Australian children in LSAC

Child's age (years)	Dimension 1: Health		Dimension 2: Family relationships		Dimension 3: Community connectedness	Dimension 4: Material well-being		Dimension 5: Educational well-being		Dimension 6: Emotional well-being	Dimension 7: Risky behavior
	Body weight	Medical care	Home activities	Outdoor activities	Community activities	Extra-cost activities	Access to computer	Talk about school	School perform.	Bullied	Drug/Alcohol
4–5	0.2142	0.0869	0.0866	0.0956	0.0104	0.3247	0.1982	0.2353	0.3452	0.1782	0.0402
	(0.2136)	(0.0880)	(0.0885)	(0.0955)	(0.0112)	(0.3352)	(0.2106)	(0.2420)	(0.3594)	(0.1869)	(0.0406)
6–7	0.1923	0.0973	0.0860	0.1451	0.0276	0.1968	0.1012	0.0020	0.0554	0.3048	0.0194
	(0.1953)	(0.0993)	(0.0881)	(0.1452)	(0.0278)	(0.2042)	(0.1085)	(0.0018)	(0.0605)	(0.3083)	(0.0197)
8–9	0.2423	0.1127	0.0683	0.1718	0.0439	0.0919	0.0692	0.0020	0.0624	0.3306	0.0236
	(0.2452)	(0.1117)	(0.0704)	(0.1760)	(0.0471)	(0.0983)	(0.0707)	(0.0020)	(0.0641)	(0.3293)	(0.0230)
10–11	0.2733	0.0964	0.0655	0.2828	0.0433	0.0841	0.0267	0.0025	0.0723	0.2935	0.0281
	(0.2799)	(0.0974)	(0.0653)	(0.2835)	(0.0451)	(0.0873)	(0.0314)	(0.0025)	(0.0721)	(0.2936)	(0.0286)
12–13	0.2783	0.0914	0.0793	0.3984	0.0773	0.2100	0.0225	0.0039	0.0866	0.2595	0.0318
	(0.2802)	(0.0918)	(0.0801)	(0.3985)	(0.0785)	(0.2140)	(0.0246)	(0.0040)	(0.0875)	(0.2637)	(0.0328)

Note Headcount rates denote the proportion of children who are deemed disadvantaged for the particular indicator relative to the total sample. Numbers in parenthesis are headcount rates of disadvantage computed for the unbalanced panel sample. Sample size for the balanced panel: 3557 per age group. Sample size for the unbalanced panel: 4012 for 4–5 years; 3918 for 6–7 years; 3948 for 8–9 years; 3951 for 10–11 years; and 3747 for 12–13 years. *Source* Longitudinal Study of Australian Children (LSAC) collected biennially from 2004 to 2012, following children from the age of 4–5 years to 12–13 years
Source Mishra et al. (2018)

Table 11.15 Child disadvantage headcount rates, disaggregated by indicator and age for Indigenous children in LSIC

Child's age (years)	Dimension 1: Health	Dimension 2: Family relationships		Dimension 3: Community connectedness		Dimension 4: Material well-being		Dimension 5: Educational well-being		Dimension 6: Emotional well-being	Dimension 7: Risky behavior
	Body weight	Home activities	Outdoor activities	Community safety	Community suitability	Housing size	Housing quality	School attendance	Educ. resources	Bullied	Drug/Alcohol
3½–5	0.1034	0.0034	0.0207	0.1276	0.1000	0.5034	0.3310	0.2310	0.0759	0.4517	0.2138
	(0.1131)	(0.0064)	(0.0175)	(0.1704)	(0.1338)	(0.5207)	(0.3933)	(0.2357)	(0.0701)	(0.5064)	(0.2627)
4½–6	0.2922	0.0097	0.0195	0.1201	0.1104	0.5617	0.3247	0.0812	0.0877	0.4091	0.1364
	(0.2837)	(0.0121)	(0.0225)	(0.1419)	(0.1280)	(0.5692)	(0.3408)	(0.1003)	(0.0744)	(0.4291)	(0.1817)
5½–7	0.2918	0.0066	0.0197	0.1246	0.1148	0.5770	0.2656	0.2164	0.1836	0.4230	0.1672
	(0.2899)	(0.0042)	(0.0231)	(0.1429)	(0.1218)	(0.5840)	(0.3256)	(0.2500)	(0.1849)	(0.4601)	(0.1996)
6½–8	0.3259	0.0288	0.5048	0.1022	0.1054	0.6230	0.2620	0.2173	0.1693	0.4473	0.2428
	(0.3100)	(0.0349)	(0.5044)	(0.1092)	(0.1157)	(0.6550)	(0.3384)	(0.2336)	(0.1812)	(0.4738)	(0.2445)
7½–9	0.3439	0.0510	0.4204	0.1019	0.0955	0.5860	0.3185	0.2389	0.1720	0.2962	0.2197
	(0.3410)	(0.0628)	(0.4435)	(0.1151)	(0.1067)	(0.5900)	(0.3473)	(0.2259)	(0.2364)	(0.3159)	(0.2427)
8½–10	0.4581	0.0613	0.0194	0.1161	0.1032	0.6226	0.3484	0.2581	0.2097	0.4581	0.2226
	(0.4442)	(0.1284)	(0.0358)	(0.1242)	(0.1074)	(0.6126)	(0.3389)	(0.2611)	(0.2232)	(0.4758)	(0.2632)

Note Headcount rates denote the proportion of children who are deemed disadvantaged for the particular indicator relative to the total sample. Numbers in parenthesis are headcount rates of disadvantage for the unbalanced panel. Sample size for the balanced panel: 321 per age group. Sample size for the unbalanced panel: 706 for 3½–5 years; 655 for 4½–6 years; 591 for 5½–7 years; 534 for 6½–8 years; 529 for 7½–9 years; and 488 for 8½–10 years. *Source* Longitudinal Study of Indigenous Children (LSIC) collected annually from 2008 to 2013, following children from the age of 3½–5 years to 8½–10 years

Source Mishra et al. (2018)

Using the multidimensional measure of deprivation presented earlier in Eq. (11.4) for a single time period ($T = 1$), Figure 11.3 compares the multidimensional disadvantage scores of indigenous and non-indigenous children in Australia. Figure 11.4 provides a similar comparison between indigenous children living in areas of 'high isolation' and 'low isolation'. Figure 11.3 shows that the differential between Indigenous and non-Indigenous children widens as we assign greater weighting to children who are disadvantaged in more dimensions through the parameter α, indicating that the Indigenous children are more profoundly affected by the effect of multiple instances of disadvantage. Figure 11.4 shows that Indigenous children living in highly isolated geographic regions face higher levels of disadvantage than those in relatively less isolated regions, with this ratio inflating

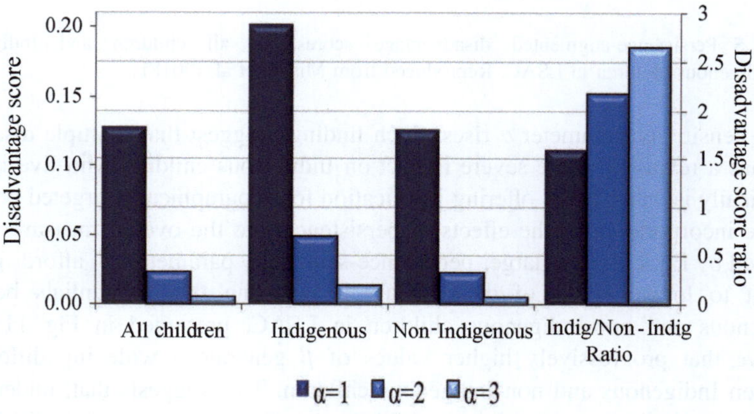

Fig. 11.3 Disadvantage scores of all children and Indigenous/non-Indigenous subgroups in LSAC. Reproduced from Mishra et al. (2018)

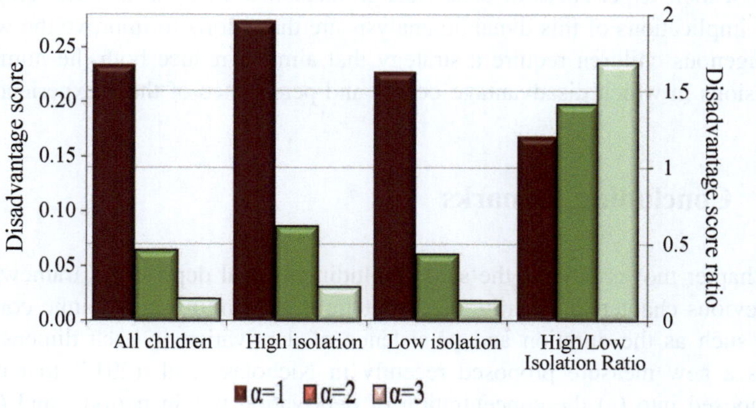

Fig. 11.4 Disadvantage scores of all Indigenous children and high/low isolation subgroups in LSIC. Reproduced from Mishra et al. (2018)

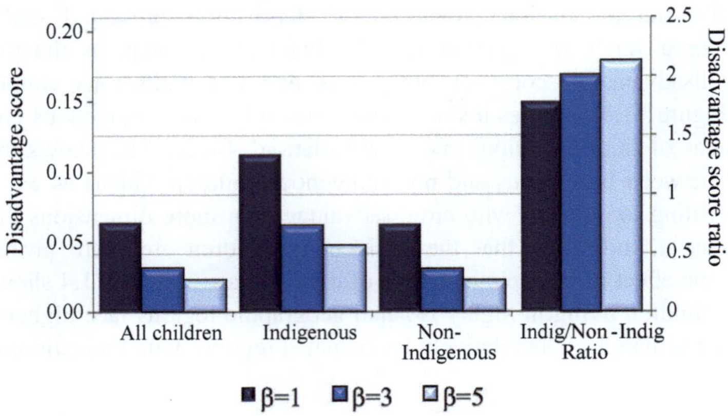

Fig. 11.5 Persistence-augmented disadvantage scores for all children and Indigenous/non-Indigenous children in LSAC. Reproduced from Mishra et al. (2018)

as the sensitivity parameter α rises. Such findings suggest that multiple disadvantage has a relatively more severe impact on Indigenous children who live in geographically isolated areas, offering justification for geographically targeted policies.

The incorporation of the effects of persistence into the overall measure is represented by Eq. (11.4). A larger persistence-sensitivity parameter (β) affords greater weight to longer spells of disadvantage. Examining the differentials between Indigenous and non-Indigenous children in LSAC, presented in Fig. 11.5, we observe that progressively higher values of β generate a widening differential between Indigenous and non-Indigenous children. This suggests that, under these parameters, Indigenous children in LSAC are affected more profoundly by the impact of persistence than non-Indigenous children. The dynamic framework therefore shows that not only are levels of disadvantage already higher among Indigenous children to begin with, but there are circumstances in which the ongoing nature of their experiences of disadvantage intensifies this gap in well-being. The policy implications of this dynamic analysis are that efforts to improve the welfare of indigenous children require a strategy that aims to reduce both the number of dimensions in which disadvantage occurs and persistence of these experiences.

11.5 Concluding Remarks

This chapter moves beyond the static multidimensional deprivation framework of the previous chapter to describe recent attempts at bringing in dynamic considerations such as the duration and persistence of deprivation in each dimension. It reports a new measure proposed recently in Nicholas et al. (2017) that can be decomposed into (a) the concentration of deprivation within periods, and (b) the concentration of deprivations within dimensions. The dynamic measures considered in this chapter exploit the subgroup decomposability property to identify population subgroups that endure longer spells of deprivation than others along with the dimensions where the deprivation spells are the most acute. The illustrative applications in the chosen studies on the data sets of Australia and China confirm the policy friendliness of the proposed measures by identifying sub-groups and dimensions that need targeted intervention. While this chapter should serve to point to great potential in further development of these dynamic multidimensional measures, their application requires panel data covering a reasonably long period of time to render meaningful estimation of duration and persistence of deprivation. Unfortunately, such panel data sets are still difficult to find especially ones that provide information on the household's access to a range of dimensions. The central message of this chapter is the need to collect and make available more such data sets since there is great potential for their use in policy.

References

Alkire S, Foster J (2010) Designing the inequality-adjusted Human Development Index (HDI). Oxford Poverty and Human Development Initiative (OPHI), Working Paper, No. 37

Alkire S, Foster J (2011) Counting and multidimensional poverty measurement. J Public Econ 95:476–487

Alkire S, Foster J (2016) Dimensional and distributional contributions to multidimensional poverty. OPHI Working Paper 100, University of Oxford

Atkinson A (2003) Multidimensional deprivation: contrasting social welfare and counting approaches. J Econ Inequality 1:51–65

Atkinson A, Cantillon B, Marlier E, Nolan B (2002) Social indicators. The EU and social inclusion. Oxford University Press, Oxford

Ayala L, Jurado A, Perez-Mayo J (2011) Income poverty and multidimensional deprivation: lessons from cross-regional analysis. Rev Income Wealth 57(1):40–60

Bardhan P (2010) Awakening giants, feet of clay. Princeton University Press, Princeton

Bossert W, Chakravarty S, D'Ambrosio C (2009) Multidimensional deprivation poverty and material deprivation. ECINEQ Working paper no. 2009-129

Bossert W, Chakravarty S, D'Ambrosio C (2010) Poverty and time. UNU-WIDER Working paper no. 2010/74

Bossert W, D'Ambrosio C, Peragine V (2007) Deprivation and social exclusion. Economica 74 (296):777–803

Bourguignon F, Chakravarty S (2003) The measurement of multidimensional poverty. J Econ Inequality 1:25–49

Calvo C, Dercon S (2007) Chronic poverty and all that: the measurement of poverty over time. Working paper 89 of Chronic Poverty Research Centre, Manchester

Chakravarty S, D'Ambrosio C (2006) The measurement of social exclusion. Rev Income Wealth 52(3):377–398

Datt G (2013) Making every dimension count: multidimensional poverty without the dual cut off. Monash Economics Working Papers 32–13, Monash University

Dutta I, Pattanaik P, Xu Y (2003) On measuring deprivation and the standard of living in a multidimensional framework on the basis of aggregate data. Economica 70:197–221

Eurostat (2000) European social statistics, income poverty and social exclusion. THEME 3, population and social conditions, Luxembourg

Fan S, Kanbur R, Wei S, Zhang X (eds) (2014) Oxford companion to the economics of China. Oxford University Press, Oxford, p 2014

Foster JE (2007) A report on Mexican multidimensional poverty measurement. OPHI Working Paper, No. 40
Foster JE (2009) A class of chronic poverty measures. In: Addison T, Hulme D, Kanbur R (eds) Poverty dynamics: interdisciplinary perspectives. Oxford University Press, Oxford, pp 59–76
Foster JE, Greer J, Thorbecke E (1984) A class of decomposable poverty measures. Econometrica 52:761–766
Gradin C, del Rio C, Canto O (2012) Measuring poverty accounting for time. Rev Income Wealth 58(330–354):2012
Hoy M, Zheng B (2011) Measuring lifetime poverty. J Econ Theory 146:2544–2562
Jayaraj D, Subramanian S (2010) A Chakravarty-D'Ambrosio view of multidimensional deprivation: some estimates for India. Econ Polit Wkly XLV(60):53–65
Klasen S (2000) Measuring poverty and deprivation in South Africa. Rev Income Wealth 46 (1):33–58
Labar K, Bresson F (2011) A multidimensional analysis of poverty in China from 1991 to 2006. China Econ Rev 22(646–668):2011
Lahoti R, Jayadev A, Reddy S (2015) The global consumption and income project (GCIP): an introduction and preliminary findings. UN/DESA Working Paper No. 140
Minujin A, Nandy S (eds) (2012) Global child poverty and well-being: measurement, concepts, policy and action. The Policy Press, Bristol
Mishra A, Ray R (2012) Multidimensional deprivation in the awakening giants: a comparison of China and India on micro data. J Asian Econ 23:454–465
Mishra A, Ray R, Risse L (2018) A multidimensional dynamic measure of child disadvantage: a methodological tool for policymakers. Soc Indic Res. https://doi.org/10.1007/s11205-017-1742-x (Forthcoming)
Nicholas A, Ray R (2012) Duration and persistence in multidimensional deprivation: methodology and Australian application. Econ Rec 88:106–126
Nicholas A, Ray R, Sinha K (2017) Differentiating between dimensionality and duration in multidimensional measures of poverty: methodology with an application to China. Rev Income Wealth (Forthcoming)
Nicholas A, Ray R, Valenzuela R (2010) Evaluating the distributional implications of price movements: methodology, application and Australian evidence. Econ Rec 86(274):352–366
Park A, Wang S (2014) Poverty. In: Fan S, Kanbur R, Wei S, Zhang X (eds) Oxford companion to the economics of China. Oxford University Press, Oxford
Paul S (1992) An illfare approach to the measurement of unemployment. Appl Econ 24(7):739–743
Popkin BM, Du S, Zhai F, Zhang B (2010) Cohort profile: the China health and nutrition survey-monitoring and understanding socio-economic and health change in China, 1989–2011. Int J Epidemiol 39:1435–1440
Ray R, Sinha K (2015) Multidimensional deprivation in China, India and Vietnam: a comparative study on micro data. J Human Dev Capabilities 16:69–93
Scutella R, Kostenko W, Wilkins R (2009) Estimates of poverty and social exclusion in Australia: a multidimensional approach. Melbourne Institute of Applied Economic and Social Research, Working Paper Series, Working paper No. 28/09
Sengupta M (2009) Unemployment duration and the measure of unemployment. J Econ Inequality 7:273–294
Shapley L (1953) A value for n-person games. In: Kuhn HW, Tucker AW (eds) Contributions to the theory of games, vol II, Annals of mathematical studies vol 28. Princeton University Press, Princeton, pp 307–317
Shorrocks AF (2013) Decomposition procedures for distributional analysis: a unified framework based on the Shapley value. J Econ Inequality 1:99–126
Shorrocks A, Foster J (1987) Transfer sensitive inequality measures. Rev Econ Stud 54(3):485–497

Stiglitz JE, Sen A, Fitoussi JP (2009) Report by the commission on the measurement of economic performance and social progress. Available at http://www.insee.fr/fr/publications-et-services/dossiers_web/stiglitz/doc-commission/RAPPORT_anglais.pdf

UNICEF (United Nations International Children's Emergency Fund) (2007) UN General Assembly adopts powerful definition of child poverty. https://www.unicef.org/media/media_38003.html

Ware JE, Snow KK, Kosinski M, Gandek B (2000) SF-36 health survey: manual and interpretation guide. Quality Metric Inc., Lincoln

Yalonetzky G (2014) Conditions for the most robust multidimensional poverty comparisons using counting measures and ordinal variables. Soc Choice Welfare 43:773–807

You J, Wang S, Roope L (2014) Multi-dimensional intertemporal poverty in rural China. (University of Oxford Centre for the Study of African Economies Working Paper Series No. WPS/2014-36), 2014

Chapter 12
Food Consumption, Poverty, Hunger and Undernourishment

12.1 Introduction

In this penultimate chapter of this volume, the discussion turns to poverty and undernourishment in India. Besides providing evidence on the magnitudes and trend in the rates of poverty and undernourishment, this chapter describes and reports the principal findings from Ray (2007) that examine the link between the two during the period from the late 1980s to the first part of the new millennium. Attention is focussed in this study on the mismatch in India between the estimates of poverty rates and of prevalence of undernourishment and of the contradictory trends between the two. Since a crucial element in the link between poverty and undernourishment is Food consumption and its effect on nutritional intake, we provide estimates of the two over this period. A result of much significance is the feature that there has been a decline in cereal consumption that is associated with a decline in calorie intake. This study also highlights the role of government welfare schemes such as the Public Distribution Scheme (PDS) in the government's poverty eradication programme and shows that the importance of the PDS varies between regions and between female-headed households and others.

As the most important target group from a policy viewpoint is children, this chapter reports the estimates of malnourished children in India with the rates of 'stunted' and 'wasted' children being used as the measures of child malnourishment. We report the principal findings from Maitra et al. (2013) that examine the relationship, if any, between child nutritional outcomes and calorie intakes. A significant result obtained in this study is that declining calorie intake in India is associated with a deterioration in the short-run nutritional outcome as measured by the rates of 'wasted' children, but this does not extend to long-run child health outcomes measured by the rates of 'stunted children'. It is now well documented that India's record on the health outcomes is quite dismal and does not match with her impressive performance on growth rates and declining poverty rates and that child health outcomes in India are much inferior compared to that of China.

R. Ray, *Household Behaviour, Prices, and Welfare*, Themes in Economics,
https://doi.org/10.1007/978-981-13-1930-3_12

This chapter also reports the spatial differences in child health outcomes in India as obtained in a recent study by Maitra and Ray (2013) comparing the state of child health in the State of West Bengal with that in the other regions. Some regions have performed much better than others, and this needs to be examined and explained to devise effective policy intervention in the laggard States. They reinforce the point made earlier in different contexts that it is misleading to make all-India generalisations. The study by Maitra and Ray (2013) that provides evidence on the regional differences in child health outcomes in India is described in some detail later in this chapter. This chapter describes in some detail the above-mentioned studies that share a common focus on Food consumption, calorie intake, undernourishment, poverty and child health outcomes in India. Recently, a group of leading Indian economists have favoured a move to cash transfers to take the place of in-kind transfers such as the Public Distribution System (PDS) and Midday Meal Scheme (MDMS).

This chapter examines the nutritional implications of such a move and compares the role of direct cash transfer in reducing undernourishment with that of the existing welfare schemes, PDS and the MDMS. The results from an ongoing study by the author with Kompal Sinha on the 68th round of the NSS, the latest large sample survey available, have been presented later in the chapter. The rest of the chapter is organised as follows. The study by Ray (2007) on changing Food consumption in India is described in Sect. 12.2, the link between calorie intake and nutritional outcomes on children that is explored in Maitra et al. (2013) is discussed in Sect. 12.3, and the spatial heterogeneity in child health outcomes is reported in Sect. 12.4 following the investigation in Maitra and Ray (2013). The possible move to a 'universal basic income' to be transferred directly to the recipient's bank account is explored in relation to the MDMS and PDS in Sect. 12.5. Section 12.6 concludes the chapter.

12.2 Food Consumption, Calorie Intake and Undernourishment in India

12.2.1 Summary

Ray (2007) examines the changes in the nature and quantity of Food consumption in India during the reform decade of the 1990s and analyses their implications for calorie intake and undernourishment. The study documents the decline in cereal consumption, especially in the urban areas, and provides evidence that suggests an increase in the prevalence of undernourishment over the period 1987/88 to 2001/2002. The results also point to a significant number of households, even in the top expenditure decile, suffering from undernourishment. This calls for a reassessment of the current strategy of directing the Targetted Public Distribution System (TPDS) exclusively at households 'below the poverty line'. This study shows that, both as a source of subsidised calories and as a poverty reducing instrument, the PDS is of much greater importance to female-headed households than it is to the rest of the population. Another important result is that, notwithstanding the sharp decline in their expenditure share during the 1990s, rice and wheat continue to provide the dominant share of calories, especially for the rural poor. The overall message is that, especially in a period of significant economic change, one needs to go beyond the standard expenditure-based money metric measures to assess the changes in the living standards of households.

12.2.2 Background and Motivation

The 1990s witnessed widespread economic reforms and liberalisation in India. Much of the discussion on the effects of these reforms has centred on the temporal movement in poverty and inequality magnitudes (see, e.g. Bhalla 2003; Dubey and Gangopadhyay 1998; Meenakshi and Ray 2002; Ray and Lancaster 2005; Sen and Himanshu 2004). Relatively little attention has been paid, until recently, to changes in the magnitude and pattern of Food consumption over the reform period, in spite of the links between consumption changes and poverty movements which is suggested by the calorie basis of the original definition of the poverty line in India (Dandekar and Rath 1971). As Ray and Lancaster (2005) have shown, this link has weakened to the extent that the official poverty line in India today is quite out of step with that based on the household's minimum calorie requirements. This is reflected in a dissonance, even contradiction, between expenditure-based poverty estimates and the calorie-based measures of hunger or undernourishment (Coondoo et al. 2005).

During a period of significant changes in the nature of Food consumption, which have serious implications for a household's calorie intake, expenditure and income-based poverty magnitudes do not give a true picture of Food and nutritional security. This points to the need to analyse trends in Food consumption, especially for cereals, over the reform period in India. Ray (2007) pays special attention to the calorie intake of two minority groups, namely female-headed households and the backward classes. Evidence is presented on the role of the Public Distribution System (PDS) in providing cheap calories to households, especially those of these two minority groups. This is a topic of some policy importance in the Indian context in view of recent discussions on the effectiveness of the PDS as an anti-hunger strategy, and the efforts to target the PDS exclusively at households 'below the poverty line' (BPL). The results of this study suggest that such a strategy may be counterproductive since a lot of households that are 'above the poverty line' (APL), especially in the rural areas, nevertheless suffer from undernourishment. Such APL households are missing out on the provision of subsidised rice and heat, via the PDS, because they fall outside the purview of this system.

12.2.3 Data Sets

The data sets used in this analysis are from the 43rd (July 1987 to June 1988), 50th (July 1993 to June 1994), 55th (July 1999 to June, 2000) and 57th (July 2001 to June 2002) rounds of the National Sample Survey (NSS) in India. The 55th round data provides information, at the household level, on calorie intake. These, in conjunction with the conversion factors of Indian Foods provided in Gopalan et al. (1999), were used to calculate calorie consumption figures in the other rounds. In the present study, the distinction between the 'availability' and the actual 'intake' of calories has to be disregarded, due to the absence of necessary information. Another potential complication that cannot be corrected is the possible non-comparability of the thirty-day Food expenditure figures in NSS round 55 with those in the other rounds, because of the inclusion of questions on the seven-day recall figures on Food expenditure in that questionnaire (see Sen 2000).

12.2.4 Results

Tables 12.1 and 12.2 report the State-level changes in the monthly per capita consumption (in kgs) of the principal Food items between 1987/88 (Round 43) and 2001/2 (Round 57) in rural and urban areas, respectively. The following features are worth noting. First, cereal consumption is generally much higher in rural than in urban areas, mainly due to the higher consumption of rice by rural households. The reverse is the case for meat/fish/eggs and fruits/vegetables. Second, there has been a marked decline in the consumption of all the cereal items over the period 1987/88–2001/2 in nearly all the States and in both rural and urban areas, with the reduction being particularly sharp for the smaller cereal items, namely barley, maize and cereal substitutes such as tapioca. Third, there has been a switch in preferences towards non-cereal items such as meat/fish and fruits/vegetables and, once again, this picture holds generally.

These features are confirmed in Table 12.3 which presents the all-India average values of both the (monthly) Food consumption quantities and the Food expenditure shares at the beginning (1987/88) and end (2001/2) of our sample period. The Engel Food share in total expenditure also registered a sharp decline over this period, especially in the urban areas. While some, including Rao (2005), have interpreted these movements as evidence of urbanisation and increased household affluence, others like Mehta and Venkatraman (2000) have argued that such changes have been involuntary, reflecting the loss in access to common property resources of the rural poor. Whatever the underlying factors causing these changes, they have led to significant declines in calorie consumption, due to the switch from calorie-intensive cereal items to non-cereals, which are more expensive sources of calories.

The PDS in India is quite unique in terms of the extent and intensity of its coverage. With a network of about 4.75 lakh Fair Price Shops (FPSs) in 2004, the

Table 12.1 Per capita Food consumption (kg/30 days) in rural areas (Ray 2007)

States	Food items													
	Rice		Wheat		Other cereals[a]		Pulses		Dairy		Edible oils		Meat/fish/eggs	
	1988	2002	1988	2002	1988	2002	1988	2002	1988	2002	1988	2002	1988	2002
Andhra Pradesh	11.8	11.2	0.1	0.2	2.3	0.9	0.8	0.7	2.5	3.7	0.4	0.5	1.7	2.3
Assam	13.7	12.7	0.9	0.7	0.0	0.0	0.8	0.7	1.5	1.7	0.3	0.5	1.9	2.8
Bihar	9.1	7.9	5.6	6.1	1.1	0.5	1.1	0.7	1.7	2.4	0.3	0.4	0.5	0.7
Gujarat	2.0	2.1	4.8	4.1	5.6	3.5	1.0	0.9	4.7	6.1	0.7	1.0	0.3	0.4
Haryana	0.8	0.7	13.5	8.8	0.5	0.3	0.9	0.6	12.6	12.8	0.3	0.4	0.3	0.1
Himachal Pradesh	4.3	4.8	7.3	5.9	4.5	1.9	1.6	1.4	8.5	8.9	0.6	0.7	0.6	0.8
Karnataka	5.3	5.7	0.8	1.1	7.9	4.5	1.0	0.9	2.9	3.3	0.3	0.5	0.9	1.8
Kerala	9.9	8.6	0.6	0.9	2.0	1.0	0.5	0.5	2.4	3.2	0.3	0.5	3.4	4.8
Madhya Pradesh	6.9	2.9	5.9	6.8	2.9	1.7	1.3	0.9	2.4	3.6	0.3	0.5	0.3	0.3
Maharashtra	3.0	3.6	2.4	3.0	7.7	4.5	1.2	1.1	2.5	2.8	0.5	0.7	1.0	1.5
Orissa	14.7	13.3	0.6	0.4	0.9	0.5	0.5	0.5	0.8	0.6	0.2	0.3	0.5	0.8
Punjab	0.8	0.9	11.2	9.2	0.4	0.3	1.1	0.8	13.6	11.8	0.5	0.7	0.8	0.6
Rajasthan	0.2	0.2	12.5	8.2	4.4	4.4	0.7	0.6	7.2	10.7	0.4	0.5	0.2	0.5
Tamil Nadu	10.1	10.0	0.2	0.3	2.5	0.4	0.8	0.8	1.6	2.1	0.3	0.5	1.1	2.3
Uttar Pradesh	3.9	3.8	10.7	8.4	1.0	0.4	1.3	0.9	4.5	4.4	0.4	0.5	0.4	0.6
West Bengal	13.6	12.0	1.5	1.1	0.0	0.0	0.5	0.5	1.4	1.8	0.3	0.5	1.9	3.9

States	Food items									
	Vegetables/fruits		Sugar/spices		Processed Food		Beverages		Total Cereals	
	1988	2002	1988	2002	1988	2002	1988	2002	1988	2002
Andhra Pradesh	6.2	9.0	1.4	1.3	1.1	2.1	2.3	8.0	14.3	12.3
Assam	10.0	13.0	1.2	1.1	0.7	1.1	2.8	3.2	14.5	13.3
Bihar	6.7	9.7	1.0	0.9	0.3	0.8	0.9	3.2	15.8	14.5

(continued)

Table 12.1 (continued)

States	Food items									
	Vegetables/fruits		Sugar/spices		Processed Food		Beverages		Total Cereals	
	1988	2002	1988	2002	1988	2002	1988	2002	1988	2002
Gujarat	6.2	9.4	1.9	1.8	0.3	1.3	1.4	2.5	12.4	9.7
Haryana	7.0	10.7	2.5	1.9	0.3	3.0	2.9	4.2	14.8	9.8
Himachal Pradesh	6.1	8.8	1.9	1.8	0.2	1.7	2.5	4.6	16.1	12.5
Karnataka	7.3	10.1	1.8	1.5	0.8	1.2	4.1	7.7	14.0	11.2
Kerala	11.5	15.5	1.6	1.6	0.3	2.7	9.7	7.9	12.5	10.5
Madhya Pradesh	5.6	7.1	1.5	1.3	0.3	1.1	1.2	2.5	15.7	11.3
Maharashtra	6.2	9.9	1.7	1.7	0.3	4.6	2.4	3.2	13.2	11.1
Orissa	6.8	7.8	1.1	0.9	0.3	2.7	0.5	1.6	16.1	14.3
Punjab	8.4	9.3	3.0	2.3	0.2	0.8	3.9	2.7	12.4	10.3
Rajasthan	4.0	6.8	2.2	1.8	0.2	1.0	2.1	2.1	17.0	12.8
Tamil Nadu	6.7	9.7	1.5	1.3	0.9	1.8	4.4	11.7	12.9	10.7
Uttar Pradesh	7.7	8.6	1.7	1.3	0.2	1.6	0.9	2.3	15.6	12.7
West Bengal	8.5	11.3	1.1	1.1	0.3	2.6	1.7	4.7	15.1	13.1

Note [a]Other cereals consist of smaller cereal items such as barley, maize and cereal substitutes (e.g. tapioca)
Source Author's calculations based on NSS Rounds 43, 57

Table 12.2 Per capita Food consumption (kg/30 days) in urban areas (Ray 2007)

States	Food items													
	Rice		Wheat		Other cereals[a]		Pulses		Dairy		Edible oils		Meat/fish/eggs	
	1988	2002	1988	2002	1988	2002	1988	2002	1988	2002	1988	2002	1988	2002
Andhra Pradesh	10.3	9.2	0.7	0.8	0.5	0.3	0.9	0.8	3.9	4.1	0.5	0.6	2.5	2.9
Assam	10.5	9.4	1.3	1.4	0.0	0.0	1.1	0.8	2.1	1.8	0.5	0.7	3.0	3.7
Bihar	7.7	5.8	5.8	6.0	0.2	0.0	1.2	0.9	2.5	3.9	0.4	0.6	1.1	1.6
Gujarat	2.3	1.8	5.7	4.9	1.6	1.2	1.2	0.9	6.2	7.5	1.0	1.1	0.7	0.8
Haryana	6.8	1.0	10.1	7.9	0.1	0.0	1.1	0.7	8.7	9.3	0.6	0.7	1.4	2.9
Himachal Pradesh	3.8	3.5	6.2	5.7	0.4	0.2	1.6	1.2	7.7	8.8	0.6	0.7	2.3	1.9
Karnataka	5.6	5.1	1.4	1.8	3.1	2.2	1.0	1.0	3.9	5.1	0.4	0.6	1.7	2.2
Kerala	7.9	7.2	0.9	1.0	0.6	0.4	0.6	0.6	3.5	4.2	0.4	0.5	4.9	5.3
Madhya Pradesh	3.9	2.3	7.3	7.5	0.5	0.2	1.4	0.9	4.5	4.8	0.6	0.7	1.3	1.0
Maharashtra	2.9	3.2	4.3	4.0	2.4	1.2	1.2	1.0	4.8	5.3	0.7	0.9	2.4	2.4
Orissa	10.6	10.2	2.3	2.1	0.1	0.0	0.8	0.8	2.3	2.7	0.4	0.5	1.8	2.2
Punjab	1.2	1.3	8.7	7.8	0.1	0.0	1.2	0.9	10.1	10.6	0.7	0.7	1.3	2.2
Rajasthan	0.6	0.6	11.4	9.2	0.8	0.9	0.9	0.7	7.3	7.7	0.6	0.7	0.7	1.0
Tamil Nadu	8.9	8.1	0.7	0.6	0.2	0.1	0.9	0.9	3.3	4.0	0.4	0.5	2.9	3.7
Uttar Pradesh	2.5	2.5	8.9	7.3	0.1	0.1	1.2	0.9	5.3	5.9	0.5	0.6	1.0	1.5
West Bengal	8.3	7.3	2.9	2.4	0.0	0.0	0.7	0.6	2.8	2.9	0.5	0.7	3.3	5.0

States	Food items									
	Vegetables/fruits		Sugar/spices		Processed Food		Beverages		Total cereals	
	1988	2002	1988	2002	1988	2002	1988	2002	1988	2002
Andhra Pradesh	10.0	12.8	1.5	1.3	2.0	3.3	5.9	12.6	11.5	10.2
Assam	12.3	13.8	1.3	1.1	0.4	6.8	6.4	16.0	11.9	10.8
Bihar	10.0	14.3	1.2	1.1	0.2	3.4	2.7	10.4	13.7	11.8

(continued)

Table 12.2 (continued)

States	Food items									
	Vegetables/fruits		Sugar/spices		Processed Food		Beverages		Total cereals	
	1988	2002	1988	2002	1988	2002	1988	2002	1988	2002
Gujarat	8.9	11.3	1.8	1.6	0.2	3.0	3.5	7.9	5.2	7.9
Haryana	12.6	15.3	1.9	1.9	0.3	1.8	8.5	6.2	17.0	8.9
Himachal Pradesh	13.6	11.7	1.8	1.5	0.3	9.2	6.3	13.8	10.3	9.4
Karnataka	9.7	14.1	1.6	1.5	2.3	4.4	6.2	11.5	10.1	9.0
Kerala	14.1	16.5	1.6	1.6	0.2	9.5	9.7	13.4	9.4	8.6
Madhya Pradesh	10.6	10.5	1.8	1.6	0.3	1.8	5.9	6.9	11.7	10.0
Maharashtra	13.4	14.2	1.7	1.5	0.7	5.1	6.6	12.9	9.6	8.4
Orissa	11.5	15.3	1.5	1.2	0.4	4.1	3.4	8.0	13.0	12.4
Punjab	12.5	13.0	2.3	2.0	0.3	4.9	8.6	13.0	10.0	9.1
Rajasthan	9.9	11.3	2.1	1.6	0.2	2.0	6.4	6.5	12.7	10.7
Tamil Nadu	11.2	12.5	1.6	1.4	1.7	5.5	6.6	12.5	9.8	8.8
Uttar Pradesh	13.0	13.4	1.7	1.4	0.4	2.2	4.4	7.0	11.5	9.9
West Bengal	11.9	16.6	1.2	1.1	0.7	8.0	5.5	15.3	11.3	9.7

Note [a]Other cereals consist of smaller cereal items such as barley, maize and cereal substitutes (e.g. tapioca)

Source Author's calculations based on NSS Rounds 43, 57

Table 12.3 All-India mean consumption and expenditure shares (Ray 2007)

Food items	Urban			Rural		
	1998 (Round 43)	2002 (Round 57)	Change (%)	1998 (Round 43)	2002 (Round 57)	Change (%)
Consumption/capita (kg/days)						
Rice	5.65	4.85	−14.2	7.35	6.79	−7.7
Wheat	4.57	4.03	−11.70	4.80	4.05	−15.7
Other cereals	0.83	0.56	−32.5	2.59	1.38	−46.8
Total cereals	11.05	9.44	−14.5	14.74	12.22	−17.2
Pulses	1.06	0.86	−18.8	0.97	0.77	−20.9
Dairy	4.52	5.25	16.2	3.34	3.94	17.9
Edible oils	0.56	0.69	23.6	0.35	0.51	45.4
Meat/fish/eggs	2.01	2.49	23.8	0.91	1.50	65.6
Vegetables/fruit	11.46	13.44	17.3	6.99	9.48	35.6
Sugar/spices	1.63	1.46	−10.4	1.53	1.34	−12.7
Share of total Food expenditure (%)						
Rice	16.33	14.06	−13.9	24.97	21.32	−14.6
Wheat	9.07	8.70	−4.1	10.99	9.58	−12.8
Other cereals	1.80	1.18	−34.4	5.87	2.83	−51.7
Total cereals	27.20	23.94	−12.0	41.83	33.73	−19.3
Pulses	6.16	5.66	−8.1	6.48	6.31	−2.6
Dairy	13.23	15.71	18.7	9.87	12.02	21.8
Edible oils	8.65	6.55	−24.4	7.41	6.53	−11.9
Meat/fish/eggs	5.37	5.58	4.0	4.27	5.34	25.1
Vegetables/fruit	12.29	15.03	22.3	10.32	14.56	41.1

(continued)

Table 12.3 (continued)

Food items	Urban			Rural		
	1998 (Round 43)	2002 (Round 57)	Change (%)	1998 (Round 43)	2002 (Round 57)	Change (%)
Sugar/spices	8.12	7.44	−8.4	8.73	8.36	−4.2
Processed Food	13.59	13.49	−0.7	8.28	9.31	12.5
Beverages	5.38	6.61	22.8	2.83	3.83	35.5
Share of total expenditure (%)						
All Food	66.1	50.0	−24.4	72	60.9	−16.1

PDS is possibly the largest distribution network of its type in the world. It is a major instrument in the government's anti-poverty programme and serves as a safety net for the poor. Responding to criticisms that the PDS has an urban bias and fails to serve the poor, in June 1997 the government introduced the targetted PDS (TPDS) which distinguished between 'below the poverty line' (BPL) and 'above the poverty line' (APL) families in setting the quantity and issue price of the subsidised Food grain items. In a further tightening of the Public Distribution System, the *Antyodaya Anna Yojana* (AAY) scheme was introduced on 25 December 2000, which makes the TPDS more focussed by targeting the very poor, that is the destitute, who form a population of one crore families out of a total of 6.52 crore BPL families covered under TPDS.

The role of the PDS has figured prominently in discussions on the economic reforms undertaken in India in the 1990s. Table 12.4 presents some evidence on this issue by reporting the share of the household's intake of calories that is contributed by the PDS. The calculations were performed not only at State level and for all households but also, separately, for the female-headed households and the backward classes. Table 12.4 shows that the importance of the PDS in supplying inexpensive calories to the household varies sharply between the constituent States of the Indian Union. For example, a much larger share of the total calorie intake is supplied through the PDS in the southern States, especially Kerala and Tamil Nadu, than in the northern States such as Punjab, Rajasthan, Haryana and Bihar. This is partly due to the caste-based discrimination and exclusion prevailing in the northern States that allow the backward classes very limited access to the PDS. Another feature that is apparent from Table 12.4 is that in the calorie-poor States—although not everywhere—the female-headed households and the backward classes obtain a greater share of their total calories from their PDS Food rations than the rest of the population. Since these minority groups are more poverty-prone than the others (see, e.g. Meenakshi and Ray 2002; Ray and Lancaster 2005), it is important to keep this in mind in the ongoing debate on the future of the PDS.

A comparison of the calorie shares of the PDS items between NSS rounds 50 (1993/94) and 55 (1999/2000) reported in Table 12.4 shows that, notwithstanding the market-driven agenda of economic reforms and the sharp rise in the issue prices of rice and wheat (see Rao 2005: 190), there is not much evidence of any significant decline in the importance of PDS in supplying calories to the household especially at the all-India level. Evidence on the role of the PDS in the government's poverty eradication programme is provided in Table 12.5. For NSS round 55 (1999/2000), in rural areas, this table compares the household POU rates in the presence and absence of PDS. While the former are the POU rates actually prevailing in round 55, the latter are the POU estimates in the hypothetical case of no PDS, that is, with the PDS calorie estimates assumed to be zero. Note that in the absence of a satisfactory modelling strategy, it was necessary to ignore the increase in the non-PDS calories, due to a switch from PDS to Food purchases in the open market, thus exaggerating the rise in POU due to the hypothetical abolition of the PDS.

These hypothetical calculations suggest that the PDS plays a significant role as an anti-poverty programme in the calorie-poor southern States such as Andhra

Table 12.4 Calorie share of PDS items in rural households (Ray 2007)

State	All households		Female-headed households		SC/ST households	
	NSS Round 50 (1993/94)	NSS Round 55 (1999/00)	NSS Round 50 (1993/94)	NSS Round 55 (1999/00)	NSS Round 50 (1993/94)	NSS Round 55 (1999/00)
Andhra Pradesh	0.177	0.153	0.251	0.191	0.207	0.184
Assam	0.051	0.058	0.076	0.089	0.037	0.058
Bihar	0.022	0.022	0.021	0.027	0.022	0.026
Gujarat	0.093	0.076	0.108	0.094	0.126	0.105
Haryana	0.025	0.019	0.022	0.018	0.022	0.027
Himachal Pradesh	0.143	0.140	0.126	0.118	0.143	0.165
Karnataka	0.084	0.111	0.123	0.158	0.104	0.141
Kerala	0.303	0.280	0.325	0.313	0.345	0.392
Madhya Pradesh	0.038	0.042	0.043	0.052	0.041	0.050
Maharashtra	0.070	0.085	0.092	0.125	0.075	0.094
Orissa	0.021	0.112	0.021	0.150	0.020	0.123
Punjab	0.018	0.014	0.018	0.012	0.023	0.017
Rajasthan	0.067	0.024	0.062	0.049	0.074	0.027
Tamil Nadu	0.157	0.242	0.199	0.292	0.170	0.280
Uttar Pradesh	0.027	0.026	0.047	0.052	0.030	0.030
West Bengal	0.028	0.035	0.031	0.037	0.028	0.038
All India	0.071	0.078	0.114	0.126	0.067	0.083

Source Author's calculations based on NSS Rounds 50, 55

Pradesh, Kerala and Tamil Nadu, but is less significant in the relatively calorie-affluent States such as Punjab and Rajasthan in the north and Bihar in the east. The policy message here is to warn against arriving at generalised conclusions, at the all-India level, on the future role of the PDS. The policy prescriptions need to be tailored to the changing realities of the individual States. Also, the small hypothetical drop in the POU rates in some of the northern States seems to justify the TPDS strategy of targeting the BPL households with a higher Food price subsidy, rather than the earlier PDS practice of supplying inexpensive and subsidised calories to all, including the APL households. However, as Ray (2007) reports, a significant number of APL households are also undernourished and they will miss out if the PDS is restricted entirely to BPL households.

The Indian poverty lines for the rural and urban populations are based on calorie norms of 2400 and 2100 kcal per capita per day, respectively. These estimates are close to, though not exactly the same as, the energy allowances recommended by an Export Group of the Indian Council of Medical Research (ICMR 2002). A household is classified as calorie-poor (non-poor) if its observed calorie intake

Table 12.5 Rural calorie-based POU[a] rates (%) in NSS round 55 in the presence and absence of Public Distribution System (PDS) (Ray 2007)

State	All households		Female-headed households		SC/ST households	
	With PDS	No PDS	With PDS	No PDS	With PDS	No PDS
Andhra Pradesh	64.3	80.3	50.1	72.7	68.9	87.4
Assam	75.5	80.9	71.0	78.1	75.0	80.9
Bihar	56.5	59.3	46.5	49.5	65.6	68.4
Gujarat	66.1	74.5	51.7	60.9	74.8	82.6
Haryana	42.2	44.9	33.5	34.7	61.3	63.3
Himachal Pradesh	35.5	55.0	19.7	37.9	42.1	66.2
Karnataka	66.5	77.6	54.3	73.4	78.0	87.7
Kerala	66.6	83.0	63.8	81.9	77.7	93.3
Madhya Pradesh	62.5	67.2	50.5	55.9	68.7	73.1
Maharashtra	65.4	74.6	43.0	62.2	71.9	78.7
Orissa	58.9	72.7	40.3	63.1	64.2	77.7
Punjab	43.5	45.7	30.0	31.8	56.1	58.5
Rajasthan	35.2	38.9	29.3	36.4	42.1	45.6
Tamil Nadu	75.9	89.0	62.3	81.8	82.9	93.0
Uttar Pradesh	41.8	45.6	33.8	40.7	51.4	55.3
West Bengal	60.4	65.2	54.0	57.9	61.1	66.7
All India	57.7	65.5	47.5	60.3	64.4	71.8

Note [a]POU measures the prevalence of undernourishment
Source Ray and Lancaster (2005)

turns out to be less (more) than the required amount. The prevalence of undernutrition (POU) is, then, measured as the percentage of households who are unable to meet their daily calorie requirement. The estimates of POU in rural and urban India in NSS rounds 43 (1987/88) and 57 (2001/2) are presented in Tables 12.6 and 12.7, respectively. These estimates are much higher than the expenditure-based poverty estimates using the official poverty line (see Ray and Lancaster 2005). Many argue that the POU and the expenditure-based poverty estimates are not directly comparable, since while the former measures hunger, the latter measures the failure to buy a minimum bundle of items, both Food and non-Food, which are necessary for survival. The POU measure has been used extensively by the FAO in worldwide calculations of hunger (FAO 1992) and in some individual countries and regions (Harriss 1990). Tables 12.6 and 12.7 suggest that in India over the period 1987/88–2001/2, there has been rising hunger, that is, an increasing failure to meet the calorie requirement at the household level. For example, at the all-India level, the rural POU rate increased from 48.16% in 1987/88 to 66.90% in 2001/2. The rise in hunger or undernourishment stands in sharp contrast to much of the evidence from the expenditure-based poverty literature used routinely in poverty debates on India, suggesting a decline in poverty over this period.

Table 12.6 Percentage of rural households undernourished (POU)[a] (Ray 2007)

State	Head count poverty rates (%) in NSS Round 43 (1987/88)[b]	POU rates (%) in NSS Round 43 (1987/88)	POU rates (%) in NSS Round 57 (2001/2002)
Andhra Pradesh	40.0	52.34	73.50
Assam	27.7	60.57	73.06
Bihar	48.7	49.14	50.91
Gujarat	28.4	56.56	77.31
Haryana	13.9	24.80	63.23
Himachal Pradesh	NA	22.46	40.83
Karnataka	41.2	54.52	77.39
Kerala	19.7	65.85	71.04
Madhya Pradesh	49.6	45.78	77.61
Maharashtra	40.6	56.35	67.10
Orissa	53.0	56.22	68.60
Punjab	9.6	31.45	54.53
Rajasthan	31.8	31.74	53.85
Tamil Nadu	44.3	67.31	84.03
Uttar Pradesh	42.9	36.30	56.94
West Bengal	36.6	53.58	68.90
All India	39.0	48.16	66.90

Notes [a]POU measures the prevalence of undernutrition

[b]These poverty rates were calculated using national poverty line and reported in Sen and Himanshu (2004: Table 1a)

Source Author's calculations based on NSS Rounds 43, 57

Table 12.7 Percentage of urban households undernourished (POU)[a] (Ray 2007)

State	Head count poverty rates (%) in NSS Round 43 (1987/88)[b]	POU rates (%) in NSS Round 43 (1987/88)	POU rates (%) in NSS Round 57 (2001/2002)
Andhra Pradesh	45.7	37.35	57.70
Assam	28.7	34.65	47.84
Bihar	57.9	30.46	43.58
Gujarat	32.1	43.04	57.58
Haryana	36.9	29.03	56.31
Himachal Pradesh	NA	12.08	26.05

(continued)

Table 12.7 (continued)

State	Head count poverty rates (%) in NSS Round 43 (1987/88)[b]	POU rates (%) in NSS Round 43 (1987/88)	POU rates (%) in NSS Round 57 (2001/2002)
Karnataka	45.1	37.71	50.63
Kerala	38.2	48.00	49.02
Madhya Pradesh	40.9	34.28	58.63
Maharashtra	30.6	38.66	51.47
Orissa	39.2	29.39	39.94
Punjab	21.0	31.97	41.35
Rajasthan	36.9	30.37	41.55
Tamil Nadu	38.9	51.19	63.84
Uttar Pradesh	48.6	32.80	52.30
West Bengal	39.7	41.17	50.68
All India	38.7	36.97	51.00

Notes [a]POU measures the prevalence of undernutrition
[b]These poverty rates were calculated using national poverty line and reported in Sen and Himanshu (2004: Table 1b)
Source Author's calculations based on NSS Rounds 43, 57

12.3 Evidence on the Link Between Food Consumption and Malnourished Children in India

Despite its economic success, India has made little progress towards meeting its Millennium Development Goal targets of reducing undernourishment, particularly among children. Maitra et al. (2013) use nationally representative data sets, the *National Family Health Surveys* (NFHS II and NFHS III) and the *National Sample Survey* (55th and the 61st rounds) to analyse the link, if any, between child nutritional outcomes and calorie intakes. Their analysis finds evidence of an improvement in the height-for-age z scores, but a worsening in weight-for-height z scores for children aged 0–3 over the period 1998/1999–2005/2006. There is also a worsening of calorie intake over this same period, with some of the most noticeable declines taking place in households with children aged 0–3. Table 12.8 (from Maitra et al. (2013)) compares the expenditure patterns and nutrient intake of households with at least one child in the age category 0–3 years with that of households without a child in this age category (or *other* households). These comparisons could potentially provide important insights on the observed nutritional outcomes of children aged 0–3 years.

The presence of a young child reduces the mean household expenditure on rice, pulses, eggs, fish and meat, vegetables and fruit, items that are typically consumed by adults and older children. The differences in the expenditure figures on these

Table 12.8 Differences in Food expenditures between households with and without a child aged 0–3 years (Maitra et al. 2013)

	55th Round			61st Round		
	Households with children aged 0–3	Other households	*p* value of diff.	Households with children aged 0–3	Other households	*p* value of diff.
Per adult equivalent consumption of						
Rice (kg/month)	8.139	9.332	0.000	7.699	8.904	0.000
Wheat (kg/month)	6.313	5.249	0.000	5.657	4.863	0.000
Other cereals (kg/month)	2.009	2.005	0.957	1.911	1.807	0.000
Pulses (kg/month)	1.091	1.173	0.039	0.929	1.017	0.000
Milk (kg/month)	7.776	8.026	0.445	7.194	7.952	0.000
Milk Products (kg/month)	0.909	1.055	0.286	0.646	0.688	0.614
Egg, Fish, Meat (kg/month)	0.987	1.192	0.000	0.899	1.124	0.000
Vegetables (kg/month)	7.255	7.576	0.000	6.634	7.045	0.000
Fresh fruits (kg/month)	1.846	2.428	0.000	1.630	2.187	0.000
Calorie (kcal/day)	2092.6	2163.7	0.013	2002.5	2097.3	0.000
POU rates	0.89	0.86	0.378	0.91	0.89	0.001
Poverty rates	0.31	0.18	0.000	0.30	0.17	0.000
Household size	6.9	4.7	0.000	6.8	4.5	0.000
Household size (as adult equivalent)	5.1	3.8	0.000	4.9	3.7	0.000

Notes POU rates are the fraction of people who are undernourished. Calculation of POU rates is based on the criterion of 'actual calories < required calories'. *P* values refer to *p* values of mean comparison *t* test between households with at least one child aged 0–3 and those households without any child in that age group

Food items between these two household types are highly significant. Moreover, contrary to expectations, this is also true for milk, a product consumed by young children, although the expenditure difference is not significant for milk in NSS 55. From Table 12.8, we also observe that households with one or more children in the age group 0–3 years have lower calorie intakes and higher prevalence of undernourishment (POU) rates compared to the *other* households. To obtain those figures, Maitra et al. (2013) adjust for the household's size and the age and gender-specific calorie requirements of individuals in the household.

Not only are households with young children spending less on Food on an adult equivalent basis in both years, but also their situation worsened over the period 1999/2000–2004/2005. In particular, households with children aged 0–3 were not only observed to have lower expenditures on milk in NSS 61, compared to NSS 55, but the gap with other households has also widened with respect to milk expenditures, an important item in child consumption. Similarly, the difference in calorie intake between households with and without young children is highly significant in both survey rounds and increases in size and significance between the two survey years. The difference in POU rates between households with children aged 0–3 and *other* households is also statistically significant in NSS 61. Disaggregated calculations also show that at all levels of monthly per capita expenditure, households with young children have lower calorie intakes compared to *other* households.

Based on evidence from the National Family Health Surveys (NFHS), Maitra et al. (2013) report a worsening in the weight-for-height z scores, but an improvement in height-for-age z scores for young children between 1998/99 and 2005/06. Given their NSS-based evidence reported in Table 12.7 above, Maitra et al. (2013) draw a link, though not necessarily a causal one, between lower calorie intake and worsening of the child's short-run health, but this does not translate to a similar link with the child's long-run health status since other factors may have come into play.

12.4 Child Health in West Bengal

Maitra and Ray (2013) provide evidence on regional differences in the State of child health in India with special reference to child health in West Bengal. While there are several studies at the all-India level, there are relatively few studies that compare the State of child health between the various States, and hardly any that looks exclusively at West Bengal. This study attempts to address this limitation. The study analyses four interrelated child health indicators in West Bengal, namely child malnourishment (measured by the rates of stunting and wasting), prenatal, infant and child mortality rates. This paper also provides evidence on how these rates vary with the gender of the child, parental education and the wealth status of the household. West Bengal does not fare badly on child health in relation to the all-India figures, does better than the rest of East India, but lags considerably behind South India. Its performance on mortality rates is much better than the all-India figures, and, quite significantly, West Bengal does quite well in relation to South India.

However, during the period of this study, the mortality rates in West Bengal hardly showed any improvement, in sharp contrast to the all-India picture. Another result of significance is that, while improving parental education can play a strong role in reducing the mortality rates in West Bengal, the wealth effects are weak and statistically insignificant. The importance of mother's health for that of her offspring is underlined by the result that the child of a malnourished mother in West Bengal is at increased risk from wasting which often leads to death. Policy interventions are required to delink maternal health from child health. In view of the dismal picture on child health and the high mortality rates that West Bengal recorded in this study, the importance of devising new and effective policies cannot be overstated. And that can only start once we have reliable and updated information on child health in West Bengal. The study by Maitra and Ray (2013) is now reported in somewhat greater detail.

The three most commonly used measures of child health[1] are height for age, weight for height and weight for age. Low values of these variables define, respectively, stunting, wasting and underweight. The height for age is expressed as a z score defined as the difference between the child's height and a recommended norm for a child of that age divided by the standard error of the height values. The weight for height is similarly measured by the z score defined as the difference between the child's weight and that recommended for a child with that height divided by the standard error. Traditionally, the recommended norm has been based on anthropometric data collected in the USA by the National Center for Health Statistics (NCHS). In response to criticisms of basing the norm on the health data of US children, in recent years the WHO has based the norm on a more representative sample.

Children whose z scores for height for age and weight for height fall below −2 are considered to be stunted and wasted, respectively. While height for age is a measure of the long-run health status of a child, weight for height and weight for age are measures of the short-term health status. Economists have usually taken the weight measures more seriously since low weight is regarded as exposing the child to death.[2] A child is said to be undernourished if her/his z score is less than −2, and severely undernourished if her/his z score is less than −3. A child's status on undernourishment will depend on the z score that is being used. Svedberg (2000) argues that the reliance on only one measure will lead to an underestimate of undernourishment, since it misses children who are considered undernourished by other indices. Svedberg (2000) proposes a composite index of anthropometric failure (CIAF) that incorporates all undernourished children, be they wasted and/or stunted and/or underweight. Nandy et al. (2005) have shown that for India, the use

[1]See Svedberg (2000) for a comprehensive discussion of the measures of undernutrition.

[2]Between the two weight measures, weight for age will show higher rate of malnourishment than weight for height since the latter, unlike the former, controls for age.

of CIAF suggests that 59.8% of children in India in 1998/99 are undernourished, while 45.2, 15.9 and 47.1% children are found to be stunted, wasted and underweight, respectively. In this study, however, Maitra and Ray (2013) follow the tradition of using the conventional measures of stunting and wasting to measure undernutrition.

Neonatal mortality (NM) is defined as the number of deaths during the first 28 completed days of life per 1000 live births in a given year or period. Mortality during neonatal period is considered a good indicator of both maternal and newborn health and care. Infant mortality (IM) is defined as the number of deaths (1 year of age or younger) per 1000 live births. IM reflects the state of medical services at the time of the birth of the child. Child mortality (CM) is defined as the number of deaths of children (5 years of age or younger) per 1000 live births. Maitra and Ray (2013)'s study was based on the information contained in the second and third rounds of the National Family Health Surveys (NFHS 2, NFHS 3). NFHS 2 was conducted in 1998–99 in 26 States of India with extensive information on population, health and nutrition with an emphasis on women and young children. NFHS 3 was carried out in 2005–6 with added information on the anaemic status of children. The study takes advantage of the disaggregated information by States to pay special attention to the nutritional status of women and infant children in West Bengal over the period spanned by NFHS 2 and NFHS 3 and compare the State's performance with that in the rest of India.

The NFHS data sets also provide information on the educational status of the child's mother and the wealth status of the child's household. These are used to provide evidence on the questions on whether maternal education and household affluence have any impact on the child's health status. Figure 12.1 compares the average z scores of children (0–3 years) in West Bengal with India (overall) and the different regions[3] Figure 12.2 presents and compares the corresponding stunting and wasting rates between the various regions in India with special attention paid to how West Bengal fares with respect to the rest of the country. It is clear that, along with the rest of India, West Bengal experienced an improvement in child stunting and a worsening in child wasting during the period, 1998–1999 to 2005–2006. Neither in terms of stunting nor in terms of wasting, does West Bengal fare any worse than the all-India average. Indeed, West Bengal fares much better than the rest of Eastern India on stunting, though less so on wasting. Southern India fares the best among the regions especially on stunting, Eastern and Northern India fare the worst.

Table 12.9 presents the 'height-for-age' and the 'weight-for-height' z scores in the various regions along with that in West Bengal and the country as a whole. Table 12.10 presents the corresponding rates for child stunting and wasting in the last two rounds of NFHS. These tables confirm the pictures portrayed in

[3]To be specific: *North* consists of Haryana, Himachal Pradesh, Madhya Pradesh, Punjab, Rajasthan and Uttar Pradesh; *South* consists of Andhra Pradesh, Karnataka, Kerala and Tamil Nadu; *East* consists of Assam, Bihar, Orissa and West Bengal; and finally *West* consists of Gujarat and Maharashtra.

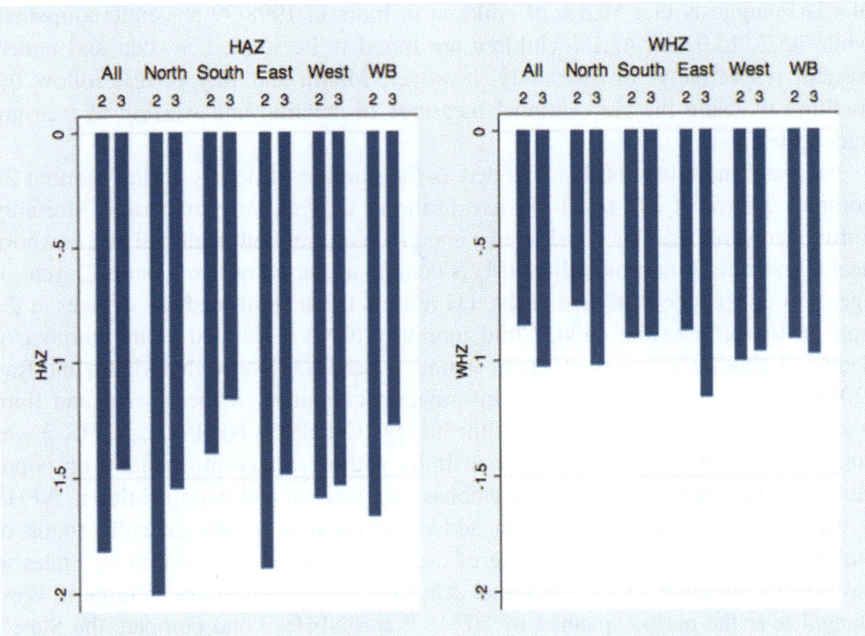

Fig. 12.1 Mean HAZ and WHZ, NFHS II and NFHS III. Note: 2 = NFHS II; 3 = NFHS III. Reproduced from Maitra and Ray (2013)

Figs. 12.1 and 12.2 in showing a statistically significant improvement in child stunting in most regions including West Bengal, and a statistically significant worsening in child wasting in most regions again including West Bengal. The improvement in stunting and the deterioration in wasting in West Bengal during this most recent period, 1998/99–2005/6 was highly significant (at 1% significance level), consistent with the all-India picture. Note, however, from Table 12.10 that, in terms of magnitude, while West Bengal's improvement in stunting was lower than that in the Eastern region as a whole, the deterioration in wasting outstripped that in the East and in India (as a whole).

Table 12.11 presents a more disaggregated picture of the extent of malnutrition, captured by stunting and wasting rates by gender, rural/urban, wealth quintile and mother's education. In West Bengal, there is a gender divide in child stunting (against girls) in NFHS II; however, this pro-male bias appears to have diminished over the period (and is not statistically significant in NFHS III). Rural children do much worse than urban children in stunting in West Bengal but not in child wasting. This essentially implies that the long-term health of children is considerably worse in rural areas compared to that in urban areas. Both stunting and wasting rates diminish as households become richer—we find evidence of strong wealth effects in that stunting and wasting rates both decline as we move up the wealth distribution. There is a large reduction in the stunting rate as we move from Q4 to Q5: stunting rates drop from 29 to 9% in NFHS II and from 23 to 10% in NFHS III

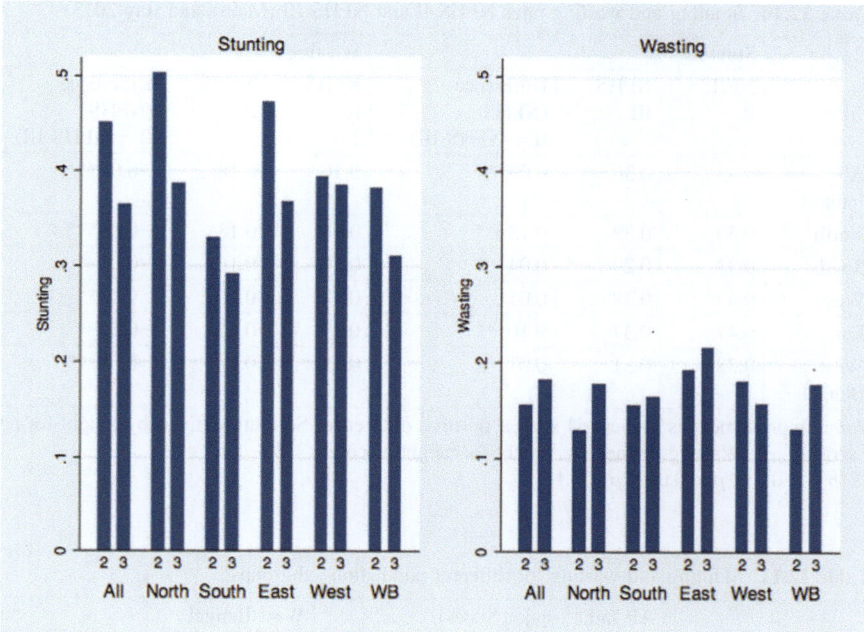

Fig. 12.2 Proportion stunted and wasted, NFHS II and NFHS III. *Note* 2 = NFHS II; 3 = NFHS III. Reproduced from Maitra and Ray (2013)

Table 12.9 Height-for-age and weight-for-height *z* scores NFHS II and NFHS III (Maitra and Ray 2013)

	Height-for-age *z* scores			Weight-for-height *z* scores		
	NFHS II	NFHS III	Difference (NFHS II − NFHS III)	NFHS II	NFHS III	Difference (NFHS II − NFHS III)
All India	−1.82	−1.46	−0.35***	−0.84	−1.03	0.18***
North	−2.00	−1.55	−0.46***	−0.76	−1.02	0.26***
South	−1.39	−1.16	−0.24***	−0.90	−0.90	−0.01
West	−1.59	−1.53	−0.06	−1.00	−0.96	−0.04
East	−1.89	−1.48	−0.41***	−0.87	−1.16	0.29***
West Bengal	−1.67	−1.27	-0.39***	−0.91	−0.97	0.07

Notes Improvement is associated with a negative difference
***$p < 0.01$, **$p < 0.05$, *$p < 0.1$

as we move from Q4 to Q5. The drop is not as dramatic in the case of wasting, but even here there is a large wealth effect. Mother's education has strong and positive effects on the health of her children.

Table 12.10 Stunting and wasting rates NFHS II and NFHS III (Maitra and Ray 2013)

	Stunting			Wasting		
	NFHS II	NFHS III	Difference (NFHS II − NFHS III)	NFHS II	NFHS III	Difference (NFHS II − NFHS III)
All India	0.45	0.36	0.09***	0.16	0.18	−0.03***
North	0.50	0.39	0.12***	0.13	0.18	−0.05***
South	0.33	0.29	0.04***	0.16	0.16	−0.01
West	0.39	0.38	0.01	0.18	0.16	0.02**
East	0.47	0.37	0.10***	0.19	0.22	−0.02**
West Bengal	0.38	0.31	0.07***	0.13	0.18	−0.05***

Notes Improvement is associated with a positive difference. Stunting defined by height-for-age z score < −2; Wasting defined by weight-for-height z score < −2
***$p < 0.01$, **$p < 0.05$, *$p < 0.1$

Table 12.11 Stunting and wasting for different population subgroups

	All India (major States)			West Bengal		
	NFHS II	NFHS III	Difference	NFHS II	NFHS III	Difference
Panel A: stunting						
Male	0.44	0.36	0.08***	0.34	0.30	0.04
Female	0.46	0.37***	0.10***	0.43	0.32	0.11***
Rural	0.49	0.40	0.09***	0.45	0.38	0.09***
Urban	0.35	0.30	0.05***	0.25	0.23	0.03
Hindu	0.46	0.37	0.09***	0.34	0.27	0.07***
Other religion	0.42	0.36	0.06***	0.48	0.37	0.11***
Wealth quintile 1	0.57	0.50	0.08***	0.58	0.45	0.14***
Wealth quintile 2	0.53	0.45	0.08***	0.43	0.36	0.08*
Wealth quintile 3	0.48	0.38	0.10***	0.35	0.28	0.07
Wealth quintile 4	0.40	0.32	0.08***	0.29	0.23	0.06
Wealth quintile 5	0.26	0.19	0.07***	0.09	0.10	−0.00
Mother: no education	0.54	0.47	0.08***	0.54	0.39	0.15***
Mother: primary school	0.45	0.39	0.06***	0.41	0.37	0.04
Mother: secondary school	0.31	0.26	0.04***	0.18	0.20	−0.02
Panel B: wasting						
Male	0.16	0.19	−0.03***	0.14	0.17	−0.03
Female	0.15	0.18	−0.02***	0.12	0.18	−0.06***
Rural	0.16	0.19	−0.03***	0.14	0.20	−0.06***

(continued)

Table 12.11 (continued)

	All India (major States)			West Bengal		
	NFHS II	NFHS III	Difference	NFHS II	NFHS III	Difference
Urban	0.13	0.16	−0.03***	0.11	0.14	−0.03
Hindu	0.16	0.19	−0.03***	0.13	0.17	−0.04**
Other religion	0.14	0.17	−0.03***	0.14	0.20	−0.06**
Wealth quintile 1	0.21	0.24	−0.02***	0.20	0.22	−0.02
Wealth quintile 2	0.18	0.21	−0.03***	0.11	0.23	−0.11***
Wealth quintile 3	0.16	0.18	−0.02**	0.12	0.13	−0.01
Wealth quintile 4	0.13	0.16	−0.03***	0.11	0.12	−0.01
Wealth quintile 5	0.10	0.13	−0.03***	0.07	0.14	−0.07**
Mother: no education	0.18	0.21	−0.03***	0.16	0.23	−0.07**
Mother: primary school	0.16	0.20	−0.04***	0.15	0.15	−0.00
Mother: secondary school	0.12	0.15	−0.03***	0.09	0.15	−0.06**

Comparing West Bengal to the major States of India (Maitra and Ray 2013)

Here as well, the effect is monotonic and interestingly the effect of mother's education on the health of children is stronger in West Bengal compared to India (as a whole). For example, in West Bengal, NFHS 2 records a sharp drop in child stunting rates from children of mothers with no education (54%) to those with secondary education (18%). At all-India level, the corresponding stunting rates decrease from 54 to 31%. In contrast to stunting, the decrease in wasting rates with increased education of the mother is much less. In West Bengal, NFHS 3 records no change in the wasting rates (15%) between primary and secondary educated mothers, though there was a noticeable drop in NFHS2 from 15 to 9%. Two further (and interesting) observations are: first, the improvement in child stunting in West Bengal has been statistically significant in the bottom three quintiles (Q1, Q2 and Q3), but not in the top two wealth quintiles (Q4 and Q5). Second, the improvement in child stunting in West Bengal over the period, 1998–1999 and 2005–2006, took place only in households where the mother had no education. This contrasts sharply with the all-India results which record improvement in stunting for children regardless of the level of the mother's education.

The neonatal, infant and child mortality rates in the two NFHS rounds, at all-India level and disaggregated by regions along with that in West Bengal, have been reported in Table 12.12. The all-India figures show a statistically significant improvement (i.e. decline) in all the three types of mortality rates between 1998/9 and 2005/6, as do North, South and East India. However, West Bengal is an exception. There was no noticeable change in either neonatal or infant mortality rates, and a very weak improvement in child mortality during this period. The silver lining was that for all the three types of mortality, the rates in West Bengal were much lower than in the country as a whole. It is interesting to note that, while South outperformed the rest of the country, especially, West Bengal on child health, the mortality rates in the South with respect to NM, IM and CM are no better than in West Bengal—in fact, marginally worse. This suggests that while the quality of medical services in the form of neonatal and post-natal care in West Bengal compared quite favourably with the rest of the country recording some of the lowest mortality rates in all three categories, the same cannot be said of the state of child health in West Bengal vis-a-vis the rest of India, especially South India. Figure 12.3 confirms the picture that is contained in Table 12.12. It shows that the mortality rates in West Bengal are no worse than in the rest of India—in fact, most significantly, they are marginally better than in South India which reverses the result on child health. Note, however, that while the South witnessed a sharp improvement in the mortality rates during the period spanned by the NFHS 2 and NFHS 3, there was hardly any change in West Bengal. There was a small increase in neonatal mortality rates in West Bengal.

12.5 Cash Transfers Versus In-Kind Transfers

Earlier in this chapter, we have provided evidence on the role that the PDS plays in protecting household welfare by supplying subsidised calories to the household seen in Table 12.4 and reducing the rate of 'prevalence of undernourishment' in Table 12.5. The discussion is now extended to Midday Meals Scheme (MDMS) which is another example of a large programme of in-kind transfers in India. Unlike the PDS, the MDMS only applies to households with school-going children, though the nutritional effect can spread to adults in the household by freeing resources that would have been spent on school meals. The Midday Meal Scheme[4] in India is the largest school meal programme in the world, covering an estimated 139 million children. India also has the largest early child development programme in the world (the Integrated Child Development Services or ICDS), which provides free meals as part of a nutritional programme.

The Midday Meal Scheme has bold objectives: it aims to enhance enrolment, retention and attendance among primary school children while simultaneously improving their nutritional levels. Although the scheme officially started as a centrally sponsored initiative in 1995, it was limited to providing dry rations and was not fully implemented in most States until 2002. Following a Supreme Court ruling in November 2001, all State Governments were mandated to introduce cooked school meals, and by 2003, most States had started providing school meals. Crucially, in 2004 a Supreme Court order made it mandatory to provide midday

[4]This description of the MDMS has been taken from Porter et al. (2010) that is available in https://assets.publishing.service.gov.uk/media/57a08b06e5274a31e000090c/the-impact-of-the-midday-meal-scheme-on-nutrition-and-learning.pdf.

Table 12.12 Neonatal, infant and child mortality rates for NFHS II and NFHS III (Maitra and Ray 2013)

	Neonatal mortality			Infant mortality			Child mortality		
	NFHS II	NFHS III	Diff	NFHS II	NFHS III	Diff	NFHS II	NFHS III	Diff
All India	0.045	0.040	0.005***	0.075	0.060	0.015***	0.091	0.070	0.021***
North	0.051	0.044	0.006***	0.088	0.069	0.019***	0.106	0.081	0.025***
South	0.037	0.032	0.005**	0.054	0.045	0.009***	0.064	0.050	0.014***
West	0.036	0.037	−0.001	0.054	0.050	0.004	0.065	0.056	0.009***
East	0.045	0.041	0.004*	0.072	0.061	0.011***	0.090	0.074	0.016***
West Bengal	0.030	0.036	−0.005	0.049	0.049	0.001	0.060	0.057	0.003

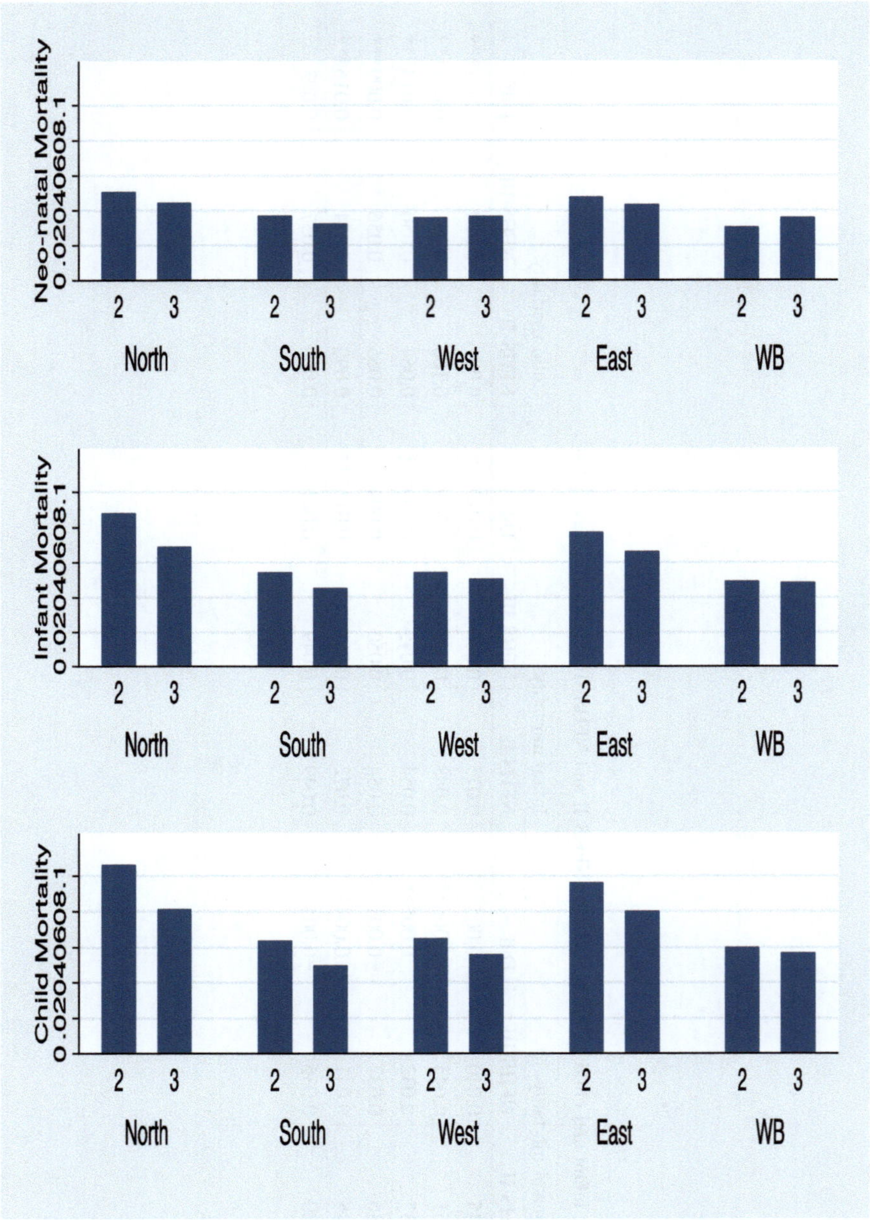

Fig. 12.3 Neonatal, infant and child mortality. Reproduced from Maitra and Ray (2013)

meals during summer vacations in 'drought-affected areas'. This was an important intervention, as drought has affected large sections of India's rural population.

In India, there has been considerable interest from State Governments in the performance of the Midday Meal Scheme, particularly in relation to the benefits it brings marginalised children. While there is evidence from a number of other studies that the scheme exerts a positive influence on enrolment and may increase daily calorific intake on school days, the impact on longer-term nutritional status has not been clear. Evidence on the effectiveness of the MDMS is provided in Tables 12.13 and 12.14 which compare the intakes of calorie, protein and fat between households that report some participation in MDMS and those that do not.[5] One can see that the MDMS is associated with higher intake of calorie, protein and fat in nearly all the States, with the size of the increase varying between States. There is no obvious regional pattern in the size of the effect of MDMS on the intakes. It is also worth noting that in nearly all the States the MDMS seems to be more effective as a nutrient enhancing programme in the urban areas compared to the rural, with the size of the increase in intake recording much higher magnitudes in the former.

12.6 Universal Basic Income

12.6.1 Background

The idea of direct and unconditional cash transfers, of which universal basic income (UBI) is the best example, has been gathering support in recent years. UBI is a rare example of an idea that has support from both sides of the political divide and, at the same time, has dissenters that cross that divide as well. The idea of UBI originated in the developed country context with Europe's first trials of the UBI taking place in Finland and with very encouraging results. UBI is a very attractive idea since it allows the household to spend the money as it desires and not dictated to by the State, is easy to administer since the cash is directly transferred to the recipient's bank account, avoids leakages and is not prone to corruption unlike the PDS. Recently, the idea has found favour in India with a group of leading economists, including successive Chief Economic Advisers (CEAs) of the Government of India, writing and speaking in favour of cash transfers and UBI. UBI received official recognition as a possible action plan when it featured in the Economic Survey of India, 2016–17.

There is very little evidence on the UBI in India, and that makes the increasing support for it difficult to understand. The only trial of the UBI idea in India was carried out as a randomised control trial in a pilot project in eight villages in Madhya Pradesh with favourable results. The results include the following observations: 'Many used money to improve their housing, latrines, walls and roofs, and to take precautions against malaria… Nutrition was improved, particularly in scheduled caste (SC) and scheduled tribe (ST) households. Perhaps the most important finding was the significant improvement in the average weight-for-age of young children (World Health Organization *z*-score), and more so among girls'—

[5]See Ray and Sinha (2018a) for a more complete treatment.

Table 12.13 Average per capita monthly nutrient consumption for MDMS and non-MDMS rural households—NSS 68th Round (2011–12) (Ray and Sinha 2018a)

State	Calorie		Protein		Fat	
	Non-MDMS	MDMS	Non-MDMS	MDMS	Non-MDMS	MDMS
Andhra Pradesh	57,319	60,935	1445	1550	1103	1268
Assam	59,185	59,233	1503	1517	761	823
Bihar	60,323	64,422	1718	1845	1021	1172
Chhattisgarh	56,509	62,365	1356	1531	800	960
Gujarat	52,120	56,317	1384	1495	1554	1845
Haryana	58,758	68,772	1732	2108	1538	1950
Himachal Pradesh	66,795	74,189	1957	2183	1539	1886
Jharkhand	55,951	60,101	1461	1573	770	910
Karnataka	51,485	55,924	1360	1483	1108	1272
Kerala	45,369	51,579	1367	1584	769	1009
Madhya Pradesh	56,862	60,880	1707	1800	1095	1282
Maharashtra	56,688	61,885	1534	1688	1491	1727
Orissa	56,744	60,918	1368	1499	600	716
Punjab	60,937	71,236	1742	2068	1627	2139
Rajasthan	60,029	68,324	1836	2071	1461	1865
Tamil Nadu	47,501	52,306	1233	1404	878	1061
Uttar Pradesh	59,443	62,435	1713	1798	1059	1262
Uttaranchal	67,333	71,372	1874	2004	1472	1678
West Bengal	57,057	61,371	1432	1564	866	1011
All India	57,179	62,345	1564	1724	1132	1360

Table 12.14 Average per capita monthly nutrient consumption for MDMS and non-MDMS urban households—NSS 68th Round (2011–12) (Ray and Sinha 2018a)

State	Calorie		Protein		Fat	
	Non-MDMS	MDMS	Non-MDMS	MDMS	Non-MDMS	MDMS
Andhra Pradesh	44,915	57,078	1107	1476	912	1340
Assam	51,846	58,464	1288	1513	737	1005
Bihar	53,824	62,415	1519	1758	857	1236
Chhattisgarh	51,282	58,707	1252	1508	833	1177
Gujarat	48,132	56,634	1284	1476	1396	2043
Haryana	50,231	62,364	1434	1803	1151	1905
Himachal Pradesh	56,070	69,015	1623	1997	1288	1892
Jharkhand	50,851	59,938	1391	1688	698	1235
Karnataka	46,408	54,820	1219	1465	1055	1418
Kerala	43,239	51,675	1235	1620	776	1100
Madhya Pradesh	50,648	60,002	1508	1721	1033	1485

(continued)

Table 12.14 (continued)

State	Calorie		Protein		Fat	
	Non-MDMS	MDMS	Non-MDMS	MDMS	Non-MDMS	MDMS
Maharashtra	55,221	57,087	1527	1593	1582	1777
Orissa	51,581	57,168	1240	1501	583	963
Punjab	52,791	61,651	1482	1779	1356	1882
Rajasthan	56,710	62,087	1718	1831	1398	1812
Tamil Nadu	44,565	50,965	1162	1385	836	1161
Uttar Pradesh	52,620	59,413	1529	1716	967	1385
Uttaranchal	57,560	68,112	1636	1915	1140	1701
West Bengal	50,671	55,632	1302	1513	845	1231
All India	51,009	59,117	1392	1645	1023	1460

see http://sewabharat.org/wp-content/uploads/2015/07/Report-on-Unconditional-Cash-Transfer-Pilot-Project-in-Madhya-Pradesh.pdf. It is doubtful if RCT is appropriate for evaluating the effectiveness of UBI since one needs to allow a simultaneous contraction of the subsidised welfare schemes such as the Public Distribution Scheme (PDS) and Midday Meals Scheme (MDMS) to pay for the UBI. It is therefore misleading to assess UBI by studying the effect of cash transfer in isolation from what happens to in-kind transfers as the experimental project in Madhya Pradesh has done.

12.6.2 Universal Basic Income and Undernourishment

In this section which reports ongoing work with Kompal Sinha,[6] we provide speculative evidence from the 68th round of the NSS (2011/12) on the effectiveness of the UBI in increasing calorie intake in India. According to the FAO, India is one of the most calorie-poor countries in the world and ranked 126 on average per capita calorie intake in a list of 172 countries. India has consistently recorded a very high rate of prevalence of undernourishment (POU) which has refused to decline even as her poverty rate fell. In their study, Ray and Sinha (2018a) have used a daily per capita intake of 2400 kcals in rural areas and 2100 kcals in urban areas as cut-off for defining undernourishment. Using calorie conversion factors on Indian Foods, Ray and Sinha (2018b) calculated the per capita calorie intake of every household and in each of the major States, and from them the mean POU rates. Ideally, one would have preferred to examine the effect of income increase of the poor via UBI on anthropometric outcomes but, unfortunately, the NSS data does not contain anthropometric indicators, while the NFHS 4 data which does contain

[6]Ray and Sinha (2018b).

anthropometric information contains no information on household income or expenditures.

Column 2 in Tables 12.15 (rural) and 12.16 (urban) provides the mean POU rates for all households below the Tendulkar poverty line (BPL). The remaining columns provide the mean POU rates for households between the poverty line (PL) and 20% above the PL, between 20 and 40% above the Pl, etc. The idea is to treat these columns as providing evidence of what the mean POU rate will be if UBI is set at 1.2 times the PL, 1.4 times the PL etc., with the last column recording the POU rates if the UBI is set at twice the PL. There is nothing 'experimental' in these numbers since these are based on actual NSS consumption data. The figures below each Tables 12.15 and 12.16, Figs. 12.4 and 12.5 provide a graphical representation of the numbers in the Table. The three key features of these tables are as follows: (a) the rural POU rates are generally greater than the urban and, somewhat surprisingly, the rural areas of the southern States of Karnataka, Kerala and Tamil Nadu record very high rates of POU; (b) as the graphs confirm, the spatial variation in the POU rates between States is much greater in the urban areas than the rural; and (c) the UBI secures only a modest decline in the POU rates, especially in the rural areas where a UBI that is set at twice the PL still leaves one in two households undernourished. The effect of UBI is larger in the urban areas but even here with a UBI of this magnitude one in three households still remains undernourished. The UBI generally does better in the urban areas. This discussion is summarised in Fig. 12.6 which plots the relationship, at the level of all the States, between POU and UBI. To secure a POU rate that is 'acceptable' at around 25% in the urban areas, one requires an UBI that is set at 4 times the PL, and much more than that in the rural areas. Note, incidentally, that the numbers in Tables 12.15 and 12.16 are an overestimate of the POU decline with UBI increase since they do not factor in the nutrient intake declines as the PDS and MDMS have to be curtailed, if not disbanded altogether, to make room for the increasing UBI.

12.6.3 PDS, MDMS and Undernourishment

This raises the question: how calorie enhancing are the Midday Meal Scheme (MDMS) and the Public Distribution System (PDS)? Table 12.17 (rural) and Table 12.18 (urban) contain evidence on this from the NSS, 68th round, as it contains information on the participation or otherwise of every household in either welfare programme. PDS is more effective in enhancing the calorie intake in the urban areas, while MDMS is more effective in the rural areas. This result is perhaps not unexpected since a much greater percentage of children go to private schools in the urban areas where MDMS is not operational. The effectiveness of the MDMS in rural areas is consistent with existing evidence—for example, from Young Lives data—see https://www.younglives.org.uk/content/impact-midday-meal-scheme-nutrition-and-learning. This result complements the result on UBI in Tables 12.15 and 12.16 which showed that UBI is more calorie enhancing in the urban areas.

Table 12.15 POU for BPL cut-offs—NSS 68 Rural (entire sample) (Ray and Sinha 2018b)

States	POU for BPL households (with UBI = 0) (%)	POU (with UBI = 1.2 PL) (%)	POU (with UBI = 1.4 PL) (%)	POU (with UBI = 1.6 PL) (%)	POU (with UBI = 1.8 PL) (%)	POU (with UBI = 2.0 PL) (%)
Andhra Pradesh	89.09	71.92	65.18	59.41	55.11	50.56
Assam	78.93	64.82	55.72	53.93	50.15	47.82
Bihar	56.02	37.07	32.78	30.32	28.12	26.66
Chhattisgarh	70.34	44.94	43.68	39.72	38.27	37.43
Gujarat	98.51	82.20	78.75	73.68	70.80	67.33
Haryana	90.00	64.44	65.49	58.65	48.97	44.84
Himachal Pradesh	59.46	33.33	28.17	24.73	21.76	19.43
Jharkhand	67.46	45.28	41.67	38.02	35.99	34.41
Karnataka	98.77	90.32	85.21	79.65	74.77	70.90
Kerala	100.00	100.00	99.35	97.90	95.61	92.97
Madhya Pradesh	68.20	50.00	44.88	41.67	37.91	35.68
Maharashtra	88.76	79.11	72.28	64.62	59.15	55.03
Orissa	60.00	41.27	38.26	37.02	34.97	33.50
Punjab	100.00	75.00	67.50	64.42	57.20	51.67
Rajasthan	58.87	52.97	43.66	36.34	33.08	29.64
Tamil Nadu	96.27	92.51	92.79	89.70	84.05	81.33
Uttar Pradesh	54.40	36.75	33.17	29.79	27.81	26.66
Uttaranchal	70.00	35.71	26.99	20.20	17.96	15.65
West Bengal	76.94	64.68	60.96	56.34	53.06	50.65
All India	78.00	61.18	56.66	52.43	48.67	45.90

PL = Tendulkar poverty line, BPL = Below poverty line and UBI = 'universal basic income'

Table 12.16 POU for BPL cut-offs—NSS 68 urban (entire sample) (Ray and Sinha 2018b)

States	POU for BPL households (with UBI = 0) (%)	POU (with UBI = 1.2 PL) (%)	POU (with UBI = 1.4 PL) (%)	POU (with UBI = 1.6 PL) (%)	POU (with UBI = 1.8 PL) (%)	POU (with UBI = 2.0 PL) (%)
Andhra Pradesh	61.31	48.14	45.68	42.23	39.90	37.52
Assam	56.63	42.59	39.81	33.33	28.70	27.27
Bihar	33.52	18.88	15.33	13.88	13.18	12.35
Chhattisgarh	40.54	28.74	33.10	34.21	31.90	29.96
Gujarat	72.62	58.50	57.56	53.71	49.32	45.54
Haryana	47.54	41.82	39.62	34.55	30.77	28.22
Himachal Pradesh	25.00	20.00	25.93	20.00	18.03	13.92
Jharkhand	50.97	29.47	27.16	24.66	23.02	24.05
Karnataka	83.49	71.76	61.45	57.46	53.28	50.96
Kerala	92.78	84.72	83.58	81.45	78.61	75.78
Madhya Pradesh	47.94	27.14	25.87	23.59	20.47	20.67
Maharashtra	60.31	41.76	41.24	40.50	38.15	35.25
Orissa	42.70	29.17	25.56	25.21	25.25	24.17
Punjab	65.00	61.96	49.42	40.43	34.96	32.45
Rajasthan	49.62	35.92	30.88	25.00	22.37	20.67
Tamil Nadu	78.41	77.25	73.15	67.25	61.14	56.47
Uttar Pradesh	41.43	26.57	22.22	20.89	19.87	19.17
Uttaranchal	20.00	14.89	13.40	13.57	12.15	10.67
West Bengal	67.92	55.24	50.39	46.62	45.20	45.93
All India	54.62	42.87	40.07	36.76	34.01	32.16

PL = Tendulkar poverty line, BPL = Below poverty line and UBI = 'universal basic income'

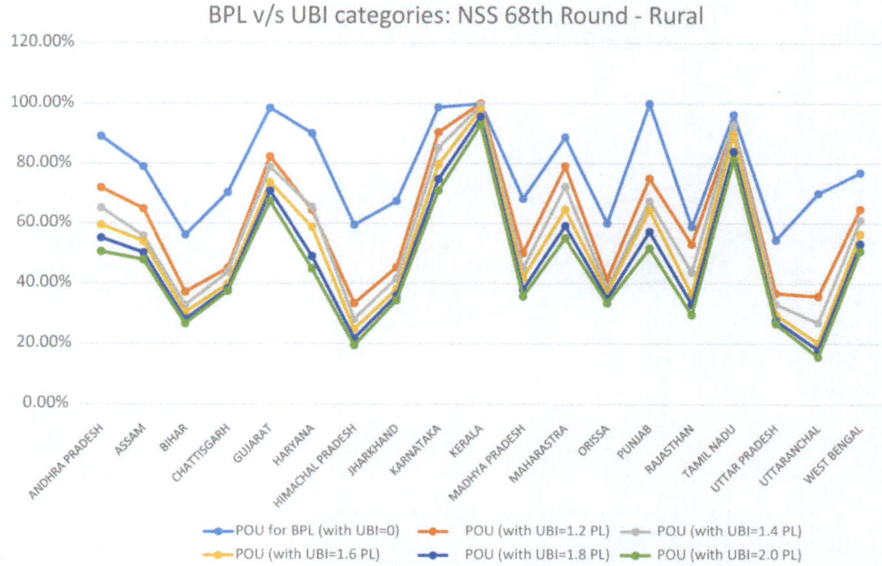

Fig. 12.4 Proportion of undernourished corresponding to different levels of UBI by States—rural. Reproduced from Ray and Sinha (2018b)

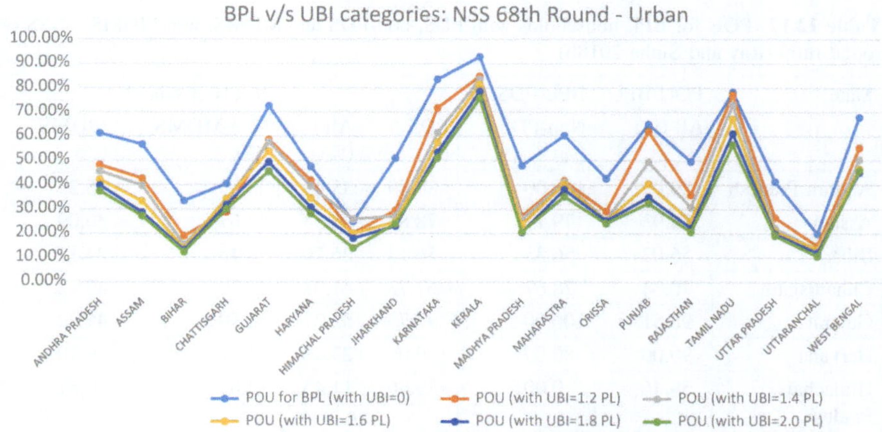

Fig. 12.5 Proportion of undernourished corresponding to different levels of UBI by States—urban. Reproduced from Ray and Sinha (2018b)

If UBI is to be introduced, then it should be initially done in the urban areas and extended to the rural areas later.

The purpose of this discussion is not to argue against the introduction of UBI in India which has considerable merits, but to warn against the danger of looking at UBI in isolation from the other welfare programmes that currently exist. Several

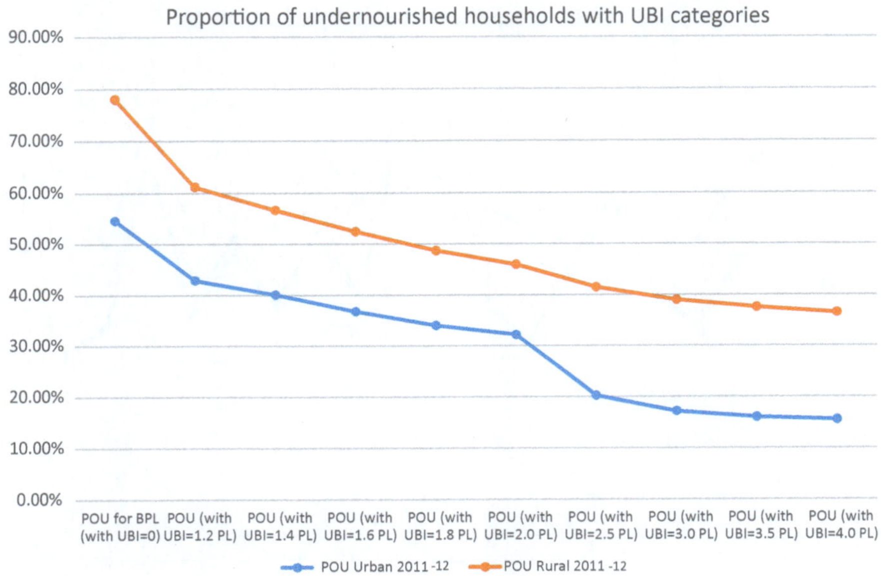

Fig. 12.6 Proportion of undernourished corresponding to various levels of UBI, over all the States. Reproduced from Ray and Sinha (2018b)

Table 12.17 POU for BPL households with PDS, non-PDS and MDMS, non-MDMS—NSS 68 round rural (Ray and Sinha 2018b)

State	POU-BPL	BPL-PDS			Meals at school	
	All (%)	Non-PDS (%)	PDS (%)	All (%)	Non-MDMS (%)	MDMS (%)
Andhra Pradesh	89.09	100.00	88.89	35.45	35.53	35.29
Assam	78.93	79.17	78.87	40.53	45.67	30.09
Bihar	56.02	56.35	56.13	26.76	28.45	24.15
Chhattisgarh	70.34	78.67	67.73	41.08	41.29	40.92
Gujarat	98.51	100.00	97.73	52.27	53.50	49.72
Haryana	90.00	80.00	100.00	23.48	22.21	29.70
Himachal Pradesh	59.46	0.00	59.46	11.43	12.07	10.81
Jharkhand	67.46	68.52	66.53	38.69	41.94	36.45
Karnataka	98.77	100.00	98.63	58.48	57.41	59.51
Kerala	100.00	100.00	100.00	68.15	65.59	75.26
Madhya Pradesh	68.20	79.22	61.44	37.99	39.94	35.46
Maharashtra	88.76	88.89	88.64	39.04	40.42	37.40
Orissa	60.00	68.34	57.44	38.24	39.21	37.36
Punjab	100.00	0.00	100.00	22.77	19.65	30.18

(continued)

Table 12.17 (continued)

State	POU-BPL	BPL-PDS			Meals at school	
	All (%)	Non-PDS (%)	PDS (%)	All (%)	Non-MDMS (%)	MDMS (%)
Rajasthan	58.87	67.80	52.44	21.72	20.78	23.45
Tamil Nadu	96.27	100.00	96.23	66.85	65.35	70.69
Uttar Pradesh	54.40	57.68	50.66	27.30	28.21	24.92
Uttaranchal	70.00	100.00	67.86	12.35	13.55	11.14
West Bengal	76.94	88.28	72.05	41.69	45.58	37.67
All States	78.00	74.36	76.88	37.07	37.70	36.85

commentators have also noted this, and some have suggested that the UBI should be paid for by dismantling the 'regressive subsidy programmes' such as fertiliser and LPG subsidies which cost much more than the 'progressive subsidy programmes' such as the PDS and MDMS. But that requires a political will that is not in evidence going by the track record of successive governments. Clearly, more exploratory research has to be undertaken on the UBI before it is introduced.

12.7 Concluding Remarks

This chapter focusses attention on the interrelated topics of Food consumption, undernourishment, poverty rates and child health with special reference to changes in their indicators during one of the most significant periods in independent India. It provides evidence on decline in Food consumption and calorie intake. The evidence on child health is mixed with deterioration in some of the anthropometric indicators, improvement in the others. A result of significance is the mismatch between expenditure-based poverty rates and the prevalence of undernourishment rates with the decline in the former standing out in sharp contrast with an increase in the latter. The poverty rates are consistently lower than the rates of undernourishment raising questions on the way poverty is quantified in India. The need to have a fresh look at poverty measurement prompted the government of India to set up an expert committee under the chairmanship of the noted economist, C. Rangarajan, to examine the issue and provide recommendations on possible changes. The Rangarajan Committee's report has been critically reviewed in Ray and Sinha (2014).

The report has several positive features such as the return to the calorie norm, the anchoring of the non-Food requirements to a normative basket based on the median non-Food expenditures and the use of unit values from household expenditure unit records instead of the conventional aggregate price indices used previously. However, it missed the opportunity to go beyond the expenditure-based poverty rates and examine the possibility of a wider multidimensional view of deprivation.

Table 12.18 POU for BPL households with PDS, non-PDS and MDMS, non-MDMS—NSS 68 round urban (Ray and Sinha 2018b)

State	POU-BPL	BPL-PDS			Meals at school	
	All (%)	Non-PDS (%)	PDS (%)	All (%)	Non-MDMS (%)	MDMS (%)
Andhra Pradesh	61.31	79.41	57.58	24.71	23.04	36.96
Assam	56.63	66.04	53.10	24.49	24.23	25.49
Bihar	33.52	38.12	29.89	16.63	16.69	16.41
Chhattisgarh	40.54	62.07	35.29	24.17	24.86	22.39
Gujarat	72.62	76.00	67.65	27.21	26.81	31.03
Haryana	47.54	51.52	42.86	16.79	15.81	34.29
Himachal Pradesh	25.00	25.00	25.00	9.95	7.64	20.59
Jharkhand	50.97	50.64	52.00	27.52	26.10	32.19
Karnataka	83.49	95.35	80.47	38.57	34.85	48.81
Kerala	92.78	100.00	92.31	53.16	49.66	66.84
Madhya Pradesh	47.94	51.32	44.72	22.71	21.26	30.57
Maharashtra	60.31	64.56	57.02	26.54	28.40	19.43
Orissa	42.70	52.22	38.22	25.43	24.68	26.98
Punjab	65.00	66.67	61.11	17.74	16.42	29.41
Rajasthan	49.62	48.00	51.72	15.52	15.55	15.24
Tamil Nadu	78.41	92.31	77.70	42.52	40.72	52.77
Uttar Pradesh	41.43	45.87	34.90	19.09	19.08	19.18
Uttaranchal	20.00	50.00	15.38	8.11	7.45	11.76
West Bengal	67.92	75.34	63.11	33.46	33.46	33.45
All States	54.62	62.65	51.58	24.96	24.04	30.20

The TOR of this committee was wide ranging and invited such an investigation. Its summary dismissal of the multidimensional approach is a disappointment, especially when there has been significant methodological advancement in the area. Unfortunately, we will have to wait for the next expert committee to question and examine the concept of an absolute and one-dimensional view of poverty that has dominated the poverty measurement literature in India. The same comment applies to the Rangarajan Committee's failure to recognise the large increase in inequality in India during the 1990s and beyond that should have encouraged a rethink of the 'absolute' view of poverty that has characterised the working of successive expert committees.

References

Bhalla SS (2003) Recounting the poor: poverty in India, 1983–99. Econ Polit Wkly 38(4):338–349

Coondoo D, Majumder A, Lancaster G, Ray R (2005) Alternative approaches to measuring temporal changes in poverty with application to India'. University of Tasmania, Hobart. Available online: www.utas.edu.au/economics

Dandekar VM, Rath N (1971) Poverty in India: I. Econ Polit Wkly 6(1):25–48

Dubey A, Gangopadhyay S (1998) Counting the poor: where are the poor in India? Sarvekshana, analytical report no 1. Government of India, Department of Statistics, Delhi

FAO (1992) World food supplies and prevalence of chronic undernutrition in developing regions as assessed in 1992. FAO (mimeo), Rome

Gopalan C, Rama Sastri BV, Balasubramanian SC (1999) Nutritive value of Indian foods. National Institute of Nutrition, ICMR, Hyderabad

Harriss B (1990) The intra-family distribution of hunger in South Asia. In: Dreze J, Sen A (eds) The political economy of hunger. vol. 1: entitlements and well-being. Clarendon Press, Oxford, pp 351–424

ICMR (2002) Nutrient requirements and recommended dietary allowances for Indians: a report of the expert group of the Indian Council of Medical Research. ICMR, New Delhi

Maitra P, Ray R (2013) Child health in West Bengal: comparison with other regions in India. Econ Polit Wkly 49:50–58

Maitra P, Rammohan A, Ray R, Robitaille MC (2013) Food consumption patterns and malnourished Indian children: is there a link? Food Policy 38:70–81

Meenakshi JV, Ray R (2002) Impact of household size and family composition on poverty in rural India. J Policy Model 24:539–559

Mehta J, Venkatraman S (2000) Poverty statistics: bermicide's feast. Econ Polit Wkly 35 (27):2377–2381

Nandy S, Irving M, Gordon D, Subramanian SV, Smith DV (2005) Poverty, child nutrition and morbidity: new evidence from India. Bull World Health Organ 83(3):210–216

Porter C, Singh A, Sinha A (2010) The impact of the midday meal scheme on nutrition and learning. Young Lives Policy Brief 8. 4pp. Available in https://assets.publishing.service.gov.uk/media/57a08b06e5274a31e000090c/the-impact-of-the-midday-meal-scheme-on-nutrition-and-learning.pdf

Rao CHH (2005) Agriculture, food security, poverty and environment: essays on post-reform India. Oxford University Press, Delhi

Ray R (2007) Changes in food consumption and the implications for food security and undernourishment: India in the 1990s. Dev Change 38(2):321–343

Ray R, Lancaster G (2005) On setting the poverty line based on estimated nutrient prices: condition of socially disadvantaged groups during the reform period. Econ Polit Wkly 40 (1):46–56

Ray R, Sinha K (2014) The Rangarajan expert committee report on poverty measurement: another lost opportunity. Econ Polit Wkly XLIX(32):43–48

Ray R, Sinha K (2018a) Food consumption, calorie intake and undernourishment in India: the recent evidence on the role of welfare schemes. Monash University, Melbourne, mimeographed

Ray R, Sinha K (2018b) Can cash transfers help the poor? A note of scepticism based on NSS evidence. Monash University, Melbourne, mimeographed

Sen A (2000) Estimates of consumer expenditure and its distribution: statistical priorities after NSS 50th round. Econ Polit Wkly 35(51):4499–4518

Sen A, Himanshu (2004) Poverty and Inequality in India: I. Econ Polit Wkly 39(38):4247–4263

Svedberg P (2000) Poverty and undernutrition: theory, measurement and policy. Oxford India Paperbacks, New Delhi

Chapter 13
Summary and Conclusion

As stated in the introduction, this volume seeks to bring together a collection of essays covering a diverse set of topics but with a shared focus on household behaviour and welfare. The emphasis in the chosen studies is on the interplay of methodology and empirical work with a view to understanding the behaviour in a way that can lend itself to policy formulations that can improve household welfare. Much of the empirical studies that have been reported in detail here have been on India which provides an interesting setting given the size and diversity of the country, the spatial nature of the intra-country comparisons involved in rural–urban comparisons and that between States, and the availability of rich data sets in India that contain a variety of information that is matched by few other countries. Not surprisingly, India has seen some of the earliest studies on consumer demand behaviour and welfare analysis.

Much of the early work on the enumeration and analysis of poverty by Indian social scientists involved close collaboration between economists, statisticians, nutritionists and experts from related disciplines. The setting of poverty lines in India is an early example of this in the form of a proposal by Indian statisticians and economists to anchor such lines on calorie norms to avoid the arbitrariness in identifying the poor. The proposal was first introduced and implemented in India back in the 1960s. Though this approach to poverty measurement has its share of critics in recent years, one cannot deny the contribution that the thinkers and planners in India made through their impact on subsequent thinking on poverty and distributional issues that are visible even today. The volume edited by Banerjee et al. (2017) which is a revised version of the classic volume, Poverty and Income Distribution edited by Srinivasan and Bardhan (1974), traces the early work of Indian statisticians and economists that shaped our thinking in subsequent years.

As the essays in the volume illustrate, there is no better example of the interrelation between analytical specification, data collection, analysis of household behaviour and evidence-based policy formulation than in the early work of the Indian researchers mostly based at the Indian Statistical Institute which operated in tandem with the Planning Commission. The National Sample Surveys, which

R. Ray, *Household Behaviour, Prices, and Welfare*, Themes in Economics,
https://doi.org/10.1007/978-981-13-1930-3_13

provided a rich source of information that has been extensively used by researchers and has been the basis of several of the studies described in this volume, was the result of a collaborative effort between the Indian Statistical Institute and the Planning Commission in the early days of Indian planning. Some of the earliest studies of expenditure patterns on household budget data were carried out by researchers based at the Indian Statistical Institute and provided input to work by the Planning Commission.

In course of time, the way we view poverty has changed and so has the mode of identification of the poor. Poverty and, more generally, deprivation is now viewed as multidimensional. The traditional procedure of counting the poor based on the income or expenditure-based poverty line has given way to multidimensional poverty measurement which requires an array of information at the household level on access to facilities considered essential for a decent life. The Indian Planning Commission has operationalised the idea of multidimensional poverty by defining 'poor' households not just as those living below the poverty line but those that are denied access to a range of living facilities as specified by the Planning Commission. As the discussion in Chaps. 10 and 11 showed, this has increased the data requirements for conducting poverty enumeration and welfare analysis. The data side has also kept pace with this methodological development by making available through the Demographic and Health (DHS) surveys for various countries, a range of information that was not available even a decade ago. However, India is lagging behind in this area since the National Family and Health Surveys (NFHS) which are the Indian equivalent of the DHS are available infrequently, and the latest NFHS, namely NFHS-4, has been made publicly available only very recently.

As the discussion in Chap. 11 showed, the literature on multidimensional poverty measurement has seen the introduction of persistence and duration in the poverty measures which require the availability of longitudinal data. From a policy viewpoint, it is important to not only measure poverty, but also to identify those who suffer long spells of poverty, the duration of such spells and the dimensions where the spells are particularly acute. This is another area of data collection where India is now lagging behind since the country lacks a large-scale panel data of the type that is available in several other countries such as CHNS in China and the HILDA in Australia. The National Sample Surveys of India which have few parallels elsewhere in terms of the quantity of information they contain are also slipping in terms of reliability, sampling biases and their increasing divergence from the national accounts. There is clearly scope for work to improve the quality and availability of information on which much of policy-driven work depends so crucially. There is also need for some coordination between the NSS and NFHS. While the former provides data on household expenditures disaggregated by items but no anthropometric information on the household members, the latter provides such information but none on household income or expenditures.

The present volume reports studies that involve cross-national comparisons such as in the work carried out by the International Comparison Project (ICP) on estimating Purchasing Power Parities (PPPs). Until India and China joined the list of countries that are included in the PPP estimations, the ICP did not have much of a profile that changed when India and China came into the ICP exercise. At the same time, their entry showed one of the main limitations of the ICP exercise, namely, ignoring the spatial differences within a country in estimating the purchasing power of that country's currency. As the studies reported in this volume showed, India is a good example of a country where it is not meaningful to come up with a single number as the PPP of the Indian Rupee. It is worth noting that the ICP has signalled its intention to provide more importance to the estimation of subnational PPPs in its future exercises. The need to recognise spatial differences in price movements between the constituent States of a large heterogeneous country such as India, and the fact that the spatial picture may change over time, pointed to the need for a framework and methodology that simultaneously measures both temporal and spatial price changes. The methodology proposed in Chap. 6 provides a possible basis for further work in the area. Earlier, the discussion in Chap. 4 underlined the close nexus between price indices, price measurement and welfare comparisons and illustrated that discussion by providing evidence of the link between price movements and inequality.

The importance of price measurement in welfare analysis was further underlined in the discussions in Chap. 6 which described how the spatial price differences can be measured and used in welfare-based rankings of the States in India. The discussion was further advanced in Chap. 9 which showed that the PPPs can have a significant effect on estimates of global poverty. As that discussion showed, we need to move beyond the ICP PPPs and experiment with alternative sets of PPPs, not just ICP PPPs, to get a robust picture of world inequality and poverty. The issue of commodity tax design and tax reforms in India that was discussed in Chap. 7 has recently attracted media attention in India and has figured extensively in discussions due to the move to a countrywide GST. While this is a welcome move due to its administrative simplicity compared to the myriad of State sales taxes in the previous system, the spatial differences in the expenditure pattern between the different States and regions in India which was the theme of several of the studies described in this volume has posed a particular challenge to the move to the new system which prescribes a set of taxes that will be uniformly set across the entire country. There is no evidence of any systematic and rigorous quantitative study of commodity taxation behind the particular set of GST rates that have been proposed. There have been ad hoc announcements of GST that are designed as compromises to various State interests and are not grounded on sound principles of tax design and tax reform. Not surprisingly, we see a succession of frequent announcements changing the GST rates leading to uncertainty. This is another area where there is need for policy prescriptions to be better informed by sound analytical considerations grounded in rigorous empirical exercise.

The penultimate chapter drew attention to the paradox that, notwithstanding its satisfactory performance on indicators such as growth rates, income increase, poverty reduction and the size of its aggregate GDP, India does abysmally on indicators such as maternal and child health, infant mortality rates and the prevalence of hunger measured by the rate of 'prevalence of undernourishment' (POU).

India's POU rates, which are among the highest in the world, have refused to decline even as her poverty rates fell. As the Indian experience shows, increased prosperity at the aggregate level does not necessarily translate to increased Food security. This has underlined the need for targeted in-kind transfer programs such as the Public Distribution System (PDS) and the Midday Meals Scheme (MDMS). As the evidence presented in Chap. 12 showed, several of the households above the poverty line suffer from high levels of undernourishment, and the PDS is playing a significant role in providing Food security to large sections of the vulnerable. Though the latest NSS data set still records very rates of POU for households below the poverty line (BPL), upwards of 80% in several cases, undernourishment is not limited to BPL households. This suggests that far from directing the PDS, which offers subsidised calories, to BPL households in the targeted PDS (TPDS) scheme that is operational in several States, it should be made available to all households. The PDS should also be expanded to include Food items that have high nutritional content, especially in micronutrients, such as iron that have been a source of anaemic deficiency in Indian women and children. There is a view among many Indian economists that favours a move to cash transfers in the form of a 'universal basic income' (UBI) to take the place of subsidised welfare schemes such as the PDS. The preliminary results presented in Chap. 12 suggest that it is still too premature to make such a move.

References

Banerjee A, Bardhan P, Somanathan R, Srinivasan TN (2017) Poverty and income distribution in India. Juggernaut Books, New Delhi, India

Srinivasan TN, Bardhan P (1974) Poverty and income distribution in India. Statistical Publishing Society, Calcutta

Author Index

R. Ray, *Household Behaviour, Prices, and Welfare*, Themes in Economics,
https://doi.org/10.1007/978-981-13-1930-3

Subject Index

R. Ray, *Household Behaviour, Prices, and Welfare*, Themes in Economics,
https://doi.org/10.1007/978-981-13-1930-3

MIX
Papier aus verantwortungsvollen Quellen
Paper from responsible sources
FSC® C105338

If you have any concerns about our products,
you can contact us on
ProductSafety@springernature.com

In case Publisher is established outside the EU,
the EU authorized representative is:
Springer Nature Customer Service Center GmbH
Europaplatz 3, 69115 Heidelberg, Germany

Printed by Libri Plureos GmbH
in Hamburg, Germany